D1568196

The Roots and Consequences of 20th-Century Warfare

The Roots and Consequences of 20th-Century Warfare

Conflicts That Shaped the Modern World

Spencer C. Tucker

 ABC-CLIO™

An Imprint of ABC-CLIO, LLC
Santa Barbara, California • Denver, Colorado

Library of Congress Cataloging-in-Publication Data

Names: Tucker, Spencer, 1937– author.
Title: The roots and consequences of 20th-century warfare : conflicts that shaped the modern world / Spencer C. Tucker.
Other titles: Roots and consequences of twentieth century warfare, conflicts that shaped the modern world
Description: Santa Barbara, California : ABC-CLIO, [2016] | Includes index.
Identifiers: LCCN 2016001807 | ISBN 9781610698016 (alk. paper) |
    ISBN 9781610698023 (ebook)
Subjects: LCSH: Military history, Modern—20th century. | War—History—20th century.
Classification: LCC D431 .T83 2016 | DDC 355.009/04--dc23 LC record available at http://lccn
    .loc.gov/2016001807

ISBN: 978-1-61069-801-6
EISBN: 978-1-61069-802-3

20 19 18 17 16   1 2 3 4 5

This book is also available as an eBook.

ABC-CLIO
An Imprint of ABC-CLIO, LLC

ABC-CLIO, LLC
130 Cremona Drive, P.O. Box 1911
Santa Barbara, California 93116-1911
www.abc-clio.com

This book is printed on acid-free paper ∞
Manufactured in the United States of America

For Dr. Juris and Ingrid Simanis,
dear friends who understand from personal experience
the cruel costs of World War II and the Cold War

About the Author

Spencer C. Tucker, PhD, has been senior fellow in military history at ABC-CLIO since 2003. He is the author or editor of more than 58 books and encyclopedias, many of which have won prestigious awards. Tucker's last academic position before his retirement from teaching was the John Biggs Chair in Military History at the Virginia Military Institute, Lexington, VA. He has been a Fulbright scholar, a visiting research associate at the Smithsonian Institution, and, as a U.S. Army captain, an intelligence analyst in the Pentagon. His recently published works include *American Civil War: A State-by-State Encyclopedia*, *Wars That Changed History: 50 of the World's Greatest Conflicts*, and *U.S. Conflict in the 21st Century: Afghanistan War, Iraq War, and the War on Terror*, all published by ABC-CLIO.

Contents

Chronological Entry List

Alphabetical Entry List

Introduction

The century just past was a very productive one for Mars, the Roman god of war; it saw what were arguably the two greatest wars in history and a spate of comparatively minor conflicts. The first conflict covered here is the Russo-Japanese War of 1904–1905. As the first modern victory for an Asian power over a major European state, it had a profound impact on Russian history and also helped to set up the confrontation between the United States and Japan in 1941. The First and Second Balkan Wars of 1912–1913 were the precursors to World War I. Indeed, tensions in the Balkans began the Third Balkan War, which almost immediately became World War I.

In many ways, World War I was the most important war of the century. Total military and civilian deaths were on the order of 18.4 million. The war also brought finis to the German, Russian, Austro-Hungarian, and Ottoman Empires. World War II also set in motion the process of decolonization and, at the same time, drew arbitrary borders for much of the former Ottoman Empire in the Middle East, creating the problems that are still working themselves out today. The war also made the United States the world's leading financial and industrial power.

The peace settlement following the war certainly sowed the seeds for World War II, not because it was too harsh or too lenient (it was in fact a compromise) but because it was never enforced. Many Germans believed the lie that they had been cheated out of victory in World War I by the collapse of the home front by Jews, pacifists, and communists. It was none of these but instead the German military that had been in charge of German affairs that was responsible for the decisions that cost Germany victory.

U.S. president Woodrow Wilson's cherished League of Nations turned out to be of little use. Lacking compulsory membership and its own military establishment, it also had little in the way of enforcement powers. The League of Nations proved utterly incapable of keeping the peace in the interwar years. Only the small powers truly championed it. The major powers largely ignored it, and the United States even refused to join it, which the other powers would cite as an excuse for their own refusal to do what was right. This was painfully obvious in the major test of the Second Italo-Ethiopian War (1934–1935), when in an act of clear aggression Italy defied the League of Nations and invaded Ethiopia with virtual impunity.

The principal powers that had put together the peace settlement—Britain, France, and the United States—never enforced it. The French wanted to craft a truly effective treaty, but even without this, peace might have lasted had the British and Americans supported the French. As it turned out, both the United States and Britain retreated into isolationism and appeasement. This was plain in the Italian invasion of Ethiopia but also in the Spanish Civil War (1936–1939), when the British warned the French that if they intervened to assist the legitimately elected Republican government of Spain and this led to a general European war, Britain would not support France. At the same time, the British were the first to condone a direct violation of the Versailles Treaty when in 1935 they signed a treaty with Germany that allowed that country to exceed naval construction limits imposed at the end of World War I. The British people have much to be proud of in World War II, but war might have been averted had their government been prepared to support the French and stand up to German chancellor Adolf Hitler earlier.

The Soviet Union also bears much responsibility for World War II. Soviet leader Joseph Stalin's nonaggression pact with Hitler on August 23, 1939, made possible the latter's invasion of Poland on September 1, which precipitated the war. Stalin was no fool. He understood Hitler's desire to secure much of Eastern Europe as *Lebensraum* (living space) but hoped to purchase time and have war with Germany on his terms when the Soviet Union was ready militarily. Thus, Stalin agreed to divide Poland and the Baltic States with Hitler and to assist the German war machine with vast quantities of key raw materials. That changed in 1941, of course, with Hitler's monumental mistake of invading the Soviet Union. Securing control of Eastern Europe had, of course, been one of Germany's goals in World War I.

Many scholars point out that World War II actually began first in Asia, when

the Japanese sought to take advantage of the Chinese Civil War of 1927–1949. That conflict continued at a lower level during World War II and was only resolved afterward. The Second Sino-Japanese War of 1937–1945 is covered here as a part of World War II.

The effects of World War II were immense. It touched more of the world than World War I. The human costs of World War II were also greater: 65 million to 80 million killed. The Soviet Union's losses alone were on the order of 27 million dead (U.S. deaths totaled some 419,000, including 9,500 members of the merchant marine). Strategic bombing ensured that physical damage was also more widespread and costly. Far from crushing the Soviet Union and communism as he had anticipated, Hitler in fact greatly strengthened both, as at war's close the Soviet Union came to control most of Central and Eastern Europe. World War II also saw the emergence of a second superpower, the United States. If the American Century did not begin at the close of World War I, it certainly did with World War II. The war also marked the effective end of colonialism as the British, French, Dutch, and Portuguese Empires came under increased pressure from nationalists determined that their countries would be free from foreign control. Many of these colonial powers refused to recognize the inevitable, however, ushering in a number of conflicts in Asia and Africa.

As soon as World War II ended, a new war began in the contest between the United States and the Soviet Union. Known as the Cold War, it is so named because thankfully there was no actual warfare between the two superpowers, both of which came to possess sufficient numbers of nuclear weapons to destroy the world many times over. Rather, it was a series of smaller conflicts and proxy wars. Actual fighting in the Cold War can be said to have first begun in Greece. The civil war there during 1946–1949 saw the communist states of Yugoslavia, Bulgaria, and Albania aiding the Greek communists as they battled Greek government forces supported by Britain. That country's inability financially to carry on the struggle brought the United States into the fray. This led in turn to the Truman Doctrine, the Marshall Plan, the North Atlantic Treaty Organization, and the Containment Doctrine.

While the British Labour Party, which had come to power in the closing days of World War II, recognized that the days of colonialism were at an end, French leaders did not. It is hard for the weak to be generous, and France had suffered greatly in the war. Only with its vast overseas empire could it be considered a Great Power. French leaders therefore refused to grant real independence to Vietnam, and the result was the costly Indochina War of 1946–1954. The Geneva Conference of 1954 temporarily divided Vietnam at the 17th parallel pending elections in two years to reunify the country. The Containment Doctrine and rampant anticommunist hysteria in the United States, fueled by the track record of communists in power not allowing free elections, led the U.S. government to support the new leader of South Vietnam, Ngo Dinh Diem, in his refusal to hold the reunification elections. This brought on the costly Vietnam War (1957–1975), which for the first time exposed the limits of American military power in the face of strident nationalism.

The Korean War of 1950–1953 was one of the century's most interesting. It began when Kim Il Sung, leader of the communist Democratic People's Republic of Korea (North Korea), sent his army south in an invasion of the U.S.-backed Republic of Korea (South Korea). He did so with the full support of Stalin and Chinese Communist leader Mao Zedong (Mao Tse-tung). Without their consent and support there would have been no war. Kim was confident that he could reunify Korea before the United States could intervene in force. (Korea, like Germany and some other states, had been divided into occupation zones at the end of World War II, and this had become permanent.) Kim was almost proved correct, for South Korea was largely unarmed. But U.S. military forces from Japan bought sufficient time, and other countries furnished aid. U.S. president Harry S. Truman authorized a counterinvasion of North Korea, and China then entered the war. Although the fighting seesawed back and forth, it came to an end in an armistice approximately where it had begun, at the 38th parallel. The Korean War was the first war for the United Nations and can be seen as the first modern-day limited war. Indeed, neither side was willing to risk a catastrophic nuclear exchange in order to prevail in Korea. The Korean War also greatly enhanced the prestige of Communist China. Unfortunately, the Korean Peninsula remains today one of the world's major flash points.

Other wars in Asia included the Indo-Pakistani wars in the period 1947–1999, fought over Kashmir following independence; the Malayan Emergency of 1948–1960; the Soviet-Afghan War (1979–1989); and the quarter-century-long Sri Lanka War (1983–2009).

There were many wars in Africa. The Algerian War of 1954–1962 saw the French professional army almost immediately transplanted there from Indochina. Settlement of the conflict was complicated by the large minority European population, and the war ended only with the return to power of General Charles de Gaulle and his realization that independence for Algeria was the only viable option. A large European settler population played the key role in the start of the Rhodesian Bush War (Zimbabwe War of Independence) of 1964–1979. Other African wars covered here are the Angolan War, or War for Zimbabwe Independence (1961–1974), and the Nigerian Civil War (Biafran War) of 1967–1970, which was especially costly in human terms, claiming at least 2 million dead.

There were also important wars in Latin America. Those covered here are the Mexican Revolutionary War of 1910–1920, which some argue is ongoing; the Cuban Revolutionary War of 1956–1959; and the Nicaraguan Revolution (1961–1979).

The three important Arab-Israeli wars in the period are treated here in some depth as one long section. Certainly they have been of immense importance in shaping the modern Middle East, and the Arab-Palestinian issue remains unresolved today. Other important Middle East conflicts covered here are the Iran-Iraq War (1980–1988) and the Persian Gulf War of 1991. The 20th century ended amid new fighting in the Balkans in the Yugoslav Wars of 1991–1999.

There were, of course (and unfortunately), an abundance of choices, but I have attempted to include wars from each continent. Of course this work is not complete, as many conflicts have necessarily been omitted due to publishing limitations, but I trust that what is here will be representative. Each selected conflict has sections treating causes, course, and consequences as well as a timeline and list of books for further reading. While I have written most of the entries, some are by others. I am especially grateful to Drs. Richard Hall, Paul Pierpaoli Jr., and Pedro Santoni for their assistance in this project. I take full responsibility for any possible errors, however.

SPENCER C. TUCKER

Russo-Japanese War (1904–1905)

Causes

Identified as the first great war of the 20th century, the Russo-Japanese War of 1904–1905 resulted from the clash of imperial ambitions between Russia and Japan to see which power would dominate the Far East. The interest of Czar Nicholas II (r. 1894–1917) in the Far East was hardly a secret. Indeed, for centuries Russian czars had sought to secure a warm-water year-round outlet on the high seas. In the Crimean War (1853–1856), Britain and France had blocked Russian efforts to obtain access to the Mediterranean from the Black Sea at the expense of the Ottoman Empire, while in the 1880s the British had stymied the Russian attempt to secure Afghanistan and push southward to the Indian Ocean.

In the 1890s Russia's leaders temporarily set aside ambitions in the Balkans in favor of a warm-water port in the Far East. Britain and France had gained spheres of influence in China as a consequence of the Opium Wars (1839–1842 and 1856–1860), while Japan had defeated China in the Sino-Japanese War of 1894–1895 and secured de facto control of Korea. Nicholas II saw no reason why, if the Great Powers were bent on dismembering China, Russia should not also secure a share, especially since by pushing southward through Chinese territory it might obtain an ice-free port. He marked out for acquisition the Chinese territories of Manchuria and Korea. If these were annexed to the Russian Empire or converted into Russian spheres of influence, they would provide excellent ports to supplement that of Vladivostok ("Rule the East") in the Far East, which was closed part of each year.

Control of Manchuria would also provide a shorter and more direct rail connection to Vladivostok. In 1891 Russia had begun construction of the Trans-Siberian Railway. (Not completed until 1916, it is the world's longest rail line.)

Japan, however, wanted to acquire Manchuria's considerable natural resources for itself. Japan is an island nation without substantial natural resources, and mountains make up some 70 percent of the country. Japan's leaders were determined to reverse what they regarded as an accident of history by wresting control from China of the hermit kingdom

Nicholas II was czar of Russia from 1894 to 1917. His desire to secure control of Manchuria for Russia and failure to anticipate the Japanese reaction to this led to the Russo-Japanese War of 1904–1905. (Library of Congress)

of Korea across the Tsushima Straits and also an opening in Manchuria. In 1894 Japan went to war with China in order to secure these ends.

While the Japanese secured de facto control of Korea following their victory in the Sino-Japanese War, they were denied a foothold in Manchuria. One of the provisions of the peace settlement imposed by Japan was that China surrender the Liaotung (Liaodong) Peninsula in southern Manchuria, but Russian leaders had marked out that territory for themselves and therefore opposed the Japanese acquisition. For reasons of their own, France (which had signed a treaty of alliance with Russia in 1894 and was eager to strengthen that bond) and Germany (seeking to court Russia) agreed to support the Russian position. The governments of all three pressed the Japanese leaders to surrender the territory. Faced with the opposition of a coalition of major European powers, its leaders eventually ceded their claim to territory on the Asian mainland in return for an additional indemnity from China.

Russia then advanced its own position in China under the pretense of defending Chinese territorial integrity. On June 3, 1896, the Li-Labonov Treaty signed in Moscow provided that Russia would aid China if it were attacked by a third power. Russia also secured economic concessions, including the right to build the Chinese Eastern Railway across Manchuria to Vladivostok. This railway, to be protected by Russian troops, would connect Vladivostok in the Far East with inland Siberia and European Russia by a much shorter and more direct route than the Trans-Siberian Railway. In a convention of March 27, 1898, Russia also secured a lease of about 500 square miles of territory—including part of the land surrendered by Japan in 1895—at the

end of the Liaotung (now Liaodong) Peninsula and the right to construct a branch line to connect this territory with the Chinese Eastern Railway at Harbin. Subsequently the Russians improved the harbor of Darien and constructed a powerful fortress and naval base at Port Arthur. Russia now had a warm-water port/outlet for the Trans-Siberian Railway, and it appeared that Manchuria would pass under Russian control.

Both Russia and Japan took part in the eight-nation international force that intervened in China in 1900 during the Boxer Rebellion (Boxer Uprising) to relieve the international legations under siege in the Chinese capital of Peking (now known as Beijing). Russia had already sent 177,000 soldiers to Manchuria, supposedly to protect its railways under construction there but with the real aim of detaching Manchuria from China. Although the Russian government assured the other powers that it would vacate the area after the crisis was over, by 1903 Russia had yet to establish a schedule for its withdrawal. This brought Japanese anger and diplomatic protests by Japan.

Japan had opened negotiations with the British government, which was also worried about Russian expansion in the Far East, and on January 30, 1902, the two governments concluded an agreement. This treaty, the first between a European power and an Asiatic state on the basis of equality, ensured that in the event of war between Japan and Russia, Great Britain would remain neutral. The treaty also stipulated that if any power assisted Russia in such a war, Great Britain would fight on the side of Japan.

Their position now considerably strengthened, in 1903 Japanese leaders offered the Russians a compromise. Japan agreed to recognize Russian ascendancy

Approximate Casualty Statistics for Key Battles of the Russo-Japanese War

	Russia	Japan
Battle of Sha-Ho (October 5–17, 1904)	41,351 killed/wounded	20,345 killed/wounded
Battle of Sandepu (January 26–27, 1905)	12,241 killed/wounded	9,000 killed/wounded
Battle of Mukden (February 21–March 10, 1905)	100,000 killed/wounded	70,000 killed/wounded
Naval Battle of Tsushima (May 27, 1905)	4,830 killed	110 killed

Sources: Michael Clodfelter, *Warfare and Armed Conflict: A Statistical Reference to Casualty and Other Figures, 1618–1991* (Jefferson, NC: McFarland, 1992); Denis Warner and Peggy Warner, *The Tide at Sunrise: A History of the Russo-Japanese War, 1904–1905,* 2nd ed. (London: Routledge, 2004).

in the greater part of Manchuria if Russia withdrew its troops from Manchuria, recognized Japan's right to intervene in Korea, and gave Japan the right to build a railroad from Korea into Manchuria that would connect with the Chinese Eastern Railway. When Russian leaders hesitated, the Japanese broke off diplomatic relations. Japanese leaders believed with considerable justification that Russia was merely trying to postpone war until it had completed its strategic rail net in the region. While Czar Nicholas II and his advisers anticipated war with Japan, they also believed that it would occur in circumstances favorable to Russia and that Japan certainly would never begin it.

The sole voice of reason in the Russian cabinet was Minister of Finance Sergei Witte. During the summer of 1902 Witte traveled in the Far East to study the Chinese Eastern Railway, and he returned with the conviction that Russia should regard Manchuria as "unconditionally and forever lost." He called for the evacuation of Manchuria and securing Russian influence in the Far East "by peaceful means exclusively." As Witte noted later, "The report failed to impress His Majesty. Had

he followed my advice, we would have avoided the unhappy war with all its disastrous consequences." Witte's outspoken opposition to the czar's Manchurian policy led in 1903 to his removal from his post. (In 1905 Nicholas recalled Witte to salvage the wreckage of the czar's failed Far Eastern policies and arrange a peace agreement with Japan.)

Witte's sage advice had come up against Czar Nicholas's ambition and contempt for and ignorance of the Japanese, which was shared by most Russians. The Trans-Siberian Railway had been extended through Manchuria against the advice of the Russian military. Now that it had been built, the military argued that it had to be protected. Minister of War Aleksei Kuropatkin even presented a plan whereby Russia would sell China all of southern Manchuria—which was, of course, its own territory—in exchange for China's concession to Russia of northern Manchuria. In addition, Kaiser Wilhelm II of Germany was encouraging Nicholas's Asian ambitions in order to distract Russia's attention from Europe.

Japanese leaders, however, decided not to wait for Russia's convenience. Their answer was the preparation of a preemptive strike in order to secure control of the seas, essential if troops were to be transported from Japan to Manchuria and Korea.

War between Russia and Japan in 1904 appeared to be a mismatch. Although Russia was vastly superior in resources and manpower (on paper its army numbered some 4.5 million men), it would be seriously handicapped at the outset of fighting because it would be unable to immediately bring its full strength to bear. The conflict was far distant from the heart of Russia, and troops and supplies would have to be shipped 5,500 miles over the single-track Trans-Siberian Railway. A gap in the line imposed by Lake Baikal complicated Russia's logistical problems.

The Russian Navy was divided into three main squadrons, again widely separated—the Baltic, the Black Sea, and the Pacific—and it was difficult to concentrate them. Russian troops lacked enthusiasm for the war, the purpose of which they either did not understand or did not approve. Indeed, the war never did receive the wholehearted support of the Russian people. Inefficiency and corruption, which had so often undermined Russian armies in the past, again appeared in this conflict. Finally, it was Russia's misfortune to have a supreme command lacking both initiative and strategic ability.

Japan, on the other hand, had a highly disciplined, efficient, and enthusiastic army and navy. Its military establishment was well trained and ably led and was loyally supported by the Japanese people. Many of the more powerful ships of the Japanese Navy were new. Furthermore, Japan was in close proximity to the seat of hostilities, and assuming control of the

sea, it could place its forces in the field with a minimum of difficulty.

SPENCER C. TUCKER

Course

On February 6, 1904, Japanese vice admiral Tōgō Heihachiro's Combined Fleet sailed from Japan to attack the Russian fleet based at Port Arthur (now Lüshunkou District), while at the same time Admiral Uryu Sotokichi departed with a squadron of four heavy cruisers for Chemulpo (now Incheon) Bay in western Korea, there to ensure the safe landing of Japanese troops. Outside the harbor of Chemulpo in the early afternoon of February 8, Uryu joined a flotilla of Japanese torpedo boats and three transports carrying 3,000 men and horses and equipment of the army's 12th Division. Another Japanese cruiser had been keeping close watch on the harbor where three Russian ships—a cruiser, a gunboat, and a transport—lay at anchor.

The opening shots of the war occurred at about 2:15 p.m. on February 8 between the Japanese ships and the Russian gunboat *Koreetz,* which had put to sea with dispatches and mail for Port Arthur. Although this seems unlikely, the Japanese claimed that the *Koreetz* fired its one gun first. A Japanese torpedo boat attack having failed, the *Koreetz* was able to return to port. That evening the Japanese troops began coming ashore, and the next morning a number of them set off to capture the Korean capital of Seoul. Uryu then sent an ultimatum to the Russians demanding that their ships take to the sea or be attacked in the harbor, a violation of international law.

The Russians decided that honor dictated that they fight, although the cruiser *Varyag* was their only ship capable of battle. In the late morning of February 9, the

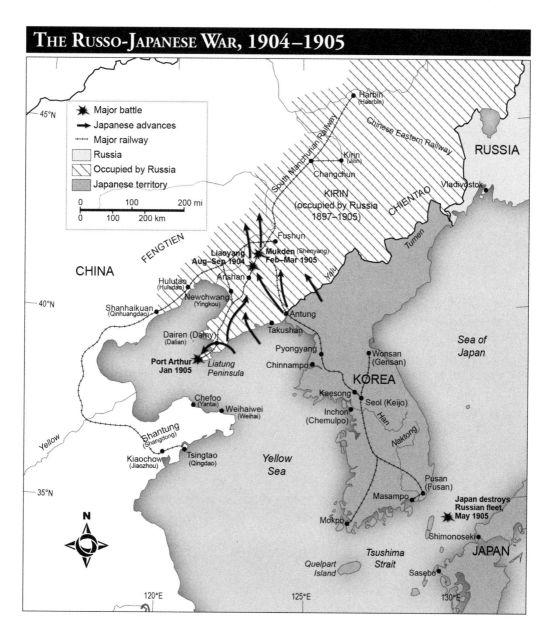

THE RUSSO-JAPANESE WAR, 1904–1905

two Russian warships exited the harbor. In an hour-long battle both ships were heavily damaged but were able to regain the harbor, whereupon the Russians scuttled all three. The Japanese claimed that they suffered no casualties and no damage to their ships.

Aside from the warships at Chemulpo, the Russians had at Vladivostok 4 heavy cruisers and 17 torpedo boats, but their most powerful naval force—7 battleships and 4 cruisers—was at Port Arthur. Because early on February 7 the Japanese had cut the cable between Port Arthur and Korea, the Russian authorities at Port Arthur were unaware of the start of the war.

During the night of February 8–9, 1904, Tōgō launched a surprise torpedo attack against Port Arthur. It badly damaged two battleships and a cruiser. With daylight Tōgō brought up his heavy ships and shelled at long range the shore batteries, the town, and Russian ships. Although four Russian ships were damaged, in the exchange of fire most Japanese vessels were also struck, and Tōgō reluctantly ordered the Combined Fleet to withdraw. There were no pangs of conscience in Tokyo regarding the surprise Japanese attacks of February 8, and not until February 10 did Japan formally declare war.

On February 17, Japanese general Kuroki Tamemoto's First Army began coming ashore at Chemulpo. After reorganizing, the Japanese troops began moving northward. In mid-March other members of Kuroki's army landed at Chinnampo, midway between Chemulpo and the Yalu, and advanced north to Pyongyang and then to the Yalu.

Tōgō, meanwhile, was frustrated at his inability to destroy the Russian naval forces at Port Arthur in the initial attack, and he was now obliged to keep up the pressure and adopt attrition tactics. Vice Admiral Stepan Ossipovitch Makarov took over command at Port Arthur and initiated a series of sorties to harass the Japanese cruisers while avoiding contact with Tōgō's battleships. Both sides also laid minefields, but Makarov was killed and his battleship lost when it encountered a Japanese minefield in April. The Japanese also lost two battleships to mines, but Japan now rushed troops to southern Manchuria. General Nogi Maresuke and his Third Army cut off Port Arthur from the land and drove back northward Russian forces attempting to relieve the fortress.

Following the first Japanese land assault on Port Arthur, Czar Nicholas II ordered Admiral Vilgelm Vitgeft, Makarov's successor, to break free and steam to Vladivostok. Determined to take his entire squadron, Vitgeft departed on August 10 with 18 ships. That afternoon Tōgō closed on the Russians with 34 ships and 29 torpedo boats. In the ensuing Battle of the Yellow Sea, although themselves struck hard, the Japanese ships scored two hits late in the day that killed Vitgeft and put his flagship out of control and the Russian battle line into complete confusion. The Russian squadron then scattered. No Russian ships were destroyed or taken in the battle, however. Five battleships, a cruiser, and 3 destroyers regained Port Arthur. Most others were interned in Chinese ports and Saigon.

News of the Battle of the Yellow Sea reached Vladivostok on August 11, but not until the 13th did three cruisers under Rear Admiral Nikolai von Essen steam to the assistance of the Port Arthur Squadron. On August 14 they ran into Admiral Kammimura Hikonojo's four armored cruisers. In the resulting Battle of Ulsan, the Japanese sank one of the Russian cruisers. The others were able to regain Vladivostok, but Japan now had complete control of the sea.

That autumn in Manchuria, Japanese land forces under General Oyama Iwao engaged the main Russian forces under General Alexsei Kuropatkin. In the great Battle of Liaoyang (August 25–September 3, 1904), 127,000 Japanese faced off against 245,000 Russians. The battle claimed 23,000 Japanese casualties against only 19,000 Russians lost. Kuropatkin had repulsed three days of Japanese assaults, but believing that he had been defeated, he began a well-managed, systematic withdrawal toward Mukden. During October 5–17 the two sides fought another battle at the Shao-Ho (Shaho, Sha River). In it the Russians lost some 40,000 men, the Japanese 20,000.

Wrecked Russian warships in Port Arthur harbor in December 1904 during the Japanese siege of that Russian base. (Library of Congress)

On January 2, 1905, Port Arthur, now blockaded by land and sea, surrendered. This released the bulk of Nogi's Third Army for deployment northward. During January 26–27 another land battle occurred in Manchuria at Sandepu (Heikoutai). The Russians, now reinforced to 300,000 men, took the offensive against Oyama's 220,000 Japanese. Kuropatkin was close to victory but failed to press his advantage, and the battle ended in stalemate.

By the third week in February the Russians were drawn up along a 47-mile line south of the important rail center of Mukden (present-day Shenyang). The Russians deployed three armies, the Japanese four. Estimates of strength vary widely, but each side fielded as many as 310,000 men. This battle, during February 21–March 10, 1905,

saw the Japanese attacking the entrenched Russians. The Russians blunted the initial Japanese attacks but in heavy fighting on March 6–8 were driven back to the point that Kuropatkin feared that his lines of communication northward might be cut. On March 10 Kuropatkin carried out an orderly withdrawal northward toward the cities of Teih-ling (Tieling) and Harbin.

Casualty figures for the Battle of Mukden vary widely, but the Russians lost something on the order of 100,000 men and considerable equipment. Japanese casualties may have totaled 70,000 men. Kuropatkin's forces were still largely intact. Nonetheless, the heavy losses sustained at Mukden and in prior battles, coupled with increasing domestic unrest in Russia, culminated in the start on January 22 of the

Russian Revolution of 1905 and gave the czar and his advisers pause.

Russia's leaders, however, were determined on one more toss of the dice by their Baltic Fleet, renamed the 2nd Pacific Squadron, that had been sent around the world to the Far East. If the Russians could gain control of the sea, they could cut off Japanese forces in Manchuria and bombard Japanese coastal cities, forcing Japan from the war.

On October 15, 1904, Rear Admiral Zinovi Petrovitch Rozhdestvenski's 36 warships had set out on what would be a seven-month odyssey. The most powerful units were the four new Borodino-class battleships: the *Borodino, Alexander III, Orel,* and *Kniaz Suvarov.* The voyage went badly from the start. On October 21, off the Dogger Bank in the North Sea, jittery Russian crews opened fire on their own cruiser, the *Aurora,* and the British Hull fishing fleet, mistaking them for Japanese torpedo boats and sinking several trawlers. This incident almost brought war with Britain.

After the fleet rounded Portugal, some ships proceeded eastward through the Mediterranean and the Suez Canal, while the main detachment continued south around Africa. With Japan's ally Britain refusing to supply coal, the Russians were forced to secure it from German colliers. The lack of coaling stations led Rozhdestvenski to order the ships to take on whatever they could, placing it in every possible space and precluding training and gunnery practice.

Reunited at Madagascar, on March 16 the fleet started across the Indian Ocean, refueling five times at sea—an unprecedented feat. Following one last stop to take on supplies and coal at Cam Ranh Bay in French Indochina, the Russian ships slowly made their way north through the South China Sea and up the Chinese coast.

Rozhdestvenski hoped to get to Vladivostok without battle. He sent most of his auxiliary vessels to anchor at the mouth of the Yangtze River, and he timed his advance through the Tsushima Straits to be at night. He also sent two cruisers toward the east coast of Japan in a vain attempt to persuade the Japanese that the entire fleet would follow.

Tōgō gambled that Rozhdestvenski would choose the most direct route to Vladivstok by means of the Tsushima Straits and planned a trap there. The Japanese also had cut off Vladivosotok by sowing 715 mines at the entrance to Peter the Great Bay.

On the night of May 26–27, Japanese picket ships sighted the Russian fleet in the straits, and Tōgō's ships immediately left their bases, dumping coal as they went to increase their speed. Tōgō relied on radio messages to keep informed of the location of the Russian ships (Tsushima was the first naval battle in which radio was used in action). The total Russian fleet consisted of eight battleships, eight cruisers, nine destroyers, and several smaller vessels. The firepower of the two fleets was slightly to the Russian advantage, but this was offset by the fact that the Japanese crews were far superior to the Russians in gunnery.

Tōgō had 4 battleships, 8 cruisers, 21 destroyers, and 60 torpedo boats. His ships had been recently overhauled and repaired. They also possessed superior speed; they were, on average, about 50 percent faster than the Russian ships, even the newest of which were fouled from the long voyage. Tōgō's men were battle-tested and were led by highly skilled officers.

On the afternoon of May 27, trailed by Japanese cruisers, the 2nd Pacific Squadron sailed past Tsushima Island. When the Russian ships came out of some fog at 1:19 p.m., Tōgō in the battleship *Mikasa* to the northeast at last sighted his prey. The Russian ships were steaming in two columns. Rozhdestvenski had his flag in the *Suvarov,* the lead ship in the starboard column.

The Russians assumed that Tōgō would turn south and bridge the gap, allowing his battleships to fire on the weaker Russian divisions, but this would have left the Russian ships headed toward Vladivostok, with the Japanese moving in the opposite direction. Instead, Tōgō made a daring move, ordering his cruisers to make a 270-degree turn to the northeast to cut the Russians off from Vladivostok. This brought the Japanese ships onto a course paralleling the Russians; with their superior speed they would turn east and cross the Russian "T" at leisure.

This maneuver carried grave risks, because during the long turn Tōgō exposed in succession his entire line of ships to the full broadsides fire of the Russian fleet. Seconds after the *Mikasa* began its turn, the *Suvarov* opened fire. Other Russian ships followed suit. As the fleets formed into two converging lines, each blasted away at the other. Rozhdestvenski altered course slightly to port, reducing the range, but the Russian fire rapidly deteriorated as the range closed.

Russian fire damaged three Japanese ships and forced a cruiser out of the battle line. But soon the *Suvarov* was on fire, and another battleship, the *Oslyabya,* was holed. The Japanese concentrated their fire on the crippled battleships, and their superior gunnery told.

By nightfall the Japanese victory was nearly complete. Rozhdestvenski, wounded in the battle, yielded command to Rear Admiral Nicholas Nebogatov. That night

Tōgō sent his destroyers and torpedo boats to finish off those Russian vessels not already sunk or escaped. Isolated fighting continued throughout the night, but by the next day the Japanese had sunk, captured, or disabled eight Russian battleships.

Of 12 Russian ships in the battle line, 8 were sunk, including 3 of the new battleships; the other 4 had been captured. Of the cruisers, 4 were sunk and 1 was scuttled; 3 limped into Manila and were interned; another made it to Vladivostok. Of the destroyers, 4 were sunk, 1 was captured, 1 was interned at Shanghai, and 2 reached Vladivostok. Three special service ships were sunk, 1 was interned at Shanghai, and 1 escaped to Madagascar.

Tōgō lost only three torpedo boats. All Japanese ships remained serviceable. The Russians had 4,830 men killed or drowned and just under 7,000 taken prisoner. Japanese personnel losses were 110 killed and 590 wounded. The Battle of Tsushima was of immense importance. In just one day Russia ceased to be a major Pacific power; fully a half century would pass before it regained major status at sea.

The battle led Czar Nicholas to seek peace. Although Russia, with its vast resources and manpower, might possibly have sent new armies to continue the war, popular discontent and political unrest at home alarmed the czar's ministers, who were therefore willing to consider peace proposals. On the other hand, its military efforts had nearly bankrupted Japan (a fact that Japanese leaders had carefully concealed from the Japanese people), so its leaders were also ready to halt military operations.

Both Kaiser Wilhelm II and U.S. president Theodore Roosevelt had urged peace upon the belligerents. Both sides agreed to peace talks to be held at the Portsmouth

Navy Base in New Hampshire, where peace was concluded on September 5, 1905.

SPENCER C. TUCKER

Consequences

On the invitation of U.S. president Theodore Roosevelt, a peace conference opened at the unlikely venue of the U.S. Navy Yard at Portsmouth, New Hampshire. Czar Nicholas II recalled to government service the able Sergei Witte, who had opposed the czar's Manchurian policies that had brought war and revolution, and charged him with salvaging what he could. Witte played a key role in saving his country from the worst consequences of the defeat.

The September 5, 1905, Treaty of Portsmouth transferred Russia's cessions in southern Manchuria to Japan, converting that area into a Japanese sphere of influence. Russia also recognized Japan's preponderant interest in Korea and its right to control and "protect" the Korean government. In addition, Russia surrendered to Japan the southern half of Sakhalin Island, which Japan had occupied during the war. The treaty, favorable as it was to Japan, was not popular in that country, for Japanese leaders had not obtained the indemnity they wanted, and the Japanese people were unaware of how close the country was to bankruptcy.

The Russo-Japanese War had profound domestic impact in Russia. The outbreak of fighting had greatly increased popular discontent because most Russians had no clear idea why it was being fought and because of the corruption and inefficiency revealed from the onset of fighting with the lack of adequate equipment, munitions, and supplies for the troops at the front. Mounting unrest at home found confirmation in the July 28, 1904, assassination in St. Petersburg of reactionary minister of the interior Vyacheslav von Plehve. It appeared that Nicholas II might follow a less reactionary course when he appointed to succeed Plehve liberal noble Prince Pyotr Dmitrievich Svyatopolk-Mirsky. Then in November 1904 Nicholas permitted representatives of the rural and urban assemblies, the zemstvos and dumas, to meet informally in a national congress.

This congress petitioned Nicholas to guarantee individual liberties and establish a national parliament. Although the czar agreed to some reforms, he refused to take any step that might bring the creation of a national parliament. Popular unrest thus continued. Russian military reverses and food shortages in the cities, which were not unrelated to the war, brought demonstrations, and early in 1905 St. Petersburg was paralyzed by a great general strike.

Russian Orthodox priest Father Georgi Gapon persuaded the workers of St. Petersburg that their best course was to present a petition to the czar in person, and on Sunday, January 22, 1905, he led as many as 200,000 men, women, and children to the Winter Palace to present the petition. Gapon had written to Nicholas beforehand stressing the demonstration's peaceful character and urging him to accept the petition. Nicholas's response was to leave the city while armed police and mounted Cossack soldiers protected the palace. The crowd was peaceful and arrived at the palace with no indication of hostile intent. Nonetheless, the guards ordered them to disband, and when they failed to move quickly enough the Cossacks and police opened fire. Several hundred people were killed and nearly 3,000 were wounded in what came to be called "Bloody Sunday."

Additional strikes and political demonstrations then swept Russia. Nicholas dismissed Mirsky and ordered the reactionary

General Dimtri Trepov to restore order in the capital. Trepov's brutal measures failed to end the unrest, however, and a number of prominent people were assassinated in what now became a revolution. Workers in nearly every industry went on strike, and peasants in the countryside attacked and burned noble residences. Subject nationalities in Poland and the Caucasus demonstrated for national rights, and even the crew of the battleship *Potemkin* joined the revolutionary movement.

With the greater part of his armed forces thousands of miles distant in Manchuria, Nicholas II was in no position to use force and was therefore obliged to give way. He issued a number of reform decrees, dismissed Trepov, and recalled Witte, who had just negotiated the Treaty of Portsmouth.

Nicholas's reform measures proved insufficient, obliging him to issue on October 30, 1905, what became known as the October Manifesto. It granted freedom of speech, the press, and association and also promised a national Duma (legislature) for Russia to represent the will of the people. He also pledged that no future law would be binding without the Duma's consent. Other reform decrees followed.

Eventually, with the gradual return of Russian troops from the Far East after the signing of the Treaty of Portsmouth, the fear that had forced Nicholas to make his liberal concessions passed. In spite of Witte's opposition, Nicholas now set out to restore as much of the old autocratic system as possible. Troops put down nationalistic revolts in Poland and the Caucasus and restored order in the countryside, and the government unleashed a wave of terror in pogroms and in the activities of the so-called Black Hundreds, gangs encouraged to attack those opposing the regime.

Thousands of Russians were arrested or executed, with the czar taking an active role in this activity. In March 1906 he felt secure enough to annul most of the important provisions of the October Manifesto. Then in May, shortly before the first Duma met, Nicholas dismissed Witte as prime minister and replaced him with a reactionary.

The czar now reserved for himself the right to alter at any time the constitutional form of the government, and state ministers continued to be responsible to him alone. The aristocracy weathered the Russian Revolution of 1905 with scant effect. This situation continued because of a loyal army, financial and moral support from foreign governments, and divisions among the revolutionaries. It would change dramatically as a consequence of World War I, however.

Militarily, defeat in the Russo-Japanese War did point out the major shortcomings in the Russia Army and brought reforms that helped prepare it for the greater challenge to come in World War I. The failure to address social and economic inequities, however, brought another revolution in March 1917 and the abdication of Nicholas II. The new government's decision to continue Russian participation in World War I brought a second revolution—really a coup d'état by the Bolsheviks—in November.

Militarily, the Russo-Japanese War demonstrated the importance of the machine gun on the modern battlefield, but the European powers, with the exception of the Germans, did not take proper notice. Tsushima also led the Japanese to believe that wars could be turned by one big battle. Only the heavy guns had counted in the battle, vindicating proponents of an all big-gun battleship, of which HMS *Dreadnought* in 1906 was the first. Ironically, Tsushima was also the only major decisive fleet action in the history of the steel battleship. In the future, underwater or aerial weapons would often exercise the dominant influence at sea.

Internationally, the Russo-Japanese War showcased the high stakes involved in Great Power rivalry in East Asia. The 1890s had seen a significant imperial push in the Far East, exemplified by the Sino-Japanese War of 1894–1895, the Spanish-American War of 1898, and the Philippine-American War of 1898–1902. Coming on the heels of turn-of-the-century expansionism and the Boxer Rebellion, the Russo-Japanese War capped off a feverish scramble for hegemony in the Far East driven by a search for markets, imperial aspirations, and military and geostrategic concerns.

In the Russo-Japanese War, the Japanese had not only halted Russian expansion in the Far East but also shown the world that a new Great Power had arisen in Asia. Indeed, the war confirmed Japan as the premier military power of the Far East. The Japanese victory also rocked all Asia in the sense that the myth of European military supremacy had been forever shattered, which helped set the stage for the showdown between Japan and the United States in 1941.

SPENCER C. TUCKER

Timeline

1894–1895

Japan is victorious over China in the Sino-Japanese War.

1896

June 3

The Li-Lobanov Treaty is signed in Moscow between Russia and China.

1898

March 27

In a convention of this date between Russia and China, Russia secures a lease of about 500 square miles of territory—including part of the land surrendered by Japan in 1895—at the end of the Liaotung (now Liaodong) Peninsula and the right to construct a branch line to connect this territory with the Chinese Eastern Railway at Harbin.

1900

The Great Powers, including Russia and Japan, intervene in China during the Boxer Rebellion to relieve the siege of the foreign legations. Russian forces introduced into Manchuria fail to depart after the end of the rebellion, despite Japanese protests.

1902

January 30

Japan concludes an alliance with Great Britain.

1903

Japanese leaders offer the Russians a compromise that would create spheres of influence regarding Manchuria and Korea, but when the Russians hesitate, the Japanese break off negotiations.

August 16	Russian minister of finance Sergei Witte's opposition to Czar Nicholas II's Manchurian policy leads to Witte's removal from his post.

1904

February 6	Japanese vice admiral Tōgō Heihachiro sails from Japan with the Combined Fleet for Port Arthur (present-day Lüshunkou District), while Vice Admiral Uryu Sotokichi sails with four heavy cruisers for Chemulpo (Incheon) Bay in western Korea.
February 8	The Russo-Japanese War begins with the Japanese victory over Russian warships at Chemulpo (present-day Incheon).
February 8–9	With the Russians unaware of the Chemulpo attack, the Japanese launch a surprise night attack against Russian warships just outside the harbor at Port Arthur.
February 10	Japan formally declares war on Russia.
February 17	The Japanese First Army begins coming ashore at Chemulpo (Incheon), Korea.
Mid-March	Japanese troops land at Chinnampo, Korea, and advance north to Pyongyang and then to the Yalu River.
July 28	Russian minister of the interior Vyacheslav von Plehve is assassinated in St. Petersburg.
August 10	The Japanese defeat the Russians in the naval Battle of the Yellow Sea.
August 14	The Japanese defeat the Russians in the naval Battle of Ulsan. Japan now has complete control of the sea.
August 25–September 3	In the Battle of Liaoyang in Manchuria, the Russians hold off the Japanese and inflict more casualties than they themselves sustain, but Russian commander Alexsei Kuropatkin, believing himself defeated, withdraws.
October 5–17	Japanese forces engage the Russians in the indecisive Battle of the Shaho (Sha-Ho, Sha River) in Manchuria.
October 15	The Russian Baltic Fleet, commanded by Rear Admiral Zinovi Rozhdestvenski, sets out on what will be a seven-month voyage to the Far East.
October 21	Off the Dogger Bank in the North Sea, jittery Russian crews open fire on one of their own ships and the British Hull fishing fleet, mistaking them for Japanese torpedo boats and sinking several trawlers. This incident almost brings war with Britain.

1905

January 5	Russian forces at Port Arthur, blockaded by land and sea, surrender to the Japanese.
January 22	"Bloody Sunday" in St. Petersburg, Russia, marks the beginning of the Russian Revolution of 1905.
January 26–27	In the Battle of Sandepu (Heikoutai), Manchuria, Russian forces attack the Japanese, but the fighting ends in stalemate.
February 21–March 10	Both sides suffer heavy casualties in the great Battle of Mukden (present-day Shenyang) in Manchuria, but the Russians are forced to withdraw.
May 27	Japanese admiral Tōgō's combined fleet annihilates Russian admiral Rozhdestvenski's Baltic Fleet in the decisive Battle of Tsushima Straits.
September 5	The Treaty of Portsmouth, signed in New Hampshire, officially ends the Russo-Japanese War.
October 30	Czar Nicholas II issues the October Manifesto, promising a national legislature (Duma) for Russia.

SPENCER C. TUCKER

Further Reading

Busch, Noel F. *The Emperor's Sword.* New York: Funk and Wagnalls, 1969.

Connaughton, R. M. *The War of the Rising Sun and the Tumbling Bear: A Military History of the Russo-Japanese War, 1904–5.* New York: Routledge, 1998.

Corbett, Julian S. *Maritime Operations in the Russo-Japanese War, 1904–1905.* 2 vols. Rockville, MD: Sidney Kramer, 1994.

Date, John C. *Battle of Tsushima, 1905.* Garden Island, New South Wales: Naval Historical Society of Australia, 1993.

Evans, David C., and Mark R. Peattie. *Kaigun: Strategy, Tactics, and Technology in the Imperial Japanese Navy, 1887–1941.* Annapolis, MD: Naval Institute Press, 1997.

Forczyk, Robert. *Russian Battleship vs Japanese Battleship, Yellow Sea 1904–05.* New York: Osprey, 2009.

Grove, Eric. *Big Fleet Actions: Tsushima, Jutland, Philippine Sea.* London: Arms and Armour, 1995.

Hough, Richard. *The Fleet That Had to Die.* New York: Viking, 1958.

Jentschura, Hansgeorg, Dieter Jung, and Peter Mickel. *Warships of the Imperial Japanese Navy, 1869–1945.* Translated by David Brown and Antony Preston. Annapolis, MD: United States Naval Institute, 1977.

Jukes, Geoffry. *The Russo-Japanese War, 1904–1905.* Oxford, UK: Osprey, 2002.

Malozemoff, Andrew. *Russian Far Eastern Policy, 1881–1904.* Berkeley: University of California Press, 1958.

Matsumura Masayoshi. *Baron Kaneko and the Russo-Japanese War (1904–1905): A Study in the Public Diplomacy of Japan.* Translated by Edmund Morris. Morrisville, NC: Lulu, 2009.

Nish, Ian Hill. *The Origins of the Russo-Japanese War.* New York: Longman, 1985.

Novikov-Priboy, Aleksei. *Tsushima.* London: George Allen and Unwin, 1936.

Okamoto Shumpei. *The Japanese Oligarchy and the Russo-Japanese War.* New York: Columbia University Press, 1970.

Olender, Piotr. *Russo-Japanese Naval War, 1904–1905.* 2 vols. Sandomierz, Poland: Stratus, 2009–2010.

Paine, S. C. M. *The Sino-Japanese War of 1894–1895: Perceptions, Power, and Primacy.* New York: Cambridge University Press, 2003.

Papastratigakis, Nicholas. *Russian Imperialism and Naval Power: Military Strategy and the Build-Up to the Russo-Japanese War.* New York: I. B. Tauris, 2011.

Pleshakov, Constantine. *The Tsar's Last Armada: The Epic Voyage to the Battle of Tsushima.* New York: Basic Books, 2002.

Steinberg, John W., et al., eds. *World War Zero: The Russo-Japanese War.* Boston: Brill, 2007.

Tikowara, Hesibo. *Before Port Arthur in a Destroyer: The Personal Diary of a Japanese Naval Officer.* Translated by Robert Francis Sidney Grant. London: John Murray, 1907.

Tomitch, V. M. *Warships of the Imperial Russian Navy.* San Francisco: BT Publishers, 1968.

Warner, Denis, and Peggy Warner. *The Tide at Sunrise: A History of the Russo-Japanese War, 1904–1905.* Portland, OR: Frank Cass, 2002.

Watts, Anthony J. *The Imperial Russian Navy.* London: Arms and Armour, 1990.

Westwood, J. N. *Russia against Japan, 1904–05: A New Look at Russo-Japanese War.* Albany: State University of New York Press, 1986.

Mexican Revolution (1910–1920)

Causes

Throughout the summer of 1910, Mexicans prepared for an elaborate monthlong celebration of the centennial anniversary of the wars of independence that September. President Porfirio Díaz was elected to his eighth term in office, having already served for a 30-year period characterized by unprecedented political stability and economic prosperity. Díaz had faced, for the first time, a formidable challenge from an opposition candidate, Francisco Madero, but Madero's arrest and the usual electoral fraud produced an overwhelming victory for the 80-year-old president. Few observers could have predicted that Díaz would be swept from office the following May by tens of thousands of armed Mexicans who responded to Madero's call for "effective suffrage and no reelection." How did such an apparently stable and long-standing regime fall so quickly?

For decades after achieving independence from Spain in 1821, Mexico suffered from chronic political instability, economic stagnation, civil wars, and foreign interventions. In the absence of a central state capable of exercising sovereign political authority throughout the territory of Mexico, regional military strongmen, or caudillos, seized and lost power through military coups. Between 1821 and 1855, Mexicans witnessed 55 different presidencies, each lasting an average of less than one year, 35 of them held by military men. The most notable of the 19th-century caudillos, General Antonio López de Santa Anna, seized the presidency himself on nine different occasions.

Throughout this period, liberals and conservatives—the two main political factions in 19th-century Mexico, as elsewhere in Latin America—struggled to establish a central state capable of providing for political stability and economic development. The crux of the difference between the two groups was whether the state would be secular, limited in its powers, and federal in organization, as the liberals would have it, or centralized, powerful, and closely linked to the Catholic Church, as advocated by the conservatives. The liberals gained ascendancy in the Revolution of Ayutla (1854–1855), after ousting Santa Anna from the presidency for the final time and in the wake of Mexico's disastrous loss of half of its national territory to its northern neighbor in the Mexican-American War (1846–1848).

Beginning in 1855, the liberal government issued a series of far-reaching reforms designed to spark economic growth, radically curtail the power and activities of the Catholic Church, and foster a common national identity rooted in liberal citizenship. The most notable of these reforms was the 1856 Lerdo Law. It mandated that almost all property owned by civil and ecclesiastical corporations—including the Catholic Church, Indian villages, and municipalities—be privatized through sales to occupants and tenants.

The Church's extensive properties were ultimately nationalized and sold off in the context of the civil war generated by the liberal reforms. The privatization of municipal and village lands was a much longer, contested, and incomplete process. Liberals intended this property to remain in the hands of its mainly peasant cultivators, but in many regions and villages, wealthier residents and outsiders were able to acquire municipal and village lands through various types of sales, procedural irregularities, and fraud, giving rise to one of the central grievances that would later fuel the revolution.

The promulgation of the liberal constitution of 1857 set off a civil war between liberals and conservatives known as the War of the Reform (1858–1861). Just as the liberals, under the leadership of President Benito Juárez, defeated their conservative opponents, they faced intervention by the French (1862–1867) and the installation of Austrian archduke Ferdinand Maximilian as emperor of Mexico by Napoleon III. With the defeat and ouster of the imperial armies and the execution of Maximilian in 1867, leading liberals then began to fight among themselves. Díaz, a popular liberal general and hero in the war against the French, attempted to oust the increasingly autocratic Juárez from the presidency in the failed Rebellion of La Noria in 1872. Four years later, Díaz successfully unseated Juárez's successor, President Sebastián Lerdo de Tejada, in the 1876 Rebellion of Tuxtepec and assumed the presidency himself, although he did not take formal control until early 1877. Díaz ushered in a period of unprecedented political stability and economic development.

The period from 1876 to 1911 is known as the Porfiriato. Apart from a four-year period (1880–1884), Díaz held the presidency throughout. The famed Pax Porfiriana (Porfirian Peace) was achieved and maintained through a combination of coercion and patronage politics. The national police force (*rurales*), established by Juárez but greatly expanded by Díaz, maintained order in the countryside

through the suppression of both banditry and unruly peasants. Well aware of the dangers posed to his own rule by a large and politicized military, Díaz quickly brought the Federal Army under his control through a sweeping reorganization of the command structure and significant reductions in the numbers of both soldiers and officers. While this much smaller army was well trained and supplied during the Porfiriato, it proved incapable of defeating the revolutionary armies of 1910–1913.

The Porfiriato was a period of both constitutional and authoritarian rule. Díaz simply had the 1857 constitution amended by a compliant legislature whenever it suited his purposes to do so. Elections were held regularly for all levels of government, but in reality it was Díaz who appointed governors, members of the national legislature, and judges. Governors, meanwhile, controlled the state legislatures and appointed the all-important *jefes políticos,* local political bosses charged with implementing laws and maintaining order at the district and municipal level. Díaz thus ruled through complex patron-client networks held together by patronage, pragmatism, and personal loyalties. This order could not be maintained indefinitely, however. Toward the end of the Porfiriato, Díaz became much less adroit in his handling of these personalistic networks, imposing unpopular, abusive, and corrupt authorities on an increasingly resentful population. Furthermore, these networks were exclusionary, leaving large numbers of provincial elites and a growing rural and urban middle class with no means of competing for political power and few channels for expressing their grievances and demands.

Political stability, together with a massive influx of foreign capital, made possible a remarkable period of rapid economic growth in Mexico. Foreign companies, attracted by the very generous concessions offered to them by the Díaz government, invested heavily in railroads, mines, and textile mills. Mexican investors, meanwhile, took advantage of Porfirian land laws and the liberal Lerdo Law of 1856 to acquire vast new holdings, often at the expense of peasant villagers. On their new properties, they expanded production of agricultural export crops such as cotton, sugar, henequen, coffee, and beef. Both foreign and Mexican companies invested in the development of new industries producing for domestic and international markets, including textiles, shoes, cement, and glass.

The Porfirian economic boom brought great prosperity to many Mexicans (and foreigners), but it left the majority of the population—working country people—in precarious straits, landless or land poor, increasingly reliant on insecure wage labor, and unable to provide for their own subsistence in the face of declining food production and rising prices for basic goods. Furthermore, the model of export-oriented development adopted by the Díaz government rendered Mexico quite vulnerable to the vicissitudes of the international economy, as became readily apparent after 1907, when an economic downturn in the United States, corn and cotton crop failures in northern Mexico, falling international silver prices, and a reduction in the U.S. import quota for Mexican sugar all contributed to a deep economic crisis.

This economic crisis contributed to a political crisis, which in turn generated a revolution. Political opposition to Díaz had been growing for some time on the part of provincial landowners and middle-class groups that were excluded from political power and resented the intrusions of the Porfirian state into local and regional affairs. One of the more radical sources of opposition was the Mexican Liberal Party (PLM), founded by Ricardo Flores Magón in 1906 and home to numerous anarchists and socialists as well as anti-Díaz liberals. The PLM called for armed resistance to the Díaz government and encouraged labor militancy; PLM-backed strikes in the Cananea copper mines and the Rio Blanco textile mills in 1906 and 1907 resulted in the deaths of hundreds of workers, shot by the Federal Army. However, it was the (initially) far more moderate antireelectionist movement of Madero, a wealthy landowner and industrialist from the northern state of Coahuila, that would spearhead the first phase of the Mexican Revolution.

Running against Díaz in the presidential elections of 1910, Madero drew widespread support from Mexicans across social classes and regions. Recognizing the threat posed by his opponent, Díaz had Madero arrested in the summer of 1910 on the charge that he was fomenting rebellion; subsequently, Díaz declared himself to be the overwhelming winner of blatantly fraudulent elections. In response, Madero fled to the United States, where he issued the Plan of San Luis Potosí, declaring the recent elections void, designating himself as interim president, making a passing reference to the need for social reforms, and calling on all Mexicans to rise up in arms against the government on November 20, 1910.

A little more than five months later, Díaz was ousted from the office he had held for more than 30 years by the tens of thousands of Mexicans, mainly poor and mainly rural, who responded to Madero's call to revolution. Upon leaving for exile in Paris, Díaz was reported to have said,

Population Decline in Mexico during the Mexican Revolution

Year	Estimated Population	Life Expectancy at Birth (years)		Crude Birth Rate (per 1,000)		Crude Death Rate (per 1,000)	
		Male	Female	Male	Female	Male	Female
1910	15,160,000	28	31	49	46	35	33
1911	15,083,000	25	28	48	45	40	36
1912	15,007,000	18	22	52	48	53	46
1913	14,931,000	16	18	44	41	57	50
1914	14,855,000	15	17	44	41	59	52
1915	14,780,000	17	19	44	40	54	47
1916	14,705,000	19	22	44	40	49	42
1917	14,630,000	28	28	44	40	34	34
1918	14,556,000	25	26	44	40	38	36
1919	14,482,000	33	34	48	44	29	28
1920	14,409,000	30	31	50	46	34	32
1921	14,335,000	30	32	50	46	34	32
1922	14,566,000	30	32	50	46	34	31
1923	14,801,000	31	33	50	45	34	31

Sources: Robert McCaa, *Missing Millions: The Human Cost of the Mexican Revolution* (Minneapolis: University of Minnesota Population Center, 2001); B. R. Mitchell, *International Historical Statistics,* 3rd ed. (New York: Palgrave Macmillan, 1992).

"Francisco Madero has unleashed a tiger; now let's see if he can tame it." As would soon be apparent, Madero could not.

JENNIE PURNELL

Course

In 1910 Francisco Madero, a wealthy young landowner from a prominent Coahuila family in northern Mexico, announced his intention to challenge Díaz in the upcoming Mexican presidential election. Recognizing Madero as a threat, Díaz had Madero arrested at Monterrey and imprisoned in San Luis Potosí. Madero escaped, however, and declared the election, which had certainly been rigged, to have been a fraud. On October 5, 1910, Madero issued his Plan de San Luis Potosí, the thrust of which was a call for free suffrage and no reelection for the presidency (Díaz had espoused such in 1876 in the Plan of Tuxtepec but then had served multiple terms).

Declaring the Díaz regime illegal and himself as president pro temp until new fair elections could be held, Madero called for a revolution beginning on November 20 to oust Díaz from power. In his appeal, Madero also hinted at, but did not precisely spell out, land reform.

Madero's vague promises resonated with the Mexican peasantry, and in response to his appeals, uprisings occurred among a number of working-class groups, including agricultural laborers and miners. Much of the impoverished Indian population also rose up in support. Among rebel leaders rallying to Madero were Francisco "Pancho" Villa, Ricardo Flores Magón, Emiliano Zapata, and Venustiano Carranza.

Rebels took control of Mexicali and Chihuahua City, and there was a revolt in Baja California. On May 8–10, forces led by Villa and Pascual Orozco attacked and defeated Mexican federal troops at Ciudad Juárez across the Rio Grande from El Paso, Texas, as hundreds of El Pasoans watched from rooftops and train cars.

On May 21, 1911, Díaz signed the Treaty of Ciudad Juárez in which he agreed to abdicate in favor of Madero. Madero insisted on a new election as validation of his rule, which he won overwhelmingly in October 1911.

Although Madero had the support of the U.S. government and a number of revolutionary leaders, including Villa and Zapata, he proved to be a weak leader and incapable of instituting the demands for sweeping change awakened by the revolution. When Madero failed to honor his promise of land reform, on November 25, 1911, Zapata, leader of the Indian communities in the central state of Morelos, broke with the president and announced the Plan de Ayala. It called for an end to land "usurped" by the owners of the haciendas and the restoration of the *ejidos,* land farmed communally in a state-supported system.

Shortly thereafter, General Victoriano Huerta, head of the Federal Army that Madero had left intact, forced Madero to resign the presidency. Huerta had Madero executed on February 22, 1913, and then set about restoring Díaz's system of personal dictatorship.

Forces in the north led by Pancho Villa and Zapata were now joined by the army of General Venustiano Carranza, who emerged as the political leader of the renewed revolutionary effort.

The United States also entered the picture. Since August 1913 the idealistic President Woodrow Wilson had been trying to force Huerta from power, and from October U.S. warships were stationed off the Gulf of Mexico port of Tampico for the purpose of intimidation and as a show of force to protect U.S. lives and the considerable U.S. financial interests in Mexico. In this turbulent situation, an incident occurred at Tampico on April 9 when a boat party of seamen was mistakenly seized and then detained by Mexican authorities. Although the seamen were released and the local Mexican military commander expressed regret over the incident, U.S. rear admiral Henry Mayo, commanding the Fourth Division of the Atlantic Fleet, demanded a formal apology and a 21-gun salute to the U.S. flag. On April 11, Huerta apologized for the temporary arrest of the boat party, but he rejected Mayo's demand for a salute to the American flag.

President Wilson was determined that the salute be rendered. The Huerta government then agreed to the salute, providing that it was answered round for round. Although Mayo had stated in his original ultimatum that this would be the case, Wilson rejected this stipulation, and the U.S. Atlantic Fleet was ordered to concentrate off the east coast of Mexico. Meanwhile, Wilson learned of the scheduled arrival on April 21 at the principal Mexican port of Veracruz of the German freighter *Ypiranga* with a cargo of arms and ammunition for the Huerta government. Determined to stop the arms shipment from reaching Huerta and with the final U.S. deadline for the Mexican salute having expired, on April 18 Wilson went before a joint session of Congress to request a resolution authorizing him to employ force against Mexico. While the House of Representatives passed the resolution, a vote in the Senate was delayed until April 22.

Mexican revolutionary Pancho Villa (center) with a group of his men in 1910. (Time Trip/ Alamy Stock Photo)

Informed early on April 21 that the *Ypiranga* was scheduled to dock at Veracruz that morning and that trains were already in the port ready to move the arms to the Mexican interior, Wilson instructed Rear Admiral Frank Fletcher to land men and seize control of the customhouse at Veracruz in order to avert a possible diplomatic crisis with Germany over seizure of the ship. The Americans could thus take possession of the arms as they were landed.

The U.S. landing party of marines and seamen went ashore on the morning of April 21. Hopes that fighting could be averted were in vain, and additional U.S. forces then went ashore as the *Ypiranga* entered the harbor and anchored. (The ship departed Veracruz on May 3 and subsequently unloaded its arms southeast of Veracruz at Puerto [now Coatzacoalcos], Mexico.) U.S. forces ashore, now organized as a naval brigade of nearly 4,000 men and supported by naval gunfire, took control of Veracruz on April 22. The U.S. side suffered 17 dead and 63 wounded; at least 126 Mexicans were killed and 195 wounded. The next day, the U.S. Senate finally authorized Wilson to employ force against Mexico.

On July 15, Wilson achieved his goal when Huerta, his chief source of revenue in customs duties at Veracruz now cut off, resigned the presidency and fled abroad. (The seven-month U.S. occupation ended on November 23, with the withdrawal of the last U.S. troops.)

On August 15, 1914, Carranza's principal field commander, General Álvaro Obregón, signed a number of treaties in Teoloyucan in which the last of Huerta's forces surrendered to him and recognized Carranza. On August 20, Carranza entered

Mexico City in triumph and set himself up as head of the new government.

Despite recognition of Carranza by the major Latin American countries, unrest continued, with other rebel leaders claiming power for themselves and inflicting further suffering on the Mexican people. Carranza's principal opponents were Zapata, who resented Carranza's shift to the Right politically and sought to secure land for the peasants, and Villa, who came to dominate northern Mexico.

At the beginning of October, Carranza issued a call for a meeting of commanding military chiefs and governors. It took place in Aguascalientes in north-central Mexico during October 10–November 9, 1914, but Zapata did not attend, and the meeting failed in its goal of resolving the differences between the rivals for power. After the meeting, Villa and Zapata reconciled and agreed to collaborate against Carranza. On December 6, 1914, they entered Mexico City with a combined force of some 60,000 men. Carranza and his supporters fled to Veracruz.

Carranza's chief general Álvaro Obregón retook Mexico City on January 28, 1915. Departing Mexico City on March 10, he then engaged Villa in a series of battles, the principal one being near the city of Celaya in Guanajuato during April 13–15, 1915. Employing a defense in depth strategy that included trenches and machine guns, gleaned from his study of the fighting in Europe, Obregón rebuffed his opponent's headlong cavalry charges. In the battle Villa suffered some 4,000 men killed and 6,000 captured along with 32 guns taken. After the battle, 120 of Villa's officers who had been taken prisoner were executed.

Although Villa escaped and engaged Obregón's forces again into July, the Battle of Celaya effectively ended any hopes Villa had of taking power. Both Villa and Zapata continued small-level guerrilla operations. Meanwhile, Zapata's supporters were defeated in his base of Morelos.

Villa remained active, however, and once again the fighting in Mexico embroiled the United States. On November 26, Villa's forces, having occupied Nogales in Sonora, opened fire on U.S. Army soldiers in Nogales, Arizona. The two sides exchanged fire for some two hours until a Mexican force loyal to Carranza arrived and attacked the Villistas. Later that day, the Carranzaistas accidentally opened fire on the American soldiers, and another short skirmish was fought. The battle resulted in the deaths of several Mexicans and was the first significant engagement fought between Villistas and the U.S. military. Worse was to follow.

On January 11, 1916, Villistas stopped a train near Santa Isabel southwest of Chihuahua City and shot all 17 American mining engineers on board. Only 1 survived. On January 13, angry residents of El Paso attacked Mexicans and murdered a number of them. Then, on the night of March 9, Villa and some 600 of his followers crossed the border into the United States with the intent to seize weapons and ammunition at Camp Fulong, an army base three miles north of the border and just south of Columbus, New Mexico. Villa encountered more U.S. soldiers than expected and was forced to beat a hasty retreat, with more than 100 men killed. During the brief occupation of Columbus, however, Villa burned its central business district. Eighteen Americans, including 10 civilians, were killed in the raid.

President Wilson responded by ordering a large part of the U.S. Army and the entire National Guard of 110,000 men to the border. On March 15, under Wilson's directive, Brigadier General John J. Pershing led some 10,000 U.S. regulars into northern Mexico to hunt down Villa. The U.S. force reached some 300 miles into Mexican territory, but Villa escaped, and Carranza demanded that U.S. forces withdraw immediately. Wilson refused and countered with a demand for the release of 23 American soldiers captured by Mexican government forces. The Mexicans yielded on this point, but with war with Germany looming, Wilson withdrew all U.S. troops from Mexico by February 5, 1917, without their having captured Villa. A failure in its stated object, the so-called Punitive Expedition exacerbated tensions between the United States and Mexico.

In September 1916, meanwhile, Carranza issued a call for the election of deputies to a constitutional convention to convene in Querétaro on December 1, 1916. The convention produced the Constitution of 1917, which became the founding document of the new Mexican nation. It included a number of progressive ideas that, however, were not enacted right away. Violence abated somewhat following the assassination of Zapata in a government ambush at Chinameca in Morelos on April 10, 1919. Villa surrendered to government forces on July 28, 1920.

As his presidential term came to an end in 1920, Carranza supported Ignacio Bonillas to succeed him against the candidacy of General Obregón. This action earned the enmity of many in the army as well as Obregón, General Plutarco Elías Calles, and Sonoran governor Adolfo de la Huerta. They then led a rebellion against the government. On April 8 an aide to Obregón attempted to kill Carranza, who then fled Mexico City for Veracruz. Betrayed en route, he was assassinated at Tlaxcalantongo on May 21 by the forces of General Rodolfo Herrero. Felipe Adolfo de la Huerta served as provisional president until November, when Obregón was elected. Obregón commenced a period of stabilization during which the Constitution of 1917 was implemented, albeit selectively, and peace was restored.

SPENCER C. TUCKER

Consequences

The Mexican Revolution was the first of the major social revolutions of the 20th century and became a point of reference for all subsequent Mexican history. Though the fighting caused untold damage and cost nearly 1 million lives, the revolutionary leadership brought Mexicans together under new ideologies that included all social groups. Until very recently, all Mexican presidents have sought to identify with the revolution as the touchstone of Mexican politics. After its military phase of 1910–1920, the revolution was followed by two decades of reconstruction, revolutionary state formation, and, in the 1930s, radical reform.

The basic institutions of the postrevolutionary state were established between 1920 and 1940, and important aspects of Mexican society were transformed through the partial implementation of the 1917 Mexican Constitution—most notably its provisions regarding land redistribution, subsoil wealth, and the Catholic Church.

Some scholars point to continuities between the Porfirian and postrevolutionary states and argue that Mexico did not really experience a genuine revolution. Both states were highly centralized and interventionist, with powerful presidencies and compliant legislatures and courts. Both took an active role in promoting economic development: the Porfirian state directed foreign investment toward the agricultural and mining sectors, and the postrevolutionary state provided generous incentives for Mexican industrialists to produce for domestic markets and engaged in significant economic production itself in key sectors of the economy. (Carlos Salinas, president between 1988 and 1994, radically changed the role of the state in the economy when he adopted economic liberalism.)

Like the Porfirian state, the postrevolutionary state was, until quite recently, authoritarian, but it was authoritarian in a different way. The Partido Revolucionario Institucional (Institutional Revolutionary Party, PRI) monopolized political power at all levels and in all branches of government until the 1980s; it did not lose the presidency until the 2000 victory of Vicente Fox of the Partido Acción Nacional (National Action Party, PAN), making the PRI the longest-ruling party of the 19th century. But since the Lázaro Cárdenas administration, the PRI has been a very inclusive and pragmatic organization. While it has certainly served to control the demands of workers and peasants, it has also afforded them minimal representation and a fair amount of patronage. Co-optation through inclusion and patronage, rather than repression, has been the norm in dealing with opposition movements in postrevolutionary Mexico.

Mexican presidents since the revolution have wielded great powers, both constitutional and otherwise, but since 1934 they have wielded them for a limited period of time. Every six years the presidency has changed hands (reelection remains prohibited), bringing about wholesale changes in government personnel and thus providing many opportunities for elites who hanker after political power. Civilians have exercised firm control over the military since the 1940s, precluding the pattern of military

coups and brutal large-scale repression so common elsewhere in Latin America.

The most dramatic reforms of the revolutionary period occurred during the presidency of Cárdenas. Cárdenas, like Plutarco Elías Calles before him, implemented the many anticlerical policies of the 1917 constitution, drastically reducing the Catholic Church's role in education and preventing clergy, as individuals and as representatives of the Church, from participating in politics. Most Mexicans continue to identify themselves as practicing Catholics, but the Church has played only a minor role in Mexican politics since the revolution, in striking contrast to its importance in other Latin American countries.

In 1938, Cárdenas expropriated all foreign oil companies in Mexico, following a two-year dispute between oil workers and their U.S. and British employers, and created a state-owned oil company called Petróleos Mexicanos, or Pemex. The move was wildly popular in Mexico and was applauded throughout Latin America, although it caused considerable tension between Mexico and the United States until the matter of compensation was resolved. Public ownership of oil wealth remains a vital symbol of Mexican nationalism and sovereignty, even as Mexico has opened up some aspects of the petroleum industry to foreign investment and ownership.

Finally, Cárdenas carried out a sweeping redistribution of land that transformed property rights in the Mexican countryside. The political capital accrued through this reform helped to sustain the PRI through the 1980s. Over the course of his six years in office, Cárdenas distributed some 50 million acres of land to 11,000 agrarian reform communities, or *ejidos*. In contrast to his predecessors and successors, Cárdenas expropriated some of the richest and most productive land in the country, including vast cotton estates in the northern region of La Laguna, coffee plantations in Chiapas, and henequen plantations in Yucatán. The National Ejido Credit Bank was created to provide the new peasant beneficiaries (*ejidatarios*) with financing. By the time Cárdenas left office in 1940, almost half of the cultivated land in Mexico was held by 20,000 *ejidos* with more than 1.6 million peasant members.

Since 1940, most Mexican presidents have ignored the reformist provisions of the 1917 constitution (not to mention the democratic ones), but the very existence of the constitution, together with the PRI's adherence to a revolutionary discourse and its glorification of Mexico's revolutionary past, has always served to legitimize claims for redistributive justice and democratization. Repression has been real but limited; elections have been fraudulent but held on a regular basis and sometimes genuinely contested. With the emergence of a wide variety of social movements and opposition parties in the 1980s and 1990s (joining the much older PAN), Mexico has gradually undergone a profound, if still partial, process of democratization, even as many of the important redistributive provisions of the constitution have been eliminated.

JENNIE PURNELL

Timeline

1876

November	Mexican politician Porfirio Díaz forces President Sebastián Lerdo de Tejada to resign and early the next year formally assumes the presidency himself. The next three decades see unprecedented order and prosperity in Mexico.

1910

October 5	Francisco Madero issues his Plan de San Luis Potosí, calling for free suffrage and no reelection for the presidency. He also hints, but does not spell out, social change for the millions of disadvantaged rural Mexicans. Declaring the Díaz regime illegal, Madero calls for a revolution, beginning on November 20.
November 14	Madero supporter Toribio Ortega takes up arms and leads a group of followers at Cuchillo Parado, Chihuahua.
November 20	Official starting date for the Mexican Revolution.

1911

May 8–10	In the Battle of Juárez, troops supporting Madero, led by Francisco "Pancho" Villa and Pascual Orozco, attack and defeat Mexican federal troops in Ciudad Juárez.
May 21	Following successful revolts in a number of cities in northern Mexico and Baja California and a string of Mexican

Army defeats in battle, Díaz signs the Treaty of Ciudad Juárez in which he agrees to resign the presidency in favor of Madero. Díaz then goes into exile in France.

1911

October 11   Madero handily wins the Mexican presidential election.

November 25   With President Madero having failed to honor his promise of land reform, Emiliano Zapata, leader of the Indian communities in the central state of Morelos, announces his Plan de Ayala, which calls for the return to the peasantry of lands "usurped" by the owners of the haciendas and declares war on the government.

1913

February 18   Mexican general Victoriano Huerta topples the regime of President Madero in a coup d'état.

February 22   Huerta has Madero executed and then establishes an authoritarian regime similar to that of Díaz. Huerta is soon challenged in turn by a number of rivals, chief among them liberal politician Venustiano Carranza.

1914

April 9   Eight U.S. Navy sailors in a boat are mistakenly arrested at Tampico but are subsequently released.

April 22   Following the Tampico Incident, there is an impasse regarding a demand that the Mexican government order a salute to the U.S. flag, on which U.S. president Woodrow Wilson (who has been seeking to oust Huerta) insists. This and the expected arrival of a shipment of German arms at the port of Veracruz for the Huerta government lead Wilson to order U.S. forces to occupy the customhouse at Veracruz. On April 21 a landing force of marines and sailors goes ashore, but there is fighting. Following their reinforcement and shelling by U.S. ships offshore, U.S. forces establish control of Veracruz on April 22.

April 24   The U.S. government accepts an offer by the governments of Argentina, Brazil, and Chile (the ABC Powers) to mediate the dispute with the Huerta government, and U.S. forces are ordered not to undertake further offensive action at Veracruz.

May 4   Seventy-one U.S. Navy warships are operating in Mexican waters.

July 15	With U.S. forces having cut off Mexican president Huerta's chief source of revenue in the port of Veracruz, Huerta resigns the presidency of Mexico and flees abroad.
August 15	Leading Carranza general Álvaro Obregón signs treaties in Teoloyucan in which the last of Huerta's forces surrender to him and recognize Carranza.
August 20	Carranza enters Mexico City in triumph and sets himself up as head of the new government.
October 10–November 9	Carranza issues a call for a meeting of commanding military chiefs and governors, which occurs at Aguascalientes in north-central Mexico. Zapata does not attend, and the meeting fails in its goal of resolving the differences between the rivals for power.
November 23	The seven-month occupation of Veracruz comes to an end with withdrawal of the last U.S. troops.
December 6	Villa and Zapata, having reconciled, enter Mexico City with some 60,000 men. Carranza flees to Veracruz.

1915

January 6	Carranza's principal general Álvaro Obregón retakes Mexico City.
March 10	Obregón departs Mexico City to do battle with Villa.
April 13–15	Following a series of earlier inconclusive engagements, Mexican Army forces under Obregón defeat those under Villa in a major battle near the city of Celaya in Guanajuato. Although Villa escapes and continues to engage Obregón's men, the Battle of Celaya effectively ends any chance of Villa taking power.
November 26	Villa's forces, having occupied Nogales in Sonora, open fire on U.S. Army soldiers in Nogales, Arizona. The two sides exchange fire until forces loyal to Carranza arrive and attack the Villistas. The battle is the first significant engagement between Villistas and the U.S. military.

1916

January 11	Villa's forces stop a train and murder 16 American mining engineers at Santa Isabel in northern Mexico.
January 13	A race riot occurs in El Paso, Texas, in which a number of Hispanics are killed.
March 9	Villa and some 500 of his men raid Columbus, New Mexico, hoping to secure arms. Before withdrawing, they set fire to and destroy much of the business district

and kill 18 civilians and soldiers. Villa's own losses are perhaps 100 men.

In response to the raid, President Wilson orders a large part of the regular army and the entire National Guard of 110,000 men to the border.

March 15   The U.S. Punitive Expedition into northern Mexico begins. Some 10,000 U.S. regulars under Brigadier General John J. Pershing go into northern Mexico to hunt down Villa. Pershing moves some 300 miles into Mexican territory, but Villa escapes, and Mexican president Venustiano Carranza demands an immediate U.S. withdrawal. Wilson refuses and counters with a demand for the release of 23 American soldiers captured by Mexican government forces. The Mexicans yield, but with war with Germany now looming, Wilson withdraws all U.S. troops from Mexico by February 5, 1917, without having captured Villa.

December 1   A constitutional convention convenes in Querétaro. It produces the Mexican Constitution of 1917.

1917

March 1   The U.S. press publishes the Zimmermann Telegram. This January 19, 1917, communication from German state secretary for foreign affairs Arthur Zimmermann to German ambassador to Mexico Heinrich von Eckhardt calls on Eckhardt to approach the Mexican government about joining the war on Germany's side should the United States enter the war and also seek Mexican assistance in getting Japan to switch sides in the war. In return, Germany promises financial assistance and, following a German military victory, the return to Mexico of lands that it lost to the United States in 1848.

Publication of the Zimmerman Telegram creates widespread support, especially in the western part of the United States, for intervention on the Allied side in World War I.

1919

April 10   Zapata is killed in a government ambush at Chinameca in Morelos.

1920

April–July   With his presidential term coming to a close, Carranza supports a civilian, Ignacio Bonillas, to succeed him against General Álvaro Obregón. This earns the enmity of many in the army as well as Obregón, General Plutarco Elías Calles, and Sonoran governor Adolfo de la Huerta. They now lead a rebellion against the government. On April 8, 1920, an aide to Obregón attempts to assassinate Carranza, who flees Mexico City for Veracruz. He is betrayed en route and is assassinated at Tlaxcalantongo on May 21 by the forces of General Rodolfo Herrero. De la Huerta is provisional president until November, when Obregón is elected, beginning a period of stabilization.

1920

May 28   Felipe Adolfo de la Huerta becomes interim president.

July 28   Mexican bandit and revolutionary Pancho Villa surrenders to government forces.

November   General Obregón is elected president of Mexico, implementing the Mexican Constitution of 1917 and restoring peace.

SPENCER C. TUCKER

Further Reading

Benjamin, Thomas. *La Revolución: Mexico's Great Revolution as Memory, Myth and History.* Austin: University of Texas Press, 2000.

Brading, David, ed. *Caudillo and Peasant in the Mexican Revolution.* Cambridge: Cambridge University Press, 1980.

Brunk, Samuel. *Emiliano Zapata: Revolution & Betrayal in Mexico.* Albuquerque: University of New Mexico Press, 1995.

Cumberland, Charles C. *Mexican Revolution: Genesis under Madero.* Austin: University of Texas Press, 1952.

Fallaw, Ben. *Cárdenas Compromised: The Failure of Reform in Postrevolutionary Yucatán.* Durham, NC: Duke University Press, 2001.

Garner, Paul. *Porfirio Díaz.* White Plains, NY: Longman, 2001.

Gilly, Adolfo. *The Mexican Revolution.* New York: Norton, 2005.

Gonzales, Michael J. *The Mexican Revolution, 1910–1940.* Albuquerque: University of New Mexico Press, 2002.

Hart, John M. *Revolutionary Mexico: The Coming and Process of the Mexican Revolution.* Berkeley: University of California Press, 1987.

Joseph, Gilbert M., and Daniel Nugent, eds. *Everyday Forms of State Formation: Revolution and the Negotiation of Rule in Mexico.* Durham, NC: Duke University Press, 1994.

Katz, Friedrich. *The Life and Times of Pancho Villa.* Stanford, CA: Stanford University Press, 1998.

Knight, Alan. *The Mexican Revolution.* 2 vols. Lincoln: University of Nebraska Press, 1990.

Meyers, William K. *Forge of Progress, Crucible of Revolt: Origins of the Mexican Revolution in La Comarca Lagunera, 1880–1911.* Albuquerque: University of New Mexico Press, 1994.

Perry, Laurens Ballard. *Juárez and Díaz: Machine Politics in Mexico.* DeKalb: Northern Illinois University Press, 1978.

Quirk, Robert E. *The Mexican Revolution and the Catholic Church, 1910–1919.*

Bloomington: Indiana University Press, 1973.

Roeder, Ralph. *Hacia El México Moderno: Porfirio Díaz.* [Toward Modern Mexico: Porfirio Díaz]. Mexico City: Fondo de Cultura Económica, 1973.

Ruiz, Ramón Eduardo. *The Great Rebellion: Mexico, 1905–1924.* New York: Norton, 1980.

Smith, Robert Freeman. *The United States and Revolutionary Nationalism in Mexico, 1916–1932.* Chicago: University of Chicago Press, 1972.

Smith, Stephanie J. *Gender and the Mexican Revolution: Yucatán Women and the Realities of Patriarchy.* Chapel Hill: University of North Carolina Press, 2009.

Tutino, John. *From Insurrection to Revolution in Mexico: Social Bases of Agrarian Violence, 1750–1940.* Princeton, NJ: Princeton University Press, 1986.

Villegas, Daniel Cosío. *The United States versus Porfirio Díaz.* Translated by Nettie Lee Benson. Lincoln: University of Nebraska Press, 1963.

Womack, John. *Zapata and the Mexican Revolution.* New York: Vintage Books, 1970.

Balkan Wars (1912–1913)

Causes

The First Balkan War (1912–1913) was a sharp and bloody conflict in Southeastern Europe that led to World War I. Most of Southeastern Europe had come under Ottoman domination by the end of the 14th century. Afterward, Montenegro maintained a precarious autonomy from Ottoman rule. By the first half of the 19th century, Greece, Serbia, and Romania established independent regimes. After their defeat of the Ottoman Empire in the Russo-Turkish War of 1877–1878, the Russians established a large Bulgarian state in the Treaty of San Stefano of March 3, 1878.

Objections from Austria-Hungary and Great Britain caused a revision of the settlement at the Congress of Berlin in July 1878. San Stefano, Bulgaria, was trisected into a Bulgarian principality under the nominal suzerainty of the Ottoman sultan, the Ottoman province of Eastern Rumelia with an Orthodox Christian governor, and Macedonia under the direct rule of the Ottoman sultan. Montenegro, Romania, and Serbia received formal Great Power recognition as states independent of all ties to the Ottoman Empire. Thereafter all the Balkan states sought to overturn the Berlin settlement to realize their nationalist goals within the Ottoman Empire. The political elite of all of these states were convinced that only by attaining their nationalist objectives could they develop as modern states. In this line of thinking, Germany and Italy served as examples.

These states, including Bulgaria, Greece, Montenegro, and Serbia, all harbored irredentist aspirations against the Ottomans. Many of these aspirations overlapped, especially in Macedonia. Bulgarian, Greek, and Serbian nationals all claimed Macedonia as a part of their national irredentas. All of the Balkan states sponsored cultural efforts as well as armed bands in Macedonia. For some time these rivalries precluded the formation of a Balkan alliance directed against the Ottomans. The Young Turk Revolution in 1908 and its objective of an Ottoman revival, however, engendered closer cooperation among these Balkan states.

An opportunity for the realization of their nationalist objectives arose when the weakness of the Ottomans became apparent during the Italo-Ottoman War of 1911–1912. The Albanian uprisings that had begun in 1910 also demonstrated the feeble condition of the Ottoman state. With the support of Russia, which sought to regain the position lost in Southeastern Europe during the Bosnian Crisis of 1908–1909, Bulgaria and Serbia signed an alliance on March 13, 1912. This alliance contained provisions for the rough division of Ottoman territories. It recognized Bulgarian claims in Thrace and Serbian claims in Albania. It also included a provision for a partition of Macedonia into a Bulgarian zone and a "contested zone" in northwestern Macedonia to be arbitrated by the Russian czar if Macedonian autonomy proved to be unworkable. Bulgaria and Serbia then signed bilateral agreements with Greece and Montenegro during the spring and summer of 1912. Other than the Bulgarian-Serbian agreement, the Balkan allies made little effort to arrange division of any territories conquered from the Ottomans. The Bulgarians in particular had little confidence in the Greek Army and were convinced that they could realize their objectives in Macedonia ahead of the Greeks. Bulgaria's failure to delineate its claims in Macedonia with Greece led to great complications after the First Balkan War and was a major cause of the Second Balkan War.

While the First Balkan War arose from the strong desire of the Orthodox Christian governments in the Balkans to realize their nationalist claims to Ottoman territory, the Second Balkan War came about because of conflicting claims to Ottoman territory, especially Macedonia. During the initial phase of the First Balkan War, Serbian troops overran northern Albania and most of Macedonia. In December 1912 Austria-Hungary made its opposition to a Serbian presence in northern Albania clear.

The recognition that they could not realize their claims to northern Albania made the Serbs determined to hold on to the parts of Macedonia they had occupied, despite the 1912 treaty with Bulgaria. In 1913, the Serbs requested a revision of the 1912 treaty. The Bulgarians, still fighting at Adrianople, ignored the Serbian request. By March 1913, Bulgarian and Greek soldiers were skirmishing in contested regions of Macedonia.

On May 5, Greece and Serbia concluded an alliance directed against Bulgaria. Meanwhile, the Romanians pressed their claims for compensation from Bulgaria. As the largest Orthodox Christian state in Southeastern Europe, the Romanians regarded themselves as the "gendarme" of the Balkans. As the extent of the Balkan League victories became clear, the Romanians sought to maintain their position in the Balkans by seeking compensation in Bulgarian Dobrudzha. After their military successes against the Ottomans, the

Bulgarians were reluctant to part with any of their own territory.

The Protocol of St. Petersburg on May 8, 1913, awarded the northeastern Bulgarian town of Silistra to Romania. This decision left both Bulgaria and Romania dissatisfied. When the Bulgarians became embroiled in conflict with their allies, the Romanians utilized the circumstances to seize not only Silistra but all of Bulgarian Dobrudzha.

After the signing of the Treaty of London, the Bulgarians quickly transferred the bulk of their army from Thrace to Macedonia to enforce their claims against the Greeks and Serbs. Discontent at the long time of service without respite emerged in the Bulgarian ranks. The command urged the government to use the army or send it home. On the night of June 29–30, Czar Ferdinand ordered General Mihail Savov to take action. Savov then ordered the army to undertake local attacks to improve its tactical position. These attacks against the Greeks and Serbs began the Second Balkan War.

RICHARD C. HALL

Course

The First Balkan War began on October 8, 1912, with fighting between Montenegro and the Ottoman Empire. Bulgaria, Greece, and Serbia entered the war on October 18. Each of the Balkan allies separately confronted their common enemy. In many ways the armies of the Balkan League were similar. They all followed European models for staff work, training, logistics, communication, and sanitation. Many officers had received education at Great Power military schools. They all depended on conscripted peasants to fill their ranks. They all had a variety of equipment from European sources.

A disabled and abandoned artillery piece during the Second Balkan War in 1913. (Hulton-Deutsch/Corbis)

The Bulgarians had the largest army among the Balkan allies, with around 350,000 men after mobilization. Volunteers from the Macedonian revolutionary organizations supplemented the Bulgarian ranks. The Greeks were able to field around 110,000 men. Alone among the Balkan allies, the Greeks possessed a substantial navy that, in addition to 8 destroyers, 19 torpedo boats, and 1 submarine, included the formidable armored cruiser *Georgios Averov.* The Montenegrin Army essentially was a partially trained militia consisting of most of the males of military age in the country. This amounted to around 36,000 men. Montenegrin immigrants in the United States returned home to add to the Montenegrin force. The Serbian Army had a mobilized strength of 230,000 men.

The Ottomans had the largest single army, with the potential of 450,000 men. This army, however, lacked the homogeneity of the Balkan forces. Armenian, Greek,

and Slavic soldiers in the Ottoman army could not be expected to fight loyally for the Ottoman sultan. Although the Young Turk regime had implemented some reforms after 1908, these were not yet fully realized. Also, the Ottoman forces were distributed throughout the empire. Some were fighting an insurgency in Yemen, some were still in Ottoman North Africa, and others were in Anatolia, Mesopotamia, and Syria. At the beginning of the war the Ottomans had approximately 300,000 in their European provinces. The Ottomans also had a navy that included a modern light cruiser, the *Hamidiye*; a modern armored cruiser, the *Mecidiye*; and a number of other vessels.

The Ottoman armies were deployed as the First (Eastern or Thracian) Army under the command of Abdullah Pasha and the Second (Macedonian or Western) Army led by Ali Risa Pasha. The most important theater was in Thrace. The Bulgarians committed the majority of their forces to confront the main Ottoman army that was in position to defend the Ottoman capital. Unwisely, the Ottoman commander initiated an offensive, which the Bulgarians easily deflected. They responded with a strong offensive through northeastern Thrace. The Bulgarian armies were under the nominal command of Czar Ferdinand but were led by deputy commander in chief General Mihail Savov. The Bulgarian First Army, led by General Vasil Kutinchev, and General Radko Dimitriev's Third Army overcame Ottoman resistance at Kirk Killase (Lozengrad) and at a massive battle raging from Buni Hisar (Pinarhisar) to Lyule Burgas (Lule Burgaz). This later event was the largest European battle between the Franco-Prussian War and World War I.

At the same time, General Nikola Ivanov's Second Army first masked and then surrounded and besieged the Ottomans at Adrianople (Edirne). The Second Army did not immediately attempt to take the well-fortified former Ottoman capital. The Bulgarian offensive thrust the Ottomans to their final defensive positions at Chataldzha (Catalca), about 20 miles outside of Constantinople. The presence of the Bulgarian First and Third Armies outside of Constantinople caused some disconcertion among the Great Powers, especially the Russians. Only on November 16–17 did Ottoman forces rally to defeat a Bulgarian attempt to cross the Chataldzha lines and seize their capital. Smaller Bulgarian units, meanwhile, proceeded against little opposition into the Rhodopes and western Thrace and on toward Salonika.

In the western theater, Greek Army troops advanced in two directions against slight opposition. The main thrust of the Greek advance was directed at Salonika. The Army of Thessaly under the command of Crown Prince Constantine soon overran its namesake region, defeating a small Ottoman force at Yanitsa on November 1. After negotiations with the Ottoman commander of Salonika, Hassan Tahsin Pasha, the Greeks entered Salonika on November 8, only a day ahead of the Bulgarian unit moving south from Bulgaria across the Rhodopes with the same objective. An uneasy condominium ensued in that city.

The Army of Epirus, led by General Constantine Zapundsakis, moved into Epirus and besieged the important town of Janina (Ioannina). A unit of Italian volunteers led by Ricciotti Garibaldi, the son of Giuseppe, participated in this campaign. The Greeks did not immediately surround the town, so it was able to withstand their initial assaults. The Greek Navy seized the Aegean Island of Tenedos on October 20. This effectively closed the straits. The Greeks then held the Ottoman fleet at bay and occupied most of the rest of the Aegean Islands, including Chios and Mytilene.

The Montenegrins had two objectives: the Sandjak of Novi Pazar and the northern Albanian town of Scutar (Shkoder). In pursuit of these objectives they divided their forces into three groups. The nominal commander of all the Montenegrin forces was King Nikola. The Eastern Division, commanded by Brigadier Janko Vukotich, advanced into the Sandjak of Novibazar, while most of the rest of the Montenegrin forces advanced toward the northern Albanian town of Scutari (Shkoder). The Zeta Division, led by Crown Prince Danilo, moved along the eastern shore of Lake Scutari toward its objective, while Brigadier Mitar Martinovich's Coastal Division proceeded along the western shore of the lake. Despite several direct assaults, Scutari held firm. The Montenegrins fought bravely but without many of the apparatuses of a

Balkan Wars: Estimated Deaths

Country	Estimated Population	Estimated Armed Forces	Estimated Deaths
Bulgaria	4,430,000	607,000	30,000
Serbia	2,910,000	175,000	5,000
Greece	2,630,000	90,000	4,750
Montenegro	247,000	30,000	2,000
Turkey	23,000,000	400,000	50,000

Source: Valery Kolev and Christina Koulouri, eds., *The Balkan Wars,* 2nd ed. (Thessaloniki, Greece: Center for Democracy and Reconciliation in Southeast Europe, 2009).

modern army. This undoubtedly hampered their ability to take Scutari.

The Serbian chief of staff, Vojvoda Radomir Putnik, planned an all-out attack on the Ottomans. He arrayed their forces in four main groups. The largest group, the Serbian First Army, commanded by Crown Prince Alexander, advanced from the north into Macedonia. Meanwhile, the Serbian Second Army, the main part of the Serbian army, moved south into Macedonia. The Second Army easily defeated the Ottomans at Kumanovo in northern Macedonia on October 23–24 and then after engagements at Prilep and Bitola (Monastir) proceeded to occupy most of the rest of Macedonia. Meanwhile, the Serbian Second Army, under General Stepa Stepanovich, invaded Macedonia from Bulgarian territory in order to cut off any Ottoman units retreating south.

The Serbian Third Army, commanded by General Bozhidar Jankovich, overran Kosovo, the emotional center of Serbian nationalism. The Third Army proceeded on to Skoplje and from there crossed over the Albanian Alps into Albania. On November 28, elements of the Serbian Third Army reached Durres (Durazzo) on the Adriatic coast. This was the cause of great disconcertion for the Austro-Hungarians and Italians. Two smaller Serbian units

entered the Sandjak of Novi Pazar. Having achieved their initial aims quickly and without heavy losses, the Serbs agreed to a Bulgarian request to send troops to participate in the siege of Adrianople and to a Montenegrin plea for help at Scutari. The Serbian Second Army went to Thrace to help the Bulgarians at the end of October 1912. Elements of the Serbian Third Army had assisted the Montenegrins at Scutari since December 1912. In February 1913, the Serbs sent an additional 30,000 man force and some artillery to help the Montenegrins.

By the time the warring parties agreed to an armistice on December 3, the only territories in Europe remaining to the Ottomans were the besieged cities of Adrianople, Janina, and Scutari; the Gallipoli Peninsula; and the part of eastern Thrace behind the Chataldzha lines.

While the Balkan allies and the Ottomans assembled in London on December 16 to negotiate a peace settlement, the ambassadors of the Great Powers credentialed to Great Britain convened nearby to direct the course of the peace settlement and protect their own interests. The London Ambassadors' Conference, on the insistence of Austria-Hungary and Italy, recognized the independence of an Albanian state that some Albanian notables had proclaimed in Vlore (Valona) on November 28, 1912. This state blocked Serbian and Montenegrin claims to territories on the eastern shore of the Adriatic Sea. These claims had the strong support of Russia.

At the same time, the Austrians demanded that Serbian troops evacuate those portions of northern Albania occupied that autumn. The Great Powers were able to forestall the outbreak of war between Austria-Hungary and Russia over this issue. Talks between the Balkan allies and the Ottomans soon stalled, mainly over the issue of Adrianople, and hostilities resumed on February 3, 1913.

Fighting during this second round mainly occurred at the three besieged cities of Adrianople, Janina, and Scutari. On March 6, Janina fell to the Greeks. On March 26, the Bulgarians, with some Serbian help, took Adrianople. The Montenegrins and assisting Serbian units bogged down around Scutari. A major assault in February failed. Only on April 23, after the departure of the Serbs under pressure from the Great Powers, did the Montenegrins succeed in entering the city after three days of negotiations with the exhausted defenders. The major powers, especially Austria-Hungary, refused to sanction a Montenegrin occupation of Scutari because the London Ambassadors' Conference had assigned it to the new Albanian state. After threats and a show of force, together with the promise of generous subsidies, the Montenegrins evacuated Scutari.

Elsewhere elements of the Serbian First Army fought with the remnants of the Ottoman Second Army in central Albania. Also, the Bulgarians deflected Ottoman attacks at Bulair on the Gallipoli Peninsula and an Ottoman landing at the port of Sharkoi on the Sea of Marmara. The Ottomans intended these efforts to take the pressure off the defenders of Adrianople and possibly even to break through to them. Also, fighting resumed at the Chataldzha positions. After the fall of the three besieged cities, both sides were exhausted.

On Ottoman initiative, the Bulgarians agreed to an armistice on April 15. The other Balkan allies did not participate in this second armistice. On May 30, 1913, the Balkan allies and the Ottomans signed a peace treaty in London. With the Treaty of London, the Ottoman Empire ceded its European territories west of a straight line drawn between Enos and Media (Enez-Midye). This result clearly was preliminary. By the time of the signing of the Treaty of London, friction among the Balkan allies over the division of Macedonia had risen to a great degree. The Second Balkan War ensued soon thereafter.

The Second Balkan War began on the night of June 29–30, 1913, when Bulgarian deputy commander in chief General Mihail Savov, frustrated by Russian inactivity and worried about growing discontent in the army's ranks, launched probing attacks on the orders of Czar Ferdinand against Greek and Serbian positions in Macedonia. This order was given without the direct knowledge of the Bulgarian government, which was struggling to persuade the Russians to uphold their arbitration obligations from the March 1912 Bulgarian-Serbian Treaty.

Bulgarian prime minister Stoyan Danev countermanded the attack order, and General Savov complied. This caused Czar Ferdinand to fire Savov and replace him with First Balkan War hero Radko Dimitriev. The retraction of orders and change of command, however, had the effect of causing great initial confusion in the Bulgarian Army. While some units fought, others stood aside.

The Greeks and Serbs utilized the Bulgarian attacks to implement their alliance, and the Second Balkan War ensued. In southern Macedonia near Shtip, from July 1–4 the Serbian First and Third Armies inflicted heavy casualties on the Bulgarian Fourth Army and forced it back to the Bergalnitsa River. At the same time, King Constantine's Greek Army defeated General Nikola Ivanov's Bulgarian Second Army at Kilkis and squeezed it out of much of southeastern Macedonia. Greek forces quickly overran and captured Bulgarian troops stationed in Salonika to enforce Bulgarian claims to that city. Bulgarian forces retreated from the Greeks and Serbs toward their prewar frontiers. At the Battle of Kalimantsi on July 18, 1913, Bulgarian troops gained a defensive success and prevented the Serbian Army from entering the territory of prewar Bulgaria.

By this time, however, the situation for Bulgaria had worsened to the east and the north. Taking advantage of the situation, Romanian and Ottoman troops joined in the attack on Bulgaria. The Romanians objected to the establishment of a strong Bulgaria on their southern frontier and sought compensation in the town of Silistra and in southern Dobrudzha. The Ottomans sought to recover Adrianople.

The Bulgarians found themselves attacked on all sides. With their entire army committed to the fight against the Greeks and Serbs, they lacked forces with which to oppose the invading Ottomans and Romanians. The Ottomans reoccupied Adrianople on July 23 without firing a shot. Romanian units advanced against no opposition almost all the way to Sofia.

The result was a Bulgarian catastrophe. In the subsequent Treaty of Bucharest (August 10, 1913) with Greece, Montenegro, and Serbia and the Treaty of Constantinople (September 30, 1913) with the Ottoman Empire, the Bulgarians had to acknowledge complete defeat and the loss of much of the gains from the First Balkan War.

RICHARD C. HALL

Consequences

The two Balkan wars changed the map of Southeastern Europe. A fragile Albanian state emerged, largely dependent on the Great Powers. They did not determine its final borders until the Council of Florence in February 1914. Even then, Greek and Serbian armed bands encroached on the territory of the new state. The big winners were Greece and Serbia. Greece obtained clear title to Crete and also obtained Epirus, including the city of Janina; a large portion of southern and western Macedonia, including Salonika; and the Aegean Islands. These areas added around 2 million people to the Greek population.

Serbia acquired Kosovo and much of Macedonia, almost doubling its territory and adding almost 2 million to its population. Significantly, much of this new population was not Serbian. Serbia and Montenegro divided the Sandjak of Novibazar between them. Montenegro also gained small areas on its southern border with the new Albanian state.

Bulgaria, even after defeat in the Second Balkan War, gained the Rhodope region; central Thrace, including the insignificant Aegean port of Dedeagach; and a piece of Macedonia around Petrich. Much of the population of these regions was not Bulgarian. These people included Greeks, Pomaks (Bulgarian-speaking Muslims), and Turks. Romania obtained southern (Bulgarian) Dobrudja (Dobrudzha). In this region of mixed ethnicity there were relatively few Romanians. The Ottoman Empire, which had held large European territories since the 14th century, was almost totally eliminated from Europe by the Treaty of London. In the Second Balkan War, the Ottomans managed to regain eastern Thrace, which remained its only possession in Europe.

The Balkan wars created major population movements. Victorious Bulgarian armies in Thrace and Serbian armies in Kosovo and the Sandjak of Novi Pazar committed atrocities against the Muslim populations of these regions. This caused some Muslims to seek safety in Constantinople and Albania. After the Second Balkan War, pro-Bulgarian Macedonians moved out of Greek- and Serbian-controlled areas. Some Bulgarians also left southern Dobrudzha after the Romanian occupation.

The Balkan wars were the first armed conflicts on European soil in the 20th century and in many ways presaged World War I. Mass attacks against entrenched positions, concentrated artillery barrages, and military use of airplanes made their first appearances in European warfare. Losses to disease among both civilians and military personnel were significant. These presaged the great influenza epidemic of World War I.

The larger European powers mainly ignored the lessons of the Balkan wars. There was not enough time between the end of the Second Balkan War and the opening of World War I to process information. Nor did many of the General Staffs of the Great Powers think that the experience of the Balkan states had anything to teach them.

The two wars resulted in at least 150,000 military dead, with the Bulgarians and Ottomans suffering the heaviest losses. Many more soldiers were wounded or missing. The armies of the Balkan League killed thousands of mainly Muslim civilians during the First Balkan War. Ottoman armies in retreat vented their frustration on local Orthodox Christian populations. During the Second Balkan War, Bulgarian troops killed Greek civilians, and Greek and Serbian soldiers killed Bulgarian and pro-Bulgarian Macedonian civilians. These wars also brought about the deaths from disease of tens of thousands of civilians.

The Balkan wars left a legacy of frustration for the Bulgarians and the Ottomans, providing a basis for continued conflict in World War I. For the Bulgarians, the loss of Macedonia for a second time was especially frustrating. San Stefano and Bucharest became conflated. They sought redress on the side of the Central Powers in World War I, where they would lose Macedonia for a third time. Likewise, the Ottomans sought to regain some of their lost possessions and contemplated war against Greece in the spring of 1914. They too found themselves fighting on the side of the Central Powers in World War I.

Montenegro had almost doubled its population and territory in the Balkan wars. Montenegrin gains, however, were not the result of the success of Montenegrin arms. The wars had demonstrated the antiquated nature of King Nikola's personal regime and the deficiencies of the Montenegrin Army. In the competition between the Montenegrin Petrovich dynasty and the Serbian Karageorgevich dynasty for leadership of the Serbian national cause, the Karageorgeviches emerged as the clear winners as a result of the Balkan wars.

The Balkan wars also imparted a sense of inflated national success among the Greeks, Romanians, and Serbs. On two occasions during the Balkan wars, Austria-Hungary had resorted to threats of force against Serbia to protect Albania.

The Austrians would make one more such threat in October 1913 before finally resorting to force. Less than a year after the signing of the Treaty of Bucharest, war again erupted in Southeastern Europe after the assassination of Archduke Franz Ferdinand in Sarajevo by a Bosnian Serb terrorist. The resulting Third Balkan War metamorphosed into World War I.

The Second Balkan War left Serbia as Russia's only important client on the Balkan Peninsula. It also reoriented Bulgaria from Russian patronage toward Austria-Hungary and Germany. Both of these consequences were important in the development of World War I. Russia had to support Serbia in July 1914 or risk exclusion from the Balkan Peninsula, while Bulgaria joined the Central Powers in September 1915.

Within the next five years, all of the participants in the Balkan wars would become involved in further disastrous and costly conflicts. Many of the same battlefields of the Balkan wars, such as Gallipoli and Doiran, again saw fighting. During World War I, the populations of Southeastern Europe again made great sacrifices for the nationalist aims of the political elite.

RICHARD C. HALL

Timeline

1878

March 3   Created from territory of the Ottoman Empire, a large Bulgaria comes into being under the terms of the Treaty of San Stefano.

1910   Uprisings against Ottoman rule occur in Albania.

1912

March 13   Bulgaria and Serbia conclude an alliance.

May 5   Greece and Serbia conclude an alliance directed against Bulgaria.

October 8   The First Balkan War (1912–1913) begins with a declaration of war by Montenegro against the Ottoman Empire. Bulgaria, Serbia, and Greece follow suit. Fighting begins on October 18, with the allied Balkan states invading Ottoman territory.

October 20   Greek naval forces take the island of Tenedos in the Aegean.

October 22   Bulgarian forces are victorious over the Ottomans at Kirk Kilissé in Thrace.

October 23–24   Serbian forces defeat the Ottomans in the Battle of Kumanovo.

October 28–November 3   The Bulgarians defeat the Ottomans in the important Battle of Lule Burgas. The Bulgarians then advance to the Chataldzha lines, the last Ottoman defense before

Istanbul (Constantinople). The Russian government warns the Bulgarians not to occupy Istanbul.

November 8	Greek forces enter Salonika. Bulgarians enter the next day.
November 10	Serbian forces, having overrun southern Albania, reach the Adriatic Sea.
November 16–18	The Serbs defeat the Ottomans in the Battle of Monastir, and the remaining Ottoman forces fall back on Florina. The Serbs now control southwestern Macedonia.
November 17–18	Bulgarian forces attack the Ottoman Chataldzha line before Istanbul, but their assault fails.
November 24	Austria-Hungary, determined to block Serbian access to the Adriatic Sea, threatens military intervention. This announcement triggers an acute international crisis. Vienna calls for the creation of an independent Albania. Italy supports the Austrians, while Russia backs Serbia. France promises assistance to Russia in the event of war with Germany, while Germany reluctantly promises its support to Austria if that country is attacked while defending its legitimate interests. Britain, sympathetic with the Austrian position, seeks to work with Germany to produce a settlement while at the same time seeking to avoid alienating France and Russia. The crisis reaches a head in late November–early December when both Austria and Russia begin to mobilize. It recedes when Russia, clearly unready for war, withdraws its support of Serbian territorial claims.
November 28	Serbian forces reach Durazzo on the Adriatic.
December 3	An armistice is concluded between the Ottoman Empire, Bulgaria, and Serbia. Greece does not participate, however.
December 16	The London Peace Conference opens. An attempt to end the war, it breaks up on January 23, 1913, with a coup d'état in Istanbul.

1913

January 23	A day after representatives of the Great Powers convince the Ottoman government to yield Adrianople, a coup d'état occurs in Istanbul (Constantinople). Kamil Pasha is overthrown by Turkish nationalists known as the Young Turks, headed by Enver Bey. The new government refuses to yield Adrianople, the Aegean Islands, and Crete.

February 3	The First Balkan War resumes.
March 4–6	The Greeks defeat the Ottomans in the Battle of Bazini.
March 21	Greek forces capture Janina from the Ottomans.
March 26	Bulgarian forces capture Adrianople.
April 16	Bulgaria and the Ottoman Empire conclude an armistice, to which the other warring Balkan powers soon accede.
April 22	Montenegrin troops capture Scutari despite protests from the major powers, which had assigned it to Albania. In early May under threat of war from Austria-Hungary, the Montenegrins abandon Scutari, and the Serbs evacuate Durazzo.
May 8	In the Protocol of St. Petersburg, the major powers award Silistra to Romania, to compensate Romania for Bulgarian gains elsewhere.
May 30	Peace talks having resumed on May 20, 10 days later under a British ultimatum the Balkan states accept the settlement arranged by the Great Powers and sign the Treaty of London, ending the First Balkan War. Under its provisions, the Ottoman Empire cedes to the Balkan states its territory in Europe beyond a line drawn from Enos near the mouth of the Maritza River on the Aegean Sea to Midia on the Black Sea. The Sanjak of Novi Pazar is divided between Serbia and Montenegro, while Bulgaria receives Thrace north of the line between Enos on the Aegean Sea and Midia on the Black Sea. There is no definitive decision regarding the division of Macedonia because of disagreements among the Balkan states. Albania is declared independent, with Serbia, Montenegro, and Greece to withdraw their forces and the boundaries of Albania to be decided by the Great Powers. The Ottoman Empire cedes Crete to the Balkan allies, renouncing all rights of sovereignty. The Great Powers are to decide the fate of the islands in the Aegean Sea (except for Crete) and the status of Mount Athos.
June 1	The Balkan states having fallen to quarreling among themselves over the spoils of the war, Greece and Serbia conclude an alliance against Bulgaria, following the latter's refusal to grant them more of Macedonia than had been agreed to in the treaty of March 13, 1912. Bulgaria is willing to submit this to arbitration by Russia, but Serbia evades this.

June 29	The Second Balkan War begins. With Greece and Serbia planning war against Bulgaria, the major territorial winner in the First Balkan War, Bulgarian Army commander General Mihail Savov orders a preemptive attack on Greek and Serbian positions without informing Bulgarian premier Stojan Danev. Although the Bulgarian government disavows Savov's action, the Serbs and Greeks take advantage by mounting their long-prepared attack on Bulgaria. They are joined by Romania and even the Ottoman Empire. Bulgaria is defeated by July 30.
July 1–4	The Serbs defeat the Bulgarians in eastern Macedonia at the Bergalnitsa River, while the Greeks defeat the Bulgarians in southern Macedonia at Kilkis.
July 18	In the Battle of Kalimantsi, the Bulgarians win a defensive victory and prevent the Serbs from entering Bulgarian territory.
July 23	Ottoman forces reoccupy Adrianople.
August 10	The Second Balkan War officially comes to an end with the Treaty of Bucharest. Romania receives northern Dobrudja; Serbia and Greece take those parts of Macedonia that they occupied during the war, including Monastir and Ochrid to Serbia and Salonika (today Thessaloniki) and Kavalla to Greece. Bulgaria retains only a small bit of Macedonia. Along the Aegean Sea, Bulgaria keeps only a small stretch of land between the Mesta and Maritza Rivers, along with the small port of Dedeagatch.
September 23	Following Albanian raids into territory assigned to Serbia under the Treaty of London, the Serbian Army invades Albania.
September 29	The Treaty of Constantinople is concluded between the Ottoman Empire and Bulgaria. Under its terms, the Ottoman Empire recovers in Europe Adrianople and territory up to the Maritza River.
October 18	Austria-Hungary threatens to intervene in Serbia unless the Serbs withdraw from Albania within eight days. The Serbs reluctantly comply.
October 30	Austria-Hungary and Italy demand that Greece withdraw its troops from southern Albania by December 31.
December 13	British foreign secretary Sir Edward Grey proposes that southern Albania be divided between Greece and Albania, with Greece to receive compensation in the Aegean

Islands. Although this is finally accepted, the Greeks do not evacuate southern Albania until the end of April 1914, after which the dispute over the Aegean continues. By June 1914 there is a real danger of war between Greece and the Ottoman Empire. Both Balkan wars and their aftermath have threatened to draw in the big powers and bring world war.

SPENCER C. TUCKER

Further Reading

Despot, Igor. *The Balkan Wars in the Eyes of the Warring Parties.* Bloomington, IN: iUniverse, 2012.

Erickson, Edward J. *Defeat in Detail: The Ottoman Army in the Balkans, 1912–1913.* Westport, CT: Praeger, 2003.

Hall, Richard C. *The Balkan Wars, 1912–1913: Prelude to the First World War.* London and New York: Routledge, 2000.

Hellenic Army General Staff. *A Concise History of the Balkan Wars, 1912–1913.* Athens: Army History Directorate, 1998.

Helmreich, E. C. *The Diplomacy of the Balkan Wars, 1912–1913.* Cambridge, MA: Harvard University Press, 1938.

International Commission to Inquire into the Causes and Conduct of the Balkan Wars. *The Other Balkan Wars.* Washington, DC: Carnegie Endowment, 1993.

Kiraly, Bela K. *East Central European Society and the Balkan Wars.* New York: Columbia University Press, 1987.

Thadden, Edward C. *Russia and the Balkan Alliance of 1912.* University Park: Pennsylvania State University Press, 1965.

Vachkov, Alexander. *The Balkan War, 1912–1913.* Sofia: Angela, 2005.

World War I (1914–1918)

Causes

Impetus for a general European war had been building for decades, and all the major European powers bore some measure of responsibility for the war that began in 1914. Historians usually identify five underlying causes: nationalism (the triumph of statism over internationalism but also the desire of subject minorities to have their own nation-states), two hostile alliance systems, imperialist and trade rivalries, an arms race, and economic and social tensions.

Nationalism was the major impetus, and nowhere was this more obvious than in Austria-Hungary, a mélange of at least a dozen minorities. Germans (23 percent) and Magyars (19 percent) dominated, but early in the 20th century Slavic nationalism, championed by neighboring Serbia, threatened the Dual Monarchy. Enjoying the support of Russia, Serbia had long sought to be the nucleus of a large state embracing all the southern Slavs. In 1908, in an effort to diminish Serb influence and cut it off from access to the sea, the Dual Monarchy annexed Bosnia-Herzegovina. This almost brought war with Russia. Austria-Hungary also insisted on the creation of an independent Albania.

Germany—Europe's preeminent military power—was Austria-Hungary's closest ally and supported its action in Bosnia-Herzegovina. The German Empire had come into being as a consequence of the Franco-Prussian War of 1870–1871. Having imposed a draconian peace settlement on France, German chancellor Otto von Bismarck sought to isolate that country, which was bent on revenge. An arrangement with both Austria-Hungary and Russia (the Dreikaiserbund, or Three Emperors' League) shattered on their competition in the Balkans. Forced to choose, Bismarck in 1879 selected Austria-Hungary as Germany's principal ally. This Dual Alliance was the bedrock of German foreign policy into World War I. Not prepared to cast Russia adrift, however, in 1887 Bismarck concluded the so-called Reinsurance Treaty with it, which he kept secret from Austria.

As long as Bismarck was chancellor France remained isolated, but in 1888 Wilhelm II became emperor. Young, rash, and headstrong, he soon clashed with Bismarck and in 1890 dropped him as chancellor and dramatically changed Germany's foreign policy. Relations with Russia were already frayed, but the situation was made worse when in 1890 Wilhelm ordered that the Reinsurance Treaty not be renewed. Russia was rapidly industrializing and seeking foreign capital, and France stepped into the breach. By 1894 the two had forged a military alliance against Germany.

Thus, by 1914 there were two mutually antagonistic alliance systems in Europe. The first consisted of Germany and Austria-Hungary. Separate from it was the Triple Alliance of 1882 of Germany, Austria-Hungary, and Italy, made possible because of Italian anger over France's seizure of Tunis, but Italy was an increasingly reluctant ally.

France and Russia formed the second alliance, to which Britain was informally linked. During World War I the latter three (with Japan and then Italy after 1915) became known as the Entente Powers, the

Entente, the Allied Powers, or simply the Allies. Germany and Austria-Hungary (later the Ottoman Empire and Bulgaria) were, for their geographical location, the Central Powers.

Wilhelm II was not content with Germany being the preeminent European power; he wanted it to be the preeminent world power. He reversed Bismarck's wise policy of not building a strong navy so as not to antagonize Britain, and the result was a naval-building contest between the two powers beginning in the mid-1890s. Wilhelm II and Grand Admiral Alfred von Tirpitz saw Germany challenging Britain on the seas for world mastery. Wilhelm II's bellicose actions alienated would-be allies and created a climate of uncertainty. Many Germans, however, saw themselves encircled and denied their rightful place in the sun.

The economic transformation experienced by Germany after 1871 brought social change and worker unrest, the rise of socialism, and the antagonism of most political parties toward the government, which despite a democratic veneer was controlled by the kaiser and the military. Some German leaders saw a general European war as a means to unite the country.

France also looked forward to war. In addition to an indemnity of more than twice the cost of the war to Prussia, the Treaty of Frankfurt of 1871 had stripped France of Alsace and Lorraine. French foreign policy after 1871 is said to have been dominated by one word: revenge. France had found immediate gratification in empire building, but this almost brought war with Britain. In 1904, however, the two ended decades of rivalry in an agreement on colonial issues. Britain and Russia concluded a similar arrangement in 1907.

Russia was beginning to enter the modern age, although Czar Nicholas II would

The headstrong Wilhelm II became kaiser, or German emperor, at age 29 in 1888. Determined to make Germany the leading world power, he had profound influence in bringing about World War I. (Library of Congress)

make no concessions to political change. Russia sought ascendancy in the Balkans and control of the straits to ensure free access from the Black Sea into the Mediterranean. Humiliated in the Russo-Japanese War (1904–1905), Russia had expended considerable resources in rebuilding its military. Russian industrial and military growth, which included the construction of new strategic railroads, raised alarm bells in Berlin. Chief of the German General Staff Colonel General Helmuth von Moltke said in May 1914 that in several years Russia would be rearmed and the Entente Powers would then be so powerful that it would be difficult for Germany to defeat them. Germany therefore had no alternative but to seek a preventive war while there was a chance of victory.

Britain followed its traditional pattern of involving itself in continental affairs only to preserve vital national interests or the European balance of power, but Germany's decision to build a powerful navy drove Britain to the side of France. The British also viewed growing German industrial might and trade as a threat. Although aligned with France and Russia, Britain had as its sole military responsibility in 1914 a 1912 pledge to protect France's coasts from German naval attack.

Several crises almost brought general European war in the decade before 1914. Two, in 1905–1906 and 1911, involved Morocco when Germany, with no vital interests at stake, threatened war to block a French takeover. In 1908 war almost erupted over Austria's annexation of Bosnia-Herzegovina, but Russia backed down. In 1911 Italy went to war with the Ottoman Empire to secure present-day Libya and the Dodecanese Islands. Then in 1912 and 1913 two regional wars raged in the Balkans, both of which had threatened to draw in the big powers and bring world war.

In 1914 a Serb nationalist organization linked to the Serbian military undertook the assassination of Archduke Franz Ferdinand, heir to the Austrian throne and believed to favor greater rights for Slavs within the Dual Monarchy. This was a threat to Serbian aspirations. On June 28, 1914, in Sarajevo, Bosnia, young Bosnian Serb nationalist Gavrilo Princip shot to death Franz Ferdinand and his wife as they rode in an open car. This event touched off World War I, also known as the Great War.

Austrian leaders sought to use the assassination to advantage, envisioning a localized Balkan conflict in which the Serbian question would be settled "once and for all." But Austria required German support, as this might bring on a general European war. Russia had backed down in 1908, but this made a second retreat less likely. German leaders were well aware that Austria-Hungary intended to attack Serbia, but because the Dual Monarchy was its only reliable ally, on July 6, 1914, Berlin again pledged its support in the famous blank check.

On July 7 Vienna proposed a surprise attack on Serbia, but the Hungarians insisted on diplomacy first. To cloak the intention to crush Serbia, the Austro-Hungarian council of ministers approved an ultimatum couched so that Serbia must reject it. On July 22 Germany approved the terms, and a day later the ultimatum was sent to Belgrade with the demand for a reply within 48 hours.

To the world's surprise, Serbia responded within the time limit, accepting all the Austrian demands except those directly impinging on its sovereignty but offering to accept arbitration by the Hague Court or a decision of the big powers regarding these. Vienna declared the response unsatisfactory, severed diplomatic relations with Serbia, and ordered partial military mobilization; Serbia had already mobilized.

In St. Petersburg the Russian government hoped to bluff Vienna into backing down by ordering "preparatory measures" for a partial military mobilization. This step on July 26 had the support of the Russian General Staff, which believed that war was inevitable.

On July 28 the Third Balkan War began when Austria-Hungary formally declared war on Serbia; later that day it commenced shelling Belgrade. On July 29 Russia ordered actual mobilization in four Russian military districts. Czar Nicholas II made the decision only with great difficulty and after an exchange of telegrams with Kaiser Wilhelm. On July 30 Russia ordered a general mobilization. This ensured that the Balkan war would become a general European conflict, for military timetables came into play.

In planning for the possibility of a two-front war against France and Russia, General of Cavalry Alfred von Schlieffen, chief of the German General Staff during 1891–1906, envisioned sending most German military strength against France with a holding action against a slowly mobilizing Russia. Following the rapid defeat of France, Germany would then deal with Russia. Implicit in this was that Germany could not allow the Russians to mobilize and still win the war. The German government therefore demanded that Russia halt its mobilization. With no answer forthcoming, on August 1 Germany ordered general mobilization.

The French cabinet had refused to mobilize the army but did order troops to take up position on the frontier, although far enough from it so as to convince British public opinion that France was not initiating hostilities. The Schlieffen Plan, however, mandated that there be no delay in opening an attack against France. Thus, on August 1 the Germans demanded to know how France would respond to war between Germany and Russia. Berlin insisted that even if France pledged neutrality, it would have to surrender certain eastern fortresses as proof of sincerity. No French government could agree to this, and Premier René Viviani replied that France would act in accordance with its interests. That same day France ordered military mobilization. On August 3, Germany declared war on France.

SPENCER C. TUCKER

Course

Chief of the German General Staff Field Marshal Count Alfred von Schlieffen believed that the quickest way to defeat France was to invade through Belgium. When the Belgians rejected a demand for the right of transit through their country, on August 4 the Germans invaded. This brought Britain into the war. Italy declared its neutrality, but within a few weeks the Ottoman Empire joined the Central Powers, while Japan sided with the Allies.

For the Allies, the most potent weapon was the British Royal Navy. Britain also had the world's largest merchant marine, vital for transporting war materials. With 19 million tons of shipping, it counted half the world's total.

On land, the advantage lay with the Central Powers. Germany had the world's largest army and the second-largest reserve of male citizens (Russia had the largest). France had the next-largest army but was weak in reserves because its population was 25 million less than that of Germany, although it could draw on its colonial population.

Considering everything, the Allies were stronger than the Central Powers. The Allies had a larger military force and a far larger population (279 million to 120 million). The Allies were also better placed economically. If the war could be prolonged and other factors remained equal, economics and demography would give the Allies victory.

The Germans had no intention of fighting a prolonged war, however. Their advance into Belgium occasioned only a delay of several days. Schlieffen's successor, General Helmuth von Moltke, made significant modifications to the original plan, however. Moltke reduced the heavy balance in favor of the right wing in order

WESTERN FRONT, 1914

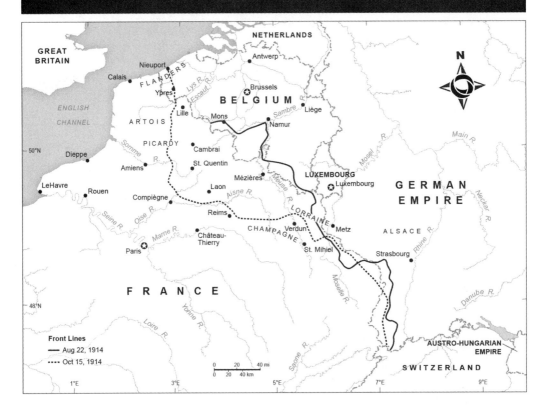

to strengthen the left wing against an expected French offensive. Then, because the Russians moved faster than anticipated, Moltke detached some 80,000 men from the right wing and sent them east. Given the excellent French rail net that allowed rapid troop movements, the Schlieffen Plan might not have worked in any case, but Moltke gave it no chance.

Meanwhile, French Army chief of staff General of Division Joseph Joffre committed three of his five armies to a massive offensive to retake Alsace and Lorraine. Only one army, the Fifth Army, was in the critical area of the Belgian frontier. Joffre's offensive met quick defeat, but thanks to the railroads, he was able to quickly shift forces northward.

The small but well-trained British Expeditionary Force (BEF) arrived in France, but soon it and the French were forced to withdraw. By September 4 five German armies pressed along a line that sagged below the Marne River only some 25 miles east and northeast of Paris. The city's fall seemed certain.

Joffre ordered a stand. The ensuing Battle of the Marne (September 5–12) involved more than 2 million men and was the most important of the war. The Allies were able to exploit a gap between two German armies, but the Germans then withdrew in good order. What the French would call the "Miracle of the Marne" had denied Germany the quick victory it needed to win the war, and on September

14 General of Infantry Erich von Falkenhayn replaced Moltke as chief of the German General Staff.

A race to the sea ensued, with each side endeavoring to turn the other's flank and the Germans trying to capture the English Channel ports. The sanguinary First Battle of Ypres (October 22–November 22) marked the end of the war of movement on the Western Front and began that of trenches and stalemate.

The front extended some 350 miles from the English Channel to the Swiss frontier. Both sides constructed dugouts and laid barbed wire. Trenches were necessary for protection against the machine guns and quick-firing artillery. From the end of 1914 until early 1918, there was no change of more than 10 miles in the front lines, with the sole exception of a 1917 voluntary German withdrawal from the Noyon salient. Joffre was convinced that his armies could break through and pressed the offensive. Large-scale attacks that winter and the next spring targeting the Noyon salient that pointed toward Paris were all costly failures.

There was also heavy fighting on the Eastern Front. Owing to the length of the front, combat here was much more fluid. The Russians agreed to strike early to divert German strength east, but they also chose to make a major effort against Austria-Hungary. Still, Russian forces enjoyed a manpower advantage of three to one over the Germans in East Prussia. The Russians, however, were deficient in weapons and logistical support, and the Germans knew Russian plans through intercepted radio communications.

Two large Russian armies invaded East Prussia in mid-August, but they were separated by the physical barrier of the Masurian Lakes. Colonel General Paul von Beckendorff und Hindenburg assumed command in East Prussia, with Major General Erich Ludendorff as his chief of staff. Leaving a single cavalry division to oppose the northern Russian army, they sent the rest south by train and won an overwhelming victory in the Battle of Tannenberg (August 26–31), then returned north and defeated the other Russian army in the First Battle of the Masurian Lakes (September 7–13).

The Russians did enjoy success against Austria-Hungary, defeating it in eastern Galicia and pushing more than 100 miles to the Carpathian Mountains. In late September the Russians laid siege to the Austrian fortress of Przemyśl and were in position to outflank Germany's major industrial center of Silesia.

Hindenburg took the offensive in Poland and reached almost to Warsaw before withdrawing to counter the anticipated Russian offensive in Silesia, defeating the Russians in the battles at Łódź and Łowicz in November and forcing their withdrawal. The Austrians captured Belgrade on December 2, but the Serbs counterattacked and by the end of the year had cleared Serbia of the invaders.

At sea, the Royal Navy chased down German merchant ships or drove them into neutral ports. Two naval battles occurred off South America. In the Battle of Coronel (November 1), the German East Asia Squadron destroyed a British squadron in the first defeat for the Royal Navy at sea in a century. A more powerful British squadron turned the tables on December 8 in the Battle of the Falklands. The submarine became Germany's most effective weapon at sea. On September 22, one German submarine sank three old British cruisers off the Dutch coast, marking a new era in naval warfare.

The Ottoman Empire's entry into the war brought fighting in the Middle East and Caucasia. The British sent Indian Army forces to protect oil facilities in Mesopotamia and to Egypt to guard the Suez Canal. There was also heavy fighting between Russian and Ottoman forces in Caucasia, where the Russians generally had the upper hand until 1917.

In Asia, Japan capitalized on the preoccupation of the Western powers with Europe to further its imperial ambitions. Japanese troops captured the German holdings in China and the German Pacific islands north of the equator. Japan also sought, unsuccessfully, to establish a protectorate over China.

Fighting occurred in Africa, where French, British, and imperial (South African) forces moved against the German colonies. Despite initial Allied success, German colonel Paul von Lettow-Vorbeck, with only some 14,000 German and native African troops, tied down 300,000 British, South African, Belgian, and Portuguese troops in German East Africa, Mozambique, and Rhodesia until the end of the war.

The Germans employed poison gas in the Second Battle of Ypres (April 22–May 25), although the defenders managed to seal the breach it created. Thereafter the Allies developed their own poison gas, and both sides introduced gas masks.

Italy joined the war in 1915. Both sides courted Italy, but the Allies could offer territory at the expense of Austria-Hungary, and on May 23 Italy declared war on the Dual Monarchy. Italian Army commander General Luigi Cadorna made his major efforts along the Isonzo River, but the Austrians beat back four Italian offensives there in the second half of the year.

In 1915 on the Eastern Front, the Germans defeated the Russians in the Second Battle of the Masurian Lakes and also turned back the Russian Silesian offensive. However, in March the fortress of Przemyśl and its 110,000-man garrison surrendered to the Russians, who then resumed their Carpathian advance. German reinforcements helped halt them in late April. In early May the Central Powers retook Przemyśl and occupied Lviv. The Russians then withdraw all the way to the Bug River. The Central Powers had retaken all territory lost in 1914.

The Central Powers resumed their southern offensive in July and captured Lublin. In August the Russians abandoned both Warsaw and Brest-Litovsk. By early September the Polish salient ceased to exist, and the Germans stood on Russian soil. Vilnius (Vilna) fell on September 19.

Yet another front opened in 1915 in the Dardanelles Campaign. British leaders, chiefly First Lord of the Admiralty Winston Churchill, sought to use their sea power advantage in what was one of the war's most controversial campaigns and great missed opportunities. Churchill planned to force the straits, open a southern supply route to Russia, and threaten a bombardment of Constantinople to drive the Ottomans from the war. He assumed that this could be accomplished by ships alone.

The British and French assembled a powerful naval force off the Dardanelles. Only two Ottoman infantry divisions were in position to oppose a landing, and had Allied troops been sent, the operation probably would have been successful. The Allied March 18 naval effort to force the Dardanelles ended in failure, because Ottoman howitzers ashore prevented the minesweepers from doing their work and the ships encountered a small, recently laid minefield.

The campaign continued, but as a land operation. Both sides committed additional resources, but Ottoman reinforcements

Estimated Casualty Statistics of World War I

	Total Mobilized	Killed in Action or Died of Wounds	Wounded	Captured	Missing	Civilian Dead	Ships Lost
United States	4,355,000	126,000	234,300	7,500	116,700	750	3
United Kingdom	8,904,467	908,371	2,090,212	140,000	51,650	292,000	162
France	8,410,000	1,375,800	4,266,000	175,300	361,700	500,000	35
Russia	12,000,000	1,700,000	4,950,000	2,417,000	1,221,300	1,500,000	46
Italy	5,615,000	650,000	947,000	569,000	31,000	1,021,000	23
Japan	800,000	300	907	0	3	0	5
Austria-Hungary	7,800,000	1,200,000	3,620,000	1,344,700	855,300	700,000	6
Germany	11,000,000	1,773,700	4,216,058	1,049,800	103,000	692,000	291
Ottoman Empire	2,850,000	325,000	400,000	145,000	95,000	2,150,000	5

Sources: Michael Clodfelter, *Warfare and Armed Conflict: A Statistical Reference to Casualty and Other Figures, 1618–1991* (Jefferson, NC: McFarland, 1992); Joan Ellis and Michael Cox, *The World War I Databook* (n.p.: Aurum, 2002); Susan Everett, *The Two World Wars,* Vol. 1, *World War I* (n.p.: n.p., 1980); Boris Urlanis, *Wars and Population* (n.p.: University Press of the Pacific, 1971).

prevented the Allied troops sent ashore at Gallipoli from breaking free. The subsequent Allied evacuation (completed on January 9, 1916) was the only well-executed part of the campaign.

In 1915 also, the Austrians opened a new offensive against Serbia, aided by Bulgaria's entry in the war. The Central Powers promised Bulgaria Macedonia, and on October 11 Bulgaria attacked. The British and French made only a halfhearted effort to aid Serbia before withdrawing to Salonika and evacuating the 75,000 Serb survivors who made it to Albania. In the Middle East, largely Indian Army forces advanced on Baghdad, only to be forced back, besieged, and forced to surrender at Kut-al-Amara (December 7–April 29, 1916).

Meanwhile, the Royal Navy tightened its blockade of Germany. In February 1915 Germany responded with unrestricted submarine warfare, declaring the waters around Great Britain and Ireland a war zone and every ship including neutral vessels subject to attack. On May 7 a German submarine torpedoed the British passenger liner *Lusitania* off southwestern Ireland. At least 124 of the 1,201 dead were Americans, but U.S. president Woodrow Wilson set himself against war.

Continued loss of American lives in other attacks did bring heavy American pressure and a temporary halt to unrestricted submarine warfare. In March the Germans pledged that merchant ships would not be sunk without warning and provision for the safety of those aboard.

Airplanes came into their own in 1915. Since they proved invaluable for reconnaissance and artillery observation, fighter aircraft were developed to shoot down the enemy reconnaissance planes. By 1917, aircraft had become an integral part of ground operations. Both sides also employed strategic bombing: the Germans used lighter-than-air zeppelins and then twin-engine bombers to strike London. Aircraft also saw service at sea, although the Royal Navy was the only nation to employ aircraft carriers in combat.

The year 1916 saw the war's two biggest land battles and its largest sea battle. Falkenhayn was well aware that time was working against Germany. He reasoned that one big push might drive France from the war. His objective was the fortress city of Verdun in a narrow salient protruding into German-controlled territory. Believing that the French would commit all available manpower to defend Verdun, Falkenhayn planned a battle of attrition.

The Germans struck on February 21. General of Division Henri Philippe Pétain assumed command. As Falkenhayn anticipated, Verdun became a matter of national honor for the French, but this also kept the Germans from breaking off their attack. The French held and in the fall were able to take the offensive. The battle claimed some 1,220,000 casualties, 420,000 of them killed.

On July 1, meanwhile, the British initiated the Battle of the Somme. The attackers encountered a sophisticated German defense in depth and, by the end of the first day, had sustained 57,470 casualties (19,240 of them killed), almost half of their force. German losses were about 8,000. Confident of eventual success, BEF commander General Douglas Haig continued the offensive. On September 15 he employed tanks for the first time in the war. The offensive finally ended on November 19. It was the war's costliest battle.

The British suffered some 420,000 casualties, the French 195,000, and the Germans 650,000.

The Battle of Jutland of May 31–June 1, 1916, was the biggest naval engagement of the war. Both sides had anticipated a major fleet encounter in the North Sea that might decide world mastery. This almost occurred when the British and German fleets met off the Jutland Peninsula. The entire German High Seas Fleet of 101 ships was at sea. Its commander, Admiral Reinhard Scheer, hoped to catch and destroy part of the British Grand Fleet, but unknown to him the entire Grand Fleet of 151 ships under Admiral Sir John Jellicoe was at sea. When Scheer realized the odds, he turned for home. The Germans claimed victory, as the British suffered far higher casualties and lost 14 ships to only 11 for the Germans, but the blockade remained in place, and the Germans now halted major surface operations in favor of submarines.

The Italian front remained inconclusive in 1916, despite five more Italian Isonzo offensives and the Austrian Trentino or Asiago Offensive. In the Battle of Lake Naroch (March 18–April 14) on the Eastern Front, the Germans blunted a Russian drive to relieve pressure on Verdun. The Austrian Trentino Offensive brought an appeal from Italy, and the Russians then approved a new offensive against Austria-Hungary. Commanded by General Aleksei Brusilov, it was aimed at Galicia and western Ukraine. When the Central Powers moved resources there, General Aleksei Evert's powerful northern army group was to launch the main Russian drive toward Vilnius.

Brusilov instituted a number of new procedures to ensure surprise, and his offensive of June 4–September 20 achieved spectacular early success before running

EASTERN FRONT, 1914–1918

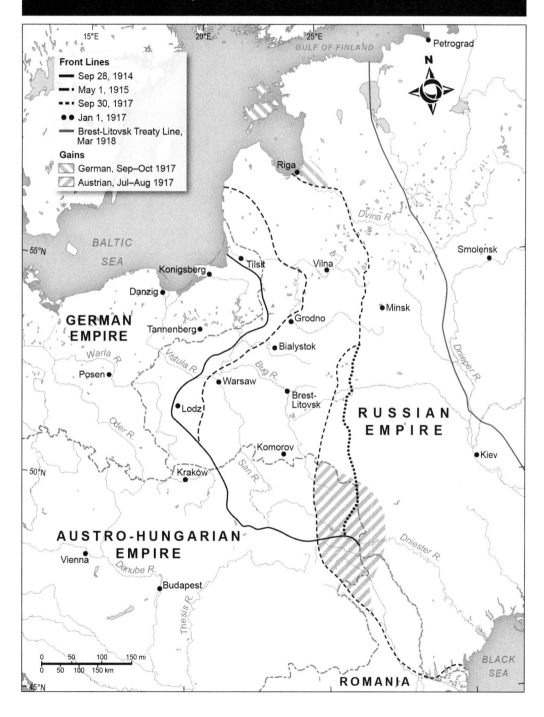

Front Lines
— Sep 28, 1914
–·– May 1, 1915
--- Sep 30, 1917
●● Jan 1, 1917
▬ Brest-Litovsk Treaty Line, Mar 1918

Gains
German, Sep–Oct 1917
Austrian, Jul–Aug 1917

GULF OF FINLAND

Petrograd

15°E   20°E   25°E

N

Riga

Dvina R.

Smolensk

BALTIC SEA

55°N

Tilsit

Vilna

Konigsberg

Danzig

Minsk

GERMAN EMPIRE

Tannenberg

Grodno

Bialystok

Warla R.

Vistula R.

Bug R.

Posen

Warsaw

Brest-Litovsk

RUSSIAN EMPIRE

Lodz

Oder R.

Komorov

Kiev

50°N

San R.

Kraków

AUSTRO-HUNGARIAN EMPIRE

Dniester R.

Vienna

Danube R.

Budapest

Thesis R.

BLACK SEA

0   50   100   150 mi
0   50   100   150 km

45°N

ROMANIA

Dnieper R.

afoul of supply shortages and lack of reserves. Evert, however, although enjoying a superiority of three to one in men and guns, failed to move in time, dooming any chance for success.

The Germans insisted that the Austrians transfer forces from the Italian front, and they sent their own troops south, checking Brusilov and eventually forcing him to abandon his gains. Nonetheless, this was Russia's greatest feat of arms of the war. It marked the end of the Dual Monarchy as a military power, may have saved the Italians, and weakened the German attack at Verdun.

The Brusilov Offensive brought Romania into the war. Its leaders had long coveted Hungarian Transylvania. Fearing that it might now fall to the Russians, they signed a secret treaty whereby the Allies promised them Transylvania and other territory. The Allies also pledged a simultaneous Russian advance and an offensive from Salonika. On August 27, 1916, Romania invaded Hungary. Romania's army was, however, poorly trained and led and short of equipment. Russian assistance also did not materialize.

Romania's entry into the war brought Falkenhayn's dismissal and his replacement with Hindenburg, who shifted the major German effort to the Eastern Front. By the end of the year Romania had been defeated, giving the Central Powers its agriculture. They also could now hold their eastern lines with fewer troops.

At the end of 1916 the Allies agreed to continue the Western Front as the critical sector of war, with the French Army to mount the major offensive in 1917. General of Division Robert Nivelle replaced Joffre in December 1916, but Nivelle's plan for massive frontal assaults against well-fortified defensive positions was essentially the same failed tactic of the preceding two years. Also, in the spring of 1917 the Germans shortened their front by withdrawing 20 miles and eliminating the Noyon salient in favor of the excellent new defensive positions of the Siegfried Stelling, known to the Allies as the Hindenburg Line.

The Germans were well aware of Nivelle's intentions, having captured a set of plans in a trench raid. Nivelle persisted nonetheless. The Nivelle Offensive, also known as the Second Battle of the Aisne and the Third Battle of Champagne, began on April 16 and involved some 1.2 million French soldiers but produced few gains. Nivelle had promised to halt it immediately if it was unsuccessful, but he did not do so. The attacks continued until May 9, resulting in widespread French Army mutinies. Pétain now replaced Nivelle as commander of the army. Pétain visited the disaffected units, promised to address complaints, and pledged no future attacks without real hope of success.

Meanwhile, the United States entered the war. In probably the most fateful decision of the entire conflict, the German government resumed unrestricted submarine warfare on February 1. Without this Russia would still have collapsed, and Germany would have had to deal with only France and Britain on the Western Front in 1918, conceivably giving it victory.

Britain imported more than half its food and raw materials, and the German high command believed that an all-out submarine offensive would force it from the war. If this occurred, France would have to give up. The Germans accepted the fact that unrestricted submarine warfare would bring the United States into the war, but they reasoned that the war would be over before this could have major impact.

With German torpedoes claiming American lives, on April 6 the United States declared war. In addition to being a tremendous morale boost for the Entente, this meant immediate financial assistance in the form of loans as well as food and significant industrial assistance. (U.S. annual steel production was three times that of Germany and Austria-Hungary combined.)

It would take time for U.S. resources to count. The navy was ready; the army was not. Including the National Guard, it numbered just 200,000 men. Wilson appointed General John J. Pershing to command the American Expeditionary Forces, but only four U.S. divisions reached France by December 1917.

German submarines were soon sinking ships faster than they could be built. Allied technology in antisubmarine detection, depth charges, and mines played roles, but the main factor in the defeat of the U-boats was the institution of the convoy system. The submarines still registered kills, but the proportion of ships sunk to those sailing was far less than that of merchant ships traveling singly. Submarine losses also rose.

Fighting on the Western Front resumed in the summer of 1917. Haig took the initiative, hoping to achieve a breakthrough and outflank the German defenses from the north. Although the British captured much of Messines Ridge on June 7, the next phase, a series of battles collectively known as the Third Battle of Ypres and the Passchendaele Campaign (July 31–November 10, 1917), ended with no breakthrough. Deepening the Ypres salient by some five miles cost the British a quarter million casualties.

There was near disaster on the Italian front. Cadorna's Tenth and Eleventh Battles of the Isonzo led the Austrians to request German assistance. This led to a Central Powers offensive, the Twelfth Battle of the Isonzo, better known as the Battle of Caporetto (October 24–November 12, 1917).

Germans constituted nearly half of the attacking forces, and they employed surprise and new infiltration tactics. Deserters warned of the assault, but Cadorna expected it to occur elsewhere. He did order defense in depth along the entire line with only light forces in forward positions, but the Second Army commander failed to implement this, bringing disaster.

The Italians were driven first back across the Tagliamento River, then beyond the Piave, the bridges of which were then blown. Cadorna was sacked, replaced by General Armando Diaz. The attackers, however, had outrun their supply lines and artillery support, and Diaz now had a shorter front. Still, Italy had sustained some 320,000 casualties, most of them prisoners, and lost immense quantities of equipment. Central Powers losses were only about 20,000 men. Surprisingly, the Italian Army quickly recovered, and an important result of the fiasco was the Allied decision to create the Supreme War Council, the first real Allied effort to bring about unity of command.

Although Italy continued in the war, Russia did not. What happened in Russia was attributable more than anything else to the failed leadership of Czar Nicholas II. Political ineptitude, economic disarray, and general war weariness brought revolution; Nicholas's forced abdication on March 15, 1917; and the establishment of a provisional government. Its decision to continue the war, more than anything else, brought the Bolsheviks to power.

As Bolshevik Party leader Vladimir I. Lenin, financially supported by the German government, worked to topple the government and end Russian participation in the war, Minister of War Alexander Kerensky planned a great offensive in Galicia. Russia's last great military effort of the war, this Kerensky or Second Brusilov Offensive, opened on July 1. The Russians initially made significant gains, but these ended on the arrival of German reinforcements.

German general of infantry Max Hoffmann launched a counterstrike on July 19, resulting in widespread Russian withdrawals. By early August the Russians had evacuated Galicia and Bukovina. The entire Southwestern Front collapsed, and the gains of 1916 were wiped out.

Kerensky and new Russian Army commander General Lavr Kornilov soon quarreled, and Kornilov attempted a coup d'état in September, leading Kerensky to arm the Bolsheviks to defend the capital. Although the coup attempt fizzled, Kerensky was now at the mercy of the radical Left. Conditions continued to deteriorate, especially in the cities, where there were major food shortages. On the night of November 6–7, 1917, the Bolsheviks seized power.

In Mesopotamia, after repelling Ottoman efforts to capture the Suez Canal, the British took the offensive in the Sinai. Following two failed efforts to capture Gaza, Lieutenant General Edmund Allenby assumed command and captured Gaza and Beersheba on October 31. Allenby's forces entered Jerusalem on December 9.

At the beginning of 1918, both sides were reeling. The Allied blockade was, however, strangling Germany. If Germany was to win the war it would have to be in 1918, with its army bearing the brunt of the effort. This, however, hinged on peace on the Eastern Front and transferring forces before American manpower could count.

The Germans and Russians opened negotiations at Brest-Litovsk on December 3 and two weeks later concluded an armistice. Peace talks followed, but the Russians sought to delay, anticipating a communist revolution in Germany that would drive that country from the war. The Russians also naively expected negotiations on the basis of no annexations or indemnities. Hoffmann disabused the Russians of this when he presented Germany's crushing demands.

With the Russians balking, on February 18, 1918, Hoffmann set his forces in motion. The Bolsheviks had destroyed the Russian Army in coming to power and were in no position to fight. Lenin convinced the party leaders to agree to peace, assuring them that the most important thing was to consolidate Bolshevik power in Russia. Lost territory could be recovered later.

On March 3, 1918, the Bolsheviks signed the Treaty of Brest-Litovsk. Russia lost Poland, Courland (western Latvia), and Lithuania. In addition, Russia had to evacuate Livonia, Estonia, Finland, and the Åland Islands; quit Ukraine; recognize the treaty between the Ukrainian People's Republic and the Central Powers; and surrender Ardahan, Kars, and Batum to the Ottoman Empire. Russia also had to agree to pay Germany an indemnity of 4–5 billion gold rubles. Russia lost nearly 1.3 million square miles of territory and 62 million people, a third of its population. In view of subsequent German protestations regarding the 1919 Treaty of Versailles, it is worth remembering that the Treaty of Brest-Litovsk was far harsher. It was also approved by the German Reichstag, which in 1917 had passed a resolution calling for peace with no territorial annexations.

On May 7 the Central Powers forced Romania to sign the equally punitive Treaty of Bucharest. Romania had to cede territory to Bulgaria and Hungary, while Germany secured a 90-year lease on its oil wells and mineral rights.

Ludendorff now shifted forces westward to win the war before U.S. forces could turn the balance. He erred in retaining 1 million soldiers in the east. Although half of these were ultimately ordered west, they might have given Germany victory had they been available at the onset.

The Ludendorff Offensive, also known as the 1918 Spring Offensive and the Kaiserschlacht (Kaiser's Battle), was a series of drives aimed primarily at forcing the British from the war, whereupon the French would have to give up.

Begun on March 21, 1918, the offensive enjoyed great initial success, but Ludendorff's mishandling of objectives meant that the Germans were unable to exploit tremendous advances. The Germans also sustained heavy casualties, particularly among their elite assault forces. The German drives clearly revealed the lack of Allied coordination, and they now entrusted overall command to French general of division Ferdinand Foch. Also by now there were some 325,000 American troops in France. By the end of the war the U.S. Army had 2.1 million men in France, with 1.3 million on the firing line.

Austria-Hungary, meanwhile, made its last major military effort, attacking the Piave line. Although the attackers got 100,000 men across the river, Diaz counterattacked. Soon the Italians had retaken the territory south of the river.

On the Western Front, Ludendorff reequipped and reinforced for a final effort. A month's delay, however, enabled the Allies to bring more U.S. troops into the line. At dawn on July 15 Ludendorff launched the Champagne-Marne Offensive (July 15–18), also known as the Second Battle of the Marne. Ludendorff committed 50 divisions to capture Reims and the vital Paris-to-Nancy rail line. He expected to then return to Flanders and finish off the British. There was, however, no guarantee that the Germans would not continue up the Marne Valley to Paris.

German deserters betrayed most of the plan and its timing, enabling Foch to order counterbattery fire against the German assembly areas during the night of July 14–15. The German advance was soon halted, and the strategic initiative passed to the Allies. Foch had assembled a strong reserve, and on July 18 he launched his counteroffensive. Although Allied casualties were heavy, it succeeded brilliantly. On July 20 Ludendorff called off his planned Flanders drive in order to hold the area to the south, rejecting sound advice that he withdraw to the Siegfried Line.

Foch now planned a series of attacks to occur all the way from Ypres to Verdun and intended to allow the Germans no respite. The first of these, the British Amiens Offensive (August 8–September 4), succeeded brilliantly, with many Germans simply surrendering after at best token resistance. Soon the Allies had retaken all the territory lost in the spring German offensives.

During September 12–15, U.S. and French forces pinched out the Saint-Mihiel salient south of Verdun. Then on September 26 the French and Americans launched their massive Meuse-Argonne Offensive, which continued until the end of the war.

The Italians also resumed the offensive. With Austria-Hungary breaking apart,

French soldiers in the ruins of a church on July 15, 1918, during the Second Battle of the Marne. (National Archives)

Italian leaders sought a strong negotiating position at the peace conference. The Battle of Vittorio-Veneto (October 24–November 4) saw Austro-Hungarian soldiers deserting en masse. Some 427,000 were taken prisoner, along with 5,000 guns. An armistice on the Italian front was signed on November 3, and fighting ceased the next day.

Bulgaria was actually the first Central Power to break. The Allies defeated the Bulgarians in the Battle of the Vardar (September 15–24), Skopje fell on September 19, and an armistice was concluded the next day. The Allies recaptured Belgrade on November 1, and on November 10 they crossed the Danube. Allied troops also crossed into Romania, and on November 10 it reentered the war.

British forces advanced in Mesopotamia and in Palestine, winning a major victory at Megiddo (September 19). Operating with Arab forces, Allenby captured Damascus (October 1) and Aleppo (October 25). In Caucasia, the disintegration of Russian forces produced a virtual vacuum. Although the Ottomans were hardly capable of major offensive operations, they recovered the territory lost to Russia earlier and then captured Kars, moved into Persia and Azerbaijan, and took Baku. All of this was rendered meaningless with the Ottoman surrender on October 30, however.

Hindenburg and Ludendorff knew that the war was lost. Indeed, on September 29 they called for a new German government and immediate armistice negotiations. Although they had been in complete control of German policy for the past two years, the Duo eschewed any responsibility for the defeat.

On October 3, Prince Max of Baden became chancellor of a new liberal German government. On October 28, a mutiny broke out in the High Seas Fleet at Kiel on word that the admirals planned a last-ditch naval foray. With revolution threatening and with Wilhelm II refusing to act on his own, Prince Max simply announced on November 9 that the kaiser had abdicated. Wilhelm then went into exile in the Netherlands.

Allied leaders discussed whether to continue the war until Germany surrendered. An armistice would merely halt the fighting, with peace negotiations to follow. Foch believed that two weeks would have forced a German surrender, but general war weariness and French and British fears of growing American influence worked in favor of an armistice. The Germans were forced to agree to evacuate all captured territory as well as the left bank of the Rhine and Alsace-Lorraine and surrender the bulk of their navy and significant quantities of other weapons to preclude resumption of fighting. The armistice went into effect at 11:00 a.m. on November 11. The war was over at last.

SPENCER C. TUCKER

Consequences

The Allied failure to insist on German surrender undoubtedly saved lives but had momentous consequences. Because Germany was spared invasion and the German armies marched home in good order with battle flags flying, many Germans believed in the "stab in the back" legion posited by the political Right that the German armies had not been defeated in the field but had been betrayed by corrupt politicians, Jews, war profiteers, and disaffection on the home front. Later this provided considerable grist for Adolf Hitler, especially when leading German generals testified that it was fact.

On January 18, 1919, the Paris Peace Conference opened. Russia did not take part. Civil war was then raging, and efforts to cobble together a united Russian delegation proved fruitless. Although five delegations (those of Britain, France, the United States, Italy, and Japan) played important roles, the conference was dominated by the Big Three of Britain, France, and the United States. U.S. president Woodrow Wilson and British prime minister David Lloyd George stood together on most issues, meaning that French premier Georges Clemenceau was the odd man out.

On April 28, the conferees approved creation of the League of Nations. Wilson's cherished project, it emerged not as a binding international organization with its own military force, as the French and many smaller powers desired; instead, it was based on voluntary membership with emphasis on moral suasion. Sanctions were its strongest enforcement weapon. Unfortunately, many people saw the League of Nations as a cure-all for the world's security problems when other guarantees were what really mattered.

The peace treaties, all named for Paris suburbs, were as follows: the Treaty of Versailles with Germany (June 28, 1919), the Treaty of Saint-Germain with Austria (July 20, 1919), the Treaty of Neuilly with Bulgaria (November 27, 1919), the Treaty of Trianon with Hungary (March 21, 1920), and the Treaty of Sèvres with the Ottoman Empire (August 10, 1920), superceded by the Treaty of Lausanne (July 24, 1923).

The most important of these treaties was that with Germany. France sought to detach the entire Rhineland from Germany and make it independent with a permanent Allied occupation force. Britain and the United States opposed this and wanted all troops to depart on the signing of the treaty. To break this impasse, Britain and

The so-called Council of Four: (from left) British prime minister David Lloyd George, Italian prime minister Vittorio Orlando, French premier Georges Clemenceau, and U.S. president Woodrow Wilson at the Paris Peace Conference, May 27, 1919. (National Archives)

the United States offered France a guarantee that they would come to its support should it ever be attacked by Germany. Clemenceau was forced to yield, but the U.S. Senate never approved this Anglo-American Treaty of Guarantee, and the British government claimed that its agreement was contingent upon American acceptance. The French thus lost the security guarantee they had so desperately sought.

The Treaty of Versailles restored Alsace and Lorraine to France and gave Belgium the small border enclaves of Moresnet, Eupen, and Malmédy. In recompense for the deliberate destruction of French coal mines by the withdrawing Germans, France was to receive the coal production of the Saar region of Germany for 15 years.

The Saar itself would be under League of Nations administration, with Saarlanders to vote at the end of the period whether to continue that status or join Germany or France.

Plebiscites were to decide the future of northern and southern Schleswig. Germany was also to cede most of Posen and West Prussia to the new state of Poland, with a plebiscite to be held in districts of Upper Silesia. Gdansk (Danzig) would be a free city under the League of Nations but within the Polish customs union to provide that new state with a major seaport. Germany ceded Klaipėda (Memel, now part of Lithuania) to the Allies, and all the German colonies were to be organized as mandates under League of Nations supervision.

The Rhineland and a belt east of the Rhine 18 miles (30 kilometers) deep were to be permanently demilitarized. The Allies were allowed to occupy the Rhineland for up to 15 years, with Germany to bear the costs. The Kiel Canal was to be open to the warships and merchant ships of all nations, and Germany's rivers were internationalized. The German Army was restricted to 100,000 officers and men, and it was denied all military aircraft, heavy artillery, and tanks. Its navy was limited to six predreadnought battleships in capital ships and was not permitted submarines.

In the highly controversial Article 231, Germany accepted responsibility for having caused the war, establishing the legal basis for reparations. Germany was to pay for all civilian damages in the war. (The bill, presented in May 1921, was $33 billion.) In the meantime, Germany was to pay $5 billion. Germany was also to hand over much of its merchant ships and fishing fleet. It was also to build 200,000 tons of shipping for the Allies annually for a period of five years. While the other major signatories approved the Treaty of Versailles, the U.S. Senate never ratified it.

The treaties with the other defeated powers imposed restrictions on their military establishments and demanded reparations. That with Austria confirmed the breakup of the former Dual Monarchy. Hungary, Czechoslovakia, Yugoslavia, and Poland were all independent. Austria was forced to cede from its own territory Eastern Galicia to Poland as well as the Trentino, Trieste, and Istria to Italy. Italy also secured the South Tirol (Tyrol), even though this violated Wilson's "self-determination of peoples" because of its German-speaking population of some 240,000 people. Shorn of its raw materials and food-producing areas, Austria was hard-hit economically,

and many Austrians favored union with Germany (Anschluss), which was, however, forbidden.

Hungary lost almost three-quarters of its pre–World War I territory and two-thirds of its people. Czechoslovakia gained Slovakia, Austria secured western Hungary, and Yugoslavia took Croatia and Slovenia and part of the Banat of Temesvar. Romania received the remainder of the Banat and Transylvania, with its large Magyar population, along with part of the Hungarian plain.

Bulgaria was forced to yield territory to the new Yugoslavia and to cede Western Thrace to Greece and thus port facilities on the Aegean Sea. Bulgaria gained minor territory at the expense of the Ottoman Empire.

The Ottoman Empire renounced all claim to non-Turkish territory. The Kingdom of the Hejaz in Southwest Asia became independent. France secured a mandate over a new state of Syria (to include Lebanon), while Britain gained a mandate over Mesopotamia (the future Iraq, to include Mosul) and Palestine. Smyrna (present-day Izmir) in eastern Anatolia and the hinterland was to be administered by Greece for five years, after which a plebiscite would decide its future, while Italy gained the Dodecanese Islands and Rhodes. Greece received the remaining Ottoman islands in the Aegean as well as Thrace. Armenia was made independent. The treaty also established an autonomous Kurdistan under the League of Nations. The straits were internationalized, and territory adjacent to them was demilitarized.

Turkish nationalists such as General Mustafa Kemal were outraged by this treaty, and they set out to drive the Greeks from Anatolia. As a result of their military successes, the dictated Treaty of Sèvres was superceded by the negotiated settlement of the Treaty of Lausanne in 1923. Although Turkey still gave up all claim to the non-Turkish areas, it recovered much of Eastern Thrace as well as Imbros and Tenedos. The remainder of the Aegean Islands went to Greece. Italy retained the Dodecanese Islands, and Turkey recognized British control of Cyprus. The Kurds and the Armenians lost out. There was no mention of autonomy for Kurdestan and no independent Armenia. The straits were to be demilitarized and open in times of peace to ships of all nations and in times of war if the Ottoman Empire was neutral. If Turkey was at war, enemy ships but not those of neutral nations might be excluded.

There was much debate about the Paris settlement in subsequent years. Critics on the Right claimed that World War II would not have occurred had the French been allowed to write the settlement, while those on the Left maintained that the Treaty of Versailles was too harsh to conciliate the Germans. However, the peace settlement was a compromise, and the reality is that it did not significantly diminish German power. In any case, Britain, France, and the United States failed to cooperate on enforcement of the treaty in the postwar period, and there is no reason to suppose that they would have done any better with a different treaty. The United States almost immediately withdrew into isolation, while the British had little interest in postwar collective security arrangements binding them to France and Europe. This left enforcement of the peace settlement to France, a burden that it proved incapable of bearing alone.

SPENCER C. TUCKER

Timeline

1879

October 7	The Dual Alliance is concluded between Germany and Austria-Hungary.

1882

May 20	The Triple Alliance is concluded between Germany, Austria-Hungary, and Italy.

1887

June 18	The Reinsurance Treaty is concluded between Germany and Russia.

1890

June	Germany refuses to renew the Reinsurance Treaty.

1894

January 4	France and Russia conclude a military alliance.

1904

April 8	The Entente Cordiale is concluded between France and Great Britain.

1907

August 31   The Triple Entente of France, Russia, and Great Britain becomes reality with the signing of the Anglo-Russian Entente.

1908

October 6   Austria-Hungary annexes Bosnia-Herzegovina.

1914

June 28   Archduke Franz Ferdinand of Austria-Hungary and his wife Sophie are assassinated in Sarajevo.

July 6   Germany extends the "blank check" to Austria-Hungary, agreeing to support it unconditionally.

July 23   Austria-Hungary delivers an ultimatum to Serbia.

July 25   Serbia accepts most of the Austro-Hungarian ultimatum and agrees to arbitration on the rest.

July 26   Russia commences "steps preparatory to mobilization."

July 28   Austria-Hungary declares the Serbian response unacceptable and declares war.

July 29   Russia orders partial mobilization.

July 31   Germany warns Russia to halt its mobilization.

August 1   Germany orders general mobilization.

August 3   Germany declares war on France.

August 4   German troops enter neutral Belgium.

August 5   Great Britain declares war on Germany.

August 5–16   The Germans besiege and capture the Belgian fortress city of Liège.

                         Austro-Hungarian troops invade Serbia.

August 14–25   Battle of the Frontiers on the Western Front.

August 17   Russian forces invade East Prussia.

August 18   Russian forces invade Austro-Hungarian Galicia.

August 20   The German siege of Antwerp begins. It falls on October 10, 1914.

August 22   The British Expeditionary Force arrives in France.

August 23   Japan declares war on Germany.

                         Battle of Mons.

August 26–31   Battle of Tannenberg.

August 28   Naval Battle of Heligoland Bight.

September 3	The Russians take Lvov (Lemberg) in Galicia.
September 5–12	First Battle of the Marne.
September 7–13	First Battle of the Masurian Lakes.
September 29–October 17	German offensive in Poland.
October 18–November 30	Battle of the Yser.
October 22–November 22	First Battle of Ypres.
October 29	Ships of the Ottoman Navy shell Russian bases on the Black Sea.
November 1	Naval Battle of Coronel.
November 2	Russia declares war on the Ottoman Empire.
November 16–25	Battles of Łódź and Łowicz.
December 8	Naval Battle of the Falklands.
December 17	The First Battle of Artois begins; it ends on January 4, 1915.
December 20	The First Battle of Champagne begins; it ends on March 17, 1915.
December 22	The Battle of Sarikamish begins; it ends on January 17, 1915.

1915

January 24	Naval Battle of the Dogger Bank.
February 7–22	Second Battle of the Masurian Lakes.
February 14	Germany institutes a "war zone" around the British Isles, with every ship there subject to attack.
February 19	Allied ships commence a bombardment of the outer forts of the Dardanelles.
March 10–12	Battle of Neuve Chapelle.
March 14	A German submarine sinks the French passenger ship *Sussex*. The Germans then agree not to sink merchant ships without providing for the safety of those on board.
March 18	In an attempt to force the Dardanelles, the British and French fleets lose three battleships.
March 22	Przemyśl surrenders to the Russians.
April 5–30	Battle of Woëvre.
April 22–May 25	Second Battle of Ypres.
April 25	Allied troops land at Cape Helles on the Gallipoli Peninsula and on the Asian side of the Dardanelles.

May 7	A German submarine sinks the British passenger liner *Lusitania.*
May 8–June 18	Second Battle of Artois.
May 23	Italy declares war on Austria-Hungary.
June 3	The Central Powers retake Przemyśl.
June 23–July 7	First Battle of the Isonzo.
July 18–August 3	Second Battle of the Isonzo.
August 4–7	The Russians abandon Warsaw.
August 6–7	British forces land at Suvla Bay on the Gallipoli Peninsula.
August 25	The Germans capture Brest-Litovsk.
September 25–October 14	Battle of Loos.
September 25–October 16	Third Battle of Artois.
September 25–November 6	Second Battle of Champagne.
October 11	Bulgaria joins the war on the side of the Central Powers.
October 18–November 4	Third Battle of the Isonzo.
November 10–December 2	Fourth Battle of the Isonzo.
December 7	The Ottoman siege of Kut-al-Amara begins; it ends with a British surrender on April 29, 1918.
December 8	British forces begin their evacuation of the Gallipoli Peninsula; it is completed on January 9, 1916.

1916

January 13–February 3	The Ottomans fail to capture the Suez Canal.
February 16	Battle of Erzurum.
February 21–July	Battle of Verdun.
March 11–19	Fifth Battle of the Isonzo.
March 18–April 14	Battle of Lake Naroch.
May 15–June 17	Austro-Hungarian Trentino or Asiago Offensive.
May 31–June 1	Naval Battle of Jutland.
June 4–September 1	Russian Brusilov Offensive.
July 1–November 19	Battle of the Somme.
August 6–17	Sixth Battle of the Isonzo.
August 27	Romania declares war on Austria-Hungary.
September 14–20	Seventh Battle of the Isonzo.

September 15	Tanks are employed for the first time in the war, by the British, in the Battle of the Somme.
October 10–12	Eighth Battle of the Isonzo.
November 1–14	Ninth Battle of the Isonzo.
December 6	The Germans capture Bucharest.

1917

February 1	Germany resumes unrestricted submarine warfare.
March 16	A provisional government takes power in Russia.
March 16–April 5	German forces in the Noyon salient withdraw to their new Siegfried Line (Hindenburg Line).
April 6	The United States declares war on Germany.
April 9–15	Battle of Arras.
April 16–May 9	The Nivelle Offensive (Second Battle of the Aisne).
May 12–June 8	Tenth Battle of the Osonzo.
May 24	The Allies institute the convoy system.
June 7–14	Battle of Messines Ridge.
June 27	Greece declares war on the Central Powers.
July 1–19	Kerensky Offensive (Second Brusilov Offensive).
July 31–November 10	Third Battle of Ypres (Passchendaele Campaign).
August 18–September 15	Eleventh Battle of the Isonzo.
September 3	German forces capture Riga.
October 24–November 12	Twelfth Battle of the Isonzo (Battle of Caporetto).
October 31	British Empire forces capture Gaza and Beersheba.
November 5	The Rapallo Conference leads to the creation of the Supreme Allied War Council.
November 6–7	The Bolsheviks seize power in Russia.
November 20–December 5	Battle of Cambrai.
December 15	An armistice goes into effect on the Eastern Front.

1918

March 3	The Russians sign the Treaty of Brest-Litovsk, ending their participation in the war.
March 21–July 18	The Ludendorff Offensive.
May 7	The Romanians sign the Treaty of Bucharest, ending their participation in the war.

June 15–22	Battle of the Piave.
July 15–18	Second Battle of the Marne.
August 8–September 4	The British Amiens Offensive.
September 12–14	American and French forces reduce the Saint-Mihiel salient.
September 15–24	Battle of the Vardar.
September 19	Battle of Megiddo.
September 26–November 11	The Allied Amiens Offensive.
September 29	Field Marshal Paul von Hindenburg, knowing that the war is lost, calls for a new German government and immediate negotiations for an armistice.
September 30	Bulgaria agrees to an armistice.
October 24–November 4	Battle of Vittorio-Veneto.
October 28	Mutiny occurs in the German High Seas Fleet at Kiel.
November 3	An armistice takes effect on the Italian front.
November 10	Romania reenters the war.
November 11	An armistice takes effect on the Western Front.
1919	
January 12	The Paris Peace Conference opens. It officially ends on January 21, 1920.
June 21	The German fleet is scuttled at Scapa Flow.
June 28	The Treaty of Versailles is signed between the Allied Powers and Germany.
November 9	The U.S. Senate rejects the Treaty of Versailles and the League of Nations Covenant.
November 27	The Treaty of Neuilly is signed between the Allies and Bulgaria.
1920	
March 8	The U.S. Senate rejects the Treaty of Versailles and the League of Nations Covenant for a second and final time.
June 4	The Treaty of Trianon is signed between the Allies and Hungary.
August	The Treaty of Sèvres is signed between the Allies and the Ottoman Empire.

SPENCER C. TUCKER

Further Reading

Chickering, Rodger. *Imperial Germany and the Great War, 1914–1918.* Cambridge: Cambridge University Press, 2004.

Doughty, Robert A. *Pyrrhic Victory: French Strategy and Operations in the Great War.* Cambridge, MA: Belknap, 2005.

Falls, Cyril Bentham. *The First World War.* London: Longmans, 1960.

Farwell, Byron. *The Great War in Africa, 1914–1918.* New York: Norton, 1989.

Gilbert, Martin. *The First World War: A Complete History.* New York: H. Holt, 1994.

Halpern, Paul G. *A Naval History of World War I.* New York: Routledge, 1995.

Herwig, Holger H. *The First World War: Germany and Austria-Hungary, 1914–1918.* New York: Arnold, 1997.

Herwig, Holger H., and Richard F. Hamilton. *The Origins of World War I.* New York: Cambridge University Press, 2003.

Kennett, Lee. *The First Air War, 1914–1918.* New York: Free Press, 1991.

Lyons, Michael J. *World War I: A Short History.* 2nd ed. New York: Prentice Hall, 1999.

Meyer, Gerald J. *A World Undone: The Story of the Great War, 1914 to 1918.* New York: Random House, 2006.

Neiberg, Michael S. *Fighting the Great War: A Global History.* Cambridge, MA: Harvard University Press, 2005.

Sachar, Howard Morley. *The Emergence of the Middle East, 1914–1924.* New York: Knopf, 1969.

Strachan, Hew. *World War I: A History.* New York: Oxford University Press, 1998.

Tucker, Spencer C. *The Great War, 1914–18.* Bloomington: Indiana University Press, 1998.

Tucker, Spencer C., ed. *World War I: The Definitive Encyclopedia and Documents Collection.* 5 vols. Santa Barbara, CA: ABC-CLIO, 2014.

Russian Civil War (1917–1922)

Causes

Russia's participation in World War I brought great suffering, and its 3,750,000 dead in the war were the most of any participating nation. Widespread war weariness accompanied by the horrific casualties, inept leadership coupled with resistance to all reform, corruption, and economic dysfunction—especially in the major cities—all combined to topple the czarist regime of Nicholas II. On March 8, 1917, strikes and riots occurred in the Russian capital of Petrograd (formerly St. Petersburg), and on March 10 there was a general mutiny of troops there. On March 11, members of the Duma (parliament) refused to obey an imperial order to disband, and on March 15 the March Revolution occurred (it was a month earlier in the Julian calendar then in use in Russia and is thus also known as the February Revolution). Nicholas abdicated at the urging of his general staff. Duma leaders immediately organized a provisional government headed by liberal Prince Georgy Lvov. It was composed of moderate to conservative Duma leaders, with the sole exception being Alexander F. Kerensky, a socialist deputy who became minister of justice.

Allied leaders were not displeased with the news, convinced that the change of regime would stimulate the Russian people to even greater sacrifices in the war. To ensure this, however, they made loans to Russia contingent on its continuation as a belligerent. This was not an issue for the new Russian leaders, who were determined to fight on to victory and justify Russia's tremendous sacrifices and to realize its war aims. They also believed that the war effort would shift attention away from pressing domestic concerns. As it worked out, however, this decision proved to be a fatal blunder; more than anything else, it made possible the subsequent Bolshevik seizure of power.

The provisional government initiated reforms, to include freedom of expression and a political amnesty, but the country was soon swept up in lawlessness with a soaring crime rate, the closing of factories, the collapse of army discipline, and increasing numbers of desertions.

The provisional government did secure the agreement of the many Russian political parties, including the small militant Marxist Bolshevik Party, to a political truce. But among exiles returning to Russia under the general political amnesty was Bolshevik leader Vladimir I. Lenin. His return from exile in Switzerland was made possible by the German government, which also provided him considerable financial assistance to help him destabilize the new government and bring the Bolsheviks to power because they were the only Russian party opposing the war. This German aid, kept secret by the Bolsheviks, was of immense importance in their seizure of power.

On the evening of his return to Petrograd on April 16, 1917, Lenin proclaimed what came to be known as "The April Theses." These outlined the Bolshevik program but also called for a complete break with the provisional government and an end to what Lenin characterized as the "predatory war."

Kerensky, meanwhile, had become the key figure in the new government, and he staked all on a great military offensive planned by Russian Army commander in chief General Mikhail Alekseyev and carried out by General Aleksei A. Brusilov and known as the Second Brusilov or Kerensky Offensive. Designed to drive Austria-Hungary from the war, it occurred during July 1–19. Although the Russian army registered major gains, it soon ground to a halt because Brusilov lacked reserves and his armies outran their supply lines. The Germans also came to the relief of their ally, and soon the Russian Army underwent a breakdown in discipline with the men deserting in droves, encouraged by Bolshevik "truth squads."

Meanwhile, in the so-called July Days (July 16–18) in Petrograd, radicals egged on by the Bolsheviks attempted to seize control of the government. It responded with the arrest and imprisonment of most Bolshevik leaders, although Lenin escaped and went into hiding in Finland.

Promonarchist elements in Russia now attempted to undo the March Revolution. That August, Kerensky replaced Brusilov as commander of the army with General Lavr Kornilov. Military discipline had all but disappeared, and many hoped that Kornilov could restore it and right the situation. Meanwhile, on September 1 the Germans captured the city of Riga. This opened the Baltic coast to a German advance, uncovering Petrograd.

In these circumstances, Kornilov demanded a free hand and an end to political discussion groups formed to spread democratization in the army. Kornilov's demands brought a clash with Kerensky, and when Kerensky dismissed him, Kornilov attempted a coup d'état, apparently with the support of most army officers and the Russian middle and upper classes. On September 9 Kornilov ordered a march on Petrograd.

Betrayed by the army but overestimating its threat and underestimating that posed by the Bolsheviks, Kerensky turned for assistance to the extreme Left and the shadow government of the Petrograd Soviet. The soviets were the local socialist councils that had sprung up all over Russia in imitation of those of the Russian Revolution of 1905. Kerensky ordered the release of Bolshevik leaders from prison and the arming of socialist leader Leon Trotsky's Petrograd Red Guard of soldiers, sailors, and workers sympathetic to the Bolsheviks. (The Bolsheviks would later use these weapons against the government.)

Kerensky's move proved unnecessary, as revolutionary workers and Bolshevik propagandists halted the trains carrying Kornilov's troops before they could reach Petrograd and persuaded the men to simply go home. On September 12 Kornilov was arrested. (He later escaped and became a leader of the White forces in the subsequent Russian Civil War.) Although the right-wing attempt to seize power had been halted, Kerensky now was at the mercy of the radical Left.

Conditions in Russia continued to deteriorate, especially in the cities, which were swept by chronic food shortages and rampant inflation. In late September, buoyed by an infusion of German funds, the Bolsheviks advanced their program of "peace, bread, and land" and "all power to the Soviets." More than any other Russian political leader, Lenin sensed the great longing of the Russian people for peace at virtually any price.

To fend off the Bolshevik surge, on September 27 Kerensky declared Russia a republic and called for the election of a

Approximate Allied Forces in the Russian Civil War

Russian Region	Allied Country	Number of Troops	Dates of Intervention
Murmansk	United Kingdom	7,400	June 1918–October 1919
	France	1,000	June 1918–October 1919
	Italy	1,350	June 1918–October 1919
	Serbia	1,200	June 1918–October 1919
Arkhangelsk	United Kingdom	2,420	April 1918–September 1919
	France	900	April 1918–September 1919
	United States	4,800	May 1918–August 1919
	Serbia	350	June 1918–September 1919
Ukraine/Odessa/ Transcaucasus	United Kingdom	22,000	December 1918–August 1919
	France	30,000	December 1918–April 1919
	Greece	30,000	December 1918–April 1919
Siberia and the Far East	United Kingdom	2,000	1918–1920
	France	3,000	1918–1920
	Canada	4,000	1918–1920
	United States	8,358	August 1918–April 1920
	Japan	70,000	December 1917–October 1922
	Czechoslovakia	50,000	June 1918–1920

Sources: Michael Clodfelter, *Warfare and Armed Conflict: A Statistical Reference to Casualty and Other Figures, 1618–1991* (Jefferson, NC: McFarland, 1992); Richard Ullman, *Intervention and the War* (Princeton, NJ: Princeton University Press, 1961).

constitutional assembly. In early October, Trotsky, now allied with Lenin, was elected chairman of the Petrograd Soviet. Lenin, meanwhile, secretly returned to Petrograd. Meeting with the Bolshevik Party leadership, he called for a coup d'état and assured them it would succeed. There was considerable reluctance to undertake this, and the party leaders approved the attempt by a majority of a single vote.

The Bolshevik coup occurred on the night of November 6–7. (It was October by the Russian calendar, hence the name October Revolution.) It was timed to coincide with a meeting of the All-Russia Congress of Soviets in Petrograd. Trotsky was the key figure in the operation, as revolutionary soldiers, sailors, and Red Guards occupied strategic points in the city and arrested members of the provisional government. Kerensky escaped abroad. It was an amazing occurrence. The Bolsheviks counted only a very small percentage of the total Russian population. Keeping power would be a considerable challenge.

On the evening of November 7 the last remnants of the government opposition, having taken refuge in the Winter Palace, surrendered to the Bolsheviks, and Lenin was able to announce to the Congress of Soviets the establishment of the new government. The congress approved the Bolshevik takeover and passed a resolution assuming the reins of government. Russia was now proclaimed a "Soviet Republic." Yet power, for all practical purposes, remained in Bolshevik hands, for on November 8 the same congress authorized a provisional government, known as the Soviet of People's Commissars. Lenin was chairman, Trotsky was commissar for foreign affairs, and Joseph Stalin was commissar for national minorities.

The Bolsheviks were not slow to implement their reorganization of Russia. On November 7, they decreed the breaking up of the large estates, with the land to be distributed among the peasants. (On February 19, 1918, they would abolish private ownership in land. It was to belong to the state, and only those willing to cultivate it were to be permitted to use it.) The Bolsheviks also ordered the nationalization of the banks and confiscation of private accounts. In January 1918 they repudiated the national debt.

A Bolshevik decree of November 28, 1917, gave factory workers control over their enterprises, and by the summer of 1918 the Bolsheviks had nationalized all larger factories. Soon this was also applied to the smaller plants. Workers were forced into government-controlled labor unions and denied the right to strike. Private trade was gradually suppressed, and the government undertook to distribute food and other commodities among the urban populations. Rationing was soon introduced. The Bolsheviks also moved against the Russian Orthodox Church. A decree of December 17, 1917, confiscated all church property and ended religious instruction in the schools.

This radical Bolshevik program brought great opposition from many Russians: the monarchists, the great noble landowners, propertied middle classes, the church, and the deeply religious among the population. Russian nationalists of all political persuasions also opposed Lenin's plan to withdraw Russia from the war. At the same time, of course, Ukrainians were happy for the war to end, as were most people in the Central Asian and Caucasian republics and the Baltic States and most elements in Finland and Poland.

Securing peace with Germany in order to allow the Bolsheviks to concentrate on defeating those opposing the revolution was a priority for Lenin. Indeed, Lenin's first action on assuming power had been to declare that Russia was withdrawing from the war. He called for an immediate peace on the basis of "no indemnities, no annexations." Less than a month after seizing control of the government, on December 3 the Bolsheviks opened talks with the Germans in the Polish city of Brest-Litovsk, and on December 17 an armistice was declared.

Bolshevik expectations of peace on a "forgive and forget" basis were quickly dashed, however, when the Germans presented their demands. The Bolsheviks then adopted a policy of "neither war nor peace." The German response came on February 18, 1918, in the resumption of offensive military operations, and by the end of the month the German Army was within 100 miles of Petrograd. Russian lead representative to the talks Trotsky called for "revolutionary war," but having largely destroyed the army in their pursuit of power, the Bolsheviks were in no position to do so.

Lenin assured the Bolshevik leadership that Germany was on the brink of a communist revolution and that any peace signed with the present German government would not last. The chief consideration, he said, must be the preservation of communism in Russia. Lenin's position prevailed, albeit narrowly.

On March 3, 1918, the Russians signed with Germany the Treaty of Brest-Litovsk.

By any standard, it was a disaster for Russia, which lost some 1.3 million square miles of territory with 62 million people and more than 50 percent of its industry, along with the bulk of its iron and coal as well as grain production. Russia was forced to yield Poland, the Baltic provinces, eastern Ukraine, Finland, and Transcaucasia. Azerbaijan, Georgia, and Armenia all established themselves as independent states. The treaty was immensely unpopular, and Lenin had to use all of his skills and pressure to get it approved by the leadership. Even so, the vote was 7 to 6.

Not until 1940 was Joseph Stalin able, with German chancellor Adolf Hitler's help, to recover most of the 1914 frontier. The sole advantage to the Bolsheviks of the treaty was that it allowed them to concentrate on the Whites, for civil war was now raging in Russia.

SPENCER C. TUCKER

Red Army soldiers pose for their photograph in Petrograd (now Saint Petersburg) before their departure for the front during the Russian Civil War. (Fine Art Images/Heritage Images/Getty Images)

Course

The Russian Civil War of 1917–1922 was amazingly complex, both because of the multitude of groups contesting the future course of Russia and because it involved fighting between Russian forces and neighboring states as well as military intervention by Russia's former allies.

The two largest combatant groups were the Red Army, the military force of the Bolshevik government of Russia, and the loosely allied forces of the White Army. The Whites were a quite diverse grouping. They ranged politically from antidemocratic Far Right monarchists to staunchly democratic and moderate socialists. The Whites also included much of the landowning and commercial middle class who wanted a Western-style democratic government. Also opposing the Bolsheviks were the devoutly religious Russians who

opposed Bolshevik policies regarding the Russian Orthodox Church. Alongside the two major groupings of the Reds and the Whites was a far smaller group known as the Greens. Made up of militant socialists, it fought both the Reds and the Whites. There was even a Black Flags force of anarchists.

The armies of a number of nations also fought the Reds. Imperial Russia had been a collection of many different nationalities, and many of these peoples saw the chaos of 1917 as a chance to establish their own nation-states. These included the breakaway republics of Finland, Estonia, Latvia, Lithuania, and Poland. There was even a force of Czechs. In addition, the Allied nations of Britain, France, the United States, and Japan all sent armed forces into Russian and on occasion clashed with the Reds.

Revolutionary activity also expanded beyond Russia's prewar borders. The

Bolsheviks rightly believed that their hold on Russia would be more secure if there were like states on Russia's borders. They were therefore quite active in trying to stir up like revolutions in a number of other states, including Germany, Hungary, the Ottoman Empire, Mongolia, and Persia.

Various dates are given for the Russian Civil War. Some historians date the beginning of the conflict from the Bolshevik seizure of power. Certainly it was under way with the Bolshevik expropriation of the lands and the end of special privileges for the Don Cossacks.

To protect its hold on power and crush opposition, on December 20 the Bolsheviks organized the Extraordinary Commission to Combat Counter-Revolution, also known as the Cheka. It was soon about the task of liquidating opposition to the regime through a campaign of explicit terror. There was also the problem of the other political parties, for the November 25 elections for a constituent assembly that Kerensky had called earlier returned 420 Socialist Revolutionaries (SRs) to only 225 Bolsheviks. Accordingly, when the assembly met in Petrograd on January 18, 1918, Red troops dispersed it. Many of the SRs now joined the anti-Bolshevik movements.

The Bolsheviks began the war with nothing resembling a trained force except the Red Guard. It was certainly small and limited to the cities but was trained and enthusiastic. During the first period of the civil war the government suffered one reverse after another, but gradually Trotsky, as people's commissar for military and naval affairs, organized the Red Army. The Reds seem to have gotten the best commanders, most of them junior officers hastily promoted on the basis of ability. The Bolsheviks also co-opted many

Russian revolutionary Leon Trotsky, shown here in 1920, was one of the key figures in the Bolshevik Revolution of November 1918 and then foreign minister of the new regime. Subsequently commissar of war, he directed the effort against the White forces in the Russian Civil War of 1917–1922. (Underwood Archives/Getty Images)

of the better czarist commanders, such as Brusilov, as "military specialists." Under Trotsky's leadership, the Red Army developed into a regular army based on conscription and subject to strict discipline. Trotsky was dedicated, ruthless, tireless, and supremely confident; he proved to be a revolutionary general of high caliber.

Geography also benefited the Reds. Initially the territory firmly in their control coincided approximately with that of medieval Muscovy. Here the Bolsheviks enjoyed the advantage of interior lines, with short supply lines radiating out from Moscow that enabled the rapid movement of men and supplies. The Reds also derived a certain measure of support from the fact that they were defending Russian territory against foreign armies.

The Whites never could coordinate their efforts or their ideology. Neither did they win the support of the Don, Kuban, or Siberian Cossacks or the numerous nationalities of the empire; as centralists they persistently rejected the idea of autonomy. The White forces were also widely scattered on the periphery: in the northwest (Baltic provinces), the south (Ukraine, Caucasus), and the east (Siberia). This made coordination between the various White forces difficult, if not impossible. The Reds also had the considerable stocks of arms and munitions that had been produced by 1917 under the czarist war effort, while the Whites secured much of their arms and munitions from the Allies, chiefly France (the principal White supporter) and Britain.

The lack of cohesion among the counterrevolutionary movements and the shifting attitudes of the Allied governments constantly hampered the White military operations. Many Russians regarded the Whites as mere tools of the Allies, and the fact that their prominent commanders had been associated with the czarist regime made them suspect for many. The contest that ensued was a fight to the death by hungry and ragged soldiers, with neither side asking or giving quarter and with both sides committing horrible atrocities.

The Russian Empire had been the world's largest country, and in faraway provinces in Siberia and Central Asia where the Bolsheviks were poorly organized, local authorities held on to power. In November 1917, Russian Army officer Alexander Dutov led a revolt by the Don Cossacks, who had enjoyed special privileges under the czars but saw them disappear under the Bolsheviks. On January 10, 1918, the rebels declared the Republic of the Don. Here, as elsewhere, the situation became complicated when Don Cossacks under Pyotr Krasnov opened negotiations with the Germans; the anti-Bolshevik movement in the Don region ultimately split into pro-German and pro-Allied factions.

Peripheral portions of the former Russian empire sought to break free. On January 12, 1918, the Latvians declared their independence from Russia. Finland, Estonia, and Lithuania did the same. On March 12 the Bolsheviks moved the capital from Petrograd to Moscow. This was partly because of Petrograd's exposed position in relation to the German military and Germany's satellite states and partly due to threats from counterrevolutionary forces in the border areas.

With the signing of the Treaty of Brest-Litovsk, German forces moved into the Baltic region in April 1918, German troops landed in Finland, and Kaiser Wilhelm II offered its throne to his brother-in-law, Prince Karl of Hesse. That same month German and Austro-Hungarian troops occupied western Ukraine, vital for its grain production, and there established a military dictatorship under Pavlo Skoropadski. The kaiser also accepted the "invitation" of the Estonians to be their king, and in July Lithuania offered its throne to Prince Wilhelm of Urach, a younger member of the ruling family in Württemberg.

The Germans actively supported the Finns in their war against Bolshevik forces. Major General Rüdiger von der Goltz's 9,500-man Baltic Division landed at Hangö on April 3, then moved inland and took Helsingfors (Helsinki) from the Bolsheviks on April 18. At the same time, General Karl Mannerheim's Finnish forces secured the Karelian Isthmus. On April 29, 12,000 Russian troops at Vyborg surrendered, giving the Finns considerable military equipment. By the end of April Finland was freed of the Russians, and the bulk of the German troops departed at the end of May.

The Bolsheviks also did battle with the Estonians, Latvians, and Lithuanians during 1918–1920. This fighting ended with Moscow conceding their independence.

The Allied governments, especially the French and British, intermittently encouraged and supported those opposed to Bolshevik rule. The Allies sent supplies, money, and troops to help the White forces. Some initially and naively hoped that if the Bolsheviks were overthrown Russia would reenter the war against Germany. The Allies also wanted to keep the considerable quantities of war supplies they had given the Russians from falling into German hands. Toppling communism was another goal.

There was, however, no coordination to the Allied effort. On June 23, 1918, British troops landed at Murmansk, and in early August British and French forces took control of Arkhangelsk (Archangel) and agreed to support a puppet Government of Northern Russia. U.S. forces also soon arrived. By the spring of 1919, there was considerable fighting between the Allied troops and the Bolsheviks.

Some 45,000 Czechs also joined the White side. They had constituted the Czech Legion in the Russian Army. The legion was formed of Czechs living in Russia but also of those taken prisoner by the Russians in World War I. The Czech Legion fought against Austria-Hungary in the expectation that an Allied victory would bring Czech independence. The members of the Czech Legion now endeavored to leave Russia and join the Western Allies still fighting the Germans.

Their way blocked by the Bolsheviks, the Czechs formed an alliance with the anti-Bolsheviks and fought their way across Siberia along the Trans-Siberian Railway, eventually controlling much of it. They reached Vladivostok in May 1918 and there allied themselves with Admiral Aleksandr Kolchak's White army.

The situation in the Far East was confused with the establishment there of several independent Siberian governments in September 1918. In November Kolchak set up an autonomous Siberian government at Omsk and attempted to unify the White forces in Siberia. He proved to be an ineffective commander as well as an inept politician.

The situation was further complicated when the Japanese sent troops to Vladivostok in August. Ultimately this force grew to as many as 50,000 men. The Japanese saw the possibility of securing the Russian maritime provinces. American forces also soon arrived at Vladivostok, in part to prevent the Japanese from realizing this aim. Meanwhile, Kolchak's Siberian White army, supported by the Czechs, advanced west from Siberia into eastern Russia, taking Perm and Ufa in December.

Leading commander of the counterrevolutionary White forces General Lavr Kornilov, former commander of the Russian Army, was killed early in the civil war, on April 13, 1918, at Krasnodar, north of the Black Sea. General Anton Denikin then took command in southern Russia, where he carried the brunt of the fighting. The last commander in the south was Russian Army general Baron Pyotr N. Wrangel.

Fears that nearby White forces might free former czar Nicholas II and his family led to the Bolsheviks' execution of Nicholas, his family, and their remaining retainers on July 17, 1918, at Ekaterinburg in the Urals, where they were being held. For 70 years the Soviet government held that the deaths were the work of panicked local Bolsheviks. Not until 1990 did Moscow admit that Lenin had known all about the plan and that the Ekaterinburg Soviet cleared the execution with Moscow first.

In September 1918 the various White factions met in conference at Ufa in the Urals, but the effort to unify the many factions failed on the issue of autonomy for the Cossacks and national minorities. The Whites, moreover, put off laying out a detailed program for fear it would antagonize one or more groups of supporters.

During May–October 1919, Denikin mounted a major offensive, driving north and taking Kiev from the Bolsheviks on September 2. Baron Wrangel's drive on Tsaritsyn (the future Stalingrad) on the Volga to link up with White forces under Kolchak was delayed by logistics problems, and by the time he had secured Tsaritsyn on June 17, Red forces under General Mikhail N. Tukhachevsky had driven back Kolchak.

On October 6, White Russian general Nikolai Yudenich, having assembled a counterrevolutionary army of 20,000 men in southern Estonia, crossed the border and marched on Petrograd in a bold effort to capture the city. He reached the Petrograd outskirts on October 19, but Trotsky was able to assemble sufficient forces to halt the drive and force Yudenich to retire to Estonia.

Following the blunting of Denikin's offensive, Tukhachevsky took the offensive in southern Russia. He recaptured Kiev on December 17 and pushed the Whites back on the Black Sea. On March 27,

1920, British ships evacuated most of the remaining White troops in southern Russia, principally from the port of Novorossisk. The only remaining White force in the south was a small army under General Wrangel in the Crimea.

When the civil war brought the cities and armies into danger of starvation, in December 1920 the Bolsheviks ordered the peasants to turn over to the government their entire surplus. As the peasants were reluctant to do so and saw no chance of any return in consumer goods for the food, the government was driven to adopt forced rationing. On Lenin's directive, it also introduced requisition squads that created famine wherever they operated. Such policies caused widespread unrest. Ironically, the peasants were probably the key factor in the outcome of the fighting. Despite their great suffering, no doubt the vast majority believed that if the Whites triumphed they would lose the land they had gained from the revolution.

The Russian Civil War was further complicated by a separate simultaneous conflict between Russia and Poland. One of the thorniest issues to resolve during the Paris Peace Conference following World War I was the frontier between these two states. Toward that end, Allied leaders established a commission headed by George Curzon, 1st Marquess Curzon of Kedleston. The resulting Curzon Line generally followed lines of ethnicity and the 1797 border between Prussia and Russia. The Bolsheviks refused to accept the line, however, and the Poles used the fighting in Russia to their advantage by occupying areas of mixed Polish-Russian population in the undefined frontier area bordering Belorussia and the Ukraine.

In 1919 the Red armies might have been crushed if Poland had moved at the same time as the White offensive in southern Russia, but Polish policy was aimed at continuation of civil strife in Russia, or so Denikin claimed in his memoirs.

There had already been fighting between the two sides in 1919, but in 1920, with the Red armies subduing the remaining White forces, the Bolshevik government turned its attention to the Poles and presented them with an ultimatum that would have effectively given Russia a protectorate over Poland. The Poles rejected this, and Russian forces massed for an invasion. Rather than waiting to be attacked, the Poles took the initiative.

Following conclusion of an alliance with the Ukrainians under Hetman Simon Petlyura, Polish head of state General Józef Piłsudski launched Operation KIEV on April 24, driving on the city of Kiev with Ukrainian forces on his right flank. Capturing Kiev on May 7, Piłsudski then planned to turn north, behind the Pripet Marshes, to take Marshal Tukhachevsky's Red army in the rear but lacked the logistical support to carry this out. Tukhachevsky then struck southward with his army, while Red forces under General Semën M. Budënny drove north against Piłsudski's right flank. By mid-June the Poles were in full retreat.

Seeking to take advantage of the Russo-Polish War, White general Peter Wrangel in June 1920 launched a surprise offensive north from the Sea of Azov region. It proved too little, too late, and Red forces led by General Mikhail Frunze drove the Whites back to the Crimea. The British evacuated the remaining White forces by sea in mid-November.

In the Russo-Polish War, the military advantage now appeared to lie with the Russians, with Tukhachevsky on the verge of taking Warsaw. Because the Polish intelligence service was able to read the Russian ciphers, Piłsudski knew the Russian troop dispositions and ordered a daring counterattack against Tukhachevsky's left, which signal intercepts revealed as the Russian weak point. Fought during August 16–25, the Battle of Warsaw ended in an overwhelming Polish victory. The Poles suffered some 50,000 casualties but inflicted some 150,000 Russian casualties, including 66,000 taken prisoner. The Poles also captured more than 230 artillery pieces, 1,000 machine guns, and 10,000 vehicles. The battle was one of the most decisive of the century and marked the first check to Bolshevik westward expansion.

Piłsudski continued a broad offensive on each side of the Pripet Marshes, and the Poles inflicted additional major defeats on the Russians, who were forced to withdraw to Minsk. The war came to a close with the Treaty of Riga on March 18, 1920. The Russians yielded to the Poles some 52,000 square miles of territory in Belorussia and Ukraine east of the Curzon Line.

Bolshevik forces continued to advance elsewhere, and on October 25, 1922, Japanese forces evacuated Vladivostok, which then reverted to Bolshevik control. In Bolshevik historiography this marks the official end of the civil war, but the last White enclave was that of the Ayano-Maysky district on the Pacific coast under General Anatoly Pepeliayev, which surrendered on June 17, 1923. Sporadic armed resistance continued in Central Asia until 1934.

SPENCER C. TUCKER

Consequences

Millions of Russians died in the Russian Civil War, and large areas of the country were laid waste. Bolshevik Russia found itself isolated internationally. Nonetheless, their rule would have immense

ALLIED INTERVENTIONS IN WESTERN RUSSIA, 1918–1922

consequences for Russia and for the world. The Bolsheviks were able to recover all the territories lost as a consequence of the Treaty of Brest-Litovsk, with the exception of Finland, Poland, and the new Baltic republics. Ukraine and Transcaucasia were reintegrated into the new Bolshevik political entity thanks to the forcible creation of governments in these states along the soviet model. Nominally independent, these states entered into close relations with the new Russian Soviet Federated Socialist Republic to form a federation.

The Union of Soviet Socialist Republics (Soviet Union) came into being in July 1923. Although the name implies a federative structure, the Soviet Union was highly centralized, with only the industrial workers and poor peasants having access to political power. In Marxist thought, this period, known as the Dictatorship of the Proletariat, was to bring about the end of economic classes and thus the causes of class conflict.

The proletariat hardly had power, however, as a system of indirect representation prevailed by which the peasants, who constituted some 80 percent of the population, were six steps removed from the central organs of power, and the urban workers were four steps removed. This arrangement of indirect representation enabled the central authorities to control affairs.

In effect power flowed downward, as the Communist Party paralleled and was closely woven into the governmental structure. Higher offices in the government and the party were interlocking, and the head of the party effectively controlled the state. No political parties other than that of the Bolsheviks (the Communist Party) were permitted. Freedom of speech and the press were abolished. No opposition to the regime was allowed, and the judicial

system was not independent but merely an organ of the government charged with enforcing its policies. Because members of the Communist Party were only a small minority of the population, the Bolsheviks reverted to force to ensure their rule.

Those critical of repression under the czars were shocked by the violence and scale of what now occurred under communist rule. Many members of the nobility and the upper classes were "liquidated," but the determination to stamp out all opposition applied to peasants and urban workers alike. All opposition to the regime was crushed by arbitrary imprisonment, execution, or exile to forced labor camps known as gulags. It used to be assumed that this terror emerged under Soviet leader Joseph Stalin. Recent scholarship has shown, however, that the gulags were set up under Lenin, although Stalin did vastly expand them.

Lenin was absolutely ruthless in liquidating opposition. He was the father of domestic Russian terrorism and was merciless in its execution. Although the number will never be known with any certainty because many of its victims simply vanished without public notice, by 1922 perhaps 50,000 people had perished in the so-called Red Terror.

Worse was to come. The attempt by the Bolshevik leadership to introduce pure communism in one fell swoop during 1919–1921 (war communism) proved a disaster. Chaos ensued, especially in the industrial sector. Production by 1921 was only 17 percent of 1913 figures.

The peasants resisted the communist economic plan to turn over all agricultural production beyond a bare minimum needed for their families and for seed purposes in exchange for industrial goods that never arrived. When the government seized their crops, the peasants resorted to passive resistance by reducing the acreage planted. There was active resistance as well. Indeed, this was among the most violent components of the civil war. The peasants also slaughtered their livestock en masse rather than turn them over or watch them starve for lack of fodder. These developments, coupled with shortages of tools and fertilizer and an untimely drought, created a great reduction in food supplies and a widespread famine that claimed hundreds of thousands of additional lives.

With the government unable to provide food for the urban workers, unrest grew, and outright resistance to the government occurred. In March 1921 there was a great revolt of sailors, soldiers, and workers at the major Russian naval base at Kronstadt on Kotlin Island in the Baltic near Petrograd. It took a 50,000-man Red Army force to crush the revolt.

With the communist experiment in danger of collapse, in 1921 Lenin introduced concessions in what became known as the New Economic Policy. Lenin himself said it would "be easier to change the policy than the peasants," and he described the change as "one step backward to take two steps forward." Its most important element was the scrapping of agricultural requisitions in favor of an incentive system of a fixed tax on surplus production, with the peasants free to dispose of this on the open market. Land policies were also changed to allow the renting of land and the hiring of agricultural laborers. A few peasants, known as kulaks (money grabbers), became quite wealthy as a result.

In industry, firms employing fewer than 20 workers were denationalized. Foreign corporations were also granted concessions in various industries and agriculture. Under these new policies the economy showed vast improvement, and by 1927 industrial production at last surpassed pre–World War I levels.

Lenin died in January 1924. A succession struggle had already been under way following a stroke in 1921 and Lenin's consistently declining health thereafter. Following a prolonged period of leadership triumvirates, by 1929 Stalin held complete power. A master of power politics, he was also paranoid and extraordinarily cruel. Stalin carried out a reversal of the New Economic Policy and instituted a program of rapid industrialization through a series of five-year plans with rigid centralization and the establishment of fantastically high production goals for every aspect of the economy. Its emphasis was on heavy industry. Agriculture was to be reorganized on a large-scale mechanized basis through great state and collective farms. Resistance was crushed, with the kulaks liquidated.

Peasant opposition to the changes brought widespread famine once again. Reliable casualty figures of the human cost are unavailable, but including famine fatalities, the number of those who died in Stalin's collectivization of agriculture may have reached 10 million or more. For what it is worth, that is the figure Stalin cited to British prime minister Winston Churchill in Moscow in August 1942.

Stalin continued to push heavy industry, and although Russia registered major advances in production, the gains were uneven, and many Russians suffered immensely. In fact, 1932–1933 saw severe famine in parts of Russia.

Beginning in 1934, Stalin instituted a series of purges and show trials that resulted in the deaths of most all of the old guard Bolshevik leadership. Twelve members of the first Soviet government lived in

1937. Stalin killed 11 of them; he was the 12th. Soviet ambassadors overseas were even called home and shot. But the trials were only the tip of the iceberg. Tens of thousands of Russians were summarily shot or murdered without benefit of judicial proceedings. The trials were, in fact, a massive charade covering what became known as the Great Purge (also known as the Deep Comb-Out).

A second series of trials in 1937 reached into the Russian military. Ultimately some 30,000 officers were arrested and implicated in a specious plot organized by Marshal Mikhail Tukhachevsky to overthrow the government. Most of those arrested were shot or imprisoned, some with their entire families. As a consequence of his purge of the military leadership, Stalin was nearly the architect of his country's defeat in World War II.

How many people perished in the Great Purge? According to one source, declassified Soviet documents show that during the period 1937–1938 the Soviet secret police detained 1,548,366 persons, and 681,692 of these were shot. Historian Robert Conquest posits a figure twice that, with the secret police having falsified numerous death certificates. Historian Michael Ellman puts the toll during 1937–1938 at 950,000 to 1.2 million. Whatever the precise tally, there can be no doubt that the show trials and the Great Purge accomplished all that Stalin desired in making him perhaps the most powerful of rulers in history.

In foreign policy, Lenin had expended considerable sums and effort trying to bring about communist revolutions in Germany, Hungary, and elsewhere. The agency for this was the Third International, or Communist International (Comintern), formed in March 1919. After 1926, with the Soviet Union still largely isolated in Europe, Stalin became interested in collective security. The Soviet Union joined the League of Nations and entered into security pacts with other powers, including France and Czechoslovakia.

Disillusioned with the failure of Britain and France in 1938 to prevent the German dismemberment of Czechoslovakia, Stalin became convinced that the Western governments were attempting to turn Hitler's aggression toward Russia. Stalin anticipated war with Germany at some point (after all, Hitler had proclaimed in *Mein Kampf* that "New soil is to be found only in the East"). But he also believed that he could postpone it until such point as the Soviet Union could win such a contest.

In these circumstances Moscow signed a nonaggression pact with Nazi Germany in August 1939. This permitted Hitler to unleash World War II a week later with an invasion of Poland. From Stalin's perspective, the pact, which also involved the shipment of substantial Soviet goods for the German war machine and the Soviet Union's acquisition of eastern Poland and the Baltic States, also had the advantage of giving Russia time to perfect its military preparations and hopefully weaken Germany by the latter's involvement in a war with Great Britain and France.

In 1940 the Soviet Union was well on the way to becoming the second most important industrial country in the world. Its gross industrial output was 5 times as large as 1929 and 12 times as large as 1913. It produced 4 times as much oil as the rest of Europe put together and stood first in iron ore, copper, and phosphates and second in Europe only to Germany in the production of steel. The Soviet Union was also a leading producer of foodstuffs.

In 1941 the Soviet Union had a total population of 193 million people. During the previous 15 years some 11 million men had received full military training, and a like number had partial training. In 1941 the Soviet Union was far better prepared in leadership, manpower, military equipment, and industrial and agricultural resources to withstand attack than it had been in 1914. On the outbreak of war with Germany in June 1941, the Soviet Union outnumbered the Germans six to one in tanks, five to one in aircraft, and two to one in submarines. But the war with Germany, the Great Patriotic War as it came to be known in Russian history, would also lead to the deaths of as many as 27 million Russians.

SPENCER C. TUCKER

Timeline

1917

March 8	Strikes and riots occur in Petrograd.
March 10	A general mutiny of troops occurs in Petrograd.
March 11	Members of the Russian Duma (parliament) refuse to obey an imperial order to disband.
March 15	Czar Nicholas II abdicates both for himself and his son in favor of his brother Michael, who in turn abdicates to the provisional government, pending election of a constituent assembly. The new provisional government, headed by the liberal Prince Georgy Lvov, decides to continue the war. The government also initiates reforms that include freedom of expression and political amnesty, but Russia is swept by lawlessness and unrest.
April 16	Bolshevik leader Vladimir I. Lenin returns to Petrograd and announced his "April Theses," which include a socialist program but also an end to support of the provisional government and to Russian participation in the war.
July 1–16	The Russian Army mounts its last great military effort of World War I. Known as the Second Brusilov Offensive for army commander General Aleksei A. Brusilov and the Kerensky Offensive for Alexander F. Kerensky, now minister of war and the key figure in the government, it is centered in Galicia and seeks to drive Austria-Hungary from the war. Although the Russians register great gains, the Germans prevent an Austro-Hungarian collapse. Order now breaks down in the Russian Army, and troops desert in droves.
July 16–18	The Bolsheviks and other radical groups attempt to seize control of the Russian government. The provisional government responds by jailing most Bolshevik leaders. Lenin goes into hiding in Finland.

September 1	German forces capture Riga on the Baltic. The way to Petrograd is now open.
September 9–14	New Russian Army commander General Lavr Kornilov demands a free hand over the army. Kerensky refuses and dismisses him. Kornilov then attempts a coup d'état supported by most of the army's officers, the middle class, and the Allied governments. Kornilov orders a march on the capital. In this crisis, Kerensky turns to the extreme Left, releasing Bolshevik leaders from prison and arming Leon Trotsky's Red Guard of soldiers, sailors, and workers sympathetic to the Bolsheviks. This step was unnecessary, as Bolshevik agitators halt the trains before they can reach Petrograd and persuade Kornilov's soldiers to go home. Kornilov is arrested, although he soon escapes.
November	The Russian Civil War commences with the revolt of the Don Cossacks.
November 6–7	Armed Bolsheviks seize power in Petrograd in a coup d'état and arrest members of the provisional government, although Kerensky escapes. The communist era in Russia has begun.
December 3	Russia opens armistice talks with the Germans in the Polish city of Brest-Litovsk.
December 17	An armistice goes into effect between Germany and Russia.

1918

January	White general Anton Denikin drives Bolshevik forces from the oil fields in the Caucasus region.
January 9	Peace talks open at Brest-Litovsk between Russian and German negotiators.
January 22	Ukraine declares its independence from Russia.
January 28	The Bolshevik Council of People's Commissars creates a Workers' and Peasants' Red Army. Originally military service is voluntary.
	In Finland, with Bolsheviks already in control of Helsingfors (Helsinki), a minority of radical Reds try to take power throughout Finland. That same day Finnish forces under Karl Mannerheim take Vasa (Vsasa), securing a large quantity of Russian arms. Mannerheim's subsequent drive south is checked in mid-March by Red forces, however.

February 3	Bolshevik forces capture Kiev.
February 13	White general A. M. Kaledin commits suicide following a military defeat.
February 16	Lithuania, still under German occupation, declares its independence from Russia. Bolshevik troops invade but are soon driven out. When German troops are withdrawn in November, Bolshevik forces move back in.
February 18	Following the breakdown of peace talks between German and Bolshevik negotiators, German troops resume hostilities. Crossing the Dvina River, they capture Pskov.
February 24	Estonia declares its independence from Russia.
March 3	Bolshevik negotiators accept the draconian German terms, and peace is concluded in the Treaty of Brest-Litovsk.
March 12	The Bolsheviks transfer the Russian capital from Petrograd (St. Petersburg) to Moscow, owing to the proximity of Petrograd to German forces and their satellite states but also because of the threat posed by the White forces.
March 26	Leon Trotsky switches positions in the Bolshevik government from commissar for foreign affairs to commissar for war.
April 3	German forces intervene in Finland on the side of Finns fighting the Bolsheviks.
April 13	The leading White general in the civil war, Lavr Kornilov, former commander of the Russian Army, dies in battle. Denikin then takes command of counterrevolutionary White forces in southern Russia.
April 18	German forces in Finland secure Helsingfors (Helsinki).
April 22	Transcaucasians declare their independence from Russia, forming the Transcaucasian Republic.
April 29	Bolshevik forces at Vyborg in Finland surrender, with the Finns securing substantial stocks of military equipment. By the end of April, Finland is free of the Russians.
May 26	The Transcaucasian Republic splits into three separate states of Georgia, Armenia, and Azerbaijan, all of which declare their independence from Russia.
May 29	Trotsky orders the members of the 45,000-man Czech Legion to surrender their arms. They refuse. The Czech Legion of the Russian Army wanted to join the Western Allies still fighting the Germans in the expectation that

an Allied victory would bring an independent Czechoslovakia. The Czechs will form an alliance with anti-Bolshevik forces and fight their way across Siberia along the Trans-Siberian Railway, eventually controlling much of it and allying themselves with Kolchak's White Army.

June 7	An armed clash occurs between members of the Czech Legion and the Red Army at Chelyabinsk.
June 23	British forces land at Murmansk. The Western Allies intend their intervention to hold German forces at bay and prevent extensive Allied military stores from falling into German hands. They also naively hope that if the Bolsheviks can be overthrown, the Russians will reenter the war against Germany.
July 4–10	The meeting of the Fifth All-Russian Congress of Soviets occurs. The Socialist Revolutionaries, who had previously participated in the Bolshevik government, are expelled, and on July 10 the congress adopts the constitution of the Russian Soviet Federated Socialist Republic.
July 16	With White forces and the Czech Legion nearby, the Bolsheviks kill Czar Nicholas II, his wife Alexandra, their children, and their attendants at Ekaterinburg on the approval of Lenin in Moscow.
August 2	British and French forces land at Arkhangelsk (Archangel).
August 11	The Japanese land troops at Vladivostok on the Pacific. Ultimately they will send as many as 50,000 men, far more than any other Allied power, with the hope of taking advantage of the Russian Civil War to annex the Russian maritime provinces.
August 15–22	U.S. forces land at Vladivostok.
September 4	U.S. troops join the British at Murmansk.
September 5–10	Some 11,000 Red troops battle 6,000 Whites and Czechs at Kazan, with the Reds victorious and recapturing Kazan.
September 23	The Whites create a new government, known as the Provisional All-Russian Government, at Omsk.
November 7–9	A Soviet government is organized in Bavaria in Germany.
November 11	An armistice between the Western Allies and Germany goes into effect on the Western Front, and World War I effectively comes to an end.

November 18	Latvia declares its independence from Russia.
	Following the establishment of an autonomous Siberian government at Omsk, a coup brings Admiral Kolchak to power, proclaimed as "Supreme Leader of Russia," in effect a military dictator.
November 22	German forces withdraw from Estonia, and the Bolsheviks invade.
December 18	French troops occupy Odessa.
December 24	Admiral Kolchak's Siberian White Army, supported by the Czech Legion, advancing westward from Siberia into eastern Russia, captures Perm and Ufa.

1919

January	Estonian troops, aided by British naval forces in the Baltic, force a Bolshevik withdrawal from Estonia.
	Bolshevik commissar for war Leon Trotsky commits major resources to halting a drive west into eastern Russia by White forces under Admiral Kolchak. Late this month the Reds retake Ekaterinburg and force Kolchak back into Siberia.
January 4	Bolshevik troops, having invaded Latvia, capture the city of Riga and set up a Bolshevik republic.
January 5	Bolshevik troops capture Vilna (now Vilnius), capital of Lithuania. This action sparks Polish intervention, leading to war between Russia and Poland.
February 3	Red forces capture Kiev.
March	With the approval of the Allies, a combined German-Latvian force drives Red forces from Latvia.
March 22	A communist government, headed by Bela Kun, is established in Budapest, Hungary.
April 19	Poland seizes Vilna.
May 21	British forces move into northern Persia, and in the Battle of Alexandrovsk on the Caspian Sea, a British flotilla defeats a Bolshevik naval force. The British then turn their ships over to the White Russians, but the Whites are defeated by the Reds in 1920, and the ships are lost.
May 22	The Red Army takes Ufa, and Kolchak's army retreats.
May–October	In a major White offensive, commander in the south General Denikin strikes north and retakes Kiev from the Bolsheviks on September 2. But General Peter

	Wrangel's drive on Tsaritsyn (the future Stalingrad) on the Volga to link up with forces under Admiral Kolchak is delayed by logistics problems, and by the time Wrangel takes Tsaritsyn on June 17, Red forces under General Mikhail N. Tukhachevsky have driven back Kolchak.
August	U.S. forces evacuate northern Russia.
August 18	White forces under Denikin capture Odessa.
September 30–October 12	Remaining British and French forces quit Arkhangelsk on September 30 and Murmansk on October 12. These areas of northern Russia are promptly retaken by the Bolsheviks.
October	Renewed fighting occurs in Latvia between Latvian and German forces against the Bolsheviks. The Western Allies insist that provisions of the Treaty of Versailles be enforced, and the Germans withdraw in late November.
October 6–19	White general Nikolai Yudenich, having assembled 20,000 men in southern Estonia, on October 6 crosses the border and marches on Petrograd in a bold effort to capture the city. He reaches the outskirts of the city on October 19, but Bolshevik commissar of war Trotsky is able to assemble sufficient forces to halt the drive and force Yudenich to retire to Estonia.
October 20	Red forces capture Orel.
November 14	Red forces retake Omsk.
December 17	Following the blunting of White general Denikin's offensive, Red Army general Mikhail N. Tukhachevsky retakes Kiev on this date and pushes the Whites back on the Black Sea.
	White commander Kolchak is forced to yield authority in Siberia to General Nicholas Semnënov.

1920

January	Latvian forces again expel Bolshevik troops.
February 1	Latvia and Russia conclude an armistice.
February 2	Bolshevik Russia and Finland and Estonia conclude the Treaties of Tartu, whereby Russia recognizes the independence of Finland and Estonia.
February 7	White general Kolchak is captured and executed by the Bolsheviks. Meanwhile, the members of the Czech Legion fight their way east and are evacuated from Vladivostok by Allied ships.

March 27	Allied ships evacuate most of the remaining White troops in southern Russia, principally from Novorossisk. The only remaining White force is a small army under General Wrangel in the Crimea.
April	U.S. expeditionary forces quit Siberia.
April 1	The last U.S. troops depart Vladivostok.
April 24	Fighting has been occurring between Polish and Bolshevik forces since 1919, but in early 1920 the Bolshevik government is able to turn its full attention to the Poles. Having rejected the Bolshevik ultimatum that would have established a Russian protectorate over Poland and with Russian forces then massing against his country, Polish leader General Jósef Piłsudski commences Operation KIEV, supported by Ukrainians under Hetman Simon Petlyura, with the goal of taking Kiev.
April 28	A Red Army offensive in the Caucasus captures Baku, but British warships prevent the Bolsheviks from securing control of the Caspian Sea.
May 7	Polish forces capture Kiev.
May 15–June 25	Red Army forces under Marshal Tukhachevsky strike southward against General Piłsudski's Polish left flank, while Red general Semën M. Budënny drives northwest against Piłsudski's right flank. By June 13 the Polish left is also in full retreat, and Red cavalry troops reach the outskirts of Lwów (Lemberg, today L'viv in Ukraine).
May 18	Bolshevik naval forces land on the Caspian coast and capture Enzeli (Pahlevi) and then Resht. The British then withdraw from the north Persian Gulf/Caspian Sea region.
June–November	Taking advantage of the Russo-Polish War, White general Wrangel launches a surprise offensive north from the Sea of Azov region, but Red forces led by General Mikhail Frunze drive the Whites back to the Crimea. The British evacuate the remaining White forces by sea in mid-November.
July 12	Lithuania concludes with Russia the Treaty of Moscow, whereby Russia recognizes Lithuanian independence.
July 15	Red Army troops capture Vilna from the Poles.
July 19–20	Red Army marshal Tukhachevsky captures Grodno in present-day Belarus.

August	Persian forces retake Resht from the Russians but are then driven out again and forced to retreat southward.
August 11	Russia and Latvia sign the Treaty of Riga, whereby Russia recognizes Latvian independence.
August 16–25	Polish forces under General Piłsudski defeat the Russians under Marshal Tukhachevsky in the Battle of Warsaw. One of the decisive battles of the 20th century, the Battle of Warsaw marks the first check to Bolshevik westward expansion.
September 2	White forces under Denikin capture Kiev.
September 12–October 10	The Poles continue their broad offensive on each side of the Pripet Marshes.
September 15–25	Polish forces under General Piłsudski defeat Russian marshal Tukhachevsky's Third Army in the Battle of the Niemen River.
September 18	Polish forces under General Wladisław Sikorski capture Tarnopol.
September 26	Polish forces under General Piłsudski recapture Grodno.
September 27	Polish forces under General Piłsudski again defeat Russian forces under Marshal Tukhachevsky in the Battle of the Shchara (Szczara). The Russians withdraw to Minsk.
October	Independent warlord and monarchist Baron Roman von Ungern-Sternberg leads renegade White Russian forces into Outer Mongolia, driving out the Chinese occupiers and setting up an independent monarchist state with the plan of recreating the old Chinese Empire.
October 9	Polish irregulars drive Lithuanian forces from Vilna. Subsequent efforts by the League of Nations to adjudicate the dispute with a plebiscite to the satisfaction of both Poland and Lithuania are unsuccessful. A state of war continues between Poland and Lithuania until December 1927.
October 14	In the Treaty of Tartu, Russia formally recognizes the independence of Finland. The treaty also calls for Lake Ladoga to be demilitarized.
October 19	The Bolsheviks and Poles agree to an armistice.

1921

January	With the Bolshevik government of Russia and the Persian government having negotiated a treaty, British forces withdraw entirely from northern Persia.

March	The Bolsheviks set up a Mongolian government in exile at Kiakhta across the border in Siberia, and a Red Army force under pro-Soviet Mongolian leader Damdin Süh-baatar invades Mongolia and defeats Ungern-Sternberg's forces.
March 18	In the Treaty of Riga, the Russo-Polish War is officially ended. The Russians yield to the Poles large areas of Belorussia and Ukraine: almost 52,000 miles of territory east of the Curzon Line. With the exception of Lithuania, this is roughly the Polish eastern border before the partition of 1797.
May	Ungern-Sternberg initially enjoys success in leading Mongolian forces in an invasion of Russian territory in the vicinity of Troitskosavsk (now Kyakhta, Buryatia).
August	Red Army forces defeat Mongolian forces under Ungern-Sternberg. Handed over by his own men to the Red Army on August 21, Ungern-Sternberg is quickly tried and shot. Russian troops then occupy Mongolia.
October 23	The Ottoman Empire and the Bolshevik government of Russia conclude peace in the Treaty of Kars. Russia secures Batum, while the Ottoman Empire obtains Kars and Ardahan.

1922

April 16	Russia and Germany conclude the Rapallo Pact. Germany extends de jure recognition of the Soviet government, and each renounces all war claims and prewar indebtedness. In the following years, the relationship sees the Soviet Union securing needed manufactures from Germany. The German Army also dispatches officers and technicians to help train the Red Army and is able to experiment with tanks and aircraft (both of which are forbidden to it under the Treaty of Versailles) as well as other new weapons and military equipment.
October 25	Japanese forces evacuate Vladivostok, and the Bolsheviks reestablish control. Russian historians regard this as marking the official end of the Russian Civil War.
December 30	A treaty signed in Moscow establishes the Soviet Union. It brings together in a federation the Russian Soviet Federative Socialist Republic and similar republics in the Ukraine, White Russia (Belorussia), and Transcaucasia. Known as the Union of Soviet Socialist Republics (Soviet Union), it goes into effect in July 1923.

1923

June 17   Ayano-Maysky District, the last White enclave under General Anatoly Pepelyayev on the Pacific coast, surrenders to the Bolsheviks.

SPENCER C. TUCKER

Further Reading

Bradley, John F. N. *Civil War in Russia, 1917–1920.* London: Batsford, 1975.

Brinkley, George A. *The Volunteer Army and Allied Intervention in South Russia, 1917–1921: A Study in the Politics and Diplomacy of the Russian Civil War.* Notre Dame, IN: University of Notre Dame Press, 1966.

Brovkin, Vladimir N. *Behind the Front Lines of the Civil War: Political Parties and Social Movements in Russia, 1918–1922.* Princeton, NJ: Princeton University Press, 1994.

Bullock, David. *The Russian Civil War, 1918–22.* New York: Osprey, 2008.

Chamberlain, William Henry. *The Russian Revolution, 1917–1921.* New York: Macmillan, 1957.

Foglesong, David S. *America's Secret War against Bolshevism: U.S. Intervention in the Russian Civil War, 1917–1920.* Chapel Hill: University of North Carolina, 1995.

Holquist, Peter. *Making War, Forging Revolution: Russia's Continuum of Crisis, 1914–1921.* Cambridge, MA: Harvard University Press, 2002.

Kenez, Peter. *Civil War in South Russia, 1918: The First Year of the Volunteer Army.* Berkeley: University of California Press, 1971.

Kenez, Peter. *Civil War in South Russia, 1919–1920: The Defeat of the Whites.* Berkeley: University of California Press, 1977.

Khvostov, Mikhail, and Andrei Karachtchouk. *The Russian Civil War (I): The Red Army.* London: Osprey, 1996.

Lebovich, Dimitry V. *White against Red: The Life of General Anton Denikin.* New York: Norton, 1974

Lincoln, W. Bruce. *Red Victory: A History of the Russian Civil War.* New York: Simon and Schuster, 1989.

Luckett, Richard. *The White Generals: An Account of the White Movement and the Russian Civil War.* New York: Viking, 1971.

Mawdsley, Evan. *The Russian Civil War.* Boston: Allen and Unwin, 1987.

Read, Christopher. *From Tsar to Soviets.* New York: Oxford University Press, 1996.

Silverlight, John. *The Victors' Dilemma: Allied Intervention in the Russian Civil War.* New York: Weybright and Talley, 1971.

Stewart, George. *The White Armies of Russia: A Chronicle of Counter-Revolution and Allied Intervention.* New York: Russell and Russell, 1970.

Strod, Ivan I. *Civil War in the Taiga: A Story of Guerilla Warfare in the Forests of Siberia.* Moscow: Progress, 1933.

Swain, Geoffrey. *The Origins of the Russian Civil War.* New York: Longman, 1996.

Wade, Rex A. *The Bolshevik Revolution and Russian Civil War.* Westport, CT: Greenwood, 2001.

Williams, Beryl. *The Russian Revolution, 1917–1921.* London: Blackwell, 1987.

Irish War of Independence and Civil War (1919–1923)

Causes

The English conquered Ireland in 1172 and immediately subjected the Irish to harsh rule. After a period of virtual Irish independence in the 15th century, Great Britain reestablished its control in the 17th and early 18th centuries. The great contest between Catholicism and Protestantism then sweeping Europe had major consequences for Ireland, where the English disestablished the Catholic Church and established the (Protestant) Church of Ireland, which the Irish people were obliged to support financially. Because the hated English were Protestant, the Irish clung to their Catholic faith. The English also tightened their political control; the Test Act of 1672 prevented all those not taking communion in the Church of England—that is, Catholics and nonconforming Protestants—from holding public office. It was not repealed until 1829. The Irish also found themselves deprived of other rights, including ownership of hereditary property. By the 19th century Ireland was largely ruled by wealthy Anglican landowners, many of them absentee, while most Irishmen were reduced to agricultural labor.

Natural disasters also inflicted a heavy toll. Severe winters of 1739–1741 destroyed the potato crop and other staples, resulting in the Famine of 1740. Perhaps some 200,000 people, an eighth of the population, died. The great Irish Potato Famine (1845–1852) added another 1 million deaths and led more than that number to emigrate (many to the United States).

In 1782 Ireland was granted legislative independence from Great Britain, although the British government still controlled Irish affairs. In 1798, abetted by revolutionary France, the Society of United Irishmen mounted a revolt with the goal of establishing an independent Irish republic. It was easily crushed and helped bring about the Act of Union (1800), by which Ireland was joined with Great Britain to constitute the United Kingdom of Great Britain and Ireland.

The continued sectarian divide, absentee British landlords, and the religious issue all fueled demands in Ireland for home rule and independence. Hatred of the English was now part of the Irish psyche, thanks to the centuries of economic exploitation and religious and political oppression.

Ireland was now also somewhat divided along other lines as well, for in the course of the 17th century the British government had taken much of the land of northeastern Ireland and granted it to Scottish and English settlers to form the "Plantation of Ulster." This northern Protestant majority, the so-called Unionists, was fearful of being engulfed in a sea of Catholic Irish and wanted to continue as part of Britain. They strongly opposed home rule for Ireland, seeing it as only a step toward Irish independence.

The gulf between Ireland and Great Britain was now deep. Whereas England and Scotland were predominantly Protestant, Ireland was largely Catholic. Whereas

Great Britain had become chiefly industrial, Ireland remained largely agricultural.

In the first quarter of the 19th century, the Catholic Association came to the fore. Its leader, Daniel O'Connell, was successful in his campaign to secure repeal of the Test Act. This action enabled Catholics to hold seats in the British Parliament. O'Connell failed to end the Act of Union, however. A more radical Irish organization then formed. Known as Young Ireland and mirroring other similarly named organizations throughout Europe, it attempted a revolt on July 29, 1848, during the wave of European revolutions that year, but it was easily put down by the British authorities.

In the 1850s the Fenian Brotherhood came to the fore. Formed among Irish in the United States, it attracted most of its support from abroad but did produce rioting in the English cities of Lancashire in 1867, which led the government to call out troops. In 1870 a new threat arose to British rule in Ireland with the formation that year of the Irish Nationalist Party, led by Charles Stewart Parnell. It took its place in the British Parliament alongside the dominant Conservative and Liberal Parties.

By 1870 there were some 600,000 Irish tenants working the lands of the great English landlords, who had the right to impose on them whatever rents they wished. To maximize their own returns, the landlords increasingly raised rents. They were able to do this because of the expanding Irish population. With the native Irish having virtually no other alternative except farming, the landlords could extract virtually any rent they wished. They could also evict tenants with no legal obligation to compensate them for any improvements they had made during their tenancy.

The short-term demands of the Irish Nationalist Party included the so-called "three F's" of fair rents, fixity of tenure, and "free sale," or the right to sell their successors any improvements they might have made. The ultimate Irish demand, however, was an end to landlordism and the return of the land that had once been theirs.

The so-called Irish question now dominated British domestic politics. In 1868, William Gladstone, leader of the Liberal Party, became prime minister and made reform in Ireland a priority. In his first ministry (1868–1874), Gladstone in 1869 pushed through an act that disestablished the Church of Ireland. This largely removed complaints by the Irish people regarding religion. Another act, the Land Act of 1870, prohibited the arbitrary increase of rents and stipulated that an evicted tenant had to be compensated for any improvements. The state was also to help peasants seeking to buy land. Unfortunately, the act largely failed because the landlords were able to take advantage of legal loopholes.

In his second ministry (1880–1885), Gladstone again sought to deal with the Irish problem. Parnell was determined to secure home rule, and in 1877 in the House of Commons he began a policy of obstructing all legislation until this was achieved. Although Parnell was opposed to violence, it occurred in Ireland and brought repressive measures. In 1881, however, Gladstone secured passage of a new land act that provided for a fixed 15-year period for rent as well as tenant safe tenure on the land and the right to sell any improvements.

Gladstone's third ministry, in 1886, was of short duration largely because of his support of home rule by a bill to give Ireland a separate parliament for its own affairs. But more than a quarter of Gladstone's own Liberal Party members of Parliament

Irish War of Independence and Civil War (1919–1923)

Approximate Number of Deaths Due to the Great Potato Famine (1845–1852)
1,000,000

Approximate Number of Landless Irish Tenants Working for English Landlords (1870)
600,000

Approximate Casualty Figures for the Easter Rising (April 24–29, 1916)

British Government Forces	Irish Insurgents	Civilians
132 killed, 397 wounded	64 killed, 200 wounded	254 killed, 2,127 wounded

Aftereffects of the Easter Rising

Number of Irish Rendered Homeless or Destitute	Number of Irish Imprisoned
100,000	3,500

Approximate Number of Deaths, Irish War of Independence (January 1919–July 1921)

British Government Forces	Irish Republican Army	Civilians
714	550	750

Sources: Tim Pat Coogan, *The Irish Civil War* (Boulder, CO: Roberts Rinehart, 1998); Michael A. Hopkinson, *The Irish War of Independence* (Ithaca, NY: McGill-Queen's University Press, 2002); Charles Townshend, *Britain's Civil Wars: Counterinsurgency in the Twentieth Century* (London: Faber and Faber, 1986).

opposed home rule. Led by John Bright and Joseph Chamberlain, they established the Liberal Unionist Party and joined with the Conservatives in defeating the Home Rule Bill. Parliament was then dissolved to allow the electorate to pass on the issue, and the Liberals went down to defeat.

Gladstone returned to power for a fourth and last time during 1892–1894. Home rule in Ireland was the chief issue. Support from the Irish Nationalists allowed the Liberals to form a government and, in 1893, pass Gladstone's Government of Ireland Bill (or Second Home Rule Bill). Promptly rejected by the House of Lords, it therefore failed to become law.

Following passage of the Parliament Act of 1911 that restricted the power of the House of Lords to veto legislation, in January 1913 the House of Commons passed a bill establishing an Irish parliament, although not with complete autonomy. The House of Lords immediately rejected it. Again it was passed by the Commons, and again the Lords rejected it. Under the provisions of the Parliament Act of 1911 it appeared that nothing could prevent the eventual enactment of the law in 1914 if the Commons passed it a third time. By this time, however, the Protestant Ulsterites were determined to do whatever was necessary to prevent Irish home rule. In addition to fearing rule by a majority Catholic Irish parliament, there was deep concern in the more industrial and wealthier Ulster that the views of rural and poorer Ireland would prevail and legislation would be enacted harmful to the economic life of that region. Ulsterites insisted that Ireland remain part of the United Kingdom.

Sir Edward Carson, leader of the Ulsterites, believed that the Liberal government might be frightened into dropping the home rule project if Ulster showed its determination not to submit. Mass meetings and demonstrations occurred, and on January 13, 1913, a military organization of 100,000 men, known as the Ulster Volunteer Force, was organized. Also, more than 237,000 Unionist men made a solemn covenant never to submit to an Irish parliament.

All of this caused Prime Minister Herbert H. Asquith to seek a compromise, which greatly angered Redmond, who on November 25, 1913, began to raise a force of Irish Volunteers to support home rule for all Ireland. Civil war appeared in the offing. The situation was made all the more difficult for the government in the so-called Carragh Mutiny of March 20, 1914, when a number of British Army officers chose to submit their resignations rather than be obliged to force Ulster to accept home rule.

Despite this threatening situation, the Commons passed the Home Rule Bill for a third time in May 1914. In July, with conditions in Ireland growing constantly more menacing, King George V called a conference of representatives of all sides to meet at Buckingham Palace, but no agreement could be reached.

In August 1914 World War I began. It led all sides to reach a compromise. The Home Rule Bill became law on September 18, but the Ulster Unionists teamed with the British Conservatives to secure simultaneous passage of the Suspensory Act that delayed enactment of the Home Rule Bill for the duration of the war. In 1913 the Irish nationalists had established the Irish National Volunteers of some 100,000 men to counter the formation the year before of the Ulster Volunteers. At the start of the war, most of the Irish National Volunteers joined the British Army. A minority of no more than 14,000 chose not to fight for Britain and formed the Irish Volunteers. All told, some 180,000 Irishmen served in the British Army during the war.

The Irish Republican Brotherhood, the Irish Volunteers, and the Irish Citizen Army established to protect Irish workers now resolved to revolt against British rule and establish an Irish republic. Patrick Pearse led what became known as the Easter Rising or Easter Rebellion of April 24–29.

Irish-born Sir Roger Casement agreed to seek German support, necessary for the endeavor to succeed. The Germans sent 20,000 rifles in the Norwegian trawler *Aud* to Ireland. Intercepted by the Royal Navy, it was scuttled by its commander. Casement, meanwhile, returned to Ireland aboard a U-boat but was almost immediately captured. The plotters had planned to use a parade by the Irish Volunteers in Dublin on Easter Day as cover for the risings. These setbacks and dissension in the leadership caused the rebellion to be put off until Easter Monday. While this made it a surprise to the British, it also meant that few Irish Volunteers took part, and the rebellion was confined largely to Dublin.

On April 24, 1916, some 1,500 rebels (1,200 Irish Volunteers and 300 members of the Citizen Army, including 90 women), seized strategic points throughout Dublin, and Pearse proclaimed establishment of the Irish republic. Although taken by surprise, the British rushed in reinforcements and sealed off the city while cutting off rebel units from one another. On April 29 Pearse surrendered.

In the so-called Easter Rising, government forces lost 132 killed and 397 wounded, while 64 insurgents were killed and perhaps 200 wounded. A total of 254 civilians perished, and 2,127 were wounded. Some 200 buildings in central Dublin were destroyed by the fighting and accompanying looting, and 100,000 people were left homeless or in need of public relief.

The surviving rebels were booed as they were marched off to prison, but the public attitude changed when the British placed all Ireland under martial law, and some 3,500 people, most of whom had not participated in the insurrection, were imprisoned. The authorities tried 161 participants. Sixty-six were sentenced to death, and 15, including Pearse, were executed by firing squad during May 3–15 before Asquith had the good sense to halt the remainder. Casement was later tried for treason and hanged in London. These actions, however, turned much of Ireland against the British and destroyed any hope of reconciliation.

In Britain the Easter Rising weakened Prime Minister Asquith, while in Ireland it led to the demise of the Irish Parliamentary Party and the rise of the separatist party Sinn Féin (Ourselves Alone), which explains why the Easter Rising was sometimes called the "Sinn Féin Rebellion," although that party had no part in it. Members of Sinn Féin who were interned for taking part in the insurrection were eventually released, and most of them, notably Michael Collins and Eamon de Valera, assumed leadership positions in the republican movement.

Sinn Féin's strength was clearly shown in the December 1918 British parliamentary elections, when it secured some 70 percent of the Irish seats in the British Parliament. Sinn Féin asserted that the elections constituted a mandate in favor of independence, and on January 21, 1919, the 27 newly elected Sinn Féin members of the British Parliament, calling themselves

the Teachtaí Dála (TDs), assembled at the Mansion House in Dublin and there established an Irish parliament known as the Dáil Éireann (Assembly of Ireland). Cathal Brugha was proclaimed president, as Sinn Féin leader Éamon de Valera had been rearrested in May 1918 and was then imprisoned in Lincoln Gaol in England.

SPENCER C. TUCKER

Course

The Irish War for Independence or Anglo-Irish War of 1919–1921 can be said to have begun on January 21, 1919, when the members of Sinn Féin elected to the British Parliament met in Dublin and organized themselves as an Irish parliament, the Dáil Éireann (Assembly of Ireland). Several hours later, members of the Irish Volunteers ambushed the transport of a cartload of explosives bound for the quarry at Soloheadbeg, County Tipperary, and killed two members of the Royal Irish Constabulary (RIC), the Irish police force. The fighting gradually spread. It was more a struggle for control of the Irish people than for territory and remained a low-intensity insurgency, consisting largely of acts of intimidation, ambushes, and assassinations.

Sinn Féin leader Éamon de Valera, having escaped prison in England in February 1919, on April 1 replaced Cathal Brugha as president of the Dáil Éireann (Assembly of Ireland), the self-proclaimed Irish parliament. The newly reconstituted Irish Volunteers, now known as the Irish Republican Army (IRA) and commanded by Michael Collins and Richard Mulcahy, concentrated on freeing political prisoners and attacking the RIC, the symbol of British authority in Ireland and a ready source of weapons.

With the British cabinet reluctant to employ military force, the job of restoring peace in Ireland largely fell to the RIC. The IRA applied social and economic pressures against the police and their families, and sometimes this turned violent. In republican areas, the campaign worked well; in Unionist areas, it failed. This strategy was sufficiently effective, however, that by the end of 1919, the RIC had lost almost 20 percent of its numbers through resignation and retirement. The recruiting pool also shrank.

When the RIC began to close its outlying stations to concentrate police power in the larger towns, the British government finally authorized recruitment of World War I veterans from Britain into the force. They became known as the "Black and Tans," after their polyglot uniforms. For this reason the War of Irish Independence is sometimes called the Black and Tan War or simply the Tan War. Sent directly into the existing force with little training, the Black and Tans began to arrive in March 1920. Their numbers proved insufficient, however. The British government then recruited, beginning in the summer of 1920, another police group, known as the Auxiliary Division of the RIC (ADRIC). They soon earned a reputation for brutality and atrocities.

With British Army support, in the autumn of 1920 the reinforced police struck out into the countryside they had abandoned months before. This put many IRA leaders on the run, but it also forced them into the role of full-time insurgents. Although fighting was sporadic, the IRA struck back in November and December 1920. On November 21, 1920, known as "Bloody Sunday," the IRA assassinated 14 British intelligence agents in Dublin. That afternoon members of the RIC opened fire at a soccer match, killing 14 civilians and wounding another 65. A week later the IRA

ambushed and killed 17 ADRIC members at Kilmichael in County Cork. London declared martial law throughout much of southern Ireland. The fighting now intensified, with no apparent end in sight. Most of the worst combat occurred in Dublin, Belfast, and Munster; these three locations accounted for some three-quarters of the casualties.

In December 1920 the British Parliament passed a fourth Home Rule Bill. It set up two parliaments in Ireland—one for the six counties in northeast Ulster and another for the rest of the island. Ireland's army, navy, foreign relations, customs, and tariffs all were to remain under control of the Parliament in London. Both divisions of Ireland would still be represented in the British Parliament as well, although in fewer members than before. Northern Ireland accepted the plan at once and proceeded to carry it out. The rest of Ireland repudiated it, however. Sinn Féin rejected outright anything to do with an act that would appear to permanently partition Ireland.

The year 1921 brought little change, except that the British Army received a mandate to engage in combat operations against the IRA, but this had little effect beyond adding to the violence. Both sides were preparing for increased fighting when on July 11, 1921, the leaders on both sides agreed to a truce. Negotiations during the next five months resulted in the Anglo-Irish Treaty that officially ended the war on December 6, 1921. The fighting had claimed some 550 dead on the IRA side and 714 dead for the United Kingdom forces; 750 civilians were also killed.

The treaty provided for the establishment of the Irish Free State, which would have the same constitutional status in the British Empire as the self-governing dominions. The Irish Free State would also have its own military forces and its own armed vessels for the protection of revenue and fisheries, although some harbor facilities were conceded to the British, and the Royal Navy would have responsibility for defending the Irish coast, pending an arrangement to be negotiated later. Much to the chagrin of the IRA, Northern Ireland was not to be included in the Irish Free State if it declared its desire to continue under the act of 1920.

In effect, the treaty partitioned Ireland. Southern Ireland became independent as the Irish Free State, while the six northern, primarily Protestant, counties were formed into the state of Northern Ireland and continued as part of the United Kingdom.

The treaty created a schism in the IRA. The treaty was not a month old when hardline republicans began to agitate against it in the Dáil Éireann ratification debates. De Valera took the lead in denouncing the treaty and urged its rejection. The IRA hard-liners opposed it because the new Irish state did not include Northern Ireland and because it did not make Ireland a republic and kept it within the British Commonwealth. The moderates, such as Michael Collins, who had headed the delegation to negotiate a settlement, asserted that despite failings, the treaty laid the basis for peace and friendship with England and brought to a close the centuries-old conflict. On January 7, 1922, however, the Dáil Éireann approved the treaty in a vote of 64 to 57, whereupon de Valera resigned the presidency. Collins succeeded him as chairman of the provisional government.

De Valera and his followers withdrew from the parliament and now plunged the new Irish Free State into civil war. The "Irregulars," as the IRA hard-liners came to be known, subjected Ireland to an orgy of destruction. As the Free Staters formed

a government, the IRA prepared to fight. Both sides took provocative actions, but neither seemed eager to engage in battle with their former comrades.

On April 14, 1922, some 200 antitreaty IRA members led by Rory O'Connor seized the Four Courts (the site of the Supreme Court, the High Court, the Dublin Circuit Court, and, until 2010, the Central Criminal Court) in the middle of Dublin and began to fortify it. Their aim was to spark a new armed conflict with the British that would unite the two IRA factions and bring about the scrapping of the Anglo-Irish Treaty and the institution of a republic encompassing the whole of Ireland.

The British then still had thousands of soldiers in Dublin awaiting evacuation. Despite heavy pressure from the British, the provisional government initially did nothing. This was an act of rebellion against the legally constituted Irish government, and Collins was determined that it be put down, but by Irishmen, not the British.

Elections to the Dáil Éireann occurred on June 16, and an overwhelming 73 percent of the vote went to protreaty candidates, but this seemed to make little difference to antitreaty IRA members who rejected the result. Two events now prompted Collins to move against the militants. The first was the assassination of British field marshal Sir Henry Wilson, who had played an important role in the Irish War of Independence and was gunned down by IRA militants on the steps of his private residence in London. The second was the kidnapping by the militants at the Four Courts on June 27 of Irish Free State Army deputy chief of staff General J. J. O'Connell.

Collins took action the next day, initiating the Battle of Dublin, a week of street battles during June 28–July 5 that also

A barricade during the fighting of the Battle of Dublin (June 28–July 5, 1922) that marked the beginning of the Irish Civil War. (Brooke/Topical Press Agency/Getty Images)

marked the commencement of the Irish Civil War. Dislodging the antitreaty forces from their Dublin stronghold entailed much destruction. The government forces suffered 16 killed and 122 wounded, while the militant IRA defenders sustained 49 killed, 158 wounded, and more than 400 taken prisoner.

The protreaty government's control over the main cities of Ireland and the lack of coordination between the different antitreaty military units meant that the latter's forces, which did not command the support of the predominantly rural Irish people or the Catholic Church, had no chance of winning the civil war. The conflict was nonetheless intense and bloody, with atrocities on both sides. On August 22 at Béal na Bláth in County Cork, antitreaty IRA members ambushed and assassinated Collins, who was determined to visit County Cork despite pleas by his advisers that it was too dangerous. There was never an official investigation into the assassination, and the circumstances surrounding his death remain mysterious. De Valera disclaimed any role in the event. O'Connor and three others were executed by the government on December 8 as a reprisal for the murder of a Dáil member.

William Cosgrave succeeded Collins as president of the provisional government. The deputies also adopted a constitution. The British king had nominal executive authority, represented in Ireland by a governor-general, but actual executive power was in the hands of an executive council, directly responsible to the lower house of the legislature. On December 6, 1922, the Irish Free State came into being by royal proclamation. Soon Ireland had been admitted to the League of Nations and had dispatched diplomatic representatives abroad.

The fighting escalated for several months before the antitreaty IRA began losing popular support. In the spring of 1923 de Valera finally admitted the impossibility of continuing the struggle, and in late April 1923 he first issued an order to his men to cease the struggle and then a proclamation ordering a cease-fire. The final death toll in the Irish Civil War was about 5,000 on the antitreaty side and some 800 for the government. The war formally ended on May 24, 1923, although the bitterness lasted for decades thereafter, and the divide between Northern Ireland and Eire continues to the present.

WILLIAM H. KAUTT AND
SPENCER C. TUCKER

Consequences

Sporadic violence continued in Ireland, including assassinations. In 1927, Éamon de Valera—who had refused to take the oath of allegiance to the British king and had therefore been excluded from the Chamber of Deputies—announced that he would take the oath and become head of a constitutional opposition.

Despite real gains that came to the Irish Free State during the administration of president of the Executive Council William Cosgrave (1923–1932), the worldwide economic depression inevitably affected his government's popularity. As in other countries, the voters turned against the party in power. De Valera, meanwhile, appealed to Irish nationalism by taking a decidedly anti-British approach. This included a demand for abolishing the oath of allegiance to the king. De Valera also won the support of small landowners with his

pledge to withhold the payments they were obliged to make to the British government under the prior land-purchase agreements.

In the Irish parliamentary election of February 16, 1932, de Valera's Fianna Fáil party triumphed over Cosgrave's Cumann na nGaedheal, winning 72 seats to 57. De Valera was then elected president of the Executive Council, and in July he withheld the payments to Britain on the land annuities. The British Parliament retaliated by empowering the government to levy a duty of up to 100 percent on Irish goods coming into Britain in order to secure funds equal to the defaulted land annuities. De Valera then imposed his own almost prohibitive duties on British imports. This crippling tariff war continued until 1936, when de Valera admitted failure and negotiated a trade agreement with London.

Meanwhile, de Valera had been taking steps intended to emphasize the political independence of the Irish Free State. The oath of allegiance to the king was abolished, and de Valera also made it unnecessary to secure approval of the British governor-general in Ireland for acts passed by the Irish parliament. Then in December 1936, the Chamber of Deputies abolished the office of governor-general altogether.

In April 1937 a new constitution was promulgated that proclaimed the Irish nation's "indefeasible and sovereign right to choose its own form of government, to determine its relations with other nations and to develop its life, political, economic and cultural, in accordance with its own genius and traditions." Nowhere in the document was there mention of Britain or the British king. The constitution provided for a two-house legislature. It also called for a president, although real executive power was vested in a prime minister and a cabinet responsible to the lower house of the Chamber of Deputies. The constitution was approved by 56 percent of those casting votes in a national referendum on December 29, 1937. The constitution took effect immediately, and the name of the Irish Free State was officially changed to Eire (Gaelic for Ireland).

Irish nationalism found expression in official promotion of the use of the Irish language, known as Gaelic, which is spoken as a first language by only a minority of the Irish people. The constitution of Ireland recognized Gaelic as the national and first official language of the Republic of Ireland (with English being another official language), although most business is conducted in English. From the establishment of the Irish Free State in 1922, the government required proficiency in Irish for new appointments to any civil service position and for lawyers (although this was modified in 1974). The Irish representative to the League of Nations was even instructed to make his speeches in it. Family names and place-names were Gaelicized. The great difficulty of the language, however, has prevented its widespread adoption.

In April 1938, de Valera concluded agreements with London that removed British naval installations and troops from the Irish republic, making Eire responsible for its own defense. Other agreements provided for Ireland to pay a final settlement of the land annuities as well as annual payments to compensate Britain for losses sustained in the violence of the 1920s. Each nation also accorded the other most favored nation status in trade. All matters of contention between the two states were thus removed except the vexing question of partition. His success in concluding these agreements helped de Valera's Fianna Fáil win a decisive majority in the June 1938 elections.

The outbreak of World War II provided de Valera an opportunity to show that Eire was independent of Great Britain. In contrast to other members of the British Commonwealth, Eire declared its neutrality, a decision that had considerable public support. With an army of only 7,500 men, two naval patrol craft, and four fighter aircraft, Eire was hardly in a position to make a major commitment of military forces. The inability to utilize Eire's ports for its naval ships, however, imposed a major strain on the Allies in the vital Battle of the Atlantic. During the war, de Valera steadfastly and foolishly turned down British offers, even by Prime Minister Winston Churchill, to resolve partition in return for an end to Irish neutrality. However, Eire did allow British overflights of its territory, and it returned downed Allied pilots to Northern Ireland instead of interning them; it also allowed British patrol craft in its waters. Thousands of Irishmen also volunteered for service in the Allied armies. During the war, more than 180,000 people left Eire for Northern Ireland or the United Kingdom, and 38,544 Irish citizens volunteered for service with the British armed forces.

There was some pro-German sentiment among the Irish, however. Anti-Semitic bills were brought before the Dáil, and de Valera refused to expel Axis diplomats. Perhaps more shocking, on Adolf Hitler's death in 1945, de Valera went in person to the German embassy to express his condolences.

Acts of violence by the illegal IRA against Northern Ireland were a problem for the Eire government, which feared that the British might use them as an excuse to intervene. To forestall such a possibility, during the war de Valera sharply increased the size of the Irish Army and auxiliary forces to some 250,000 men (albeit poorly armed and trained). Ireland suffered economically during the war, but de Valera doggedly pursued his policies.

On the other hand, Northern Ireland was an important base for Allied operations during the war. Soon after the Japanese attack on Pearl Harbor, U.S. president Franklin D. Roosevelt and Churchill agreed that Northern Ireland and Scotland would provide bases for training and the Allied troop buildup for the invasions of North Africa in 1942 and France in 1944. The Americans took over the defense of Northern Ireland, thus allowing British soldiers to be deployed elsewhere. The Eire government officially protested this agreement.

On December 21, 1948, the Government of Ireland Act was signed into law. Under it Eire became the Republic of Ireland. The act entered into force on Easter Monday, April 18, 1949, the 33rd anniversary of the beginning of the Easter Rising.

This action ended Ireland's technical link with the British Commonwealth, which at the time precluded republics from membership.

Unfortunately for the people of Ireland, sectarian violence continued in the island, as the IRA sought to bring about the union of Northern Ireland with the Republic of Ireland. The British and Irish governments sought to bring about a peaceful resolution to 30 years of sectarian violence in Northern Ireland during 1968–1998, widely known as "The Troubles," between the majority Protestant and the minority Catholic paramilitaries, while the British Army sought to keep order. Not until 1998 was a peace settlement secured; the Good Friday Agreement was approved in referendums both in Northern Ireland and the Republic of Ireland. As part of the peace settlement, the Republic of Ireland's territorial claim to Northern Ireland expressed in Articles 2 and 3 of its constitution was removed from that document.

SPENCER C. TUCKER

Timeline

1172	The English conquer Ireland.
1672	The English Test Act of 1672 prevents Catholics and nonconforming Protestants from holding public office. The act is not repealed until 1829.
1739–1741	Severe winters bring the deaths of some 200,000 Irish.
1782	Ireland is granted legislative independence from Great Britain, although the British government still controls Irish affairs.
1798	The Society of United Irishmen mounts a revolt hoping to establish an independent Irish republic, but it is easily put down by the British.
1800	The British Parliament enacts the Act of Union, by which Ireland is joined with Great Britain to constitute the United Kingdom of Great Britain and Ireland.

1845–1852
The Great Irish Potato Famine brings the deaths of some 1 million Irish. More than 1 million others leave Ireland altogether.

1848

July 29
The Irish republican Young Ireland organization attempts a revolt against British rule, but it is easily crushed.

1867
British Army troops are called out to put down riots by the Irish in cities in Lancashire, England.

1869
British prime minister William Gladstone secures passage by Parliament of an act disestablishing the Church of Ireland.

1870
A new threat arises to British rule in Ireland with the formation of the Irish Nationalist Party, led by Charles Stewart Parnell. Its elected representatives take their place in the British Parliament.

Gladstone also secures passage by Parliament of the Land Act. It prohibits arbitrary increases in rents and provides that evicted tenants be compensated for any improvements they have made. The state also is to help peasants seeking to buy land. Landlords are quick to take advantage of loopholes in the legislation.

1877
Parnell's Irish Nationalists begin obstructing all legislation in the British House of Commons until Irish home rule is achieved.

1881
Gladstone secures passage of a new land act with a fixed 15-year period for rent as well as tenant safe tenure on the land and the right to sell any improvements.

1886
Gladstone's attempt to pass a bill granting home rule to Ireland is stymied when more than a quarter of his Liberal Party breaks away and forms the National Liberal Party, joining the Conservatives in opposition and killing the legislation.

1893
Gladstone secures passage in the House of Commons of his Government of Ireland Bill (or Second Home Rule Bill), but it is promptly rejected by the House of Lords and therefore does not become law.

1913
The House of Commons passes a bill establishing an Irish parliament, although not with complete autonomy. The House of Lords immediately rejects the bill. Again passed by the Commons, it is again rejected by the Lords. Under provisions of the Parliament Act of 1911 it

appears that nothing can prevent the eventual enactment of the law in 1914 if the House of Commons passed it a third time, but the Protestant Ulsterites are determined to do whatever is necessary to prevent Irish home rule, and on January 13, 1913, they create the Ulster Volunteer Force, a military formation of some 100,000 men.

1913

November 25   The Irish National Volunteers, which grows to some 100,000 men, is established to counter the force being raised by the Protestants in Ulster.

1914

March 20   With civil war in Ireland looming, what is known as the Carragh Mutiny occurs. British Army officers at Carragh, Ireland, submit their resignations rather than being obliged to force the population of Ulster to accept home rule under separatists in southern Ireland. The officers are subsequently reinstated.

May   The British Parliament passes the Irish Home Rule Bill for a third time.

July   King George V calls a conference at Buckingham Palace to discuss the Irish situation, but it ends without resolution.

August 4   Britain declares war on Germany in World War I.

September 14   The Irish Home Rule Bill becomes law, but the Suspensory Act delays its implementation until the end of World War I.

1916

April 24–29   Encouraged by the German government, on Easter Monday, April 24, militant Irish nationalists seize strategic points throughout Dublin. The leader of this so-called Easter Rising or Easter Rebellion, Patrick Pearse, issues a proclamation declaring an Irish Republic. Events are largely confined to Dublin, and although caught off guard, British authorities respond swiftly and crush the insurrection by April 29.

May 3–15   British authorities, having placed Ireland under martial law and arrested thousands of people—many of them quite innocent—execute by firing squad 15 members of the Easter Rising, including Pearse. The harsh British reaction helps turn what had been perceived as a humiliating nationalist defeat into a patriotic triumph.

1918

December | The Irish republican Sinn Féin (Ourselves Alone) party wins a sweeping victory in elections in Ireland for the British Parliament, capturing most seats outside of the Protestant stronghold of Ulster. Sinn Féin considers this a mandate for an independent Irish republic.

1919

January 21 | Twenty-seven newly elected Irish Sinn Féin members of the British Parliament meet in Dublin. They form the Dáil Éireann (Assembly of Ireland) and declare independence from the United Kingdom. Because Sinn Féin leader Éamon de Valera is in prison in England, Cathal Brugha is proclaimed president. Several hours later members of the Irish Volunteers kill two members of the Royal Irish Constabulary (RIC). These actions begin the Irish War of Independence.

April 1 | Éamon de Valera, having escaped from prison in England in February, takes office as the president of the Dáil Éireann (Assembly of Ireland).

1920

March | British veterans of World War I, recruited to serve in Ireland against the Irish republicans and known as the "Black and Tans," begin arriving in Ireland.

November 21 | On this day, known as "Bloody Sunday," the IRA assassinates 14 British intelligence agents in Dublin. In the afternoon members of the RIC open fire at a soccer match, killing 14 civilians and wounding another 65.

December | The British Parliament passes a fourth Home Rule Bill for Ireland. It establishes two parliaments: one for the six counties in Ulster and one for the rest of the island. Ireland's army, navy, foreign relations, customs, and tariffs are to remain under London's control. Both divisions of Ireland are to be represented in the British Parliament. Northern Ireland accepts the plan, but the rest of Ireland repudiates it as appearing to make permanent the partition of the island.

1921

July 11 | Both sides agree to a truce in the fighting in order to commence peace negotiations.

December 6 | The Anglo-Irish Treaty is signed. It formally ends the Irish War of Independence, and Britain recognizes the

Irish Free State with the same constitutional status within the empire as the self-governing dominions.

1922

January 7
: The Dáil Éireann approves the Anglo-Irish Treaty in a vote of 64 to 57, whereupon de Valera resigns the presidency. Michael Collins, who had helped negotiate the treaty, succeeds him as chairman of the provisional government. De Valera and his followers then begin a civil war against the Irish Free State.

April 14
: Some 200 hard-line IRA members led by Rory O'Connor seize control of the Four Courts in central Dublin and begin to fortify it, hoping to draw the British into the civil war and reunite the two IRA factions.

June 16
: Elections to the Dáil Éireann on this date produce an overwhelming 73 percent vote for protreaty candidates, but the hard-line IRA members refuse to accept the verdict and continue the civil war.

June 28–July 5
: Borrowing artillery from the British Army, Collins sends the Irish Free State Army against the hard-line IRA members holding the Four Courts. The government forces prevail in the so-called Battle of Dublin.

August 22
: Collins is ambushed and murdered by IRA militants opposed to the treaty with Britain. He is succeeded by William Cosgrave as president of the provisional government.

December 6
: The Irish Free State comes into being.

1923

April
: Concluding that he cannot win the civil war, de Valera enters into a truce with the Irish Free State government.

May 24
: The Irish Civil War formally ends.

1932

February 16
: De Valera's Fianna Fáil party triumphs over Cosgrave's Cumann na nGaedheal in the Irish parliamentary elections, and de Valera becomes the president of the Executive Council.

July
: De Valera withholds payments owed to Britain on the land annuities, initiating a trade war with Britain that lasts until 1936.

1935

July
: Riots by the Protestant majority in Belfast, Northern Ireland, against Catholics lead to the expulsion of

Catholic families there. These actions bring reprisals by the Irish Free State government, heightening friction with Britain.

1937

April   A new constitution for the Irish Free State is announced.

December 29   The new constitution is approved by 56 of the electorate, and the Irish Free State is replaced by Eire.

1938

April   De Valera concludes agreements with the British government that remove British military installations and naval bases from the Irish republic and settles other issues such as payment for the land annuities and compensation for British losses sustained in the fighting in Ireland in the 1920s.

June   De Valera's success in securing the treaties with Britain helps his Fianna Fáil party win a decisive majority in the Irish parliamentary elections.

1939

September   Ireland declares its neutrality in World War II.

1949

April 18   The Government of Ireland Act goes into effect. Ireland officially becomes a republic and leaves the British Commonwealth.

1968–1998   Violence in Northern Ireland, known as "The Troubles," occurs in Northern Ireland between its Protestant majority and the Catholic minority. The British Army, seeking to maintain the peace, is also involved.

SPENCER C. TUCKER

Further Reading

Beaslai, Piaras. *Michael Collins and the Making of the New Ireland.* Dublin, Ireland: Phoenix, 1926.

Bowman, John. *De Valera and the Ulster Question, 1917–1973.* New York: Clarendon, 1982.

Collins, Michael. *The Path to Freedom.* Dublin, Ireland: Talbot, 1922.

Coogan, Tim Pat. *Eamon de Valera: The Man Who Was Ireland.* New York: HarperCollins, 1995.

Coogan, Tim Pat. *The Irish Civil War.* Boulder, CO: Roberts Rinehart, 1998.

Coogan, Tim Pat. *The Man Who Made Ireland: The Life and Death of Michael Collins.* Niwot, CO: Roberts Rinehart, 1992.

Dwyer, T. Ryle. *Big Fellow, Long Fellow: A Joint Biography of Collins and de Valera.* New York: St. Martin's, 1999.

Fergusson, Sir James. *The Curragh Incident.* London: Faber and Faber, 1964.

Foster, R. F. *Modern Ireland, 1600–1972.* London: Penguin, 1988.

Gregory, Adrian, and Senia Paseta, eds. *Ireland and the Great War: A War to Unite Us All?* Manchester, UK: Manchester University Press, 2002.

Hennessey, Thomas. *Dividing Ireland: World War I and Partition.* London: Routledge, 1998.

Hopkinson, Michael A. *The Irish War of Independence.* Ithaca, NY: McGill-Queen's University Press, 2002.

Jeffery, Keith. *Ireland and the Great War.* New York: Cambridge University Press, 2000.

Kautt, W. H. *Ambushes & Armour: The Irish Rebellion, 1919–1921.* Dublin, Ireland: Irish Academic Press, 2010.

Lydon, James F. *The Making of Ireland: From Ancient Times to the Present.* New York: Routledge, 1998.

McGarry, Fearghal. *The Rising: Ireland, Easter 1916.* Oxford: Oxford University Press, 2010.

Stewart, A. T. Q. *The Ulster Crisis: Resistance to Home Rule, 1912–14.* London: Faber and Faber, 1967.

Townshend, Charles. *Britain's Civil Wars: Counterinsurgency in the Twentieth Century.* London: Faber and Faber, 1986.

Townshend, Charles. *The British Campaign in Ireland, 1919–1921: The Development of Political and Military Policies.* Oxford: Oxford University Press, 1975.

Younger, Calton. *Ireland's Civil War.* New York: Taplinger, 1968.

Chinese Civil War (1927–1949)

Causes

The Chinese Civil War, which is generally divided in two phases—1927–1936 and 1946–1949—was an internecine conflict between the government of the Republic of China (ROC), led by the Guomindang (GMD; Kuomintang, Nationalists), and the supporters of the Chinese Communist Party (CCP). The war ended with the defeat of the GMD and the establishment of the People's Republic of China (PRC).

On October 10, 1911, a revolution commenced in China against the Qing dynasty that had ruled China since 1644. It is known as the Xinhai Revolution (Hsinhai Revolution and also the Revolution of 1911) because it occurred in 1911, the year of the Xinhai, or stem-branch, in the cycle of the Chinese calendar. The revolution began as a mutiny among troops at Wuchang in Hubei Province and quickly spread throughout western and southern China. On October 14 the court appointed General Yuan Shikai (Yuan Shih-kai) to head the Imperial Army and crush the rebellion, a task he accepted only after forcing the court to appoint him prime minister, which occurred on November 1, 1911.

Yuan made a few perfunctory efforts against the rebels but on December 4 signed a truce with them. Then on December 30 a revolutionary provisional assembly meeting in Nanjing (Nanking) elected Chinese Nationalist Sun Yixian (Sun Yat-sen), who had recently returned from exile, president of the Provisional Republic of China. He held that post from January 1 through March 12. On February 12, meanwhile, Qing child emperor Henry Puyi abdicated, and on February 15 Yuan secured for himself the position of president of the Provisional Republic of China by the national assembly. Sun resigned in order to unite the country. Yuan, however, soon ran roughshod over the new republican institutions in a bid to strengthen his personal power.

China was neutral at the onset of World War I in August 1914, but Japan, which came into the war early on the Allied side, sought to take advantage of the preoccupation of the major European powers with fighting in Europe to further its holdings in China. In November 1914 Japan captured the German base of Qingdao (Tsingtao) on Kiautschou Bay. Not content with this, on January 18, 1915, the Japanese secretly presented to Yuan a diplomatic note with 21 provisions, known as the Twenty-One Demands. On May 8 Yuan agreed to a modified acceptance of the first four groups of demands. These called for the transfer of Germany's rights in Shandong (Shantung) to Japan, extension to 99 years of Japanese rights in southern Manchuria, joint control by Japan of certain key Chinese industries, and a declaration that China's coasts would not be leased or ceded to any power. Yuan, however, rejected a fifth set of demands calling for Japanese advisers in key areas and railroad concessions in the Changjiang (Yangtze, Yangxi) River Valley.

Yuan, meanwhile, sought to become emperor. On December 9, 1915, following a carefully orchestrated monarchist campaign and the election of a handpicked assembly, he accepted the position of emperor, to commence on January 1, 1916.

Faced with an immediate rebellion in Yunnan in December 1915, however, Yuan announced on March 22, 1916, that he was canceling his imperial aspirations. He then organized a new republican cabinet. Yuan, however, died on June 6.

Because there was no successor capable of commanding the loyalty of the many disparate military forces across China, a period now began in which regional warlords controlled various parts of China, leaving the central government in Beijing with little real authority over domestic affairs. The warlord period lasted from 1916 to 1927. The term "warlord" is perhaps misleading, as many of them were in fact capable and intelligent men.

On August 14, 1917, China declared war on Germany and Austria-Hungary. The Chinese government took this step on urging by the United States, which itself had entered the war in April, in order to secure a place at the peace conference that would end the conflict. U.S. president Woodrow Wilson hinted that the principle of self-determination of peoples should apply to China. Many Chinese put their trust in Wilson and assumed that U.S. pressure would bring an end to the Japanese military presence in China.

Although it did not send combat units, China supplied considerable manpower in labor battalions sent to France, the Middle East, and Africa. As a consequence, China secured an end to the German and Austrian extraterritoriality and Boxer Uprising indemnity payments and the return of its cessions at Tianjin (Tientsin) and Hankou (Hankow). China's chief goal at the Paris Peace Conference was, however, to regain control of the Shandong Peninsula. In this it was to be disappointed. The leaders of Britain, France, and the United States ultimately supported Japan's position that it should continue in control of Shandong, which it had taken from Germany. Japan did, however, promise to return control of Shandong to China. This was accomplished in February 1922, although Japan retained economic control of the railway there and of the province as a whole.

The Allied decision at Paris infuriated the Chinese, and a great demonstration was held in Tiananmen Square in Beijing on May 4, 1919, protesting the peace treaty, which the Chinese delegates to the Paris Peace Conference then refused to sign. Disillusionment with the settlement and the West in general was an important factor behind the formation of the CCP.

Meanwhile, the GMD and Sun Yixian, who was president of the ROC from October 10, 1919, to March 12, 1925, sought to secure assistance from the major Western powers to defeat the warlords and reunify China. It had, however, been in the interest of most of these governments to see China weak, and in any case they were wrestling with their own major problems after the war. As a result, nothing came of Sun's effort. In 1921 Sun turned to the new Soviet Union, which agreed to support his efforts while at the same time aiding the newly established CCP.

The CCP was founded in Shanghai in 1921 by Chen Duxiu and Li Dazhao. While there had been informal communist groups in China and among Chinese overseas in 1920, the first CCP Congress was held in Shanghai in July 1921, attended by 53 men. Soviet representative of the Communist International (Comintern) Adolph Joffe advised the CCP early on to collaborate with other political groups supporting the Chinese Revolution, especially the GMD.

On January 26, 1923, in Shanghai, Sun and Soviet representative Joffe concluded what became known as the Sun-Joffe

Important Conflicts in the Chinese Revolution and Civil War

Name of Conflict	Dates	Principal Combatants	Primary Generals	Victor
Zhili-Anhui War	July 14–July 23, 1920	Zhili clique vs. Anhui clique	Wu Peifu, Duan Qirui	Zhili clique
First Zhili-Fengtian War	April 10–June 18, 1922	Zhili clique vs. Fengtian clique	Wu Peifu, Zhang Zuolin	Zhili clique
Second Zhili-Fengtian War	September 15–November 3, 1924	Zhili clique vs. Fengtian clique	Wu Peifu, Zhang Zuolin	Fengtian clique
Northern Expedition	1926–1928	Kuomintang vs. Fengtian clique and Zhili clique	Chiang Kai-shek; Wu Peifu and Zhang Zuolin	Kuomintang
Central Plains War	May–November 4, 1930	Chiang Kai-shek's forces vs. Coalition forces	Chiang Kai-shek; Yan Xishan, Feng Yuxiang, and Li Zongren	Chiang Kai-shek's forces
Battle of Shanghai	August 13–November 26, 1937	Nationalists and Communists vs. Imperial Japanese forces	Chiang Kai-shek and Chen Cheng; Kiyoshi Hasegawa	Japan
Battle of Nanjing	December 9, 1937–January 31, 1938	China vs. Japan	Tang Shengzhi, Matsui Iwane	Japan
Hundred Regiments Offensive	August 20–December 5, 1940	China vs. Japan	Peng Dehuai and Zhu De; Hayao Tada	China
Battle of Changsha	December 24, 1941–January 15, 1942	China vs. Japan	Xue Yue, Korechika Anami	China
Operation ICHIGO	April 17–December 11, 1944	China and United States vs. Japan	Tang Enbo, Shunroku Hata	Japan
Second Guangxi Campaign	August 4, 1945	China vs. Japan	Zhang Fakui, Yukio Kasahara	China
Xinghua Campaign	August 29–September 1, 1945	Nationalists vs. Communists	Liu Xiangtu	Communists
Shandang Campaign	September 10–October 12, 1945	Nationalists vs. Communists	Yan Xishan; Liu Bocheng and Dcng Xiaoping	Communists
Campaign to Suppress Bandits	November 1945–April 1947	Nationalists vs. Communists	Li Huatang, Lin Biao	Communists

Name of Conflict	Dates	Principal Combatants	Primary Generals	Victor
Battle of Siping	March 15–March 17, 1946	Nationalists vs. Communists	Liu Handong, Wan Yi	Communists
Meridian Ridge Campaign	August 13–August 18, 1947	Nationalists vs. Communists	Ma Jiyuan, Wang Shitai	Nationalists
1947 Autumn Offensive	September 14–November 5, 1947	Nationalists vs. Communists	Chen Cheng, Lin Biao	Communists
Siege of Changchun	May 23–October 19, 1948	Nationalists vs. Communists	Zheng Dongguo, Xiao Jingguang	Communists
Huai-Hai Campaign	November 6, 1948–January 10, 1949	Nationalists vs. Communists	Liu Chih, Liu Bocheng	Communists
Shanghai Campaign	May 12–June 2, 1949	Nationalists vs. Communists	Tang Enbo, Chen Yi	Communists
Battle of Kuningtou	October 25–October 27, 1949	Republic of China vs. People's Republic of China	Tang Enbo, Su Yu	Republic of China

Sources: Trevor N. Dupuy, *The Military History of the Chinese Civil War* (New York: F. Watts, 1969); E. R. Hooton, *The Greatest Tumult: The Chinese Civil War, 1936–49* (London: Brassey's, 1991); Odd Arne Westad, *Decisive Encounters: The Chinese Civil War, 1946–1950* (Stanford, CA: Stanford University Press, 2003).

Manifesto. In it the Soviet Union pledged assistance for China's unification. Comintern agent Mikhail Borodin arrived in China in 1923 to aid in the reorganization and consolidation of the GMD. The CCP also joined the GMD in what was known as the First United Front.

Chinese nationalism continued to be fueled by the foreign concessions in the country. On May 30, 1925, British police at Shanghai employed gunfire to end a Chinese student demonstration against the unequal treaties and the British presence. This May Thirtieth Incident and a similar occurrence at Guangzhou (then Canton) on June 23 resulted in a widespread boycott of British goods and shipping that continued until October 1926.

The Soviet Union, meanwhile, provided considerable assistance to the training of the new Nationalist Army and its military academy, established at Whompoa and headed from 1924 by Sun's trusted lieutenant, Jiang Jieshi (Chiang Kai-shek). A fervent Chinese Nationalist who opposed the Communists, Jiang had joined the Chinese Army in 1908 and had received military training in Japan. The CCP was also at Whompoa; one of the political instructors was Zhou Enlai, future foreign minister of the PRC. The CCP was quite small at this time, however; in 1922 it had only some 300 members, while GMD strength was some 50,000.

Unfortunately for China, revered Sun Yixian died on March 12, 1925. Jiang succeeded him and immediately moved to eliminate all potential rivals. On July 9, 1926, Jiang initiated the Northern Expedition, an effort by some 100,000 National Revolutionary Army soldiers to march from Guangzhou, defeat the warlords, and unify China.

Jiang's first objective was territory held by the warlord Wu Peifu. The National Revolutionary Army captured Hankou (Hankow) on September 6. Following a siege, the army took Wuchang (Wuch'ang) on October 10. Jiang then transferred the capital from Guangzhou to Hankou. He next moved east against the warlord Sun Chuanfang in the lower Changjian (Yangxi, Yangtze) River Valley, centered on the city of Nanjing (Nanking), which GMD forces captured on March 24, 1927.

Although his campaign against the northern warlords had gone well, Jiang became alarmed about the rising power of his allies, the Communists. The CCP had staged bloody although unsuccessful uprisings in several industrial cities, most notably Shanghai. Jiang now purged CCP members from GMD institutions, and on April 12, 1927, he ordered his troops to seize control of the Chinese portion of Shanghai and break the back of the CCP there. An estimated 3,000–4,000 Communists in Shanghai and neighboring areas were killed. Another 30,000 suspected Communists, peasant association members, and leftists died in purges from April through August 1927. Understandably, this action brought a split in the GMD. Denounced by the Hankou government for his actions in Shanghai, Jiang established his own government at Nanjing.

During April–June 1927, the two rival ROC governments each mounted campaigns against the northern warlords, now supported by Marshal Zhang Zuolin (Chang Tso-lin), the warlord of Manchuria and northeastern China. Hankou government forces, however, enjoyed only mixed success in northern Hubei (Hu-pei) and southern Henan (Ho-nan) Provinces, while the Nanjing forces under Jiang advanced through Anhui (Anhwei) Province against Sun Chuanfang in Xuzhou (Hsuchow). In June the warlord Feng Yuxiang, known as the Christian General, moved southwest from Shaanxi (Shan-hsi) against Jiang, who then withdrew into northern Henan. On June 21, however, Feng met with Jiang and agreed to support him.

In July 1927 Jiang's government in Hankou, having discovered a Communist plot to seize control, forced all known Communists from government posts and expelled the Soviet political and military advisers. Following this action, on August 1, communist elements in the Hankou Army stationed in the city of Nanchang in Jiangxi (Kiangsi) Province mutinied, hoping that this would trigger a communist revolution throughout China. Proposed by communist leader Li Lisan, the mutiny was led by Generals Ye Ting, He Long, and Zhu De.

Nationalist troops loyal to the Hankou government crushed the rebellion. Although most of the rebel troops were caught or dispersed, Zhu De escaped with a small force into the mountains of western Jiangxi. This Nanchang Uprising, however, is usually recognized as the beginning date for the Chinese Workers and Peasants Red Army (the future People's Liberation Army) as well as the long civil war between the Nationalists and Communists in China.

SPENCER C. TUCKER

Course

With the beginning of the Chinese Civil War on August 1, 1927, GMD leader Jiang refused to try for an agreement with more

GMD radical leaders at Hankou and, in order to restore unity, resigned a week later and traveled to Japan. The two GMD factions then reunited at Nanjing.

On September 7, in what is known as the Autumn Harvest Uprising, Communist leader Mao Zedong (Mao Tse-tung) led a peasant insurrection in Hunan and Jiangxi Provinces, establishing the short-lived Hunan Soviet. GMD forces defeated Mao's small force, but Mao and Red Army founder Zhu De established a rural strategy, placing the peasantry as the center of revolutionary activity. Heretofore traditional communist theory had called for revolution based on industrial workers.

Seeking to take advantage of the split in GMD ranks and the communist uprisings in central China, in September 1927 the warlord Sun Chuanfang led 70,000 men across the Changjiang but was met and defeated by GMD general Li Zongren (Li Tsung-jen) in the five-day Battle of Longtan (Lung-tan). Li lost some 5,000 dead, while Sun suffered as many as 20,000 dead and perhaps 30,000 taken prisoner. Sun then withdrew back into northern China. In December GMD troops also put down a communist uprising in Guangzhou.

Jiang returned to China in January 1928 and was reappointed commander of the ROC Army and chairman of the reunited Nationalist government. He then prepared to renew operations against the warlords of northern China to reunify the country while at the same time continuing the struggle against the Communists. On April 1, he launched some 700,000 troops against the northern warlords. GMD forces crossed the Huang He (Yellow River) and advanced on Beijing (Peking), taking the former imperial capital on June 8. Prominent warlord in northeastern China and Manchuria Marshal Zhang Zuolin tried to

Jiang Jieshi (Chiang Kai-shek), leader of the Chinese Nationalists (Guomindang), shown here in 1928. (FPG/Getty Images)

withdraw into Manchuria but, having rejected cooperation with the Japanese, was assassinated by them on June 4. He was succeeded by his son Zhang Xueliang, who acknowledged Nationalist authority over Manchuria.

The Japanese presence, however, rendered Jiang's efforts to control all China very difficult. The Japanese had secured the German concession in China in World War I, and the GMD northern offensive led them to rush troops to Jinan (Tsinan), capital of Shandong (Shantung), in order to establish their control over that entire province. Fighting followed, with GMD forces obliged to withdraw from Jinan on May 11. China appealed to the League of Nations, which took no action. On March 28, 1929, however, the Japanese and Chinese reached agreement, and Japanese troops withdrew from Jinan, ending the immediate crisis over Shandong.

In 1929 a dispute arose between the Soviet Union and the ROC regarding ownership of the Chinese Eastern Railroad, and in October Moscow sent troops into Manchuria. This action forced the Chinese and Zhang Xueliang to acknowledge that the Soviets had indeed inherited the assets belonging to the former imperial Russia. Russian troops then withdrew in January 1930.

In 1930, CCP chairman Li Lisan ordered a communist uprising among the urban proletariat of the principal cities of central China. Mao opposed this but was overruled. The sole communist success came at Changsha (Ch'ang-sha) in Hunan Province, and it was brief. Li was called to Moscow. Mao now established a rural base in southern China, the Jiangxi Soviet Republic, which by 1933 had some 200,000 men under arms.

Jiang now regarded the Communists as an even greater threat than the Japanese, and during December 1930–September 1934 he waged five campaigns against their Ruijin (Juichin) base in Jiangxi. Jiang referred to these as bandit suppression (or extermination) campaigns. The Communists easily turned back the first two (December 1930–January 1931 and April–May 1931). Jiang commanded the third campaign (July–September 1931) in person, and his forces were converging on Ruijin when word was received of the Mukden Incident. This caused him to break off the offensive and withdraw.

The Mukden Incident of September 18, 1931, saw Japanese officers set off an explosion near the South Manchuria Railway near Mukden (present-day Shenyang) in southern Manchuria, then blame it on nearby Chinese soldiers. The Japanese military then began the conquest of all Manchuria. Presented with this fait accompli, the Japanese government supported the action. On February 18, 1932, Japan proclaimed the "independence" of Manchuria as Manchukuo (Manzhouguo), headed by former Qing emperor Henry Puyi, who had been deposed in 1912. On September 15, 1932, a protocol established a Japanese protectorate over Manchukuo.

The Chinese responded with a boycott of Japanese goods, and to break this the Japanese sent 70,000 troops into Shanghai on January 28, 1932. In what is known as the First Battle of Shanghai (January 28–March 4, 1932), GMD forces put up surprisingly effective resistance before being driven out after a month of fighting. The Chinese government then agreed to end the boycott.

Jiang then resumed action against the Communists. His summer 1932 offensive in the Anhui-Henan-Hubei border area was largely successful. The Fourth Bandit Suppression Campaign in Jiangxi during January–May 1933 was, however, again disrupted by increased Japanese activity in northern China. Claiming that this Inner Mongolian province was actually part of Manchuria, the Japanese sent troops into Rehe (Jehol) and added it to their Manchurian holdings. In early April they also moved against Chinese forces south of the Great Wall to within a few miles of Beijing and Tianjin. In May, GMD forces evacuated Beijing, now controlled by pro-Japanese Chinese.

On May 31, 1933, the Beijing leaders concluded the Tanggu Truce with Japan. The truce required that all Chinese troops be withdrawn south and west of a line running roughly from Tianjin to Beijing, while Japanese troops would withdraw north of the Great Wall. This created a zone administered by the Demilitarized Peace Preservation Corps, controlled by Chinese friendly to Japan.

Jiang's carefully prepared Fifth Bandit Suppression Campaign (December 1933–September 1934) greatly benefited from German military advisers. This well-planned and methodical operation by some 300,000 GMD troops was slowly closing on Ruijin when the communist leadership decided on a breakout. This began with a diversionary attack by some 130,000 communist troops, allowing 86,000 others, 11,000 political cadres, and many thousands of civilian porters to escape. The troops left behind were to fight a delaying action, then disperse as best they could.

Although the escaping Communists easily broke through the first Nationalist strongpoints and began the Long March (October 1934–October 1935), they lost some 40,000 troops and virtually all the porters in fighting at the Xiang (Hsiang) River in Hunan Province (November 30–December 1, 1934). The remaining Communists now had to fight their way across some of the most difficult terrain of western China before proceeding north. The trek lasted 370 days, with the Communists under near-constant attack from the ground and air. Counting those who joined en route, about 100,000 people reached the remote northwestern Chinese province of Shaanxi. The Long March of some 3,700 miles was an extraordinary feat and confirmed Mao as leader of the CCP.

During 1935–1936 Jiang ordered troops commanded by allied warlord Zhang Xueliang to attack and eliminate the remaining Communists. The soldiers refused, insisting that the Chinese should be fighting the Japanese and not each other. In the December 1936 Xi'an Incident, Zhang forced Jiang to agree to a united front with the Communists against the Japanese. The GMD-CCP relationship remained strained, however.

Japan, meanwhile, continued its efforts to control all of China. On the night of July 7, 1937, an unplanned clash occurred west of Beijing at the Lugouqiao (Lukouch'iao), or Marco Polo Bridge, between Japanese and Chinese troops. Known as the China Incident, it marked the beginning of the Second Sino-Japanese War (1937–1945), which merged into World War II.

Later that month, after the Chinese government at Nanjing rejected their ultimatum, the Japanese invaded the coveted northern provinces, and by the end of December they controlled the five provinces north of the Huang He. In mid-December Japan installed a new government in Beijing. Japan never declared war, enabling it to avoid U.S. neutrality legislation and purchase raw materials and oil. But this also allowed the U.S. government to aid China. Japanese expansionary policies in China and Southeast Asia brought increasing U.S. resistance, culminating in American economic sanctions and the Japanese attack on Pearl Harbor (December 7, 1941).

Jiang gradually abandoned northern and eastern China, withdrawing to Chongqing in the far southwestern China province of Sichuan. Meanwhile, the Communists controlled northwestern China. The buildup in their military strength led the Communists to try to drive the Japanese from northern China. In the Hundred Regiments Offensive (August 20–December 5, 1940), Communist forces attacked Japanese installations and Japanese-held cities. The better-equipped Japanese North China Army responded in force, defeating CCP forces in pitched battles and convincing Mao to go over to guerrilla operations behind Japanese lines. This policy provoked ferocious Japanese reprisals against both the Communists and the civilian population in the so-called Three Alls Campaign ("burn all, loot all, kill all"), but it helped disrupt Japanese control and enhanced the reputation of the Communists as dedicated opponents of Japanese rule.

In December 1940 Jiang ordered the Communist New Fourth Army, operating south of the Changjiang in Anhui and Jiangsu (Kiangsu) Provinces, to withdraw north of the river. Its commander, General Ye Ting, refused, evidently because it conflicted with Mao's orders. Jiang then dispatched GMD troops. Ye finally obeyed, and at the end of December his troops began to cross the river. When most of the men were across, a far larger GMD force attacked the remainder, killing or capturing some 7,000 men, including Ye. Communist bitterness regarding this was perhaps the final blow to CCP-GMD collaboration against the Japanese, although an uneasy alliance continued until 1944.

Throughout the Second Sino-Japanese War, both Jiang and Mao focused on a postwar military confrontation. Jiang drove his U.S. advisers to distraction with his reluctance to commit his troops and the substantial military equipment provided by the Americans against the Japanese. Jiang's refusal and his failure to deal with the vast corruption that characterized many top ROC officials eroded his hold on popular loyalties. It was a different story in the Communist areas. The idealistic communist rhetoric, the Spartan living conditions of their leaders, the willingness to use troops to help the peasants, and small-scale partisan operations against the Japanese all aided the communist cause.

World War II ended in August 1945 with Japan's surrender, but some 1.45 million Japanese troops remained in central China, and 900,000 more remained in Manchuria. The Communists now controlled much of northwestern China, with some 90 million people and an army of some 1 million. Jiang insisted that the Japanese surrender only to GMD forces, then about 2.7 million men. During the war the Japanese had stockpiled substantial arms in Manchuria in order to hold that resource-rich area. Despite objections from Jiang, Soviet forces that had invaded Manchuria in early August 1945 turned over much of this equipment to the CCP. To forestall a communist takeover of all of northern China, beginning in August 1945 the United States provided aircraft and ships to transport some 500,000 Nationalist troops to Manchuria.

At the same time, U.S. leaders, especially Ambassador Patrick J. Hurley, urged Jiang to strengthen his political position by carrying out meaningful reforms. Jiang refused, saying that this must await the defeat of the Communists. Increasingly, many Chinese saw the CCP rather than the GMD as the only hope for long-overdue change. Hurley's efforts to encourage GMD-CCP reconciliation and the formation of a coalition government failed, and Hurley resigned.

Communist forces under Lin Biao now moved into southwestern Manchuria. Beginning on November 15, GMD troops attacked them in areas not controlled by the Soviet army. The much better armed GMD forces made steady progress, winning control of much of Manchuria.

The last and most sustained American effort to bring about a reconciliation between the two sides came in the 13-month mission to China of former U.S. Army chief of staff General George C. Marshall. Arriving in China in December 1945, he secured a temporary cease-fire in January 1946. It was broken later that spring when, as Soviet units withdrew, GMD forces attacked CCP troops moving into formerly

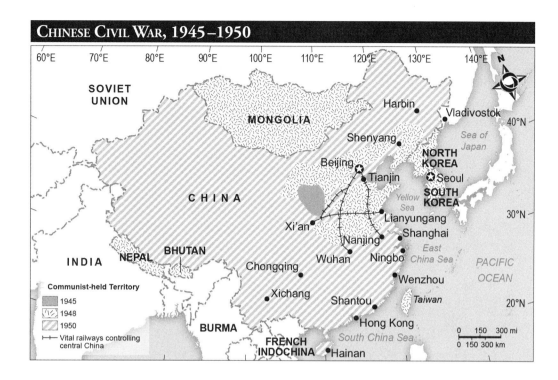

CHINESE CIVIL WAR, 1945–1950

Soviet-occupied areas in Manchuria. In January 1946 also the Communists renamed their military forces the People's Liberation Army (PLA).

Full-scale fighting resumed on July 20, 1946, when Jiang launched more than 100 brigades against Communist-held areas in Hubei and Henan Provinces. Although Washington provided massive loans and large amounts of military equipment, it refused to commit American troops.

In early November Jiang ordered a unilateral cease-fire and informed Marshall that he was willing to resume negotiations with the Communists. They rejected this, and the fighting continued. Marshall departed China in January 1947, blaming both sides for the failure to secure an agreement.

By 1947, with inflation and corruption rampant in GMD-controlled areas, large numbers of the Chinese middle class deserted the GMD; many left China altogether. Meanwhile, the CCP's introduction of land reform was a powerful incentive for peasant support. By 1947 also, the Communists were strong enough to commence offensive operations, and during January–March Lin Biao launched three separate offensives across the Songhua (Sungari) River. GMD forces, which had assumed a defensive posture with the end of U.S. military assistance in July 1946, repulsed all three.

During May–June 1947 PLA troops converged on the Manchurian population centers of Changchun (Ch'angch'un), Jilin (Kirin), and Siping (Szeping). With these cities cut off, Nationalist forces had to be supplied by air, and the GMD abandoned its bridgehead across the Songhua. Jiang rushed two additional armies northward. In the Third Battle of Siping (June 14–30), the GMD repulsed PLA efforts to take the city. A lull in the fighting then occurred as both sides reinforced.

Meanwhile, a successful GMD offensive in Shaanxi Province brought the capture of the communist capital of Yan'an on March 19, 1947. The PLA continued its offensives elsewhere, however, as Mao refused to pull back troops to defend his capital. (The PLA retook Yan'an on April 19, 1948.)

In Manchuria, in September 1947 the PLA began its Liaoxi Corridor Offensive to cut off Shenyang (Mukden) from northern China. GMD forces managed to secure the corridor in early October, however. In January and February 1948, the PLA mounted a second offensive. Jiang assumed command, and in February 1948 the GMD again secured the corridor, whereupon Jiang returned to Nanjing.

Constant PLA pressure in Manchuria brought a GMD withdrawal from Jilin in order to defend the large city of Changchun. The GMD's continued defensive posture and withdrawals were now adversely affecting morale. In May PLA forces opened an offensive in the Huang He Valley of north-central China, taking GMD positions north of the river. The offensive culminated in the Battle of Jinan during September 14–24, with 80,000 GMD troops captured or having defected.

On September 12, meanwhile, the PLA renewed its campaign against the Liaoxi Corridor, seizing control of it on September 12. Repeated GMD efforts failed to reopen it. With the military situation in Manchuria now hopeless, Jiang ordered his forces there to fight their way south. A substantial portion of the GMD forces at Changchun defected to the Communists, however, and many remaining units surrendered. In the Battle of Shenyang (October 17–30) the PLA attacked the withdrawing Nationalists. Shenyang itself fell on November 1, and by the end of the year the PLA controlled all of Manchuria. Jiang's effort to reclaim Manchuria had resulted in 380,000 GMD casualties.

The largest major Communist offensive of 1948 came in east-central China on November 7, at Kaifeng and Xuzhou, known as the Huaihai (Huai-Hai) Offensive for the Huai River and the Longhai (Lung-hai) Railroad that roughly paralleled the river. Each side ultimately committed some 600,000 men. General Chen Yi had overall command of the PLA forces. A rapid PLA advance and further Nationalist defections brought the encirclement of the 7th Army Group east of Xuzhou. Jiang ordered 15 divisions to relieve the surrounded troops, but the 7th Army Group surrendered on November 22, with only about 3,000 of its original 90,000 men escaping. Meanwhile, on November 16, PLA forces surrounded the GMD 13th Army Group at Xuzhou. Jiang ordered the 12th Army Group and the Eighth Army to advance to assist its escape, but PLA forces caught and defeated both. Jiang then abandoned Xuzhou. Some 200,000 men of the 13th Army Group were surrounded at Yongcheng (Yung-ch'eng), and most simply defected. The offensive ended on January 10, 1949. Nationalist casualties totaled about 327,000 men. This broke the back of the GMD forces and removed the principal Nationalist defensive line north of the Changjiang, opening the way to the capital of Nanjing.

On January 21, 1949, Jiang resigned. Vice President Li Zongren became acting president. On January 31 PLA forces entered Beijing, and on March 25 Mao proclaimed it again the capital of China.

On April 1, Li Zongren offered a peace settlement, suggesting a division of the country at the Changjiang. The Communists rejected this and called for the GMD to surrender. On April 20 PLA troops began crossing the Changjiang, and two days later they took Nanjing. What remained of the GMD government withdrew to

Red Army troops on the march during the assault on Shanghai in the Chinese Civil War, May 21, 1949. (Keystone/Hulton Archive/Getty Images)

Guangzhou. Shanghai fell on May 25. During the next month, many GMD troops and their commanders simply defected. The GMD capital was relocated to Chongqing.

On October 1, 1949, in Beijing, Mao announced the establishment of the PRC. This date is generally accepted as the end of the Chinese Civil War. The PLA took Ghangzhou on October 15 and Chongqing on November 30. The last GMD capital was at Chengdu (Ch'eng-tu).

On December 7, 1949, GMD forces completed their evacuation of the Chinese mainland to the island of Taiwan (Formosa), where the government of the ROC had already relocated. Some fighting continued on the mainland into 1950.

SPENCER C. TUCKER

Consequences

The communist victory in the long Chinese Civil War was complete. Zhou Enlai became premier and foreign minister. The Soviet Union and its satellites immediately recognized the PRC, followed by Burma, India, and Great Britain.

Remaining Chinese GMD forces who could escape, along with government officials and many ordinary Chinese, fled to the island of Taiwan, where Jiang Jieshi established the ROC government. The Nationalists also retained control of the islands of Jinmen (Quemoy) and Mazu (Matsu) and several dozen smaller islands off the Chinese coast. Jiang then carried out a program of reforms in Taiwan that, had they been enacted on the mainland earlier, might have won the support of the Chinese population during the civil war.

The ROC claimed to represent all China, a position supported by the United States. (The ROC continued to represent China on the United Nations [UN] Security Council until 1971, when a UN

General Assembly resolution recognized the PRC as the legal government of China and gave it the UN Security Council seat held by the ROC and indeed expelled the ROC from the UN altogether. Both governments officially claimed one another's territory, but increasingly few countries officially recognized ROC sovereignty over mainland China.)

Most observers expected to see Jiang's government on Taiwan soon fall to a Communist invasion from the mainland, and initially there was little interest in Washington in preventing this from occurring. This position changed dramatically with the decision by PRC leader Mao Zedong to take his country into the Korean War in the fall of 1950. U.S. president Harry S. Truman, having been already falsely charged by Republican Party leaders in the United States of having "lost China," found it politically necessary to prevent a Communist invasion of Taiwan. UN commander in Korea U.S. Army general Douglas MacArthur called for the employment of Chinese Nationalist troops in Korea or "unleashing" Jiang's forces on mainland China. Truman was not prepared to allow either, but he did order the U.S. Seventh Fleet into the Taiwan Strait to prevent a Communist invasion of Taiwan and also to prevent any ROC assaults from Taiwan against the mainland.

The Korean War was costly for China in human terms. Chinese deaths during the war from all causes approached 1 million. But Soviet assistance during that conflict brought the creation of the Chinese Air Force, and having fought the United States and allied UN forces to a stalemate, the war marked the emergence of the PRC on the world stage as a Great Power.

Successive U.S. administrations sought without success to isolate China diplomati-

cally and also enacted restrictive trade legislation against the PRC. The Indochina War (1946–1954) and the Vietnam War (1957–1975), during which time the PRC strongly supported efforts by the Democratic Republic of Vietnam (North Vietnam) to reunite all Vietnam under its rule, as well as the Southeast Asia Treaty Organization of 1954, two Taiwan Strait crises, and the PRC's growing desire to secure modern military hardware and nuclear technology all led to close cooperation between the PRC and the Soviet Union. The 1950s saw massive Soviet arms sales, economic aid, and technical assistance to the PRC.

After the United States and the ROC signed a mutual security treaty in 1954, cooperation between the PRC and the Soviet Union again increased, ending only in the so-called Sino-Soviet Split of 1960–1989 when the leaders of the two nations quarreled over who should lead the worldwide communist movement and the PRC leadership sharply criticized post–Joseph Stalin leaders for their de-Stalinization campaign and for the policy of peaceful coexistence with the United States. The PRC leadership was also upset over Soviet handling of the 1962 Cuban Missile Crisis and the Kremlin's neutral stance during a military clash between India and China in 1962. Indeed, at the low point in Sino-Soviet relations, there were even military clashes along the common border between the two countries. This period also saw the Chinese in 1964 explode their first nuclear bomb, with the PRC becoming the fifth nation in the world to possess such a weapon.

Relations between the United States and China remained tense after the Korean War and only began to improve in 1971, when U.S. secretary of state Henry Kissinger secretly visited China, followed the next year by U.S. president Richard

Nixon, which opened the way for the normalization of relations. The United States formally recognized the PRC in 1978, and in 1979 the two nations exchanged diplomatic legations. The vexing problem of the ROC on Taiwan remained, however.

Domestically, on taking over China the PRC instituted highly centralized political and economic control. There was considerable physical destruction from the civil war, and the government initially encouraged a degree of private enterprise to get the economy going again. This increasingly gave way, however, to large centrally controlled and inefficient government enterprises. By the end of the Cold War in 1991, however, there was an increasing mix of state-run and private enterprises. A burgeoning population helped drive the Chinese economy. During 1945–1991 the population doubled to more than 1 billion people, the world's largest.

This was not to imply that this process was an even one, however. In the Agrarian Law of 1950 the government seized privately held land and redistributed it to the peasants. In the process, largely completed by 1952, some 300 million peasants acquired more than 113 million acres (46 million hectares) of land. By 1953, however, the PRC increased agricultural collectivization, and under the so-called Great Leap Forward of 1958, some 20,000 farming cooperatives became People's Communes, with a decidedly mixed result.

In May 1956 the government launched its Hundred Flowers Movement, inviting differing views from Chinese intellectuals. An immediate outpouring of criticism followed, leading to a hasty retreat by the regime and the institution of the Anti-Rightist Campaign of 1957. In 1958 Mao launched the Great Leap Forward, a nationwide industrialization effort in which individual

Chinese were encouraged to set up their own backyard iron forges and steel mills. It was a disastrous failure. In May 1963, Mao began the Socialist Education Campaign to counter the growing influence of capitalism. It gave way to the Cultural Revolution (1966–1976), aimed at eradicating those accused of deviating from an ultraleftist approach. Numerous CCP leaders were removed from their posts, publicly humiliated, and, in many cases, killed.

The year 1975 saw the Four Modernizations Program of opening China to the outside world. The four modernizations were agriculture, industry, science and technology, and defense. The program instituted special policies and flexible measures to attract foreign investment and technology sharing. Also, special economic zones in the coastal regions for wholly owned or joint enterprises were established to promote exports.

In 1976 both Zhou and then Mao died, and new leaders came to the fore. Deng Xiaoping, who led the CCP from 1978, began the introduction of pragmatic policies based on "seeking truth from facts" and extensive economic reforms that reversed the collectivization and communalization process. This included household land contracts whereby private households could control land use, rural industrialization, incentives for private enterprises to hire private labor, and increased competition in international markets. These reforms were widely credited with making the PRC one of the world's fastest-growing economies and sharply raising the standard of living for hundreds of millions of Chinese.

Yet rising prices, growing corruption in the CCP leadership, and the increasing alienation of many young well-educated Chinese brought prodemocracy protests, leading to the Tiananmen Square Incident of June 4, 1989, when many of the students were killed in an army intervention. Deng stepped down from a number of his government posts, and an antibourgeois liberalization campaign ensued. Nonetheless, Deng's influence continued, and he was generally considered to be the country's "paramount leader" until his retirement in 1993. The reforming Chinese leadership ushered in by Deng introduced an increasingly mixed economy subject to market forces, and China enjoyed unprecedented economic growth, in large part thanks to an aggressive approach in world markets.

In sum, the Chinese Civil War unified China, and some six decades later China had the world's second-largest economy, behind only the United States, and had taken what many consider to be its rightful place on the world stage.

SPENCER C. TUCKER

Timeline

1911

October 10	The Xinhai (Hsin-hai) Revolution begins against the ruling Qing dynasty.
December 30	A provisional assembly meeting in Nanjing (Nanking) elects Sun Yixian (Sun Yat-sen) president of the Provisional Republic of China.

1912

February 12	The boy emperor Henry Puyi abdicates, bringing to an end the Qing dynasty.
February 15	General Yuan Shikai secures the position of president of the Provisional Republic of China. Hoping to unite the country, Sun Yixian resigns.

1915

January 18	Japan presents its Twenty-One Demands to Yuan, seeking to secure de facto control of China.

1916

June 6	Chinese president Yuan Shikai dies.
1916–1928	This period in Chinese history is often identified as the Warlord Era. It is marked by the emergence of powerful individuals ruling large swaths of northern China. The Warlord Era ends with the Northern Expedition of 1927–1928, but new warlords continue to exercise local control until the end of the Chinese Civil War in 1949.

1917

August 14	The Republic of China (ROC) declares war on Germany and Austria-Hungary.

1919

May 4

A great demonstration occurs in Tiananmen Square in Beijing against the Paris peace settlement, which confirms Japanese control of the Shandong Peninsula.

October 19

Sun Yixian becomes president of the ROC.

1921

July

The First Congress of the Chinese Communist Party (CCP) is held in Shanghai, attended by 53 men.

1923

January 26

President Sun Yixian and Soviet representative Adolph Joffe conclude the Sun-Joffe Manifesto, in which the Soviet Union pledges assistance for China's unification.

1924

Sun Yixian lieutenant Jiang Jieshi assumes command of the new military academy at Whampoa.

1925

March 12

President Sun Yixian dies and is succeeded by Jiang Jieshi.

1926

July 9

Jiang initiates the Northern Expedition, an ambitious military effort to defeat the warlords in northern China and reunify the country.

September 6

Jiang's GMD forces capture Hankou (Hankow).

October 10

Jiang's troops take Wuchang (Wuch'ang).

1927

March 24

Nationalist troops capture the city of Nanjing (Nanking).

April 12

Fearful of the Communists, Jiang orders GMD troops to seize control of the Chinese portion of Shanghai and destroy the Communist Party there. An estimated 3,000–4,000 Communists are slain. Another 30,000 suspected Communists and leftists are killed in purges from April through August 1927. Denounced by the Hankou government for his actions in Shanghai, Jiang establishes his own government at Nanjing.

August 1

Communist elements in the Hankou Army stationed in Nanchang mutiny. They hope to start a general Communist uprising throughout China, but troops loyal to GMD leader Jiang crush the revolt. The Nanchang Uprising is, however, recognized as the beginning of the Chinese Workers and Peasants Red Army (the future PLA) and the start of a long civil war between the Nationalists and Communists in China.

August 7

Owing to a split in the Nationalists, Jiang resigns and leaves China for Japan.

September

Nationalist troops defeat an offensive led by warlord Sun Chuanfang in the Battle of Longtan (Lung-tan).

September 7

In the August Harvest Uprising, communist leader Mao Zedong leads a short-lived peasant insurrection in Hunan and Jiangxi Provinces.

December 11–15

Nationalist forces put down a Communist uprising in Guangzhou.

1928

January 6

Jiang returns to China from Japan and is made head of both the Nationalist Army and a reunited Nationalist government.

April 1

The Nationalist offensive against the northern warlords begins.

May 3

Fighting between Nationalist and Japanese troops occurs in Shandong Province in eastern China, with the Nationalists forced to withdraw on May 11.

June 8

Beijing falls to the Nationalist forces.

1930

July 28

Communist uprisings occur, ordered by CCP chairman Li Lisan, in cities of central China. The only success, and it is temporary, comes at Changsha. This failure strengthens Mao's position in the CCP.

December 1930–January 1931

Jiang launches his First Bandit Suppression Campaign against the Communists at Jiangxi.

1931

April–May

Jiang mounts his Second Bandit Suppression Campaign in Jiangxi.

July–September

Jiang carries out his Third Bandit Suppression Campaign in Jiangxi.

September 18

The Mukden Incident occurs in which the Japanese forces plant a bomb on the railroad line near Mukden, then blame it on the Chinese and use this as an excuse to take all of Manchuria.

1932

January 28–March 4

In the First Battle of Shanghai, Japanese forces invade Shanghai to break a Chinese boycott of Japanese goods, ultimately defeating Chinese Nationalist forces there.

February 18

Japan proclaims the independence of Manchuria as Manchukuo (Manzhouquo).

September 15

A protocol establishes Manchukuo as a Japanese protectorate.

1933

January–May

Jiang carries out his Fourth Bandit Suppression Campaign in Jiangxi.

May 31

Japanese forces having resumed offensive operations in northern China and forcing Nationalist troops to evacuate Beijing, pro-Japanese Chinese in the capital conclude the Tanggu Truce with Japan. The truce creates a demilitarized zone controlled by Chinese friendly to Japan.

December–September 1934

Jiang mounts his carefully prepared Fifth Bandit Suppression Campaign in Jiangxi.

1934

October 1934–October 1935

Communist forces in Jianqxi break out of the Nationalist encirclement, and in the epic Long March, the survivors reach Shaanxi Province in northwestern China.

November 30–December 1

Nationalist forces inflict a major defeat on the escaping Communist forces in the Battle of the Xiang River in Hunan Province.

1936

December 12–24

In the Xi'an Incident, Manchurian warlord Zhang Xueliang forces Jiang Jieshi to agree to a united front with the Communists against the Japanese.

1937

July 7

A clash between Chinese and Japanese troops at the Lugouqiao, or Marco Polo Bridge, west of Beijing begins the Second Sino-Japanese War (1937–1945), and the Japanese invade the northern provinces of China. By the end of December they control all five Chinese provinces north of the Huang Ho (Yellow River).

1940

August 20–December 5

In what is known as the Hundred Regiments Offensive, Communist forces attack the Japanese in northern China but are ultimately defeated.

Late December	Nationalist troops attack part of the Communist New Fourth Army crossing the Changjiang River and destroy it in perhaps the final blow to CCP-GMD collaboration against the Japanese in World War II.

1941

December 7	Japanese forces attack Pearl Harbor, bringing war between the United States and Japan.

1945

August 15	Japan announces its surrender. The formal surrender ceremony ending World War II occurs on September 2. Communist forces now control much of northwestern China, with some 90 million people and an army of 1 million.
Mid-October	U.S. forces help move half a million Nationalist troops to begin the struggle with the Communists for control of Manchuria.
Mid-November	GMD troops attack Communist forces in areas of Manchuria not held by Soviet forces. The United States provides substantial assistance to the GMD but refuses to commit American troops.

1946

January	The CCP renames its military forces the People's Liberation Army.
July	The United States ends military assistance to the ROC.
July 20	Full-scale fighting in the civil war resumes when Jiang launches an offensive by more than 100 brigades against Communist-held areas in Hubei and Henan Provinces.
November	Jiang proclaims a unilateral cease-fire and proposes peace talks, which the Communists reject. The fighting then resumes.

1947

January–March	PLA commander in Manchuria General Lin Biao launches three separate offensives with his Fourth Field Army across the Songhua River, but ROC forces repulse all three.
March 19	GMD forces capture the CCP capital of Yan'an.
April 19	The PLA recaptures the CCP capital of Yan'an.
June 14–30	In the Third Battle of Siping, GMD forces turn back PLA efforts to take the city.
September 14–24	The Battle of Jinan ends in a PLA victory.

October 17–30	The PLA is victorious in the Battle of Shenyang, and the city falls to the Communists on November 1. By the end of the year the PLA controls all of Manchuria.

1948

March 12–14	In the Fourth Battle of Siping, GMD forces again rebuff the PLA.
November 7	The great PLA Huaihai (Huai-Hai) Offensive begins. It ends on January 10 in a resounding PLA victory, opening the way to their capture of the ROC capital of Nanjing.

1949

January 21	ROC president Jiang Jieshi resigns, and Vice President Li Zongren becomes acting president.
January 31	PLA forces enter Beijing.
March 25	Mao proclaims Beijing the capital of China.
April 1	ROC acting president Li offers a peace settlement based on a division of China at the Chongjiang. The Communist side rejects this and calls on the ROC to surrender.
April 22	The PLA captures the ROC capital of Nanjing.
May 25	The PLA takes control of Shanghai.
October 1	In Beijing, Mao proclaims the People's Republic of China. This date is usually given as the end of the Chinese Civil War, although some fighting continues into 1950.
October 15	The PLA captures Ghangzhou.
November 30	The PLA captures the latest ROC capital of Chongqing.
December 7	GMD forces complete their evacuation of mainland China to the island of Taiwan, where the government of the ROC had already relocated.

Spencer C. Tucker

Further Reading

Bianco, Lucien. *Origins of the Chinese Revolution, 1915–1949.* Stanford, CA: Stanford University Press, 1971.

Chen, Jian. *Mao's China and the Cold War.* Chapel Hill: University of North Carolina Press, 2001.

Crozier, Brian. *The Man Who Lost China: The First Full Biography of Chiang Kai-shek.* New York: Scribner, 1976.

Dreyer, Edward L. *China at War, 1901–1949.* New York: Longman, 1995.

Eastman, Lloyd E., ed. *The Nationalist Era in China, 1927–1949.* Cambridge, MA: Harvard University Press, 1991.

Fairbank, John King. *China: A New History.* Cambridge, MA: Harvard University Press, 1994.

Fairbank, John K., and Albert Feuerwerker, eds. *The Cambridge History of China,* Vol. 13, *Republican China, 1912–1949,* Part 2. Cambridge: Cambridge University Press, 1986.

Feigon, Lee. *Mao: A Reinterpretation.* Chicago: Ivan R. Dee, 2002.

Fenby, Jonathan. *Chiang Kai-shek: China's Generalissimo and the Nation He Lost.* New York: Carroll and Graf, 2004.

Furuya, Keiji. *Chiang Kai-shek: His Life and Times.* New York: St. John's University Press, 1981.

Hsiung, James C. *China's Bitter Victory: The War with Japan, 1937–1945.* New York: M. E. Sharpe, 1992.

Hutchings, Graham. *Modern China: A Guide to a Century of Change.* Cambridge, MA: Harvard University Press, 2001.

Lary, Diana. *China's Republic.* New York: Cambridge University Press, 2007.

Liu, F. F. *The Military History of Modern China, 1924–1949.* Princeton, NJ: Princeton University Press, 1956.

Lynch, Michael J. *China: From Empire to People's Republic, 1900–49.* London: Hodder and Stoughton, 2006.

Lynch, Michael. *The Chinese Civil War, 1945–49.* New York: Osprey, 2010.

Lynch, Michael J. *Mao.* New York: Routledge, 2004.

Pogue, Forrest C. *George C. Marshall,* Vol. 4, *Statesman, 1945–1959.* New York: Viking Penguin, 1987.

Short, Philip. *Mao: A Life.* New York: Henry Holt, 2000.

Spence, Jonathan D. *Mao Zedong.* New York: Viking, 1999.

Tanner, Harold. *The Battle for Manchuria and the Fate of China.* Bloomington: Indiana University Press, 2012.

Tanner, Harold. *Where Chiang Kai-shek Lost China: The Liao-Shen Campaign, 1948.* Bloomington: Indiana University Press, 2015.

Terrill, Ross. *Mao: A Biography.* Revised and expanded ed. Stanford, CA: Stanford University Press, 1999.

Truman, Harry S. *Memoirs,* Vol. 2, *Years of Trial and Hope, 1946–1953.* New York: Doubleday, 1956.

Westad, Odd Arne. *Cold War and Revolution: Soviet-American Rivalry and the Origins of the Chinese Civil War, 1944–1946.* New York: Columbia University Press, 1993.

Westad, Odd Arne. *Decisive Encounters: The Chinese Civil War, 1946–1950.* Stanford, CA: Stanford University Press, 2003.

Westad, Odd Arne. *Restless Empire: China and the World since 1750.* New York: Basic Books, 2012.

Zarrow, Peter Gue. *China in War and Revolution, 1895–1949.* London: Routledge, 2005.

Chaco War (1932–1935)

Causes

The Chaco War of 1932–1935 between Bolivia and Paraguay was both the bloodiest and most important military conflict in 20th-century South American history. The war was fought over possession of the northern Chaco. The Gran Chaco is a vast, arid area of some 250,000 square miles (estimates of its size differ) occupying the area of roughly 17° to 33° South latitude and between 65° and 60° West longitude located west of the Paraguay River, east of the Andes Mountains, and north of the Rio Pilcomayo. The Chaco is a sparsely settled, flat, alluvial, sedimentary plain with a subtropical climate. It can be divided into three principal regions, with most of the fighting in the war taking place in the semiarid Chaco Boreal, or Northern Chaco, which constitutes some 100,000 square miles of territory north of the Rio Pilcomayo to the Brazilian Pantanal. Today most of this land lies within Paraguay.

Bolivia and Paraguay were among South America's poorest countries. Both had claimed the Chaco since the Latin American Wars of Independence from Spain during 1810–1826. The Gran Chaco was supposed to have been divided among Argentina, Bolivia, and Paraguay, with the large part west of the Rio Paraguay to be joined to Paraguay. Argentina had claimed only the territory south of the Rio Bermejo. But the War of the Triple Alliance (1864–1870)—the bloodiest conflict in Latin American history, fought between Paraguay and the three allied countries of Argentina, Brazil, and Uruguay—had pushed Argentina's border farther north.

Both Bolivia and Paraguay are landlocked nations. Bolivia became especially interested in the Chaco region following the War of the Pacific (1879–1883), when it lost its seacoast to Chile. The first confrontation between Bolivia and Paraguay regarding the Chaco region came in 1885, when Bolivian Miguel Araña Suarez set up a trading post on the upper Paraguay River south of Bahía Negra. Suarez assumed it to be Bolivian territory, but Bolivia had earlier recognized Bahía Negra as belonging to Paraguay, and on learning of the situation, Paraguay dispatched a gunboat and forcibly evicted the Bolivians. In 1902, Bolivia set up two new outposts in the Chaco, both along the Pilcomayo River, ignoring a Paraguayan government protest.

World War I made oil a geostrategic resource, and its discovery in the Andean foothills and the subsequent growing importance of oil exports to the Bolivian economy increased the importance of the Chaco region as a route for shipping the oil to the Atlantic Ocean via the Paraguay and Paraná Rivers and eventually the Rio de la Plata. In the early 1920s, Bolivians were settling in the Chaco in larger numbers, encouraged by the belief that there were large oil reserves there. Foreign oil companies were also involved. Indeed, the Chaco War is sometimes attributed to the rivalry between Royal Dutch Shell in Paraguay and Standard Oil of New Jersey in Bolivia. Standard Oil was already producing oil from the Andes discoveries.

As more Bolivians settled in the Chaco, they came into conflict with the native Guarani-speaking tribesmen there and began to push them out. Although these natives shared strong ties with Paraguay, which claimed the Chaco, the Paraguayans were slow to settle there. Both sides then began sending military probes into the territory settled by the other. Small armed clashes ensued beginning in 1927, and these soon escalated.

The first major fighting between the armed forces of Bolivia and Paraguay occurred on December 5, 1928, when a Paraguayan cavalry unit overran the Bolivian outpost of Fortin Vanguardia, a few miles northwest of Bahía Negra on the northern part of the Paraguay River. The Paraguayans captured 21 Bolivian soldiers and burned the outpost. The Bolivians retaliated by securing Paraguayan military posts in the Pilcomayo area to the south. But with neither side then prepared for outright war, the leaders of both countries were willing to accept outside mediation in the form of a truce put together under the auspices of the League of Nations. A Pan-American conference then attempted to settle the question through arbitration but failed to achieve that end. Meanwhile, both Bolivia and Paraguay, having noted military deficiencies as a result of the 1928 fighting, sought to improve their organizational and mobilization schemes and acquire more modern weaponry from abroad. Bolivia used oil revenues to purchase arms from the British firm of Vickers.

Both countries also continued their penetration of the Chaco region to include the establishment of forts at key locations. Without a formal declaration of war,

Bolivian forces invaded the Chaco and on June 15, 1932, captured the Paraguyan Fort Carlos Antonia López. The Chaco War was on.

SPENCER C. TUCKER

Course

The Chaco War saw the first South American combat employment of modern 20th-century weaponry such as machine guns, motor vehicles, aircraft, and even a few tanks. All of these had been used by the belligerents in World War I. The Chaco War was in fact the first international conflict in the Americas in which both sides employed aircraft. The lessons of World War I were, however, little understood and only imperfectly applied. Infantry carried the brunt of the fighting in costly frontal attacks. The Chaco region also presented considerable physical challenges for the combatants. Its barren, arid nature forced both sides to pay considerable attention to logistics, and the Paraguayans proved much more adept at this than the Bolivians—a key factor in their ultimate victory.

Bolivia enjoyed a number of advantages. Its population of some 2,150,000 vastly outnumbered that of Paraguay, with 800,000. With 9,400 officers and men at the start of the war, the Bolivian Army was more than twice as large as that of Paraguay, but Bolivia never mobilized more than 60,000 men at one time, and never more than two-thirds of the army served in the Chaco. At the start of the war Bolivia had 88 aircraft, a surprisingly large number for Latin America at the time.

At the beginning of the war, Paraguay's army numbered some 4,000 men. On mobilization, its military force grew to some 24,000 men formed in two divisions under the command of Lieutenant

Chaco War (1932–1935)

Approximate Size of Opposing Armies (1932)	
Bolivia	**Paraguay**
9,400	4,000

Approximate Total Number of Men Mobilized (1932–1935)	
Bolivia	**Paraguay**
60,000	150,000

Approximate Death Figures (all causes) for Chaco War (1932–1935)	
Bolivia	**Paraguay**
52,000	36,000

Sources: Adrian J. English, *The Green Hell: A Concise History of the Chaco War between Bolivia and Paraguay, 1932–1935* (Stroud, Gloucestershire, UK: Spellmount, 2007); Bruce Farcau, *The Chaco War: Bolivia and Paraguay, 1932–1935* (Westport, CT: Praeger, 1996).

Colonel (later general) José Félix Estigarribia. By 1935, widened conscription to include 17 year olds meant that some 150,000 Paraguayans served in the army during the course of the war. Paraguay also had a small navy of 668 officers and men including naval infantry and artillery, both of which were subsequently assigned to one of the army divisions. The navy's principal role during the war was the riverine transport and supply of army forces and the evacuation of wounded. Paraguay had 25 aircraft at the start of hostilities.

The Bolivians had put together a detailed war plan, the principal objective of which was to control the west bank of the Paraguay River, thus giving Bolivia the entire Chaco Boreal. The Bolivian plan was to draw Paraguayan forces to the southwest, then outflank them to the north and secure the major upper Paraguay River port of Puerto Casado and the lesser ports of Bahía Negra and Fuerte Olimpo. Bolivia's leaders believed that no more than 6,000 troops could be sustained logistically in the Chaco at any one time. This, however,

nullified their considerable advantage in manpower over Paraguay. The Bolivians planned to conduct military operations in the Chaco with five strong infantry battalions supported by five artillery batteries. This force proved hopelessly inadequate, however, and considerable blame for what transpired must therefore rest with Bolivian president Daniel Salamanca Urey. Also holding the title of captain-general of the nation's armed forces, Salamanca consistently underestimated the resources that would be required for Bolivia to secure a military victory.

Lieutenant Colonel Juan B. Alaya, chief of staff of the Paraguayan Army, was the principal military strategist for Paraguay. He posited a defensive strategy at first, with a slow withdrawal of his forces to the Paraguay River while using cavalry and guerrillas to wear down the advancing Bolivian forces. After the Bolivians were extended logistically, he planned to go over to offensive operations by conventional units.

Bolivian forces invaded the Chaco Boreal without having formally declared war, and on June 15, 1932, they captured Fort Carlos Antonia López in the central region. This action secured Bolivian access to the Atlantic Ocean via the Paraguay River. On July 15 Paraguayan forces retaliated by capturing Fort Mariscal Santa Cruz, but in the first months of the war, it was the larger and better-trained Bolivian Army that enjoyed the most success. On July 29, the Bolivians launched their first major offensive of the war with the intention of threatening the main Paraguayan supply ports of Puerto Casado and Concepción on the Paraguay River. The Bolivian I Corps in the north took Fort Corrales, which had been occupied by the Paraguayans earlier, while the Bolivian II Corps captured Fort Lopez. The Bolivian I Corps then took Fort Toledo before going on to seize the strategically important Fort Boquerón on July 31.

On August 14, 1932, Eusebio Ayala was elected president of Paraguay, and deputy chief of staff Lieutenant Colonel José Félix Estigarribia convinced him of the need for Paraguay to gather all possible assets and strike quickly before Bolivia could take advantage with its considerably greater military resources. Indeed, Paraguay responded with a full mobilization, which enjoyed wide popular support for Paraguayans who considered the Chaco their homeland. Bolivia, on the other hand, carried out only a partial mobilization.

The Bolivians paused, planning to renew offensive action on September 11, but the Paraguayans, now commanded by Estigarribia, learned the timing of the Bolivian offensive and mounted a preemptive strike with some 13,000 men on September 9 against Fort Boquerón. Following the failure of four days of frontal assaults, Estigarribia changed his tactics to cutting off and isolating Bolivian garrisons

in order to force their surrender. Boquerón was taken on September 29, and Estigarribia was rewarded with command of the Paraguayan Army.

Following this success, on October 1 Estigarribia launched a general offensive. By October 10 the Paraguayans had retaken Forts Corrales and Toledo. Bolivian resistance at Acre was stout, but Estigarribia cut the road to it from the south, and the Bolivians then withdrew to Alihuati. The Paraguayan pursuit was so swift that the Bolivians could not hold there and were again forced to withdraw. Although Paraguayan success was more limited in the southern part of the front, Estigarribia had good reason to be pleased. The Paraguayans had taken some 15 Bolivian positions, defeating the Bolivian II Corps and separating it from the Bolivian I Corps.

Wet winter weather then closed in, precluding large-scale operations by both sides, although on December 13 the Bolivians did manage to retake Platanillos. This brought finis to major operations until March 1933. During the respite in the fighting, Bolivia organized a third army corps. President Salamanca also brought in German general Hans Kundt to command the army. As a German Army major in 1911, he had commanded a small military mission to Bolivia. Returning to Germany on the beginning of World War I, he had risen to major general. In 1921 he returned to Bolivia and became chief of staff of the army and in 1923 was appointed minister of war until a coup in 1930 forced him into exile. Now in 1932 he returned to Bolivia as commander in chief.

Unfortunately for Bolivia, Kundt was unable to reverse the situation. Although he resumed offensive operations, he was unable to take advantage of his superior numbers, better equipment, and more numerous aircraft. He also failed to establish an effective logistical network to supply his men in the Chaco. Kundt also persisted in employing his troops in costly frontal assaults against well-defended Paraguayan positions, although he was hardly the only commander during the war guilty of such.

In 1933 the Paraguayans, ably led by Estigarribia, succeeded in cutting off and destroying or at least forcing the withdrawal of one Bolivian Army unit after another. The Paraguayan 1st Division defeated the Bolivian 4th Division in the Battle of Gondra during July 11–15, 1933, although the Bolivians managed to withdraw with their heavy equipment. A major clash took place at Campo Grande during August 30–September 15 when Estigarribia's forces successfully encircled two Bolivian regiments defending two of the three flanks of Fort Alihuatá and forced a Bolivian surrender.

On March 1, 1933, the fighting resumed, with Kundt ordering a general offensive in the Coralles sector in order to relieve pressure on Saavedra. This forced Estigarribia to withdraw men from Camp Jordan to meet the offensive, which in turn enabled the Bolivian I Corps to take the weakened Camp Jordan. The Bolivian offensive soon ground to a halt, however.

Thus far, the major offensives in the war—two Bolivian and one Paraguayan—had brought only small gains. This changed with Estigarribia's second Paraguayan offensive, beginning on December 13. It enjoyed immediate success, with the Paraguayans forcing the surrender of the Bolivian 4th and 9th Infantry Divisions, which together sustained some 10,000 killed, wounded, or captured. These two divisions were half of the Bolivian I Corps. Estigarribia's great success in largely driving Bolivian forces out of the eastern Chaco, coupled with Bolivian logistical failures, had all but ended the war.

Displeased with the state of affairs, in December Bolivian president Salamanca removed Kundt from command. Kundt then returned to Germany. The far more capable General Enrique Peñaranda del Castillo replaced Kundt, but the damage had been done. Before long, Salamanca was quarreling with Peñaranda regarding military plans and appointments, asserting his authority as commander in chief.

With Paraguay apparently on the verge of victory, on December 20, 1933, its leaders unwisely accepted a Bolivian offer of an 18-day armistice for the purpose of peace negotiations. These went nowhere, but the halt in fighting worked greatly to Bolivian advantage and allowed Bolivian forces to complete their withdrawal and consolidate on Fort Ballivián, where they worked feverishly to improve its defenses. These came to resemble those of World War I, with dugouts, barbed-wire entanglements, and reserve and support trenches. Fighting resumed in early January 1934, but 11 months would pass before the Paraguayans captured Fort Ballivián.

By early 1934, Paraguay had 80,000 men committed to the offensive, and for the first time in the war its army was on undisputed Bolivian territory. General Peñaranda now reorganized his defeated troops, continued to improve the strong defenses around Ballivián, and restored Bolivian morale. For the first time in the war, the Bolivians also enjoyed the benefit of interior lines. A serious threat loomed, however, in that the Bolivian forces were backed up against the Rio Pilcomayo and the Argentine border. Were the Paraguayans to break through, they would be in position to cut off thousands

Paraguayan soldiers on patrol near Bolivian positions during the Chaco War. (Ullstein Bild via Getty Images)

of Peñaranda's men from the remainder of Bolivian territory.

Estigarribia slowly followed the Bolivian army as it had withdrawn. He put his men to work improving existing roads and building new ones in order to be certain that his extended supply system over hundreds of miles by water and land could sustain a major operation against Fort Ballivián. On April 25, with some 40,000 men in place, Estigarribia launched a general frontal assault, apparently forgetting the earlier costly lesson of such tactics at Fort Boquerón. With its failure, he attempted an envelopment of the Bolivian left flank, but this incurred heavy casualties of some 5,000 men taken prisoner.

On May 10, Paraguay formally declared war. Estigarribia, meanwhile, came up with a brilliant strategy. Noting that the Bolivians showed no inclination to leave

their defenses, he gambled that he could contain them at Ballivián with fewer than their number of men. He sent a division northeastward toward the valuable Bolivian oil fields of Santa Cruz Province in order to force the withdrawal of some Bolivian troops from Ballivián. Peñaranda took the bait, detaching some 12,000 men rather than the 10,000 Estigarribia had anticipated.

Estigarribia then struck on the afternoon of November 14, and by nightfall the next day the Paraguayan forces were within a few miles of Ballivián. By dawn on November 16 they were at the Pilcomayo River, and Bolivian Forts Ballivián and Guachalla had both fallen. The trap had closed on the Bolivians. While some of them managed to make it through the Paraguayan lines and others made it into Argentina, the vast majority were forced to surrender. The Paraguayans took some 8,000 prisoners, including 2 divisional commanders. Another 7,000 Bolivians had been killed. The Paraguayans also secured substantial quantities of weapons and military supplies. All of this was at a cost of 3,000 Paraguayan casualties.

By the end of this second phase of the war, Paraguay had taken 130 Bolivian forts and some 34,750 square miles of territory. Bolivia had now suffered some 45,000 casualties to only 20,000 for Paraguay. Bolivia's field army was down to 15,000 men, while that of Paraguay numbered 35,000.

The League of Nations now attempted to bring the war to an end, but the Bolivian government rejected the effort on the grounds that the proposed settlement did not submit the entire territorial dispute to arbitration. Despite the Bolivian military's desire to end the war, President Salamanca was determined to continue it. His poor relations with the military proved to be his downfall, however. Salamanca blamed Peñaranda for the recent military reversals and decided to replace him and a number of his subordinate commanders. But when the Bolivian president traveled to army headquarters at Villamontes (Villa Montes) to explain his decision, Peñaranda and other officers arrested him. In order to keep democratic appearances, they replaced Salamanca with Vice President José Luis Tejada, who may himself have been a party to the coup.

The third and final phase of the war commenced in December 1934. Paraguay now effectively controlled the Chaco Boreal. Bolivian territory there was limited to a small strip some 150 miles in length and 30 to 60 miles in width. With the Paraguayan field army now twice the size of their own forces, the new Bolivian government ordered a general mobilization

on December 9. This ultimately produced 125,000 replacements. Although the Paraguayan Army ultimately penetrated some 300 miles into Bolivia, Estigarribia failed to capture Villamontes in April, and effective Bolivian counterattacks finally drove the Paraguayans back.

By now, both sides were exhausted and tired of war. A cease-fire was arranged for noon on June 10, 1935. Then on January 21, 1936, five other South American countries (Argentina, Brazil, Chile, Colombia, and Peru) and the United States arranged a truce that included the renewal of diplomatic relations between Bolivia and Paraguay and the release of all prisoners of war.

SPENCER C. TUCKER

Consequences

Paraguay captured about 23,000 Bolivian soldiers during the war, along with some 10,000 civilians. Many of those captured chose not to return home, however. Paraguay returned some 17,000 prisoners of war. Bolivia released 2,500 Paraguayans. The war claimed some 52,000 Bolivian deaths: 25,000 in battle and 27,000 from sickness and disease. Paraguayan dead totaled some 36,000: 12,000 in battle and 24,000 from sickness and disease. The effects of the Chaco War on the region were felt for decades afterward.

The war was formally settled in the Treaty of Buenos Aires of July 21, 1938. It awarded Paraguay some three-quarters of the disputed territory but gave Bolivia access to the Atlantic Ocean by means of the Paraguay and Parana Rivers and the use of Puerto Casado as a free port. A final treaty delineating the border between the two countries was signed in Buenos Aires on April 28, 2009.

The war had profound effects on both countries. In Bolivia, government mishandling of the conflict discredited the national leadership. It also led to heightened political consciousness among the indigenous peoples, who constituted perhaps two-thirds of the population but worked in deplorable conditions in the mines and on the great estates. Their service in the army during the war brought their political awakening, along with a demand for reform.

The so-called Chaco Generation of malcontents included much of the middle class, intellectuals, and younger military officers. The latter took the lead, and on May 17, 1936, the Bolivian Army overthrew the government with the goal of effecting genuine change. In 1941 the Movimiento Nacionalista Revolucionario (Revolutionary Nationalist Movement, MNR) was established. A leftist political party, it favored reform and espoused mild nationalism while rejecting Marxist ideology. The MNR supported the regime of the mild reformer President Gualberto Villarroel López (1943–1946).

Wealthy Bolivian mining interests financed conservatives who opposed Villarroel, however. Workers, meanwhile, used their new political rights to demand additional concessions. Villarroel responded with excessive repression, which brought a large-scale revolt. On July 21, 1946, crowds invaded the Palacio Quemado. Although Villarroel announced his resignation, this proved insufficient for the rioters, who assassinated him and some of his aides, then hanged Villarroel's body from a lamppost.

The mining interests and the Marxist pro–Soviet Union Partido Izquierda Revolucionario (Party of the Revolutionary Left, PIR) now held power, while the MNR leaders fled into exile. After reorganizing their movement, in October 1949 the MNR began a brief but bloody civil war, which ended in their defeat. However,

the MNR won the 1951 national elections, only to have the PIR declare these fraudulent.

On April 9, 1952, the MNR seized power, beginning what is known as the Bolivian National Revolution. Initially led by Victor Paz Estenssoro, president during 1952–1956, the MNR introduced universal adult suffrage, instituted land reform, promoted rural education, and, in 1952, nationalized the country's largest tin mines. In 1964, a military junta overthrew President Paz. The military then held power for nearly two decades, when more political turmoil followed.

The Chaco War was also a catalyst for change in Paraguay. The soldiers who had sacrificed so much and had been forced to fight with so little in the way of military equipment resented what they regarded as the failure of the Liberal Party in power. There was also great anger regarding the failure to establish pensions for those who had won the war for Paraguay while General José Félix Estigarribia had been rewarded with a pension of 1,500 gold pesos a year. Colonel Rafael de la Cruz Franco Ojeda was the leader of the malcontents, who included students. When the government exiled Franco for having criticized President Eusebio Ayala, on February 17, 1936, army units marched on the Presidential Palace and forced Ayala to resign, bringing to an end 32 years of rule by the Liberals.

The Partido Revolucionario Febrerista (Revolutionary Febrerista Party), known as the Febreristas, brought Franco back from exile in Argentina as president. Franco then proceeded to deliver on the pledge of social and economic change. The new government guaranteed the right to strike and instituted an eight-hour workday. His government also expropriated a half million acres of land and distributed it to some 10,000 peasant families.

Franco's embrace of totalitarianism mimicking Benito Mussolini in Italy, however, brought reaction. In 1937, the army revolted and returned the Liberals to power. Unhappiness with the 1938 peace with Bolivia that saw Paraguay yielding some of the territory it had conquered in the war led the Liberals to install General Estigarribia as president.

Estigarribia understood that national stability demanded the institution of a number of the Febrerista policies. In order to circumvent opposition by die-hard Liberals in the National Assembly, Estigarribia assumed "temporary" dictatorial powers in February 1940. He then carried out reforms in land ownership, banking, and education while balancing the budget. In August 1940 a national plebiscite approved a new constitution. It gave the president enhanced powers, which in the wrong hands would be a threat to democracy.

Unfortunately for Paraguay, Estigarribia was killed in a plane crash in September 1940. War Minister Higinio Moríñigo succeeded him. A shrewd politician, Moríñigo nonetheless soon clamped down on individual rights and installed a military dictatorship that was openly pro-Axis.

He remained in power owing to his political abilities and a growing economy fueled by the wartime demand for Paraguayan products.

The Allied victory in the war led Moríñigo to liberalize his regime somewhat but not enough to prevent both a failed coup d'état in December 1946 and full-scale civil war in March 1947. Moríñigo was saved by the forceful actions of Paraguayan Army lieutenant colonel Alfredo Stroessner Matiauda. The rebellion came to an end in August, with the Colorados Party, which had been out of power since 1904, now having near total control. In 1950 a group of Colorados army officers, including Stroessner, installed Federico Chaves as president. The army was in effect the key player in Paraguayan politics. In May 1954, Stroessner seized power. He ruled Paraguay with a heavy hand until February 1989.

Incidentally, no commercial amounts of oil or gas were discovered in the Chaco region until 2012, when supposedly substantial deposits were located in the Paraguayan portion of the Chaco just north of the Pirity River. Bolivia also gained what turned out to be substantial natural gas reserves in its portion of the Chaco, with these second only to those of Venezuela.

SPENCER C. TUCKER

Timeline

1928

December 5 — Paraguayan forces attack and capture the Bolivian outpost of Vanguardia in the Chaco region. Bolivia retaliates by taking Paraguayan military posts to the south in the Pilcomayo area.

1932

June 15 — The Chaco War begins with the Bolivian capture of Fort Carlos Antonia López, thereby securing Bolivian access to the Atlantic Ocean via the Paraguay River.

July 15	Paraguayan forces capture Fort Mariscal Santa Cruz.
July 31	Bolivian forces capture the strategically important Fort Boquerón.
August 14	Eusebio Ayala is elected president of Paraguay.
September 29	Paraguayan forces retake Fort Boquerón.
October 1	Paraguayan forces launch a general offensive.
December 13	The Bolivian Army retakes Platanillos.

1933

March 1	New Bolivian Army commander General Hans Kundt launches an offensive in the Corrales sector of the front.
July 11–15	The Paraguayan 1st Division defeats the Bolivian 4th Division in the Battle of Gondra.
August 30–September 15	Paraguayan forces encircle two Bolivian regiments defending two of the three flanks of Fort Alihuatá and force a Bolivian surrender.
December	Mounting Bolivian military reverses lead Bolivian president Daniel Salamanca Urey to replace Bolivian Army commander General Kundt with General Enrique Peñaranda del Castillo.
December 13	General Estigarribia launches his second Paraguayan offensive.
December 20	Paraguay accepts a Bolivian offer of an 18-day armistice to conduct peace negotiations.

1934

May 10	Paraguay formally declares war on Bolivia.
November 16	The Paraguayans capture the key Bolivian installation of Fort Ballivián.
November 27	The Bolivian Army overthrows President Salamanca.
December 9	The Bolivian government declares a general mobilization.

1935

June 10	A cease-fire goes into effect.

1936

January 21	Six neutral nations (Argentina, Brazil, Chile, Peru, Uruguay, and the United States) secure a truce between Bolivia and Paraguay that leads to a diplomatic solution and brings the release of all prisoners of war.
May 17	Bolivian military officers, led by Colonel David Tora Ruilova, overthrow the government in a coup d'état.

1938

July 21   The Treaty of Buenos Aires officially ends the war. Paraguay receives three-quarters of the disputed territory, but Bolivia is awarded access to the Atlantic Ocean by means of the Paraguay and Parana Rivers as well as the use of Puerto Casado as a free port.

2009

April 28   A final treaty establishing the definitive border between Bolivia and Paraguay is signed in Buenos Aires.

SPENCER C. TUCKER

Further Reading

English, Adrian J. *The Green Hell: A Concise History of the Chaco War between Bolivia and Paraguay, 1932–1935.* Stroud, Gloucestershire, UK: Spellmount, 2007.

Estigarribia, José Félix. *The Epic of the Chaco: Marshal Estigarribia's Memoirs of the Chaco War, 1932–1935.* Austin: University of Texas Press, 1950.

Farcau, Bruce. *The Chaco War: Bolivia and Paraguay, 1932–1935.* Westport, CT: Praeger, 1996.

Finot, Enrique. *The Chaco War and the United States.* L&S Print, 1934.

Garner, William. *The Chaco Dispute: A Study in Prestige Diplomacy.* Washington, DC: Public Affairs, 1966.

Hagedorn, Dan, and Antonio L Sapienza. *Aircraft of the Chaco War, 1928–1935.* Atglen, PA: Schiffer Publishing, 1997.

Klein, Herbert S. *The Impact of the Chaco War on Bolivian Society.* Chicago: University of Chicago Press, 1963.

Morales, Waltraud Q. *A Brief History of Bolivia.* New York: Facts on File, 2003.

Quesada, A. M. *The Chaco War, 1932–1935: South America's Greatest Modern Conflict.* New York: Osprey, 2011.

Ronde, Philip de. *Paraguay, a Gallant Little Nation: The Story of Paraguay's War with Bolivia.* New York: Putnam, 1935.

Schey, Lida von. *Estigarribia and the Chaco War.* St. Andrews, Scotland: University of St. Andrews, 1984.

Zook, David H. *The Conduct of the Chaco War.* New York: Bookman Associates, 2006.

Second Italo-Ethiopian War (1935–1936)

Causes

The Second Italo-Ethiopian War (1935–1936), also known as the Second Italo-Abyssinian War, was a major colonial conflict in the lead-up to World War II that conclusively demonstrated the inability of the League of Nations in carrying out collective action to preserve international security. Italy's interest in colonizing Ethiopia, also known historically as Abyssinia, reached back to the late 19th-century imperialism and general effort by many European states to carve out holdings in Africa. Italy's interest was centered in the area along the Red Sea, the importance of which had increased with the opening of the Suez Canal in 1869. Another powerful motive behind the Second Italo-Ethiopian War was the desire to avenge an earlier humiliating defeat suffered by the Italians at the hands of the Ethiopians.

In 1869 an Italian trading company acquired the small port of Assab at the mouth of the Red Sea, purchasing it from one of the several rulers of a divided Ethiopia. In 1881 the Italian government took over control of Assab, and in 1885 it added Massawa. Italian imperialists then sought to expand these small holdings into an empire in Northeast Africa, and toward that end most coveted Ethiopia.

Italy's efforts to expand from Massawa into the interior brought war with Ethiopia, and in 1887 Italy suffered its first colonial disaster when on January 26 some 7,000 Ethiopians surprised a far smaller Italian force of some 500 men at Dogali; 420 Italians were killed, and the remaining 80 were taken prisoner.

This reverse did not deter the Italian government, now headed by Francesco Crispi. In 1900 Italy's East African holdings were organized as Eritrea. In 1889 also the Italian government had established another colony on the east coast of Africa, Somaliland, to the east and south of Ethiopia. That same year the Italians aided Menelek, a local Ethiopian chieftain, in seizing control of the Ethiopian Empire and persuaded him to agree to a treaty of friendship. Menelek was no fool, and seeing the treaty for what it was—an effort by the Italians to gain full control—he soon renounced it, whereupon the Italian government decided to employ force to secure a protectorate over Ethiopia in what became the First Italo-Ethiopian War (1895–1896).

In 1895 some 9,000 Italian troops began an invasion of northern Ethiopia from Eritrea. A paucity of resources and superior Ethiopian numbers, however, forced the Italians to withdraw into the fortress of Magdala, where they were besieged for nearly two months until their surrender in January 1896. In another action, almost an entire Italian garrison of 2,000 men was wiped out. These military reversals were a major blow to Italian pride, and Crispi ordered the recall of the governor of Eritrea, General Oreste Baratieri.

Goaded by his official disgrace or ordered by Crispi to advance (accounts differ) but convinced that well-armed, well-trained reinforcements who had recently arrived at Massawa from Italy would ensure victory, Baratieri decided on a major offensive into Tigre, the northernmost

Second Italo-Ethiopian War (1935–1936)

Approximate Casualties for the Battle of Amba Aradam (February 10–19, 1936)

	Ethiopians	Italians
Killed	8,000	300
Wounded	12,000	500

Approximate Casualties for the Battle of Ogaden (April 14–25, 1936)

	Ethiopians	Italians
Killed/Wounded	15,000	200

Total Deaths for Second Italo-Ethopian War (1935–1936)

Ethiopians (Military and Civilian)	Italians (Military)
760,000	2,000

Sources: John Gooch, *Mussolini and His Generals* (Cambridge: Cambridge University Press, 2007); David Nicolle, *The Italian Invasion of Abyssinia, 1935–1936* (London: Osprey, 1997).

Ethiopian province. On March 1, the invading Italian and Eritrean force of 20,000 men was met at Adowa and defeated by an army of 90,000 Ethiopians. The battle claimed half the invading force: 6,000 killed and 4,000 taken prisoner. Menelek, however, made no attempt to invade Eritrea. The victory consolidated his position as emperor, and he said that there had been sufficient slaughter. The wounded were left to die, the prisoners were emasculated, and native troops who were found to have been branded after Magdala and told not to fight with the Ethiopians again had their right hands and left feet amputated. In the ensuing Treaty of Addis Ababa (October 23, 1896), Italy recognized Ethiopian independence and promised to restrict itself to Eritrea.

In Italy, Adowa was regarded as nothing short of a national disgrace. Crispi was forced to resign, and the surviving soldiers were booed on their return to Italy. Although the Italian government then set aside imperial ambitions for the time being, many Italians wanted their country to emulate other European states in building an empire in Africa. They also wanted to avenge Adowa, which it was said was written on Italian hearts.

Benito Mussolini came to power in Italy in 1922 and within a few years had set up a fascist dictatorship. Mussolini liked to conjure up ancient Roman glories, and building an overseas empire was an important foreign policy goal. He took advantage of Adowa as a humiliating event to stir nationalist sentiment against Ethiopia and endeavored to make that independent African state part of a greatly expanded Italian African empire. Mussolini claimed that this would provide prestige but would also create a place for Italy's surplus population to settle rather than see Italians immigrate to the United States or Latin America. He saw the areas as a market for Italian goods, and he also hoped to discover there and be able to exploit strategic raw materials.

On December 5, 1934, Italian and Ethiopian border patrols clashed at Walwal (Ualual in Italian), an oasis in a disputed area between Ethiopia and Italian

Somaliland. Ethiopia immediately filed a protest with Italy and requested that the affair be arbitrated under terms of an Italo-Ethiopian treaty from 1928. Italy refused and demanded a formal apology, an indemnity, and the arrest and punishment of the Ethiopians involved.

On January 3, 1935, Ethiopia formally appealed to the League of Nations under Article 11 of its covenant. This decision by the Ethiopian government probably sealed Mussolini's intention to invade Ethiopia. In its January meeting, the League Council postponed consideration of the incident, hoping that it might in the meantime be settled by an arbitration commission and urging direct negotiation between the two governments. The arbitration commission's unanimous decision, announced on September 3, 1935, found that neither side was to blame for the Walwal clash, since each believed it was fighting on its own soil.

Meanwhile, the British and French governments, who sought a formal alliance with Mussolini against Adolf Hitler's Germany, began negotiations with Italy to reach a solution, but Mussolini rejected an Anglo-French proposal that would have secured for Italy an economic mandate under the League of Nations for the financial and administrative organization of Ethiopia. Instead Mussolini proceeded to build up Italian manpower, military equipment, and supplies in Africa. On March 28, he appointed General Emilio De Bono as the commander in chief of Italian forces in East Africa. On October 3, 1935, Italian forces again invaded Ethiopia.

SPENCER C. TUCKER

Course

On October 3, 1935, Italian dictator Benito Mussolini sent his forces into Ethiopia. He did so on his own authority without consulting with the Fascist Grand Council and without a formal declaration of war, expecting an easy victory that could be presented as a personal triumph. Four days later on October 7, the League of Nations Council decided that "the Italian government has resorted to war in disregard of its covenants under Article 12 of the Covenant of the League of Nations." This was the first time that the League of Nations had declared a European Great Power to be an aggressor. The League Council then referred the matter to the League of Nations Assembly for action. The League Assembly concurred in the verdict and appointed a committee to consider measures to be taken under Article 16, which dealt with sanctions.

The sanctions selected, which were adopted by most member states, included an immediate arms embargo against Italy, financial restrictions, a ban on the importation of Italian goods, a ban on the exportation to Italy of key war materials, and a call on member states to try to replace imports from Italy with imports from states that normally had profitable markets in Italy.

The sanctions were never applied with full force, and a ban on the export of oil to Italy—the one export commodity that might actually have halted Italy by bringing its war machine to halt (Italy had no oil of its own)—was approved but held in abeyance. Indeed, French foreign minister Pierre Laval and British foreign secretary Sir Samuel Hoare agreed to limit the sanctions even before they were applied. The two were, in fact, playing a double game, hoping not to drive Mussolini into the arms of Hitler. Publicly, the diplomats argued that sanctions on oil would not be effective because Germany and the United States were not bound by them. Furthermore, Mussolini had announced that the extension of sanctions to include petroleum products would be regarded as an unfriendly act—that is, an act involving war.

The sanctions voted by the League of Nations went into effect on November 18. The Italian government proclaimed November 19 as the "Black Day." Indeed, most Italians did not understand why their nation should be branded an outlaw state and rallied behind Mussolini.

While incomplete sanctions were being applied to Italy, the French and British governments were, in fact, trying to appease Mussolini. The result was the notorious December 1935 Hoare-Laval Proposals, with the planned cession to Italy of areas in Ethiopia in the vicinity of Eritrea and Somaliland and the establishment of an extensive zone of expansion and colonization in southern Ethiopia in which Italy should have a monopoly of economic rights. In effect, Hoare and Laval were prepared to cede most of Ethiopia to Italy. However, public knowledge and condemnation of the plan was so widespread and vigorous in Britain and France that both men were forced to resign.

In January 1936 new British foreign secretary Anthony Eden urged the adoption of sanctions on oil, but action was deferred while the League of Nations made one final effort at mediation. Before such could be taken, however, on March 7 German chancellor Adolf Hitler sent troops to reoccupy the Rhineland. Hitler's decision violated the Treaty of Versailles and the Locarno Pacts and raised the threat of a European war, further complicating the Ethiopian situation and definitely ending the possibility that France would support an oil embargo.

While the diplomats talked, Italian forces had been carrying out military operations in Ethiopia. Before the war, Emperor Haile

Selassie had done what he could with very limited national resources to improve his military forces. Belgian military advisers were at work to train the army, and Swedes ran an Ethiopian officer cadet school, but time was too short for either to accomplish much. The Ethiopians had a few radios, but this worked to their disadvantage in that the Italians intercepted the Ethiopian communications and were thus fully aware of all their tactical moves as they were occurring. More than any other single factor, this helped win the war for the Italians.

The Ethiopian Air Force numbered only 12 aircraft at the outbreak of the war. Complete Italian command of the air was another decisive factor. Italian military engineering was also a key to their victory. It helped overcome considerable natural obstacles in advancing the Italian war machine. The Italians also exploited the tribalism and factionalism of Ethiopia. Neither side bothered too much about taking prisoners.

General Emilio De Bono commanded Italian troops in East Africa and personally commanded the forces invading Ethiopia from Eritrea. This force numbered nine divisions in three corps: the Italian I and II Corps and the Eritrean Corps. General Rodolfo Graziani commanded a secondary southern front of two divisions and assorted other forces that invaded Ethiopia from Italian Somaliland.

At 5:00 a.m. on October 3, the Italian ground forces crossed the March River and invaded Ethiopia. Haile Selassie ordered Ras (Duke) Seyum Mangasha, commanding the Ethiopian Army of Tigre, to withdraw a day's march from the river. Other Ethiopian forces also fell back, and the Italians occupied Adigrat on October 5. Adowa, the site of the Italian Army's humiliating defeat in 1896, was taken by the

Italian soldiers during the fighting in Eritrea in 1935 during the Second Italo-Ethiopian War (1935–1936). (Galerie Bilderwelt/Getty Images)

Italians the next day. The Italians secured the holy city of Axum without resistance on October 15, with the Italian soldiers looting the Obelisk of Axum. Makale fell on November 8, and on November 16 De Bono was rewarded with promotion to the rank of marshal of Italy. The Italian advance was deliberate but too slow for Mussolini, and when De Bono refused to advance beyond Makale to Amba Alagi as Mussolini demanded, Mussolini replaced him with Marshal Pietro Badoglio.

In December, Haile Selassie mounted what came to be known as the Christmas Offensive. Four Ethiopian armies totaling some 190,000 men advanced against the Italians with the goal of splitting the enemy forces on the northern front and invading Eritrea. Although the Ethiopians enjoyed modest success and succeeded in destroying a number of the small Italian

tanks, they were unable to overcome the advantage in modern weaponry held by the Italians.

On December 26, Badoglio requested and received permission from Mussolini to employ poison gas. This took the form of a mixture of different gases, including mustard gas. Because it was absorbed through the skin, it severely affected the Ethiopian soldiers, most of whom went barefoot. The Italian Air Force also bombed a Swedish Red Cross hospital, which was plainly marked with red crosses, and also employed mustard gas there.

Upon receiving reinforcements from Italy, Badoglio resumed the northern offensive in late January 1936. Three important northern front battles followed. The First Battle of Tembien (January 20–24) ended in a draw, but the Italians ended the threat of an invasion of Eritrea by

Ethiopian forces under Ras Kassa. In early February the Italians captured Amba Aradam, and in the battle of that same name (also known as the Battle of Enderta, as it occurred over most of that province), Badoglio's 70,000 Italians destroyed as a fighting force Ras Mulugeta Yeggazu's army of 80,000 men, inflicting some 8,000 killed and 12,000 wounded on the Ethiopians while suffering only 800 casualties themselves. On February 27–29 the Italians won decisively the Second Battle of Tembien, in which they destroyed the Ethiopian armies commanded by Ras Kassa and Ras Seyoum.

Indeed, the northern front saw unrelieved Ethiopian defeats. In the Battle of Shire (February 29–March 2) the Italians defeated an Ethiopian army under Ras Imru, and on March 31 in the Battle of Maythew they defeated an Ethiopian counteroffensive led in person by Emperor Haile Selassie, with the Italian Air Force attacking the Ethiopian survivors at Lake Ashangi with mustard gas. The Italians sustained 400 casualties and the Eritrean forces fighting with them suffered 873, while the Ethiopians sustained some 11,000 casualties.

Meanwhile, on the southern front, General Graziani also attacked on October 3, 1935, in a series of probes designed to test Ethiopian defenses along the border with Italian Somaliland while also securing Ethiopian frontier posts. As on the northern front, the Ethiopians took the offensive in December in hopes of recovering lost territory and then invading Italian Somaliland. In the ensuing Battle of Genale Doria (January 2–16, 1936), however, Graziani's Italians turned back the Ethiopians under Ras Desta Damtu advancing on Dolo. A lull in ground combat then ensued. Nonetheless, the Italian Air Force remained active, and on March 22, despite the fact that

Harar, Ethiopia's second-largest population center, had been declared an open city in January and there was no military activity there, Italian Air Force planes bombed both it and Jijiga, greatly damaging both cities. The Italians occupied Harar on March 26.

On April 14, Graziani launched a ground offensive, initiating the Battle of the Ogaden (April 14–25) against defenses manned by the last Ethiopian force of any size on the southern front, that commanded by Ras Nasibu Emmanual. The Italians were completely victorious, with the Ethiopians sustaining some 15,000 killed or wounded and the Italians only 200. Mussolini promoted Graziani to marshal of Italy for his actions, and Graziani replaced Badoglio as viceroy of Ethiopia in late May 1936.

Emperor Haile Selassie, his armies defeated and demoralized and his retreat to the west cut off by disaffected tribal chiefs, fled by train on May 2 to French Somaliland. There he boarded a British warship.

Meanwhile, convinced that major Ethiopian resistance was at an end, on April 26 Badoglio began his "March of the Iron Will" from Dessie to the Ethiopian capital city of Addis Ababa. Some 30,000 Italian troops, in perhaps the greatest motorized military column organized to that point in history, moved by two main routes toward Addis Ababa, which they entered on May 5. In Rome that same day, Mussolini announced that "Ethiopia is Italian," and on May 9 he decreed that all of Ethiopia was under Italian sovereignty and that King Victor Emmanuel III was now the emperor of Ethiopia. On June 1, 1936, Italian East Africa was reorganized as Africa Orientale Italiana, an area of some 666,000 square miles with a population estimated at some 12 million people in 1939.

The one-sided nature of the Second Italo-Ethiopian War conflict can be seen in the casualty totals. In the war, Ethiopia lost 760,000 dead, both military and civilian, whereas the Italian government claimed losses of some 2,000 dead, with another 1,600 lost from among its Eritrean allies.

SPENCER C. TUCKER

Consequences

The Second Italo-Ethiopian War had proven the powerlessness of the League of Nations. For all it accomplished, the league might as well never have met on the issue. Italy's triumph in Ethiopia presented a new problem: Should the league recognize Italy's conquest as a fait accompli that it had failed to prevent and remove the sanctions, or should it maintain that Italy had gone to war in disregard of league obligations and continue economic sanctions against Italy, regardless of its victory? The British government favored a "common-sense" approach of abandoning sanctions. On the other hand, the Little Entente, the Balkan Entente, and the so-called neutrals all favored continuing the sanctions.

The British government took the lead in dismantling the sanctions. In early June 1936 Prime Minister Neville Chamberlain described the continuance of sanctions as the "very midsummer of madness." This pronouncement was followed on June 18 by a statement from Foreign Minister Anthony Eden confirming the cabinet's decision to propose to the League of Nations that sanctions should be abandoned. On June 23 Home Secretary Sir John Simon stated, "The point is that, with the present situation in Europe and the great dangers surrounding us here at home, I am not prepared to see a single ship sunk even in a successful naval battle in the cause of Abyssinian independence." The French government announced that "consideration of fact" called for the abolition of sanctions. Other nations followed suit, with impetus provided by an announcement by U.S. president Franklin Roosevelt on June 20 that he was cancelling restrictive measures adopted by his government on Italy.

When the League Assembly met in Geneva on June 30, 1936, the decision to close the book on Ethiopia had been all but settled. Nonetheless, the floor and galleries of the Assembly Hall in Geneva were packed on June 30 for an address by Haile Selassie. As he rose to speak, Italian correspondents in the press gallery produced whistles and blew them, while others hooted and screamed insults. After their ejection from the hall, the deposed emperor announced that he was there "to claim that justice which is due to my people, and the assistance promised to it eight months ago, when 50 nations asserted that aggression had been committed in violation of international treaties." He went on to describe the horrors of the war, including the use by the Italians of a "death-dealing rain" of mustard gas. He then discussed the diplomatic negotiations and Ethiopia's betrayal by the League of Nations, pointing out the lack of assistance given by the league members to Ethiopia and the implications of this for world security. Haile Selassie also placed the war in its proper perspective:

It is not merely a question of the settlement of Italian aggression. It is collective security: it is the very existence of the League of Nations. It is the confidence that each State is to place in international treaties. It is the value of promises made to small States that their integrity and independence shall be respected and ensured. . . . In a word it is international morality that is at stake. . . . God and history will remember your judgement.

As he stepped down from the podium to muted applause, Haile Selassie remarked prophetically, "It is us today; it will be you tomorrow!"

On July 4, 1936, the League Assembly adopted a resolution that, while "remaining firmly attached to the principles of the Covenant . . . excluding the settlement of territorial questions by force," nonetheless recommended an end to the sanctions. Italy had won. None of the big powers had been prepared to use force, and another blow had been dealt to the principle of collective security to halt aggression. The Second Italo-Ethiopian War also served to give Mussolini an exaggerated sense of Italy's military effectiveness.

Ethiopian resistance to Italy continued, however. In July 1936 Ethiopian insurgents attacked Addis Ababa, but their attempt to seize power failed, and most of them were caught and executed. Intermittent Ethiopian resistance and the Italian pacification effort claimed perhaps several hundred thousand Ethiopians killed.

On June 10, 1940, with the German defeat of France presumed imminent, Italy formally entered World War II. The British government was now faced with the task of defending its own possessions in East Africa from the Italians. This would, of course, be best accomplished by invading and taking over Italian East Africa. The task fell largely to South African and African colonial troops, supported by Ethiopian guerrillas. Colonel Orde Wingate had

charge of coordinating Ethiopian forces in support of the Allied campaign, but Haile Selassie arrived in Gojam in northwestern Ethiopia on January 20, 1941, and immediately undertook to unite the various Ethiopian resistance groups under his authority.

The Allied plan called for an offensive against Italian Somaliland and eastern Ethiopia in the Harer and Dire Dawa area in order to isolate Italian troops in the highlands and cut the rail link between Addis Ababa and Djibouti. At the same time, British forces from Sudan would invade Eritrea and cut off Italian forces from the Red Sea, while the Royal Navy moved against Italian naval assets. The land campaign in the north ended with the lengthy and costly Battle of Keren (February 5–April 11, 1941) and the defeat of Italian troops in Eritrea. British forces secured Italian Somaliland by March 3, and soon thereafter the Italians initiated negotiations for the surrender of their remaining forces. On May 5, 1941, Haile Selassie reentered Addis Ababa, but the last of the Italian forces, cut off near Gonder, did not surrender to the British and Ethiopians until January 1942.

The British left responsibility for internal affairs in the emperor's hands, with all actions that might affect the Allied war effort requiring British approval. In January 1942 a new agreement was concluded with a military convention that called for British assistance in training a new Ethiopian Army. Meanwhile, the emperor used the British presence to strengthen his own control over the provincial governors. The British helped with the establishment of a new national bureaucracy for the country, and British-trained police also strengthened the central government as they gradually replaced the provincial police forces that had in the past served the interests of the governors.

The 1942 agreement confirmed Ethiopia as a sovereign state, but the Ogaden and certain strategic areas, such as the French Somaliland border, the Addis Ababa-Djibouti railroad, and other "Reserved Areas," remained under British administration. In 1942 a U.S. economic mission arrived in Ethiopia, a step that would significantly affect the country's subsequent direction.

In 1943 there were revolts in two regions of Ethiopia: Tigray, which had traditionally enjoyed a fair degree of independence from the central government, and the Ogaden, inhabited largely by Somalis. British aircraft from Aden assisted by ground troops put down the Tigray rebellion, while two battalions of Ethiopian troops suppressed the Ogaden uprising.

The British government rejected Haile Selassie's effort to secure for Ethiopia after the war substantial portions of the former Italian East Africa. The Ethiopians claimed that Eritrea was racially, culturally, and economically part of Ethiopia, but the British were well aware of growing Eritrean national sentiment. The British also rejected Ethiopian demands for Italian Somaliland, which the British held to be part of a greater Somalia. On December 19, 1944, however, Britain and Ethiopia concluded the Anglo-Ethiopian Accords whereby Britain recognized full Ethiopian sovereignty.

SPENCER C. TUCKER

Timeline

1869	An Italian trading company acquires the port of Assab on the southern Red Sea in Eritrea.
1881	The Italian government takes control of Assab.
1885	The Italian government acquires Massawa, also on the Red Sea in Eritrea.
1887	
January 26	With Italian forces having invaded Ethiopia, at Dogali in eastern Eritrea on this date some 7,000 Ethiopians destroy an Italian Army force of 500 men. The Italians suffer 420 dead and the remainder prisoners.
1889	Italy organizes a new colony in Somaliland on the Horn of Africa to the east and south of Ethiopia.
1893	Judging his position secure, new Ethiopian emperor Menelek repudiates his treaty with Italy.
1895	The First Italo-Ethiopian War begins, with an invasion of northern Ethiopia from Eritrea by some 9,000 Italian troops.
1896	
January	Following a siege of nearly two months, the Italian fortress of Magdala surrenders to the Ethiopians.

March 1	Some 20,000 Italian and African troops are defeated by 90,000 Ethiopians in the Battle of Adowa. Half the Italian force is either killed or taken prisoner.
October 23	The Treaty of Addis Ababa is signed, whereby Italy recognizes the independence of Ethiopia and promises to restrict itself to Eritrea.
1900	Italy's holdings on the Red Sea are organized as Eritrea.
1922	
October	Benito Mussolini comes to power in Italy.
1934	
December 5	Ethiopian and Italian forces clash at Walwal (Ualual in Italian).
1935	
January 3	Ethiopia appeals to the League of Nations for resolution of its border dispute with Italy, probably sealing Mussolini's decision to invade Abyssinia. Mussolini seeks to take advantage of the Italian desire for revenge to add Ethiopia to the Italian empire, and he hopes to discover minerals there and secure an outlet for Italy's surplus population.
January 7	French foreign minister Pierre Laval travels to Rome and there concludes with Italian premier Benito Mussolini the Franco-Italian Accords. In addition to agreements regarding Europe aimed to contain Adolf Hitler's Germany, Laval agrees to transfer some 44,015 square miles (114,000 square kilometers) of land to Italy's colonies of Libya and Eritrea. He also apparently promises Mussolini that France will not oppose Italian interests in Ethiopia.
April 11–14	In the Stresa Conference following Adolf Hitler's announcement that Germany will rearm, French foreign minister Pierre Laval, British prime minister Ramsay MacDonald, and Italian premier Benito Mussolini agree "to oppose unilateral repudiation of treaties which may endanger the peace of Europe." The last two words are added at the request of Mussolini in order to avoid compromising his designs on Ethiopia.
September 3	The arbitral board of the League of Nations finds unanimously that neither side is to blame for the Walwal incident, concluding that each believed that it was fighting on its own territory.

October 3	Italian forces invade Ethiopia from both Eritrea and Italian Somaliland, initiating the Second Italo-Ethiopian War.
October 5	Italian forces occupy Adigrat.
October 6	Italian forces take Adowa, the site of the Italian Army's humiliating defeat in 1896.
October 7	The League of Nations Council votes that Italy has resorted to war in disregard of Article 12 of the League of Nations Covenant, the first time in its history that the League of Nations has declared a European Great Power an aggressor.
October 15	Italian forces secure Axum.
November 8	Italian forces take Makale.
November 18	Limited sanctions imposed by the League of Nations go into effect against Italy.
December 13	Foreign ministers Pierre Laval of France and Sir Samuel Hoare of Britain set out to appease Italian dictator Benito Mussolini, laying before the League of Nations proposals that call for the cession to Italy of areas in Ethiopia in the vicinity of Eritrea and Somaliland as well as an extensive area in southern Ethiopia in which Italy is to have an economic monopoly. These would have given Italy most of Abyssinia. Public condemnation of the plan is immediate and widespread, especially in Britain and France; Hoare and Laval are both forced to resign.

1936

January 2–16	In the Battle of Genale Doria on the Southern Front, Graziani's Italians turn back an Ethiopian offensive under Ras Desta Damtu advancing on Dolo with the aim of invading Italian Somaliland.
January 20–24	In the First Battle of Tembien, Italian forces on the Northern Front neutralize the threat of an invasion of Eritrea by Ethiopian forces commanded by Ras Kassa.
February 10–19	On the Northern Front, the Italians attack and decisively defeat the Ethiopians in the Battle of Amba Aradam, destroying the Ethiopian army commanded by Ras Mulugeta.
February 27–29	On the Northern Front, the Italians win a decisive victory in the Second Battle of Tembien, destroying

	Ethiopian armies commanded by Ras Kassa and Ras Seyoum.
February 29–March 2	In the Battle of Shire on the Northern Front, Italian forces defeat Ethiopian forces under Ras Imru.
March 22	On the Southern Front, despite the fact that Harar has been declared an open city, Italian Air Force planes bomb both it and Jijiga, reducing both cities to rubble.
March 26	Italian forces enter Harar, Ethiopia's second-largest city.
March 31	In the Battle of Maythew on the Northern Front, the Italians defeat an Ethiopian counteroffensive commanded by Emperor Haile Selassie.
April 14–25	On the southern front, Italian general Graziani launches a ground offensive, initiating the Battle of the Ogaden and completely destroying the defenders under Ras Nasibu Emmanual, the last Ethiopian force of any size on this front.
April 26	Marshal Badoglio begins his "March of the Iron Will," the movement of 30,000 Italian troops from Dessie to the Ethiopian capital of Addis Ababa.
May 2	Emperor Haile Selassie flees Ethiopia to French Somaliland and then to a British warship.
May 5	Italian forces enter Addis Ababa. This same day in Rome, Mussolini announces that "Ethiopia is Italian."
May 9	Mussolini announces that all of Ethiopia is under Italian sovereignty and that Italian king Victor Emmanuel III is now emperor of Ethiopia.
July 4	The League Council recommends the lifting of sanctions against Italy for its invasion of Ethiopia.
1941	In the course of the East Africa Campaign, British Empire forces liberate Ethiopia.
1944	
December 19	Britain and Ethiopia conclude the Anglo-Ethiopian Accords whereby Britain recognizes full Ethiopian sovereignty.

SPENCER C. TUCKER

Further Reading

Baer, George W. *Test Case: Italy, Ethiopia, and the League of Nations.* Stanford, CA: Hoover Institute, Stanford University, 1976.

Barker, A. J. *The Civilizing Mission: A History of the Italo-Ethiopian War of 1935–1936.* New York: Dial, 1968.

Barker, A. J. *Rape of Ethiopia, 1936*. New York: Ballantine Books, 1971.

Baudendistel, Rainer. *Between Bombs and Good Intentions: The Red Cross and the Italo-Ethiopian War, 1935–1936*. New York: Berghahn Books, 2006.

Burgwyn, James. *Italian Foreign Policy in the Interwar Period: 1918–1940*. Westport, CT: Praeger, 1997.

De Bono, Emilio. *La preparazione e le prime operazioni*. Rome: Istituto Nazionale Fascista di Cultura, 1937.

Dugan, James, and Laurence Lafore. *Days of Emperor and Clown: The Italo-Ethiopian War, 1935–1936*. Garden City, NY: Doubleday, 1973.

Gentilli, Roberto. *Guerra aerea sullíEtiopia, 1935–1939*. Florence, Italy: Ed. A.I., 1992.

Giannini, Filippo. *Benito Mussolini, l'uomo della pace: Da Versailles al 10 giugno 1940*. Rome: Editoriale Greco e Greco, 1999.

Gooch, John. *Mussolini and His Generals*. Cambridge: Cambridge University Press, 2007.

Graziani, Rodolfo. *Fronte del Sud*. Milan: A. Mondadori, 1938.

Haile Selassie I. *My Life and Ethiopia's Progress: The Autobiography of Emperor Haile Selassie I, King of Kings and Lord of Lords*, Vol. 2. Edited by Harold Marcus et al. and translated by Ezekiel Gebions et al. Chicago: Research Associates School Times Publications, 1999.

Lamb, Richard. *Mussolini as Diplomat*. New York: Fromm International, 1999.

Mack Smith, Denis. *Mussolini*. New York: Knopf, 1982.

Mack Smith, Denis. *Mussolini's Roman Empire*. New York: Viking, 1976.

Matthews, Herbert Lionel. *Eyewitness in Abyssinia: With Marshal Bodoglio's Forces to Addis Ababa*. London: M. Secker and Warburg, 1937.

Mockler, Anthony. *Haile Selassie's War: The Italian-Ethiopian Campaign, 1935–1941*. New York: Random House, 1984.

Nicolle, David. *The Italian Invasion of Abyssinia, 1935–1936*. Oxford, UK: Osprey, 1997.

Spanish Civil War (1936–1939)

Causes

The Spanish Civil War of 1936–1939 was both hard-fought and sanguinary. It came about because of the determined efforts of Spanish Republicans to eliminate an entrenched feudalism in Spain and the effort of the long-established power groups there, known as the Nationalists, who sought to destroy the newly elected government that threatened traditional Spanish values. The fighting that began in 1936 was not left to the Spaniards themselves, for soon outside forces became involved. The struggle continued until 1939. Both sides were equally ruthless, and there were millions of casualties. Nationalist reprisals continued for years after their victory.

In order to understand the passions loosed in the Spanish Civil War, it must be remembered that Spain was late to catch up with the rest of Western Europe in political and economic development. In 1936 Spain had a population of some 24 million, but most of the country's land and wealth were concentrated in the hands of fewer than 5,000 powerful families. The Catholic Church also played a major role, being bound up in the Spanish identity since the Reconquesta, the retaking of the country from the Moors completed at the end of the 15th century. To be Spanish was to be Catholic. The Catholic Church in Spain was not a progressive instrument for human rights and change, however. It was part of the establishment, opposing reform and even popular education. While the average Spaniard had deep affection for his or her parish priest and the Catholic faith, this did not extend to high Church officials or the Church establishment,

which were correctly seen as part of a governing elite that had little concern for the peasants, who made up the majority of the population. Certainly this resentment became manifest during the civil war, when there was considerable violent anticlerical activity.

The Industrial Revolution that had taken place in Western Europe was slow to arrive in Spain, but this had accelerated during World War I. Spain had remained neutral in the conflict, but the war had seen trade with both sides and enhanced industrial development to meet demand. This economic upturn disappeared with the return of peace and slackened demand, and labor unrest occurred with frequent strikes.

On September 15, 1923, Spanish king Alfonso XIII (r. 1886–1931) called on trusted confidant Miguel Primo de Rivera, Marquis of Estella, to become prime minister and establish an authoritarian corporate state. In effect, de Rivera became, with the king's approval, a military dictator. De Rivera was something of a playboy, personally charming and courtly and constantly in the news with his sports, women, and rakish style of living. Certainly his government did little to ameliorate Spain's deep-seated social and economic problems. Criticism of the government was treated as disloyalty and met with harsh punishment. Liberals and intellectuals were removed from positions of influence, and the press was heavily censored. De Rivera boasted that he was determined to eliminate what he called "the disastrous mania of thinking." The vast majority of Spaniards already had a very low standard of living, and when the worldwide economic depression that began in 1929 reached Spain, it had an immediate and decided impact. Strikes ensued, accompanied by considerable violence. Spain was soon teetering on the brink of revolution.

With the dictatorship having failed, Alfonso XIII went in the opposite direction. On January 28, 1930, he dismissed Primo de Rivera, who then took himself to Paris and drank himself to death in March. His replacement as prime minister was former colonial administrator General Dámaso Berenguer y Fusté, who repealed some of the harsher measures of the previous administration, earning for his administration the name *dictablanda* (toothless dictatorship) as opposed to Primo de Rivera's *dictadura* (hard dictatorship). Censorship was relaxed, some exiles were allowed to return, and the Spanish Cortes (parliament) was recalled. These reforms were too little, too late, however, for Spain was now in turmoil. Labor unrest continued, coupled with a military uprising and increasing demands for an end to the monarchy. Berenguer resigned as prime minister on February 14, 1931, and was replaced by Admiral Juan Bautista Aznar-Cabañas.

The Spanish municipal elections of April 12, 1931, were such a repudiation of the monarchy that Alfonso's advisers suggested that he go abroad into temporary exile. Two days later, without formal abdication, Alfonso departed, and the Second Spanish Republic was proclaimed (the First Spanish Republic had lasted only from 1873 to 1874). There were high hopes that this would begin a new era that would see Spain transformed into a modern, progressive state.

The first election for the revived Cortes occurred on June 28, 1931, and was an overwhelming endorsement of the Republic. The Socialist-Republican coalition triumphed, and the leader of the Liberal Democratic Right, Niceto Alcalá-Zamora, became acting prime minister of the provisional government. In light of later charges by Adolf Hitler and Benito Mussolini that they had intervened in Spain to prevent it from going communist, it should be remembered that of 473 elected deputies to the first Cortes, not a single member was a declared communist. The Republican majority in the Cortes was made up of liberals and socialists from a wide range of political parties who were basically no more liberal than the New Dealers of President Franklin Roosevelt in the United States or the Labour Party of Ramsay MacDonald in Great Britain. Indeed, the new government enjoyed widespread support in Spain. On October 14, 1931, Manuel Azaña Diaz, leader of the Republican Action Party, became the first prime minister of the Second Spanish Republic.

But in a sign of what was to come, extremists on both sides had committed excesses during the election campaign. The reactionaries resorted to hoodlum tactics by their privately funded paramilitary forces, while militant leftists burned churches and convents and committed outrages against priests and nuns. Azaña Diaz was impatient with slow change, and he did not help matters by being reluctant to punish violence by the Left. Archbishop of Toledo Pedro Segura y Sáenz, who by virtue of his position was also primate of Spain, was on the other side of the spectrum. A staunch conservative who opposed toleration of Protestants, found merit in the Spanish Inquisition, and opposed virtually anything modern including public education and giving the vote to women, Segura certainly inflamed the situation by his incendiary speeches and

Spanish Civil War

Spanish Civil War (July 1936–March 1939)	
Died (All Causes, Including Civilians)	600,000+
Wounded (Including Civilians)	750,000–1,000,000
Approximate Number of Spanish Refugees	500,000–550,000

Casualties for Ebro Offensive (July 24–November 16, 1938)		
	Republicans	Nationalists
Killed/Missing	30,000	6,500–10,000
Wounded	45,000	30,000–40,000

Sources: Raymond Carr, *Modern Spain, 1875–1980* (Oxford: Oxford University Press, 2001); Helen Graham, *The Spanish Republic at War, 1936–1939* (New York: Cambridge University Press, 2002).

railings against the new republic as both anti-Spanish and anti-Christian.

The years that followed saw continued unrest in Spain. When the Republicans were in power, they pushed through reforms to benefit the workers and the peasants. These included changes already in place in most of Europe, such as insurance rights for the unemployed, the sick, the disabled, and the elderly. Unions also received legal recognition and protection, and hours of labor were fixed. The Republicans also moved against the special privileges enjoyed by the Catholic Church and wealthy Spaniards. A new constitution was enacted, and women received the right to vote.

On November 19, 1933, new national elections were held. A new voting system had come into effect, and the governing leftist parties were divided. The election resulted in a victory for the center and right-wing political parties. Alejandro Lerroux, leader of the Radical Republican Party, became prime minister. The new government curtailed previously enacted reforms and restored certain special privileges enjoyed by the establishment. The governing coalition also removed leftists and liberals from key posts in the administration and in the next two years jailed some 30,000 dissidents. The government also purged the ranks of the army of leftists. With both sides largely intolerant of the other and Spain increasingly polarized between Right and Left, it became clear to most observers that the struggle was unlikely to be resolved at the polls and that the losing side would be unwilling to peaceably accept the democratic verdict.

The next national election took place on February 16, 1936. Learning the lesson of their division in the last election, the leftist parties (Republicans, socialists, Syndicalists, and communists) established a Popular Front and beat the coalition of conservative republicans, clericals, and monarchists. Azaña returned to the premiership and formed a cabinet that immediately undertook the restoration of autonomy in Catalonia, a social reform program that included distribution of land to the peasants and the development of public education, coupled with an anticlerical policy. On May 10, Azaña was elected president of the republic.

As expected, the Nationalists defied the election result. Extremists among them joined the Spanish fascist party, the Falange

Española (Spanish Phalanx), known as the Falange. It had been founded in 1934 by José Antonio Primo de Rivera with the aim of vindicating the dictatorship established by his father. It had as its insignia a bundle of arrows and the slogan "Arriba España" (Spain Arise). Demonstrations gave way to violence. The Nationalists assassinated a prominent Republican leader. The Republicans responded by kidnapping and murdering a prominent rightist leader.

Meanwhile, those on the political Right had been preparing to seize power. The plotters were forced to launch their effort prematurely, however, because the government learned that something was about to occur. The Right made its move on July 18, 1936, in a revolt of army regiments in Spanish Morocco. The putsch was led by the senior officers in the army determined to prevent the Republicans from destroying the character and traditions of ancestral Spain. The issues were clear. As historian Herbert Matthews has put it, the central question of the Spanish Civil War was "whether the Catholic, traditional, agrarian, and centralized rule of the past centuries should continue, or whether the great issues that the French Revolution had resolved for France and much of the Western world should be accepted. These included democratic government, capitalism, civil freedoms, separation of church and state, and land reform."

SPENCER C. TUCKER

Course

At the outset of the civil war, the two sides appeared pretty evenly matched. The Nationalists, also known as the Fascists, had some two-thirds of the army and 90 percent of the officers. They also could count on the support of the Catholic Church, diehard monarchists, and the conservative old-line families who possessed the bulk of the country's wealth. In addition, they had the Spanish Foreign Legion and the many powerful armies of the paramilitary groups, the Carlists and the Falange.

The government side was known as the Republicans or Loyalists. It had the navy, which was solidly Republican, and most of the air force. It also had strong support from the peasants and workers in the most industrialized part of Spain, the Madrid-Valencia-Barcelona triangle. The loyalties of the middle class were fairly evenly divided. Families were split. Thus, Nationalist general Francisco Franco Bahamonde's brother Ramón Franco was the ace fighter pilot of the Spanish Republic's air force and died fighting on the Republican side.

The Nationalists were led by General José Sanjurjo y Sacanell, but he was killed in a plane crash on July 20 while on his way from Lisbon to Burgos, and leadership devolved to General Franco, who would emerge as the caudillo (leader) and the most durable of 20th-century dictators. Opinions differed as to which side would have won the civil war had it been left to the Spaniards themselves, but the Republicans must be given the edge. Certainly the war would have been over much more quickly. Foreign military intervention greatly prolonged the suffering and augmented the death toll.

German and Italian aid came early. On July 26, 1936, with the war only a week old, Nationalist emissaries met with German chancellor Adolf Hitler, seeking to buy 10 transport aircraft to ferry Franco's troops from Morocco to Spain. Getting these men across the Mediterranean was crucial to Nationalist success, and Republican control of the navy blocked access by water. Hitler responded by loaning 30 aircraft with full German aircrews. Beginning on July 29, these flew 20,000 Spanish and Moroccan troops to Nationalist-controlled Seville in southern Spain.

Hitler recognized the possibility of a general war but was willing to risk it. In addition to hoping to tie the Western democracies down in Spain, he wanted to distract attention from the German military buildup. Were the Nationalists to win, it would guarantee Germany supplies of Spanish iron ore and other strategic materials. Spain could also prove to be a useful testing ground for new weapons being adopted by the German military.

In November 1936 the Germans formed the Kondor (Condor) Legion. It numbered about 6,000 men with more than 100 aircraft, but 19,000 men and 300–400 aircraft served in all. The men were not volunteers but rather regular German military personnel, largely aircrew and support personnel, assigned to Spain. Spain proved to be not only a test platform for German aircraft in combat conditions but also the training school for the coordination of ground troops and tactical air that was to be so devastatingly effective early in World War II. The Kondor Legion proved decisive in the outcome. Some 330 members of the unit died in Spain, and 1,000 were wounded.

Italian leader Benito Mussolini wanted to involve Italy in Spain early, but Marshal Pietro Badoglio warned that sending regular ground troops might spark a general war for which Italy was not prepared. At first Italy provided only secret aid in the form of equipment and technicians. Later Mussolini sent regular army troops. The Italian intervention was both larger and less effective than that of the Germans. Some 40,000 Italians served in Spain, along with several hundred aircraft. About

3,100 Italians died there, and 1,000 more were permanently disabled.

The attitude of the Soviet Union was quite different. Soviet leader Joseph Stalin believed that an all-out victory by either side was undesirable. A Republican victory would produce a left-wing Spanish government that was unlikely to be under Kremlin control. Even the emergence of a wholly communist Spain would have given him only a weak ally at the other end of Europe. On the other hand, success by Franco would—and indeed did—weaken France, thus freeing the anticommunist Hitler to concentrate on aggression in the east. Stalin's position thus became one of not helping the Republic win while not allowing it to lose (although this policy did not keep Franco from winning). Stalin hoped that a long war might even bring a world war in which France, Britain, Germany, and Italy would destroy one another, with Russia emerging as the dominant power in Europe.

The first Soviet military aid did not reach the Republican side until October 1936. The aid was always limited in scope and subject to many restrictions, and no Soviet fighting units were ever sent to Spain. Stalin sent only some Soviet pilots, flight instructors, and tank experts. The Russians also supplied arms and ammunition, food, and medical aid to the Republic. But the logistics of getting the aid there were immense. Stalin also insisted on payment in cash for goods rendered. Spain had the fourth-largest gold reserves in the world, and the Republican government shipped several hundred million dollars of it to Odessa.

Their assistance, of course, gave the Soviets more and more influence. Gradually the more moderate Republican leaders were bypassed and ousted. On September

4, 1936, Francisco Largo Caballero, one of the leaders of the Spanish Socialist Workers' Party (PSOE), became both prime minister and minister of war. He resigned on May 17, 1937, and was succeeded by another PSOE leader, Juan Negrín, who as prime minister collaborated closely with the communists until April 1, 1939, and the end of the war.

In the lineup, a great deal depended upon the reaction of the Western democracies. The French government and most of the French people sympathized with the Republicans, and Premier Léon Blum, a socialist, promised to supply 20 bombers, 50 machine guns, and eight 75mm guns as well as rifles, bombs, and ammunition. The British government was then led by Stanley Baldwin and in 1937 by Neville Chamberlain. Appeasement was well under way, as the year before London had concluded a naval agreement with Germany in defiance of the Treaty of Versailles and had also failed to support the French in undertaking military action against Germany when Hitler remilitarized the Rhineland in March 1936. Chamberlain was unwilling to run the risk of a wider war and insisted on a policy of nonintervention, that is, embargoing military supplies to both sides. At the British government's request, Blum flew to London on July 23, when Foreign Minister Anthony Eden made it clear that the British government's pledge to come to the aid of France if it was attacked by Germany would be null and void if French aid to the Spanish government gave Germany the excuse to invade France.

Having to fight Germany alone was clearly unacceptable to the French. France itself was also sharply divided politically, and the April–May 1936 national elections in France won by the Popular Front had been the most bitterly contested since World War I. There was even concern that France itself might dissolve into civil war. But the overriding consideration was that France had to have British support against Germany. Blum now halted military assistance to the Spanish Republic although quietly permitting a few aircraft to be smuggled out.

Hopes that the other powers could be convinced to stay out of the struggle proved groundless. Although 27 nations, including all the Great Powers, signed the nonintervention agreement, men and supplies continued to flow to the Fascist side from Germany and Italy. Apart from the Soviet Union, Mexico was the only Western country to help the Loyalists. It sent 18,000 rifles. As late as January 1939 Chamberlain said that he saw no need to lift the arms embargo, which "would inevitably lead to the extension of the conflict with consequences which cannot accurately be foreseen but would undoubtedly be grave."

President Franklin Roosevelt declared U.S. neutrality and nonintervention. His sympathies were with the Republicans, but 1936 was an election year, and he did not want to offend the millions of conservative Catholic voters who, swayed by Nationalist propaganda and Republican atrocities against members of the clergy in Spain, supported that side. Thus, the United States technically enforced the embargo, but large quantities of oil supplied by American companies managed to make their way to Spain to fuel fascist planes and tanks.

Many people in the Western countries were appalled by the attitude of their governments, and a number volunteered to go to Spain to fight. The vast majority of these "Internationals" fought on the Republican side. Some 40,000 men from 54 nations came to Spain, and 8,000 died there. There were 3,000 from the United States formed in the Lincoln and Washington Brigades; 1,000 of them died, and during the Cold War the survivors were all branded as communists.

It was almost a miracle that the Republicans were able to hold on as long as they did. At the end of July 1936, Madrid remained republican, thwarting plans for a quick coup. Barcelona also stayed loyal, as did Valencia and most other major cities.

Battles raged everywhere. Wherever the Nationalists were in control they slaughtered members of the Popular Front as a matter of official policy. On July 19 Nationalist general Emilio Mola told a meeting of mayors near Pamplona that "It is necessary to spread an atmosphere of terror. We have to create the impression of mastery. . . . Anyone who is overtly or secretly a member of the Popular Front must be shot." There was also terror in Republican Madrid as self-appointed Chekas (for the Russian secret police) set about trying real and suspected rebels. Thousands, including many wealthy Spaniards, were summarily executed following drumhead trials. President Azaña and other leaders were appalled but powerless to stop it. The wealth thereby secured often went to the parties and trade unions or was simply pocketed. But at Badajoz after the Fascists took the city, 2,000 people were rounded up and shot in its bullring, and during Franco's advance from Seville on Madrid thousands of prisoners were murdered. Franco did not mourn their deaths as did Azaña. Clearly the Nationalist killings were directed by the authorities. Those who died on the Republican side were the victims of individuals acting without official authority.

The rebels had hoped to take Madrid at the offset, believing that its capture would bring the war to a speedy conclusion. But the Republicans held the city of Toledo, about 75 miles south-southwest of the capital, although the rebel force there had barricaded itself in the large Alcázar of Toledo and were refusing to surrender. For 72 days (July 21–September) the Republicans laid siege to the alcazar (fortress) in what was certainly one of the most dramatic episodes of the entire war. The alcazar was a formidable structure with 10-foot walls and was situated on high ground that dominated the city. It was also the home of the Spanish Military Academy, commanded in July 1936 by Colonel José Moscardó Ituarte.

On July 21, there were some 1,500 people inside the Alcázar of Toledo. Moscardó probably commanded 150 officers and noncommissioned officers assigned to the Spanish Military Academy, 650 members of the Guardia Civil, and 7 cadets (the others being on vacation). There were also more than 500 military dependents. In addition, the colonel had taken about 100 civilian hostages. The defenders were well armed. Toledo was home to an important arms factory, and the rebels removed its stocks to the fortress. Unfortunately for the Republicans, they lacked the modern heavy artillery necessary to breach the fortress walls.

On July 23, in what is perhaps the most celebrated single incident of the war, Republican militia leader in Toledo Candido Cabello talked by telephone with Moscardó and informed him that unless he surrendered the fortress within 10 minutes, Cabello would shoot Moscardó's 17-year-old son Luis. Cabello put the boy on the phone, and the colonel told him that he should commend his soul to God, shout "Long live Spain," and prepare for a hero's death. Moscardó then informed Cabello that he would never surrender. (The Republicans indeed executed young

Moscardó, although on August 23 in reprisal for an air raid.)

On September 18 the attackers exploded a large mine that collapsed the tower on the southeast corner of the fortress and opened a breach in the wall. General José Enrique Varela Iglesius and a force of Moroccans were then about 25 miles from Toledo but headed for Madrid. Franco decided on September 19 to divert them to Toledo. He realized that this decision might well cost him Madrid, but he believed that relieving the Toledo garrison was more important, probably because of the arms factory. On September 23 Varela set out, and three days later his men cut the road between Toledo and Madrid.

On September 27, before the Nationalists could arrive, the Republicans exploded another mine on the northeast side of the fortress. But at sunset that same day the Nationalist relief force arrived and entered the alcazar, which was in flames. The Moroccan troops, meanwhile, massacred all Republicans in Toledo they could find, including the wounded in San Juan Hospital. Madrid, however, remained in Republican hands until March 1939.

Madrid's resistance became legendary. On November 6, as four Nationalist columns under General Mola commenced a loose siege of the city (the Republican government fled to Valencia), Mola famously remarked to an English journalist that a "fifth column" would rise up inside the city, the origin of this term for subversive activity.

The Nationalists attacked Madrid on November 8 but were repulsed. The city held out despite air strikes, its defenders led by General José Miaja. The defenders vowed "No pasaran" (They shall not pass).

The fighting continued, and on April 26, 1938, there occurred a signal event in the war, the bombing of the Basque city of Guernica in northern Spain. Colonel Wolfram von Richthofen, chief of staff of the Kondor Legion, planned an attack on the Renteria bridge near Guernica. With Nationalist troops moving on Bilbao, Richthofen hoped that destruction of the bridge would trap sizable Basque forces. Richthofen had earlier secured an agreement with the Nationalist leadership that allowed German and Italian aircraft to act independent of Nationalist control and attack Republican troop concentrations "without regard for the civilian population."

Some aircraft were Italian, but most of those taking part were German. The bombs—a mix of incendiaries and high-explosive bombs dropped from high altitude—fell not on the bridge but on Guernica itself, setting much of the city on fire and destroying two-thirds of its buildings. German fighter aircraft strafed civilians trying to flee. Casualty figures from the attack vary from 250 to as many as 1,654 dead and 889 wounded. Richthofen wrote in his diary, "Guernica, city of 5,000 inhabitants, literally leveled." Although the raid on Guernica was not an experiment in the terror bombing of civilians, much of the world perceived it as such and drew false lessons from it as to the effectiveness of airpower in attacks on civilian centers. In that sense the bombing of Guernica must be regarded as one of the defining moments in the development of modern airpower.

News reports of the bombing horrified much of the world and gave the Republicans a powerful propaganda weapon. The Nationalists and the German government in Berlin claimed that there had been no attack and that the destruction had been arranged by the Republicans themselves to discredit the Nationalists. The event served

Destruction in the Basque city of Guernica three days after the attack by German and Italian aircraft on April 26, 1937. (Daily Herald Archive/SSPL/Getty Images)

as inspiration for Spanish artist Pablo Picasso's painting *Guernica,* one of the most famous artworks of the 20th century.

On April 1, Nationalist troops invested Bilbao. Following weeks of heavy fighting that included Nationalist air attacks, the city fell on June 18. The Nationalists captured Santandar on August 25 and Gijon on October 21, completing their conquest of northwestern Spain. A week later, the Spanish government relocated from Valencia to Barcelona. On December 5, the Republicans opened a large offensive around Teruel in Aragon. Although they captured Teruel on December 19, the poorly equipped and supplied Loyalist forces were soon brought to a halt. The Nationalists recaptured Teruel in February 1938.

On July 25, 1938, the Republicans staked all on a great counteroffensive from Catalonia along the Ebro River, committing 100,000 men of their 400,000-man army in an effort to reestablish communication with Castile and draw the Nationalists away from Valencia. The initial crossing of the Ebro caught the Nationalists by surprise and went well, but within a week the drive was halted, largely by Nationalist airpower and artillery. The Nationalist side now enjoyed near total air superiority, and this was the difference in the war. Nonetheless, it took the Nationalists until November 16 to push the Republican troops back across the Ebro. The Republican side lost some 30,000 dead, 20,000 wounded, and 20,000 taken prisoner. Nationalist casualties were 6,500 dead, 30,000 wounded, and 5,000 prisoners. The failure of their offensive marked the beginning of the end for the Republicans in the war.

On January 26, 1939, the Nationalists captured Barcelona. They then overran all Catalonia, and some 200,000 Loyalist troops fled across the border into France, where they were disarmed and interned. In early March, ships of the Republican Navy escaped to the Tunisian port of Bizerte, where they were interned. On February 27, the British and French governments recognized the Nationalist government without conditions. The Spanish Civil War officially ended on March 28, when Nationalist troops entered Valencia and Madrid.

SPENCER C. TUCKER

Consequences

The Nationalists took their revenge for months after the formal end of the war. Those suspected of being Loyalists or having aided the Republican side were ferreted out and shot. The human toll of the Spanish Civil War has never been accurately determined, but the best estimates are about 600,000 Spaniards killed on both sides, with another 100,000 perishing after the war at Nationalist hands. Half a million more Spaniards fled the country and lived as refugees in wretched camps opened by the French on the other side of the Pyrenees.

The Spanish economy was in ruins, its gold reserves gone. Agricultural and industrial output was far below that of 1935. Much of Spain's infrastructure was gone. Half a million buildings had been destroyed or damaged. The transportation system was hit hard, with bridges and railroads in need of replacement or repair. Some 60 percent of the rolling stock had been lost, and 40 percent of the country's merchant fleet had been sunk or damaged. Franco immediately established a dictatorship. An edict gave him sole authority to take emergency measures without consulting his council of ministers, and his one-man rule continued. The Catholic Church was restored to its full pre-Republican

prominence. Land taken under the Second Republic was returned to the original owners. Strikes were banned, and rigid censorship was introduced. The government demanded complete loyalty. Swift punishment was the lot for those who refused to comply. Some 200 special prisons held anywhere from 367,000 to 500,000 political prisoners.

Franco's Spain may not have been the equal of Nazi Germany or the Soviet Union, but it was nevertheless a stifling dictatorship, and the deep wounds of the Spanish Civil War were long in healing. An entire generation of Spaniards grew up in a nation unaccustomed to words such as "democracy," "freedom," "liberty," "justice," and "compassion."

The Western world lost a great deal in Spain. Now it would be difficult if not impossible to work up international enthusiasm or commitment for a just cause. As Hungarian author, journalist, and former communist Arthur Koestler put it, "Spain was the last twitch of Europe's dying conscience." A succession of Western concessions to the dictators followed in the civil war's wake.

Perhaps the most dramatic effect of the Spanish Civil War on the international level was to bring the two fascist partners in aggression, German and Italy, together in what came to be known as the Rome-Berlin Axis. This came about during the war on November 6, 1937, when Italy adhered to the Anti-Comintern Pact. The stated aim of this pact between Germany and Japan was to counteract the activities of the Communist International (Comintern) based in Moscow. Italy's adherence completed the Axis triangle (Berlin-Rome-Tokyo) of states opposed to the status quo and determined to reshape the post–World War I settlement. Certainly the Spanish

Civil War was an important link in the chain of events that led to World War II.

On the beginning of World War II, Franco sided with Hitler and Mussolini. Franco did not bring Spain into the war because he believed that his cause was better served if he posed as a technical neutral. This attitude of nonbelligerency as opposed to neutrality nonetheless infuriated Hitler, who considered invading Spain. Franco succeeded in putting off Hitler, congratulating the führer after each of his early victories. Franco did send troops, under the guise of volunteers, to fight Russia after Hitler's invasion of the Soviet Union. This was the Blue Division, so named for its blue Falange shirts; the uniform also included red Carlist berets and brown Foreign Legion trousers. A force of 18,000 men, it had an excellent combat record. Franco intended it as a sop to Hitler but also to demonstrate his hatred of communism, get rid of Falange hotheads in Spain, and show Hitler that Spaniards would fight a German invasion of Spain and fight well.

Throughout the war, Franco provided the Germans with observation posts in Spanish Morocco to monitor Allied ship movements and allowed German submarines to be serviced in Spanish ports. After the Allied landings in North Africa, Franco shifted to a neutral stance, but when the war was over Spain became a primary refuge for leading Nazis and their collaborators.

After the war the Allies punished Franco's wartime conduct with quarantine treatment. Spain was kept out of the United Nations (UN) and was condemned for "its origins, its nature, its record, and its close association with the aggressor states." But then came the Cold War with the Soviet Union. With this, alliances and their rationales shifted sharply. Spain was now seen as a welcome bulwark against communism. The boycott of Franco was lifted, and Spain was admitted to the UN. The history of the Spanish Civil War was rewritten to conform to the transformation of yesterday's enemies into today's allies. In this revisionist version, Franco became the shining knight who had saved Europe from atheist communism. U.S. air and naval bases were established in Spain, and U.S. aid propped up the regime. Spanish democrats remembered with bitterness this embrace of Franco.

Franco died in 1975. He had arranged for the grandson of Alfonso XIII to assume the throne as Juan Carlos (r. 1975–2014). Juan Carlos I proved to be an adroit leader. He stifled a rightist attempt to seize power and oversaw Spain's transition to democratic government.

SPENCER C. TUCKER

Timeline

1886

May 17	Alfonso XIII becomes king of Spain.

1931

April 12	Municipal elections result in an overwhelming repudiation of the monarchy.
April 14	King Alfonso III goes into exile, and the Second Spanish Republic is established.

June 28	Moderate republicans score a victory in the Spanish general election.
October 14	Manuel Azaña Diaz, leader of the Republican Action Party, becomes the first prime minister of the Second Spanish Republic.

1933

November 19	Center and right-wing candidates win the new elections for the Cortes (parliament).

1933–1936

	Spain is increasing divided politically into Left and Right, with each intolerant of the other and neither willing to accept a democratic outcome peaceably.

1936

February 16	Learning the lesson of their division in the last election, the leftist parties establish a Popular Front and in the national elections of this date defeat a rightist coalition. Azaña then returns to the premiership.
May 10	Azaña is elected president of the Spanish Republic.
June 18	The political Right (the Nationalists) launches its effort to overthrow the Second Republic by force.
June 20	The leader of the rebellion, Spanish Army general José Sanjurjo y Sacanell, is killed in a plane crash. General Francisco Franco becomes the rebellion's leader.
June 26	German chancellor Adolf Hitler, approached by Nationalist emissaries, agrees to loan transport and fighter aircraft in order to ferry Foreign Legion troops from Spanish Morocco to Spain.
July 21–September 28	In one of the most dramatic episodes of the war, Republican forces lay siege to Nationalist troops in the Alcázar of Toledo. The Nationalist decision to relieve the siege may have saved Madrid at this point in the war.
July 29	Italian military assistance to the Nationalist side is revealed when an Italian bomber flying to Spanish Morocco makes a forced landing in French Morocco.
September 4	Francisco Largo Caballero, one of the leaders of the Spanish Socialist Workers' Party (PSOE), becomes prime minister and minister of war in the Republican government.
November	The Germans establish the Kondor (Condor) Legion in Spain. It proves critical to the Nationalist victory.

1937

March 8–16	In a surprise attack, two Italian infantry divisions, supported by light tanks, penetrate Loyalist lines at Guadalajara but are then caught by Republican aircraft and scattered. Most of the Italian forces regain their own lines, however.
March 18	Loyalist forces are victorious over the Italians and capture large quantities of stores in the Battle of Brihuega.
April 1	Nationalist troops invest Bilbao.
April 26	In one of the signal events of the war, German and Italian aircraft bomb the Basque city of Guernica in northern Spain. The event greatly contributes to the myth of airpower as a war-winning weapon.
April 30	Republican aircraft attack and sink the Nationalist battleship *España*.
May 17	Juan Negrín, one of the leaders of the PSOE, becomes prime minister of the Republican government. He collaborates closely with the communists until April 1, 1939, and the end of the war.
May 31	German warships shell Almeria. On May 29, two Loyalist aircraft attacked the German pocket battleship *Deutschland* at Iviza. The warship was part of the Non-Intervention international naval patrol force. On May 31 in reprisal, the German pocket battleship *Admiral Scheer* and four escorting destroyers shell the city of Almeria in Andalucia for one hour, killing 24 civilians and injuring another 100 as well as inflicting extensive damage on the city.
June 18	Nationalist forces capture Bilbao.
August 25	Nationalist forces capture Santandar.
October 21	Nationalist troops seize Gijon, completing their conquest of northwestern Spain.
October 28	The Republican government relocates from Valencia to Barcelona.
December 5	Loyalist forces launch a major offensive around Teruel in Aragon. Although Teruel is taken on December 19, the poorly equipped and supplied Loyalists are soon brought to a halt. Nationalist forces retake Teruel in February 1938.

1938

July 25–November 16	The Republican side stakes all on a great counteroffensive from Catalonia, along the Ebro River. They commit

100,000 of their 400,000-man army in an effort to reestablish communication with Castile and draw the Nationalists away from Valencia. The initial crossing of the Ebro catches the Nationalists by surprise and goes well, but the offensive is soon halted, thanks largely to Fascist airpower and artillery. Fighting is fierce, and it takes the Nationalists more than three and a half months to push the Republican troops back across the Ebro. The failure of their offensive marks the beginning of the end for the Republican side in the war.

1939

January 26   Nationalist forces capture Barcelona. Loyalist resistance collapses. The Nationalists then overrun all of Catalonia, and some 200,000 Loyalist troops flee across the border into France, where they are disarmed and interned.

February 27   The British and French governments recognize the Nationalist government without conditions.

March   Early this month, the ships of the Republican Navy escape across the Mediterranean to the Tunisian port of Bizerte, where they are interned by the French.

March 28   Nationalist troops enter the cities of Valencia and Madrid, bringing the war to an end.

1939–1945   During World War II, Spain is a nonbelligerent but is friendly to the Axis powers and clandestinely assists their war effort.

1975

October 30   Franco concedes full power to Juan Carlos.

November 20   Franco dies.

November 22   The Cortes proclaims Juan Carlos I as king of Spain.

SPENCER C. TUCKER

Further Reading

Alpert, Michael. "The Clash of Spanish Armies: Contrasting Ways of War in Spain, 1936–1939." *War in History* 6(3) (1999): 331–351.

Alpert, Michael. *A New International History of the Spanish Civil War.* Basingstoke, UK: Palgrave Macmillan, 2004.

Alpert, Michael. *The Republican Army in the Spanish Civil War, 1936–1939.* New York: Cambridge University Press, 2013.

Beevor, Antony. *The Battle for Spain: The Spanish Civil War, 1936–1939.* London: Weidenfield and Nicolson, 2006.

Bolloten, Burnett. *The Spanish Revolution: The Left and the Struggle for Power during the Civil War.* Chapel Hill: University of North Carolina Press, 1979.

Bowen, Wayne H., and José Alvarez, eds. *A Military History of Modern Spain.* Westport, CT: Praeger Security International, 2007.

Brenan, Gerald. *The Spanish Labyrinth: An Account of the Social and Political Background of the Civil War.* Cambridge: Cambridge University Press, 1993.

Buchanan, Tom. *Britain and the Spanish Civil War.* Cambridge: Cambridge University Press, 1997.

Carr, Raymond. *Modern Spain, 1875–1980.* Oxford: Oxford University Press, 2001.

Coverdale, John F. *Italian Intervention in the Spanish Civil War.* Princeton, NJ: Princeton University Press, 1975.

Ealham, Chris, and Michael Richards. *The Splintering of Spain.* New York: Cambridge University Press, 2005.

Elstob, Peter. *Condor Legion.* New York: Ballantine Books, 1973.

Graham, Helen. *The Spanish Civil War: A Very Short Introduction.* New York: Oxford University Press, 2005.

Graham, Helen. *The Spanish Republic at War, 1936–1939.* New York: Cambridge University Press, 2002.

Howson, Gerald. *Arms for Spain.* New York: St. Martin's, 1998.

Jackson, Gabriel. *The Cruel Years: The Story of the Spanish Civil War.* New York: John Day, 1974.

Jackson, Gabriel. *The Spanish Republic and the Civil War, 1931–1939.* Princeton, NJ: Princeton University Press, 1965.

Kowalsky, Daniel. *Stalin and the Spanish Civil War.* New York: Columbia University Press, 2008.

Laureau, Patrick. *Condor: The Luftwaffe in Spain, 1936–1939.* Crowborough, UK: Hikoki, 2001.

Matthews, Herbert L. *Half of Spain Died: A Reappraisal of the Spanish Civil War.* New York: Scribner, 1973.

Othen, Christopher. *Franco's International Brigades: Foreign Volunteers and Fascist Dictators in the Spanish Civil War.* London: Reportage Press, 2008.

Payne, Stanley G. *A History of Spain and Portugal.* Madison: University of Wisconsin Press, 1973.

Payne, Stanley G. *The Spanish Civil War, the Soviet Union, and Communism.* New Haven, CT: Yale University Press, 2004.

Preston, Paul. *The Coming of the Spanish Civil War.* London: Macmillan, 1973.

Preston, Paul. *A Concise History of the Spanish Civil War.* London: Fontana, 1986.

Preston, Paul. *Franco: A Biography.* New York: Basic Books, 1994.

Preston, Paul. *The Spanish Civil War: Reaction, Revolution, and Revenge.* New York: Norton, 2006.

Proctor, Raymond L. *Hitler's Luftwaffe in the Spanish Civil War.* Westport, CT: Greenwood, 1983.

Radosh, Ronald, Mary Habeck, and Grigory Sevostianov. *Spain Betrayed: The Soviet Union in the Spanish Civil War.* New Haven, CT: Yale University Pres, 2001.

Seidman, Michael. *The Victorious Counter-Revolution: The Nationalist Effort in the Spanish Civil War.* Madison: University of Wisconsin Press, 2011.

Taylor, F. Jay. *The United States and the Spanish Civil War, 1936–1939.* New York: Bookman Associates, 1971.

Thomas, Hugh. *The Spanish Civil War.* Revised ed. New York: Modern Library, 2001.

Whealey, Robert H. *Hitler and Spain: The Nazi Role in the Spanish Civil War, 1936–1939.* Lexington: University Press of Kentucky, 1989.

World War II (1939–1945)

Causes

World War II was the most wide-ranging, destructive, and costly conflict in human history. Ultimately it involved virtually every major country and region. The war pitted the totalitarian Axis states of Germany, Italy, and Japan against the Allied nations, with the principal powers being Britain, France, the United States, and the Soviet Union. Some historians date the war as beginning with the Japanese invasion of China in 1937. Japanese official histories, however, start with 1931, when their forces overran Manchuria. Most histories of the war, however, begin with September 1939 and the German invasion of Poland.

World War II was in many respects a continuation of World War I. The Versailles Treaty with Germany of 1919 is often depicted as a piece of French villainy too harsh on Germany. Too harsh to conciliate and too weak to destroy, it also was not enforced. This, rather than its severity or lack thereof, is what made possible the renewal of World War I by Germany 20 years later. Germans, however, keenly felt the modest territorial losses imposed on them, although Germany was still the most powerful state of Europe.

The Treaty of Versailles limited the German Army to 100,000 men. Germany was also denied heavy artillery, tanks, and military aviation, and the General Staff was to be abolished. The German Navy was sharply limited in size and could not have submarines. Right from the start Germany violated these provisions, arranging with other states, notably the Soviet Union, for the development of new weapons and the training of military personnel. Article 231,

the so-called war guilt clause, fixed blame for the war on Germany and its allies and was the justification for reparations, which were set at $33 billion.

The new German democratic government, the Weimar Republic, had to bear the shame of Versailles. Many Germans came to believe the "stab in the back" lie perpetuated by the German Right that their army had not been defeated in the field but had been forced to surrender because of a collapse of the home front.

The breakup of the Austro-Hungarian Empire as a consequence of World War I brought the creation of new states in Poland, Czechoslovakia, and Yugoslavia. They sought refuge in an alliance known as the Little Entente and were linked to France through a 1925 treaty of mutual assistance between that country and Czechoslovakia. The Soviet Union refused to recognize Poland's new eastern border, the Curzon Line. But Poland won the Soviet-Polish War (1919–1921) fought over this.

Allied unity disappeared almost immediately with the end of the war. The United States withdrew into isolation, and Britain disengaged from European affairs. This left France to enforce the settlement. Yet France was weaker in both population and economic strength than Germany, despite the latter's 1919 losses. In effect this meant that it was up to the Germans themselves to decide whether they would abide by the treaty provisions.

The German government initially adopted obstructionist policies to break the treaty, and by 1923 it halted major reparations payments. French premier Raymond

Poincaré responded by sending troops into the Ruhr, the industrial heart of Germany. German chancellor Wilhelm Cuno's government then adopted a policy of passive resistance, urging workers not to work and promising to pay their salaries in order to buy time for the United States and Britain to pressure France into withdrawal. Poincaré stood firm, however, and the result was catastrophic German inflation. By November 1923 the mark had fallen to 4.2 trillion to the dollar. This wiped out the savings of the German middle class and caused many Germans to lose all faith in democracy.

Seemingly Poincaré had won. Germany agreed to pay reparations under a scaled-down schedule, and French troops were withdrawn from the Ruhr in 1924. Although the French people approved of Poincaré's action, its high financial cost coupled with the opposition of Britain and the United States helped bring the Left to power in 1924; it reversed Poincaré's go-it-alone approach.

The new German government of Chancellor Gustav Stresemann embarked on a policy of living up to its treaty obligations. "Fulfillment" and "conciliation" replaced "obstruction" and brought the Locarno Pacts of 1925, in which Germany voluntarily guaranteed its western borders as final, promised not to resort to war with its neighbors, and promised to resolve disputes through arbitration. Britain, while it promised at Locarno in 1925 to defend France and Belgium in the event of German attack, refused to make any such pledge regarding the states of Central and Eastern Europe.

By the 1930s, however, the leaders of Germany, Italy, and Japan were not satisfied with the 1919 settlement, and the Western powers seemed unable to resist their demands. This was partly the result of the heavy human costs of World War I, but in Britain some influential figures were sympathetic toward fascism and dictators seen as opposing communism. British governments avoided commitments to continental Europe and embraced appeasement, the notion that meeting the more legitimate demands of the dictators would obviate the need for war. Prime Minister Neville Chamberlain (1937–1940) was its principal architect. There was also great concern in Britain, as elsewhere, about air attacks on cities in any future war.

The United States had greatly benefited from World War I. At modest human cost, the United States had become the world's leading financial power. Yet Americans believed that they had been misled by wartime propaganda and drawn into the war by the arms merchants. Congress enacted legislation preventing loans or the sale of arms to combatants in a war. Such legislation, of course, benefited the already well-armed aggressor states and handicapped their victims, who were not well armed. But most Americans eschewed involvement in world affairs.

The Soviet Union was largely absorbed in internal matters. Soviet leader Joseph Stalin did not accept the new frontiers in Eastern Europe as final. Poland was a particular concern; it had been partially carved from former Russian territory, and more land had been lost to Poland in the 1921 Treaty of Riga ending the Soviet-Polish War.

Stalin was, however, quite concerned about Germany after Adolf Hitler came to power in 1933, for the German leader openly expressed his hatred of communism and his intention to secure *Lebensraum* (living space) in Eastern Europe. Stalin thus pursued an internationalist

Adolf Hitler in 1933. In January of that year, by entirely legal means, Hitler became chancellor of Germany. His determination to reverse the outcome of World War I led directly to World War II. (Print Collector/Getty Images)

course, even while carrying out unprecedented actions against his own people that may have brought the deaths of 20 million people, including the vast majority of the military leadership.

The chain of events that culminated in World War II began in Asia in 1931, when Japan seized Manchuria. In World War I, Japan had secured the German colonial possessions in China, and Japanese nationalists sought to take advantage of the worldwide economic depression and continuing upheaval in China to rectify their nation's lack of natural resources. They wanted to secure Manchuria but also to control Mongolia, China, and South Asia.

The Japanese Army had little sympathy for civilian rule, and in the 1930s it dominated the government and even resorted to political assassination. On September 18, 1931, officers of the elite Japanese Kwantung Army in southern Manchuria set off an explosion near the South Manchuria Railway near Mukden. Blaming this on the Chinese, the Japanese then began the conquest of all Manchuria. Presented with this fait accompli by its military, Tokyo supported the action.

China appealed to the League of Nations. The League Council was reluctant to embark on tough action without the collaboration of the United States (not a League of Nations member), which was not forthcoming. The British also opposed drastic action. Without them, the League of Nations could do little. Japan ignored League of Nations calls for both sides to withdraw their troops and continued military operations. Then in February 1932 Japan proclaimed Manchuria independent as Manchukuo, although a protocol established it as a Japanese protectorate.

The League of Nations Lytton Commission condemned the Japanese move, recommended an autonomous government under Chinese sovereignty that would recognize Japan's special economic interests, and urged nonrecognition of Manchukuo. On February 24, 1933, of 42 members of the League Assembly, only Japan voted against the report. The Japanese delegation then walked out, and in March Tokyo gave notice that it would withdraw from the League of Nations.

Manchukuo was larger than France and Germany combined, but in March 1933 Japanese troops added the Chinese province of Jehol. Early in April they moved to within a few miles of Beijing and Tianjin (Tientsin). In May Chinese forces evacuated Beijing, controlled by pro-Japanese Chinese leaders who then concluded a truce with Japan, creating a demilitarized zone administered by Chinese friendly to Japan.

The economic depression and general Western indifference to the plight of Asians precluded Western military action, but a worldwide financial and commercial boycott in accordance with Article 16 of the League of Nations Covenant might have brought Japanese withdrawal. Even this was beyond Western will, however. The failure to enforce collective security here encouraged other states with similar goals.

Germany was next to take advantage. Hitler, who came to power in January 1933 by entirely legal means, precipitated a series of crises. In October 1933 he withdrew Germany from the League of Nations and the Geneva Disarmament Conference. In response, in June 1934 the Soviet Union, Poland, and Romania mutually guaranteed their existing frontiers, and that September the Soviet Union joined the League of Nations.

On July 25, 1934, Austrian Nazis attempted to seize power in Vienna in order to achieve Anschluss, or union with Germany, forbidden by the 1919 peace settlement. Although Chancellor Engelbert Dollfuss was assassinated, Austrian authorities put down the coup attempt. Italian dictator Benito Mussolini rushed troops to the Brenner Pass. Germany, still largely unarmed, was in no position to oppose Italy, and Hitler, who had initially expressed his support, now disavowed the coup attempt.

To prevent Germany from annexing Austria, in January 1935 France secured a pact with Italy. The pact called for close cooperation between the two powers regarding Central Europe and reaffirmed the independence and territorial integrity of Austria. In secret provisions, Italy promised to support France with its air force in the event of a German move to remilitarize the Rhineland, and France agreed to provide troops to aid Italy should the Germans threaten Austria. France also transferred some of its African territory to the Italian colonies of Libya and Eritrea, and French foreign minister Pierre Laval apparently pledged that France would not oppose Italy's colonial ambitions.

In January 1935 the Saar voted overwhelming to rejoin Germany. On March 16, Hitler announced that the Reich would reintroduce compulsory military service and increase its army to more than 500,000 men. Paris, London, and Rome protested but took no action to compel Berlin to observe its treaty obligations. On May 2, 1935, France and the Soviet Union signed a five-year mutual assistance pact, but the French never did agree to a military convention to coordinate an actual response to German aggression. On May 16 the Soviet Union and Czechoslovakia signed a similar pact, but the Soviet Union was not obligated to provide armed assistance unless France first fulfilled its commitments, already extended to Czechoslovakia.

Britain took the first step in the appeasement of Germany. On June 18, 1935, Britain signed a naval agreement with Germany that violated the Versailles Treaty. In spite of having promised the French in February that it would take no unilateral action toward Germany, London agreed to Germany building a surface navy of up to 35 percent the tonnage of the Royal Navy. In effect this permitted Germany a navy larger than those of either France or Italy. London also allowed Germany 45 percent of the Royal Navy in submarines, which had specifically been prohibited. The Anglo-German Naval Agreement was the first occasion when any power sanctioned Germany's misdeeds.

In October 1935 Mussolini invaded Ethiopia (Abyssinia). The outcome was a foregone conclusion, and in May 1936 Italian forces captured Addis Ababa, and Mussolini proclaimed the annexation of Ethiopia. The League of Nations voted to condemn Italy, but British foreign secretary Sir Samuel Hoare and French foreign minister Laval worked behind the scenes in their infamous Hoare-Laval Proposals to broker away Ethiopia to Italy in return for Italian support against Germany. When this became known, public anger forced both men to resign.

The League of Nations voted to impose sanctions but not on oil, which would have severely crippled Italy. The argument was that Italy could always turn to the United States, which was not bound by League of Nations decisions. In the end, even the ineffectual sanctions were lifted. Another blow had been dealt to collective security.

The seminal event on the road to World War II was Hitler's remilitarization of the Rhineland. On March 7, 1936, he sent 22,000 German troops, armed with little more than rifles and machine guns, into the Rhineland. This violated the Treaty of Versailles but also the Locarno Pacts voluntarily entered into by Germany. The operation occurred while France was in the midst of a bitterly contested election campaign that brought the leftist Popular Front to power.

Incredibly, France had no contingency plan, and its intelligence services grossly overestimated the size of the German forces involved and believed Hitler's false claims that the Luftwaffe (German Air Force) had achieved parity with the French Armée de l'Air. Paris appealed to London, which made it clear that Britain would not

fight for the Rhineland. Had the French acted alone, their forces would have rolled over the Germans, and this probably would have been the end of Hitler.

Remilitarization of the Rhineland provided protection for the industry of the Ruhr and a springboard for invading France and Belgium. It also had another important effect, for Belgium now renounced its treaty of mutual assistance with France and again sought security in neutrality. Germany promptly guaranteed that state's inviolability and integrity.

Almost immediately another international crisis erupted in Spain, where civil war began on July 18, 1936. The leftist Popular Front won a narrow victory in the elections of 1936, and Spanish traditionalists, known as the nationalists, took up arms. Germany and Italy aided the nationalists, with German aviation, known as the Kondor Legion, a key factor in the ultimate nationalist victory.

The Western democracies cut the Spanish republic adrift. France wanted to help, but Britain threatened that if this led to a general European war it would not honor its pledge of military support, forcing France to back down. British leaders came up with a noninterventionist policy, but although all the Great Powers promised to abide by it, only the Western democracies did so.

Among major powers, only the Soviet Union assisted the republic. Stalin apparently hoped for a protracted struggle entangling the Western democracies and Germany at the other end of the continent. Aid from the Soviet Union, paid for in gold by the republican sides, eventually brought a communist takeover of that government. In March 1939 nationalist forces took Madrid, and by April hostilities ended. Some 600,000 Spaniards had died in the fighting; the nationalists executed another 200,000

Estimated Casualty Statistics of World War II

	Total Mobilized	Killed in Action or Died of Wounds	Wounded	Civilian Dead	Jewish Dead (5.7 million total)	Cost (billions 1945 US$)
United States	12,300,000	292,000	671,800	6,000	N/A	$288.0
United Kingdom	5,120,000	264,000	300,000	91,000	N/A	$82.6
Soviet Union	12,500,000	7,500,000	18,000,000	9,000,000	1,000,000	$93.0
France	5,000,000	250,000	350,000	350,000	83,000	$111.3
China	5,000,000	1,310,000	1,793,000	10,000,000	N/A	$41.9
Germany	10,200,000	3,500,000	5,000,000	1,400,000	160,000	$212.3
Japan	6,095,000	1,750,000	4,000,000	672,000	N/A	$41.3
Italy	3,750,000	250,000	66,000	100,000	8,000	$21.0

Sources: The American War Library, http://members.aol.com/veterans; John S. Bowman, ed., *Facts about the American Wars* (n.p.: H. W. Wilson, 1998); John R. Elting, "Costs, Casualties and Other Data," Grolier. com, http://members.aol.com/forcountry/ww2/wc1.htm; Martin Gilbert, *Atlas of the Holocaust* (New York: William Morrow, 1993); Joseph V. O'Brien, "World War II: Combatants and Casualties," John Jay College of Criminal Justice, http://web.jjay.cuny.edu/~jobrien/reference/ob62.html; Boris Urlanis, *Wars and Population* (n.p.: University Press of the Pacific, 1971).

after the war, and it is likely that a similar number died of starvation and disease.

The Spanish Civil War brought together Germany and Italy. On October 25, 1936, they formed the Rome-Berlin Axis. On November 25 Germany and Japan signed the Anti-Comintern Pact to oppose activities of the Comintern (Third International), created by Moscow to spread communism. On November 6, 1937, Italy joined the Anti-Comintern Pact.

Shortly afterward Mussolini announced that Italy would not act to prevent Anschluss. Italy also withdrew from the League of Nations and recognized Manchukuo as an independent state in November 1937. (Germany followed suit in May 1938.) By 1938 the Great Powers were again divided into two antagonistic groups.

Japan, meanwhile, asserted its right to control China. Tokyo demanded an end to Western assistance to China, threatening force should it continue. In 1935 Japan also began encroaching upon several of China's northern provinces. The Chinese government at Nanjing, headed by Generalissimo Jiang Jieshi (Chiang Kai-shek), was more concerned with the Chinese Communists and initially favored appeasement, but students and the Chinese military demanded action. The Chinese Communists also expressed a willingness to cooperate against Japan.

On July 7, 1937, a clash occurred near Beijing between Japanese and Chinese troops. Later that month after the Nationalist government rejected their ultimatum, the Japanese invaded the coveted northern provinces. In a few days they had occupied both Tianjin and Beijing, and by the end of the year Japan controlled all five Chinese provinces north of the Yellow River.

In mid-December Japan installed a pro-Japanese government in Beijing. Japan never declared war against China, however. This enabled it to avoid U.S. neutrality legislation and purchase raw materials and oil, but this also allowed Washington to aid China.

The fighting was not confined to northern China, for in August 1937 the Japanese attacked the great commercial city of Shanghai. It fell in November. Japanese forces then advanced up the Yangtse and in December took Nanjing, where they committed wide-scale atrocities. China again appealed to the League of Nations, which again condemned Japan. But the Western powers failed to withhold critical supplies and financial credits from Japan. By the end of 1938 Japanese troops controlled the great commercial cities of Tianjin, Beijing, Shanghai, Nanjing, Hankow, and Guangzhou (Canton), and the Nationalist government had relocated to the interior city of Chongqing (Chungking).

Japanese troops also clashed with the Soviet Union. Fighting began in 1938 in the poorly defined triborder area of Siberia, Manchukuo, and Korea. Although no state of war was declared, significant battles occurred, no doubt giving Tokyo a new appreciation of Soviet fighting ability and helping to influence the 1941 decision not to strike north into Siberia but instead to proceed against the European colonial possessions of Southeast Asia.

In Western Europe, by 1938 the situation was such as to encourage Hitler to embark upon his own territorial expansion. Austria was first. On February 12, 1938, Hitler demanded that Austrian chancellor Kurt von Schuschnigg appoint Austrian Nazis to key cabinet positions. On March 9 Schuschnigg attempted an end run by announcing a plebiscite on Anschluss only

four days hence. Hitler was determined that there be no plebiscite and demanded Schuschnigg's resignation and postponement of the vote under threat of invasion. Schuschnigg gave way and resigned. Austrian Nazi leader Arthur Seyss-Inquart then took power and invited in German troops "to preserve order," although they had already crossed the border.

On March 13 Berlin declared Austria to be part of the Reich, and the next day perhaps 1 million Austrians welcomed Hitler to Vienna. France and Britain lodged formal protests, but that was the extent of their action. After the war Austrian leaders denied culpability by successfully positing that their country was the first victim of Nazi aggression.

Anschluss greatly strengthened Germany's strategic position, as Germany was now in direct contact with Italy, Yugoslavia, and Hungary. Czechoslovakia was the next target. It was almost isolated, with its trade largely at German mercy, and Germany outflanked the powerful western Czech defenses.

Some 3.5 million Germans lived in Czechoslovakia. They had long complained about discrimination in a state in which Czechs were only the largest minority. Czechoslovakia was the keystone of Europe. It had a military alliance with France, a well-trained 400,000-man army, the important Skoda munitions complex at Pilsen, and strong western fortifications. Unfortunately for the Czechs, the latter were in the Erzegeberge (Ore Mountains), where the population was almost entirely German. Also, Bohemia-Moravia, almost one-third German in population, now protruded into the Reich. Hitler pushed the demands of the Sudetendeutsch (Sudeten German) Party to address legitimate complaints into outright union of the German regions with Germany.

In May 1938, during key Czechoslovakian elections, German troops massed on the border and threatened invasion. Confident in French support, Czechoslovakia mobilized. France and the Soviet Union stated their willingness to go to war to defend Czechoslovakia, and in the end nothing happened. Hitler then ordered the construction of fortifications along the German western frontier. Called by the Germans the West Wall, it was clearly intended to prevent France from supporting its eastern allies.

Western leaders now pondered whether Czechoslovakia, formed only in 1919, was really worth a general European war. By mid-September Hitler was insisting on "self-determination" for the Sudeten Germans and threatening war if this was not granted. If Germany intervened militarily, France would have to decide whether to honor its pledge to defend Czechoslovakia. If it did so, this would bring on a general European war.

In this critical situation Chamberlain flew to Germany to meet with Hitler. Hitler informed him that the Sudeten Germans must be able to unite with Germany and that he was willing to risk war to accomplish this. London and Paris then decided to force self-determination on Prague.

The British and French decision to desert Czechoslovakia resulted from many factors. Both countries dreaded a new general war with the threat of air attacks against London and Paris. Britain had begun to rebuild the Royal Air Force (RAF) only the year before, and the Germans succeeded in duping the French as to actual Luftwaffe strength. The Western Allies also believed that they could not count on the Soviet Union, the military of which was still recovering from Stalin's purges. In France and especially in Britain there

were also those who viewed Nazism as a bulwark against communism and hoped to encourage Hitler to move against Russia so that communism and fascism might destroy one another.

Chamberlain desperately hoped to prevent a general European war. A businessman before entering politics, he believed in the sanctity of contracts and, despite evidence to the contrary, could not accept that the leader of the most powerful state in Europe was a blackmailer and a liar. But the West had in 1919 championed "self-determination of peoples," and by this Germany had a right to all it had hitherto demanded. The transfer of the Sudetenland to the Reich did not seem too high a price for a satisfied Germany and a peaceful Europe. Finally, there were Hitler's statements that once his demands upon Czechoslovakia had been satisfied he would have no further territorial ambitions in Europe.

Under heavy British and French pressure, on September 21 Czechoslovakia accepted the Anglo-French proposals. Chamberlain again traveled to Germany and so informed Hitler. To his surprise Hitler upped the ante, demanding that all Czechoslovak officials be removed from the Sudeten area within 10 days and that all military and economic establishments be left in place.

Hitler's demands led to the most serious international crisis in Europe since 1918. Prague informed London that Hitler's demands were unacceptable, as they would not allow Prague time to organize its military defense. London and Paris agreed with the Czech position and decided not to pressure Prague to secure its acceptance. A general European war appeared inevitable.

U.S. president Franklin Roosevelt urged an international conference, and Mussolini secured Hitler's reluctant agreement. Chamberlain, French premier Edouard Daladier, and Mussolini traveled to Munich and met with Hitler on September 29. The Soviets were not invited, and Czechoslovakia itself was not officially represented. The object was simply to give Hitler what he wanted and avoid war.

The Munich agreement of September 30 gave Hitler everything he demanded, and on October 1 German troops marched across the frontier. Poland and Hungary now demanded and also received Czechoslovakian territory that contained their national minorities.

Even though France and Britain were far from ready for war, it would have been better to have fought Germany in September 1938. Even if the Soviet Union and Poland had not joined in, the German Army would have been forced to fight against France, Britain, and Czechoslovakia. Germany was not then ready for war. The Luftwaffe would have had to fight on two fronts and was short of bombs. Also, only 12 German divisions were available to hold against eight times that number of French divisions. And there would be 35 well-trained and well-equipped Czechoslovak divisions, backed by substantial numbers of artillery, tanks, and aircraft. Later those responsible for the Munich agreement claimed that it bought a year for the Western democracies to rearm, but in fact a year later Britain and France were in a much worse position than they had been at the time of the Munich crisis.

The Munich agreement had far-reaching international effects. It effectively ended the French security system. Poland, Romania, and Yugoslavia now questioned the worth of French commitments. Stalin saw the Western surrender to Hitler as an effort by the Western powers to encourage

Germany's *Drang nach Osten* (Drive to the East) and precipitate a war between Germany and the Soviet Union.

Despite Hitler's assurance that the Sudetenland was his last territorial demand, events soon proved the contrary. Seizing upon internal dissension in Czechoslovakia, in March 1939 under German goading, Slovakia and Ruthenia declared their independence. The Germans then threatened Czechoslovak president Emil Hácha with the immediate destruction of Prague from the air unless Bohemia and Moravia became German protectorates. Hácha signed, and on March 15 Nazi troops occupied what remained of Czechoslovakia. Slovakia became a vassal state of the Reich, and Hungary soon seized Ruthenia. On March 21 Germany demanded that Lithuania return Memel, with its mostly German population, secured after World War I to provide Lithuania access to the sea. The Lithuanian government complied.

In the former Czechoslovakia the Wehrmacht secured 1,582 aircraft, 2,000 artillery pieces, and sufficient equipment for 20 divisions. This more than offset any increase in armaments that Britain and France had achieved. Between August 1938 and September 1939 Skoda produced nearly as many arms as all British arms factories combined.

Hitler's actions, however, proved that his demands were not limited to Germans. The British were now finally convinced that they could no longer trust Hitler. Indeed, Britain and France responded with a series of guarantees to the smaller states now threatened by Germany.

With Poland obviously Hitler's next target, on March 31, 1939, Great Britain and France extended a formal guarantee to support that country in the event of a German attack. At the 11th hour and under the worst possible circumstances, with Czechoslovakia lost and the Soviet Union alienated, Britain reversed its East European policy and agreed to do what the French had sought in the 1920s.

Mussolini took advantage and strengthened Italy's position in the Balkans by seizing Albania in April 1939. Britain and France then extended guarantees to defend Greece and Romania. On April 28 Hitler reiterated earlier demands for the Baltic port city of Gdansk (Danzig) and insisted that Germany receive extraterritorial rights in the Polish Corridor. Poland refused. On May 23 Hitler met with his leading generals and stated his intention to attack Poland at the first suitable opportunity.

In April, Britain and France initiated negotiations with the Soviet Union for a mutual assistance pact. But their guarantee to Poland gave the Soviet Union protection on its western frontier. Although negotiations continued until August, they failed to produce agreement. Poland, Latvia, Lithuania, and Estonia all feared the Russians as much as or more than the Germans, and all were unwilling to allow Soviet armies within their borders to defend against German attack. Polish leaders also refused to believe that Hitler would risk war with Britain and France. In the end, the British and French negotiators refused to give Poland and the Baltic States to Stalin the way they had handed Czechoslovakia to Hitler.

While the Kremlin negotiated more or less openly with Britain and France, it also sought an understanding with Germany. Stalin held equal suspicion for all foreign governments; his preoccupations were remaining in power and what was in the best interest of the Soviet Union. Signals from Stalin convinced Hitler that Stalin truly wanted an agreement.

Stalin personally negotiated with German foreign minister Joachim von Ribbentrop in Moscow on August 23, and a Soviet-Nazi agreement was signed that night. It consisted of an open 10-year non-aggression pact, but there were two secret protocols, not publicly acknowledged by Moscow until 1990. The first partitioned Eastern Europe between Germany and the Soviet Union. The Soviet sphere included eastern Poland, Romanian Bessarabia, Estonia, Latvia, and Finland. Lithuania and western Poland went to Germany. A month later Hitler traded Lithuania to Stalin in exchange for further territorial concessions in Poland. The second secret provision was a trade convention whereby the Soviet Union would supply vast quantities of raw materials to Germany in exchange for military technology and finished goods. This was of immense assistance to the German war machine early in World War II.

Although Hitler's and Stalin's interests coincided over Poland, Stalin failed to understand the danger of the alliance. He expected that the Germans would face a protracted war in the west, which would allow the Soviet Union time to rebuild its military. Stalin assumed that an eventual clash would occur with Germany but not before 1943, and by then the Red Army would be ready to meet it.

The Nazi-Soviet Non-Aggression Pact shocked the West. Communism and Nazism, supposed to be ideological opposites on the worst possible terms, had come together. The German invasion of Poland was originally set for August 26 but was delayed owing to Italy's decision to remain neutral. Uncertain of German victory, Mussolini insisted on armaments and raw materials that he knew Germany could not supply. He did agree to keep secret the decision to remain neutral and continue military preparations so as to fool the British and French. The weight of Italy in the German calculus was so slight that it took only a few days for Germany to reset its military plans and go it alone.

SPENCER C. TUCKER

Course

On September 1, 1939, German forces invaded Poland. Two days later, Britain and France declared war on Germany. World War II had begun.

France and Poland together had the equivalent of 150 divisions. Germany had only 98 divisions, and 36 of these were being organized. Hitler, however, had supported the creation of 14 new armored, mechanized, and motorized infantry divisions. The armored divisions were to break through weak points, followed by motorized infantry and mobile antitank guns, all supported by flying artillery in the Ju-87 Stuka dive-bomber. The Polish campaign was the first example of blitzkrieg (lightning war).

The Germans were able to invade from three directions simultaneously. The bulk of the Polish forces were dispersed forward along the 800-mile western frontier and could thus be cut off and surrounded. German aircraft prevented concentration and spread panic by attacking cities, including Warsaw. Then on September 17, the Soviets invaded from the east in accordance with secret provisions of the Nazi-Soviet Non-Aggression Pact. The Red Army also proceeded into Estonia, Latvia, and Lithuania. Warsaw surrendered on September 27, and organized Polish resistance ceased on October 5.

In the west the French had an overwhelming strength on the ground and, with the RAF, in the air. The Allies had promised the Poles immediate air attacks

and a French invasion of Germany, but the best the French could do was a slight advance of some 5 miles on a 16-mile front. Despite light casualties, the French halted and, when Warsaw surrendered, withdrew. Had they undertaken a major offensive, it would have reached the Rhine and greatly impacted the war. Britain did even less. The British Expeditionary Force (BEF) had not even completed its assembly by early October, and Polish pleas for the bombing of Germany met no response.

Germany annexed outright about half of the territory taken. The remainder was exploited for cheap labor. Special extermination squads moved in to kill potential leaders and Jews. Poland ultimately became a vast network of work camps and extermination centers, with Jews shipped there from all over Europe. During the war some 6 million Jews were slaughtered in what was called the "Final Solution of the Jewish Question" but is better known as the Holocaust. The Russians also imposed a brutal regime in their part of Poland, executing some 15,000 Polish Army officers and intellectuals.

The Poles made an important technological contribution. The Germans had adopted for transmission of classified messages an electromechanical rotor encrypting device christened Enigma. Japan also used the machine. Enigma enabled encoding in some 150 million combinations, with settings typically changed daily. The Germans believed that such messages were unbreakable. The Poles, however, achieved some success in decoding Enigma and shared this with their allies. The British then assembled a team of experts and developed additional refinements that, with German operator errors, greatly reduced the delay. If it did not enable the Allies to win the war, Enigma intelligence (code-named Top Secret Ultra) undoubtedly shortened it.

Stalin now demanded territory from Finland to provide security for Leningrad. He offered in return more Russian land but in the north. When the Finns refused to yield land on the Hango peninsula for a naval base, Stalin ordered an invasion. The ensuing Soviet-Finnish War (November 30, 1939–March 13, 1940), also known as the Winter War, was a foregone conclusion but an embarrassment for Stalin. The Red Army sustained enormous casualties and took four months to defeat Finland, which then had to yield far more than the original demand.

In late November 1939 Hitler informed his military chiefs of his determination to secure *Lebensraum* (living space) at the expense of the Soviet Union. That country was then of little military threat, but Germany must first defeat France and Britain. All was then quiet on the Western Front, with the Allies content to wage a war of attrition through economic strangulation by naval blockade, as in World War I. But 1939 was not 1914, for Germany had benevolent neutrals in Italy and the Soviet Union.

Correctly convinced that the British were about to move against neutral Norway, Hitler preempted them, employing virtually the entire German Navy. Beginning on April 9, 1940, the Germans secured Oslo, other cites, and airfields. The British and French landed troops and captured Narvik, but the German invasion of France and the Low Countries on May 10 forced an Allied evacuation on June 7–8. On June 10, Norway surrendered. Denmark had been overrun on April 9.

The Germans had sacrificed half of their cruisers and destroyers but had secured protection for their northern flank as well as Norway's agriculture. Norway also provided bases from which the Germans could strike the Allied North Atlantic convoys and later the Arctic convoys bound for the Soviet Union. But the operation would severely stretch the Reich's manpower resources.

As in World War I, Germany concentrated its naval effort on submarines. In September 1939 Germany had only 55 operational U-boats, but it gradually built up the numbers. It also had success breaking the British convoy codes and developed new innovative tactics. Certainly the Battle of the Atlantic was one of the most important struggles of the war.

German surface ships carried out commerce raiding. The most spectacular engagement occurred with the sortie of the powerful German battleship *Bismarck*. It sank the British battle cruiser *Hood* and severely damaged the battleship *Prince of Wales* before itself falling prey to pursuing British warships on May 27, 1941.

After his conquest of Norway and Denmark, Hitler's next move was against France and the Low Countries of the Netherlands, Belgium, and Luxembourg. Planned for November, the invasion was repeatedly postponed owing to unusually harsh winter conditions and the Allies having secured the German invasion plans.

The original plan had called for a sweeping movement through Belgium and the Netherlands against France similar to 1914 and would have encountered the best British and French forces. The new plan massed the bulk of the German panzer divisions southward to push through the hilly and wooded Ardennes region, then drive north to the English Channel, cutting off Allied forces in Belgium. At the point of their planned breakthrough the Germans would have 44 divisions, the French 9 divisions, and the French had no reserve to contain a German breakthrough. The Allies had more tanks, but most were scattered in support of infantry. The Luftwaffe had twice the number of Allied combat aircraft and many more antiaircraft guns.

The offensive opened on May 10, 1940, and the best British and French units left their prepared defensive positions and advanced to the relief of Belgium. Although French pilots detected the German Ardennes armor buildup, reports were disbelieved, and no action was taken. On the night of May 12–13 the Germans launched their Ardennes drive. They soon crossed the Meuse, then swung northward to trap the major Allied armies in Belgium.

Hitler now intervened. On May 24 he halted the panzers for three critical days in order to allow the infantry to catch up. General Hermann Göring also assured Hitler that the Luftwaffe could destroy the BEF from the air. On May 28, despite a pledge not to act unilaterally, King Leopold III surrendered Belgian forces.

With the Allies now in great jeopardy, BEF commander Field Marshal John Vereker, Viscount Gort, rejected French appeals to attack southward against the German thrust while the French moved from the south. Believing the battle lost, Gort withdrew the BEF to the coast. During May 28–June 4 the British evacuated their own and some French troops from Dunkirk. The British were forced to abandon virtually all their equipment, but the vast bulk of the BEF escaped to fight another day.

On June 10 Mussolini, believing that Germany had won the war, cast his lot with Hitler and declared war on France and Britain. The Italians made little progress in invading southeastern France before the armistice, however. On June 16 the French cabinet voted to ask for terms.

Eighty-four-year-old Marshal Philippe Pétain became premier, and fighting in France ceased on August 25. The Germans occupied two-thirds of the country, including Paris.

On October 28 Mussolini sent Italian forces into Greece from Albania. Italy also attacked the British in Africa. Only Great Britain remained at war. Winston Churchill, who had become prime minister on May 10, appealed to U.S. president Franklin Roosevelt for material assistance.

Roosevelt believed strongly that American security was at stake, but American opinion was still strongly isolationist. American neutrality legislation was, however, amended with a repeal of a ban on arms sales, and Roosevelt ordered sharp increases in weapons production, especially aircraft and ships. In 1940 the United States adopted conscription. That September, Roosevelt agreed to provide 50 old destroyers in return for basing rights. Then on March 8, 1941, in an extraordinarily important step, Congress passed Lend-Lease, empowering Roosevelt to provide arms, raw materials, and food to countries fighting the Axis.

Roosevelt also secured bases in Greenland and Iceland and ordered American shipping convoyed as far as Iceland. When in September 1941 a German submarine fired a torpedo against a U.S. destroyer, Roosevelt issued a "shoot on sight" order. On October 31, German submarines sank the U.S. destroyer *Reuben James,* and 100 men were lost. No doubt war with Germany would have eventually come from the sinking of U.S. ships.

Britain, meanwhile, was in a perilous state. In June 1940 there was only one properly equipped division in all of Britain, and the Royal Navy ordered its ships to the far north to escape the Luftwaffe.

Hitler, however, had not anticipated the rapid defeat of France and had no plans for the logical next step of an invasion of Britain. Several key advisers urged an immediate airborne effort to secure a British toehold, but Hitler refused. Believing that the British would soon sue for peace, he let a month pass before initiating planning for a sea invasion.

The essential prerequisite was command of the air. The Battle of Britain began on July 10, 1940, and continued until October 31. German mistakes and the shortcomings of the Luftwaffe contributed to the German defeat. On November 1 the Germans shifted to area night bombing. Had Hitler concentrated on air and submarine pressure to starve Britain of resources, he could have brought about its defeat, but he pivoted toward the Soviet Union. Hitler claimed that the British continued in the war only because they hoped that Germany and the Soviet Union might come to blows: defeat the Soviet Union, and Britain would have to give up.

Hitler rejected suggestions for a far better Mediterranean option to secure the Suez Canal and the Persian Gulf oil fields. He ordered an invasion of the Soviet Union not for sound strategic reasons but instead to secure his territorial goals. In taking this decision, he grossly underestimated Soviet resources and ability.

Shocked by the rapid defeat of France, Stalin incorporated Lithuania, Latvia, and Estonia. He also annexed Bessarabia and Northern Bukovina (the latter had not been assigned to the Soviet Union). To counter these moves and secure his southern flank, Hitler pressured Romania, Bulgaria, and Hungary to join the Axis. Yugoslavia, which resisted, was conquered.

The Germans also invaded Greece, rescuing the Italians who had been driven out by the Greeks. Churchill then halted a successful British North African offensive to aid Greece. The BEF was soon defeated and evacuated to Crete, however, which Hitler then took in a successful but costly airborne invasion.

So confident was Hitler of success in the Soviet Union of one campaign of three months' duration that he did not put Germany on full wartime mobilization. Nor did he consider it necessary to coordinate plans with Japan. His Balkans campaign and heavy rains also imposed delay, perhaps the final blow to the chance of German victory. Stalin, meanwhile, received numerous warnings from Britain and the United States of German intentions but rejected them as an attempt to drive a wedge between the Soviet Union and Germany.

Early on June 22, 1941, the German Army, with Finnish, Romanian, Hungarian, and Italian contingents totaling some 3 million men, moved into the Soviet Union along a 2,000-mile front. The appallingly bad generalship of Stalin had the bulk of Red Army units in forward positions, where they were quickly cut off and surrounded. In the early fighting Stalin repeatedly ignored sound military advice. Ordering his units not to retreat cost the Red Army 665,000 men taken prisoner at Kiev and 457,000 at Smolensk.

Within a week the Germans had advanced 350 miles. By autumn they had conquered Belarus (White Russia) and most of Ukraine. In the north the Germans besieged Leningrad, in the center they were driving on Moscow, and in the south they entered the Crimean peninsula and laid siege to Sebastopol.

The blitzkrieg had worked well in short distances but broke down in the vast expanses of the Soviet Union. An appallingly primitive transportation system and winter

OPERATION BARBAROSSA, 1941–1942

temperatures plummeting to 60 degrees below zero greatly hampered German logistics. Hitler also greatly miscalculated Soviet resources. The Germans expected to meet 200 divisions. By mid-August they had defeated these but now had to contend with another 160. The Soviets also greatly outnumbered the Germans in tanks and aircraft. Stalin called on resources from Russian Asia, and in December the Soviets pushed back the Germans from the Moscow suburbs.

Hitler, disgusted by events, assumed personal command, and in the spring of 1942 he shifted the main attack to the south toward the oil fields of the Caucasus. Sebastopol soon fell. But he also sent forces against Stalingrad on the Volga and now experienced the consequences of strategic overstretch.

Major fighting was also occurring in North Africa. It had begun in September 1940 when Mussolini ordered an invasion of Egypt from Libya. Determined to maintain control of the Suez Canal, a vital supply route to India, Churchill diverted vitally needed resources. British forces secured Ethiopia, and a British counteroffensive in Egypt carried well into Libya. It could have cleared Africa of the Axis completely but was halted when Churchill decided to aid Greece.

The Italian breakdown led Hitler to send German reinforcements. Lieutenant General Erwin Rommel's Afrika Korps launched an offensive in Libya in the spring of 1941. But Hitler never did make a major effort in North Africa or the choke points of Gibraltar, Malta, and Suez. Instead, he merely opened a fresh drain on Germany's resources. The fighting in North Africa shifted back and forth, but by mid-1942 Rommel had been halted in the First Battle of El Alamein (July 1–27) in Egypt.

In December 1941 the war widened when the Japanese attacked the United States. With their own nation largely bereft of natural resources, Japan's leaders saw an opportunity to secure the rich natural resources of South Asia. In July 1940 an army-dominated government had taken power in Tokyo, determined to supplant British, French, Dutch, and American interests. The United States was the major obstacle.

On September 27, 1940, Japan entered into an alliance with Germany and Italy. This Tripartite Pact recognized Japanese leadership in "Greater East Asia" and German and Italian leadership in Europe. With their military bogged down in China, Japanese leaders saw the ideal opportunity in the defeat of France and the Netherlands as well as British weakness. In September 1940 the Japanese sent troops into northern French Indochina, ostensibly to close supply routes to Nationalist forces in China.

Germany's invasion of the Soviet Union had removed the Soviet Union as a threat, and in July 1941 Japanese forces moved into southern French Indochina, putting much of Southeast Asia, including the Philippines, within range of Japanese bombers and bringing retaliation by the United States, Britain, and the Netherlands. Roosevelt froze Japanese assets in the United States and prohibited it key exports, including oil. Japan had no oil of its own and only a two-year reserve. Tokyo branded this an "unfriendly act."

Negotiations occurred, but the United States insisted that Japan remove its troops from China and Indochina, and the Japanese refused. The reason the United States was negotiating was its own unreadiness for war. Its army was small, and American factories were only beginning to produce substantial quantities of war materials,

The Japanese attack on Pearl Harbor, Hawaii, December 7, 1941. Prominent in this photograph are the battleships *West Virginia* and *Tennessee*. (Time Life Pictures/US Navy/The LIFE Picture Collection/Getty Images)

with much of this going to Britain. The longer the delay, the better prepared U.S. forces would be.

With negotiations at an impasse, on December 7, 1941, Japan attacked without warning the U.S. Pacific Fleet at Pearl Harbor, Hawaii. This was designed to purchase time for Japan to conquer Southeast Asia and establish a defensive ring. Then when the Americans did attempt to cross the Pacific, Japanese naval aviation, submarines, and warships utilizing the deadly Long Lance torpedo would turn back the Americans and force them to recognize Japanese control of Asia.

The Pearl Harbor attack caught the Americans by surprise and inflicted terrific damage. For only slight aircraft losses of their own, the Japanese sank four of eight

U.S. battleships and severely damaged the remainder. The U.S. Pacific Fleet was now virtually hors de combat, and Japanese Southwest Pacific operations could proceed without major interference. Japan had, however, united Americans behind the war effort. Germany and Italy declared war on the United States. The Tripartite Pact did not cover acts of aggression, and if Hitler had not done this, Roosevelt might have been obliged to fight Japan only.

The Japanese now had nearly a free hand. They secured Guam and Wake Island, and they conquered the Philippines. The Japanese also moved against Hong Kong and Malaya. On February 15, 1942, they captured the great British base of Singapore. They also took the Dutch East Indies and overran Burma (present-day

Myanmar), completing their control of the western gateways to China and the Pacific. The Japanese invaded New Guinea and threatened Australia, and they sent warships into the Indian Ocean.

Still fighting in China, the Japanese were in fact stretched far beyond their capacity to hold their gains. U.S. industry dwarfed that of Japan. Japanese steel production in 1941 was only 7 million tons versus 92 million for the United States. Japan was not to have the time to exploit the resources of the conquered territory.

The United States and Britain formed the Combined Chiefs of Staff and developed a unified strategy. The defeat of Germany was the primary goal, but sufficient resources were available to permit American operations against Japan, with Australia the chief base of operations. In mid-1942 American, British, and Australian forces halted Japanese southward expansion.

The United States assumed responsibility for the Pacific area except Sumatra; the British retained responsibility for it and the Indian Ocean. China was a separate theater under American tutelage. There was, however, no unified U.S. command. General Douglas MacArthur had responsibility for the Southwest Pacific, and Admiral Chester Nimitz commanded the Pacific Ocean area.

In 1942 the United States won two naval victories. The Battle of the Coral Sea (May 4–8), the first major naval action fought by aircraft without the two fleets coming in sight of one another, was a tactical draw but a U.S. strategic victory, as it turned back a Japanese invasion of Port Moresby.

The Battle of Midway (June 4–6) is often regarded as the turning point in the Pacific war. Japanese Combined Fleet commander Admiral Yamamoto Isoroku planned to capture Midway Island with a diversionary/secondary thrust against the Aleutians. Yamamoto wanted Midway as a base for operations against Pearl Harbor and to draw out and destroy the U.S. Pacific Fleet.

Yamamoto assembled some 200 ships, including 8 carriers, and more than 600 aircraft. Nimitz could count on only 76 ships, with 2 carriers. Luck played a major role, as U.S. dive-bombers caught the Japanese carriers with their fighter cover low while dealing with torpedo bombers. Four Japanese fleet carriers were sunk, and Japan also lost 350 aircraft with their highly trained aircrews. The United States lost the carrier *Yorktown* and 150 aircraft.

In August 1942 American forces landed at Guadalcanal in the Solomons to contest Japanese construction of an airstrip. A fierce struggle ensued there and in the surrounding waters until the Japanese withdrew in February 1943. U.S. forces then embarked on a series of island-hopping operations. The U.S. Marine Corps led, assisted by the U.S. Army and made possible by the great buildup in naval forces and the fleet train concept of supply and repair vessels accompanying the battle fleet. Strong Japanese installations were on occasion bypassed and cut off.

At the same time, the U.S. Navy became history's most effective practitioner of submarine warfare. In 1941 Japan had a marginal capability of 6 million tons of merchant shipping. It built another 2 million tons during the war, but 4.8 million tons of the total were sunk by submarines. Particularly grievous was the loss of tankers. U.S. submarines also sank some 200 Japanese warships.

Meanwhile, plans to invade continental Europe had to be delayed, for U.S. forces were unready. This greatly displeased the Soviets, who understandably sought relief

Pacific Theater, 1941–1945

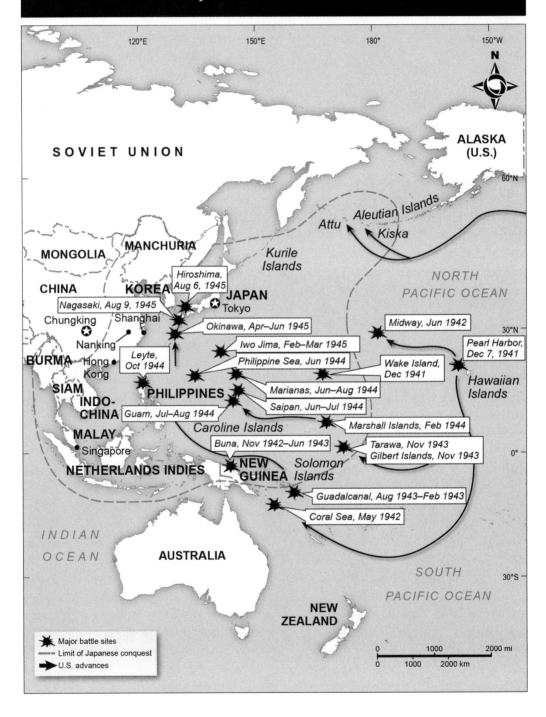

from the 300 Axis divisions on their territory. In the meantime, the Western Allies concentrated on the air bombardment of Germany.

British and American air commanders believed strongly that strategic bombing could win the war. Precision daylight bombing proving impossible, the United States in effect accepted the British argument that the way to win was to shatter morale and "unhouse" civilians in the area bombing of cities. Such arguments proved specious, although U.S. strategic bombing was much more effective in the Pacific theater.

At the end of 1942, the tide of European battle began to turn. On November 8, Anglo-American forces landed at Casablanca, Morocco, and at Oran and Algiers in Algeria. Vichy French forces contested the landings, which were, however, successful. The Allies then pushed eastward to meet British general Bernard Montgomery's Eighth Army, which broke out in the Second Battle of El Alamein (October 23–November 4), although Axis forces were able to withdraw in good order into Tunisia.

Too late, Hitler reinforced, only to see Axis forces defeated in the Battle of Tunis (May 3–13, 1943). Africa was cleared of Axis forces, and the threat to Egypt and Suez was ended. Meanwhile, by the autumn of 1943, the Allies were winning the Battle of the Atlantic, thanks to convoys, better depth charges, escort carriers, independent hunter-killer groups, new radar sets in long-range aircraft, and Ultra.

The Germans also suffered a major defeat in the Soviet Union in the Battle of Stalingrad (August 24, 1942–January 31, 1943). The Eastern Front might still have been fought to a draw but only with withdrawal and a shortened front. Hitler rejected this, insisting that there be no retreat. This only ensured that inevitable withdrawals were more costly.

By the summer of 1943 the advantage had passed to the Soviets. Increased industrial production and immense quantities of Lend-Lease aid were factors. Still, the Soviet Union bore the brunt of ground combat in the war. It lost more men at Stalingrad alone than the United States did in battle during the entire war in all theaters combined. From June 1941 the Soviets had to contend most of the time with four-fifths and never less than three-fourths of the German Army.

Hitler prepared a major offensive that became the Battle of Kursk (July 5–16, 1943). The Soviets knew the German plans through their spy apparatus in Berlin, and the attackers encountered deep, well-prepared defenses. Kursk was the largest battle of World War II, involving some 4 million Soviet and German troops, some 70,000 artillery pieces, and 12,000 planes. With 13,000 tanks engaged, it was the largest armor battle in history. On July 12 the Soviets launched a counteroffensive, making Kursk the true turning point on the Eastern Front.

U.S., British, and Canadian forces invaded and conquered Sicily during July 9–August 17, 1943. This brought finis to Mussolini's regime (the Germans subsequently rescued him and set him up as head of a rump Italian state in the north), and the new Italian government promptly opened secret talks with the Allies. On September 3 the Allies invaded Italy from the south, but the Germans took over the Italian positions. In October 1943 the Italian government declared war on Germany, but German forces blocked the advance on Rome, and the Italian campaign became a bloody stalemate as Allied resources were drawn off for the invasion of France. Rome was only liberated on June 4, 1944, and the German surrender in Italy occurred on May 2, 1945.

The Allies also continued their strategic bombing of Germany. In the summer of 1943 British and American bombers launched devastating raids against German cities. Heavy bomber losses were reversed in late 1943 with the arrival of new long-range American fighters capable of accompanying the bombers to and from their targets. Strategic bombing was important but not decisive. Germany was actually attaining its highest levels of military production at the end of the war.

General Dwight D. Eisenhower had command of the invasion of France. The Allies invaded from the sea on June 6, 1944, while airborne forces fought to prevent German reinforcements from reaching the beaches. The Germans had heavily fortified the Atlantic coastline, but the Allies brought their own artificial harbors (Mulberries). Elaborate deceptions convinced Hitler that the Allies would invade Norway and that the Normandy operation was a feint, with the main landing in France to occur in the Pas de Calais.

Some 130,000 men came ashore the first day, and 1 million came ashore within a month. Nonetheless, the going was slower than expected. Not until the end of July were the Allies able to break free. Lieutenant General George Patton's Third Army in a single month liberated most of France north of the Loire. On August 15, meanwhile, the Seventh Army invaded southern France near Cannes, then drove northeast.

The Western Allies wasted several opportunities that would have shortened the war. Failure to close a gap between Argentan and Falaise allowed some 100,000 Germans to escape. Montgomery also halted at Antwerp, and the German Fifteenth Army

was able to reach Holland. Most German leaders knew that the war was lost, but it was clear that Hitler was determined to fight to the last, even at the cost of the complete destruction of Germany. Plots to assassinate him failed, however.

Montgomery's effort to cross the Rhine at Arnheim and drive into the Ruhr failed. Meanwhile, the Soviets began a great offensive that destroyed German Army Group Center (June 22–August 19, 1944). The Red Army then halted before Warsaw. After encouraging the Poles to rise up, the Red Army then sat idly by for two months. Some 300,000 Poles died, making the subsequent Soviet subjugation of Poland far easier. In December, however, the Red Army crossed into Germany as millions of German refugees fled.

Meanwhile, Hitler planned to recapture Antwerp. Substantial German reinforcements were transferred from the Eastern Front for what would be the biggest battle on the Western Front in the war and the largest engagement ever for the U.S. Army. In the Ardennes Offensive (December 16, 1944–January 16, 1945), also known as the Battle of the Bulge, the Germans caught the Americans by surprise. Bad weather grounded Allied aircraft, and the Germans created a bulge in the lines some 50 miles deep and 70 miles wide. Clearing weather and rapid Allied reinforcement turned the tide. Then, before the Germans could shift resources eastward, the Soviets launched their great Vistula-Oder Offensive (January 12–February 2, 1945). In effect the Ardennes Offensive hastened the end of the war. Hitler, meanwhile, rejected all appeals to end the slaughter, forbidding retreat.

Soviet forces swept through the Baltic States, White Russia, Ukraine, and Poland and forced the capitulation of Romania,

NORMANDY INVASION, 1944

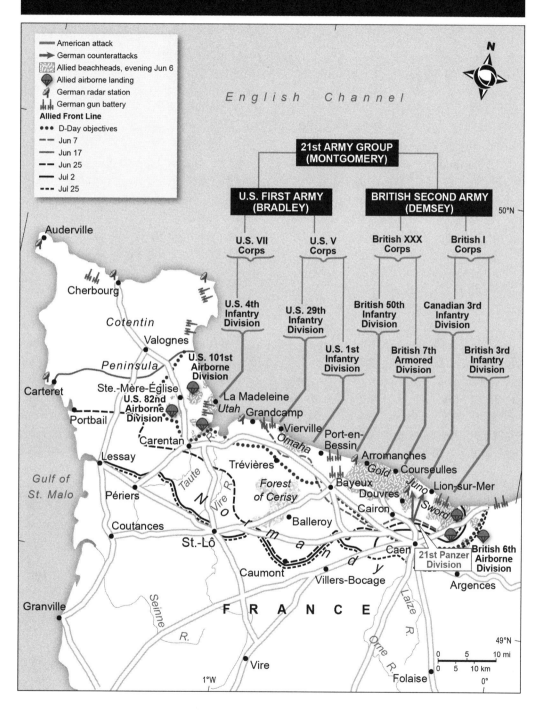

American attack
German counterattacks
Allied beachheads, evening Jun 6
Allied airborne landing
German radar station
German gun battery

Allied Front Line
••• D-Day objectives
— — Jun 7
— — Jun 17
— — Jun 25
——— Jul 2
- - - Jul 25

21st ARMY GROUP
(MONTGOMERY)

U.S. FIRST ARMY
(BRADLEY)

BRITISH SECOND ARMY
(DEMSEY)

U.S. VII Corps
U.S. V Corps
British XXX Corps
British I Corps

U.S. 4th Infantry Division
U.S. 29th Infantry Division
British 50th Infantry Division
Canadian 3rd Infantry Division

U.S. 1st Infantry Division
British 7th Armored Division
British 3rd Infantry Division

50°N
49°N

English Channel

Auderville
Cherbourg
Cotentin
Valognes
Peninsula
Carteret
Ste.-Mère-Église
Portbail
U.S. 82nd Airborne Division
U.S. 101st Airborne Division
La Madeleine
Utah Grandcamp
Vierville
Omaha
Port-en-Bessin
Arromanches
Gold Courseulles
Juno Lion-sur-Mer
Bayeux
Douvres
Sword
Cairon
Caen
21st Panzer Division
British 6th Airborne Division
Argences

Carentan
Lessay
Gulf of St. Malo
Périers
Coutances
St.-Lô
Granville
Taute
Vire R.
N
o
r
m
a
n
d
y
Trévières
Forest of Cerisy
Balleroy
Caumont
Villers-Bocage
Seinne R.
Vire
Laize R.
Orne R.
Folaise

F R A N C E

0   5   10 mi
0   5   10 km

1°W
0°

Finland, and Bulgaria. Early in 1945 the Red Army entered East Prussia, Czechoslovakia, and Hungary and began its drive into Germany. On April 16 the Soviets launched an operation to take Berlin. Eisenhower, meanwhile, sent 18 divisions to clear out the Ruhr. He also sent much of his strength southward to reduce an imagined German alpine redoubt.

Mussolini was captured in northern Italy by the antifascist resistance and shot. Hitler committed suicide in the ruins of Berlin, and the Germans surrendered unconditionally on May 8, 1945. By that time the Western Allies had met the Red Army on the Elbe and in Bohemia and Austria. The war in Europe was over.

In the Pacific, American forces had moved from the Solomons at the easternmost fringe on the Indonesian archipelago toward the Japanese home islands. The Americans assaulted and took the islands and atolls in the Middle Pacific: the Gilberts (Tarawa and Makin, November 20–24, 1943), the Marshalls (Kwajalein and Eniwetok, January 29–February 21, 1944), and the Carolines (Saipan, Guam, and Tinian, June 15–August 2, 1944). Most were desperate struggles, with the Japanese choosing to fight to the death.

U.S. naval forces inflicted major losses on the Japanese in the Battle of the Philippine Sea (June 19–21, 1944). On October 20, U.S. forces began landing on Leyte in the Philippines, triggering the largest naval battle in history in terms of men and ships. The Battle of Leyte Gulf (October 23–26) involved 218 U.S. and 64 Japanese ships and saw the end of the Japanese fleet as an organized fighting force.

During February 19–March 24, 1945, U.S. marines took Iwo Jima. Finally, in one of the war's greatest battles, the U.S. Army and U.S. Marine Corps secured Okinawa, only 300 miles from Japan itself. Meanwhile, heavy B-29 Superfortress bombers flying first from China and then from the Carolines pounded Japan. The first firebomb raid was against Tokyo on March 9–10, 1945. The single most destructive air raid in history, it destroyed 15 square miles of the city, killing more than 83,000 people and injuring 100,000. Other Japanese cities were also burned out. Carrier aviation, including the Royal Navy, and U.S. submarines shattered Japanese industry, all but destroyed intraisland shipping, and obliterated what remained of the Japanese Navy.

With the capture of Okinawa, the stage was set for an invasion of Japan, with anticipated heavy U.S. casualties. On August 6, 1945, however, the United States dropped an atomic bomb on Hiroshima. In a single instant the city of 200,000 people was destroyed, with 70,000 dead. Two days later the Soviet Union, which had pledged to enter the conflict in the Far East within three months of the surrender of Germany, declared war on Japan and invaded Manchuria. On August 9 a more powerful atomic bomb struck Nagasaki, and the Japanese cabinet decided in favor of surrender.

A number of Japanese military leaders wanted to fight on, but on August 15 Emperor Hirohito announced that Japan would surrender. Formal terms of surrender were signed on September 2, 1945. World War II was over at last.

SPENCER C. TUCKER

Consequences

World War II was immensely destructive. The butcher's bill exceeded 60 million dead. Most of continental Europe's cities were masses of rubble, and the transportation infrastructure was all but gone.

The firebombing of Japanese cities, which were largely of wood, had been especially destructive.

Among the major powers, the Soviet Union was the hardest hit. It had suffered as many as 27 million dead. Aside from the catastrophic human cost, the Germans had occupied Russia's most productive regions, and the scorched-earth policy practiced by both sides resulted in the total or partial destruction of 1,700 towns, 70,000 villages, and 6 million buildings. Perhaps a quarter of the property value of the Soviet Union was lost in the war, and tens of millions of Soviet citizens were homeless. Simply feeding the Soviet population was a staggering task. All of this goes a long way toward explaining the subsequent policies, both internal and external, of the Soviet Union.

The Soviet Union gained considerable territory. It retained control of the Baltic States of Estonia, Latvia, and Lithuania and kept territory taken from Finland in 1940 and 1944 (after Finland had reentered the war on the German side in an effort to regain the territory lost in the Winter War), which gave it the port of Petsamo and the province of Karelia. The Soviets also received land from Romania and from Poland (with the restoration of the Curzon Line). Poland received compensation in eastern Germany. Peace treaties later confirmed most of these changes. In addition, Italy gave up some territory to France, Yugoslavia, and Greece. Italian colonies in Africa (Eritrea, Libya, and Italian Somaliland) were placed under a trusteeship by the United Nations (UN). Hungary lost territory to Bulgaria and Czechoslovakia. Transylvania was restored to Romania, and Romania ceded land to Bulgaria. Japan lost its territories outside the home islands, including Korea and parts of China.

The Soviets received from Japan South Sakhalin Island and the Kuriles as well as concessions in Dalien, China, including the return of Port Arthur as a naval base. Outer Mongolia would continue to be independent of China, but China regained sovereignty over Manchuria. In effect these concessions sanctioned the replacement of Japanese imperialism with Soviet imperialism, but the Western leaders had thought these necessary to secure the timing of the Soviet entry into the Pacific war.

Far from destroying the Soviet Union and communism as he had sought, Hitler had strengthened it. Indeed, the Soviet Union emerged from the war, regarded with the United States as one of the two so-called superpowers. The Soviet armies that had liberated Eastern Europe remained in place. Obsessed as always by security concerns and with much of his western territories devastated by the fighting, Stalin was determined to establish a tier of buffer states to protect the Soviet Union from the West and its influences. The only way to have prevented this was for the United States to have gone to war with the Soviet Union, which the American public was not prepared to sanction in 1945. Indeed, American military strategy had been predicated on defeating the Germans and the Japanese at the least cost in American lives rather than securing long-range strategic goals. Churchill's plea for the Western powers to "shake hands with the Russians as far east as possible" was largely ignored.

In China, the physical destruction and loss of life had also been great, but the end of the war and a struggle over Manchuria brought a renewal of the Chinese Civil War and an eventual Communist victory.

The vast destruction in Western Europe did help to promote the movement for European integration, strongly aided by the United States in the 1947 Marshall Plan. This led to the European Common Market. The war also helped boost internationalism with the 1945 establishment of the UN, which had somewhat more power than its ineffectual predecessor, the League of Nations.

The war also greatly stimulated colonial unrest around the world. Where the colonial powers sought to hold on to their empires after August 1945, there was often fighting. France, seeking to retain its status as a Great Power, insisted on retaining its empire. This prompted the long Indochina War (1946–1954). Fighting also erupted in many other places, including Malaya,

the Netherlands Indies, Africa, and the Middle East. Even where the European powers chose to withdraw voluntarily, as in the case of Britain in Palestine and the Indian subcontinent, there was fighting as competing forces sought to fill the vacuums. Wartime decisions about postwar occupation zones led to major confrontations regarding Germany that brought the Berlin Blockade (1948–1949) and the Korean War (1950–1953). The Soviet Union and the United States and their respective allies soon clashed in what became known as the Cold War (1946–1991), a direct result of World War II and in many ways a continuation of it.

SPENCER C. TUCKER

Timeline

1931

September 18	Japanese forces detonate a bomb on the rail line near Mukden, China, and blame it on the Chinese, using this as justification for their takeover of resource-rich Manchuria. Some mark this as the beginning of World War II.

1933

January 30	Adolf Hitler becomes chancellor (prime minister) of Germany by entirely legal means.
March 23	The German Reichstag passes the Enabling Act, granting Hitler dictatorial powers.

1935

October 2	Italian troops invade Ethiopia, beginning the Second Italo-Abyssinian War.

1936

March 7	German forces remilitarize the Rhineland.
May 7	Italian dictator Benito Mussolini announces the annexation of Ethiopia.
July 18	Beginning of the Spanish Civil War.
October 25	Formation of the Rome-Berlin Axis.

| November 25 | Germany and Japan sign the Anti-Comintern Pact. |

1937

July 7	Chinese and Japanese troops clash in the Marco Polo Bridge Incident, generally held to mark the start of the Second Sino-Japanese War (1937–1945).
August 8–November 8	The Battle of Shanghai between Japanese and Chinese Nationalist forces, ending in victory for the Japanese.
November 6	Italy adheres to the Anti-Comintern Pact.

1938

March 12	German forces invade Austria.
July 29–August 11	Fighting between Japanese and Soviet forces along their common border in the Battle of Lake Khasan, also known as the Changkufeng Incident.
September 30	Conclusion of the Munich Agreement, by which Czechoslovakia is forced to cede the Sudetenland to Germany.

1939

March 15	German forces invade Czechoslovakia in violation of the Munich Agreement and establish the Czech region as the Protectorate of Bohemia and Moravia.
March 31	The United Kingdom and France extend a "guarantee" to Poland to protect it from attack.
April 1	Nationalist leader General Francisco Franco declares victory in the Spanish Civil War.
April 7	Italian forces invade Albania.
April 13	The United Kingdom and France extend a formal guarantee to protect Romania and Greece against attack.
May 11–September 16	The Nomonhan Incident (Battle of Khalkhin Gol) between Japanese and Soviet forces, ending with the defeat of the Japanese Sixth Army.
August 23	Germany and the Soviet Union sign a nonaggression pact in Moscow, with secret provisions for the division of Poland and the Baltic States between them and a pledge of Soviet raw materials to Germany.
September 1	German forces invade Poland.
September 3	On expiration of their ultimatum for Germany to withdraw from Poland, Great Britain and France declare war on Germany.
September 17	Soviet forces invade eastern Poland.

November 30	Soviet forces invade Finland.

1940

March 12	A peace treaty ends the Soviet-Finnish War.
April 9	German forces invade Denmark and Norway.
May 10	German forces invade the Netherlands, Belgium, Luxembourg, and France.
May 15	The Netherlands surrenders to Germany.
May 26–June 4	Operation DYNAMO, the evacuation of British and French forces from Dunkerque (Dunkirk), France.
June 10	Italy declares war on France and Great Britain.
	Norway surrenders to Germany.
June 14	Paris, declared an open city to spare it the fate of Warsaw and Rotterdam, falls to the Germans.
June 15	Soviet forces invade Estonia.
June 17	Soviet forces invade Latvia and Estonia.
June 22	France signs an armistice with Germany.
June 27	Soviet forces invade Romania.
June 28	Belgium surrenders to Germany.
July 3	In Operation CATAPULT, Royal Navy units secure either units of the French fleet or their neutralization in various locations including Alexandria, but when the French resist their demands, they engage and sink a number of French warships at Mers-el-Kebir, Algeria.
July 10	The Battle of Britain begins.
July 25	The United States embargoes strategic materials to Japan.
August 5–6	The Baltic States of Latvia, Lithuania, and Estonia are formally annexed to the Soviet Union.
September 3	The Destroyer for Bases Deal is concluded between the United States and Britain. Britain receives 50 World War I–vintage U.S. destroyers in return for leases on bases territory in North America.
September 13	Italian forces invade Egypt from Libya.
September 22	Vichy France is forced to allow Japanese air bases and troops in French Indochina.
September 23	British and Free French forces attack Dakar.

September 27	The Axis Tripartite Pact is signed by Germany, Italy, and Japan.
October 7	German forces enter Romania.
October 28	Italian forces invade Greece.
October 31	The Battle of Britain ends, and the Germans commence night bombing, known as "The Blitz."
November 11–12	The British stage an air attack on the Italian Fleet anchorage of Taranto, sinking one battleship and damaging two others.
November 20	Pressured by Germany, Hungary joins the Axis.
November 23	Pressured by Germany, Romania joins the Axis.
December 9	British forces commence a counteroffensive to drive the Italians from Egypt.

1941

January 19	British forces invade Italian Eritrea.
January 22	Tobruk in eastern Libya falls to Australian and British forces.
February 8	British forces take Benghazi, Libya.
March 1	Bulgaria adheres to the Tripartite Pact.
March 11	U.S. president Franklin Roosevelt signs Lend-Lease legislation, under which the United States will provide material assistance to countries fighting the Axis powers.
March 16	The British mount a counteroffensive in Somaliland and Ethiopia.
March 24	German and Italian forces under General Erwin Rommel commence an offensive against British forces in Libya.
March 25	The Yugoslav government agrees to join the Axis.
March 26	The Yugoslav government is overthrown, and the new government repudiates the Axis alliance.
March 28	British and Italian forces fight the Mediterranean naval Battle of Cape Matapan.
April 3	A pro-Axis regime is established in Iraq.
April 6	German forces invade Yugoslavia and Greece.
	British forces occupy Addis Ababa, Ethiopia.
April 11	The Axis siege of Tobruk commences.
April 13	Japan and the Soviet Union sign a nonaggression pact.

April 17	The Yugoslav Army surrenders to the Germans.
April 23	Greece signs an armistice with Germany.
May 2	British forces invade Iraq and install a pro-Allied government there on June 4.
May 20	The Germans mount an airborne assault on Crete.
May 24	The German battleship *Bismarck* sinks the British battle cruiser *Hood.*
May 27	The British sink the German battleship *Bismarck.*
June 1	Crete falls to the Germans.
June 8	British and Free French troops invade Syria and Lebanon.
June 22	Germany commences Operation BARBAROSSA, the invasion of the Soviet Union. Germany, Italy, and Romania all declare war on the Soviet Union.
June 26	Finland declares war on the Soviet Union, beginning the Continuation War.
June 27	Hungary declares war on the Soviet Union.
July 12	Great Britain and the Soviet Union sign a mutual assistance treaty.
July 24	Japanese forces occupy southern French Indochina.
August 12	British prime minister Winston Churchill and U.S. president Franklin Roosevelt meet and draw up the Atlantic Charter.
August 25	Soviet and British troops occupy Iran.
September 8	German forces lay siege to Leningrad.
September 19	German forces capture Kiev.
September 29	German forces murder nearly 34,000 Jews at Kiev.
October 3	German forces commence Operation TYPHOON, the planned capture of Moscow.
October 16	German and Romanian forces capture Odessa.
October 24	German forces capture Kharkov.
November 18	British forces launch a counteroffensive in Libya.
December 5	German forces suspend their Moscow offensive.
December 7	Japanese carrier aircraft attack Pearl Harbor, Hawaii.
December 8	The United States, Britain, and other Allied powers declare war on Japan.

	Japanese forces attack Guam, Wake, and the Philippine Islands. They also invade Hong Kong, Malaysia, and Thailand.
December 9	China declares war on Germany and Japan.
December 10	British forces relieve Tobruk.
	Japanese aircraft sink the British battleship *Prince of Wales* and battle cruiser *Repulse* off Malaya.
	Japanese forces take Guam.
December 11	Germany and Italy declare war on the United States.
December 14	Japanese forces invade Burma.
December 16	Japanese forces invade Borneo.
December 19	German chancellor Adolf Hitler assumes personal command of the German Army.
December 23	The Japanese invasion of the Philippines commences.
December 25	Japanese forces take Hong Kong.
1942	
January 1	Twenty-six nations sign the United Nations (UN) Declaration.
January 2	Japanese forces capture Manila.
January 11	Japanese forces invade the Netherlands East Indies.
January 13	German U-boats commence an offensive along the U.S. East Coast.
January 20	Japan commences an offensive in Burma.
	In Berlin, the so-called Wannsee Conference occurs to discuss procedures for the "Final Solution," the Nazi plan to exterminate the Jews.
January 21	An Axis offensive in Libya commences.
January 26	The first U.S. troops committed to the war effort in the European theater arrive in Northern Ireland.
January 28	Axis forces recapture Benghazi, Libya.
February 1	U.S. carrier aircraft strike the Marshall and Gilbert Islands.
February 8	Japanese forces take Rangoon, Burma.
February 15	Singapore surrenders to Japanese forces.
February 27–29	The naval Battle of the Java Sea.
March 7	Japanese troops enter Rangoon, Burma.

March 9	The island of Java surrenders to the Japanese.
March 13	Japanese forces land in the Solomon Islands.
April 5	Japanese naval forces raid Ceylon (Sri Lanka).
April 9	U.S. forces in the Bataan Peninsula, Philippines, surrender to the Japanese.
April 18	U.S. B-25 bombers raid Tokyo (the Doolittle Raid).
May 6	U.S. forces in the Philippines surrender to the Japanese.
May 7–8	Naval Battle of the Coral Sea.
May 20	Japanese forces complete their conquest of Burma.
May 26	Axis forces begin an offensive in Libya.
June 4–6	Naval-air Battle of Midway Island between Japanese and U.S. forces.
June 5	German forces besiege Sevastopol.
June 6	Japanese forces attack and occupy the Aleutian Islands of Attu and Kiska.
June 21	Axis forces in North Africa capture Tobruk, Libya.
July 1–3	German forces secure Sevastopol in the Crimea.
July 1–4	First Battle of El Alamein, Egypt, between Axis and British Empire forces.
July 3	Japanese forces land on Guadalcanal in the Solomon Islands.
August 7	U.S. marines land on Gaudalcanal.
August 9	German forces capture the Caucasus oil fields in the Soviet Union.
August 19	British and Canadian forces carry out a costly raid on Dieppe, France.
August 23	The Battle for Stalingrad begins.
August 31	The Battle of Alam el Halfa halts the Axis North African advance.
September 26	Australian ground forces halt Japanese land forces working overland toward Port Moresby, New Guinea.
October 23	The British Eighth Army opens the Battle of El Alamein in Egypt.
November 1	British forces break through at El Alamein, Egypt.
November 8	In Operation TORCH, British and American forces land in Morocco and Algeria.

November 11	Axis forces occupy Vichy-administered France.
November 13	British forces retake Tobruk.
November 16	Australian and U.S. forces attack Buna-Gona, New Guinea.
November 19	The Soviet counteroffensive begins at Stalingrad.
November 27	The French scuttle some 77 warships at Toulon rather than see them fall into German hands.
December 31	The naval Battle of Barents Sea occurs between German surface raiders and British warships.

1943

January 2	Australian and U.S. forces take Buna, New Guinea.
January 14–24	British prime minister Winston Churchill and U.S. president Franklin Roosevelt meet in Casablanca, Morocco.
January 23	The British Eighth Army takes Tripoli, Libya.
February 2	German forces surrender at Stalingrad.
February 8	The Red Army recaptures Kursk.
February 9	U.S. forces secure Guadalcanal.
February 14–22	Battle of the Kasserine Pass in Tunisia.
February 16	Soviet forces retake Kharkov.
March 2–4	Naval Battle of the Bismarck Sea.
March 14–15	German forces recapture Kharkov.
March 20–28	The British Eighth Army cracks the Axis Mareth Line in Tunisia.
April 19	The Warsaw Ghetto Uprising begins. It ends on May 16, crushed by the Germans.
May 11	U.S. troops land on Attu Island in the Aleutians.
May 13	Allied forces capture Tunis and secure the surrender of some 275,000 German and Italian troops.
May 16–17	The Royal Air Force (RAF) makes the Ruhr Valley dams a priority target.
May 30	U.S. forces retake Attu Island in the Aleutians.
July 5–17	The Battle of Kursk occurs, the largest tank battle in history.
July 9	U.S. and British forces invade Sicily in Operation HUSKY.
July 22	U.S. forces capture Palermo, Sicily.

July 24	RAF aircraft heavily bomb Hamburg, Germany.
August 6	Naval Battle of Vella Gulf in the Solomon Islands.
August 17	Allied forces conclude their conquest of Sicily.
	U.S. Army Air Forces (USAAF) daylight raids occur against Regensburg and Schweinfurt, Germany.
August 23	Soviet forces recapture Kharkov.
September 3	British forces land at Calabria, Italy.
September 8	The Italian government concludes an armistice with the Allies.
September 9	In Operation AVALANCHE, Allied forces land at Salerno and Taranto, Italy.
September 10–11	German forces occupy Rome.
September 18	Allied forces secure Sardinia.
September 25	Soviet forces retake Smolensk and Novorossisk.
October 1	Allied forces capture Naples.
October 4	German forces capture the Greek island of Kos.
October 5	Free French forces capture Corsica.
October 13	Italy declares war on Germany.
	A second USAAF raid occurs against Schweinfurt.
November 1	U.S. forces invade Bougainville in the Solomon Islands.
November 7	Soviet forces liberate Kiev.
November 22–26	Roosevelt, Churchill, and Nationalist Chinese leader Jiang Jieshi (Chiang Kai-shek) confer at Cairo.
November 28	Roosevelt, Churchill, and Soviet leader Joseph Stalin confer at Teheran until December 1.
December 26	U.S. forces reach Cape Gloucester, Solomon Islands.

1944

January 22	U.S. and British forces come ashore at Anzio, Italy.
January 25	The Allies begin a counteroffensive in Burma.
January 27	Soviet forces end the 900-day German siege of Leningrad.
February 3	The Allied offensive in Italy stalls at Cassino.
February 7	U.S. forces capture Kwajalein in the Marshall Islands.
February 15	Allied aircraft bomb Monte Cassino, Italy.
	Soviet forces secure Estonia.

February 18	U.S. naval forces attack the Japanese on Truk in the Caroline Islands.
February 20–26	Allied forces launch coordinated air strikes, known as "Big Week," against German factories.
March 8	Japanese forces begin an offensive in Burma.
March 15	Japanese forces invade India.
March 18	The RAF conducts a major raid on Hamburg, Germany.
April 2	Soviet troops enter Romania.
April 10	Soviet forces retake Odessa in Ukraine.
April 15	Soviet troops take Tarnopol, Ukraine.
May 9	Soviet forces recapture Sevastopol in the Crimea.
May 11	Allied forces attack the German Gustav Line south of Rome.
May 12	German forces in the Crimea surrender.
May 17–18	German troops withdraw from Monte Cassino, Italy.
May 23	Allied forces break out from the Anzio beachhead.
June 4–5	Allied troops enter Rome.
June 6	Allied forces land in Normandy, France.
June 9	Soviet forces attack Finland.
June 15	USAAF bombers strike Tokyo.
	U.S. forces invade Saipan in the Mariana Islands.
June 19–21	The Battle of the Philippine Sea occurs between U.S. and Japanese naval forces.
June 22	Soviet forces commence their great Belorussia offensive.
	Japanese forces withdraw from Kohima, India.
June 27	U.S. forces liberate Cherbourg, France.
July 4	The Allies defeat Japanese forces at Imphal in northeastern India.
July 9	British and Canadian forces capture Caen, France.
	U.S. forces declare Saipan in the Mariana Islands secured.
July 20	An assassination attempt on German leader Adolf Hitler fails, as does the associated effort by the German resistance to topple the Nazi regime.
July 21	U.S. forces invade Guam in the Mariana Islands.
July 23	Soviet forces take Lublin, Poland.

July 25	In Operation COBRA, Allied forces break out from Normandy, France.
July 28	Soviet forces retake Brest-Litovsk, Belorussia.
August 1	The Warsaw Uprising against the Germans begins.
August 4	Allied forces capture Florence, Italy.
August 10	U.S. forces secure Guam in the Mariana Islands.
August 15	In Operation DRAGOON, Allied forces land in southern France.
August 19	The French resistance mounts an uprising in Paris.
August 21	Allied forces trap 60,000 Germans in the Argentan-Falaise pocket.
August 22	All Japanese forces withdraw from India.
August 23	Romania surrenders and the next day declares war on Germany.
August 25	Free French forces liberate Paris.
	Allied forces commence an attack on the German Gothic Line in Italy.
August 28	The Allies secure Toulon and Marseilles, France.
August 30	German forces withdraw from Bulgaria.
August 31	Soviet forces take Bucharest, Romania.
September 3	German forces withdraw from Finland.
	The Western Allies liberate Brussels.
	The Soviet Union and Finland conclude a cease-fire agreement.
September 4	Allied forces liberate Antwerp, Belgium.
September 6	Allied forces liberate the southern Netherlands.
September 8	Soviet and Bulgarian forces conclude an armistice.
	Bulgaria declares war on Germany.
	German V-2 rockets hit London.
September 17–26	Operation MARKET-GARDEN, the effort by the Western Allies to secure a crossing over the Rhine River at Arnhem, ends in failure.
September 19	An armistice is concluded between the Allies and Finland.
September 25	Allied forces break through the German Gothic Line in Italy.

September 26	Soviet forces occupy Estonia.
September 28	Canadian forces liberate Calais, France.
October 2	The Warsaw Uprising ends with the surrender of the Polish Home Army to the Germans.
	Allied forces enter western Germany.
October 10–29	Soviet forces capture Riga, Latvia.
October 14	British forces liberate Athens, Greece.
October 18	Soviet forces enter Czechoslovakia.
October 20	Yugoslav Partisans and Soviet forces enter Belgrade, Yugoslavia.
	U.S. forces land at Leyte in the Philippine Islands.
October 23	Soviet forces enter East Prussia.
October 23–26	The Naval Battle of Leyte Gulf occurs between U.S. and Japanese forces.
October 24	The Japanese employ kamikaze suicide aircraft for the first time, in the Battle of Leyte Gulf.
November 4	Axis troops in Greece surrender.
November 10	Japanese forces capture Liuzhou, China.
November 20	French forces reach the Rhine through the Belfort Gap.
November 23	The first American forces reach the Rhine River.
November 24	French forces liberate Strasbourg.
	The USAAF begins systematic bombing of Japan.
November 28	The Belgian port of Antwerp is opened to Allied supply ships.
December 3–4	Civil war in Greece commences, and martial law is proclaimed in Athens.
December 16	The Germans begin their Ardennes Offensive, widely known as the Battle of the Bulge. It lasts until January 16, 1945.
December 26	U.S. forces relieve Bastogne, Belgium.
December 27	Soviet forces besiege Budapest.
1945	
January 9	U.S. forces invade Luzon, Philippines.
January 17	Soviet troops occupy Warsaw.
January 20	Hungary concludes an armistice with the Soviet Union.
January 27	Soviet forces occupy Lithuania.

January 30	A Soviet submarine sinks the German liner *Wilhelm Gustloff* in the Baltic, killing probably more than 7,000 people.
February 4–11	Churchill, Roosevelt, and Stalin meet in the Yalta Conference in the Crimea.
February 13	Remaining German forces in Budapest surrender to Soviet forces.
February 13–14	RAF and USAAF bombers destroy much of Dresden, Germany.
February 19	U.S. forces land on Iwo Jima island.
February 20	Soviet forces take Danzig (Gdansk, Poland).
March 3	Finland declares war on Germany.
March 4	U.S. forces secure Manila.
March 7	Allied forces take Cologne, Germany.
	U.S. forces seize intact the Remagen Bridge spanning the Rhine River.
March 9	USAAF B-28 bombers firebomb Tokyo in what is regarded as the single most destructive air attack in history.
March 16	U.S. forces secure Iwo Jima island.
March 20–21	Allied forces capture Mandalay, Burma.
April 1	U.S. forces land on Okinawa island.
April 7	Soviet forces enter Vienna, Austria.
April 10	Allied forces take Hanover, Germany.
April 13	Soviet forces secure Vienna, Austria.
	Allied forces take Arnhem.
April 18	German forces in the Ruhr surrender.
April 23	Soviet forces reach Berlin.
	Allied forces in Italy reach the Po River.
April 25	U.S. and Soviet forces meet at the Elbe River in northern Germany.
April 25–June 26	A Conference in San Francisco formally establishes the United Nations.
April 26	British forces capture Bremen.
April 28	Allied forces take Venice, Italy.
April 30	Adolf Hitler commits suicide in Berlin.
May 2	German forces in Italy surrender.
	Soviet forces capture Berlin.

May 3	Allied forces liberate Rangoon, Burma.
May 5	Allied forces liberate Denmark.
May 7	German forces surrender unconditionally at Rheims, France.
May 8	V-E (Victory in Europe) day.
	The Netherlands is liberated.
	Soviet forces enter Prague.
May 14	Australian troops capture Wewak, New Guinea.
June 5	The Allied Powers formally divide Germany into four occupation zones.
June 10	Australian forces invade Borneo.
June 26	The UN Charter is signed.
June 30	U.S. forces liberate Luzon in the Philippine Islands.
July 1	Allied troops move into Berlin.
July 16	An atomic bomb is successfully tested at Alamogordo, New Mexico.
July 17	The Potsdam Conference opens with Churchill, new U.S. president Harry S. Truman, and Stalin (during the conference, Churchill is replaced by new British prime minister Clement Atlee). The conference ends on August 2.
July 21–22	U.S. forces secure Okinawa.
August 6	A USAAF B-29 bomber drops an atomic bomb on Hiroshima, Japan.
August 8	The Soviet Union declares war on Japan.
August 9	Soviet forces invade Manchuria.
	A USAAF B-29 bomber drops an atomic bomb on Nagasaki, Japan.
August 14	Japan agrees to the Allied surrender terms.
September 2	The formal Japanese surrender occurs aboard the U.S. battleship *Missouri* in Tokyo Bay.
	V-J (Victory over Japan) day is celebrated.
September 5	British forces reach Singapore.
September 7	Japanese forces surrender at Shanghai.
September 9	Japanese forces in China surrender.
September 13	Japanese forces in Burma and New Guinea surrender.

September 16   Japanese forces in Hong Kong surrender.

October 24   The UN is established.

ANNETTE RICHARDSON, LAWTON WAY, AND SPENCER C. TUCKER

Further Reading

Adamthwaite, Anthony P. *The Making of the Second World War.* New York: Routledge, 1992.

Beevor, Antony. *The Second World War.* London: Weidenfeld and Nicolson, 2012.

Bellamy, Chris T. *Absolute War: Soviet Russia in the Second World War.* New York: Knopf, 2007.

Black, Jeremy. *World War Two: A Military History.* London: Routledge, 2003.

Bullock, Alan. *Hitler: A Study in Tyranny.* London: Penguin, 1990.

Davies, Norman. *No Simple Victory: World War II in Europe, 1939–1945.* London: Penguin, 2008.

Dear, I. C. B., and M. R. D. Foot, eds. *The Oxford Companion to World War II.* New York: Oxford University Press, 1995.

Drea, Edward J. *In the Service of the Emperor: Essays on the Imperial Japanese Army.* Lincoln: University of Nebraska Press, 2003.

Evans, David C., and Mark R. Peattie. *Kaigun: Strategy, Tactics, and Technology in the Imperial Japanese Navy.* Annapolis, MD: Naval Institute Press, 1997.

Evans, Richard J. *The Third Reich at War.* New York: Penguin, 2009.

Glantz, David M. *When Titans Clashed: How the Red Army Stopped Hitler.* Lawrence: University Press of Kansas, 1998.

Hastings, Max. *Inferno: The World at War, 1939–1945.* New York: Knopf, 2011.

Hsu, Long-hsuen, and Ming-kai Changai. *History of the Sino-Japanese War (1937–1945).* 2nd ed. Taipei: Chung Wu Publishers, 1971.

Keegan, John. *The Second World War.* New York: Viking, 1989.

Liddell Hart, B. H. *History of the Second World War.* New York: Putnam, 1970.

Morison, Samuel Eliot. *History of United States Naval Operations in World War II.* 15 vols. Boston: Little, Brown, 1947–1962.

Murray, Williamson, and Allan R. Millett. *A War to Be Won: Fighting the Second World War.* Cambridge, MA: Belknap, 2000.

Neillands, Robin. *The Bomber War: The Allied Air Offensive against Nazi Germany.* Woodstock, NY: Overlook, 2001.

Shirer, William L. *The Rise and Fall of the Third Reich: A History of Nazi Germany.* New York: Simon and Schuster, 1960.

Spector, Ronald. *Eagle against the Sun: The American War with Japan.* New York: Free Press, 1985.

Tucker, Spencer C. *The Second World War.* New York: Palgrave Macmillan, 2004.

Tucker, Spencer C., ed. *The Encyclopedia of World War II: A Political, Social, and Military History.* 5 vols. Santa Barbara, CA: ABC-CLIO, 2004.

Weinberg, Gerhard L. *A World at Arms: A Global History of World War II.* New York: Cambridge University Press, 1994.

Willmott, H. P. *The Great Crusade: A New Complete History of the Second World War.* Revised ed. Washington, DC: Potomac Books, 2008.

Cold War (1945–1991)

Causes

The deadlock between East and West was the single most momentous development in the post–World War II period and dominated the next half century. The term "cold war" apparently originated in 1893 with German Marxist Edward Bernstein, who used it to describe the arms race in pre–World War I Europe in which there was "no shooting" but there was "bleeding." Its usage for the East-West confrontation, however, seems to have originated with the British writer George Orwell in an article of October 19, 1945. More famously, American financier Bernard Baruch used the phrase in the course of a speech in 1947. Put in its simplest terms, the Cold War was the rivalry that developed between the two superpowers—the Soviet Union and the United States—as each sought to fill the power vacuum left by the defeat of Germany and Japan. Leaders on each side believed that they were forced to expand their national hegemony by the "aggressive" actions of the other. Misunderstandings, bluffs, pride, personal and geopolitical ambitions, and simple animosity between the two sides grew until the struggle became the Cold War.

There is no scholarly agreement on exact dates for the Cold War. Some would date it from former British prime minister Winston Churchill's speech at Fulton, Missouri, in March 1946. The most likely starting date is, however, the end of World War II in 1945. The end date for the Cold War is usually given as 1991 with the collapse of the Soviet Union.

At the end of World War II, Washington, D.C., and Moscow each had different views of the world. The United States sought a system based on the rule of law and placed high hopes on a new organization of states known as the United Nations (UN), which took its name from the victorious powers of World War II. The UN closely resembled the old League of Nations, the organization that President Woodrow Wilson had championed at the Paris Peace Conference following World War I and that the United States had then refused to join.

Typically for the United States in wartime, leaders in Washington had paid scant attention to trying to shape the postwar world. During World War II, President Franklin Roosevelt had not greatly concerned himself with postwar political problems, working on the assumption that the UN could resolve them later. Washington's preoccupation throughout the conflict was winning the war as quickly as possible and at the least cost in American lives. This frustrated British prime minister Winston Churchill, who, as was the case with his Soviet counterpart Joseph Stalin, sought to establish spheres of influence. U.S. leaders held—at least overtly—to the Wilsonian position that a balance of power and the spheres of influence were both outdated and immoral.

At the end of the war, a power vacuum existed throughout much of the world. In defeating Germany and Japan, the United States had in fact destroyed traditional bulwarks against communist expansion, although that fact was largely unappreciated at the time. In Europe there was not a single strong continental state able to bar

Soviet expansion. In the Far East there was only China, which Roosevelt had expected to be one of the Great Powers and a guarantor of a peace settlement, but China had been badly weakened by the long war with Japan and was in any case about to plunge into a full-scale civil war of its own.

Americans assumed that wars ended when the shooting stopped, and thus domestic political considerations compelled the rapid demobilization of the armed forces before the situation abroad had stabilized. Although the Soviet Union was actually much weaker in 1945 than was assumed at the time, Churchill expressed the view that only the U.S. nuclear monopoly prevented the Soviet Union from overrunning Western Europe.

In 1945, though, the Soviet Union had just emerged from a desperate struggle for survival. The armies of Germany and the Soviet Union had fought back and forth in the western Soviet Union and had laid waste to vast stretches of the region. Twenty-five million people were left homeless, and perhaps one-quarter of the total property value of the country had been lost. The human costs were staggering, with as many as 27 million dead. The effects of all of this on the people of the Soviet Union can scarcely be comprehended. Certainly for the indefinite future whatever government held power in Moscow would be obsessed with security. This, rather than expansion, was the Kremlin's paramount concern in the immediate postwar years.

Despite all the destruction, the Russians emerged from the war in the most powerful international position in their history. The shattering of Axis military might and the weakness of the West European powers seemed to open the way to Soviet political domination over much of Eurasia and the realization of long-sought aims.

Stalin, who had seen the Western powers after World War I erect a cordon sanitaire in the form of a string of buffer states against communism, now sought to do the same in reverse: to erect a cordon sanitaire to keep the West out. This was for security reasons, as Russia had been attacked across the plains of Poland three times since 1812, but was also intended to prevent the spread of Western ideas and political notions. To Western leaders, the Kremlin seemed to have reverted to 19th-century diplomacy, establishing spheres of influence, bargaining for territory, and disregarding the UN. Western leaders did not appreciate the extent to which concerns over security and xenophobia drove this policy.

Finally, there was the ideological motivation. Although its leaders had soft-pedaled it during World War II, the Soviet Union had never abandoned its goal of furthering international communism. Irrespective of security concerns, the Kremlin was ideologically committed to combating capitalism. It is thus inconceivable that Stalin would not have attempted to take full advantage of the opportunities that presented themselves at the end of the war.

As with the United States, Soviet foreign policy was closely tied to domestic needs. The Cold War would aid in enforcing authority and cooperation at home. The communist world had to appear to be threatened by encircling enemies. By the end of World War II, millions of Soviet soldiers had been in the West and had seen the quality of life and amenities there. They found their own system sadly wanting by comparison. Certainly they expected a better quality of life with the end of the war. Only a new announced threat from abroad would cause them to close ranks behind the Soviet leadership. Playing the nationalist card would enable the

Estimated Cold War Nuclear Arsenals of the United States and Soviet Union

Dates of First Nuclear Tests

	United States	Soviet Union
First Atomic Test	July 16, 1945	August 29, 1949
First Hydrogen Bomb Test	November 1, 1952	August 12, 1953

Cold War Nuclear Arsenals

	Year									
	1945	1950	1955	1960	1965	1970	1975	1980	1985	1990
Nonstrategic Warheads*										
United States	0	0	857	13,433	22,297	13,896	11,305	9,360	9,090	7,816
Soviet Union	0	5	200	1,200	5,200	9,200	15,700	22,200	28,700	21,700
Strategic Warheads										
Bomber-mounted										
United States	6	369	2,200	6,954	6,567	6,465	6,911	6,239	6,180	5,330
Soviet Union	0	0	0	372	559	596	596	596	966	1,485
Intercontinental Ballistic Missiles (ICBMs)										
United States	0	0	0	13	897	1,306	2,251	2,251	2,220	2,591
Soviet Union	0	0	0	2	295	1,546	2,277	5,630	7,154	7,285
Submarine-Launched Ballistic Missiles (SLBMs)										
United States	0	0	0	34	1,882	4,452	6,586	5,914	5,645	5,474
Soviet Union	0	0	0	32	76	301	869	1,636	2,377	3,045
Total Warheads Stockpiled										
United States	6	369	3,057	20,434	31,642	26,119	27,052	23,764	23,135	21,211
Soviet Union	0	5	200	1,605	6,129	11,643	19,443	30,062	39,197	33,515

* Short- and medium-range nuclear weapons used to support troops in the field (includes nuclear mines, gravity bombs, and cruise missiles).

Sources: Brookings Institution, *U.S. Nuclear Weapons Cost Study Project* (n.p.: Nuclear Age Peace Foundation, 1997–1998), Natural Resources Defense Council, http://www.nrdc.org.

Kremlin to mobilize public effort and suffocate dissent.

Although for different reasons, Roosevelt shared with Stalin a strong antipathy toward European colonialism, and Washington encouraged the disintegration of the European colonial empires. While idealistic and correct morally, this stance nonetheless reduced the strength of U.S. allies such as Britain, France, and the Netherlands and helped ensure that ultimately the United States would have to carry most of the burden of defense of the noncommunist world.

Roosevelt gambled his place in history in part on the mistaken assumption that he could arrange a détente with the Soviet Union. His optimism regarding "Uncle Joe" Stalin was ill-founded, however. By mid-March 1945 it was patently obvious, even to Roosevelt, that the Soviets were taking over Poland and Romania and violating at least the spirit of the Yalta agreements of February 1945 regarding multiparty systems and free elections.

Roosevelt died in April 1945. His successor Harry S. Truman insisted, despite Churchill's protests regarding the mounting evidence that the Soviets were not keeping their pledges, that U.S. forces withdraw from areas they had occupied deep beyond the lines assigned to the Soviets for the occupation of Germany. The American public clearly did not want confrontation or a global economic and political-military struggle with the Soviet Union. Americans were limited internationalists who merely wanted to enjoy their economic prosperity.

The Soviets, however, were already angry over Washington's abrupt termination of World War II Lend-Lease aid on August 21, 1945, regardless of the terms of the original law. Russian ill will was also generated by the usually smooth cooperation of the Anglo-Saxon powers and Moscow's belief that the two constantly combined against the Soviet Union. The U.S. monopoly on the atomic bomb also aroused fear in the Soviet Union as a small but vocal group of Americans demanded preventive war. Soviet concerns increased when the United States retained bomber bases within striking distance of Soviet industrial areas and undertook naval maneuvers in the Mediterranean Sea.

The Soviet Union, however, rejected a plan put forth by the United States to bring nuclear weapons under international control; instead, it proceeded with its atomic research (aided by espionage) and exploded its own bomb in September 1949. The atomic arms race was under way.

Certainly American and British attitudes toward Soviet activity in Eastern Europe and the Balkans exasperated Moscow.

Having accepted Soviet hegemony there, why did the West continue to criticize? Initially Moscow permitted political parties other than the Communist Party, and now it seemed to the suspicious leaders in the Kremlin as though the West was encouraging these parties against Soviet interests. At a minimum the Soviet Union required security, while the United States wanted democratic parties in a Western-style democracy. In only one country, Finland, did the Soviet Union and the West achieve the sort of compromise implicit in the Yalta agreements. In countries such as Poland and Hungary, noncommunist parties were highly unlikely to ensure the security that the Soviet Union desired, and Western encouragement of these groups seemed to Moscow to be a threat.

On the American side, the Russian moves kindled exasperation and then alarm as the Soviet Union interfered in the democratic processes of one East European state after another. In addition, the UN seemed paralyzed as the Soviet Union, in order to protect its interests when the majority was consistently against it, made increasing use of its UN Security Council veto. Despite this, Western pressure in the UN did help secure a Soviet withdrawal from northern Iran in 1946 in what was the first major test for the international body.

This did not mean that the West was unified. In Britain, left-wing Labourites criticized American capitalism and wanted to work with the Russian communists. The French, especially interim president Charles de Gaulle, made vigorous efforts to build a third force in Europe as a counterbalance to the Anglo-Saxon powers and the Soviet Union. It is thus tempting to conclude that only Moscow could have driven the West to the unity achieved by 1949. As Belgian diplomat Paul-Henri Spaak put it,

Stalin was the real founder of the North Atlantic Treaty Organization (NATO).

Former British prime minister Winston Churchill sounded the alarm regarding the Soviet Union. In a speech at Fulton, Missouri, on March 5, 1946, with U.S. president Harry S. Truman at his side, Churchill announced that "an iron curtain has descended across the continent." He called for a "special relationship" between Britain and the United States to meet the challenge. Americans were slow to respond, however. Ten days later Secretary of State James F. Byrnes declared that the United States was no more interested in an alliance with Britain against the Soviet Union than in one with the Soviet Union against Britain.

SPENCER C. TUCKER

Course

Germany was the principal focal point and tinderbox of the Cold War. Although in early 1947 peace treaties were concluded with other defeated states, talks regarding those for Austria and Germany deadlocked. The Soviets were busy stripping their zone of anything movable and failing to supply food to the western zones as promised. Facing increasing costs and difficulties as a result, in early 1947 the British and the Americans merged their zones, forming Bizonia.

Moscow was also pressing Turkey to return land lost by Russia at the end of World War I and to permit the Soviet Union a role in the defense of the straits connecting the Black Sea to the Mediterranean. There was also trouble in Greece, where by the end of 1946 communist guerrillas, supported by Yugoslavia, Albania, and Bulgaria, took up arms against the government.

In February 1947 London informed Washington that Britain could no longer

afford to support the Greek government. On March 12, U.S. president Harry S. Truman announced what became known as the Truman Doctrine, pledging U.S. support for "free peoples who are resisting attempted subjugation by armed minorities or by outside pressures."

In short order Congress appropriated $400 million for Greece and Turkey. The break with Moscow by Yugoslav leader Tito (Josip Broz) was also an assist. It cut off most aid to the Greek communists. By the end of 1949 the insurrection had been contained.

By the spring of 1947 the United States had expended some $16 billion in emergency relief, but there was still serious distress, and there were also fears that all Europe might fall under Soviet influence. Clearly a more robust reconstruction effort was needed. In a speech at Harvard University on June 5, 1947, Secretary of State George C. Marshall pledged U.S. financial aid if Europeans devised long-range plans and concentrated on self-help and mutual assistance. The plan was not entirely selfless; Europe was the largest U.S. trading partner, and continued American prosperity was tied to European economic revival.

Announced as open to all, the plan was actually devised so that the Soviet Union would reject it, thereby ensuring congressional passage. The Soviets insisted on bilateral agreements, with funds proportionate to that country's role in defeating Germany. They claimed that U.S. oversight constituted interference in the internal affairs of the countries involved. Fearing that economic aid to its satellites might draw them to the West, the Soviets did not permit them to participate.

In December 1947 the U.S. Congress approved $522 million and then in April 1948 approved $6.8 billion. The legislation helped stave off the communists in the April Italian elections.

On April 16, 16 noncommunist European states established the Organization for European Economic Cooperation. During the next four years, Congress appropriated $13.15 billion. With funds for Asia, it brought the total to $14.2 billion. Through 1949 this totaled $20.5 billion on economic aid and only $1.2 billion in military aid. The mix changed with the Korean War. From 1950 through 1954 the United States expended $14.1 billion on nonmilitary aid and $10.9 billion on military assistance. The Marshall Plan made the recovery of Western Europe possible and brought spectacular economic growth. It also fostered economic cooperation and the European Common Market.

In October 1947 the Soviets established the nine-nation Communist Information Bureau (Cominform) with the goal of spreading communism. In January 1949 Moscow created the Council for Mutual Economic Assistance. It was intended to integrate the national economies of the Soviet satellites with that of the Soviet Union. The Kremlin also announced its own program of economic assistance. This so-called Molotov Plan primarily benefited the Soviet Union, which received raw materials in return for shoddy and unwanted Soviet products.

In late November and early December 1947, meetings failed to resolve the deadlock regarding Germany. The Soviets tightened their control in their satellites. Surviving opposition leaders were purged, and in February 1948 Czechoslovakia fell to a communist coup d'état. This sent a shock wave through Western Europe but marked the zenith of communist expansion in Europe.

In early 1948, with the three Western powers discussing a single government for their zones, the Soviets attempted to drive the Western powers from Berlin. Beginning on April 1, the Soviets gradually cut surface access. A week later the Western governments introduced new currency for their zones, and the blockade then began in earnest. By early August it was complete.

Truman opted for an attempt to supply West Berlin by air as least likely to bring a shooting war. While it would not be difficult to supply Allied personnel, providing for more than 2 million Germans seemed impossible. Expecting the airlift to fail, the Soviets never did challenge it. Meanwhile, an Allied counterblockade of East Germany deprived the Soviet zone of essential goods and pressured the Soviets. On May 12, 1949, land traffic to Berlin resumed. The airlift had lasted 324 days and transported more than 2.326 million tons of cargo. During the blockade, a new Basic Law (an ersatz constitution) was approved for West Germany.

Soviet behavior prompted establishment of the Council of Europe and the European Common Market. Militarily it brought the Brussels Pact and NATO. France and Great Britain had signed a military alliance at Dunkirk in March 1947. A year later France, Great Britain, Belgium, Luxembourg, and the Netherlands concluded the Brussels Pact. It provided for social, economic, and cultural collaboration but was also a military alliance. Because these countries would not be able to defend themselves without U.S. assistance, talks soon began for a broader alliance.

On April 4, 1949, the North Atlantic Pact was signed in Washington by the United States, Canada, Britain, France, the Benelux states, Norway, Denmark, Iceland,

The Soviet Union's first atomic bomb test, August 29, 1949. (Sovfoto/UIG via Getty Images)

Portugal, and Italy. They declared that "an armed attack against one or more" would be "an attack against them all," with each to assist by whatever means it deemed best. The treaty went into effect on August 14, 1949. As one pundit put it, "NATO was created to keep the Americans in, the Russians out, and the Germans down."

In late August 1949 the U.S. atomic monopoly ended when the Soviet Union exploded an atomic bomb. In October 1949 the communists were victorious in China, and on June 25, 1950, war broke out in Korea.

There were two Korean states in consequence of occupation agreements. The Soviets occupied North Korea, and the United States occupied South Korea.

Soviet leader Joseph Stalin and People's Republic of China (PRC) leader Mao Zedong (Mao Tse-tung) made the war possible by supporting North Korean leader Kim Il Sung's plan to invade South Korea. Kim believed that the United States would not fight, and if it did, the war would be over before U.S. forces could intervene in strength. U.S. leaders had pointedly excluded South Korea from the U.S. defense perimeter, and South Korea was far outclassed militarily by North Korea.

Truman chose to fight, and the conflict became the first UN war. United Nations Command forces held at the Busan (Pusan) Perimeter, then broke out and began an invasion of North Korea in order to reunify Korea. China then entered the war. The fighting seesawed back and forth, and Washington concluded that it was the "wrong war, in the wrong place, with the wrong enemy" and that restoration of the prewar status quo would be sufficient. An armistice was finally concluded in July 1953, but no peace treaty has ever been signed, and the Korean Peninsula remains one of the world's most dangerous flashpoints.

The Korean War affected the Cold War in many ways. After its previous wars, the United States had disarmed, but the U.S. military had undergone considerable expansion and remained strong thereafter. In many ways Korea marked a turning point in the Cold War. The Korean War fed anticommunist paranoia in the United States and helped bring rearmament of the Federal Republic of Germany (West Germany, FRG), where there seemed to be an obvious parallel between divided Korea and divided Germany.

Both sides gained new leaders in 1953. Dwight D. Eisenhower became president of the United States. Stalin died in March and was followed by a collective leadership that ultimately gave way to rule by Nikita Khrushchev.

Fear of thermonuclear war dominated the 1950s. The Soviet Union exploded its first hydrogen bomb in 1953. Soviet leaders were particularly concerned about U.S. strategic bombing capability and the ring of overseas bases around them. A diplomacy of stalemate, based on mutual fear of nuclear destruction, held sway. In January 1954 the Eisenhower administration announced a policy of "massive retaliation" with reliance on nuclear weapons in the event of a Soviet attack. America's European allies worried about this, especially as Europe was the most likely location for a military confrontation.

The French had been fighting in Indochina since 1946, claiming it as a war against international communism rather than a defense of imperialism. In 1954,

however, France suffered a resounding defeat in the Battle of Dien Bien Phu, and French politicians used this as the excuse to extricate their nation from the war. The ensuing Geneva Accords of July 1954 provided for the independence of Laos, Cambodia, and Vietnam, with Vietnam temporarily divided at the 17th parallel pending elections in two years to reunify it.

President Ngo Dinh Diem of the Republic of Vietnam (South Vietnam, RVN) refused to permit the elections, and the Eisenhower administration supported him, arguing that the communists, who controlled the more populous Democratic Republic of Vietnam (North Vietnam), had never allowed free elections once in power. Nevertheless, Diem's decision led to a renewal of fighting in what became the Vietnam War (1957–1975).

The French Army was almost immediately again in combat in Algeria, where a rebellion against French rule began in November 1954. Fears among the large number of French settlers and professional army officers that they were going to be sold out by the Paris government led in May 1958 to a military putsch, the end of the Fourth Republic, and the return to power of General Charles de Gaulle, who established the Fifth Republic.

In the 1950s, meanwhile, a group of nations was emerging in a neutralist or nonaligned bloc known as the Third World and the developing world to distinguish it from the Western powers and the communist bloc. Indian prime minister Jawaharlal Nehru was its leader, but Tito of Yugoslavia and Gamal Abdel Nasser of Egypt were also prominent.

In Europe, deadlock continued regarding Germany and Austria. The United States insisted on free elections throughout Germany, while the Soviet Union sought direct talks between the FRG and the German Democratic Republic (East Germany, GDR). The Soviets made it clear to their Western counterparts that the price for reunification would be permanent demilitarization of both states.

Washington firmly supported creation of a West European army that would include the FRG. This became known as the European Defense Community (EDC). In August 1954, however, the French National Assembly rejected the EDC, killing it. A formula was then found for the FRG to rearm within NATO.

In 1955 the Soviets made a number of moves to ease the Cold War. They established diplomatic relations with the FRG and agreed to release the last German World War II prisoners. Finland regained Porkkala from the Soviets, who also evacuated Port Arthur. Finally, Moscow agreed to the Treaty of Belvedere, which ended the occupation of Austria and restored it to full sovereignty on the pledge of permanent Austrian neutrality and economic concessions.

In these circumstances, the leaders and foreign ministers of the United States, the Soviet Union, Great Britain, and France met in Geneva in July 1955 in a new effort to resolve the German impasse. Eisenhower issued his Open Skies Proposal to prevent surprise aerial attack, but the Soviets had no intention of opening their territory to foreign inspection and rejected it. Nor was the Soviet Union interested in a mutual security pact between NATO and the Soviet counterpart Warsaw Pact, created in May 1955. Both sides also refused to budge from their previous positions regarding Germany.

The continuing Soviet threat greatly boosted the European unification movement. The Council of Europe of 1949 was followed by the European Coal and Steel Community in 1953 and the European Economic Community in 1957. In 1959 Britain formed a counterpart European Free Trade Association.

The year 1956 saw two simultaneous watershed events: the Suez Crisis and the Hungarian Revolution. In 1956 Nasser sought funding for construction of a high dam at Aswan on the upper Nile. At the same time, however, he sought new weaponry with which to confront Israel. The Eisenhower administration pledged assistance for the dam but rejected the request for weapons. Nasser then turned to the Soviet bloc. This, along with Nasser's diplomatic recognition of the PRC, led Washington to withdraw financing for the dam. Nasser then nationalized the Suez Canal to pay for the dam construction.

Nasser's actions led to the formation of a coalition of Britain, France, and Israel against him. The leaders of each had their own reasons for wanting to topple Nasser, and they came up with a plan whereby Israel would invade the Sinai, giving Britain and France an excuse to intervene militarily to "protect" the canal. Israel struck at the end of October, and the French and British then demanded the right to occupy the canal zone. When the Egyptian government refused, on November 5 French and British forces invaded Egypt. Both the Soviet Union and the United States demanded a withdrawal. The Soviets threatened to dispatch "volunteers," but it was heavy U.S. economic pressure on Britain that brought this about, marking the effective end of Britain as a world power.

Unfortunately for the West, the crisis diverted attention from the concurrent Hungarian Revolution (October 23–November 10). This was not the first restiveness within the Soviet bloc. In June 1953 worker unrest brought rioting in East Berlin and across the Soviet zone. It was crushed by Soviet tanks. Khrushchev's moves toward de-Stalinization in early 1956, particularly his "secret speech" revealing Stalin's crimes, fomented unrest in Poland in June 1956. Demonstrations occurred in Poznań, with workers demanding redress of grievances.

Similar protests in Hungary became revolution. Encouraged by limited reforms introduced in Poland, student demonstrators in Budapest protested communist rule, bringing widespread demand for reform. New Hungarian premier Imre Nagy was swept along by the revolutionary tide and announced a number of changes, including free elections. The Soviets had already decided to intervene before Nagy's demand of a Soviet troop withdrawal and announcement that Hungary would leave the Warsaw Pact. The Kremlin correctly feared that this would spread to the other satellites. On November 4, 1956, Khrushchev sent 200,000 troops with tanks into Hungary. The Hungarians fought as best they could. Thousands died, and some 200,000 fled into Austria.

There was near universal condemnation but no action, in part because of the concurrent Suez Crisis. There was also much criticism of the United States for talk of "rolling back communism" but lack of action. The lesson of the Hungarian Revolution was that the Kremlin could do as it pleased within its sphere of influence.

In the late 1950s the Cold War appeared to spread with confrontations in the Middle East, Africa, and Asia, especially with Soviet support for so-called wars of liberation. In an effort to reassert U.S. influence in the Middle East, in early 1957 Eisenhower pledged U.S. support for the independence of Middle Eastern countries against communism.

The Soviet challenge also spread to space. On August 17, 1957, the Soviets launched the first intercontinental ballistic missile, and on October 4 they launched *Sputnik I*, the first satellite. Perceived as a sign of Soviet scientific prowess, it was especially embarrassing to the United States, which did not place its first satellite into orbit until January 1958. *Sputnik* marked the start of the space race between the two superpowers.

Many questioned whether the United States still held an edge in military technology, and talk spread of a missile gap. For NATO, the missiles posed serious problems. To offset their far smaller manpower strength, NATO states agreed to base missiles on their soil. This elicited fears of a Soviet strike that would wipe out major population centers. At the same time, Europeans questioned whether the United States would actually risk nuclear attack on its own soil in order to defend Western Europe.

At the same time Khrushchev trumpeted "peaceful coexistence," threatening on at least 150 different occasions to employ nuclear weapons against the West. Many feared that the unpredictable Khrushchev might precipitously launch a catastrophic war. In 1958 he ushered in a period of acute tension when he resumed pressure on the western zones of Berlin.

In November 1958 the Soviets informed the Western powers that they considered agreements regarding postwar Germany to be null and void. Khrushchev demanded that Berlin be turned into a demilitarized free city and gave a deadline of May 27, 1959, for a resolution. He also threatened to sign a separate peace treaty with East

Germany that would give it control of access routes into the divided city.

The Western leaders were determined not to yield. Again, a meeting of foreign ministers failed to find a solution, but the three Western powers stood united. This may have given the Soviets pause, for Khrushchev let his deadline pass without action.

Khrushchev was somewhat mollified by an invitation from Eisenhower to visit the United States. It occurred in September 1959 just as the Soviet Union landed a probe on the moon. The two leaders actually generated a cordial, friendly atmosphere—the so-called Spirit of Camp David—and agreed to a summit in Paris in May 1960 to discuss Germany, with Eisenhower scheduled to visit the Soviet Union soon afterward.

This thaw in the Cold War proved short-lived, if indeed it had existed. It was formally broken by the Kremlin following the May 1, 1960, U-2 Crisis, in which the Soviets shot down one of the U.S. reconnaissance aircraft that had been making regular overflights of the Soviet Union. Khrushchev torpedoed the Paris summit only a few hours after it began. In September 1960, Khrushchev delivered a speech at the UN in which he sharply criticized its authority and demanded changes in the composition of the secretariat.

Khrushchev's leadership also created friction within the communist bloc. By 1960, disputes between the Soviet Union and the PRC brought the Sino-Soviet split. Mao Zedong had followed Moscow's lead during the first decade of the Cold War, but after the death of Stalin in 1953 he thought he should be the spokesperson for international communism. Also, the Soviets refused to share advanced nuclear technology with China or expand military

aid. Then there was their 2,000-mile common border—the world's longest—and disputes over Mongolia. By the spring of 1961 the split was sufficiently pronounced for the Soviet Union to withdraw its technicians and cut off assistance to the PRC.

Washington was in no position to take advantage. President John F. Kennedy, who took office in January 1961, almost immediately faced a series of international challenges in civil war in Laos and the April 1961 Bay of Pigs fiasco in which U.S.-trained and -sponsored Cuban exile forces landed on Cuba in an attempt to overthrow its avowedly communist leader, Fidel Castro. Planning had begun under Eisenhower, but Kennedy allowed it to go forward while refusing air cover, which gave it no chance.

An apparently weakened Kennedy met with Khrushchev in June 1961 in Vienna, where the Soviet leader renewed his pressure on Berlin. The Soviets then began harassment of some air traffic into the city and partly closed the East-West German border. Khrushchev again threatened the use of nuclear weapons.

Khrushchev was determined to stabilize East Germany, which was hemorrhaging its population. By the summer of 1961, some 3.5 million people had fled through West Berlin to West Germany. The communist response came on August 13 with erection of the Berlin Wall.

Kennedy called for a sizable increase in defense spending and the mobilization of some military units. The only U.S. military action, however, was dispatching troops along the autobahn into Berlin. Kennedy later went to Berlin and delivered a speech there. The ugly concrete barrier became a symbol of both the failure of communism and the unwillingness of the West to take action.

U.S. president John F. Kennedy and Soviet premier Nikita Khrushchev during their meeting in Vienna, Austria, on June 3–4, 1961. (John F. Kennedy Library)

In the fall of 1961 the Soviet Union broke a three-year moratorium on nuclear testing. This set the stage for the Cuban Missile Crisis of October 1962, the single most dangerous confrontation of the Cold War and the closest the two sides came to thermonuclear war.

U.S. economic policies against Cuba designed to unseat Castro had led him to seek Soviet assistance. Cuba appeared to Khrushchev as ideal to offset the heavy advantage in long-range nuclear weaponry enjoyed by the United States. He now ordered the secret placement of missiles on the island, hoping to achieve a fait accompli. U-2 surveillance flights soon discovered the operation, however.

On October 22, 1962, in a dramatic television address, Kennedy revealed the presence of the missiles and demanded that they be removed. He ignored certain of his advisers who urged a preemptive military strike, announcing instead a naval quarantine. Meanwhile, Soviet ships carrying missiles continued toward Cuba.

On October 27 a U-2 was downed over Cuba by a surface-to-air missile, apparently on the orders of a Soviet general on the spot. This shocked even Khrushchev and may well have marked a turnabout in his thinking. U.S. contingency plans had called for an air strike if a U-2 was shot down, but Kennedy countermanded the order.

Khrushchev's hand was weak, but he arranged a face-saving compromise in which Castro, who had sought a preemptive Soviet nuclear strike on the United

States, was ignored. Khrushchev agreed to remove the missiles along with jet bombers and some Soviet troops. In return, the United States pledged not to invade Cuba and to withdraw its (obsolete) Jupiter missiles from Turkey. Massive Soviet economic assistance for Cuba continued, however.

The Cuban Missile Crisis was one of the chief causes of Khrushchev's ouster less than two years later. The crisis greatly strengthened Kennedy's hand, however, and encouraged a stronger response to communist aggression elsewhere.

The United States was now increasingly involved in Vietnam. U.S. assistance to South Vietnam was prompted by the containment policy and the domino theory, the mistaken belief that if South Vietnam fell to the communists, the rest of South Asia would automatically follow. In 1961–1962, with the communists apparently on the brink of winning the war, Kennedy dispatched both helicopters and additional advisers. Meanwhile, both the PRC and the Soviet Union were supporting North Vietnam.

The Vietnam conflict gradually escalated. In 1965, President Lyndon B. Johnson, Kennedy's successor, began bombing North Vietnam and introduced U.S. ground troops. U.S. troop strength steadily increased as North Vietnam sent its regular forces south. Following the costly but ultimately unsuccessful communist Tet Offensive of January 1968, there was a sharp drop in American public support for the war. Johnson decided not to run for reelection, and Republican Richard Nixon won the presidency in 1968.

Nixon accelerated the Johnson administration's policy of turning the war over to the South Vietnamese, but the fighting continued; indeed, there were more U.S. casualties under Nixon than during the Johnson years until a peace settlement was reached at Paris in January 1973. South Vietnam, now largely abandoned by the United States, fell to the communists in April 1975.

Other events were moving the Cold War from confrontation to cooperation, or détente. This began with de Gaulle's return to power in France in 1958. Uncertain that the United States would risk nuclear retaliation on its own soil to defend Europe, de Gaulle developed a French nuclear deterrent and the means to deliver it. He also wanted to organize Europe as a third force between the United States and the Soviet Union. In 1966, angry because the United States and Britain would not share control of nuclear weapons within NATO, he also withdrew France from the NATO military command. West Germany was the next country to venture into détente. In the late 1960s, Foreign Minister Willy Brandt instituted Ostpolitik. Brandt believed that trade and recognition would help facilitate German reunification.

Czech leader Alexander Dubček attempted to take advantage. In 1968 he introduced "socialism with a human face," reforms that ultimately included free elections and an end to censorship. Dubček, himself a communist, claimed that these would preserve communism.

The Soviet reaction was swift and decisive. In August 1968, 500,000 Warsaw Pact troops invaded Czechoslovakia, meeting only minimal resistance from a stunned population and ending the so-called Prague Spring. Soviet leader Leonid Brezhnev justified this by what became known as the Brezhnev Doctrine. It held that communist states had the right, indeed the obligation, to intervene to preserve communism where it was in power.

GLOBAL DIVISIONS AT THE HEIGHT OF THE COLD WAR, 1962

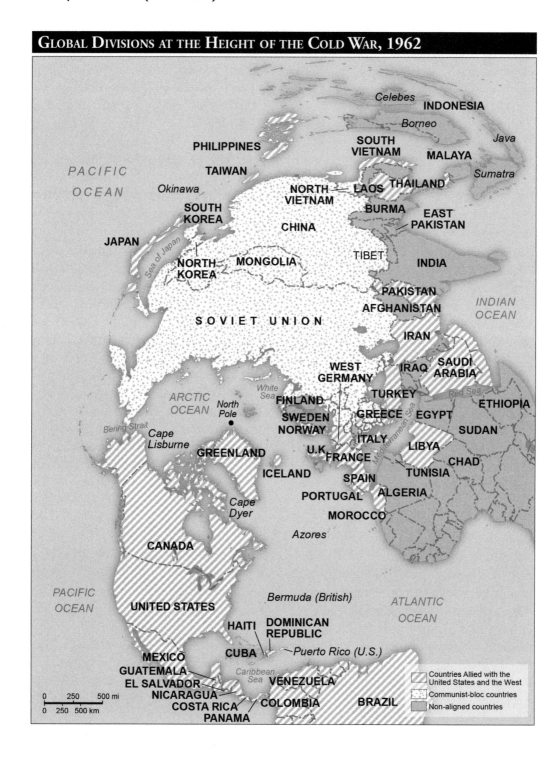

The Brezhnev Doctrine alarmed the PRC. Indeed, the Soviets assembled considerable forces along their long common border. In 1969 and 1970 there were armed clashes that easily could have become full-scale war.

Chinese concerns helped bring a thaw in relations with the United States. Since the communist victory in 1949, there had been no formal diplomatic ties between the two states. Then in February 1972 President Nixon made a dramatic trip to Beijing. The chief stumbling block was Chinese insistence on the return of Taiwan (Formosa), which Washington had regarded since the Chinese Civil War as the true representative of China. Finally, in 1978 under President Jimmy Carter, the United States severed diplomatic ties with Taiwan, although not an end to U.S. support, in order to establish full diplomatic ties with the PRC. The U.S.-PRC thaw was one of the more interesting aspects of the Cold War and helped inhibit Soviet aggressive behavior.

Another significant part of détente was the extension of Ostpolitik by Brandt. Upon becoming FRG chancellor in 1969, he decisively changed relations with the Soviet bloc. In 1970 he concluded a treaty with Moscow whereby the FRG recognized the existing border between East Germany and Poland, implicitly recognizing East Germany itself. The FRG also extended considerable loans to the communist bloc states.

Nixon did not let the Vietnam War interfere with détente. In Moscow in May 1972, he signed two major agreements with Brezhnev: the Strategic Arms Limitation Treaty (SALT I) and an agreement of principles to regularize relations between the two superpowers. The Soviets hoped to secure increased Western trade, investment, and badly needed technology while still supporting communist expansion in the developing world by means of proxy forces. Nixon, for his part, announced the Nixon Doctrine in 1973 whereby the United States would assist other nations in defending themselves against communist aggression but would no longer commit American troops. Those supporting détente hoped that it would discourage aggressive actions by the communist states.

After the Vietnam War the United States reduced defense spending to about 5 percent of gross national product (GNP), while Soviet defense expenditures rose to more than 15 percent of GNP. Certainly this played a role in the ultimate collapse of the Soviet Union. Détente sharply increased trade between the Western nations and the Soviet bloc and greatly aided the communist bloc economies. Extensive West European and Japanese loans largely went to prop up the communist regimes with short-term spending on consumer goods rather than investment in long-term economic solutions, however.

While direct diplomatic confrontation between the Soviet Union and the United States decreased in the 1970s, both sides supported proxy states, especially in the Middle East and in Africa, the scene of a number of anticolonial wars and civil wars. During the Angolan Civil War (1961–2002) the Soviets employed Cuban troops to prop up the communist regime there.

Although President Carter met with Brezhnev in Moscow in June 1979 to approve yet another strategic arms reduction agreement (SALT II), five months later Soviet leaders sent troops into Afghanistan to maintain the pro-Moscow communist government there, sending U.S.-Soviet relations plummeting.

President Carter imposed a boycott on U.S. participation in the 1980 Moscow Olympics and began a substantial U.S. military buildup that continued under his successor, Ronald Reagan. The Afghan guerrilla fighters, the mujahideen, received U.S. aid through Pakistan. U.S.-supplied Stinger shoulder-fired antiaircraft missiles soon neutralized Soviet ground-support aircraft and helicopters.

With the strain of Afghanistan, international aid commitments, and massive defense spending occasioned by the large U.S. buildup and the Strategic Defense Initiative (known to its critics as "Star Wars") initiated by President Reagan (in office during 1981–1989), the Soviets simply could not keep up. Soviet premier Mikhail Gorbachev, who took power in March 1985, had to deal with the consequences of decades of economic mismanagement.

A committed communist, Gorbachev nonetheless believed that the Soviet Union would have to embrace reform if it was to compete with the West. He hoped in his programs of glasnost (openness) and perestroika (transformation) to rebuild the economy while maintaining communist political control. His economic reforms produced scant improvement, however, and easing censorship brought civil unrest and ethnic strife as well as independence movements.

Gorbachev did score successes in foreign policy. In two summit meetings with Reagan, he offered concessions and proposed solutions that led to improved U.S.-Soviet relations and agreements on the reduction of nuclear weapons. Gorbachev also ordered the Soviet withdrawal from Afghanistan, and he promised publicly to refrain from military intervention in Eastern Europe and encouraged open elections in Central and Eastern Europe.

After the surprising collapse of the GDR government and the dismantling of the Berlin Wall in the autumn of 1989, Gorbachev also agreed to the reunification of Germany and the inclusion in NATO of the reunited Germany. Most observers credit Gorbachev, who was awarded the Nobel Peace Prize in 1990, with being the driving force behind the end of the Cold War.

Although Gorbachev's foreign policy was widely hailed abroad, the Soviet Union continued to deteriorate domestically. In 1990 several Soviet republics, including the Russian Soviet Federal Republic led by Boris Yeltsin, declared their independence. Talks between Soviet authorities and the breakaway republics resulted in a new Russian federation (or confederation) in August 1991.

In December 1991, the presidents of Russia, Ukraine, and Belarus created a loose confederation known as the Commonwealth of Independent States (CIS). Eight other republics subsequently joined, and the CIS formally came into being that same month. Gorbachev resigned as president on December 31, and the Soviet Union was officially dissolved.

The Cold War was over. Few knowledgeable observers predicted that this would occur as it did. Almost no one had perceived the fragility and weakness of one of the world's superpowers that ultimately led to its demise.

SPENCER C. TUCKER

Consequences

The Cold War was perhaps unlike any other conflict in history. It touched the lives of people around the world in unprecedented ways, and its reach went far beyond that of a traditional war or military conflict. The idea of national defense was transformed into national security, which meant that entire societies were kept perpetually mobilized.

One of the great ironies of the Cold War was the rapid rebuilding of Japan and Germany. These two well-disciplined, hard-working peoples profited handsomely from the Cold War in the sense that the Western powers needed them as allies against the Soviet Union and therefore encouraged their rapid economic development. In West Germany's case, this need was so great as to allow the rearmament of that nation in 1955, which would have been considered far-fetched in 1945. By the end of the Cold War, Germany was the dominant economic power in Europe, while Japan occupied the same position in Asia.

The space race bred in the Cold War was only part of a larger technology race between East and West that produced everything from computers to microcircuitry to global positioning satellites (GPS). Space technology was applied to advanced weapons systems that produced breakthroughs such as cruise missiles and precision-guided munitions (smart bombs). It is not possible to list even a fraction of the advances made during the space and technology races that began during the Cold War. Certainly it revolutionized human existence in the span of less than 25 years. Communications, transportation, health care, and education all were radically transformed by the technologies first used in military and space applications. And as technologies progressed—particularly in the computer field—the rate of change began to accelerate with greater speed beginning in the mid-1980s. Indeed, the lifestyles enjoyed by many today would have seemed like science fiction just a few decades ago. Never in human history has technology so rapidly changed and transformed everyday life in so short a span of time.

Of course, the end of the Cold War did not extinguish international tensions and bloodshed. Problems in the Middle East remained unresolved and became a focal point of tension and war. Although the threat of global thermonuclear war was significantly diminished, regional and civil wars proliferated. America did not reap any great peace dividend because by 1991, when the Soviet Union collapsed, it found itself the world's only military superpower, placing more burdens on its foreign and military policy. Indeed, between 1991 and 2014, the United States waged three regional wars: the 1991 Persian Gulf War, the Afghanistan War (2001–), and the 2003–2011 Iraq War. It has also been involved in other conflicts, albeit more peripherally, in places such as Somalia, the former Yugoslavia, and Libya. The end of the Cold War also resulted in the rise of failed states, in the former Yugoslavia, for example, where the removal of Soviet/communist control plunged the nation into chaos. This resulted in a decade of bloody civil war during the 1990s and the dismemberment of Yugoslavia into mutually distrustful smaller states.

Without the Soviet Union acting as counterbalance in world affairs, which included controlling and reining in its client and satellite states around the world, some areas of the globe became incubators for terrorism. Indeed, the rise of terrorism since 1991 has proven to be one of the most intractable developments of the post–Cold War era. In the past, Soviet and American pressure had managed to keep a lid on such activity; with the Soviet Union gone, controlling international terrorism has become far more difficult. The removal of Cold War dynamics has also led to a more unstable and unpredictable Middle East.

The end of the Cold War empowered rising powers such as China, Brazil, and India. This development promises to radically transform international relations and reorder the world's economic system. On the other hand, from the U.S. perspective, such a development means that American policy makers will have to adopt a wider multilateral approach to foreign policy, far more so than they did during much of the Cold War. On the positive side, the end of the Cold War has permitted real economic growth in Eastern and Central Europe and has fostered the proliferation of liberal, democratic states around the world. By the early 2000s, however, tensions between Russia, the successor state to the Soviet Union, and the United States had begun to grow. Russia refused to support the Iraq War and accused the United States of attempting to monopolize control over the oil-rich Middle East. The United States was angered by Russia's military intervention in South Ossetia (Georgia) in 2008 as well as Russia's annexation of the Crimean Peninsula in 2014 and its continued support of Ukrainian separatists. This caused U.S.-Russian relations to plunge to levels not seen since the Cold War of the early 1980s.

Yugoslavia broke apart in bloodshed that threatened to erupt into wider conflict and eventually triggered armed NATO intervention; Iran and Iraq were continuing concerns; civil war and famine remained endemic on the African continent already being ravaged by AIDS; nuclear proliferation widened, especially with the breakup of the Soviet Union, and the danger of terrorists securing nuclear weapons intensified; a quarter century–long war plagued Sri Lanka; and the dalliance with nuclear weapons by the Democratic People's Republic of Korea remained an ongoing source of concern for the West. If anything, the breakup of the bipolar world increased rather than lessened challenges facing the world's diplomats.

PAUL G. PIERPAOLI JR.

Timeline

1945

February 4–11	The Big Three Allied leaders—U.S. president Franklin D. Roosevelt, British prime minister Winston Churchill, and Soviet premier Joseph Stalin—meet at the Yalta Conference in the Crimea to hammer out final details regarding the defeat of Germany and Japan and the postwar world.
May 8	Germany surrenders unconditionally to the Allied Powers.
July 17–August 2	U.S. president Harry S. Truman, British prime minister Winston Churchill (replaced by Clement Atlee in the course of the conference), and Soviet premier Joseph Stalin meet at Potsdam, Germany. As a consequence, Germany is divided into four zones of occupation.
August 8	The Soviet Union declares war on Japan.

August 14	The Japanese government announces that it is accepting the terms of the Allied Potsdam Declaration.
September 2	The official Japanese surrender ceremony occurs aboard the U.S. Navy battleship *Missouri* in Tokyo Bay.

1946

February 9	Stalin declares that communism and capitalism are incompatible.
March 5	Churchill delivers his "Iron Curtain" speech in Fulton, Missouri.
March 10	President Truman demands that Soviet forces depart from Iran.

1947

February 22	As the Cold War intensifies, President Truman signs Executive Order 9835, known as the Loyalty Order and the Loyalty Program. The first general U.S. loyalty program, it is designed to root out communist influence in the federal government. By mid-1952, more than 4 million people have gone through security checks. Boards dismiss or deny jobs to 378, none of whom, however, are found guilty of espionage.
March 4	The leaders of France and Great Britain sign the Treaty of Dunkirk, which establishes an alliance and mutual assistance in the event of external attack.
March 12	Truman proclaims what becomes known as the Truman Doctrine, proposing U.S. aid to countries fighting communist subversion, notably Greece and Turkey.
June 5	U.S. secretary of state George C. Marshall announces what will become known as the Marshall Plan to assist war-torn Europe in recovering from World War II.
September 2	The United States and 16 Latin American countries conclude the Inter-American Treaty of Reciprocal Assistance, known as the Rio Pact, that creates a security zone around the Western Hemisphere.

1948

February 25	The communists seize power in Czechoslovakia.
March 17	As an outgrowth of the Treaty of Dunkirk the previous year, Belgium, Luxembourg, the Netherlands, Great Britain, and France sign the Brussels Pact, a mutual defense treaty aimed against the Soviet Union.

April 1	The Berlin Blockade begins, with the Soviets gradually cutting off traffic in and out of the city.
April 4	The North Atlantic Treaty, signed by 11 European states and the United States, pledges all such action as deemed necessary, including the use of armed force, to the defense of any member state that comes under external attack.

1949

May 12	The Berlin Blockade ends.
August 29	The Soviet Union explodes its first atomic bomb.
October	Chinese Communist leader Mao Zedong proclaims the establishment of the People's Republic of China (PRC).

1950

January 30	Truman approves the development of a hydrogen bomb.
February	U.S. senator Joseph McCarthy commences a witch hunt for communists in the United States, ruining the careers of many innocent people in the process.
June 24	The Korean War begins when forces of the Democratic People's Republic of Korea (North Korea) invade a largely disarmed Republic of Korea (South Korea).
April 11	Truman removes General Douglas MacArthur from command of United Nations forces in Korea.

1952

November 1	The United States explodes its first hydrogen bomb.

1953

July 27	An armistice is signed in Korea, bringing the war to a close, although no peace treaty regarding Korea has ever been signed.
August 15–19	A coup d'état sponsored by the U.S. Central Intelligence Agency (CIA) overthrows the government of Iran.

1954

March 13–May 7	The Battle of Dien Bien Phu is fought between the French and the Viet Minh (Vietnam Independence League) in eastern Tonkin, Vietnam. It ends in a Viet Minh victory.
April 26–July 20	The Geneva Conference ends in the Geneva Accords, which provide for the independence of Vietnam, Laos, and Cambodia. Vietnam is temporarily divided at the 17th parallel, with elections to be held in two years to unify the country.
June 18–27	A coup, sponsored by the CIA, overthrows the government of Guatemala.

September 8	The Southeast Asia Collective Defense Treaty, also known as the Manila Pact, is signed in Manila by seven Asian nations and the United States.
1955	
May 14	The Warsaw Pact is established, binding eight communist states of Central and Eastern Europe into a mutual defense treaty designed to counteract NATO.
1956	
June 28–30	The Poznan Riots occur in Poland, with some 100,000 people demonstrating against the communist government of Poland, which orders in some 10,000 soldiers and 400 tanks to crush the revolt. At least 57 people, and probably more than 100, are killed.
October 23–November 10	A revolution occurs in Hungary but is then crushed by Soviet military intervention. More than 2,500 Hungarians and 700 Soviet troops are killed in the fighting, and 200,000 Hungarians flee abroad.
October 29–November 7	The Suez Crisis occurs when Israel, Britain, and France attempt to topple the Egyptian government and take control of the Suez Canal. Financial pressure from the United States leads to the collapse of the scheme.
1957	Beginning of the Vietnam War.
August 21	The Soviet Union successfully launches the first intercontinental ballistic missile, designated the R-7 *Semyorka*.
October 4	The Soviet Union launches *Sputnik,* the first earth satellite to attain orbit.
November 3	The Soviet Union launches *Sputnik II.*
1958	
January 31	The United States launches its first earth satellite, the *Explorer I.*
November	Soviet leader Nikita Khrushchev demands the withdrawal of troops from the western zones of Berlin.
1959	
January 1	Insurgents led by Fidel Castro take power in Cuba.
September 15–27	Khrushchev becomes the first Soviet leader to visit the United States.
1960	
May 1	The Soviet Union downs a U-2 reconnaissance aircraft over its territory, catching the U.S. government in a lie when it produces the plane's pilot, Francis Gary Powers.

The Sino-Soviet split begins. Tensions between these two powers continue until 1969.

1961

April 17–19
The U.S.-supported Bay of Pigs Invasion occurs. An attempt to topple Castro from power in Cuba, it ends in fiasco.

August 13
The government of the German Democratic Republic (East Germany, GDR) closes the border into West Berlin and begins construction of what becomes known as the Berlin Wall.

October 14–28
The Cuban Missile Crisis occurs. Almost certainly the closest the United States and the Soviet Union come to a shooting war during the Cold War, it ends with the Soviets withdrawing their missiles from Cuba and the United States removing its missiles from Turkey.

1963

August 5
Following nearly eight years of difficult negotiations, the United States, the United Kingdom, and the Soviet Union sign a nuclear test ban treaty.

November 22
President John F. Kennedy is assassinated in Dallas, Texas.

1964

August 2, 4
The Gulf of Tonkin Incidents occur. They consist of one North Vietnamese gunboat attack on a U.S. destroyer and a presumed second attack on two U.S. destroyers off the southern coast of North Vietnam. There are no U.S. casualties.

August 7
The U.S. Congress approves the Gulf of Tonkin Resolution, giving President Lyndon B. Johnson broad authority to expand U.S. involvement in the Vietnam War.

October 16
The PRC joins the nuclear club, exploding its first atomic bomb.

1965

March 2
Operation ROLLING THUNDER, the U.S. bombing of North Vietnam, begins. It will continue, with several pauses, until November 2, 1968.

March 8
Some 3,500 U.S. marines come ashore in South Vietnam, the first U.S. ground troops to be committed to the Vietnam War.

April 28	U.S. marines are dispatched to the Dominican Republic. They remain there until July 1, 1966.
July	The U.S. government announces the dispatch of 200,000 U.S. troops to Vietnam.

1967

June 5–10	In what becomes known as the Six-Day War, Israel launches a preemptive strike against Egypt and then Syria. Jordan also enters the fray. Israel is victorious and secures the Sinai Peninsula from Egypt, the Golan Heights from Syria, and the east bank of the Jordan River from Jordan. The latter acquisition in particular will have profound implications for the lack of peace in the Middle East.

1968

January 23	North Korean forces capture in international waters the inadequately defended USS *Pueblo* reconnaissance vessel with its crew and sophisticated intelligence collection devices.
March 31	President Johnson announces that he will not stand for reelection.
August 20–21	On this night, Warsaw Pact troops, led by those of the Soviet Union, enter Czechoslovakia and there crush the liberal communist movement known as the Prague Spring.
November 5	In one of the closest presidential elections in U.S. history, Republican Richard M. Nixon defeats Democrat and sitting vice president Hubert Humphrey.

1969

March 2–September 11	A low-intensity border war occurs along the long border separating the Soviet Union and the PRC.
July 20	The United States wins the race to the moon with Apollo 11.

1970

April 29	President Nixon extends U.S. operations in the Vietnam War to Cambodia, when U.S. forces invade that country to destroy communist sanctuaries. They withdraw on July 22.

1972

February 21–28	President Nixon visits China, the first American president to do so.
May 26	The Strategic Arms Limitation Treaty (SALT I) is signed between the United States and the Soviet Union.

1973

January 27	Negotiations having begun in 1968, representatives of the United States, the Republic of Vietnam (South Vietnam), the Democratic Republic of Vietnam (North Vietnam), and the Provisional Revolutionary Government, supposedly representing communist revolutionaries in South Vietnam, sign the Agreement on Ending the War and Restoring Peace in Vietnam. The United States then withdraws from South Vietnam.
September 11	A coup supported by the U.S. CIA overthrows the Chilean government of socialist president Salvador Allende.
October 6–25	Egypt and Syria launch a surprise attack on Israel in what becomes known as the Yom Kippur War. Israel eventually defeats its opponents.

1975

April 17	North Vietnamese forces defeat South Vietnamese forces and secure Saigon, now Ho Chi Minh City, bringing to a close the long Vietnam War.

1976

February	Soviet and Cuban forces help to install a communist government in Angola.

1979

January 1	The United States and the PRC establish diplomatic relations.
January 16	Mohammad Reza Shah Pahlavi, supported by the U.S. government, quits his country for the United States. He is replaced in power on February 11 by Grand Ayatollah Ruhollah Khomeini, and an Islamic republic is proclaimed on April 1.
June 18	The United States and the Soviet Union sign the Strategic Arms Limitation Treaty II (SALT II).
December 24	Soviet forces invade Afghanistan.

1980

August 14	Polish shipyard workers go on strike and form the Solidarity Trade Union, headed by Lech Walesa.

1983

March 23	U.S. president Ronald Reagan proposes the Strategic Defense Initiative.
October 25	U.S. forces invade Grenada, defeating the Cuban troops there and overthrowing its leftist regime.

1985

March 15   Mikhail Gorbachev becomes secretary-general of the Central Committee of the Communist Party of the Soviet Union, or leader of the Soviet Union. In an effort to reform communism and save it, he institutes a campaign of openness, known as glasnost, and restructuring, known as perestroika.

1987

December 8   Reagan and Gorbachev sign a treaty agreeing to remove all intermediate nuclear missiles from Europe.

1989

February 15   The last Soviet troops are withdrawn from Afghanistan.

April 15–June 4   Led by university students, some 1 million Chinese demonstrate in Tiananmen Square in Beijing and demand reforms by the Chinese communist government until their protests are crushed by army troops. Some estimates of the number of dead range in the thousands.

August 24   Solidarity forms the first post–World War II noncommunist government in Poland.

October   Hungary shakes off communist rule.

November 10   The Democratic Republic of Germany (East Germany) allows unrestricted migration to the Federal Republic of Germany (West Germany, FRG). Tearing down of the Berlin Wall begins.

December   Communist governments fall in Czechoslovakia, Bulgaria, and Romania.

1990

March 11   Lithuania declares its independence from the Soviet Union.

May 29   Boris Yeltsin becomes the chairman of the Presidium of the Supreme Soviet of the Russian Soviet Federated Socialist Republic.

October 3   Germany is officially reunited, with the FRG absorbing the former GDR.

1991

July 10   Boris Yeltsin is elected the first president of the Russian Federation.

December 26   The Soviet Union is dissolved. The Cold War comes to an end.

SPENCER C. TUCKER

Further Reading

Acheson, Dean. *Present at the Creation: My Years at the State Department.* New York: Norton, 1969.

Ball, Simon J. *The Cold War: An International History, 1947–1991.* New York: St. Martin's, 1998.

Beschloss, Michael R., and Strobe Talbott. *At the Highest Levels: The Inside Story of the End of the Cold War.* Boston: Little, Brown, 1993.

Bullock, Alan. *Ernest Bevin: Foreign Secretary, 1945–1951.* New York: Norton, 1983.

Byrnes, James F. *Speaking Frankly.* New York: Harper and Brothers, 1947.

Chace, James. *Acheson: The Secretary of State Who Created the American World.* New York: Simon and Schuster, 1998.

Crockatt, Richard. *The Fifty Years' War: The United States and the Soviet Union in World Politics, 1941–1991.* New York: Routledge, 1995.

Crowley, Robert, ed. *The Cold War: A Military History.* New York: Random House, 2006.

Feis, Herbert. *Between War and Peace: The Potsdam Conference.* Princeton, NJ: Princeton University Press, 1957.

Fontaine, Andre. *History of the Cold War, 1917–1966.* 2 vols. New York: Pantheon, 1968.

Gaddis, John Lewis. *The Long Peace: Inquiries into the History of the Cold War.* New York: Oxford University Press, 1989.

Gaddis, John Lewis. *Strategies of Containment: A Critical Appraisal of the Postwar National Security Policy.* New York: Oxford University Press, 1982.

Gaddis, John Lewis. *We Now Know: Rethinking Cold War History.* New York: Oxford University Press, 1997.

Hogan, Michael J. *A Cross of Iron: Harry S. Truman and the Origins of the National Security State, 1945–1954.* New York: Cambridge University Press, 1998.

Kennan, George F. *Memoirs, 1925–1950.* Boston: Little, Brown, 1967.

Kuniholm, Bruce R. *The Origins of the Cold War: Great Power Conflict and Diplomacy in Iran, Turkey and Greece.* Princeton, NJ: Princeton University Press, 1994.

LaFeber, Walter. *America, Russia, and the Cold War, 1946–1996.* 8th ed. Columbus, OH: McGraw-Hill College, 1996.

Leffler, Melvyn P. *A Preponderance of Power: National Security, the Truman Administration, and the Cold War.* Stanford, CA: Stanford University Press, 1992.

McCormick, Thomas J. *America's Half-Century: United States Foreign Policy in the Cold War and After.* Baltimore: Johns Hopkins University Press, 1995.

Painter, David S. *The Cold War: An International History.* New York: Routledge, 1999.

Pierpaoli, Paul G., Jr. *Truman and Korea: The Political Culture of the Early Cold War.* Columbia: University of Missouri Press, 1999.

Seton-Watson, Hugh. *Neither War nor Peace: The Struggle for Power in the Postwar World.* New York: Praeger, 1960.

Thomas, Hugh. *Armed Truce: The Beginnings of the Cold War, 1945–1946.* New York: Atheneum, 1987.

Walker, Martin. *The Cold War: A History.* New York: Henry Holt, 1994.

Westad, Odd Arne. *The Global Cold War: Third World Interventions and the Making of Our Times.* Cambridge: Cambridge University Press, 2007.

Whitfield, Stephen J. *The Culture of the Cold War.* 2nd ed. Baltimore: Johns Hopkins University Press, 1996.

Zubok, Vladislav, and Constantine Pieshakov. *Inside the Kremlin's Cold War: From Stalin to Khrushchev.* Cambridge, MA: Harvard University Press, 1996.

Greek Civil War (1946–1949)

Causes

The threat of postwar civil war between nationalist and communist undergrounds that had fought the Axis occupiers during World War II and a real possibility in much of Europe after World War II became reality in Greece. The Greek Civil War (1946–1949), fought between the Greek Communist Party (KKE) and anticommunist Greek nationalist parties, was also the first major armed struggle of the Cold War (1945–1991). The subsequent nationalist victory over the Communists in Greece was owing primarily to the active support of first the British and then the Americans and then the geographical location of Greece, which permitted aid to be brought to bear. The outcome of the struggle would have profound impact on the Cold War well beyond that country's borders.

Greece occupies a key geographical position in the eastern Mediterranean but had long been under control of the Ottoman Empire. In the early 19th century there was widespread support for Greek independence, owing to the prominent role played by the ancient Greeks in the development of Western civilization. This sentiment found expression in what was known as Philhellenism. Western support was vital, but the struggle for independence (1821–1832) was nonetheless both protracted and sanguinary. With victory finally secured, the Greeks chose a Bavarian prince as their king.

Greek loyalties were sharply divided in World War I, and the Greeks followed a neutral stance until the Allies intervened militarily in 1917 and forced the country to join their side. In the aftermath of the war the Greeks were awarded much of eastern Anatolia from the Ottoman Empire, but this inflamed the Turks and brought war with Turkey. The Greco-Turkish War (1919–1922) ended in a Turkish victory and the expulsion and flight of Greeks from Asia Minor. The war overlapped with what the Greeks have called the Greek Genocide, a period during 1914–1922 that Greeks charge saw Turkish officials orchestrate the murder of hundreds of thousands of Greek nationals in Asia Minor.

Greece was one of the early victims in World War II. Italian leader Benito Mussolini had dreams of foreign conquest, and Greece and its Mediterranean islands seemed easy prey for his considerable war machine. In October 1940, without informing comrade-in-arms German leader Adolf Hitler in advance, Mussolini launched an invasion from Albania. Because the Italian military possessed both superior numbers and matériel, he expected an easy victory before the onset of winter.

The Greeks, however, not only held the Italians at bay but also soon mounted a counterinvasion of Albania. Having extended a guarantee in 1939 to Greece of its territorial integrity, British prime minister Winston Churchill halted a successful offensive against the Italians in North Africa and in Operation LUSTRE rushed an expeditionary force to Greece in March 1941. This threat to the Axis southern flank prior to his planned invasion of the Soviet Union prompted Hitler to dispatch German forces to Greece (Operation MARITA) in April 1941 to salvage the situation.

The combined Greek and British forces proved inadequate against the German Luftwaffe and panzers, and by early 1941 British forces had been evacuated, and the Axis powers controlled Greece. Greek king George II and his ministers accompanied the withdrawing British forces and went into exile in Egypt. The Germans then took Cyprus, and German and Italian forces occupied the smaller Greek islands. The British gamble may well have cost them early control over North Africa but also ensured that the final Allied victory there in early 1943 was more costly for the Axis side.

The Axis occupation of Greece included German, Italian, and Bulgarian troops and lasted three years in what was a very dark period in Greek history. The occupiers requisitioned resources and supplies with no concern for the survival of the Greek people, who even in the best of times had been obliged to import most of their food from abroad. Famine and disease combined to take a heavy toll.

With the Greek government in exile, various resistance groups formed and fought the Axis occupation with hit-and-run attacks. Ultimately the Greek underground tied down some 120,000 Axis troops. The occupiers responded with ruthless reprisals. (The Germans announced a policy of executing 50 Greek hostages for every 1 of their men slain.) Exact figures will never be known, but one estimate is that the Germans executed some 21,000 Greeks, the Bulgarians 40,000, and the Italians 9,000.

The Greek resistance was badly fractured during the war. The largest of these organizations was the Communist-dominated leftist National Liberation Front (EAM), with its military wing being the National Popular Liberation Army

(ELAS). As in neighboring Yugoslavia, the Communists were not reluctant to employ force against the occupiers and incur reprisals. The EAM seemed, however, to enjoy wider support than the nationalist underground.

Beginning in the autumn of 1943, there were armed clashes between the various Greek resistance organizations that had postwar political aspirations. ELAS was particularly active in this regard. For example, it moved against the National and Social Liberation (EKKA), murdering EKKA leader Dimitrios Psarros. Such actions continued until May 1944, when an agreement was reached at a meeting of representatives of the resistance groups and political parties in Lebanon under the leadership of Georgios Papandreou. Despite considerable dissension, with the EAM accusing the other organizations of collaboration with the Axis occupiers and the latter responding by accusing EAM-ELAS of violence against them and simple lawlessness, an accord was reached. This occurred in large measure because of instructions from the Soviet Union to the KKE not to harm allied unity. The conferees agreed to the National Contract that established a government of national unity of 24 ministers, 6 of whom were from the EAM. A major problem unresolved at the conference, however, was how to accomplish the disarmament of the resistance organizations.

When the Germans finally withdrew from Greece in October 1944, the EAM held the vast majority of the national territory. That same month Churchill journeyed to Moscow to meet with Soviet leader Joseph Stalin. In his memoirs Churchill describes how on October 9 he proposed a settlement for the Balkans that would give the Soviet Union 90 percent predominance

Greek Civil War (1946–1949)

Size of Opposing Forces (1946)	
Democratic Army of Greece (DSE), Communist	**Greek Army, Anti-Communist**
16,000	90,000

Approximate Amount of Select Foreign Aid for Anti-Communist Forces (1946–1949)	
United States	**Great Britain**
$775,000,000	$300,000,000

Number of Greek Refugees and Displaced Persons (1946–1949)
1,000,000

Total Casualties (Military/Civilian) during Greek Civil War (1946–1949)	
Killed	**Wounded**
80,000	400,000–420,000

Sources: Richard Clogg, *Greece, 1940–1949: Occupation, Resistance, Civil War; A Documentary History* (New York: Palgrave, 2003); John O. Iatrides, *Greece in the 1940s: A Nation in Crisis* (Hanover, NH: University Press of New England, 1981).

in Romania, 75 percent in Bulgaria, and 50 percent with the West in Yugoslavia and Hungary, with Britain to have 90 percent predominance in Greece. Stalin readily assented, but the EAM understandably failed to see the wisdom of this arrangement and chose to disregard it.

On the Axis withdrawal, the new Greek national unity government headed by left-of-center politician Georgios Papandreou was established in Athens. Fearing the strength of the Communist underground, however, Papandreou called for British troops, and they began arriving early in October 1944.

Violence erupted in Athens on December 3, 1944, when Greek gendarmes, with British troops standing by, opened fire on a large pro-EAM rally protesting the general disarmament ultimatum that had been issued by British Army lieutenant general Sir Ronald MacKenzie Scobie that,

however, excluded the right-wing Greek forces. The EAM had quit the cabinet and called for a general strike. In the ensuing melee the police shot and killed 28 demonstrators. Many others were injured.

Open warfare broke out shortly thereafter. The so-called Dekemvrianá (December Events, also known as the Battle of Athens) lasted from December 3, 1944, to January 3, 1945. British troops had to employ tanks to defeat the EAM and restore order. In this serious situation Churchill and Foreign Secretary Anthony Eden traveled to Athens and there presided over a meeting on Christmas Day 1944, at which a Soviet representative was present, in the hopes of securing a settlement. The effort failed because of excessive EAM demands. Later it was learned that the EAM had planned to blow up the hotel where the peace conference was to be held. In early January

Papandreou resigned and was replaced by General Nikolaos Plastiras. On January 15 General Scobie agreed to a cease-fire, with ELAS promising to withdraw its fighters from Patras and Thessaloniki and to demobilize in the Peloponnese.

The violence came to formal albeit temporary end with the Treaty of Varkiza, signed near Athens on February 12. Having clearly lost the first round of fighting, EAM-ELAS agreed to disarm in return for full participation in the political process. The treaty also called for the establishment of a nonpolitical national army and a plebiscite to be held within a year to establish elections and create a constituent assembly to draft a new constitution, with allied observers monitoring the elections to ensure fairness.

The Treaty of Varkiza marked the end of the EAM's political power. While ELAS did turn over a considerable quantity of weapons, the EAM soon lost its multiparty character and was thereafter completely dominated by the KKE. At the same time, tensions were heightened by the so-called White Terror of right-wing violence against EAM-KKE supporters. Members of the EAM soon took to the hills with their weapons.

In the first post–World War II national elections, held on March 31, 1946, the Royalist People's Party claimed a landslide victory in which conservatives and centrists won a two-thirds majority. A Royalist ministry was promptly installed. The election was hardly reflective of true national sentiment, however, as the KKE had called for a boycott of the election, and the KKE and many who privately sympathized with it had stayed away from the polls. With considerable justification, the KKE claimed that the election process was rigged. Having concluded that

there was no more possibility of achieving its ends through the political process, the Communists then took to arms.

SPENCER C. TUCKER

Course

The Greek Civil War commenced with the landslide victory by the right-wing Royalists in the March 31, 1946, Greek national elections, which the KKE had boycotted over quite valid charges of election fraud. The war is usually dated from March 30, the day before the actual election, when 30 former members of ELAS, the World War II National Popular Liberation Army that had fought the Axis occupation of Greece, attacked a police outpost in the village of Litrochoro and killed the policemen there. Militants in the KKE organized from ELAS a new military force known as the Democratic Army of Greece (DSE). The DSE was led by ELAS veteran Markos Vafiadis, a guerrilla leader of considerable ability who was widely known as "General Markos" and operated from a base across the border in Yugoslavia. The KKE's publicly stated goal in initiating a full-scale civil war was the restoration of a true parliamentary democracy in Greece, a claim that was seriously undermined by the establishment of Communist dictatorships throughout Central and Eastern Europe.

As fighting proceeded, in September 1946 a plebiscite was held concerning restoration of the monarchy. Some 90 percent of eligible voters went to the polls, and 69 percent of them approved King George II's return. The king was not popular in Greece, however. George II died in April 1957 and was succeeded by his son Paul, who reigned until 1964.

By the end of 1946 the Communist side was ready to attempt a comeback. In this they had strong assistance from the

Communist governments of neighboring Yugoslavia, Bulgaria, and Albania, which supplied the DSE with both arms and equipment as well as cross-border bases. The Greek government appealed to the United Nations (UN), and in May 1947 a report of the UN Balkans Investigating Committee confirmed the Greek government charges.

KKE leader Nikolaos Zachariadis visited Moscow on more than one occasion. Nonetheless, Stalin for whatever reason honored his pledge to Churchill and in fact ordered Yugoslav leader Tito (Josip Broz) to halt aid to the Greek Communists. Tito's refusal was one of the major factors behind the 1948 Yugoslav break with Moscow.

The Greek Army numbered some 90,000 men, while the DSE had only about 16,000. Nonetheless, the DSE made substantial gains in the first year of fighting. Understandably, its principal strength was in northern areas of the country bordering Albania, Yugoslavia, and Bulgaria. Fighting was particularly intense in the Vardar Valley region, but the national government was able to retain control of the major cities.

Greece was saved for the West only because the British were determined that the peninsula, with its strategic control of the eastern Mediterranean, must not fall to the Communists. But in February 1947, having spent $250 million to shore up the Greek loyalists and now deep into their own economic problems, London informed a shocked Washington that it could no longer bear the burden of maintaining Greece.

U.S. president Harry S. Truman was quick to respond. On March 12, 1947, he addressed a joint session of Congress and announced what came to be known as the Truman Doctrine. Asserting that the United States "must assist free peoples to work out their own destinies in their own way," Truman promised that the United States would "support free peoples who are resisting attempted subjugation by armed minorities or by outside pressures."

While there was trepidation in the United States over the Truman Doctrine, the alternative of giving in seemed far more perilous. In remarkably short order, in May the U.S. Congress appropriated $400 million in aid for Greece and Turkey (which itself was then under heavy pressure from the Soviet Union concerning transit rights through the Bosporus). Somewhat more than half of Truman's plan aid was in the form of military assistance. Ultimately the United States contributed about $750 million in aid for the final three years of the Greek Civil War.

The extensive rural areas of Greece bore the brunt of the war, with the peasants caught in the crossfire. When DSE partisans entered a village seeking supplies, the peasants had no means of resistance if they had wanted to do so and little choice but to comply. When government forces appeared, however, those who had furnished supplies to the partisans were branded Communist sympathizers and were often imprisoned or exiled. Government forces also often evacuated entire villages on the pretext that they were under threat of Communist attack but with the real aim of denying supplies and recruits to the Communists. This, of course, incurred considerable animosity against the government side.

Fighting intensified in 1947, with the DSE carrying out attacks on towns in northern Epirus, Thessaly, and Macedonia as well as in the Peloponnese. Government forces responded with large-scale counteroffensives, but the DSE would then be gone, with its members having returned to their mountain bases or simply moving

Greek villagers, suspected of having supported anti-government guerrillas, put to work on the roads by the government forces during the Greek Civil War, May 1948. (Bert Hardy/Picture Post/ Hulton Archive/Getty Images)

across the border into their sanctuaries in Albania, Yugoslavia, and Bulgaria. With no sanctuary to which they could withdraw, however, DSE fighters in the Peloponnese suffered disproportionally.

In September 1947, despite the opposition of Markos, the KKE leadership decided to abandon guerrilla tactics and move to full-scale conventional warfare. Then in December the KKE announced the formation of a Provisional Democratic Government, with Markos as prime minister. No foreign government recognized the self-proclaimed new government, however, while the Greek government response was to ban the KKE outright.

The change to conventional warfare led the DSE to undertake a series of attempts to take a major town and establish it as the capital of the newly proclaimed KKE government. The largest of these

efforts came at Konitsa (December 25, 1947–January 5, 1948) close to the Albanian border, in which some 1,200 DSE fighters were killed.

Nonetheless, the Communists came close to winning in Greece. The highwater mark of DSE influence came early in 1948. Now counting more than 20,000 men and women fighters with many more sympathizers, the DSE extended its military operations to Attica, reaching to within some 12 miles of the Greek capital.

The tide was turning, however. Able Greek Army commander General Alexander Papagos cleaned out incompetent officers and over time created a military force sufficient to turn the military tide. U.S. equipment and an American military assistance advisory group led by Lieutenant General James Van Fleet played an important role in his success.

The KKE was originally not overly concerned about the U.S. stance and aid and remained convinced that it could defeat the government forces even with U.S. support. The American-backed nationalist army steadily grew in strength and ability, however, and by 1948 it was clear that the DSE was in difficulty. In mid-June 1948, in Operation KORONIS the Greek Army took the offensive, with heavy fighting occurring at Mount Grammos. In the important government victory of the Battle of Grammos (June 16–August 21), some 70,000 Greek Army troops defeated 12,000 DSE fighters and caused the latter to withdraw into Albania. Desperately short of supplies and ammunition, DSE fighters in the Peloponnese also failed to capture the government ammunition depot at Zacharo in the western Peloponnese on October 13, and in Operation PERISTERA (DOVE) on December 5, 1948–January 30, 1949, some 40,000 Greek Army troops and gendarmerie forces virtually wiped out the DSE in the Peloponnese, killing some 3,500 of them and capturing another 4,000.

In January 1949 the KKE leaders took an ill-considered step and announced that their goal was no longer the restoration of true parliamentary democracy, as they had always claimed, but rather the establishment of a proletarian state. This alienated many noncommunist KKE supporters. In another mistake, the DSE again miscalculated in its military strategy, shifting from a war of attrition to a campaign to defend territory.

Certainly a key factor in the ultimate Greek government victory was the defection of Yugoslavia. Of the three Balkan states aiding the Communist guerrillas, Yugoslavia was by far the most important. The decision of the government in Belgrade to terminate military assistance followed its own split with Moscow and Yugoslavia's expulsion from the Communist Information Bureau (Cominform) in June 1948. Tito was now forced to concentrate his efforts toward resisting a possible Soviet invasion of his own country.

The Yugoslav–Soviet Union split was mirrored by internal conflict within the KKE and the DSE. The great majority of KKE members, led by party secretary Zachariadis, sided with Moscow, and in January 1949 Markos found himself accused of "Titoism" and was removed from his political and military positions, replaced by Zachariadis. In July 1949 Tito closed the border with Greece and shut down DSE camps inside Yugoslavia. Although the DSE continued to use camps inside Albania, these proved less than satisfactory, and the ideological fissures within the KKE certainly demoralized the DSE and reduced its numbers and support.

General Papagos deployed 180,000 troops in Operation TORCH (August 2–30, 1949) against only some 7,000 DSE fighters on the Grammos-Vitsi front, defeating the DSE and clearing the Communist strongholds of northern Greece. Heavy losses meant that the DSE was no longer capable of engaging Greek government forces in set-piece battles. By the beginning of September most of the DSE soldiers had either been captured, had surrendered, or had escaped across the border into Albania, which then announced that it would no longer permit DSE operations from its territory.

On October 16, 1949, a cease-fire was declared, effectively bringing the civil war to an end. Sporadic fighting continued into 1950, however. The war exacted a heavy toll. Both sides had fought without mercy, and thousands of hostages had been taken and then simply disappeared. Casualties may have been as high as half a million, with at least 80,000 dead. All were Greeks killed by Greeks. A million Greeks had also been uprooted and displaced by the fighting.

SPENCER C. TUCKER

Consequences

Western leaders chose to regard the outcome of the Greek Civil War as a Cold War victory against the Soviet Union, but the irony is that the Soviets never actively supported the KKE's effort to seize power. Nonetheless, the conflict had tremendous consequences internationally. U.S. assistance to Greece under the Truman Doctrine caused the United States to assume from Britain the burden of the world's policeman. The Truman Doctrine also led directly to the Marshall Plan and to the North Atlantic Treaty Organization (NATO), both of which would involve Greece; Greece joined NATO in February 1952.

Domestically, the civil war had great economic and political impact. Much of Greece was in ruins, and the economic consequences for the country were as great or greater than the years of the Axis occupation. Unfortunately, there was little effort in the early years after the war to introduce much-needed reforms, which had they been carried out would have substantially weakened the Communist appeal.

It was perhaps inevitable that the first few years of comparative peace would be influenced by the passions of the civil war period. Violence in the form of reprisals and punishments continued for some time. Thousands of Greeks arrested by the government during the civil war remained in prison for many years or were sent into exile on the Greek islands of Gyaros and Makronisos. A large number of Greek leftists who were able to do so emigrated.

Many from northern Greece settled in the Eastern bloc countries, especially Czechoslovakia and the Soviet Union.

In the years of fighting, Greek prime ministers and their cabinets had been drawn from the old order, and this continued afterward, with the chief objective of those in power being to make certain there would be no Communist revival. The polarization and instability of Greek politics in the mid-1960s was a direct result of the civil war and the deep divide between the leftist and rightist sections of Greek society. A major crisis attributable to this occurred in the assassination of left-wing politician Gregoris Lambraki on May 27, 1963 (the inspiration for the Costa-Gavras film *Z*). There were also a number of alleged coup plots.

Thanks to the abolition of proportional representation, the Greek Rally Party headed by war hero General Papagos, a leader of unquestioned integrity, won an overwhelming victory in the 1952 elections. During the three years of Papagos's strongman rule and eight years under his successor, economist Konstantinos (Constantine) Karamanlis (1955–1963), the government at last began to deal with pressing problems that were crippling economic development and preventing a better life for the Greek people. Efforts were made to assault the long-standing obstacles to economic improvement in the form of powerful vested interests, an entrenched bureaucracy, and chronic corruption.

The United States, meanwhile, put some $376 million in Marshall Plan assistance into Greece before this aid ended in 1962. The results provided one of the better examples of what such assistance could accomplish. American technical aid and a five-year economic plan helped increase agricultural production to a point where imports of food were unnecessary. Industrial production and international trade also grew, and tourism became a major economic boost. In 1966 the European Common Market admitted Greece as an associate member (it achieved full membership in the European Community in 1980).

Unfortunately, democratic government would soon be interrupted. In 1963 Karamanlis abruptly resigned in a dispute with King Paul over the powers of the Crown, and in July 1965 young King Constantine II, who ascended the throne in 1964, dismissed Premier Georgios Papandreou's centrist government, bringing a period of political turbulence and, on April 21, 1967, a coup d'état and the establishment of a military dictatorship.

The military junta became a considerable embarrassment for the U.S. government and NATO. The colonels running Greece were finally unseated following their mistaken decision to intervene in Cyprus. This brought an overwhelming Turkish military invasion of that island in July 1974 that led directly to the collapse of the regime in Athens. Karamanlis was invited back to Greece from Paris, where he had been living in exile for the past decade.

Greece became a republic when a 1975 referendum rejected a return to monarchy. In 1989, the Greek parliament unanimously passed a law that declared the three-year struggle of 1946–1949 as the "Greek Civil War." It also accepted the former "Communist Bandits" as "Fighters of DSE" and granted a number of them pension benefits.

SPENCER C. TUCKER

Timeline

1939

April 13	Britain and France extend a guarantee to defend Greece and Romania against external attack (read: from Germany or Italy).

1940

October 28	Italian forces invade Greece from Albania.
November 22–December 22	The Greek Army, commanded by General Alexander Papagos, mounts a counteroffensive against the Italians, opening with the capture of Koritsa. Assisted by Royal Air Force aircraft arrived from Egypt, the Greeks advance into Albania and capture large amounts of Italian war matériel. British naval units shell Valona. That winter the fighting deadlocks.

1941

March 7–27	British prime minister Winston Churchill, honoring British pledges to defend Greece, orders the best British troops in North Africa to Greece. This move, however, prevents the British from achieving complete victory this year over Italian forces in North Africa.

April 6–23	German forces conquer Greece. Alarmed over the threat to his southern flank, German chancellor Adolf Hitler orders the German military to come to the aid of the Italians in Greece simultaneous with the German invasion of Yugoslavia. The Germans catch the Greeks with 15 divisions in Albania and only 3 divisions and border forces in Macedonia. Both the Greek Army and the British Expeditionary Force (BEF) are driven back. Despite gallant resistance, the Greek Army is forced to surrender on April 23. The BEF abandons Thermopylae on April 24 for the Peloponnesus and during April 26–30 evacuates Greece altogether. Heavy equipment is simply abandoned. Many of the 43,000 troops taken off are landed on Crete.
May 20–June 1	In a large airborne operation, German forces invade and capture the island of Crete, defeating both Greek and British forces on the island.

1944

October 9	British prime minister Winston Churchill meets with Soviet leader Joseph Stalin in Moscow and concludes an agreement with him regarding the sphere of influence in Central Europe after the war. Britain is to have 90 percent influence in Greece.
October 14	British forces liberate Athens and Piraeus.
December 3	Fighting erupts in Athens when Greek government gendarmes open fire on a large pro-EAM rally called to protest a general disarmament ultimatum issued by British Army lieutenant general Sir Ronald MacKenzie Scobie that, however, excludes right-wing Greek forces. In the ensuing melee, 28 demonstrators are killed and many more are injured. This marks the beginning of the so-called Dekemvrianá (December Events, also known as the Battle of Athens). Full-scale fighting then ensues, lasting until January 3, 1945. British troops have to employ tanks to defeat the EAM and restore order. With the situation in Greece reaching crisis, British prime minister Winston Churchill and Foreign Secretary Anthony Eden confer with Greek leaders on Christmas Day in Athens, but no settlement is reached.

1945

February 12	Having lost the round of fighting in Athens, in the Treaty of Varkiza, EAM-ELAS agree to disarm in return for full participation in the political process.

1946

March 30 | Former ELAS members attack a police outpost in the village of Litrochoro and kill the policemen there, beginning the Greek Civil War.

March 31 | National elections result in a triumph for the political Right in Greece. The Greek Communist Party (KKE) had correctly pointed to a rigged election and refused to participate.

September | In a plebiscite, Greek voters approve restoration of the monarchy, and King George II returns to Greece. The voting, however, fuels animosity between the Communists and royalists.

December 3 | The Greek government complains to the United Nations Security Council that the neighboring communist states of Yugoslavia, Albania, and Bulgaria are providing military support to the communist insurgency in northern Greece.

1947

February | With its own resources exhausted and fearing that the Communist guerrilla forces might win the civil war in Greece, the British government informs the United States that it can no longer afford to support the Greek government.

March 12 | U.S. president Harry S. Truman proclaims the Truman Doctrine. Washington is shocked by the news from Britain, but on this date Truman addresses a joint session of Congress and announces what comes to be known as the Truman Doctrine, that the United States will "support free peoples who are resisting attempted subjugation by armed minorities or by outside pressures."

May | The U.S. Congress appropriates $400 million in aid for Greece and Turkey, somewhat over half this sum in military assistance.

December 25 | In the Battle of Konitsa, which ends on January 5, 1948, DSE fighters are defeated in their effort to capture a population center as the KKE seat of government.

1948

June 16–August 21 | Greek Army forces take the offensive, and in the Battle of Grammos some 70,000 Greek Army troops defeat 12,000 DSE fighters and cause the latter to withdraw into Albania.

| October 13 | Greek government forces turn back a DSE effort to capture an important ammunition depot at Zachero in the Peloponnese. |
| December 5 | The Greek government Operation PERISTERA (DOVE) commences in the Peloponnese. By the time this operations ends on January 30, 1949, some 40,000 Greek Army troops and gendarmerie forces have largely wiped out the DSE in the Peloponnese, killing some 3,500 DSE fighters and capturing another 4,000. |

1949

January	Greek Communist leaders announce that their goal is no longer the restoration of true parliamentary democracy, as they have previously stated, but instead installing a proletarian state. Its military arm, the DSE, also miscalculates, shifting from a war of attrition to a campaign to defend territory.
	In a key development also this month, Yugoslav leader Tito (Josip Broz), having split with Moscow (Yugoslavia was expelled from the Cominform the previous June), closes the border and shuts down Greek Communist camps inside his country. This is an important step, for Yugoslavia was by far the most important of the communist states supplying assistance to the Greek Communists.
August 2–30	Greek National Army commander General Alexander Papagos launches Operation TORCH, a major offensive involving some 180,000 troops against perhaps 7,000 DSE troops. The offensive largely clears northern Greece and ends in heavy DSE losses.
September	Albania announces that it will no longer permit DSE operations from its territory.
October 16	A cease-fire is declared, in effect bringing the Greek Civil War to an end, although sporadic fighting occurs into 1950.

SPENCER C. TUCKER

Further Reading

Bærentzen, Lars, John O. Iatrides, and Ole Langwitz Smith. *Studies in the History of the Greek Civil War, 1945–1949.* Copenhagen: Museum Tusculanum Press, 1987.

Carabott, Philip, and Thanasis D. Sfikas. *The Greek Civil War: Essays on a Conflict of Exceptionalism and Silences.* Burlington, VT: Ashgate, 2004.

Chandler, Geoffrey. *The Divided Land: An Anglo-Greek Tragedy.* New York: St. Martin's, 1959.

Clogg, Richard. *A Concise History of Greece.* 2nd ed. Cambridge: Cambridge University Press, 2002.

Clogg, Richard. *Greece, 1940–1949: Occupation, Resistance, Civil War; A Documentary History.* New York, 2003.

Close, David H. *The Greek Civil War, 1943–1950: Studies of Polarization.* London: Routledge, 1993.

Close, David H. *The Origins of the Greek Civil War.* New York: Longman, 1995.

Gerolymatos, André. *Red Acropolis, Black Terror: The Greek Civil War and the Origins of Soviet-American Rivalry.* New York: Basic Books, 2004.

Goulter, Christina J. M. "The Greek Civil War: A National Army's Counter-Insurgency Triumph." *Journal of Military History* 78(3) (July 2014): 1017–1055.

Goulter-Zervoudakis, Christina. "The Politicization of Intelligence: The British Experience in Greece, 1941–1944." *Intelligence and National Security* 13(1) (1998): 165–194.

Harris, William D., Jr. *Instilling Aggressiveness: U.S. Advisors and Greek Combat Leadership in the Greek Civil War, 1947–1949.* Fort Leavenworth, KS: Combat Studies Institute Press, Command and General Staff College, 2013.

Hondros, John. *Occupation and Resistance: The Greek Agony, 1941–44.* New York: Pella, 1983.

Iatrides, John O. *Greece in the 1940s: A Nation in Crisis.* Hanover, NH: University Press of New England, 1981.

Iatrides, John O. "Revolution or Self-defense? Communist Goals, Strategy, and Tactics in the Greek Civil War." *Journal of Cold War Studies* 7(3) (2005): 3–33.

Iatrides, John O., and Nicholas X. Rizopoulos. "The International Dimension of the Greek Civil War." *World Policy Journal* (March 2000): 87–103.

Kousoulas, D. G. *Revolution and Defeat: The Story of the Greek Communist Party.* New York: Oxford University Press, 1965.

Kuniholm, Bruce R. *The Origins of the Cold War: Great Power Conflict and Diplomacy in Iran, Turkey and Greece.* Princeton, NJ: Princeton University Press, 1994.

Matthews, Kenneth. *Memories of a Mountain War: Greece, 1944–1949.* London: Longmans, 1972.

Mazower, M., ed. *After the War Was Over: Reconstructing the Family, Nation and State in Greece, 1943–1960.* Princeton, NJ: Princeton University Press, 2000.

Nachmani, Amikam. *International Intervention in the Greek Civil War: The United Nations Special Committee on the Balkans, 1947–1952.* New York: Praeger, 1990.

O'Ballance, Edgar. *The Greek Civil War: 1944–1949.* New York: Praeger, 1966.

Richter, Heinz. *British Intervention in Greece: From Varkiza to Civil War, February 1945 to August 1946.* London: Merlin, 1985.

Sarafis, Stefanos. *ELAS: Greek Resistance Army.* London: Merlin, 1980.

Woodhouse, C. M. *Apple of Discord: A Survey of Recent Greek Politics in Their International Setting.* London: Hutchinson, 1948.

Woodhouse, C. M. *A Short History of Modern Greece.* New York: Praeger, 1968.

Woodhouse, C. M. *The Struggle for Greece, 1941–1949.* London: Hart-Davis, MacGibbon, 1976.

Indochina War (1946–1954)

Causes

Also known as the First Indochina War and (in contemporary Vietnam) as the Anti-French Resistance War, the Indochina War of 1946–1954 was a major event in Southeast Asian and French history. It led directly to the Vietnam War (Second Indochina War) of 1957–1975. Taken together as they should be, the two wars represent the longest conflict of the 20th century.

The European powers were interested in Indochina for reasons of religion, trade, and naval facilities. Vietnam, with its long seacoast, was especially vulnerable to European penetration. The first lasting contact between Vietnam and Europe came in 1535 with the arrival of the Portuguese. Both they and the Dutch soon established rival trading posts.

By 1615 there was also a permanent Catholic mission. French priest Alexandre de Rhodes made Catholicism a cultural force when he created *quoc ngu,* written Vietnamese with a Latin alphabet and diacritical marks. Previously Vietnamese had been written in Chinese ideographs. The French used *quoc ngu* to eliminate the political and cultural influence of Vietnamese Confucian scholars, but with it also came Western ideas of freedom and democracy.

Southeast Asia increasingly attracted European attention. The term "Indochina" is attributed to Danish cartographer Konrad Malte-Brun (1775–1826) and was applied collectively to Burma, Thailand, Tonkin, Annam, Cochinchina, Laos, and Cambodia. At the beginning of the 19th century Catholic priest Pierre Pigneau de Béhaine helped secure European mercenaries and military equipment that enabled Nguyen

Phuc Anh (from 1802, Emperor Gia Long) to reunify Vietnam. Gia Long welcomed Western military and technological assistance, but he and his successors were not interested in advancing their religion. The Vietnamese emperors regarded Catholicism as a threat to the Confucian concept of order and harmony. Catholics were not singled out, for Buddhists and Taoists were also persecuted.

The attempt by the 19th-century Vietnamese emperors to root out Christian missionaries provided the excuse for French intervention. Unfortunately for the Vietnamese, they had shown little interest in the vast improvements in weaponry since the reunification of their country, and this put them at great disadvantage in the inevitable collision with the West.

Religion may have been the excuse, but trade was a powerful motivator for the French. In the 1840s the British had taken the lead in obtaining trading concessions in China. The French soon followed suit and hoped that Vietnam might provide access to the Chinese interior by means of the Mekong and Red Rivers. In 1845 and again in 1846, French warships were sent to Vietnam to secure the release of a Catholic priest who had been imprisoned for refusing to leave the country. During the second intervention, the French sank four Vietnamese warships regarded as posing a hostile intent. Then, in August 1858, a Franco-Spanish squadron of 14 ships and 3,000 men arrived at Tourane (Da Nang). It proved to be no prize, and the expedition moved southward. On February 18, 1859, the French secured Saigon. A sleepy little

Indochina War (December 1946–July 1954)

Estimated Military Casualties

France and French Allies	Viet Minh
172,708 (94,581 dead/missing; 78,127 wounded)	520,000 (dead/missing/wounded)

Casualties for the Battle of Dien Bien Phu (March 13–May 7, 1954)

	France and French Allies	Viet Minh
Killed/Missing	1,600	7,900
Wounded	4,800	15,000

Sources: Bernard B. Fall, *Street without Joy: The French Debacle in Indochina,* revised ed. (Mechanicsburg, PA: Stackpole Books, 1994); Ted Morgan, *Valley of Death: The Tragedy at Dien Bien Phu That Led America into the Vietnam War* (New York: Random House, 2010).

fishing village, it had promise of being an excellent deepwater port. Then in 1862 the French forced Emperor Tu Duc to sign a treaty confirming their conquest. It was no accident that the French chose to penetrate Cochinchina (southern Vietnam) first; it was the newest part of the country.

By 1867 the French had conquered all of Cochinchina, and by 1887 they had control over all Indochina: Cochinchina was followed by Cambodia, Annam, and Tonkin. In 1887 they were formed into French Indochina. Laos was added in 1893. Guerrilla warfare continued in parts of the country for a time, but the last major revolt was crushed in 1913. Technically only Cochinchina was an outright colony; the others were merely protectorates. The reality was that all were ruled by a French governor-general responsible to the minister of colonies in Paris.

French administration was haphazard. Ministers of colonies and governors-general changed frequently, and with each came policy changes. Indochina also did not attract the most capable civil servants, and their salaries consumed what little money was available in the colonial budget, with little left for education or public works. The small French community

of 40,000–50,000 people dominated the economy of what was now France's richest colony.

In education the ideal was to turn the Vietnamese into a cultural copy of mainland France, but even after World War I only 10 percent of Vietnamese of school age were attending Franco-Vietnamese schools. And as late as 1940 there were only 14 secondary schools in all of Vietnam and only 1 university (at Hanoi). This produced a talented but very small native elite aspiring to positions of influence that were nonetheless closed to them. Ultimately this drove many of them to turn against France.

Vietnamese nationalist hopes were raised by the Allied victory in World War I and U.S. president Woodrow Wilson's call for self-determination of peoples. But at the Paris Peace Conference, the Vietnamese learned that this doctrine was limited to Europe. Moderate Vietnamese nationalists now took the Nationalist Party of China as their model. Their Viet Nam Quoc Dan Dang (Vietnamese Nationalist Party, VNQDD) was established in 1927.

The VNQDD led premature uprisings in 1930–1931. Although easily crushed by the French, these opened the way for the better-organized and more militant

Indochinese Communist Party (ICP), formed in 1930 in Hong Kong. By World War II the ICP, led by Ho Chi Minh, was the dominant nationalist force in Indochina.

The Japanese arrived in Indochina in 1940. Having been defeated by Germany, France was in no position to resist Tokyo's demand for bases. Ironically, this brought the United States into World War II. Japan's July 1941 move into southern Indochina meant that its long-range bombers could reach Malaya, the Dutch East Indies, and the Philippines. The United States, Great Britain, and the Netherlands imposed an embargo on scrap iron and oil to Japan, and this decision caused Tokyo to embark on war with the United States.

In May 1941, ICP leader and die-hard Vietnamese nationalist Ho Chi Minh formed the Viet Minh (Vietnam Independence League), a nationalist umbrella organization dominated by the communists, to fight the French and Japanese. The U.S. Office of Strategic Services, the forerunner of the Central Intelligence Agency, supplied limited assistance to the Viet Minh during the war.

The Japanese left the Vichy French government in Indochina in place, but as the conflict neared its end, the French were determined to liberate themselves. With these plans an open secret, the Japanese struck first. On March 9, 1945, they arrested virtually all French administrators and military personnel. Tokyo created a further problem for France by declaring Vietnam independent under Emperor Bao Dai.

With the defeat of Japan, Ho moved into the vacuum. On August 16, 1945, in Hanoi, he declared himself president of a "free Vietnam," and on September 2 he proclaimed the independence of the Democratic Republic of Vietnam (North Vietnam, DRV).

Vietnamese nationalist leader Ho Chi Minh, founder of the Indochinese Communist Party (in 1930) and president of the Democratic Republic of Vietnam, reading the proclamation of independence before an estimated half million people in Ba Dinh Square in Hanoi, September 2, 1945. (AFP via Getty Images)

World War II marked the end of European colonialism. French leaders, however, chose not to embrace the inevitable and seek accommodation with nationalist leaders. The result was a missed opportunity for orderly transition to self-rule and a close relationship with France. It is hard for the weak to be generous, and only with its empire could France hope in 1945 to continue as a Great Power.

According to the July 1945 Potsdam Agreement, the British were to take the surrender of Japanese troops south of the 16th parallel, while Chinese Nationalist troops would do the same north of that line. The British released French troops from Japanese camps, and Paris sent reinforcements to reestablish its control over southern Vietnam, Cambodia, and Laos. The French also arranged a Chinese withdrawal from North Vietnam. In October, General Jacques-Philippe Leclerc arrived in Saigon to assume command of French forces in Indochina. Reinforcements came with him.

In January 1946 Ho carried out elections in northern Vietnam. Although these were not entirely free, there could be no doubt that he had won. With the United States and the Soviet Union refusing involvement, Ho was forced, however, to deal with France, and in March 1946 he worked out an agreement with French diplomat Jean Sainteny under which the French recognized North Vietnam as a free and independent state within the French Union. France was allowed to send a limited number of troops into North Vietnam to protect its interests, although all were to be withdrawn over a five-year period. Paris also accepted the principle of a united Vietnam by agreeing to a plebiscite in southern Vietnam over whether it would join North Vietnam.

French high commissioner for Indochina Georges Thierry d'Argenlieu refused to allow the promised southern plebiscite. In a direct appeal to Paris, Ho led a delegation to France. By the time it had arrived, however, the French government had fallen. June elections weakened the Left, the socialists lost seats, and the communists, who were in the government, were trying to demonstrate their patriotism. As a result, during the ensuing Fontainebleau Conference (July 6–September 10, 1946) Paris made no concessions to the Vietnamese. D'Argenlieu had meanwhile, on his own initiative, proclaimed the independence of southern Vietnam as the "Republic of Cochinchina."

D'Argenlieu's action violated the Ho-Sainteny Agreement and left Vietnamese leaders feeling betrayed. Although there is still disagreement on this point, Ho was probably a nationalist first and a communist second. Given the long antagonistic relationship between Vietnam and China, he might have become an Asian Tito. But in September, Ho left Paris predicting war.

Tensions were already high in Vietnam when, in November 1946, the French sent a war crimes commission to Lang Son to investigate a mass grave of French soldiers killed by the Japanese in March 1945. On November 20 an armed clash occurred between French troops escorting the commission and Vietnamese. Each side blamed the other. This was overshadowed by a more ominous event the same day at Tonkin's principal part of Haiphong. The French Navy had virtually blockaded Haiphong, and a patrol vessel seized a Chinese junk attempting to smuggle contraband. Vietnamese soldiers on the shore fired on the French ship, and shooting occurred in the city itself. Peace was restored on the 22nd on a French pledge to respect Vietnamese sovereignty and the separation of forces within Haiphong.

At the time, High Commissioner d'Argenlieu was in Paris. Securing permission from Premier George Bidault to use force (Bidault probably did not realize this was imminent), d'Argenlieu cabled Vietnam and ordered a subordinate to "give a severe lesson to those who have treacherously attacked you. Use all the means at your disposal to make yourself complete master of Haiphong and so bring the Vietnamese army around to a better understanding of the situation."

On November 23, following expiration of a two-hour warning, the French opened an air, land, and sea bombardment of targets in Haiphong, with most of the firepower delivered by the cruiser *Suffren*. Estimates of the number killed in the shelling and ensuing panic vary widely, but there were probably 500 to 1,000 killed.

Although the fighting ended on November 28, whatever hopes for peace remaining had been irretrievably shattered. On December 19 the French demanded the disarmament of the Tu Ve, the Viet Minh militia in Hanoi. That night fear and mistrust, fueled by bloodshed and broken promises, erupted into all-out war.

SPENCER C. TUCKER

Course

In September 1945, before leaving Paris, Vietnamese nationalist Ho Chi Minh had talked to an American reporter and predicted both an early start of war and how it would be fought and would end. He said that it would be the war of the tiger and the elephant. The tiger could not meet the elephant in an equal contest, so he would lay in wait for it, drop on its back from the jungle, and rip huge hunks of flesh with his claws. Eventually, the elephant would bleed to death. The war played out very much along those lines.

The French did not fight the Indochina War primarily for economic reasons; indeed, by 1950 French military expenditures surpassed the total value of all French investments there. The chief reasons were political and psychological. Perhaps only with its empire could France be counted a Great Power. Colonial advocates also argued that concessions in Indochina would impact other overseas possessions, especially in North Africa, and that further losses would soon follow. French leaders also launched the domino theory. As General Jean de Lattre de Tassigny phrased it during a trip to Washington, D.C., in September 1951,

"Once Tongking [*sic*] is lost, there is no barrier until Suez." Such reasoning resurfaced during the Vietnam War.

The DRV leadership planned for a long war. The Viet Minh's chief appeal was its stated goal of ridding the country of foreigners. Vo Nguyen Giap had command of the DRV's military forces, formed in May 1945 as the Vietnam Liberation Army and later the People's Army of Vietnam (PAVN), also known as the Vietnam People's Army and the North Vietnamese Army. This former Lycée history teacher, self-taught in war, commanded the PAVN for 30 years. Ho and Giap wanted it to appeal to as many Vietnamese as possible. They imposed strict rules, including a 10-part oath that included a pledge to respect, help, and protect the people, with soldiers always to be on their best behavior. Giap believed that successful warfare grew out of correct political views.

Reportedly Giap visited Mao Zedong (Mao Tse-tung) in 1941 and learned what he could about revolutionary war from the Chinese Communist leader. Certainly Giap was much influenced by Mao's writings. Giap's *People's War, People's Army* is largely a restatement of Maoist ideas with these fighting principles added on: "If the enemy advances, we retreat; if he halts, we harass; if he avoids battle, we attack; if he retreats, we follow." Giap's strategy was, however, eclectic. If it worked, he utilized it. His chief contribution to revolutionary warfare was his assessment of political and psychological difficulties that confront a democracy in waging a protracted and inconclusive war. Public opinion would at some point, he believed, demand an end to the bloodshed, and political leaders would find themselves promising an early end to the fighting. Giap would made mistakes, chiefly in going over to the third phase of large-unit warfare too soon, but he also showed the capacity to learn from and not repeat his mistakes. Certainly he proved adroit in logistics, timing, surprise, and deception.

Giap had no shortage of recruits. Weapons were another matter. Through 1949 the PAVN had only about 83,000 of all types. Perhaps a third were homemade, another third were World War II–vintage Japanese or OSS-supplied weapons, and the other third were purchased abroad in Thailand or Hong Kong. The DRV also purchased communications equipment from the Chinese Nationalist troops before their departure from northern Vietnam. In 1946 the DRV established training schools for officers and noncommissioned officers.

French military commander in Indochina General Jacques-Philippe Leclerc had in late 1945 used his small yet mobile force of about 40,000 men to move swiftly and secure southern Vietnam and Cambodia. The Viet Minh were soon forced out into the countryside, and life returned to normal, or almost so. There were those who dreaded the Viet Minh's retreat into the jungle. Leclerc was one; he was convinced that the Viet Minh was a nationalist movement that France could not subdue militarily. Unlike most of his compatriots, he was aware of the great difficulties of jungle warfare and favored negotiations. In a secret report to Paris, Leclerc said that there would be no solution through force in Indochina.

Although the French Socialist Party showed interest in ending the war through peace talks, the steady drift to the right of the French coalition government and increasing bloodshed prevented this. French high commissioner to Indochina Admiral Georges Thierry d'Argenlieu and other French colonial administrators opposed any meaningful concessions to the nationalists, and in the summer of 1946 Leclerc departed Indochina in frustration.

Leclerc was but the first in a succession of French military commanders. He was followed by Generals Jean-Etienne Valluy, Roger Blaizot, Marcel Carpentier, Jean de Lattre de Tassigny, Raoul Salan, Henri Navarre, and Paul Henri Romuald Ely. The frequent change in commanders undoubtedly affected the overall efficiency and morale of the French Far East Expeditionary Force.

Most French leaders assumed that the conflict would be little more than a classic colonial reconquest, securing the population centers and then expanding outward in the classic "oil slick" (*tache d'huile*) method that had worked effectively in Morocco and Algeria. Meanwhile, the Viet Minh steadily grew in strength and came to control more and more territory.

In May 1947 the French did make an effort at ending the war through negotiation when Paul Mus traveled from Hanoi to meet with Ho in the latter's jungle headquarters. Mus was an Asian scholar sympathetic to the Vietnamese nationalist point of view and a personal adviser to Emile Bollaert, who had replaced d'Argenlieu as high commissioner. Mus told Ho that France would agree to a cease-fire on condition that the Viet Minh lay down some of their arms, permit French troops freedom of movement in their zones, and turn over some deserters from the French Foreign Legion. Ho rejected this offer, which was tantamount to surrender, and in May Bollaert declared that "France will remain in Indochina."

Despite its stated determination to hold on to Indochina, the French government never made the commitment in manpower necessary for the army to win. The war was essentially fought by the professional soldiers: officers and noncommissioned officers who led the French Expeditionary Corps. The French government never allowed draftees to be sent to Indochina. The small number of men available to French commanders left them very few options. A shortage of noncommissioned officers, a lack of trained intelligence officers and interpreters, and little interest in or knowledge of the mechanics of pacification all hampered the French military effort.

The French held much of Cochinchina in large part because of the powerful religious sects and Buddhists there who opposed the Viet Minh. The French also controlled the Red River Delta in the north, along with the capital of Hanoi. But the Viet Minh controlled much of the countryside, and the area they dominated grew as time went on. Initially, the Viet Minh largely withdrew into the jungle to indoctrinate and train their troops. The French invested little attention and resources to pacification efforts, and their heavy-handedness alienated many Vietnamese. The French scenario had the Viet Minh eventually tiring of their cause and giving up, but it never played out that way.

To increase available manpower, attract Vietnamese nationalist support, and quiet critics at home and in the United States, Paris sought to provide at least the facade of an indigenous Vietnamese regime as a competitor to the Viet Minh. After several years of negotiations, in March 1949 the French government concluded the Elysée Agreements with former emperor Bao Dai. These created the State of Vietnam (SVN), and Paris made the key concession that Vietnam was in fact one country.

The SVN allowed the French government to portray the war as a conflict between a free Vietnam and the communists—and

thus not a colonial war at all. Washington, which supported France in Indochina because it needed French military assistance in Europe, claimed to be convinced.

The problem for Vietnamese nationalists was that the SVN never truly was independent. The French continued to control all of its institutions, and its promised army never really materialized. France simply took the recruited soldiers and added them to the French Far East Expeditionary Corps, where they were commanded by French officers. In effect, there were only two choices for the Vietnamese: either the Viet Minh or the French. The French drove the nationalists into the Viet Minh camp.

In October 1947 the French mounted Operation LEA. Involving some 15,000 men and conducted over a three-week period, it was devoted almost exclusively to the capture of Ho Chi Minh and the Viet Minh leadership and destruction of their main battle units. Operation LEA involved 17 French battalions, and while it took Thai Nguyen and some other Viet Minh–controlled cities, it failed to capture the Viet Minh leadership and destroy the main communist units. It also showed the paucity of French resources in Indochina. The troops in LEA were badly needed elsewhere, and their employment in the operation opened up much of the countryside to Viet Minh penetration. As time went on the military situation continued to deteriorate for the French, despite the fact that by the end of 1949 Paris had expended $1.5 billion on the war.

The Indochina War changed dramatically in the fall of 1949 when the communists came to power in China. That event and the recognition of the DRV by the People's Republic of China (PRC), while helping to change Washington's attitude toward the war, in effect signaled that the war was lost for the French. The long Chinese-Vietnamese border allowed the Chinese to supply arms and equipment to the PAVN, and China provided cross-border sanctuaries where the Viet Minh could train and replenish their troops. And there were plenty of arms available from the substantial stocks of weapons, including artillery, that the United States had previously supplied to the Chinese Nationalists.

The Korean War, which began in June 1950, profoundly affected the U.S. attitude toward the war in Indochina. Korea and Vietnam came to be viewed as mutually dependent theaters in a common Western struggle against communism. Washington recognized the SVN and changed its policy of providing only indirect assistance. In June 1950 President Harry S. Truman announced that the United States would provide direct military aid to the French in Indochina and also establish a military assistance and advisory group there. By the end of the Indochina War in 1954, the United States had furnished $2.5 billion in military aid to the French and was underwriting three-quarters of the war's cost.

The French insisted that all U.S. military assistance be given directly to them rather than channeled through the SVN. Although the Vietnamese National Army was established in 1951, it remained effectively under French control, and France continued to dominate the SVN down to the end. Regardless, the Truman and Dwight D. Eisenhower administrations assured the American people that real authority had been handed over to the Vietnamese.

The Indochina War became an endless quagmire. By 1950, it was costing France between 40 and 45 percent of its entire military budget and more than 10 percent of the national budget. During September–October 1950 the Viet Minh

mounted Operation LE HONG PHONG and secured control of Route Coloniale (Colonial Highway) 4. The highway paralleled the Chinese frontier and ran from the Gulf of Tonkin to Cao Bang. In the fighting the Viet Minh captured sufficient weapons to equip an entire division. The loss of this critical frontier section gave the Viet Minh ready access to China. For all practical purposes, France had lost the war. That it was allowed to continue is proof of the lack of political leadership in Paris.

Giap now believed that circumstances were ripe for conventional large-unit warfare, and he took the offensive beginning on January 13, 1951, with Operations TRAN HUNG DAO, HOANG HOA THAM, and HA NAM NINH. These lasted until June 18 and were designed to secure Hanoi and the Red River Delta. The PAVN was, however, stopped cold by French forces led by General Jean de Lattre de Tassigny, probably the most capable of French commanders during the war. After these rebuffs, Giap simply shifted back to his phase-two strategy of engaging the French in circumstances of his own choosing.

Late that year de Lattre initiated a battle outside the important Red River Delta area. What became the Battle of Hoa Binh (November 14, 1951–February 24, 1952) was a meat-grinder battle as de Lattre envisioned but for both sides. By the end of the battle, the PAVN had paid a heavy price but had also learned how to deal with French tactics and had penetrated the French defensive ring as never before.

Giap now undertook the conquest of the Thai Highlands in northwestern Vietnam. By the end of November 1952, PAVN units had reached the Lao border. New French commander General Raoul Salan tried to halt this offensive by striking at PAVN supply lines. But Giap refused to take the bait, and Operation LORRAINE (October 29–November 8), which involved 30,000 French troops in special airborne, commando, and support formations, was soon in reverse. By December, PAVN units were still at the Lao border, and the French were back within their heavily fortified defenses in the Red River Delta.

The Viet Minh also made significant gains in central Vietnam. French control in the plateau area of the Central Highlands was narrowed to a few beachheads around Hue, Da Nang, and Nha Trang. The only areas where the French enjoyed real success were in Cochinchina and neighboring Cambodia.

In the spring of 1953, Giap assembled a powerful force to invade Laos. Laos had an army of only 10,000 men supported by 3,000 French regulars. Giap employed four divisions totaling 40,000 men and had the assistance of 4,000 communist Pathet Lao troops. Once more, the French were compelled to disperse their slender resources. They were, however, successful in preventing Giap from overrunning the Plaine des Jarres, and by late April the French halted the PAVN and inflicted heavy casualties on it. The onset of the rainy season forced the PAVN to fall back on its bases, and Laos was saved for another summer.

In July 1953, new French commander General Henri Navarre arrived in Indochina. Buoyed by pledges of increased U.S. military assistance, Navarre attempted a "general counteroffensive." The press in both France and the United States made much of the so-called Navarre Plan, but unknown to the public was Navarre's secret pessimistic assessment to his government that the war could not be won militarily and the best that could be hoped for was a draw.

With increased resources (French forces now numbered about 517,000 men against perhaps 120,000 Viet Minh), Navarre vowed to take the offensive. He ordered the evacuation of a series of small posts and gave more responsibility to the SVN's army, although this was too little, too late.

Concurrently, Giap was gathering additional resources for a larger invasion of Laos. With five divisions he hoped to secure all Laos and perhaps Cambodia, then join up with PAVN units in the south for an assault on Saigon. In the meantime, some 60,000 guerrillas and five regular regiments would tie down the French in the north. In December 1953 and January 1954, the PAVN overran much of southern and central Laos.

Navarre's response was the establishment of an airhead in far northwestern Vietnam astride the main PAVN invasion route into Laos. Navarre envisioned this either as a blocking position or as bait to draw enemy forces into a set-piece conventional battle, in which they would be destroyed by French artillery and airpower. The location that Navarre selected, the village of Dien Bien Phu, was in a large valley, with the French conceding the high ground around it to the PAVN. When he was asked later how he got into this position, Navarre said that at the time the French arrived PAVN forces did not have artillery, so there was no danger from the heights. Dien Bien Phu was also some 200 miles by air from Hanoi, and the French had only a very limited transport airlift capability of some 100 aircraft.

Giap took the bait, but he sent four divisions to Dien Bien Phu rather than the one that Navarre had envisioned. The siege of the French fortress lasted from March 13 to May 7, 1954, and its outcome was largely decided by the PAVN's ability to bring Chinese-supplied artillery to the heights thanks to an extensive supply

The March 13, 1954 successful Viet Minh assault on French outpost Beatrice (Him Lam Hill) during the Battle of Dien Bien Phu. (Apic/Getty Images)

network of coolies (the "People's Porters," Giap called them) and the inadequacy of French air support. On May 7, the French garrison surrendered. Although there was some debate in Washington over possible U.S. military intervention (Operation VUL-TURE), President Eisenhower rejected it because the British refused to go along.

The defeat at Dien Bien Phu allowed French political leaders in Paris to shift the blame to the generals and at last bring the war to an end in a conference previously scheduled in Geneva to deal with a variety of Asian problems. The war formally ended on August 1, 1954.

SPENCER C. TUCKER

Consequences

On June 17, 1954, Indochinese War critic Pierre Mendès-France became French premier and foreign minister. Three days later he imposed a 30-day timetable for an agreement by the Geneva Conference (April 21–July 20) and promised to resign if one was not reached. The Geneva Accords were signed on the last day of the deadline, July 20 (but only because the clocks were stopped; it was actually early on July 21).

The leading personalities at Geneva were Mendès-France, Chinese foreign minister Zhou Enlai, Soviet foreign minister Vyacheslav Molotov, British secretary of state for foreign affairs Anthony Eden, U.S. secretary of state John Foster Dulles, DRV foreign minister Pham Van Dong, and SVN foreign minister Nguyen Quoc Dinh. Dulles left the conference after only a few days. He saw no likelihood of an agreement regarding Indochina that Washington could approve, and he disliked the idea of negotiating with Zhou Enlai, as the

Battle of Dien Bien Phu, March 13, 1954

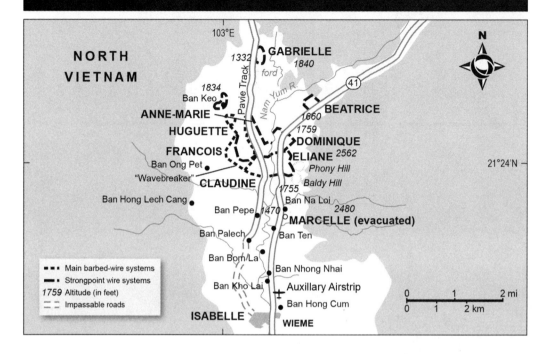

United States did not then recognize the PRC. Dulles ordered the U.S. delegation not to participate in the discussions and to act only as observers.

The Geneva Conference produced separate armistice agreements for Vietnam, Cambodia, and Laos. Pham Van Dong found himself pressured by Zhou and Molotov into an agreement that gave the Viet Minh far less than it had won on the battlefield. The conferees established Vietnam as one state, temporarily divided at the 17th parallel pending reunification. A demilitarized zone would extend three miles (five kilometers) on either side of the line in order to prevent incidents that might lead to a breach of the armistice. The final text provided that "the military demarcation line is provisional and should not in any way be interpreted as constituting a political or territorial boundary."

Vietnam's future was to be determined "on the basis of respect for the principles of independence, unity, and territorial integrity," with "national and general elections" to be held in July 1956. Troops on both sides would have up to 300 days to be regrouped north or south; civilians could also move in either direction if they so desired. The International Supervisory and Control Commission composed of representatives of Canada, Poland, and India (a Western state, a communist state, and a nonaligned state) would oversee implementation of the agreements.

Pham Van Dong was bitterly disappointed that nationwide elections were put off for two years. The DRV accepted the arrangements because of heavy pressure from the PRC and the Soviet Union and because it was confident it could control south Vietnam. There is every reason to believe that the Chinese leadership was willing at Geneva to sabotage its ally in order to prevent the formation of a strong regional power on their southern border.

The Indochina War had really been three wars in one. Begun as a conflict between Vietnamese nationalists and France, it became a civil war between Vietnamese and was also part of the larger Cold War. In the war the French and their allies sustained 172,708 casualties: 94,581 dead or missing and 78,127 wounded. These broke down as 140,992 French Union casualties (75,867 dead or missing and 65,125 wounded), with the allied Indochina states losing 31,716 (18,714 dead or missing and 13,002 wounded). French dead or missing numbered some 20,000: 11,000 French Legionnaires, 15,000 Africans, and 46,000 Indochinese. The war took a particularly heavy toll among the officers, 1,900 of whom died. PAVN losses were probably three times those of the French and their allies. Perhaps 150,000 Vietnamese civilians also perished.

One major issue throughout the war and for some years afterward was that of prisoners held by the Viet Minh, both military and civilian. Their status was always ambiguous because they were more hostages than prisoners of war, especially as the Viet Minh did not recognize the Geneva Convention regarding prisoners of war. Their prisoners were held in barbarous conditions throughout the war and beginning in 1950 were subjected to intensive political reeducation. Only a small percentage of the 36,979 reported missing during the war returned. Depending on the source, the number of confirmed prisoners in the summer of 1954 was between 21,526 and 22,474. Only 10,754 returned home, and 6,132 of them required immediate hospitalization. Some civilians were held for up to eight years.

Regroupment of the 120,000-man French Far East Expeditionary Corps from Tonkin and 140,000 PAVN soldiers and guerrillas from the south proceeded without incident. The French had 100 days to withdraw to Haiphong and an additional 200 days to reembark for the south. At the same time PAVN units in central and southern Vietnam carried out their own regroupment. Many northerners also took advantage of the article of the accords that allowed them free passage south during a 300-day regroupment period. The great majority of these were Roman Catholics from the Red River Delta area who often moved as entire communities. Minorities, such as the Nungs, also left. The U.S. Navy provided substantial sealift support in what was a considerable propaganda windfall for the SVN.

Former Vietnamese emperor Bao Dai, then in France, appointed Catholic politician Ngo Dinh Diem as premier of the SVN. Soon Diem brought a semblance of order, subduing the religious sects in the south and armed gangs in Saigon. His power base rested on the some 1 million northern Catholics who had relocated south.

Disagreements with Bao Dai led Diem to stage a referendum in October 1955 in which he called on the people of South Vietnam to choose between Bao Dai and himself. Diem won the vote handily, although this did not keep him from manipulating the result to make it a landslide. He then proclaimed the establishment of the Republic of Vietnam (South Vietnam, RVN), with himself as president. Diem held power until his assassination in November 1963. Claiming that he was not bound by the Geneva Accords, he refused to hold the promised elections and received strong support for his stand from President Eisenhower. When the date for the elections passed, Viet Minh political cadres in South Vietnam resumed the armed struggle, this time against the Diem government. Diem, meanwhile, received substantial economic aid and increasing military assistance from the United States.

In North Vietnam, Ho and other leaders were not displeased with Diem's establishment of order in South Vietnam pending the national elections. North Vietnam did face serious economic problems, for while North Vietnam contained the bulk of the industry, South Vietnam had most of the food. Ruthless moves against small landholders brought actual rebellion, crushed by PAVN troops. Then when the Viet Minh cadres left in the south to prepare for the 1956 election commenced armed struggle against Diem, the North Vietnamese leadership voted to support them, beginning the Vietnam War. The war would be extraordinarily costly to North Vietnam economically and in terms of casualties, but the desire to reunify the country overrode all other considerations. The civil war and the East-West conflict of the First Indochina War had only been suspended.

SPENCER C. TUCKER

Timeline

1615

By this date a permanent Catholic mission is established in Vietnam.

1859

February 18

The French take possession of Saigon in Cochinchina.

1862

Vietnamese emperor Tu Duc is forced to sign a treaty with the French recognizing their conquests.

1867

By this year the French have established their control over all of Cochinchina.

1887

France establishes French Indochina, consisting of Cochinchina, Annam, Tonkin (all constituting present-day Vietnam), and Cambodia.

1893

The addition of Laos completes French Indochina.

1927

December 27

Vietnamese nationalists establish in Hanoi the Viet Nam Quoc Dan Dang (Vietnamese Nationalist Party, VNQDD), modeled after the Nationalist Party of China.

1930

February 3

In a meeting in Hong Kong presided over by Ho Chi Minh, Vietnamese nationalists establish the Indochinese Communist Party (ICP), also known as the Lao Dong Party.

1930–1931

The VNQDD carries out a series of unsuccessful revolts in northern Vietnam. These failures and the arrest of participants open the way for the better-organized and more militant ICP.

1941

May

ICP leader and die-hard Vietnamese nationalist Ho Chi Minh forms the Viet Minh (Vietnam Independence League), a nationalist umbrella organization dominated by the communists, to fight the French and Japanese.

1945

March 9

With the end of World War II in the offing, the French in Indochina plan to liberate Indochina themselves. The Japanese learn of this and strike first, arresting and placing in prison camps most French administrative and military personnel.

May

The Vietnam Liberation Army is formed in northern Vietnam. Commanded by Vo Nguyen Giap, it becomes the People's Army of Vietnam (PAVN), also known as the Vietnam People's Army and the North Vietnamese Army.

August 16

In Hanoi, Ho declares himself president of a "free Vietnam."

September 2

Ho proclaims the independence of North Vietnam.

October 5

French general Jacques-Philippe Leclerc arrives in Saigon to take command of French forces in Indochina.

1946

January

Ho's supporters win elections in northern Vietnam.

March

With no support from the Soviet Union or the United States forthcoming and forced to deal with the French, Ho concludes the Ho-Sainteny Agreement with French diplomat Jean Sainteny. Paris recognizes North Vietnam as a free and independent state within the French Union and is allowed to send a limited number of troops into North Vietnam to protect its interests there, although all are to be withdrawn during a five-year period. Paris also accepts the principle of a united Vietnam by agreeing to a plebiscite in southern Vietnam as to whether it will join the Democratic Republic of Vietnam (DRV).

June 1

French high commissioner for Indochina Georges Thierry d'Argenlieu on his own initiative proclaims the formation of the "Republic of Cochinchina."

July 6–September 10	At the Fontainebleau Conference in France, the French government makes no concessions to the DRV.
November 20	Armed clashes between Vietnamese and the French occur at Lang Son and at Haiphong.
November 23	On French high commissioner for Indochina d'Argenlieu's order, French forces bombard part of Haiphong, with most of the damage inflicted by shells from the French cruiser *Suffren*.
December 19	After the French demand the disarmament of the Tu Ve Vietnamese militia, fighting begins in the capital city of Hanoi, marking the beginning of the First Indochina War. Vo Nguyen Giap commands the PAVN, the military arm of the Viet Minh.

1947

May	Peace talks between French representative Paul Mus and Ho fail to reach agreement.
October	The French mount Operation LEA, an effort to capture the DRV leadership that fails in that aim.

1949

March 8	The French government concludes the Elysée Agreements with former emperor Bao Dai. These create the State of Vietnam (SVN), with Paris conceding that Vietnam is in fact one country.
October 1	Chinese Communist leader Mao Zedong proclaims the establishment of the People's Republic of China.

1950

January 30	The Soviet Union recognizes the DRV.
June 25	The Korean War begins.
September–October	The PAVN mounts Operation LE HONG PHONG, securing much of Route Coloniale 4 in far northern Vietnam. This enables them to be supplied by China. In effect, the French have lost the war.

1951

January 13–June 18	Giap mounts a series of offensives in Operations TRAN HUNG DAO, HOANG HOA THAM, and HA NAM NINH, designed to secure Hanoi and the Red River Delta. They are halted by French forces commanded by General Jean de Lattre de Tassigny.

November 14	The Battle of Hoa Binh begins. Initiated by de Lattre, it ends on February 24, 1952, with the French proclaiming victory, but both sides suffer heavy casualties.

1952

October 29–November 8	French commander in Indochina General Raoul Salan initiates Operation LORRAINE against Viet Minh supply areas, but Giap is undeterred and continues offensive operations in northwestern Vietnam.

1954

March 13–May 7	The Viet Minh lay siege to the French strongpoint of Dien Bien Phu in northwestern Vietnam. It ends with the surrender of the French. This resounding military defeat allows the politicians in France to end the war.
April 21–July 20	An international conference held in Geneva, Switzerland, ends the Indochina War. The conference establishes Vietnam as one state, temporarily divided at the 17th parallel, pending national elections in 1956.
July 7	Emperor Bao Dai appoints Ngo Dinh Diem premier of the SVN.

1955

July	Diem announces that the SVN will not participate in the elections mandated by the 1954 Geneva Accords. He is supported in this stance by U.S. president Dwight D. Eisenhower.
October 23	Diem holds a referendum in South Vietnam in which the voters overwhelming approve the establishment of a Republic of Vietnam, with him as president.

1956

July	The date for the elections to reunify Vietnam passes without them being held.

1957

	Viet Minh cadres left in South Vietnam to prepare for the elections reject Diem's refusal to hold the election to reunify Vietnam and take up arms. They receive the support of the DRV, and by this date the Second Indochina War, better known as the Vietnam War, is under way.

SPENCER C. TUCKER

Further Reading

Buttinger, Joseph. *A Dragon Defiant: A Short History of Vietnam.* New York: Praeger, 1972.

Devillers, Philippe, and Jean Lacouture. *End of a War: Indochina, 1954.* New York: Praeger, 1969.

Duiker, William J. *The Communist Road to Power in Vietnam.* Boulder, CO: Westview, 1981.

Dunn, Peter M. *The First Vietnam War.* New York: St. Martin's, 1985.

Dunstan, Simon. *Vietnam Tracks: Armor in Battle, 1945–75.* New York: Osprey, 2004.

Fall, Bernard B. *Hell in a Very Small Place: The Siege of Dienbienphu.* Philadelphia: J. B. Lippincott, 1966.

Fall, Bernard B. *Street without Joy.* Harrisburg, PA: Stackpole, 1961.

Fall, Bernard B. *The Two Vietnams.* New York: Praeger, 1964.

Giap, Vo Nguyen. *The Military Art of People's War.* New York: Monthly Review Press, 1970.

Gras, General Yves. *Histoire de La Guerre d'Indochine.* Paris: Éditions Denoël, 1992.

Hammer, Ellen J. *The Struggle for Indochina.* Stanford, CA: Stanford University Press, 1954.

Jian, Chen. "China and the First Indo-China War, 1950–54." *China Quarterly* 133 (March 1993): 85–110.

Kelly, George A. *Lost Soldiers: The French Army and Empire in Crisis, 1947–1962.* Cambridge, MA: MIT Press, 1965.

Le Thanh Khoi. *Le Viet-Nam: Histoire et civilisation.* Paris: Éditions de Minuit, 1955.

Maneli, Mieczyslaw. *The War of the Vanquished.* New York: Harper and Row, 1969.

Marr, David G. *Vietnam 1945: The Quest for Power.* Berkeley: University of California Press, 1995.

Marr, David G. *Vietnamese Tradition on Trial, 1920–1945.* Berkeley: University of California Press, 1981.

Porch, Douglas. *The French Foreign Legion: A Complete History of the Legendary Fighting Force.* New York: HarperCollins, 1991.

Roy, Jules. *The Battle of Dienbienphu.* New York: Pyramid Books, 1963.

Schulzinger, Robert D. *A Time for War: The United States and Vietnam, 1941–1975.* New York: Oxford University Press, 1997.

Tønnesson, Stein. *Vietnam 1946: How the War Began.* Berkeley: University of California Press, 2010.

Tucker, Spencer C. *Vietnam.* Lexington: University Press of Kentucky, 1999.

Vaïsse, Maurice, and Alain Bizard, eds. *L'Armée française dans la guerre d'Indochine (1946–1954): Adaptation ou Inadaptation?* Centre d'Études d'Histoire de la Défense. Bruxelles: Complexe, 2000.

Windrow, Martin. *The French Indochina War, 1946–1954.* London: Osprey, 1998.

Indo-Pakistani Wars (1947–1949, 1965, 1971)

Causes

Immediately after the 1947 division of the Indian subcontinent into the independent states of India and Pakistan, the two countries engaged in the first of what was to be a series of wars and smaller armed clashes. There were three major wars during 1947, 1965, and 1971 as well as one undeclared war in 1999 and a series of smaller border clashes. The wars have been fought for a number of reasons, but the principal one is which country should control Kashmir.

Indian civilization can be traced back to Indus Valley settlements around Harappa and Mohenjo-daro in present-day Pakistan more than 4,000 years ago. Successive waves of invaders, from Indo-Europeans to Turko-Afghans, added linguistic and religious influences to Indian culture. Four different religions—Hinduism, Buddhism, Jainism, and Sikhism—originated on the subcontinent, while Zoroastrianism, Judaism, Christianity, and Islam were transplanted here. During 1526–1857 most of the subcontinent was under the sway of the Mughal Empire, whose rulers of Mongol and Chagati-Turkic origin were Muslim.

The Portuguese were the first Europeans to arrive. They established coastal trading posts in the late 15th century, but it was the British who came to exercise control. The British East India Company was established in the early 18th century, and in a rather amazing development, through adroit leadership and enterprise coupled with superior weaponry, this private company defeated the rival French and native princely rulers and established its control over the entire subcontinent. The 1857 Sepoy Revolt (known in India as the First Indian War of Independence), however, prompted the British Crown to assume responsibility for administering British India. On May 1, 1876, at the height of British rule, Queen Victoria took the title "Empress of India." A small but talented British administration, working largely through the native princely rulers, was able to play one against the other and dominate the affairs of the entire subcontinent.

The days of British rule were numbered, however. Western education, increased contact by Indians with the rest of the world through trade and war, and modern nationalism all worked to undermine the British position. Resistance to British rule gradually took root in the 1870s among the Western-educated Indian elite. The Indian National Congress (INC) was its principal vehicle. It was established in 1885 by British civil servants to enable a Westernized Indian elite to engage in gentlemanly discourse with their British rulers.

As with other colonial areas of the world, India experienced a wave of nationalism as a result of World War I. This was in part based on the sizable Indian Army contribution to the Allied victory but also on the concept of self-rule that gained wide currency in the developing world thanks to such declarations as the call for the "self-determination of peoples" by U.S. president Woodrow Wilson in his Fourteen Points of 1918. (As with the Chinese, the Indians were to be disappointed to learn at the Paris Peace Conference of 1919 that "self-determination" applied only to Europe.)

Indian nationalism had gained considerable strength, however, and Mohandas

Karamchand Gandhi led an increasingly successful campaign of noncooperation based on civil disobedience and passive resistance to British rule. As a result, in 1935 the British government conceded a degree of provincial autonomy in the Government of India Act. In the crisis leading up to World War II and in the conflict itself, Gandhi continued to espouse nonviolence. Gandhi, a Hindu, also insisted on India's territorial integrity, while the All-India Muslim League led by Muhammad Ali Jinnah questioned whether a Hindu-majority state would indeed protect the rights of its Muslim minority. He argued instead for an independent Muslim state.

During World War II, with Great Britain stretched to the limit and in desperate need of Indian support as the Japanese threatening an invasion of India, in March 1942 British prime minister Winston Churchill dispatched to India Sir Stafford Cripps, leader of the House of Commons. Cripps brought a pledge by the British government of what amounted to Indian independence through dominion status following the defeat of Japan. But the plan also contained a clause to the effect that no part of the Indian Empire would be forced to join the postwar dominion, and this could clearly be interpreted as supporting the creation of an independent Muslim state.

Gandhi strongly opposed the British proposal owing to the possibility of separate Hindu and Muslim states. Indeed, in August 1942 Gandhi called on the British simply to quit India immediately. This brought his arrest, along with that of most of the INC leadership. Gandhi's decision played directly into the hands of Jinnah. His Muslim League strongly supported the Allied war effort and thereby greatly advanced the possibility of the creation of a separate Muslim state in the Indian subcontinent after the war.

The Labour Party won the July 1945 British elections, and much to the chagrin of Churchill and the Conservative Party, it pledged the creation of a single independent Indian state by June 1948. To placate Muslim concerns, the new independent India was to be a federated state with a weak central government. In February 1947 Viscount Louis Mountbatten was named viceroy of India to oversee the transition.

Unfortunately for the British plan, Mountbatten could not get the Indian politicians to agree on a constitutional framework. Failing this and despite the strong opposition of Gandhi and other Hindu leaders, Mountbatten announced that there would be two states on the Indian subcontinent: a Hindu India and a Muslim Pakistan. Mountbatten was subsequently much criticized for the haste with which the partition was carried out, but on August 15, 1947, Great Britain granted independence to the Union of India and the Dominion of Pakistan.

Partition was accompanied by communal and sectarian violence on a massive scale especially in the Punjab region, where arbitrary boundary lines caused chaos, separating farms from markets and factories from the raw materials they needed to operate. The allocation of assets (settled at a ratio of four to one in favor of India) also created major problems, with Pakistan accusing India of blocking the transfer of resources to which Pakistan was due. In military assets, the partition agreement called for India to receive two-thirds and Pakistan one-third. It did not work out that way. India received the vast bulk of the armor and aircraft assets, while Pakistan secured most of the larger naval vessels. The military officers of both

Estimated Casualty Statistics of the India-Pakistan Wars

India-Pakistan War of 1947–1949

	Killed in Action	Wounded	Percentage of Kashmir Held
India	1,500	3,152	60%
Pakistan	1,500	4,668	40%

India-Pakistan War of 1965

	Killed in Action	Civilian Dead	Equipment Lost	Territory Lost
India	3,000	13,000	175 tanks 59 aircraft	300 square miles
Pakistan	3,800		200 tanks 19 aircraft	700 square miles

India-Pakistan War of 1971

	Killed in Action	Wounded	Captured
India	3,241	9,851	2,100
Pakistan	7,982	10,000	97,368
Bangladesh	at least 2 million	Unknown	Unknown

India-Pakistan War of 1999 (Kargil War)

	Killed in Action	Wounded	Captured
India	527	1,363	1
Pakistan	1,042–4,000	665+	8

Sources: "Battle Casualties of Azad Kashmir Regiment during 1947–1948," Pakistan Military Consortium, http://www.pakdef.info/pakmilitary/army/war/48warbattlecasualties.html; "Bitta Opposes Pak PoWs' Release," *The Tribune*, August 15, 1999; Michael Clodfelter, *Warfare and Armed Conflict: A Statistical Reference to Casualty and Other Figures, 1618–1991* (Jefferson, NC: McFarland, 1992); "India," Library of Congress Country Studies, http://lcweb2.loc.gov/cgi-bin/query/r?frd/cstdy:@field%28DOCID+in0189%29; Indian Ministry of Defence, "Soldiers Killed in Kargil War," Lok Sabha Starred Question No. 160, November, 28, 2002; Indian Ministry of Defence, History Division, "Official 1965 War History," Bharat Rakshak, http://www.bharat-rakshak.com/LAND-FORCES/Army/History/1965War/PDF/index.html; Thomas M. Leonard, "India-Pakistan Wars," in *Encyclopedia of the Developing World*, Vol. 2, 805–807 (Abingdon, UK: Taylor and Francis, 2006); "1965 War: Introduction," Pakistan Army, http://www.pakistanarmy.gov.pk/awpreview/textcontent.aspx?pid=196; Muralidhar B. Reddy, "Over 4,000 Soldiers Killed in Kargil: Sharif." *The Hindu*, August 16, 1999; Ruth L. Sivard, *World Military and Social Expenditures, 1987–88*, 12th ed. (Washington, DC: World Priorities, 1987–1988).

states had all been trained by the British, although few had experience at higher command. Technically, British field marshal Sir Claude Auchinleck commanded both armies.

Certainly the most appalling aspect was the postpartition uprooting of humanity.

The population of 1947 prepartition India was some 390 million people. After partition, there were perhaps 330 million people in India and 60 million in Pakistan (30 million in West Pakistan, now Pakistan, and 30 million in East Pakistan, now Bangladesh). Pakistan was also at considerable disadvantage geographically, as its two halves were separated by India. Once the international boundaries had been drawn, nearly 15 million people crossed the borders to what they hoped would be the relative safety of their religious majority. Religious hatred combined with simple greed to make the transfer of humanity tragic for many. Estimates of the numbers who died vary widely, from 200,000 to as many as 1 million. Gandhi was among the casualties. While he was able to maintain the peace in Calcutta by undertaking a fast, when he attempted the same in Delhi he was assassinated by fanatical Hindus on January 30, 1948.

A pressing issue was the future disposition of several disputed territories. The latter included Junagadh, Hyderabad, and Jammu and Kashmir. Junagadh and Hyderabad were predominantly Hindu states with Muslim leaders. They were quickly absorbed by India. The dispute over Jammu and Kashmir was not so easily resolved, however. There a Sikh, Maharajah Hari Singh, had ruled since 1925. As Kashmir was 77 percent Muslim, it was assumed that he would join the kingdom to Pakistan. However, he wanted Kashmir to remain independent and neutral, and while he was hesitating joining Pakistan, Pathan Muslims of Poonch in southeastern Kashmir rebelled against their Hindu landowners, and on October 22 Pakistan sent Muslim tribal militias into Kashmir claiming that they were needed to suppress the rebellion. These tribal militias and irregular Pakistani forces moved against the Kashmiri capital of Srinagar. They reached Uri, but Hari Singh then appealed to India for assistance. Indian prime minister Jawaharlal Nehru made this contingent on Singh signing an instrument of accession to join India, which he did on October

26. Governor-general of Pakistan Ali Jinnah rejected this, and war between India and Pakistan ensued.

SPENCER C. TUCKER

Course

The 1947 War (October 22, 1947–January 1, 1949)

Fighting in the 1947 war began on October 22 when Muslim tribal militias and Pakistani irregular forces crossed from Pakistan into Kashmir. To receive Indian assistance against Pakistan, Maharajah Hari Singh agreed to join his state to India. With this accomplished on October 26, India quickly airlifted troops to Kashmir. At first the Indians were successful, securing the Kashmiri capital of Srinagar in the Battle of Shalateng on November 7, 1947, but with Indian forces overextended, the Pakistanis triumphed at Jhangar on December 24. By the beginning of 1948 and with the war stalemated, Indian prime minister Jawaharlal Nehru requested United Nations (UN) mediation.

As the UN-brokered talks slowly progressed, India made military progress against both the Pakistani irregulars and increasing numbers of Pakistani regular forces who crossed into Kashmir to take part in the fighting. The Indian Army was victorious at Naoshera on February 6, 1948; at Gurais on May 22–27; and at Zojila on October 19. Following protracted negotiations, the fighting largely ended in December 1948, with the Line of Control dividing Kashmir into territories administered by Pakistan (northern and western Kashmir) and India (southern, central, and northeastern Kashmir). India retained the most fertile and populous regions of Kashmir, but about 30 percent of Kashmir— some 5,000 square miles—remained in

India–Pakistan: Kashmir

Pakistani hands when the cease-fire took hold on January 1, 1949. Each side had sustained about 1,500 casualties.

The UN resolution of January 5, 1949, called for a plebiscite to determine the future status of Kashmir, but India refused to permit this vote, so tensions between India and Pakistan remained high. Indeed, Kashmir remained the principal cause of animosity between India and Pakistan throughout the period of the Cold War and afterward.

The 1965 War (April–September 23, 1965)

A second Indo-Pakistani war over Kashmir broke out in April 1965 when Pakistan's president and military ruler, General Muhammad Ayub Khan, sought to test Indian resolve. Jawaharlal Nehru had died, and his successor as prime minister of India, Lal Bahadur Shastri, appeared vulnerable. Ayub had just signed a friendship pact with the People's Republic of China and began military operations in the Rann of Kutch, where the frontier was poorly defined. Within several weeks the fighting had escalated into full-scale hostilities in which the Pakistanis appeared to have had the upper hand until monsoon rains suspended the fighting. Shastri then agreed to a mediated settlement.

Emboldened by this and convinced that the Indian Army was weak, Pakistani foreign minister Zulfirkar Ali Bhutto urged a

Tribesmen from Waziristan who took up arms against India in the Indo-Pakistani War of 1965. (Hulton Archive/Getty Images)

renewal of the fighting. In August border clashes occurred in both Kashmir and the Punjab as both sides violated the Kashmir cease-fire line. On August 24, Indian forces launched a major raid across the cease-fire line.

In retaliation for the Indian raid, Ayub launched Operation GRAND SLAM on September 1, 1965, a major military offensive to cut the road linking India to Kashmir and isolate two Indian Army coups in the Ravi-Sutley corridor. Both sides also carried out air attacks against the other, not only in the Punjab but also in Indian raids on Karachi and Pakistani attacks on New Delhi. On September 6, however, India sent some 900,000 men across the border

into Pakistan. Superior numbers soon told. In one of the largest tank battles in history, the Indians defeated the Pakistanis at Chawinda (September 14–19) during their Sialkot Campaign and reached Lahore, claiming to have destroyed 300 Pakistani tanks in the process. There was no fighting at sea during the war.

On September 20, the UN Security Council passed Resolution 211 calling for an end to the fighting and negotiations to settle the issue of Kashmir. Both the United States and the United Kingdom supported the UN decision by cutting off arms supplies to both belligerents. This affected both sides, but Pakistan felt the ban more than India, since its military was weaker. The UN resolution, the halting of arms sales, and China's threat to initiate military operations against India all had their effects. Both sides accepted a cease-fire on September 27.

India then occupied a good deal of Pakistani territory, but under terms of the cease-fire both sides agreed to withdraw to the prewar boundaries.

Finally, on January 10, 1966, both sides agreed to a peace settlement at Tashkent in the Soviet Union that also included Britain and the United States. This formally reestablished the cease-fire line as it had been in 1949, restored diplomatic and economic relations between the two countries, and provided for an orderly transfer of prisoners of war. The two sides also agreed to work toward the establishment of good relations, and India again pledged to hold a plebiscite in Kashmir. Unfortunately, Indian prime minister Shastri died shortly thereafter, and his successor, Indira Gandhi, failed to implement the Kashmir plebiscite, with the result that tensions continued.

The 1971 War (December 3–16, 1971)

The third Indo-Pakistani war occurred in 1971. Since independence, the more numerous Bengali people of East Pakistan had been dominated by West Pakistan. Increasing violence and unrest in Pakistan led Ayub Khan to resign in March 1969 and turn over power to another general, Aga Mohammed Yahya Khan.

In 1970 political leader Sheikh Mujibur Rahman formed the Awami League, which sought autonomy for East Pakistan. In December 1970, the Awami League won an absolute majority in general elections for a Pakistani National Assembly called to draft a new constitution. Instead of allowing Sheikh Rahman to take power, the Pakistani government of President Yahya

Khan jailed him. Rioting then broke out in East Pakistan. Pakistani president Yahya Khan declared martial law on March 24, 1971, and began a major repression in East Pakistan that in the view of some observers amounted to genocide. Perhaps 10 million refugees fled East Pakistan into India.

With Indians demanding that their armed forces intervene, Prime Minister Indira Gandhi appealed unsuccessfully to world leaders to end the repression in East Pakistan. During June–November 1971, India and Pakistan exchanged artillery fire and conducted small raids across the border against the other. Meanwhile, on August 9, 1971, India concluded a treaty of friendship with the Soviet Union. Alarmed by West Pakistani actions in East Pakistan, the United States terminated arms shipments to Pakistan on November 8.

Meanwhile, East Pakistani refugees calling themselves the Mukti Bahini and supported by India engaged the West Pakistani forces. This goaded Pakistan into taking the first hostile action against India, a Pakistani Air Force strike against eastern India on November 22, followed by major air attacks from West Pakistan against the principal Indian air bases on December 3. The Pakistanis hoped to achieve the same surprise garnered by the Israeli Air Force against Egypt in the 1967 Six-Day War, but the Indians, well aware that they were goading the Pakistanis to war, were well prepared, and the Pakistani air strikes were largely unsuccessful.

The Pakistani air attacks on December 3 marked the official beginning of the war. India was concerned that China, with which it had fought a border war in 1962, might seek to take advantage of the situation to invade northern India. Nonetheless, Indian forces were ready and had at least three times the strength of the 90,000 West

Pakistani forces in East Pakistan. Moving swiftly and well supported by air force and naval units, the Indians launched an invasion from the north and west. During December 14–16 the Indian Army captured the East Pakistan capital of Dhaka (Dacca).

On the western front, on December 4 Pakistani forces invaded Jammu and Kashmir and registered gains of up to 10 miles into Indian territory until they were halted. During December 5–6 the Soviet Union supported its Indian ally by vetoing UN Security Council resolutions calling for a cease-fire and forcing Pakistani foreign minister Zulfikar Ali Bhutto to work through the dilatory UN General Assembly. On December 6 India officially recognized the independence of East Pakistan as Bangladesh. On December 15, with the fighting there all but over, the UN General Assembly demanded a cease-fire in East Pakistan. An embittered Bhutto left the UN and returned to Pakistan. Indian troops also recaptured some of the territory in Kashmir and the Punjab lost to the Pakistanis earlier and invaded West Pakistan in both Hyderabad and the Punjab.

Meanwhile, the Indian Navy neutralized Pakistani naval units on the first day of the war. The Indian Eastern Fleet completely controlled the Bay of Bengal, blockading East Pakistan. Indian antisubmarine warfare units sank the Pakistani submarine *Ghazi,* which tried to ambush the Indian aircraft carrier *Vikrant.* In the largest surface action in the Indian Ocean since 1945, the Indian Western Fleet sank the Pakistani destroyer *Khaibar* and a minesweeper off Karachi. Indian surface units then shelled and rocketed the naval base at Karachi. Pakistan's only naval success in the war came when the submarine *Hangor* torpedoed and sank the Indian frigate *Khukri.*

On December 16 in Dhaka, Pakistani commander Lieutenant General A. A. K. Niazi officially surrendered to Indian commander General S. H. F. J. Manekshaw, effectively ending the war. On December 17 both sides accepted a cease-fire agreement. The war saw the highest number of casualties of any of the three major India-Pakistan wars. Indian losses were some 2,400 killed, 6,200 wounded, and 2,100 taken prisoner. India also admitted that it had lost 73 tanks and 45 aircraft. Pakistan, however, lost more than 4,000 dead and 10,000 wounded, along with 93,000 prisoners (the latter figure included some of the wounded). Pakistan reportedly lost a third of its army, half of its navy, and a quarter of its air force. On December 20 Yahya Khan resigned, and Bhutto replaced him as president. Bhutto promptly placed Yahya Khan and senior Pakistani generals under arrest.

The last Indian troops were withdrawn from Bangladesh in March 1972, and on March 19 India and Bangladesh concluded a treaty of friendship. On July 2, India and Pakistan formally concluded an agreement at Simla, India. President Bhutto signed for Pakistan, and Prime Minister Gandhi signed for India. Both sides agreed to a general troop withdrawal and restoration of the prewar western border but postponed action on settlement of the dispute over Kashmir and the return of Pakistani prisoners of war. India did not agree to the release of the prisoners of war until August 1973, with the last of them returning to Pakistan in April 1974.

SPENCER C. TUCKER

Consequences

The one positive consequence for India and Pakistan of the 1971 war was the Simla Agreement, signed on July 2, 1972, in Simla, India. In the agreement, both nations pledged to resolve all future disputes through diplomatic means. Although this brought a close to major war between India and Pakistan, it did not mean a complete halt to fighting. Border incidents continued to occur regularly thereafter, threatening wider wars. In 1984, war nearly broke out over India's belief that Pakistan was involved in the Sikh insurgency of that year. This crisis was headed off by diplomacy. Fighting initiated by a local Indian commander also occurred in 1987 but was contained.

In 1999 a wider conflict occurred. Known as the Kargil War but more limited than the three previous armed conflicts, it took place during May–July 1999 in the Kargil district of Kashmir when Pakistani forces, along with Kashmiri insurgents, infiltrated across the Line of Control (the de facto border between India and Pakistan in Kashmir) into the Indian-occupied Kargil district. India responded with a major military offensive to drive out the invaders. With the real danger of another full-scale war on the Indian subcontinent, the United States, then supporting Pakistan, pressured that country to withdraw, and by the end of July organized hostilities in the Kargil district had ended.

The Kargil War is also interesting as the only instance of direct conventional warfare between two states possessing nuclear weapons. India conducted its first successful test in 1974. Pakistan, which had been developing its nuclear capability in secret for some time and had the ability to explode a nuclear weapon by 1987, conducted its first underground nuclear tests only in 1998. Pakistan has maintained that it would only employ nuclear weapons first if its armed forces were not able to halt an invasion or if a nuclear strike was initiated against Pakistan. Stated Indian policy is that it would not be the first to employ their use.

Relations between the two nuclear powers remain strained in a variety of areas, including policy toward Afghanistan. Pakistan lent strong support to the Taliban in Afghanistan during the civil war there in 1996 and afterward. India, however, strongly opposed the Taliban and criticized the Pakistani role in Afghanistan, officially establishing ties to the Northern Alliance, the chief resistance organization to the Taliban. India even recognized the Northern Alliance as the Afghan official government. Relations were further strained with the July 7, 2008, bombing of the Indian embassy in Kabul, which U.S. authorities attributed to the work of the Pakistani Inter-Services Intelligence (ISI).

Most serious were the November 26–29, 2008, terrorist attacks in Mumbai, India. During this four-day span, 10 Pakistani members of the militant Islamic Lashar-e Taiba organization carried out 12 coordinated attacks in Mumbai that resulted in the deaths of 164 people and the wounding of at least 308. Ajmal Kasab, the only attacker taken alive, later confessed to Indian interrogators that the attacks had the support of the Pakistani ISI.

Tensions regarding Kashmir remain high, and military skirmishes continue to be a common occurrence, with Pakistan accused by numerous sources of having been behind a number of terrorist attacks in Indian-occupied portions of Jammu and Kashmir. During August 30–September 1, 2011, shooting occurred along the Line of Control in the Kupwara District, resulting in the deaths of 5 Indian and 3 Pakistani soldiers. During January–October 2013 in the Mendhar sector, the beheading of an Indian soldier resulted in the worst fighting in a decade, bringing the deaths of 12

Indian and 10 Pakistani soldiers. Beginning on July 6, 2014, a series of skirmishes began in the Arnia sector. These followed the killing of a member of the Indian Border Security Force and the wounding of 3 others by Pakistan rangers.

The situation escalated, and in October 2014 India and Pakistan exchanged multiple warnings and even hints of nuclear retaliation. Heavy artillery shelling in early October resulted in the deaths of at least eight Indian and nine Pakistani civilians, with thousands of villagers forced to flee their homes. This confrontation differed from those of the previous decade in both its duration and the number of civilian casualties. It also was a significant downturn in India-Pakistan relations under new Indian prime minister Narendra Modi. Hopes had been raised when Modi invited Pakistan's embattled prime minister,

Nawaz Sharif, to attend his May inauguration ceremony.

The rising tensions along the Line of Control has raised questions regarding the widely held assumption that conflict here will not escalate into all-out conventional or even nuclear war. Kashmir has become so symbolically significant to both India and Pakistan that they are beset by zero-sum thinking. Pakistan's continued internal deterioration makes any settlement of the Kashmir dispute even more unlikely, especially with nationalist fervor drowning out any rational approach.

India continues to hold a sizable advantage over Pakistan in almost all key areas measuring national power: population (1.2 billion to 170 million), gross domestic product ($2 trillion to $237 billion), and defense spending ($36 billion to $5.1 billion).

SPENCER C. TUCKER

Timeline

1857	The Sepoy Rebellion (known in India as the First War of Indian Independence) occurs against the British East India Company, leading the British government to assume direct rule in India.
1876	
May 1	Queen Victoria takes the title "Empress of India."
1885	The Indian National Congress (INC) is established.
1914–1918	World War I, in which the Indian Army plays a major role, principally in the Middle East.
1935	Passage of the Government of India Act, whereby the British government concedes a degree of autonomy to India.
1939–1945	World War II.
1942	
March	In the Cripps Mission to India, the British government offers Indian independence after the war, but the INC rejects the conditions, which imply the possibility of partition.

1947

February 12	Viscount Louis Mountbatten is named viceroy of India. He will serve in this position until August 5, 1947, when he becomes governor-general of India until June 21, 1948.
August 15	The British grant independence to the Union of India and the Dominion of Pakistan.
October 22	Fighting commences between India and Pakistan in the 1947 war.
October 26	Maharajah Hari Singh signs the Instrument of Accession, assigning his kingdom of Kashmir, which has a majority Muslim population, to India. This touches off the First India-Pakistan War.
November 3	Indian forces win the Battle of Shalateng in Kashmir.
December 24	The Pakistanis win the Battle of Jhangar.

1948

January 30	Mahatma Gandhi is assassinated in Delhi.
February 6	Indian forces prevail in the Battle of Naoshera.
May 22–27	The Battle of Gurais sees the Indians victorious.
October 19	Indian forces win the Battle of Zojila.

1949

January 1	End of the 1947 war.

1965

April	The 1965 Indo-Pakistani War begins.
August 24	Indian forces launch a major raid across the cease-fire line in Kashmir.
September 1	Pakistan launches Operation GRAND SLAM.
September 14–19	The Indians defeat the Pakistanis in a major tank engagement at Chawinda.
September 27	A cease-fire brings the 1965 fighting to a close.

1966

January 10	Indian and Pakistani representatives meeting at Tashkent in the Soviet Union conclude the Tashkent peace agreement.

1971

March 24	Pakistani president Yahya Khan declares martial law and begins repressive measures in East Pakistan. Upwards of

	10 million residents of East Pakistan then seek refuge in India.
June–November	India and Pakistan exchange intermittent artillery fire and carry out small cross-border raids against the other.
August 9	India concludes a treaty of friendship with the Soviet Union.
November 8	Alarmed at events, the United States terminates arms to Pakistan.
November 22	Pakistani aircraft raid eastern India.
December 3	The 1971 Indo-Pakistani War begins with a major Pakistani air assault against Indian airfields that, however, registers little success.
December 4	Pakistani forces invade Jammu and Kashmir.
December 6	India recognizes the independence of East Pakistan as Bangladesh.
December 14–16	Indian forces capture Dhaka (Dacca).
December 16	Pakistani forces surrender, and the next day a cease-fire agreement enters into force.
December 19	The 1971 Indo-Pakistani War officially ends.

1972

March 19	India and Bangladesh conclude a treaty of friendship.
July 2	In the Simla Agreement, India and Pakistan renounce the use of force against the other.

1974

May 18	India carries out an underground nuclear test near Pakistan's eastern border.

1998

May 28	Although it had acquired the capability of carrying out a nuclear explosion by 1987, Pakistan announces that it has carried out five underground nuclear tests.

1999

May–July	The Kargil War occurs, with fighting in the Kargil district of Kashmir between Indian and Pakistani forces.

SPENCER C. TUCKER

Further Reading

Akbar, M. J. *India: The Siege Within; Challenges to a Nation's Unity.* New Delhi: UBSPD, 1996.

Ayub, Muhammad. *An Army, Its Role and Rule: A History of the Pakistan Army from Independence to Kargil, 1947–1999.* Pittsburgh: RoseDog Books, 2005.

Bains, J. S. *India's Territorial Disputes.* London: Asia Publishing House, 1962.

Bose, Sumantra. *The Challenge in Kashmir: Democracy, Self-Determination and a Just Peace.* Thousand Oaks, CA: Sage Publications, 1997.

Bose, Sumantra. *Kashmir: Roots of Conflict, Paths to Peace.* Cambridge, MA: Harvard University Press, 2003.

Chopra, Pran. *India, Pakistan, and the Kashmir Triangle.* New Delhi: HarperCollins, 1994.

Choudhury, G. W. *The Last Days of United Pakistan.* Bloomington: University of Indiana Press, 1974.

Choudhury, G. W. *Pakistan's Relations with India, 1947–1966.* London: Pall Mall, 1968.

Das, Chand N. *Hours of Glory: Famous Battles of the Indian Army, 1801–1971.* New Delhi: Vision Books, 1997.

Dixit, J. N. *India-Pakistan in War and Peace.* London: Routledge, 2002.

Ganguly, Sumit. *The Origins of War in South Asia: The Indo-Pakistani Wars since 1947.* Boulder, CO: Westview, 1994.

Hiro, Dilip. *The Longest August: The Unflinching Rivalry between India and Pakistan.* New York: Nation Books, 2015.

Jacques, Kathryn. *Bangladesh, India and Pakistan: International Relations and Regional Tensions in South Asia.* New York: St. Martin's, 1999.

Lifschultz, Lawrence. *Bangladesh: The Unfinished Revolution.* London: Zed, 1979.

Lyon, Peter. *Conflict between India and Pakistan: An Encyclopedia.* Santa Barbara, CA: ABC-CLIO, 2008.

Maniruzzaman, Taluder. *The Bangladesh Revolution and Its Aftermath.* Dacca: Bangladesh Press International, 1980.

Margolis, Eric S. *War at the Top of the World: The Struggle for Afghanistan, Kashmir and Tibet.* New York: Routledge, 2002.

Puri, Balraj. *Jammu and Kashmir: Triumph and Tragedy of Indian Federalism.* New Delhi: Sterling, 1981.

Wirsing, Robert. *India, Pakistan, and the Kashmir Dispute: On Regional Conflict and Its Resolution.* New York: St. Martin's, 1994.

Malayan Emergency (1948–1960)

Causes

The Malayan Emergency (also known as the Malay Emergency) was an insurgency waged by the Malayan National Liberation Army (MNLA), the military arm of the Malayan Communist Party (MCP), against British Commonwealth forces during June 16, 1948–July 31, 1960. Malaya comprises the 700-mile-long Malay Peninsula in Southeast Asia and is slightly larger than the U.S. state of New Mexico. Malaya is bordered by Thailand to the north, the South China Sea to the east and south, and the Strait of Malacca to the west and also includes Sarawak and Sabah on the northern island of Borneo. Until 1965 Malaya also included Singapore.

Malaya's multiethnic and religiously diverse population complicated development of a truly "Malaysian" identity, and like other countries in the region it underwent revolution and internal conflict. But unlike some of the nations of Southeast Asia, Malaysia emerged as one of the most stable and economically advanced countries in Asia.

The Malayan Peninsula was for centuries a crossroads of Eastern and Western civilizations. Independent sultanates traded with the Portuguese, Dutch, British, and Siamese (Thais) for nearly 300 years. The British took over the Dutch position in Malaya in 1810 and established political and administrative control over five of the sultanates (Johor, Kedah, Kelantan, Perlis, and Terenggan). In 1895 the British established a protectorate over the remaining five sultanates in the Malay Peninsula (Selangor, Perak, Negeri, Sembilan, and Pahang) as the Federated

Malaya States. Together with the Straits Settlements (Malacca, Dinding, Penang, and Singapore, the latter including Christmas Island and the Cocos Islands) and the Unfederated Malay States, they formed the Malayan Union. In the so-called residential system, the British controlled government administration, while the Malay rulers retained sovereignty. In effect, the sultans had been co-opted into the British Empire.

Malaya's economic value grew exponentially with the discovery there of significant tin deposits; ultimately Malaya became the world's largest producer of this commodity. After the turn of the 20th century, the rubber industry underwent considerable development. These two resources and Malaya's geographical location (the Strait of Malacca is one of the world's most important shipping lanes) gave Malaya considerable geostrategic importance.

Following World War I, the British government decided to develop Singapore into a major naval base, its largest in Asia. Intended as a bulwark against Japanese expansionism, the base was never completed, and in any case its defenses were designed primarily to meet an assault from the sea. The base and Malaya were primary targets of the Japanese in World War II.

On the night of December 7–8, 1941, Japanese forces commanded by General Yamashita Tomoyuki began an invasion, landing on the northeastern coast of Malaya and then working their way southward. On December 10, Japanese aircraft overwhelmed and sank at sea the

Malayan Emergency (1948–1960)

Number of British-Deployed Commonwealth Military Personnel in Malaya (1950)
40,000

Number of Malayans Forcibly Relocated to "New Villages" (1950)
470,509

Casualty Figures during Malayan Emergency (1948–1950)

Commonwealth Forces/Malayan Troops	Malayan Insurgents	Civilians
1,875 killed, 2,406 wounded	6,710 killed, 1,289 wounded	2,478 killed

Sources: Robert Jackson, *The Malayan Emergency* (London: Pen and Sword Aviation, 2008); Richard Stubbs, *Hearts and Minds in Guerrilla Warfare: The Malayan Emergency, 1948–1960* (Oxford: Oxford University Press, 1989).

British battleship *Prince of Wales* and battle cruiser *Repulse,* which had been ordered northward to disrupt the Japanese landing. Some 70,000 Japanese troops now confronted 140,000 British forces under Lieutenant General Arthur Percival, although many of the British Empire troops were poorly trained. Kuala Lumpur fell on January 11, and the ensuing defense of Singapore was badly handled. Percival surrendered Singapore and his remaining 70,000 troops on February 15.

Malaya and Singapore had fallen in only 70 days, and in the entire campaign the British sustained 138,700 casualties, mostly captured. Japanese losses were trifling by comparison: only 9,824. The Japanese capture of Singapore opened the way for Japan to secure control of the natural resources of South Asia. British prestige in Asia never recovered from the shock, as the battle signaled the end of the colonial era in Asia. British prime minister Winston Churchill was correct in his assessment of the loss of Singapore as the greatest military defeat in modern British history. Some British Empire forces did take to the jungles to carry on the fight, however.

They formed the Malayan People's Anti-Japanese Army in March 1942.

Although anticolonial movements existed before, World War II brought widespread Malaysian nationalism. The Japanese were initially welcomed by the Malay nationalists as ending British colonial rule, although the Japanese presence was far more brutal than the Malayans had expected from fellow Asians. The Japanese generally respected Islam, which was the predominant religion in Malaya, while the Sultans retained their authority and in many instances openly cooperated with the Japanese authorities.

During the Japanese occupation, the Chinese and Indians suffered the most. Many were forced into slave labor, killed, or starved to death. The radically different treatment these groups received served to aggravate already existing ethnic tensions in Malaya, for the Chinese and Indian communities considered the Malay population as complicit in Japanese occupation policies. A number, mainly Chinese, joined the MCP and resisted the Japanese. Britain and the United States supported the MCP somewhat during the war, as it was the only real organized resistance to the Japanese but was also anticolonial and opposed restoration of British rule.

By the end of the war in 1945 and the return of British control, Malaya had a population of some 6 million people. The British authorities now began reorganizing the Malay states to better address their ethnic and religious divisions. On April 11, 1946, the 11 political entities (the nine Malay states and the two British Straits Settlements of Penang and Malacca) were formed into a single British crown colony, the Malayan Union. It lasted until January 31, 1948, when the Federation of Malaya came into being. Singapore, Sarawak, and North Borneo were made crown colonies. All were under the authority of a governor-general. Malay leaders initially opposed this reconfiguration, but the British convinced them that Malay-dominated independence would be granted. Moreover, the British promised economic recovery based on Malaya's rubber and mineral wealth.

In July 1946 the British government began constitutional talks with the newly formed United Malays National Organization (UMNO). Debate centered on the authority of the sultans and British proposals to extend citizenship to all ethnic groups in a multiracial union. The talks led to the establishment of the Federation of Malaya on January 31, 1948. Britain maintained its colonial administration, while the sultans retained control of individual states. Citizenship was restrictive and heavily favored the Malays, but through this collaboration the British hoped to avoid more radical nationalist movement as witnessed in Indochina, Burma (present-day Myanmar), and especially Indonesia.

The restoration of Dutch rule in Indonesia after World War II had provoked violent revolution there, which the British feared would lead to Pan-Malay nationalism. After Indonesia won independence in 1949, the worry became communism, which gained support among its Chinese population there. Both the British and Malay rulers feared that with a large Chinese population of its own, the Federation of Malaya could face a communist insurgency like Indonesia had experienced.

With the end of World War II, the Malayan economy was in near collapse, with high unemployment, low wages, and food both scarce and expensive. These conditions led to widespread labor unrest and strikes. The British were anxious to restore the economy quickly so that Britain's own economy might benefit from the lucrative tin and rubber operations in Malaya (rubber sales exceeded in total value all other domestic exports from the United Kingdom to the United States). Any interruption of that supply would cause significant damage to the British economy. Toward that end, the British authorities opted for harsh measures, and in consequence the unrest grew more violent. In these circumstances, the MCP attempted to overthrow British colonial rule.

The Malayan Emergency dates from the murder by MCP guerrillas of three rubber plantation managers in Perak on June 16, 1948. Two days later British high commissioner Sir Edward Gent proclaimed a state of emergency. The conflict was given the misnomer "emergency" for economic reasons: London insurance companies would only cover property losses to Malayan rubber plantations and tin operations during riot or commotion in an "emergency" but not in the case of armed insurrection or civil war.

In popular Malaysian culture, the Malayan Emergency is often portrayed as a primarily Malay struggle against an international communist conspiracy, but it was far more complicated than that. Certainly the marginalization of Malaya's Chinese population and poor economic conditions played major roles. The MCP was composed mostly of ethnic Chinese who opposed both British rule and the majority Malay domination. Few Malays joined the movement, but there were recruits from Indonesia. The MCP launched its widespread insurgency through its armed wing of the Malayan Races Liberation Army. This began the 12-year period of conflict known to the British as the Malayan Emergency and to the MNLA as the Anti-British National Liberation War.

ARNE KISLENKO AND
SPENCER C. TUCKER

Course

Under the state of emergency, the MCP and other leftist parties were outlawed, and the police were given authority to arrest and detain without trial all communists and those suspected of assisting them. The MCP, led by Chin Peng, withdrew into the rural areas of Malaya and there established the MNLA.

The MNLA mounted a guerrilla campaign, targeting especially the rubber and tin industries and transportation. The fact that most of the MNLA members were ethnic Chinese helped to separate them from the majority Malay population. Their opponents referred to the MNLA as "communist terrorists," often abbreviated to "terrs," "Charlie Tango," or "Cts."

Expected to last only a few months, the insurgency continued for more than 12 years, officially lasting until July 31, 1960, 3 years after Malaya gained independence. Indeed, it became Britain's longest colonial conflict. There is no consensus as to

why the insurgency lasted so long, especially given major divisions within the MCP leadership. Clearly, British officials failed to anticipate the insurgency and were slow to react to it, but Britain was hard-pressed economically after the war, and there were other international military obligations, including the Korean War (1950–1953). In a very real sense, Malaya revealed the larger limitations of Britain's imperial power.

At first British and Commonwealth forces struggled against the insurgency. The assassination by the MCP of British high commissioner in Malaya Henry Gurney on October 6, 1951, was certainly a low point. Ultimately, the British comitted substantial resources to the Malayan effort. By October 1950, some 40,000 regular Commonwealth military personnel, including British, Australian, and New Zealand forces, were deployed in Malaya. These were in addition to some 37,000 Special Constables and 24,000 Federation Police. Despite these numbers, the insurrection proved resilient. In contrast to French Indochina, the British sent out conscripts to fight in the insurgency, but they received specialized training at the Jungle Warfare School.

The MNLA hoped to liberate areas of Malaya and set up its own administration but was unable to accomplish this. Meanwhile, the British at first concentrated on the defense of economic assets such as mines and large plantations, which, however, did nothing to sap MNLA strength.

Only in 1950 did the British initiate a more systematic and coordinated approach to the crisis when Lieutenant General Sir Harold Briggs assumed direction of military operations. Briggs introduced what became known as the Briggs Plan. Its chief hallmark was the separation of the

MALAYAN EMERGENCY, 1948–1960

insurgents from their supply sources and support bases. This was a considerable undertaking, entailing as it did the relocation, according to one estimate, of 470,509 people, some 400,000 of them ethnic Chinese Malays, into some 450 "New Villages." In most cases, the new settlements were in entirely new areas. The settlements were surrounded by barbed wire, searchlights, and other protective measures. Indeed, this would be the model for the U.S. Strategic Hamlet Program in South Vietnam during the Vietnam War.

Although there was considerable resentment at first, abetted by the destruction that accompanied the resettlement (the Geneva Conventions and international law forbid destruction of civilian property unless prompted by military necessity), the villagers came to appreciate their higher standard of living and greatly improved conditions, including schools and access to medical care. Residents of the New Villages, most of whom had been squatters, also received ownership of the land on which they now had been resettled. The New Villages succeeded in drying up MNLA supply sources and increased the vulnerability of the guerrillas to operations by the security forces.

The system of population control was prosecuted even more vigorously by General Sir Gerald Templer, who in early 1952 was appointed high commissioner with full powers over the military, police, and civilian authorities. Sir Robert Thompson, the permanent secretary of defense for Malaya who had served with the Chindits in Burma during World War II and thus had extensive knowledge of jungle warfare, was another chief architect of the British counterinsurgency plan. Templer and Thompson developed an efficient,

coordinated, and expanded intelligence apparatus. They also invented and implemented the concept of winning hearts and minds by providing medical and food aid to the Malays and other indigenous peoples.

Thompson and Templer increased the intelligence budget to provide payments to informers, and they also coordinated the use of sophisticated "black" propaganda and psychological warfare (psyops). Safe-conduct passes with pledges of monetary rewards were air-dropped over guerrilla areas to encourage defections. Aerial drops of millions of strategic leaflets, such as handwritten letters and photographs from surrendered guerrillas, were used in conjunction with voice aircraft to personalize propaganda.

British and other Commonwealth aircraft also dropped conventional ordnance on suspected MNLA camps and base areas. Airplanes and helicopters also employed chemical defoliants and napalm. The defoliants were used to deny the guerrillas cover and concealment in the jungle and to destroy their food crops. At the same time, units such as the Special Air Service (the forerunner of today's United Kingdom Special Forces), Gurkhas, and Royal Marines carried out long-range patrolling deep within guerrilla-controlled areas to destroy guerrilla bases and drive MNLA units deeper into the jungle.

Above all, reforms to citizenship helped integrate non-Malays, easing Chinese alienation. Multiracial political parties were encouraged rather than those based strictly within communities. But doubtful that this would actually happen, British administrators supported the Malayan Chinese Association (MCA) and the Malayan Indian Congress (MIC), anticommunist

An injured member of the British Special Air Service (SAS) is carried to a helicopter for evacuation during fighting in the Malayan Emergency. (Charles Hewitt/Getty Images)

groups that wrestled away the hearts and minds of non-Malays from the MCP.

By 1953 counterinsurgency operations were proving successful, and by mid-1954 the strategy of political cooperation also seemed to be working. In July 1954 the Alliance Party—uniting the UMNO, the MCA, and the MIC—was born. Dominating the Malay national elections in July 1955, the Alliance Party was fully committed to fighting the insurgency and moved quickly with the British to plan Malaya's independence. The communist strategy had clearly backfired. Rather than dividing Malaya, the emergency brought ethnic groups together in a staunchly anticommunist alliance linked to Britain.

There was only slight support for the MCP from the Soviet Union and China,

as Indonesia and Indochina received the most attention from Moscow and Beijing. Conversely, the United States supported Britain's counterinsurgency efforts, which furthered the Anglo-American special relationship.

By 1954 when Templer departed Malaya, the conflict had been largely transformed. The insurgents were now at pains to maintain themselves in the field. In 1955 the MCP offered, in vain, to negotiate a settlement. Then on August 31, 1957, Malaya was granted independence as a constitutional monarchy, removing the insurgency's appeal as a war of colonial liberation. In 1958 after mass defections, the MNLA demobilized, and by 1960 the movement was reduced to a small number of holdouts hiding in the Malay-Thai border area conducting hit-and-run raids. Chin Peng ended up in Beijing. The Malayan government declared the insurgency at an end on July 31, 1960.

SPENCER C. TUCKER AND PHILLIP DEERY

Consequences

During the period 1948–1960, the Malayan Emergency claimed the lives of 1,346 Malayan troops and 529 British Commonwealth military personnel. Another 2,406 Malayan and British Commonwealth troops were wounded. Insurgent losses have been estimated at 6,710 killed, 1,289 wounded, and 1,287 captured. Some 2,702 guerrillas surrendered voluntarily. Malayan civilian casualties have been set at 2,478 killed and 810 missing.

The Malayan Emergency cast a long shadow over the new nation. Its mythology has come to dominate the modern history of Malaya, and it became a benchmark of the Cold War in Southeast Asia. For Americans embarking on military involvement in Vietnam and wishing to apply successful British strategies, the Malayan Emergency became the quintessential counterinsurgency primer.

Malaya enjoyed considerable economic advantages. It was a leading producer of rubber, tin, and palm oil and also exported iron ore. These provided substantial resources for industrial development. Two economic plans during 1956–1960 and 1961–1965 saw heavy government investment in industry and transportation, both of which had been neglected during World War II and the Malayan Emergency. The government also sought to lessen economic reliance on commodities exports, as these were vulnerable to wide price fluctuations.

In 1963, the Federation of Malaya expanded. In 1961 Lee Kuan Yew, secretary-general of Singapore's People's Action Party, proposed to Tunku Abdul Rahman (chief minister of the Federation of Malaya during 1957–1963 and then prime minister of Malaya during 1963–1970) the establishment of a wider federation. Presumably this would allow greater government control over possible communist activities, especially in Singapore. In addition, there was concern that should Singapore, then a British crown colony, achieve independence, it might become a center for the Chinese to threaten Malayan sovereignty. Inclusion of the states of North Borneo and Sarawak would balance out the ethnic composition of the new nation. Following negotiations in July 1963 that included the British government, it was agreed that the Federation of Malaya would become Malaya on August 31, 1963, with Britain yielding North Borneo, Sarawak, and Singapore to the federation.

The governments of both the Philippines and Indonesia objected to this, each claiming North Borneo to be part of its national territory. Indonesian opposition and efforts by the Sarawak United People's Party to thwart unification delayed the formation of Malaysia. After United Nations (UN) observers affirmed that majorities in North Borneo and Sarawak did indeed wish to join Malaysia, the larger state formally came into being on September 16, 1963. The combination of states that formerly made up the Federation of Malaya is now known as Peninsular Malaysia. The total population of Malaysia was about 10 million.

The new federation was not to enjoy peace for long, for conflict soon occurred with Indonesia, led by President Sukarno. In what became known as the Konfrontasi (Confrontation), Sukarno launched his "crush Malaysia" campaign, breaking off diplomatic relations and withdrawing Indonesia from the UN. Sukarno's government supported a communist insurgency, mainly by Chinese, in Sarawak, and war between Indonesia and Malaysia seemed a real possibility, but Britain stood fast behind Malaysia, giving Indonesia pause.

The result was an undeclared low-intensity ground war that occurred in the border area between Indonesia and East Malaysia on Borneo. Combat was largely limited to platoon- or company-size light infantry on both sides of the border. The lack of roads and jungle terrain imposed serious military obstacles. British Commonwealth forces (primarily from Britain but also Australian and New Zealand troops) supported a growing Malaysian military effort and enjoyed the advantage of more effective helicopter resupply of forward military bases. In December 1964, a considerable Indonesian troop concentration along the border led the British to substantially increase their own military assets. The confrontation lasted until Sukarno's downfall in 1966. Over his objection, on August 11, 1966, Indonesia signed a formal peace agreement by which it formally recognized Malaysia.

Malaysia also faced other problems. Secessionist movements in Penang, Johor, and Kelantan were a major problem for the federation. Also, disputes involving revenue sharing and political representation led Singapore, with its largely Chinese population, to withdraw from the federation in 1965 and become an independent country. The balance of power between Malays and non-Malays remained a constant worry. Prime Minister Tunku survived these challenges by maintaining the multiracial Alliance Party. Malaysia even managed considerable foreign policy successes, such as gaining an elected seat to the UN Security Council (1965) and playing a role in the formation of the Association of Southeast Asian Nations (ASEAN) in 1967.

Following the May 1969 elections, however, violent race riots broke out, and Rahman was accused of abandoning Malay constituencies in favor of the Chinese and Indians. His UNMO, Malaysia's largest political party, was seriously divided, with some members defecting to the opposition Pan-Malayan Islamic Party. Many Chinese joined the Democratic Action Party, which became the main vehicle for political participation by non-Malays. The alliance quickly fell apart. Rahman resigned as prime minister in September 1970 and as UMNO president in June 1971.

The 1969 riots did, however, force examination of government and legal structures in Malaysia. Parliament was temporarily disbanded and replaced by the National Operations Council, a 67-member body representing the major ethnic groups, trade unions, professions, and religious bodies. The council worked to secure the rights and representation of non-Malays while guaranteeing the "special position" of Malay language and culture and the Islamic faith. Economic prosperity was considered the key to combating racial and ethnic tensions. Yet urban centers, where most Chinese and Indians lived, were better off than rural areas, where the Malay majority resided. The council therefore adopted policies to advance the *bumiputra* (sons of the soil), the predominantly Malay lower classes.

Under Prime Minister Mahatir Mohammad (1981–2003), economic development became the overriding concern. This focus, however, came at the expense of the non-Malay community, which was checked by the domination of the UMNO. Thus, although ostensibly a democracy, in effect Malaysia emerged in the 1980s as a unitary state. Behind the veneer of a multiracial federation, Malaysia had become a predominantly Malay country. Through the draconian 1960 Internal Security Act, a vestige of British law from the Malayan Emergency, Mahatir undermined all opposition. Human rights violations against non-Malay activists, particularly during the late 1980s, went largely ignored by the world community. Instead, Malaysia's moderate Islam, economic prosperity, and leading role in ASEAN lent it credibility as one of Southeast Asia's most economically successful and developed countries.

ARNE KISLENKO AND
SPENCER C. TUCKER

Timeline

1511	Malacca comes under Portuguese rule.
1641	The Dutch conquer Malacca from the Portuguese.
1810	The British establish control over a number of the sultanates of Malaya.
1867	
April 1	The Straits Settlements are established as a British crown colony.
1882	North Borneo becomes a British protectorate.
1895	The British establish a protectorate over the remaining five sultanates in the Malay Peninsula as the Federated Malaya States. Together with the Straits Settlements (Malacca, Dinding, Penang, and Singapore, and the Unfederated Malay States), they form the Malayan Union.
1941	
December 7–8	Japanese forces begin their invasion of Malaya.
1942	
January 11	The Japanese capture Kuala Lumpur.
January 15	The British surrender Singapore.
1945	
August 14	The Japanese announce their acceptance of Allied terms, ending World War II and creating power vacuums in much of the areas they had conquered, including Malaya.
1946	
April 11	The 11 British colonies on the Malayan Peninsula form a single British crown colony, the Malayan Union.
1948	
January 31	Opposition by Malay nationalists forces an end to the Malaya Union, replaced by the Federation of Malaya. It

	restores the symbolic positions of the rulers of the different Malay states.
June 16	Three rubber plantation managers are murdered in Perak, Malaya. This is given as the starting date for the Malayan Emergency.
June 18	British high commissioner Sir Edward Gent proclaims a state of emergency.

1951

October 6	British high commissioner Henry Gurney is assassinated by members of the Malayan Communist Party (MCP).

1957

August 31	Malaya becomes independent as a constitutional monarchy with the name the Federation of Malaya.

1960

July 31	The Malayan Emergency is officially declared at an end.

1963

January 20	Beginning of a confrontation between Indonesia and Malaya, with the Indonesian government announcement that it pursue a policy of *konfrontasi* (confrontation) with the Federation of Malaysia, North Borneo, and Sarawak.
September 16	The Malaysian Federation comes into being with the addition of the British crown colonies of North Borneo (which joins as Sabah), Sarawak, and Singapore.

1965

August 7	A separation agreement is signed between Malaysia and Singapore.
August 9	The Malaysian parliament votes to expel Singapore from the Malaysian Federation.

1969

May 13	Ethnic riots occur between Malays and Chinese in Kuala Lumpur.

1989

December 2	A final peace settlement in the Malayan Emergency is signed.

SPENCER C. TUCKER

Further Reading

Ahmad, Zakaria Haji, ed. *Government and Politics of Malaysia.* Singapore: Oxford University Press, 1987.

Andaya, Barbara Watson, and Leonard Y. Andaya. *A History of Malaysia.* 2nd ed. Houndmills, UK: Palgrave, 2001.

Barber, Noel. *War of the Running Dogs.* London: Collins, 1971.

Cheah, Boon Kheng. *Malaysia: The Making of a Nation.* Singapore: Institute of Southeast Asian Studies, 2002.

Chin Peng, and Ian War. *Alias Chin Peng: My Side of History.* Singapore: Media Masters, 2003.

Clutterbuck, Richard. *Conflict and Violence in Singapore and Malaysia 1945–83.* Singapore: Graham Brash, 1985.

Clutterbuck, Richard. *The Long Long War: The Emergency in Malaya, 1948–1960.* New York: Praeger, 1966.

Comber, Leon. *Malaya's Secret Police, 1945–60: The Role of the Special Branch in the Malayan Emergency.* Singapore: Institute of Southeast Asian Studies, 2008.

Hack, Karl. *Defense & Decolonization in South-East Asia: Britain, Malaya, and Singapore, 1941–1968.* Richmond, Surrey, UK: Curzon, 1971.

Hack, Karl, and Tobias Rettig. *Colonial Armies in Southeast Asia.* New York: Routledge, 2006.

Hale, Chris. *Massacre in Malaya: Exposing Britain's Mylai.* New York: History Press, 2013.

Hara, Fujio. *Malaysian Chinese & China: Conversion in Identity Consciousness, 1945–1957.* Honolulu: University of Hawaii Press, 2002.

Harper, T. N. *The End of Empire and the Making of Malaya.* Cambridge: Cambridge University Press, 1999.

Jackson, Robert. *The Malayan Emergency.* London: Pen and Sword Aviation, 2008.

Jukes, Geoffrey. *The Soviet Union in Asia.* Berkeley: University of California Press, 1973.

Neidpath, James. *The Singapore Naval Base and the Defence of Britain's Far Eastern Empire, 1919–1941.* Oxford: Oxford University Press, 1981.

Ongkili, James P. *Nation-Building in Malaysia, 1946–1974.* Oxford University Press, 1985.

Ramakrishna, Kumar. *Emergency Propaganda: The Winning of Malayan Hearts and Minds, 1948–1958.* London: Curzon, 2002.

Shome, Anthony S. K. *Malay Political Leadership.* London: Routledge, 2002.

Stubbs, Richard. *Hearts and Minds in Guerrilla Warfare: The Malayan Emergency, 1948–1960.* Oxford: Oxford University Press, 1989.

Tarling, Nicholas, ed. *The Cambridge History of Southeast Asia,* Vol. 4, *From World War II to the Present.* Cambridge: Cambridge University Press, 1992.

Arab-Israeli Wars (1948–1973)

Causes

The basic cause of the Arab-Israeli Wars had been the establishment of a Jewish state in Palestine and refusal of the neighboring Arab states to accept it. Palestine was the ancient homeland of the Jews, but revolts against the Roman Empire in the 1st century BCE and into the 2nd century CE brought a series of diasporas. The Arabs conquered Palestine in the 7th century. Rule by the Egyptian Mamluks followed in the 13th century and that of the Ottoman Turks in the 16th century. Modern times found only a remnant of Jews remaining in their original homeland. This began to change with the advent of modern nationalism, the concept that each people of distinct origin should have its own nation-state.

Jews had been subjected to widespread discrimination, segregation, and even savage persecution throughout Europe, with notable examples being Spain and Russia. Anti-Jewish violence also occurred even in France. Their manner of dress, language, and religious customs set Jews apart, and non-Jews found it easy to discriminate against them.

As a result of this persecution, many Jews came to embrace Zionism, the movement that called for the creation of a Jewish homeland or state in Palestine. In the 16th century some Jewish leaders had sought to persuade European Jews to settle in Palestine. This saw a revival in the 19th century. Justification for Zionism sprang from the account in the Old Testament of the Bible (Genesis 13:15) wherein God is described as having given the land of Israel to the Israelites in perpetuity.

Pogroms in Russia especially and blatant anti-Semitism elsewhere in Europe provided a powerful impetus to Zionism. In 1882 Leo Pinsker in Odessa, Russia, argued for reestablishment of a Jewish state in Palestine. This led to the establishment the next year of the Hovevei Zion (Lovers of Zion), promoting the settlement of Jewish farmers and artisans in Palestine. Zionists held that Jews could only be safe from prosecution in a Jewish state.

The key figure in the growth of political Zionism was Austrian Jewish journalist Theodor Herzl, who covered the trial in Paris of Captain Alfred Dreyfus, a Jewish French Army officer wrongfully accused of treason. A cause célèbre in France, the Dreyfus Affair brought considerable anti-Semitism to the fore. Herzl was moved to write a book, *The Jewish State* (1896), in which he urged the establishment of a Jewish state in Palestine. He posited a European-style democracy based on separation of church and state but rooted in Jewish values.

In August 1897 Herzl convened the First Zionist Congress in Basel, Switzerland, with more than 200 delegates from 24 states and territories. The conferees voted in favor of a "publicly recognized, legally secured homeland" for the Jews in Palestine.

Palestine was then part of the Ottoman Empire, and in 1901 and again in 1902 Herzl met with Ottoman sultan Abdul Hamid but failed to secure establishment of a Jewish state. Herzl then turned to the British government, seeking a grant of territory near the Holy Land. In 1903, in what was known as the British Uganda Programme, London offered some 5,000 square miles in what was then part of British East Africa and now Kenya. Zionists were split, but a majority opposed any territorial solution other than the Holy Land itself. Herzl died in 1904, and the next year the World Zionist Organization turned down the proposed British settlement scheme.

The World Zionist Organization now committed itself irrevocably to Palestine and reopened negotiations with the Ottoman government. These talks ran afoul of the virulent Turkish nationalism of the Young Turk Revolution of 1908. This did not, however, prevent a steadily increasing Jewish immigration to Palestine.

In 1907 the so-called practical Zionists centered in Russia established the Jewish National Fund to support Jewish settlement in the Holy Land, and the next year they set up a Zionist agency in Jaffa, Palestine. Landholdings owned by the Jewish National Fund steadily increased. Wealthy West European Jews, including French baron Edmond de Rothschild, assisted the generally financially strapped Jews wishing to relocate to Palestine. In 1914 Palestine had a population of some 657,000 Muslim Arabs, 81,000 Christian Arabs, and 59,000 Jews.

World War I brought great changes to the Middle East. The Ottoman decision to join the war on the side of the Central Powers had profound effect. In July 1915 British high commissioner in Egypt Henry McMahon opened negotiations with Arab leader Hussein, sharif of Mecca, to lead a revolt against the Ottomans in conjunction with British forces. McMahon promised on the defeat of the Ottomans the establishment of an independent Arab state, understood to include Palestine. British efforts led to the 1917 Arab Revolt.

The British were, however, playing a double game, for at the same time they were negotiating with the Arabs, they and the French had their own designs on the Middle East. In May 1916 British Middle Eastern expert Sir Mark Sykes and French diplomat François Georges Picot concluded a secret agreement, which received the subsequent concurrence of Russia, to partition much of the Middle East between them. Palestine was to fall in the British sphere. This, of course, ran counter to the British government's overture to the Arabs.

Zionists saw an opportunity in World War I, and they actively sought the support of the warring governments for a Jewish state in Palestine. The British government proved to be the most receptive. The acknowledged British Zionist leader was biochemist Dr. Chaim Weizmann, later the first president of Israel. Weizmann had developed a process for the production of acetone through bacterial fermentation, which was of immense importance to the production of munitions. His prominence gave him entrée to the highest levels of government.

The entry of the United States into the war in April 1917 was another important factor. The U.S. Jewish population was large and influential. On November 2, 1917, Foreign Secretary Arthur Balfour formally announced British government support for the establishment in Palestine "of a national home for the Jewish people." The French and U.S. governments pledged their support. U.S. president Woodrow Wilson's January 1918 Fourteen Points, aimed at shaping a postwar world, included the right of self-determination for all peoples. Many Jews and other supporters of a Jewish homeland took this to mean that Jews had an inalienable right to a Jewish state.

Estimated Force Strength and Casualty Statistics of the Arab-Israeli Wars

Israeli War of Independence (1948–1949)

	Egypt	Iraq	Israel	Jordan	Lebanon	Syria
Population	19,100,000	4,900,000	1,200,000	400,000	1,200,000	3,400,000
Men Mobilized	20,000	15,000	115,000	8,000	1,000	5,000
Men Mobilized as % of Population	0.10%	0.31%	11.67%	2.00%	<0.01%	0.15%
Total Casualties	2,000	500	6,400	300	500	1,000

Suez War (1956)

	Britain	Egypt	France	Israel
Population	51,200,000	24,400,000	43,800,000	1,900,000
Men Mobilized	13,500	50,000	8,500	45,000
Men Mobilized as % of Population	0.26%	0.20%	0.02%	2.37%
Killed in Action	22	1,000	10	189
Wounded	96	4,000	33	899
Captured or Missing	0	6,000	1	5
Aircraft Lost	0	215	0	15

Six-Day War (1967)

	Egypt	Iraq	Israel	Jordan	Syria
Population	30,900,000	8,700,000	2,700,000	2,000,000	5,500,000
Men Mobilized	400,000	250,000	200,000	60,000	300,000
Men Mobilized as % of Population	1.29%	2.87%	7.40%	3.00%	5.45%
Total Casualties	10,000	2,500	776	6,100	1,000
Military Expenditures as % of GNP	8.9%	12.1%	16.3%	13.4%	11.1%

Yom Kippur War (1973)

	Egypt	Iraq	Israel	Jordan	Syria
Population	30,900,000	8,700,000	2,700,000	2,000,000	5,500,000
Armed Forces	400,000	250,000	200,000	60,000	300,000
Armed Forces as % of Population	1.29%	2.87%	7.40%	3.00%	5.45%
Total Casualties	10,000	2,500	776	6,100	1,000
Military Expenditures as % of GNP	8.9%	12.1%	16.3%	13.4%	11.1%

Israeli Invasion of Lebanon (1982–1983)

	Israel	PLO	Syria
Men Mobilized	76,000	15,000	22,000
Number of Tanks	800	300	352
Number of Aircraft	364	Unknown	96
Killed in Action or Died of Wounds	516	1,400	1,200
Wounded	2,723	Unknown	3,000
Captured	Unknown	5,000	296
Tanks Lost	140	Unknown	334
Civilian Dead	N/A	9,583*	N/A
Civilian Wounded	N/A	16,000*	N/A

* Includes both Palestinian and Lebanese civilians.

Sources: Jewish Virtual Library, http://www.jewishvirtuallibrary.org; Michael Clodfelter, *Warfare and Armed Conflict: A Statistical Reference to Casualty and Other Figures, 1618–1991* (Jefferson, NC: McFarland, 1992); Tom Hartman, *A World Atlas of Military History, 1945–1984* (n.p.: Da Capo, 1988); Charles Issawi and Carlos Dabezies, "Population Movements and Population Pressure in Jordan, Lebanon, and Syria," *Milbank Memorial Fund Quarterly* 29(4) (October 1951): 385–403; Melvin Small and Joel David Singer, *Resort to Arms: International and Civil Wars, 1816–1980* (Thousand Oaks, CA: Sage, 1982); Spencer C. Tucker, ed., *Encyclopedia of the Arab-Israeli Wars* (Santa Barbara, CA: ABC-CLIO, 2008); U.S. Arms Control and Disarmament Agency, *World Military Expenditures and Arms Transfers* (Washington, DC: U.S. Arms Control and Disarmament Agency,1995).

The Balfour Declaration did help rally Jews behind the Entente war effort, but it also had unintended effects. In late 1922, the population of Palestine numbered 673,388 Arabs (590,890 Muslims and 82,498 Christians) and 83,794 Jews. By 1931, however, the number of Jews had sharply increased to 174,606, while the Arab population was 858,788. Tensions were heightened not only by this population influx but also by Jewish land purchases, often from wealthy absentee Arabs that necessarily brought the eviction of Arab tenants.

In July 1922, the League of Nations entrusted Britain with the mandate of Palestine. The British government soon had cause to regret this, for the British were unable to keep peace between Arab and Jews. The escalating violence was the result of the impossible British policy of permitting Jewish immigration while at the same time attempting to safeguard Arab rights. Continued immigration brought more Jewish land purchases, and these brought Arab violence and riots.

In 1920 Arabs began sporadically attacking Jewish settlements, and in response Jews formed the Haganah, a clandestine defense organization. The British attempted to create a legislative council of Arabs and Jews, but the Arabs believed that this would signal their acceptance of the mandate and refused participation. Heightened violence by 1929 led the British to halt all Jewish settlement in Palestine, but Jewish outcries caused the British to reverse this policy. In 1936, a full-fledged Arab revolt began. Lasting until 1939, it forced the British to dispatch to Palestine 20,000 additional troops and brought the deaths of some 5,000 Arabs, with many more injured. It also brought a temporary alliance between the British and the Jews.

In 1937 the British government considered partitioning Palestine into separate Arab and Jewish states but a year later rejected this as not feasible. In 1939 the British announced that Palestine would become an independent state within 10 years. The British government also sharply curtailed Jewish immigration and restricted the sale of Arab land to Jews. This policy of attempting to favor the Arabs continued during World War II, when the British even diverted naval assets to intercept and turn back ships carrying Jews attempting to escape the Holocaust. Jewish extremists now took up arms against the British in Palestine, and a three-way war ensued between Arabs, Jews, and the British.

News of the Holocaust that had brought the deaths of more than 6 million Jews dramatically changed attitudes throughout most of the world in favor of Jewish settlement in Palestine and even the creation of a Jewish state there. Most Jews now believed that the only way to prevent a new Holocaust was the creation of a Jewish state. Jewish terrorist organizations were increasingly at war with the British administration in Palestine, which was refusing to allow the resettlement in Israel from Europe of more than 250,000 Jewish survivors of the Holocaust. The official census of 1945 shows the dramatic increase in the Jewish population in Palestine, with 553,660 Jews and 1,211,100 Arabs (1,061,270 Muslims and 149,830 Christians). Jews now constituted 31 percent of the population, up from 11 percent in 1922.

On February 14, 1947, exasperated by its inability to solve the Palestinian problem, the British government turned it over to the newly created United Nations

(UN). That August the UN Special Commission on Palestine (UNSCOP) recommended terminating the British mandate and granting Palestine its independence on the basis of separate Arab and Jewish states. Although the Arab population was 1.2 million and the Jewish population just 600,000, the Jews would have had some 56 percent of the land. Jews supported the plan; understandably, the Arabs opposed it. Desperate to quit Palestine, the British government simply announced acceptance of the UNSCOP recommendation and declared in September 1947 that its mandate would terminate on May 14, 1948.

On November 29, 1947, the UN General Assembly officially approved the UNSCOP plan for the partition of Palestine in a vote of 31 to 13 with 10 abstentions, ensuring the establishment of a Jewish state in Palestine. This brought civil war in Palestine, with bombings and considerable violence. On May 14, 1948, the Jews of Palestine declared the establishment of the State of Israel a few hours before the terminations of the British mandate at midnight. The next day, the Arab armies of Egypt, Lebanon, Jordan, Syria, and Iraq invaded Palestine, beginning the Israeli War of Independence (May 15, 1948–January 7, 1949). It was only the first in a number of major Arab-Israeli wars. Smaller wars, armed clashes, and widespread animosity extend to the present.

SPENCER C. TUCKER

Course

The Israeli War of Independence (May 15, 1948–January 7, 1949)

The Arab forces ranged against Israel in 1948 included those of Egypt, Iraq, Lebanon, Syria, and Transjordan, supplemented by volunteers from Libya, Saudi Arabia, and Yemen. Officially, they were under the auspices of the Arab League, formed in 1945. King Abdullah of Transjordan was commander in chief of the Arab armies, although cooperation among these forces was almost nonexistent and a chief cause of their military failure in the war. On May 15, the Arab League announced its intention to create a unified Palestinian state to include the Jewish and Arab regions of the UN partition plan.

The Arab armies began the conflict with some 30,000 troops. This increased to only 55,000 by October 1948. Most independent observers expected the Arabs to score a quick military victory, however, largely because of their crushing superiority in heavy weapons.

On May 26, the Israeli government created the Israel Defense Forces (IDF). The IDF incorporated the irregular Jewish militias of the British mandate, to include the Haganah, led by Israel Galili, and the Palmuch, commanded by Yigel Allon. Initially numbering fewer than 30,000 troops, by the end of 1948 the IDF counted more than 100,000. At first the IDF had virtually no artillery, armored vehicles, or aircraft. As the fighting continued, the Israeli government was able to secure some arms from abroad, beginning with 25 aircraft from Czechoslovakia in late May. Czechoslovakia continued to provide the IDF with weaponry for the remainder of the war, even during UN-mandated cease-fires that prohibited arms sales to any belligerent.

During the first phase of the war of May 15–June 1, in the central part of the front Arab armies from Transjordan and Iraq advanced on Jerusalem with the aim of driving all Jews from the city. The best Arab fighting force in the war, the Transjordan Arab Legion, secured the eastern and southern portions of the new part of the city. It also occupied most of Old Jerusalem and laid siege to the remainder. Although Jewish forces, ably led by American volunteer Colonel David Marcus, failed to break through the Arab roadblock on the Tel Aviv-Jerusalem road, they constructed a new access road to Jerusalem through the mountains just before a UN-sponsored truce went into effect on June 11.

Meanwhile, Lebanese and Syrian forces invaded Palestine from the north. The Lebanese were stopped at Malkya. The Syrian invasion, which was larger and supported by tanks and artillery, was defeated by Jewish settlers at Degania, the oldest kibbutz in Palestine, although the defenders possessed only light weapons. The Israelis also blunted an ineffective Iraqi invasion across the Jordan River south of the Sea of Galilee. Soon the Iraqi Army shifted to a defensive posture around Jenin and Nablus.

Only in the south did Arab forces register significant territorial gains. Here two Egyptian brigades commanded by Major General Ahmed Ali el-Mawawi advanced into Palestine. The principal Egyptian force moved up the coastal road to take Gaza and threaten Tel Aviv. A smaller force moved inland from Abu Ageila by way of Beersheba toward Jerusalem. Although the Egyptian coastal force secured Ashdod, only 25 miles from Tel Aviv, it bogged down shortly thereafter. The inland column linked up with the Arab Legion at Bethlehem on May 22.

The first phase of the war ended with a UN-declared truce that went into effect on June 11. Although the truce included an arms embargo for all belligerents, both sides saw this as an opportunity to rest, resupply, and reequip their forces, and the Israelis were able to smuggle in arms and ammunition from Czechoslovakia during the monthlong truce.

ARAB-ISRAELI WAR, 1948

Principal Arab attacks from outside Palestine

Territory allocated to the state of Israel by the United Nations, but overrun by Arabs between May 15 and Jun 1, 1948

Territory remaining under Israeli control on Jun 1, 1948

Jewish settlements overrun by the Arabs between May 15 and Jun 1

Jewish settlements surrounded by Arab forces, but resisted repeated attempts to overrun them between May 15 and Jun 1

LEBANON

SYRIA

Malkiya
Kadesh

Mishmar
Hayarden

Nahariya

Acre

Haifa

Ein Gev

Naharayim
Afula   Degania
Gesher

IRAQI
TROOPS

Hadera

Mediterranean

Sea

Nablus

Jordan R.

Herzliya

Tel Aviv

Jaffa

Ben
Shemen

TRANSJORDAN

Atarot   Neve
Yaakov

Kfar   Mt Scopus
Menachem   Hartuv   Kallia   Bet Haarava
Nitzanim

Kedma   Massuot   Revadim
Yizhak   Ein Tzirim   The Jewish Quarter:
Old City of Jerusalem

Yad   Gat   Galon   Gush
Mordechai   Etzion   Dead
Sea

Kfar Darom

Nirim

Beersheba

Nevatim

Sodom

ISRAEL

EGYPT

SINAI   NEGEV

0   10   20 mi
0   10   20 km

33°N

32°N

31°N

34°E   35°E   36°E

During the cease-fire, UN mediator Swedish count Folke Bernadotte advanced a new partition plan, but both sides immediately rejected it. On July 9 the cease-fire collapsed, and the IDF assumed the offensive.

The primary IDF objective was to regain control of the vital Tel Aviv–Jerusalem corridor in the central sector. In heavy fighting, the IDF secured the corridor after a massive assault on Lod (Lydda) that included the first Israeli use of bomber aircraft. Defended by Transjordanian troops and supplemented by Palestinian irregulars and units of the Arab Liberation Army, Lod surrendered on July 11. The next day the IDF captured Ramle, another key location in the vital corridor.

In the north, the IDF launched Operation DEKEL, a major push against Syrian and Lebanese troops in the lower Galilee region. The IDF captured Nazareth on July 16. Only against Egyptian forces in the southern sector did the IDF fail to make significant progress. Here the IDF goals were to sever Egyptian supply lines and reopen communications with the Negev.

The second phase of the war (July 9–18) ended with another UN-brokered truce, which went into effect on July 18. Bernadotte presented yet another partition plan, this time calling for Transjordan to annex the Arab regions. It also called for the creation of an independent Jewish state and the establishment of Jerusalem as an international city. The belligerents again rejected the plan, and on September 17, the day after he had presented his plan, Bernadotte was assassinated by members of Lehi, a Zionist militia.

The truce remained in effect until October 15, when the third phase of the war (October 15–November 5, 1948) began. The IDF ended the cease-fire with a series of offensives designed to drive Arab armies completely from Israeli territory. The first strike was against Egyptian Army troops in the Negev. Operation YOAV, commanded by Yigal Allon, sought to cut off the Egyptian troops along the coast from those to the interior in the Negev. The success of this operation forced the Egyptian Army to abandon the northern Negev.

The IDF also enjoyed success in the northern sector. On October 24 Operation HIRAM commenced in the upper Galilee, with the IDF destroying remnants of the Arab Liberation Army, driving Lebanese forces completely out of Palestine, and pushing several miles into Lebanon. Shaky cease-fires were arranged in the north between Israeli and Syrian and Lebanese forces on November 30.

The fourth and final phase of the war occurred between November 19, 1948, and January 7, 1949, beginning with an Egyptian Army offensive on November 19. Although they failed in their design of relieving the Faluja pocket, the Egyptians were able to expand their coastal holdings around Gaza.

With cease-fires holding elsewhere, beginning on December 20, 1948, the IDF launched a major offensive designed to drive Egypt from the war. The IDF isolated Rafah on December 22 and secured Asluj and Auja during December 25–27. Halted by Egyptian forces in their effort to take Al-Arish, the Israelis turned to the northeast. With the IDF about to launch a major attack on Rafah, Egypt requested an immediate armistice, which the UN Security Council granted. The cease-fire went into effect on January 7, 1949.

With the cease-fire, UN mediator Dr. Ralph Bunche began armistice discussions with the two sides. Armistice agreements, but no peace treaties, were ultimately concluded between Israel and all the Arab belligerents except Iraq. The armistice with Egypt of February 24 left Egyptian troops in occupation of the Gaza Strip. In the March 23 agreement with Lebanon, Israel agreed to withdraw from territory it had captured in southern Lebanon. The Israeli-Transjordan armistice of April 3 allowed Transjordanian troops to remain in control of the West Bank and East Jerusalem. The Israeli-Syrian armistice of July 20 resulted in the creation of a demilitarized zone along the Israeli-Syrian border.

The war ended with the new Jewish state occupying about three-fourths of the former British mandate of Palestine, or about 50 percent more land than offered in Bernadotte's original partition proposal. The war claimed about 6,000 Israeli lives, one-third of them civilians. Arab losses were much higher, about 10,000 killed.

Although the figure is in dispute, as many as 1 million Arab Palestinians may have either voluntarily left or were driven from their homes and lands, forced to live in makeshift refugee camps in the adjacent Arab states, which insisted on keeping them in refugee camps until they were allowed to return. Refugee status has been passed to their descendants, who have also been denied citizenship in their host countries on the insistence of the Arab League in order to preserve their Palestinian identity "and protect their right of return to their homeland." More than 1.4 million Palestinians still live in 58 recognized refugee camps, while more than 5 million Palestinians live outside Israel and the Palestinian territories.

Some 10,000 Jews were displaced by the war. After the war many Jews either voluntarily left or were expelled by the Arab states, and a number of them and other Jews living elsewhere in the world moved to Israel to help build the new Jewish state. From May 1948 to the end of 1951 some 700,000 Jews settled in Israel, in effect doubling its Jewish population.

The relatively small and short Israeli War for Independence had immense consequences. The surprising Israeli victory humiliated the Arab states and fueled demand for revenge.

SPENCER C. TUCKER

The Six-Day War (June 5–10, 1967)

In 1954, Egyptian leader Gamal Abdel Nasser began supporting raids into Israeli territory by so-called fedayeen, or guerrilla, fighters, who almost always attacked civilians. Then in 1956 Nasser nationalized the Suez Canal. The leaders of Britain, France, and Israel came up with a plan that they hoped would topple Nasser from power and return the canal to its former management. Israel would use the fedayeen raids as the excuse to invade and occupy the Egyptian Sinai Peninsula, thus threatening the canal. Britain and France would then call for Israel and Egypt to withdraw their forces from the Suez Canal area. On the assumed refusal of Egypt to comply, British and French forces would invade Egypt.

On October 29, Israeli forces invaded the Sinai Peninsula with the announced aim of eradicating the fedayeen bases. When, as expected, Egypt rejected an Anglo-French cease-fire ultimatum, those two nations sent their forces into Egypt. Although the Egyptians were defeated, they did block the canal to shipping. U.S. president Dwight D. Eisenhower then put heavy financial pressure on the British government, and British and French forces then withdrew. Nasser's position, far from weakened, was actually strengthened. Israel did secure some of its goals, for a UN observer force took up station in the Sinai, and Israel secured freedom of navigation through the Straits of Tiran.

By the spring of 1967, however, the Middle East was poised on the brink of a new war. Although the Israeli War of Independence of 1948–1949 and the 1956 Suez Crisis had produced a reluctance on the part of Arab leaders to embark on yet a new conflict, considerable low-key fighting was occurring in the form of Palestinian raids against the Jewish state from Syria and Jordan. Israel met this undeclared war on its territory by retaliatory strikes against guerrilla camps and villages in the Golan Heights of Syria and in Jordan. The year 1965 saw an Arab attempt to divert the flow of the Jordan River, and this brought IDF attacks against the diversion sites in Syria. This in turn produced a mutual defense pact between Egypt and Syria against Israel on November 4, 1966.

On November 13, 1966, the IDF mounted a large-scale attack on Es Samu in Jordan, a Palestinian refugee camp said to be a base for Syrian terrorists. Then on April 7, 1967, two decades of sporadic raids across the Israel-Syria border exploded in an aerial battle over the Golan Heights, with IDF aircraft downing six Syrian jet fighters, after which IDF warplanes overflew Damascus in a show of force.

With Israeli's chief supporter, the United States, heavily engaged in Vietnam, the leaders of the Soviet Union saw an opportunity to alter the balance of power in the Middle East that would favor their client states of Egypt and Syria. On May 13, the Soviets provided Egypt with false information that Israel was mobilizing troops along the Syrian border. As a consequence, on May 16 Nasser, now the president of Egypt, declared a state of emergency (Israel's subsequent protestations that the

Soviet report was untrue were ignored), and the next day the Egyptian and Syrian governments proclaimed a state of "combat readiness." Jordan also mobilized.

As a consequence of this belligerency, Nasser's popularity soared in the Arab world with profound impact. On May 16, Nasser demanded that the United Nations Emergency Force (UNEF), stationed in the Sinai, depart immediately. Since the 1956 Suez Crisis the UNEF had served as a buffer between Egyptian and Israeli forces. The UNEF complied on May 19. The day before, Syria and Egypt placed their armed forces on maximum alert, while the Iraqi and Kuwaiti governments announced that their forces were also mobilizing.

In a meeting with the Arab press, Nasser announced Egypt's intention to close the Straits of Tiran to Israeli shipping. The straits were the principal avenue for Israeli trade with Asia and the transit point for 90 percent of its oil imports. Closing the straits would severely disrupt the Israeli economy. Indeed, Israel had already let it be known that it would consider such a step justification for war. Nasser knew that Israel would probably react militarily, but he assumed that the United States would not support the anticipated Israeli military response, while Egypt and its allies would have the support of the Soviet Union. The Kremlin, however, reacted negatively to Nasser's announcement. Having stirred the pot, it now urged restraint. Responding to a hotline message to Soviet leaders from U.S. president Lyndon Johnson, the Soviets on May 27 insisted that the Egyptians not strike first.

Nasser's proposal regarding the Straits of Tiran was largely bluff. He assumed that the threat of closing the straits would force Israel to withdraw its supposed increased forces along the Syrian border, greatly enhancing his standing in the Arab world. On May 22, however, Egyptian minister of defense Field Marshal Abdel Hakim Amer ordered Egyptian forces to close the straits the next day. A countermanding order would have signaled weakness on Nasser's part, and he now issued orders to the Egyptian military to prepare for war.

On May 20, meanwhile, Israel completed a partial mobilization. The Arab states were also mobilizing, and Iraqi and Algerian forces began moving to Syria and Egypt. On May 26, Nasser announced that if Israel were to strike either Egypt or Syria, this would result in a general war, with the Arab goal being "the destruction of Israel." On May 30 Jordanian king Hussein arrived in Cairo, and Egypt and Jordan concluded a mutual security pact.

On paper, the balance of forces heavily favored the Arab states. Israel had mobilized 230,000 men. It had 1,100 tanks, 200 artillery pieces, 260 combat aircraft, and 22 naval vessels. Egypt and Syria together had 263,000 men, 1,950 tanks, 915 artillery pieces, 521 combat aircraft, and 75 naval vessels. Counting Iraqi and Jordanian forces, the Arab advantage swelled to 409,000 men, 2,437 tanks, 1,487 artillery pieces, 649 combat aircraft, and 90 naval vessels.

Now certain that there would be war and unwilling to allow the Arab forces time to fully mobilize their larger resources, on June 4, despite strong U.S. opposition, Israeli prime minister Levi Eshkol authorized a preemptive strike against Egypt. Minister of defense General Moshe Dayan passed the word to Lieutenant General Yitzhak Rabin and the Israeli General Staff.

The Arab-Israeli war of 1967, known to history as the Six-Day War, commenced on the morning of June 5. For all practical purposes, the war was over by noon. The Israeli Air Force offensive of that day remains one of the most stunning successes in modern warfare.

EGYPTIAN FRONT

Destruction of the Egyptian Air Force was essential if the Israeli Army was to enjoy success on the ground, yet Israel was outnumbered by Egypt and Syria two to one in combat aircraft. It would also be difficult for Israel to defend against Egyptian and Syrian air attacks, because the attackers would come from two different directions and also because Israel was too small in area for early warning systems to provide sufficient time for Israeli fighters to scramble. The Israeli capital of Tel Aviv was 25 minutes' flying time from Cairo but only 4.5 minutes from the nearest Egyptian air base at Al-Arish.

The initial Israeli air attack plan relied on accurate, timely, and precise intelligence information. Israeli aircraft were to take off from airfields all around Israel and fly west, under radio silence and at low altitude to avoid radar out over the Mediterranean, then turn south to strike Egyptian airfields as simultaneously as possible. The strikes were to coincide with the return of Egyptian aircraft to base from morning patrols, when most Egyptian pilots would be having breakfast.

Israeli Air Force (IAF) air and ground crews were highly trained and able to reduce turnaround time between missions to a minimum. They could thus fly up to four sorties a day versus only half that number for their opponents. The operation was, however, extremely risky in that it employed almost all Israeli strike aircraft, leaving only a dozen fighters behind to fly combat air patrol in defense of Israel itself.

The IAF achieved complete tactical surprise. The first IAF attack wave struck 10

BALANCE OF FORCES, MAY 14–24, 1967

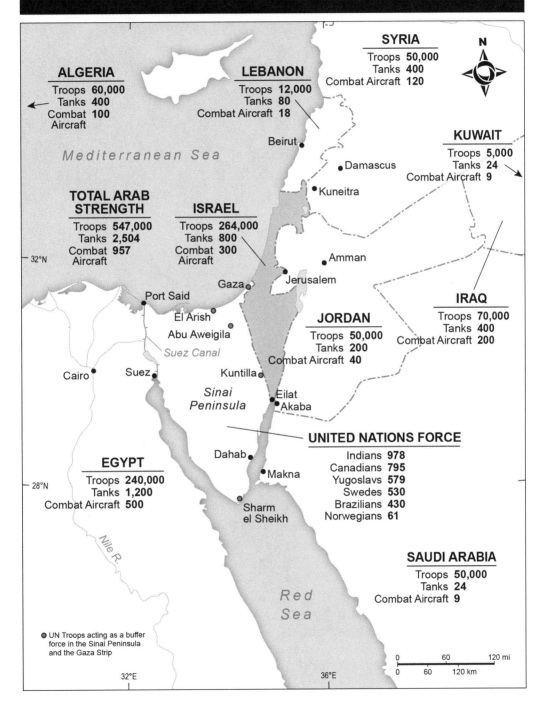

SYRIA
Troops 50,000
Tanks 400
Combat Aircraft 120

N

ALGERIA
Troops 60,000
Tanks 400
Combat 100
Aircraft

LEBANON
Troops 12,000
Tanks 80
Combat Aircraft 18

Mediterranean Sea

Beirut

KUWAIT
Troops 5,000
Tanks 24
Combat Aircraft 9

Damascus

Kuneitra

TOTAL ARAB STRENGTH
Troops 547,000
Tanks 2,504
Combat 957
Aircraft

ISRAEL
Troops 264,000
Tanks 800
Combat 300
Aircraft

32°N

Gaza

Amman

Jerusalem

Port Said

El Arish

Abu Aweigila

Suez Canal

JORDAN
Troops 50,000
Tanks 200
Combat Aircraft 40

IRAQ
Troops 70,000
Tanks 400
Combat Aircraft 200

Cairo

Suez

Kuntilla

Sinai Peninsula

Eilat

Akaba

UNITED NATIONS FORCE
Indians 978
Canadians 795
Yugoslavs 579
Swedes 530
Brazilians 430
Norwegians 61

Dahab

Makna

EGYPT
Troops 240,000
Tanks 1,200
Combat Aircraft 500

28°N

Sharm el Sheikh

Nile R.

SAUDI ARABIA
Troops 50,000
Tanks 24
Combat Aircraft 9

Red Sea

UN Troops acting as a buffer force in the Sinai Peninsula and the Gaza Strip

0   60   120 mi
0   60   120 km

32°E

36°E

A burnt out Egyptian aircraft at El Auth airport in the Sinai during the Six-Day War of June 5–10, 1967. (Express Newspapers/Getty Images)

Egyptian airfields. Only four Egyptian aircraft, all trainers, were in the air at the time, and all were shot down. Subsequent waves of Israeli aircraft arrived at 10-minute intervals. Only eight Egyptian MiGs managed to take off during the strikes, and all were shot down. In all, the IAF attacked 17 major Egyptian airfields with some 500 sorties (a sortie being one mission by one individual aircraft) in just under three hours, employing cannon fire and bombs to wipe out half of the Egyptian Air Force strength of 431 combat aircraft.

Later on June 5, Israeli aircraft struck Syria and Jordan. Following an Iraqi air strike on Israel, IAF aircraft also attacked Iraqi air bases in the Mosul area. With its opposing air forces largely neutralized, the IAF could then turn to close air support of Israeli mechanized ground forces, which had begun operations in the Sinai simultaneous with the initial air attacks. In all during the war, the Arab side lost 390 aircraft of their prewar strength of 969

aircraft (Egypt, 286 of 580; Jordan, 28 of 56; Syria, 54 of 172; Iraq, 21 of 149; and Lebanon, 1 of 12). Total IAF losses were 32 aircraft shot down of 354 at the beginning of the war, only 2 to aerial combat.

Israeli ground forces were now on the move against Egypt. The Egyptians, it should be noted, were handicapped by the fact that 50,000 of their best troops were tied down in the civil war in Yemen. Israeli ground forces sent against Egypt consisted of a mechanized brigade under Colonel Yehuda Resheff, a mechanized division commanded by Major General Israel Tal, an armored division under Major General Avraham Yoffe, and a mechanized division under Major General Ariel Sharon. Tal's division drove into the Rafah–Al-Arish area, Resheff advanced into the Gaza Strip, and Sharon moved toward fortifications in the area of Abu Ageila and Kusseima. Yoffe proceeded southward toward the central Sinai to cut off an Egyptian retreat.

On June 6, Egyptian troops in Gaza surrendered to Resheff's forces. Meanwhile, Tal's mechanized division and Yoffe's armored division linked up. Sharon sent part of his mechanized division to Rafah and Al-Arish and the remainder toward Nakhle and the Mitla Pass; Yoffe attacked the main Egyptian force at Jabal Libni in central Sinai. Egyptian Army commander Field Marshal Amer ordered all Egyptian units in the Sinai to withdraw.

On June 7 the major elements of Tal's mechanized division arrived at Bir Gifgafa, while his northern task force passed Romani. The leading brigade of Yoffe's armored division arrived at the eastern end of the Mitla Pass out of fuel and short of ammunition. Egyptian forces quickly surrounded it, but shortly thereafter Yoffe's other brigade arrived and relieved the first. Sharon's mechanized division advanced closer to Nakhle, while other units captured northeastern Sinai and Israeli air and amphibious forces secured Sharm al-Shaykh.

On June 8, Egyptian armored units attempted to provide cover for forces withdrawing from the Sinai. Tal's mechanized division drove them back, however, advancing toward the Suez Canal between Qantara and Ismailiyya. Meanwhile, Yoffe's armored division transited Mitla Pass and reached the canal opposite Port Suez, while Sharon's mechanized division captured Nakhle and moved through Mitla Pass. By the end of the day, the Sinai was firmly under Israeli Army control. Egypt had lost 80 percent of its military equipment and had some 11,500 troops killed, 20,000 wounded, and 5,500 taken prisoner. The IDF had sustained 338 killed.

On June 9, the UN Security Council called for a cease-fire. This left Israel in control of the Sinai east of the Suez Canal. While Israel immediately accepted the cease-fire, Egypt did not agree until the next day, June 10. On June 9, meanwhile, Nasser had offered his resignation as president, but it was rejected, the consequence of large Egyptian public demonstrations.

JORDANIAN FRONT

Israeli leaders had urged King Hussein of Jordan to stay out of the war, informing him at the onset of fighting that their dispute was with Egypt. Hussein wanted to avoid participation but came under heavy pressure to act. He was also deceived by early Cairo broadcasts claiming major Egyptian military successes. Hussein hoped to satisfy his allies with minimum military action short of all-out war. Jordanian 155mm "Long Tom" guns went into action against Tel Aviv, and Jordanian aircraft attempted to strafe a small Israeli airfield near Kfar Sirkin. These steps, however, led Israel to declare war on Jordan.

The Jordanians fired on Israeli territory from their part of Jerusalem, and Israeli brigadier general Uzi Narkiss commenced an offensive against Jerusalem with three brigades under Colonel Mordechai Gur. The Israelis surrounded the Old City, defended by Jordanian forces under Brigadier General Ata Ali. That same day in the Battle of Jenin-Nablus, Major General David Elazar, who headed the Israeli Northern Command, received orders to seize Jenin and Nablus and advance to the Jordan River. Elazar dispatched one division and an armored brigade toward Jenin.

On June 6, the Israelis continued their attacks on the Old City but encountered fierce Jordanian opposition. They were able, however, to prevent Jordanian forces from relieving the Old City. An Israeli tank brigade seized Ramallah, and another captured Latrun, opening the road between Tel Aviv and Jerusalem to Jewish traffic for the first time since 1947. Jenin fell to the Israelis after fierce combat.

On June 7 Gur's forces stormed the Old City, forcing a Jordanian withdrawal. That same day, the Israelis captured Bethlehem, Hebron, and Etzion. Despite Jordanian counterattacks, the Israelis also advanced on and seized Nablus. Jordanian forces then withdrew across the Jordan River, and both Israel and Jordan agreed to a cease-fire, to take effect at 8:00 p.m.

SYRIAN FRONT

At the onset of fighting, Syria had positioned on the Golan Heights six brigades on line, with six others in reserve east of Quneitra (Kuneitra). For four days Israeli commander of the Northern Front Major General David Elazar engaged in artillery duels against the Syrians, who showed no signs of wishing to initiate offensive action. On June 8, however, a UN-brokered cease-fire collapsed after artillery fire from both sides.

On June 9, with resources released from other fronts, Elazar initiated major offensive action in an advance toward the Dan-Banyas area along the foothills of Mount Hermon. The Israelis broke through the first line of Syrian defenses in the northern Golan. Other units forced their way north of the Sea of Galilee, while Elazar ordered units recently engaged in the Jenin-Nablus area to attack the Golan south of the Sea of Galilee.

Syrian defenses rapidly deteriorated on June 10. The Israelis resisted calls from the United States not to occupy the Golan Heights and to agree to a cease-fire and instead advanced on Quneitra from the north, west, and southwest. Troops from the Jordanian front pushed northeastward toward the Yarmouk (Yarmuk) Valley and occupied the southern Golan. The Israelis

then surrounded Quneitra and captured it. Only when the Golan Heights was firmly in their hands did the Israelis agree to a cease-fire. It went into effect at 6:30 p.m. on June 10.

FIGHTING AT SEA

In the last few days just before the beginning of the war, during June 3–4 the Israelis trucked landing craft by day from the Mediterranean to Eilat, then returned them at night. This led the Egyptians to believe that the Israelis were massing resources at Eilat for operations in the Gulf of Aqaba and caused them to shift naval assets into the Red Sea, redressing the Mediterranean naval imbalance.

With the start of the war, on June 5 Israeli and Egyptian naval units clashed off Port Said. An Israeli destroyer and several motor torpedo boats reached Port Said and were there met by two Egyptian Osa-class missile boats. After an inconclusive battle, the Egyptian missile boats withdrew. Israeli frogmen entered the harbors of both Port Said and Alexandria and damaged Egyptian ships at Alexandria before being taken prisoner. On June 6, as a consequence of the Israeli air attacks and land advance, Egyptian naval units withdrew from Port Said to Alexandria.

On the night of June 6–7, three Egyptian submarines shelled the Israeli coast near Ashdod and north and south of Haifa, but Israeli air and naval forces returned fire and drove them off. On June 7, with the Israeli capture of Sharm al-Shaykh, Israeli warships were able to transit the Straits of Tiran to the Red Sea unobstructed.

On June 8 the *Liberty,* a U.S. electronic intelligence-gathering ship, was in international waters some 13 miles off Al-Arish on the Sinai Peninsula when it came under attack by Israel's air force and navy.

Thirty-four American personnel died in the attack and another 172 were wounded, many seriously. Although the ship was badly damaged, its crew managed to keep the *Liberty* afloat and make Malta, escorted by ships of the U.S. Sixth Fleet. The Israeli government later apologized for the attack and paid nearly $13 million in compensation. The reasons for the attack and charges of a cover-up have been the topics of conspiracy theories, but official inquiries concluded that it was a matter of mistaken identity.

In the Six-Day War, Israel suffered some 800 dead, 2,440 wounded, and 16 missing or taken prisoner. Arab losses, chiefly Egyptian, are estimated at 14,300 dead, 23,800 wounded, and 10,500 missing or taken prisoner. Israel lost 100 tanks and 40 aircraft, while the Arabs lost 950 tanks and 368 aircraft.

The Six-Day War vastly increased the amount of territory controlled by Israel. Israel gained from Egypt all of the Sinai east of the Suez Canal, including the Gaza Strip; from Jordan, it secured the entire east bank of the Jordan River and the Old City of Jerusalem; and from Syria, it added the Golan Heights.

The territorial acquisitions by Israel as a consequence of the war have made securing a Middle East peace settlement much more difficult. Although Israel returned the Sinai to Egypt in 1978 and withdrew from the Gaza Strip in 2005, it has showed a marked reluctance to yield up the Golan Heights, the West Bank, and Old Jerusalem. Politically conservative Israelis and Ultra-Orthodox Jews consider the West Bank part of the ancient Jewish state, not to be given up on any basis. Yet some 1.7 million Arabs constitute 21 percent of the Israeli population, raising issues of Israel's survival both as a Jewish state

and a democracy. Increasing construction of Jewish settlements and Israel's determination to retain significant parts of the West Bank and all of Jerusalem constitute major barriers to any comprehensive peace settlement.

SPENCER C. TUCKER

The Yom Kippur War (October 6–25, 1973)

The Yom Kippur War of October 6–25, 1973, also known as the Ramadan War, the October War, and the 1973 Arab-Israeli War, had a profound effect on the Middle East. Egyptian president Gamal Abdel Nasser died in September 1970. His successor, Anwar Sadat, was determined to change the status quo regarding Israel. Sadat called for a gradual peace settlement that would lead to Israeli withdrawal from the Sinai but without a formal general peace agreement. Sadat resumed negotiations with the United States that Nasser had ended in 1955.

The failure of his diplomatic efforts in 1971, however, led Sadat to begin planning a military operation to break the political stalemate. Sadat believed that even a minor Egyptian military success would change the military equilibrium and force a political settlement. Israel's strength was in its air force and armored divisions, which were well trained in maneuver warfare. Egyptian strengths were the ability to build a strong defense line and new Soviet-supplied surface-to-air missiles (SAMs) deployed in batteries along the canal and deep within Egypt. Sadat hoped to paralyze the Israeli Air Force by the SAMs and counter the Israelis' advantage in maneuver warfare by forcing them to attack well-fortified and well-defended Egyptian strongholds.

In an attempt to dilute the Israeli military forces on the Sinai front, Sadat

OCTOBER WAR, 1973

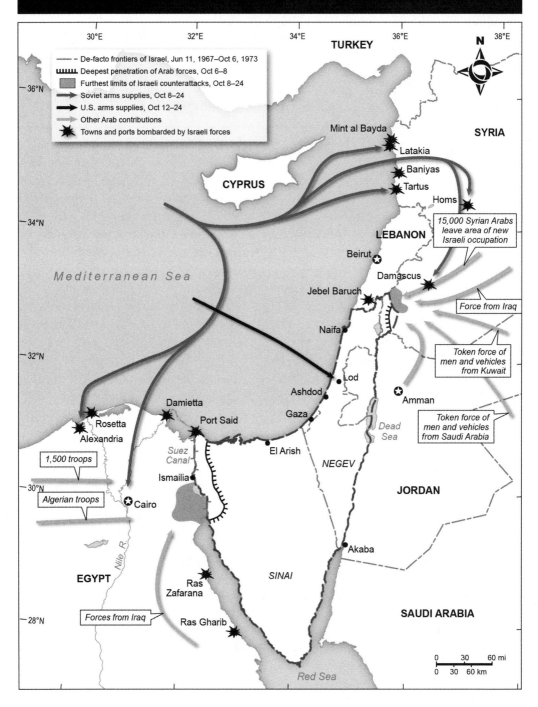

Legend:
- De-facto frontiers of Israel, Jun 11, 1967–Oct 6, 1973
- Deepest penetration of Arab forces, Oct 6–8
- Furthest limits of Israeli counterattacks, Oct 8–24
- Soviet arms supplies, Oct 8–24
- U.S. arms supplies, Oct 12–24
- Other Arab contributions
- Towns and ports bombarded by Israeli forces

TURKEY

SYRIA

CYPRUS

Mint al Bayda
Latakia
Baniyas
Tartus
Homs

15,000 Syrian Arabs leave area of new Israeli occupation

LEBANON

Beirut

Damascus

Mediterranean Sea

Jebel Baruch

Force from Iraq

Naifa

Token force of men and vehicles from Kuwait

Lod
Ashdod
Gaza

Amman

Dead Sea

Token force of men and vehicles from Saudi Arabia

Damietta
Port Said
Rosetta
Alexandria

El Arish

NEGEV

JORDAN

Suez Canal

Ismailia

1,500 troops

Algerian troops

Cairo

Akaba

Nile R.

SINAI

EGYPT

Ras Zafarana

SAUDI ARABIA

Forces from Iraq

Ras Gharib

Red Sea

0   30   60 mi
0   30 60 km

brought in Syria. A coordinated surprise attack by both states would place maximum stress on the IDF. Above all, the key to success was secrecy. Were Israel to suspect that an attack was imminent, it would undoubtedly launch a preventive attack, as in 1967. That part of Sadat's plan, at least, was successful.

A combination of effective Egyptian deceptive measures and Israeli arrogance contributed to Israel's failure to comprehend what was happening. One deception consisted of repeated Egyptian drills along the Suez Canal, simulating a possible crossing. The Israelis thus interpreted Egyptian preparations for the actual crossings as just another drill. Even the Egyptian soldiers were told that it was simply a drill. Only when the actual crossing was under way were they informed of its true nature. Even with the attack, however, the real intent of Egyptian and Syrian forces remained unclear to the Israelis, and they initially refrained from offensive action.

On the Israeli-Egyptian front, Egypt amassed nearly 800,000 soldiers, 2,200 tanks, 2,300 artillery pieces, 150 SAM batteries, and 550 aircraft. Along the canal Egypt deployed five infantry divisions with accompanying armored elements, supported by additional infantry and armored independent brigades. This force was backed by three mechanized divisions and two armored divisions. Opposing this impressive Egyptian force, Israel had only a single division supported by 280 tanks.

On October 4–5, 1973, Sadat expelled some 15,000 Soviet advisers and all their dependents. Not until the early morning hours of October 6 did Israeli military intelligence conclude that an Egyptian attack was imminent. Brigadier General Eilhau Zeira, Israeli director of intelligence, warned Lieutenant General David Elazar,

IDF chief of staff, but Prime Minister Golda Meir decided against a preemptive strike.

OPERATIONS ON THE SINAI FRONT

At 2:00 p.m. on October 6, Egypt launched a massive air strike against Israeli artillery and command positions. At the same time, Egyptian artillery shelled the Israeli Bar Lev Line fortifications along the Suez Canal. Egyptian commandos crossed the canal followed by engineers, who quickly constructed bridges, allowing the Egyptians to get sizable numbers of infantry and armor across. By October 8, the Egyptians had established a penetration three to five miles deep, with some 500 tanks, on the east bank of the canal. Two Egyptian divisions held the seized area, which was also defended by SAM batteries.

The Israelis, meanwhile, mobilized two armored divisions under Major Generals Ariel Sharon and Abraham (Bren) Adan and on October 8 launched a quick counteroffensive in an attempt to repel the Egyptians. The Israelis came up against the far larger well-organized and well-equipped Egyptian force protected by highly effective handheld antitank missiles. The Egyptians crushed the Israeli counteroffensive, and Israeli ground-support aircraft also suffered heavy losses against Egyptian antiaircraft defenses, especially SAMs. Following this setback, the Israeli General Staff decided to halt offensive actions on the Suez front and give priority to that with Syria.

Sadat now overruled his ground commander, Field Marshal Ahmed Ismail Ali, and, following Syrian pleas for assistance, ordered a resumption of the offensive in the Sinai on October 11. This, however, took Egyptian forces out of their prepared defensive positions and removed them from the effective SAM cover on the other side of the canal. On October 14 the

Israelis threw back the Egyptians and inflicted heavy losses, especially in tanks.

On October 15–16 the Israelis located a gap, unknown to the Egyptian high command, between the two Egyptian divisions defending the occupied area. Sharon's division drove through that gap, and part of the division crossed the canal. An Israeli paratroop brigade then established a bridgehead on the west bank. The Israeli high command now had two goals: establishing a SAM-free zone over which Israeli aircraft could maneuver and cutting off Egyptian troops east of the canal from their bases west of it.

The Egyptian Second Army then closed behind Sharon, isolating his division on both sides of the canal. Adan's division, however, broke through, bringing a bridge forward to the crossing point. The Egyptian Second Army, assisted by units of the Third Army, was unable to close the Israeli supply corner.

Fighting during October 16–18 was known as the Battle of the Chinese Farm for a former Japanese experimental agricultural station there, which the Israelis assumed to have been Chinese. The Egyptians suffered heavy losses, and on the night of October 17–18 Adan's division crossed the canal.

Adan's division then pushed westward, rolling up Egyptian base camps and capturing antiaircraft positions and SAM sites. On October 19, however, Sharon was unsuccessful in seizing Ismailia. During October 20–22 Sharon continued his attacks on Ismailia but encountered heavy resistance from the Egyptian Second and Third Armies. Adan, however, cut the Suez-Cairo road northeast of Suez.

On October 22 Egypt and Israel agreed to a cease-fire, to take effect that evening, but this was soon broken. Israel then sent strong reinforcements across the canal, while Adan was ordered to continue his drive southward to the Gulf of Suez. Another Israel division, commanded by Major General Kalman Magen, followed after Adan, reaching Adabiya on the Gulf of Suez.

The Egyptians turned back an Israeli effort to take Suez during October 23–24. A second cease-fire was concluded on October 24 and went into effect the next day.

OPERATIONS ON THE SYRIAN FRONT

Syrian president Hafez al-Assad's chief motivation in joining Egyptian president Sadat in the war was to regain the Golan Heights along the 45-mile Syria-Israeli border. Israel had captured it in 1967, thereby gaining security for its northern settlements from sporadic Syrian bombardment. Unlike Sadat, Assad had no intention of using the war as leverage for a settlement with Israel.

At 2:00 p.m. on October 6, simultaneous with the Egyptian air strikes to the south, Syria launched a massive air strike accompanied by a heavy artillery bombardment against Israeli positions on the Golan Heights. Syrian ground forces then advanced in an effort to recapture this area and drive on Jerusalem from the north. Syrian Army major general Yousef Chakour commanded the attacking force of some 60,000 men in two armored divisions (600 tanks) and two infantry divisions (another 300 tanks). The Syrians also had some 140 artillery batteries. Opposing them, Israeli major general Yitzhak Hofi's Northern Command numbered some 12,000 troops, 177 tanks, and 11 artillery batteries.

With the exception of one important outpost, Israeli forces were not taken by surprise. Israeli intelligence had detected the massive Syrian buildup, and Israeli forces on this front were on full alert, with the tanks in hull-down positions behind earthen barricades and with infantry in their fighting positions.

The one exception was Mount Hermon. At the very start of the war here, Syrian helicopters carried commandos to the back of the fortified Israeli observation post on Mount Hermon that provided an excellent view of the Golan Heights and the Damascus Plateau. The two-platoon Israeli garrison there was taken completely by surprise. All were slain, including those who surrendered.

The main Syrian attack by the four divisions occurred in three axes against two Israeli brigades. Israel mobilization was excellent, and reservists were soon on the scene, but it took time to ready their equipment and tanks for action and bring them forward. Nonetheless, within a day the Israelis halted the northernmost thrust by the Syrian 7th Infantry Division, destroying most of the Syrian tanks. The Israelis also repulsed an attack by the Syrian 3rd Tank Division, which was slated to pass through the 7th Infantry Division.

The two Syrian thrusts in the south nearly entered the Jordan River Valley, however. If the Syrians were able to push beyond the escarpment, they could cross the Jordan River and Galilee, cutting Israel in two. Israeli aircraft went into action immediately following the first Syrian attacks. Some 1,500 tanks of the two sides were now crammed into a relatively small space, and the Golan Heights quickly became one vast graveyard of armored vehicles, although many of the Israeli jets also fell prey to Syrian SAMs and mobile antiaircraft guns. Many Israeli tanks were also knocked out. Only the Israeli close air support, the rapid arrival of Israeli reserves, and the unimaginative Syrian

attacks prevented the Syrians from retaking the southern Golan on the second day of fighting.

During October 8–9 the Israelis counterattacked in the south, assisted by the 7th Armored Brigade brought down from the northern Golan. On October 9 the Israeli 7th Brigade halted a Syrian thrust north of Quneitra (Kuneitra), and the next day the Israelis mounted a major counteroffensive north of the Quneitra-Damascus road. Three divisions pushed the Syrian 5th Mechanized and 1st Tank Divisions back to and beyond the prewar Israeli-Syrian border.

Beginning on October 9, using the excuse of Syrian surface-to-surface missile attacks against the Hula Valley, Israel launched a major aerial campaign against Syria. Israeli aircraft struck deep within Syria, hitting the Ministry of Defense in Damascus as well as seaports, industrial sites, and fuel storage areas. These attacks profoundly impacted the Syrian economy and continued until October 21.

On October 12 the Israelis began to withdraw some units south to fight on the Sinai front. Nonetheless, by October 14 they had opened up a salient inside Syria some 10 miles deep, 30 miles wide, and only 25 miles from Damascus. The Israelis held here during October 15–19 against fierce Syrian and Iraqi counterattacks, Iraq having now entered the war. On October 15 the Israelis repulsed the Iraqi 3rd Armored Division, and on October 19 they halted another Arab counterattack against the salient, this one spearheaded by Jordanian units. The Israelis maintained these positions until the cease-fire of October 24. On October 22, following two failed assaults on October 8 and 21, Israeli helicopter-borne paratroopers and infantry recaptured Mount Hermon.

The constrained area of the Golan Heights and the large forces involved ensured both fierce fighting and heavy losses. In the fighting for the Golan Heights, Israel lost nearly 800 dead and 250 tanks put out of action, along with a number of ground-support aircraft shot down. Certainly a key factor in Israeli success was their ability to quickly return disabled tanks to battle. Syrian losses were significantly greater: perhaps 8,000 men killed, 1,150 tanks destroyed, and 118 aircraft lost.

THE WAR AT SEA

On the start of the war, the Egyptians imposed a naval blockade of Israel's coasts to disrupt its Mediterranean trade, while Egyptian destroyers and submarines at the Strait of Bab al-Mandab halted seaborne traffic to Eilat.

On the first night of the war, Israeli Saar- and Reshef-class missile boats attacked the chief Syrian Mediterranean port of Latakia (Ladhaqiyya). Syrian missile boats engaged the attackers, and in the first naval battle in history between missile-firing ships, the Israelis defeated the incoming Syrian fire-and-forget Styx missiles while using their own radar-guided Gabriel ship-to-ship missiles to destroy one Osa-class and two Komar-class missile boats and a minesweeper. The Syrian Navy then remained in port for the rest of the war. This Battle of Latakia brought new prestige for the Israeli Navy, previously regarded as only a poor relation of its highly regarded army and air force.

A second Israeli strike at Latakia on the night of October 7–8 was inconclusive, as were engagements that same night between Israeli and Egyptian naval units in the Mediterranean and Red Seas. On October 8–9, in a naval action off the Egyptian port of Damietta, Egyptian missile

boats sortied to engage an Israeli missile boat task force, which sank four of them for no losses of their own. In an action the next night off Egyptian Port Said, another Egyptian missile boat was sunk. The remaining Egyptian missile boats then withdrew to Damietta and Alexandria. Other attacks by the Israeli Navy against Syria were inconclusive, although during October 15–16 Israeli missile boats attacked the Nile Delta and sank a number of Egyptian landing craft. Finally, on October 21–22 the Israelis attacked Abu Kir (Aboukir) Bay and Alexandria and there sank two Egyptian patrol boats.

INTERNATIONAL INVOLVEMENT

Both the United States, supporting Israel, and the Soviet Union, supporting the Arab states, were caught off guard by the war, although the Soviets probably learned of the Egyptian and Syrian plans several days in advance of the actual attacks. Both the Soviets and the Americans sent supplies to their sides in the war. Between October 14 and 21, the United States airlifted some 20,000 tons of supplies to Israel, as opposed to some 15,000 tons supplied by the Soviet Union to the Arab states.

On October 24 the Soviet Union threatened intervention in announcing that it was placing seven airborne divisions on alert, presumably to be sent to Egypt if necessary to break the Israeli stranglehold on the Egyptian Third Army east of the Suez Canal. The next day, U.S. secretary of state Henry Kissinger announced that the United States had placed its armed forces—including its nuclear assets—on precautionary alert. Any possibility of a Soviet-U.S. armed clash over the Middle East ended with a UN Security Council resolution—with both the Soviet and U.S. representatives voting in the affirmative—to establish a 7,000-man UNEF to enforce the cease-fires in the Sinai Peninsula and the Golan Heights. A cease-fire concluded on October 24 went into effect the next day.

SPENCER C. TUCKER

Consequences

Casualty figures for the Yom Kippur (Ramadan) War vary depending on the source and especially for Egypt and Syria, which did not release official figures. Israel suffered 2,521–2,800 killed in action, 7,250–8,800 wounded, and 293 taken prisoner. Some 400 Israeli tanks were destroyed; another 600 were disabled but returned to service. The Israeli Air Force lost 102 airplanes and 2 helicopters. There were no navy losses.

Arab losses were much higher. Most estimates fall in the range of 5,000–15,000 Egyptians and 3,000–3,500 Syrians killed; the number of wounded is unknown. Iraq lost 278 killed and 898 wounded, while Jordan suffered 23 killed and 77 wounded. A total of 8,372 Egyptians, 392 Syrians, 13 Iraqis, and 6 Moroccans were taken prisoner. The Arab states lost 2,250–2,300 tanks, 400 of which were taken by the Israelis in good working order and added to their inventory. Arab aircraft losses are estimated at 450–512. Nineteen Arab naval vessels, including 10 missile boats, were sunk.

The Yom Kippur War revealed the vulnerability of tanks, aircraft, and ships to the new missile weapons. Although its outcome secured Israel's borders, the war shocked Israelis, who had become complacent. An investigatory agency, the Agranat Commission, led to the removal of several high-ranking officers. The commission did not assess civilian leadership responsibility, but Prime Minister Golda Meir and Minister of Defense Moshe Dayan both resigned in April 1974.

Although the Arab states lost the war, Egyptian president Anwar Sadat had achieved his aim of erasing the trauma of their rapid defeat in the Six-Day War of 1967. The Yom Kippur War also allowed him to negotiate as an equal with Israel. Yet Israel had secured additional Arab territory, and this may have helped convince many in the Arab world that the Jewish state would not be defeated militarily.

On January 18, 1974, Israel and Egypt signed a disengagement agreement by which Israel agreed to pull back its forces from west of the Suez Canal and from the length of the front to create security zones. Another agreement, known as Sinai II, of September 4, 1975, saw Israel withdrawing another 12–24 miles, with UN observer forces taking over that area. Still, Israel held more than two-thirds of Sinai.

A peace agreement between Israel and Egypt known as the Camp David Accords was finally reached in September 17, 1978, following negotiations spearheaded by U.S. president Jimmy Carter. In accordance with the treaty, Israeli forces withdrew gradually from Sinai, with the last troops exiting on April 26, 1982. Not until 1994 did Jordan become the second (and last) Arab nation to conclude a peace treaty with Israel.

On the Syrian front, from February to May 1974 Syria engaged Israel in a war of attrition along the Golan Heights, consisting of artillery fire along the cease-fire line between Quneitra (Kuneitra) and Damascus. The Syrians hoped to force Israel to agree to withdraw its troops from the Golan Heights. On May 31, the two sides agreed to disengage. An exchange of prisoners occurred, and Israel relinquished all territory taken from Syria in the Yom Kippur War, two small strips taken in 1967, and the town of Quneitra. A cease-fire line was established between the two states, patrolled by troops of the UN Disengagement Observer Force.

Finally, the Yom Kippur War brought a major worldwide economic shock. On October 17, 1973, in response to U.S. support of Israel, the Arab members of the Organization of Oil Exporting Countries, led by Saudi Arabia, decided to reduce oil production by 5 percent per month. When on October 19 U.S. president Richard Nixon authorized a major allocation of arms supplies and $2.2 billion in appropriations for Israel, Saudi Arabia declared an oil embargo against the United States, later joined by other oil exporters and extended against other states as well. Unlike the ineffective embargo of the 1967 Six-Day War, this resulted in a full-blown energy crisis in much of the West and great havoc for the Western economies. The embargo lasted five months, until March 18, 1974, but its effects endured throughout the remainder of the 1970s, as Western nations were plagued by persistent stagflation (high inflation and low growth) and considerable unemployment.

The 1973 war did not end armed clashes. Indeed, Arab frustration served as the justification for a more militant form of Islam. Israel experienced repeated terrorist attacks and two prolonged uprisings (1987–1993 and 2000–2005) by Palestinian Arabs living under Israeli occupation, known as the Intifadas. On June 6, 1982, in response to attacks by the Palestine Liberation Organization (PLO) in Lebanon against Israeli border settlements, Israel launched Operation PEACE FOR GALILEE, also known as the Lebanon War. It saw heavy casualties and the destruction of much of Beirut. The PLO agreed to leave Beirut, and Israel occupied part of southern Lebanon until 1985 and then withdrew to a security zone that it deemed essential against terrorist attacks. It did not withdraw from Lebanon completely until 2000, and the Israeli presence helped create the more radical Hezbollah organization in Lebanon as well as civil war in Lebanon until 1990 and Syrian occupation of that country until 2005.

Failure to reach a comprehensive peace settlement has seen both Israel and the Arab states spend vast sums on armaments that could have gone to infrastructure and social programs. The Arab-Israeli confrontation continued to be a constant excuse for unrest in the Middle East that would embroil the major world powers in a series of crises and conflicts. Incursions, shelling, and terror attacks against Israel continued. Unfortunately, there is insufficient space here to detail these.

In 2005 Israel abandoned its occupation of the Gaza Strip, but the establishment there of Hamas, a more militant organization than the PLO, brought three costly Gaza wars, in 2008–2009, 2012, and 2014.

The Arab-Israeli confrontation and perceived Western influence in the Arab world also helped in the creation of the Al Qaeda terrorist organization, which mounted the September 11, 2001, attacks on the United States. This in turn brought the Afghanistan War (2001–present) and was the excuse for a major U.S.-led war in Iraq (2003–2011). The Arab-Israeli imbroglio has also helped influence the West's conflict with Iran and fighting in Yemen, Egypt, Libya, and Syria. Its latest incarnation is the extremist, fundamentalist Islamic State of Iraq and Syria (ISIS), or Islamic State, which now controls much of Iraq and Syria and imperils the entire region.

SPENCER C. TUCKER

Timeline

1881–1884
The first of three major pogroms occurs in Russia (the others are in 1903–1905 and 1918–1920). In these tens of thousands of Jews in Russia and Ukraine die. More than 2 million Russian Jews emigrate in the period 1881–1920, a large number of them to the United States.

1883
The Zionist group Hovevei Zion (Lovers of Zion) is established in Russia and initiates a series of Jewish settlements in Palestine.

1890
Austrian Jewish publicist Nathan Birnbaum is credited with the term "Zionism" as the movement for the return of the Jewish people to their homeland of Israel. Zion is a hill in Jerusalem where a Jewish fortress stood.

1896
Austrian Jewish journalist Theodore Herzel publishes *Der Judenstaat* [The Jewish State], advocating the creation of a free and independent Jewish state in Palestine.

1897

August
The First Zionist Congress occurs in Basel, Switzerland, establishing the World Zionist Organization.

1917

November 2
British foreign secretary Arthur Balfour declares British government support for the establishment of "a Jewish homeland in Palestine."

1920

April 19–26
At the San Remo Conference, Britain receives the League of Nations mandate of Palestine.

1929

August 23–29
A long-running dispute between Muslims and Jews over access to the Western Wall in Jerusalem escalates into the Palestinian Riots, with considerable violence against Jews, including the Hebron Massacre in which 67 Jews are slain.

1933

January 30
Notorious anti-Semite Adolf Hitler becomes chancellor of Germany.

1939

November 9
The British government white paper of this date sets a limit of 10,000 Jewish immigrants for each year between

1940 and 1944, plus 25,000 refugees for any emergency arising during that period.

1941–1945
The Holocaust results in the methodical extermination by the Germans of nearly 6 million Jews across Europe.

1945–1948
British authorities endeavor to prevent Jews attempting to enter Palestine illegally. A three-way struggle soon ensues between the Jewish defense group Haganah and the terrorist groups Irgun and Lehi against the Arabs and the British military and administration in Palestine.

1947

November 29
The United Nations approves the creation of a Jewish state and an Arab state in the British mandate of Palestine.

1948

May 14
Prime Minister David Ben-Gurion proclaims Israeli independence just hours before the end of the British mandate.

May 15
The Israeli War for Independence begins. Arab forces from Syria, Iraq, Transjordan, Lebanon, and Egypt invade Israel. A Jewish exodus from Arab and Muslim lands results, with Jews fleeing or expelled from Muslim nations. Most settle in Israel.

1948–1949
Almost 250,000 Holocaust survivors make their way to Israel, while Operation MAGIC CARPET brings thousands of Yemenite Jews to Israel.

1956

October 29–November 7
Egyptian president Gamal Abdel Nasser nationalizes the Suez Canal. Britain, France, and Israel concoct a secret plan to restore the canal to its former administration and topple Nasser. On October 29 Israel invades the Sinai, initiating the Suez Crisis. When Egypt rejects a cease-fire ultimatum, British and French forces invade Egypt, supposedly to protect the canal. Heavy U.S. pressure causes Britain and France to evacuate. Israel also gives up the Sinai, but the Egyptian blockade of Aqaba is ended, and a UN observer force is placed along the Egyptian-Israeli border.

1967

May 16
Egyptian president Nasser demands that the UN observer force depart. It is gone by May 19.

June 5–10	With Egyptian forces preparing to invade, Israel mounts a preemptive strike and, in the Six-Day War of these dates, defeats the forces of Egypt, Syria, and Jordan, securing the Sinai Peninsula from Egypt, the West Bank of the Jordan River from Jordan, and the Golan Heights from Syria.
September 1	Arab leaders meeting in Khartoum, Sudan, go on record as opposing recognition of Israel, negotiations with Israel, and peace with the Jewish state.

1973

October 6–25	The Yom Kippur (Ramadan) War occurs. Egypt and Syria, backed up by expeditionary forces from other Arab nations, launch a surprise attack on Israel on Yom Kippur. Able to absorb the initial attacks, Israel then recaptures lost ground and pushes into both Egypt and Syria before conclusion of an armistice.
October 17	In response to U.S. support of Israel, the Arab members of the Organization of Oil Exporting Countries, led by Saudi Arabia, reduce oil production by 5 percent per month.
October 19	After U.S. president Richard Nixon authorizes major support for Israel, Saudi Arabia declares an embargo against the United States, later joined by other oil exporters and extended against other states. Lasting five months, it results in a full-blown economic crisis for the Western economies.

1978

September 18	At Camp David, Maryland, near Washington, D.C., Israel and Egypt sign a comprehensive peace treaty, the Camp David Accord, that includes the withdrawal of Israeli forces from the Sinai.

1982

June–December	In Operation PEACE FOR GALILEE, Israeli forces invade southern Lebanon to drive out the Palestine Liberation Organization (PLO).
1987	Beginning of the First Intifada against Israel.
1990	The Soviet Union permits its Jewish citizens to emigrate. Hundreds of thousands of Soviet Jews choose to leave the Soviet Union and settle in Israel.

1993

September 13	Israeli prime minister Yitzhak Rabin and PLO chairman Yasser Arafat sign the Oslo Accords.

1994

October 26   Israel and Jordan sign an official peace treaty.

2000

May 24   Israel unilaterally withdraws its remaining forces from its security zone in southern Lebanon to the internationally agreed-upon border.

September 29   The al-Aqsa (Second) Intifada begins.

2005

August   Israel withdraws its military forces and settlers from the Gaza Strip.

2006

July–August   A military conflict occurs in Lebanon and northern Israel after a Hezbollah cross-border raid into Israel.

SPENCER C. TUCKER

Further Reading

Adan, Avraham. *On the Banks of the Suez: An Israeli General's Personal Account of the Yom Kippur War.* Novato, CA: Presidio, 1980.

Bickerton, Ian J. *A Concise History of the Arab-Israeli Conflict.* Upper Saddle River, NJ: Prentice Hall, 2005.

Bowen, Jeremy. *Six Days: How the 1967 War Shaped the Middle East.* London: Simon and Schuster, 2003.

Bowyer Bell, John. *Terror Out of Zion: The Fight for Israeli Independence.* New Brunswick, NJ: Transaction Publishers, 1996.

Bregman, Ahron. *Israel's Wars: A History since 1947.* London: Routledge, 2002.

Bright, John. *A History of Israel,* 4th ed. Louisville, KY: Westminster John Knox, 2000.

Dunstan, Simon. *The Yom Kippur War, 1973.* Oxford, UK: Osprey, 2007.

Friedman, Thomas L. *From Beirut to Jerusalem.* New York: Anchor, 1990.

Gamasy, Mohamed Abdul Ghani el. *The October War: Memoirs of Field Marshal El-Gamasy of Egypt.* Translated by Gillian Potter, Nadra Morcos, and Rosette Frances.

Cairo: American University in Cairo Press, 1993.

Gawrych, George W. *The 1973 Arab-Israeli War: The Albatross of Decisive Victory.* Leavenworth Papers No. 21. Fort Leavenworth, KS: Combat Studies Institute, 1996.

Hammel, Eric. *Six Days in June: How Israel Won the 1967 Arab-Israeli War.* New York: Simon and Schuster, 1992.

Heikal, Mohammed Hasanyn. *The Road to Ramadan.* New York: Quadrangle/New York Times Book Company, 1975.

Heller, Joseph. *The Birth of Israel, 1945–1949: Ben-Gurion and His Critics.* Gainesville: University Press of Florida, 2001.

Herzog, Chaim. *The Arab-Israeli Wars: War and Peace in the Middle East.* New York: Random House, 1982.

Joseph, Dov. *The Faithful City: The Siege of Jerusalem, 1948.* New York: Simon and Schuster, 1960.

Karsh, Efraim. *The Arab-Israeli Conflict: The Palestine War, 1948.* New York: Osprey, 2002.

Krämer, Gudrun. *A History of Palestine: From the Ottoman Conquest to the Founding of the State of Israel.* Princeton, NJ: Princeton University Press, 2011.

Kurzman, Dan. *Genesis 1948: The First Arab-Israeli War.* New York: World Publishing, 1970.

Lenczowski, George. *The Middle East in World Affairs.* Ithaca, NY: Cornell University Press, 1952.

Lustick, Ian. *From War to War: Israel vs. the Arabs, 1948–1967.* New York: Garland, 1983.

Morris, Benny. *1948: The First Arab-Israeli War.* New Haven, CT: Yale University Press, 2008.

Mutawi, Samir A. *Jordan in the 1967 War.* Cambridge: Cambridge University Press, 2002.

Oren, Michael B. *Six Days of War: June 1967 and the Making of the Modern Middle East.* New York: Presidio, 2003.

Pappe, Ilan. *A History of Modern Palestine: One Land, Two Peoples.* Cambridge: Cambridge University Press, 2004.

Parker, Richard B. *The Six-Day War: A Retrospective.* Gainesville: University Press of Florida, 1996.

Pollack, Kenneth M. *Arabs at War: Military Effectiveness, 1948–1991.* Lincoln: University of Nebraska Press, 2002.

Rabinovich, Abraham. *The Yom Kippur War: An Epic Encounter That Transformed the Middle East.* New York: Schocken Books, 2004.

Rogan, Eugene L., and Avi Shlaim, eds. *The War for Palestine: Rewriting the History of 1948.* 2nd ed. Cambridge: Cambridge University Press, 2007.

Sachar, Howard M. *A History of Israel from the Rise of Zionism to Our Time.* New York: Knopf, 1967.

Sanders, Ronald. *The High Walls of Jerusalem: A History of the Balfour Declaration and the Birth of the British Mandate for Palestine.* New York: Holt, Rinehart and Winston, 1983.

Schneer, Jonathan. *The Balfour Declaration: The Origins of the Arab-Israeli Conflict.* New York: Random House, 2010.

Shazli, Saad al. *The Crossing of the Suez.* San Francisco: Mideast Research, 1980.

Shepherd, Naomi. *Ploughing Sand: British Rule in Palestine, 1917–1948.* New Brunswick, NJ: Rutgers University Press, 1999.

Smith, Charles. *Palestine and the Arab-Israeli Conflict.* Boston: Bedford/St. Martin's, 2007.

Tucker, Spencer C., ed. *The Encyclopedia of the Arab-Israeli Conflict: A Political, Social, and Military History.* 2 vols. Santa Barbara, CA: ABC-CLIO, 2008.

Korean War (1950–1953)

Causes

The Korean War was a watershed event in 20th-century history. It was both the first shooting war of the Cold War and the first limited war of the nuclear age. It was also the first United Nations (UN) war and the only time since World War II that two major powers—the United States and China—have met on the battlefield.

Situated as it was between the major powers of China, Russia, and Japan, Korea was fated to have a stormy history. The country was long the nexus of big-power confrontation and war, first between China and Japan and then between Japan and Russia. After having defeated both China in 1894–1895 and Russia in 1904–1905, Japan controlled Korea and integrated it into the Japanese economy. Korea has been a single entity during its modern history, however. The 38th parallel between the present Democratic People's Republic of Korea (North Korea, DPRK) and the Republic of Korea (South Korea, ROK) was simply an arbitrary political line dividing a country that forms a single geographic, ethnic, and economic unit.

As World War II drew to a close, U.S. president Franklin Roosevelt was determined to get the Soviet Union into the war against Japan in order to reduce anticipated heavy American casualties in an invasion of the Japanese home islands, even if the price for this might be temporary Soviet occupation of much of Northeast Asia. In endeavoring to reach some arrangement with Soviet leader Joseph Stalin on the future of Northeast Asia, Roosevelt and his advisers proposed that a postwar international trusteeship be set up for Korea under the United States, Great Britain, China, and the Soviet Union. Although there was consensus that Korea was to become "independent in due course," there was no agreement on specifics.

U.S.-Soviet relations deteriorated with the end of the war, when it became clear that for the Soviet Union the alliance had been a marriage of convenience only. This became clear when Soviet territorial and security demands became manifest in Europe. President Harry S. Truman, who took office following the death of Roosevelt in April 1945, then took a harder line toward Moscow.

On August 10, 1945, with the dropping of two atomic bombs, a Soviet declaration of war on Japan, and the Red Army already having invaded Manchuria only 60 miles from Korea (the nearest U.S. troops were 600 miles distant in Okinawa), U.S. Army colonels Dean Rusk and Charles Bonesteel were told to define an American occupation zone in Korea. They chose the 38th parallel because it divided Korea approximately in half but left the capital of Seoul in the American zone. No Korean experts were consulted. Truman approved this proposal on August 15, and it was cabled to the Soviets, who accepted it without discussion on August 16. The day before Tokyo had agreed to the Allied surrender terms, and on September 8 U.S. occupation forces began arriving at the Korean port of Incheon (Inchon).

The Korean occupiers, north and south, found a land seething with pent-up political frustration and rampant nationalism, all fueled by returning exiles. Koreans of

In one of the best known photographs of the Korean War, U.S. 1st Division marines use scaling ladders to climb over the sea wall during the September 15, 1950, Inchon invasion. (National Archives)

whatever political stripe, having suffered nearly a half century of Japanese occupation, wanted immediate independence and not a trusteeship or allied occupation. Certainly they did not want a divided nation. But few outside of Korea thought of these arrangements as anything other than temporary.

Both the Soviets and the Americans each now installed a group of Korean advisers in their two zones. These were hardly democratic and were strongly conservative in the American zone and staunchly procommunist in the Soviet zone. In December 1946 a legislative assembly opened in the American zone.

By September 1947, frustrated with the failure to settle the future of Korea by direct negotiation with the Soviet Union, the United States referred the problem to the UN. The UN General Assembly recognized Korea's right to independence and planned for the establishment of a unified government and withdrawal of the occupation forces. It established the United Nations Temporary Commission on Korea (UNTCOK) with the goal of securing a free and independent Korea. In January 1948 UNTCOK representatives arrived in Seoul to supervise elections for a national constituent assembly.

UNTCOK was refused admission to the Soviet zone, and it then recommended elections in South Korea for a new national assembly. These were held, and the Assembly duly met in May 1948; its invitation for representatives of North Korea to attend was ignored. In August 1948 the ROK was officially proclaimed in the south, with a strong presidential regime headed by the staunchly conservative former exile Syngman Rhee. He was also widely disliked by more democratic elements in Korea, and many of the ROK's key figures, including military leaders, had served the Japanese. But Washington wanted stability, although its slavish support of Rhee brought the enmity of many Korean radicals. The U.S. military government was then terminated, and the new Korean government entered into an agreement with the United States for the training of its forces.

In September 1948 the DPRK, which also claimed authority over the entire country, was inaugurated in North Korea under the presidency of veteran communist Kim Il Sung. Kim, leader of the so-called Gapsan Faction of former anti-Japanese guerrilla fighters, became the paramount leader.

In December the UN General Assembly endorsed South Korea as having the country's only lawfully elected Korean government. That same month the Soviet Union announced that it had withdrawn all its forces from North Korea. The United States completed the withdrawal of its occupation forces from South Korea in June 1949.

In September 1949, UNTCOK reported its failure to mediate between the two Korean states and warned of impending civil war. Beginning in April 1948, there had been sporadic fighting. Indeed, historian Allan Millett states unequivocally that the Korean War began on April 3, 1948, in the Jeju Island (Cheju-do) Rebellion in which communist guerrillas mounted attacks against the South Korean government. Estimates of the dead in this rebellion during 1948–1950 range from 30,000 to as many as 100,000. There were also clashes along the 38th parallel involving battalion-sized units on both sides that claimed hundreds of lives. Two of the largest were launched by the DPRK south of the 38th parallel in the Ongjin Peninsula in May and August 1949.

Both Rhee and Kim Il Sung were fervent nationalists determined to unify their country during their lifetimes. Indeed, Rhee's support for a possible military solution to the reunification question led the U.S. State Department to clearly disassociate itself from these activities. In April 1948 President Truman approved a policy statement to the effect that the United States should not become so irrevocably involved that an action taken by any faction in Korea or by any other power there could be considered a cause for war for the United States. This U.S. government attempt to adopt a hands-off policy no doubt encouraged Kim in his belief that the United States would not fight for Korea. Then on January 12, 1950, U.S. secretary of state Dean Acheson further distanced the United States when, in the course of a speech to the National Press Club, he specifically excluded both Korea and Taiwan (Formosa) from the Asian "defensive perimeter" of vital strategic interests that the United States would fight to defend.

The U.S. Joint Chiefs of Staff (JCS) reached the same conclusion, and in 1949 in two separate interviews, U.S. commander in the Far East General Douglas MacArthur had outlined a defense perimeter for the United States that excluded Taiwan as well as Korea. Republicans in Congress then demanded U.S. defense for Formosa, but no such move was made regarding Korea.

On June 25, 1950, the DPRK's armed forces mounted a massive conventional invasion of South Korea, across the 38th parallel. The communist bloc claimed steadfastly that the war had begun in a South Korean attack of North Korea and that Rhee had hoped thereby to bring about American involvement and a war in which the two Koreas would be reunited under his leadership. The communists maintained that North Korean, Soviet, and Chinese policy was merely reactive. This is false, as border clashes diminished in the period from October 1949 to the spring of 1950, because Stalin sought to prevent the possibility of a war developing before the DPRK was completely ready. Soviet foreign minister Gromyko informed ambassador to the DPRK Colonel General Terenti Shtykov that Pyongyang must cease all military operations without prior approval from Moscow, and the border between north and south remained quiet until the June invasion.

The timing of the North Korean attack was conditioned by the need to plant rice in March and then harvest it in September. At the time, many observers believed that this was a diversionary effort by the communist bloc to divert U.S. attention away from Europe, where the Soviet Union had just suffered a rebuff in the Berlin Blockade (1948–1949). Others considered it to be "soft-spot" probing to test U.S. resolve or a demonstration to show the world that America was a paper tiger. Some even saw it to be part of an elaborate plot by Stalin to unseat Mao Zedong (Mao Tse-tung) in China. Most Americans believed that Moscow had initiated events in Korea as part of some global chess move.

But the reasons behind the invasion were local, not global. Rhee's government had suffered a major reversal in what was a relatively free election. Kim Il Sung judged that Rhee might be about to fall from power, and given the announced American position and his own attitude, the moment seemed ripe. As early as September 1949 he had sought Soviet support for a military operation to seize the Onjin peninsula and perhaps territory south of the 38th parallel all the way to Kaesong. The Soviets demurred, believing that this would result in a protracted civil war that would be disadvantageous to the DPRK and the Soviet Union, allowing the United States to increase aid to the Rhee government and "agitation" against the Soviet Union.

Kim Il Sung met secretly with Stalin in Moscow in April 1950 concerning an invasion. Kim provided Stalin with what turned out to be wildly exaggerated prospects of a North Korean military success, a communist revolution in South Korea, and American abstention from intervention. He promised Stalin a concurrent communist revolution in South Korea and insisted that Washington would not intervene. Stalin himself concluded that even if the United States did move to defend South Korea, it would come too late. Soviet military aid was substantial, and its military personnel in North Korea took a key role in planning the invasion.

Stalin's approval had been contingent on the support of Chinese leader Mao Zedong, and indeed Stalin insisted that Kim meet with Mao and secure his support. As a result, Kim's Korean People's Army (KPA) included at least 16,000 members of the People's Liberation Army. These were Korean volunteers who had fought against the Japanese in World War II and in the Chinese Civil War thereafter. They joined the KPA with their weapons and equipment and played a key role in the subsequent invasion. Certainly both Moscow and Beijing were actively involved in preparations for the invasion as early as the spring of 1949.

SPENCER C. TUCKER

Course

When the Korean War began on June 25, 1950, North Korea had every military advantage. Its KPA numbered some 130,000

KOREAN WAR, 1950–1953

CHINA

MANCHURIA

SOVIET UNION

Vladivostok

N

Tunghwa

Chongjin

Yalu R.

Kanggye

Changjin (Chosin) Reservoir

Chosan

Changjin (Chosin)

Iwon

Chongchon R.

Sinuiju

Hagard

40°N

Hungnam

NORTH KOREA

Sea of Japan

Yongdok

Wonsan

Pyongyang

Imjin R.

Iron Triangle

Pork Chop Hill

Pyonggang

Ongjin Peninsula

Kumhwa

Chorwon

Yangyang

38th Parallel

Kaesong

Panmunjom

Chunchon

TAEBAEK MTS.

Inchon

Seoul

Samchok

Osan

Han R.

SOUTH KOREA

SOBAEK MTS.

Yellow Sea

Yondok

Kum R.

Taejon

Naktong R.

Kumchon

Pohang

Kunsan

Taegu

CHIRI MTS.

Masan

Pusan

35°N

Mokpo

Koje-do Island

Korea Strait

Tsushima (Japan)

Tsushima Strait

JAPAN

Limit of North Korean advance, Jun–Sep 1950

Limit of United Nations advance, Nov 1950

Limit of Chinese advance, Jan 1951

Armistice Line, Jul 27, 1953

Battle site

Principal railroads

Principal Chinese railroad supply lines

Principal roads

| 0 | 50 | 100 mi |
| 0 | 50 | 100 km |

men with heavy artillery, 151 T-34 tanks, and about 180 aircraft, including fighters and twin-engine bombers. In South Korea, the Republic of Korea Army (ROKA) was unprepared militarily because of U.S. unease about Rhee unleashing a war to reunify Korea but also because there were insufficient funds in a shrunken U.S. defense budget. In 1950 the U.S. military itself was relatively small, poorly trained, inadequately equipped, and stretched thin. The ROK military numbered about 95,000 men. No ROKA unit had progressed beyond regimental-level training, and the ROKA lacked heavy artillery, tanks, and even antitank weapons, to include mines. ROKA ammunition stocks were sufficient for only six days of combat. Its sole aircraft were trainers and liaison types.

Given these circumstances, Kim Il Sung expected to overrun South Korea quickly; indeed, the invasion plan called for this to be completed within 22–27 days. Both U.S. Far Eastern commander General Douglas MacArthur in Tokyo and Washington were taken by surprise. Fighting along the border between North and South Korea had died down, and U.S. officials did not believed that the communists would risk a nuclear war. Although Truman called it "the most difficult decision" of his presidency, U.S. intervention was certain, given the Truman Doctrine, domestic political fallout from the communist victory in China in 1949, and the belief that a communist success in Korea would embolden the communists elsewhere.

Within hours of the June 25 invasion, the UN Security Council called for an immediate cease-fire and the withdrawal of the KPA. A Soviet boycott allowed action, and on June 27 the Security Council asked member states to furnish assistance to South Korea. President Truman extended

U.S. air and naval operations to include North Korea, and he authorized U.S. forces to protect the vital port of Busan (Pusan).

Upon the recommendation of MacArthur, Truman committed U.S. ground forces in Japan to the war on June 30. The United States then had four poorly trained and equipped divisions in Japan. By cannibalizing his 7th Infantry Division, MacArthur was able to dispatch the 24th and 25th Infantry Divisions and the 1st Cavalry Division to Korea within two weeks.

Meanwhile, the war was going badly for the ROK. At the time of the invasion, four ROKA divisions were stretched out across more than 200 miles of linear front. (The remaining five ROKA divisions were engaged in training and counterguerrilla operations.) This was some 9.5 miles per regiment, far more than was possible to defend. There were also few natural obstacles to impede the KPA, and the ROKA was also forced to defend the cul-de-sac of the Ongjin peninsula. Only a valiant effort by the 6th Division on the Chunchon front allowed the remainder of the ROKA to regroup and erect the Han River defensive line, delaying the KPA offensive. Still, Seoul fell on June 28.

In one of the key strategic blunders of the war, KPA troops halted to regroup for three days. They did not begin crossing the Han until July 1. A mistaken decision by ROKA chief of staff Major General Chae Pyong Dok, however, led to its four bridges being blown hours before this was necessary, preventing thousands of troops and their heavy equipment from reaching South Korea.

On July 5 the first American ground unit—Task Force Smith of only 540 men—entered the war at Osan, 50 miles south of Seoul. The false sense of optimism that the mere presence of American troops would

Estimated Casualty Statistics of the Korean War

	Military Dead	Wounded	Missing	Captured	Civilian Dead	Civilian Missing
United States	36,914	103,284	8,177	7,140	N/A	N/A
South Korea	47,000	175,700	66,436	80,000	373,500	387,740
North Korea	215,000	303,000	101,680	83,000	406,000	680,000
China	401,000	486,000	21,211	21,000	N/A	N/A
United Kingdom	710	2,278	1,263	766	N/A	N/A
Australia	291	1,240	39	21	N/A	N/A
Canada	309	1,055	30	2	N/A	N/A
Turkey	717	2,246	167	217	N/A	N/A
France	288	818	18	11	N/A	N/A

Sources: John S. Bowman, ed., *Facts about the American Wars* (n.p.: H. W. Wilson, 1998); Michael Clodfelter, *Warfare and Armed Conflict: A Statistical Reference to Casualty and Other Figures, 1618–1991* (Jefferson, NC: McFarland, 1992); Department of Defense, *Principal Wars in Which the United States Participated: U.S. Military Personnel Serving and Casualties* (Washington, DC: Washington Headquarters Services, Directorate for Information Operations and Reports, 2003); Michael Hickey, *The Korean War: The West Confronts Communism* (n.p.: Overlook, 2000); Korean War Educator, www.koreanwareducator.org; Andrew Nahm, *Historical Dictionary of the Republic of Korea* (Lanham, MD: Scarecrow, 1993).

give the North Koreans pause was quickly dispelled when KPA tanks easily brushed the poorly equipped Americans aside.

At the request of the UN Security Council, the UN set up a military command in Korea. Washington insisted on a U.S. commander, and on July 10 Truman appointed MacArthur to head the United Nations Command (UNC). Sixteen nations contributed military assistance, and at peak strength UNC forces numbered about 400,000 ROK troops, 250,000 U.S. troops, and 35,000 personnel from other nations, the largest being the 1st Commonwealth Division from Britain and Canada, while Turkey provided a brigade. Other nations provided smaller numbers of troops or noncombat assistance in the form of medical units.

The Communist revolution predicted by Kim Il Sung for South Korea failed to materialize. Meanwhile, difficult terrain, primitive logistics, poor communication, and floods of refugees delayed the North Korean advance as much as did the defenders, but by mid-July UNC troops had been pushed back into the so-called Pusan Perimeter, an area of 30–50 miles in southeastern Korea around Busan. In desperate fighting, ROK and U.S. forces held. This may be attributed to their artillery, U.S. Air Force control of the skies, and the leadership and brilliant mobile defense instituted by the Eighth U.S. Army in Korea (EUSAK), commanded by Lieutenant General Walton Walker. The KPA also had failed early to employ its manpower advantage and mount simultaneous attacks along the entire perimeter.

Even as the Battle of the Pusan Perimeter raged, MacArthur was planning an amphibious assault behind enemy lines. Confident it could hold, MacArthur deliberately weakened EUSAK to build up an invasion force. He selected Incheon as the invasion site. Only 15 miles from Seoul, it was nearly astride the KPA's main supply line south. The recapture of nearby Seoul would also deal North Korea a major political blow.

A landing at Incheon was risky, and almost everyone except MacArthur opposed it. Mines were stacked and waiting but had not been laid. Still, the problems were daunting. On September 15 Major General Edward Almond's X Corps of the 1st Marine Division and the 7th Infantry Division commenced the invasion. Supported by naval gunfire and air attacks, the marines soon secured Inchon, and UNC forces reentered Seoul on September 24. EUSAK also broke out of the Pusan Perimeter, drove north, and linked up with X Corps on September 26. Only one-quarter to one-third of the KPA escaped into North Korea. During their retreat northward, the KPA took with it thousands of South Koreans and forced them to serve in the KPA.

By this time, there was enormous pressure in the United States on Truman to expand the war. Both Republicans and Democrats sought to defeat the Communists, not merely to "contain" them, and MacArthur was himself perhaps the most outspoken proponent of changing the war aims to include total victory. Truman, Secretary of State Dean Acheson, and new secretary of defense George C. Marshall decided to take the war into North Korea, which exceeded the UNC's mission. On October 7 the UN General Assembly passed a resolution calling for "a unified, independent, and democratic" Korea. Washington used this as justification to enter North Korea.

With Pyongyang having ignored MacArthur's call for surrender, on October 1 ROKA troops crossed into North Korea. On October 9, MacArthur ordered U.S.

forces to follow. The advance was rapid, and Pyongyang fell on October 19.

MacArthur now committed a major strategic blunder, retaining X Corps as a separate command under Almond and dividing his forces for the drive to the Yalu River. He ordered X Corps sent by sea to the east coast port of Wonsan with the task of clearing northeastern Korea, while EUSAK remained on the west coast to drive into northwest Korea. The two commands were now separated by a gap of between 20 and 50 miles. MacArthur believed, falsely as it turned out, that the Nangnim mountain range would obviate large-scale Communist operations there.

All went well at first. EUSAK crossed the Chongchon River at Sinanju, and by November 1 elements of the 24th Division were only 18 miles from the Yalu. Several days earlier a reconnaissance platoon of the ROK 6th Division reached the Yalu, the only UNC unit to get there.

China now entered the war, albeit unofficially through the guise of "volunteers." Alarmed by a U.S. military presence adjacent to Manchuria, People's Republic of China (PRC) leader Mao Zedong had issued repeated warnings about potential Chinese military intervention. Actually, he was planning to intervene even before UNC troops crossed the 38th parallel, but on September 30 Kim requested intervention. Mao was confident. He believed that the United States would be unable to counter Chinese numbers and that American troops were soft and unused to night fighting.

On October 2 Mao informed Stalin that China would enter the war. Stalin agreed to shift Soviet MiG-15 fighters already in China to the Korean border to cover the Chinese buildup and prevent U.S. air attacks on Manchuria. Soviet pilots began flying combat missions on November 1.

Stalin ordered other Soviet air units to deploy to China, train Chinese pilots, and then turn over aircraft to them. Ultimately there were some 26,000 Soviet military personnel involved. Soviet pilots bore the brunt of the ensuing air war. Although ordered to pretend they were Chinese, they soon dropped this as impractical in combat. Moscow continued to deny any Soviet involvement, however.

Stalin had no intention of using Soviet airpower for anything other than defensive purposes, but the Chinese later angrily claimed that he had promised and failed to deliver on a pledge of full air support for their ground forces. Still, Stalin had helped China establish the world's third-largest air force.

On October 25 Chinese troops entered the fighting in northwestern Korea, and Walker wisely brought the bulk of EUSAK south of the Chongchon. The Chinese offensive then slackened. The Chinese also attacked in northeastern Korea before halting operations and breaking contact there as well. The initial Chinese incursion ended on November 7.

In a meeting with President Truman at Wake Island on October 15, MacArthur had assured the president that the war was all but won but that if the Chinese intervened, their forces would be slaughtered by UNC airpower. Yet from November 1, 1950, to October 1951, MiGs so dominated the Yalu River area that U.S. B-29 bombers had to cease daylight operations. It is hard to understand how MacArthur, who touted himself as an expert on Asia, could have so misread Chinese intentions and capabilities.

The initial Chinese intervention numbered 18 divisions. In early November the Chinese moved an additional 12 into Korea, with a total of some 300,000 men.

MacArthur now ordered the destruction of the bridges over the Yalu. Washington revoked the order, but MacArthur complained of the threat to his command, and Washington gave in. The bombing on November 8 had little effect, however; most of the Chinese were already in North Korea, and the Yalu was soon frozen.

Meanwhile, American leaders in Washington debated how to proceed. The political leadership and the JCS under chairman General Omar Bradley believed that Europe had to remain the top priority. Washington decided that while Manchuria would remain off-limits, MacArthur could take other military steps that he deemed advisable, including resuming the offensive. The Democrats were especially reluctant to show lack of resolve in Korea, for the Republicans who blamed them for the "loss" of China had gained seats in the November congressional elections.

While much was made in the United States about the prohibitions of strikes on Manchuria, it should be pointed out that the Communist side also exercised restraint. With the exception of a few ancient biplanes that sporadically struck UNC positions at night, Communist airpower was restricted to north of Pyongyang. No effort was made to strike Pusan, and UNC convoys traveled without fear of air attack, even at night with lights blazing. Nor did the Communist forces attempt to disrupt UNC sea communications.

MacArthur had made X Corps dependent logistically on EUSAK instead of Japan, and Walker insisted on delaying resumption of the offensive until he could build up sufficient supplies. Poor weather was also a problem, but Walker agreed to resume the offensive on November 24. To the east, X Corps was widely dispersed.

MacArthur was oblivious to any threat, confident that this would be an occupation rather than an offensive. The offensive went well on the first day, but on the night of November 25–26 the Chinese struck EUSAK in force. On November 26 the ROKA II Corps gave way under the massive Chinese assault, exposing EUSAK's right flank. The Chinese poured 18 divisions into the gap, threatening the whole of EUSAK. In a brilliant delaying action at Kunu-ri, the U.S. 2nd Division bought time for the other EUSAK divisions to get across the Chongchon. MacArthur now ordered a retirement just below the 38th parallel to protect Seoul.

Washington directed MacArthur to pull X Corps out of northeastern Korea. Heavily outnumbered and under Chinese attack, X Corps withdrew to the coast for seaborne evacuation along with the ROK I Corps. The retreat of the 1st Marine Division and some army elements from the Changjin (Chosin was its name in Japanese maps still in use at the time) Reservoir ranks as one of the most masterly withdrawals in military history. X Corps was then redeployed to Pusan by sea. At Hungnam through December 24, 105,000 military personnel were taken off, along with some 91,000 Koreans who did not want to remain in the north.

The Korean War had entered a new phase; in effect the UNC was now fighting China. MacArthur refused to accept a limited war and publicized his views to his supporters, making reference to "inhibitions" placed upon him. UNC morale plummeted, especially with General Walker's death in a jeep accident on December 22. Not until the arrival of Lieutenant General Matthew Ridgway, Walker's replacement, did the situation improve. In the United States, meanwhile, Truman found himself under heavy pressure from Republicans to pursue the war vigorously. But fearing a wider war, possibly even a worldwide conflagration involving the Soviet Union, the administration reduced its objective to restoring the status quo antebellum.

UNC troops were again forced to retreat when the Chinese launched a New Year's offensive, retaking Seoul on January 4, 1951. But the Chinese People's Volunteer Army soon outran its supply lines, and Ridgway began a methodical limited advance designed to inflict maximum punishment rather than secure territory. Although Ridgway rejected suggestions from several of his key subordinates for an amphibious landing that might have trapped large numbers of Communist troops, by the end of March UNC forces had recaptured Seoul and by the end of April were north of the 38th parallel.

On April 11, 1951, President Truman relieved MacArthur, appointing Ridgway in his stead. Lieutenant General James Van Fleet took over EUSAK. Truman and MacArthur saw the war quite differently. MacArthur believed that it was a great anticommunist crusade that would reverse the Chinese Revolution. He sought to bomb Manchuria, employ Chinese Nationalist troops in Korea, and unleash Nationalist forces on Taiwan against the Chinese mainland. This position elicited some support from among so-called Asia Firsters in the United States, notably among Republicans, but it found little support in the UN or among West European leaders. MacArthur had made no secret of his desire to expand the war and made his case for this publicly.

Although widely unpopular at the time, MacArthur's removal was fully supported by the JCS. The general returned home to a hero's welcome, but political support soon faded, as did MacArthur's hopes, however faint, of a run for the presidency in 1952.

On April 22, the Chinese counterattacked. Rather than expend his troops in a defensive stand, Van Fleet ordered a methodical withdrawal, employing artillery firepower and air strikes against the communist forces. The Chinese pushed the UNC south of the 38th parallel, but the offensive was halted by May 19. UNC forces then counterpunched, and by the end of May the front stabilized just above the 38th parallel. The JCS now generally limited EUSAK to that line, allowing only small local advances to secure more favorable terrain.

The war now became one of position, essentially a stalemate. In these circumstances, a diplomatic settlement seemed expedient. On June 23, 1951, Soviet UN representative Jacob Malik proposed a cease-fire. With the Chinese expressing interest, Truman authorized Ridgway to open negotiations. Meetings began on July 10 at Kaesong, although hostilities continued.

UNC operations from this point were essentially designed to minimize friendly casualties, and both sides had now built deep defensive lines that would be costly to break through. In August armistice talks broke down, and later that month the Battle of Bloody Ridge began, developing into the Battle of Heartbreak Ridge, which lasted until mid-October. In late October negotiations resumed, this time at Panmunjom. The fighting continued, with half of the war's casualties occurring during the period of armistice negotiations.

On November 12, 1951, Ridgway ordered Van Fleet to cease offensive operations. Fighting now devolved into raids, local attacks, patrols, and artillery fire. In February 1953 Lieutenant General Maxwell D. Taylor took command of EUSAK. UNC air operations intensified to choke off Communist supply lines and reduce the likelihood of offensive action. By now also the burden was shifting to the ROKA, which was adding one new trained division each month and was responsible for more than half of the casualties inflicted on KPA and Chinese units. The Chinese especially targeted South Korean units. In July 1953, the last month of the war, the ROKA suffered 25,000 casualties.

In the United States, meanwhile, Truman's popularity had plummeted because of the war, and he refused to stand for reelection. In November 1952 General Dwight Eisenhower was elected president on a mandate to end the war. With U.S. casualties running 2,500 a month, the conflict had become a political liability. Eisenhower instructed the JCS to draw up plans to end the war militarily, including the possible use of nuclear weapons. Talk of this was allowed to circulate publicly. More important in ending the conflict, however, was Stalin's death on March 5, 1953.

As the armistice negotiations entered their final phase in May, the Chinese stepped up military action, initiating attacks in June and July to remove bulges in the line. UNC forces gave up some ground but inflicted heavy casualties.

Prisoner repatriation remained the chief obstacle to an agreement, and the use of prisoners as propaganda tools were the main reason the war continued. The North Koreans and Chinese had forced into their army many South Koreans, and thousands of them had subsequently been taken prisoner. If all KPA prisoners were repatriated, many South Koreans would be sent to North Korea. Also, many Chinese prisoners of war did not wish to return to China. Truman, who had seen the consequences of the forced repatriation of Russian citizens from Western Europe after World War II, was determined that none be repatriated against their will. The communist side rejected the UNC position out of hand and sought to use the prisoners to tar the UNC with the patent lie of germ warfare and immoral air operations against North Vietnam.

Following intense UNC air strikes on North Korean hydroelectric facilities and the capital of Pyongyang, the communists accepted a face-saving formula whereby a neutral commission would handle prisoner repatriation. Syngman Rhee, who was adamantly opposed to any peace settlement that did not include the reunification of the two Koreas, almost sabotaged the peace agreement with the release of some 27,000 North Korean prisoners just weeks before the final agreement. Rhee was only placated by Washington's pledge of military and financial aid in the U.S.-ROK Mutual Defense Treaty of August 1953. (Had Rhee not agreed to honor the armistice, the Eisenhower administration might have been forced to implement Operation EVERREADY, its secret but risky plan to remove him from office.) Finally, on July 27 an armistice was signed at Panmunjom, and the guns fell silent.

SPENCER C. TUCKER

Consequences

Of 132,000 North Korean and Chinese military prisoners of war, fewer than 90,000 chose to return home. Twenty-two Americans held by the communists also elected not to return home, a shock to the American public. Of 10,218 Americans captured by the Communists, only 3,746 returned; the remaining 6,472 perished. Perhaps four times that number of South Korean prisoners also died. ROK forces sustained some 257,000 military deaths, while U.S. war-related deaths numbered 36,574. Other UNC killed came to 3,960.

The DPRK has not released any casualty figures, but its military deaths are estimated at 295,000. Chinese deaths from all causes may have approached 1 million. Perhaps 900,000 South Korean civilians died during the war from all causes.

The war absolutely devastated Korea and hardened divisions between North and South Korea. Democracy was also a casualty, for the corrupt Rhee regime rode roughshod over its opposition. Certainly the war was a sobering experience for the United States, which was used to total victory. But after the war, the United States, which had disarmed after previous conflicts, kept its military establishment strong with substantial sustained increases in the national defense budget. The war also saw a considerable expansion in presidential powers.

The Korean War institutionalized the Cold War national security state and also effectively militarized U.S. foreign policy. Before the Korean War, Marshall Plan aid had been almost entirely nonmilitary. Aid now shifted heavily toward military rearmament.

The Korean War also solidified the role of the United States as the "world's policeman" and strengthened the country's relationship with its West European allies and the North Atlantic Treaty Organization. The war greatly facilitated the rearmament of the Federal Republic of Germany (West Germany) and was a tremendous boost to the Japanese economy. At the same time, the war also led Washington to extend direct military American assistance to the French fighting in Indochina, placing the United States on the slippery slope to the Vietnam War.

The Korean War had important consequences for America domestically. It ended 20 years of control by the Democratic

Party. The racial integration of the U.S. armed forces implemented during the war greatly impacted the civil rights movement of the 1960s. The war also accelerated an economic and political reorientation from the U.S. North and Northeast to the South, Southwest, and West.

The PRC gained greatly from the war, adding immensely to its prestige. China now came to be regarded as the preponderant military power in Asia. In the following decades, concerns regarding Chinese military strength were woven into the fabric of American foreign policy. These influenced subsequent U.S. policy in Vietnam.

The more than 60 years that followed the end of the Korean War have seen the ROK become a major economic power with the world's 11th-largest gross domestic product, while the DPRK became a major military power and defied the world to develop nuclear weapons and the missiles to deliver them. It is also perhaps the world's most reclusive state. No formal peace has ever been concluded in Korea, and so technically the two Koreas remain at war. The demilitarized zone and the Northern Limitation Line in the Yellow Sea today constitute one of the world's major flashpoints, with occasional military alerts and small-scale armed clashes, any one of which could sharply escalate into full-scale war.

SPENCER C. TUCKER

Timeline

1894–1895

Japan defeats China in the First Sino-Japanese War and establishes a protectorate over Korea. Japan controls Korea until 1945.

1910

August 22

Under terms of the Japan-Korea Treaty of this date, Japan annexes Korea.

1904–1905

Japan defeats Russia in the Russo-Japanese War and secures the Russian cessions in China.

1939–1945

World War II.

1943

November 22–26

At the Cairo Conference, U.S. president Franklin Roosevelt, British prime minister Winston Churchill, and Chinese leader Jiang Jieshi agree that following its period of "enslavement" by Japan, Korea should in "due course" become "free and independent."

1945

August 15

Japan announces that it is surrendering.

August 16

On August 10, 1945, U.S. Army colonels Dean Rusk and Charles Bonesteel are charged with defining an American occupation zone in Korea. They choose the 38th parallel as the dividing line between the U.S. and Soviet zones. No Korean experts are consulted. The decision is cabled to the Soviets on August 15, and they accept it the next day.

September 2 | The formal Japanese surrender occurs aboard the U.S. battleship *Missouri* in Tokyo Bay.

September 8 | U.S. occupation troops begin arriving in South Korea.

1946

December | A legislative assembly opens in the U.S. zone of Korea.

1947

September | Frustrated in its inability to settle the future of Korea in negotiations with the Soviet Union, the U.S. government refers the matter to the United Nations (UN).

1948

April | U.S. president Harry S. Truman approves a policy statement that Korean developments will not automatically be a cause for war by the United States.

April 3 | Communist guerrillas begin the Jeju Island (Cheju-do) Rebellion in South Korea. Battalion-sized clashes also occur along the 38th parallel in May and August.

May 10 | The United Nations Temporary Commission on Korea (UNTCOK), which has been denied admission to the Soviet zone, oversees elections in the American zone.

August 15 | The Republic of Korea (South Korea, ROK) is officially established, headed by Syngman Rhee.

September 9 | The Democratic People's Republic of Korea (North Korea, DPRK) is officially established. It is headed by Kim Il Sung.

December | The UN General Assembly endorses South Korea as having the country's only lawfully elected government.

1949

June | The United States completes the withdrawal of its occupation troops from South Korea.

September | UNTCOK reports its inability to mediate between the two Korean governments and warns of impending civil war.

1950

January 12 | U.S. secretary of state Dean Acheson specifically excludes Taiwan and Korea from the U.S. Asian "defensive

	perimeter." The U.S. Joint Chiefs of Staff confirm this position, as has U.S. Far Eastern Command commander General Douglas MacArthur.
April	DPRK leader Kim meets secretly in Moscow with Stalin and assures him of an easy military victory over the ROK. Kim receives a pledge of support and substantial Soviet military assistance. In May he also visits Beijing and receives the support of People's Republic of China (PRC) leader Mao Zedong.
May 30	In the ROK national elections, moderates register gains at the expense of conservatives supporting Rhee.
June 25	Korean People's Army (KPA) forces invade South Korea. Hours later the UN Security Council calls for a cease-fire and withdrawal of KPA troops from South Korea.
June 27	The UN Security Council brands the DPRK the aggressor in the war and calls on member states to furnish assistance to the ROK.
	President Truman dispatches the U.S. Seventh Fleet to the waters off Taiwan to forestall a Chinese attack on that island.
June 28	KPA forces capture Seoul.
June 30	President Truman commits U.S. ground forces to the war.
July 5	The first U.S. ground force in the war (Task Force Smith) is overwhelmed at Osan.
July 10	President Truman appoints General MacArthur to command the United Nations Command (UNC).
August 5–September 23	U.S. and South Korean forces hold in the Battle of the Busan (Pusan) Perimeter.
September 15	U.S. Army major general Edward Almond's X Corps mounts an amphibious landing to secure the port of Incheon (Inchon).
September 24	UNC forces enter Seoul.
September 26	The Eighth U.S. Army in Korea (EUSAK) driving north from the Busan Perimeter links up with X Corps.
October 1	ROKA forces cross the 38th parallel.
October 3	PRC foreign minister Zhou Enlai threatens that if U.S. forces cross the 38th parallel, China will enter the war.

October 9	U.S. forces cross the 38th parallel.
October 15	President Truman meets with General MacArthur at Wake Island. MacArthur asserts that if Chinese forces enter the war, they will be destroyed by U.S. airpower.
October 19	UNC forces capture the DPRK capital of Pyongyang.
October 25	Chinese forces enter the fighting in northwestern Korea.
November 1	Soviet pilots begin flying combat missions over North Korea.
November 7	The Republican Party gains seats in the U.S. congressional elections.
November 8	U.S. bombers strike the two main bridges spanning the Yalu River.
November 24	EUSAK resumes offensive operations in northwestern Korea.
November 25–December 2	In the Battle of the Chongchon River, Chinese forces halt EUSAK's offensive and drive EUSAK back across the river.
November 27–December 13	In the Changjin (Chosin) Reservoir Campaign, UNC forces surrounded by the Chinese fight their way out to the northeastern coast of Korea at Hungnam.
December 15	President Truman declares a state of national emergency in the United States.
December 15–24	UNC forces in northeastern Korea and Korean civilians wishing to depart are evacuated by sea from the port of Hungnam, the facilities of which are then destroyed.
December 22	EUSAK commander Lieutenant General Walton Walker dies in a jeep accident. His replacement is Lieutenant General Matthew Ridgway.

1951

January 4	Chinese forces capture Seoul.
April 11	President Truman relieves General MacArthur of his commands. Ridgway replaces him, and Lieutenant General James Van Fleet takes command of EUSAK.
April 22–May 19	The UNC contains a Chinese offensive that pushes south of the 38th parallel.
May 18	A UNC counteroffensive of this date pushes the Chinese forces back, and at the end of the month the front stabilizes along the 38th parallel, with the U.S. Joint Chiefs

of Staff limiting EUSAK offensive operations to only small advances to improve the defensive line.

July 10   Truce talks open at Kaesong but deadlock.

October 25   Truce talks resume, this time at Panmunjom.

1952

March 29   Truman announces that he will not run for reelection.

November 4   Dwight D. Eisenhower is elected president of the United States.

1953

February 11   Lieutenant General Maxwell Taylor replaces Van Fleet as commander of EUSAK.

March 5   Stalin dies in Moscow.

March 23–July 11   The Battle of Pork Chop Hill occurs.

July 27   An armistice is signed at Panmounjom, ending the fighting.

October 1   A U.S.-ROK Mutual Defense Treaty is signed.

SPENCER C. TUCKER

Further Reading

Allen, Richard C. *Korea's Syngman Rhee: An Unauthorized Portrait.* Rutland, VT: Charles E. Tuttle, 1960.

Appleman, Roy E. *United States Army in the Korean War: South to the Naktong, North to the Yalu.* Washington, DC: Office of the Chief of Military History, 1961.

Bai, Bong. *Kim Il Sung: A Political Biography.* 3 vols. New York: Guardian Books, 1970.

Bailey, Sydney D. *The Korean Armistice.* New York: St. Martin's, 1992.

Blair, Clay. *The Forgotten War: America in Korea, 1950–1953.* New York: Times Books, 1987.

Cumings, Bruce. *The Korean War.* New York: Modern Library, 2010.

Cumings, Bruce. *The Origins of the Korean War.* 2 vols. Princeton, NJ: Princeton University Press, 1990.

Edwards, Paul G. *The Inchon Landing, Korea, 1950.* Westport, CT: Greenwood, 1994.

Ent, Uzal E. *Fighting on the Brink: Defense of the Pusan Perimeter.* Paducah, KY: Turner, 1996.

Foot, Rosemary. *A Substitute for Victory: The Politics of Peacemaking at the Korean Armistice Talks.* Ithaca, NY: Cornell University Press, 1990.

Goncharov, Sergei, John W. Lewis, and Xue Litai. *Uncertain Partners: Stalin, Mao and the Korean War.* Stanford, CA: Stanford University Press, 1993.

Hermes, Walter, Jr. *U.S. Army in the Korean War: Truce Tent and Fighting Front.* Washington, DC: Office of the Chief of Military History, 1966.

Kim, Chum-Kon. *The Korean War, 1950–1953.* Seoul: Kwangmyong, 1980.

Kim, Jinwung. *A History of Korea: From "Land of the Morning Calm" to States in Conflict.* Bloomington: Indiana University Press, 2012.

Korean Institute of Military History. *The Korean War.* 3 vols. Seoul: Republic of Korea Ministry of National Defense, 1997–1999.

Li, Xiaobing. *A History of the Modern Chinese Army.* Lexington: University Press of Kentucky, 2007.

Millett, Allan R. *The War for Korea, 1945–1950: A House Burning*. Lawrence: University Press of Kansas, 2005.

Millett, Allan R. *The War for Korea, 1950–1951: They Came from the North*. Lawrence: University Press of Kansas, 2010.

Montross, Lynn, and Nicholas A. Canzona. *U.S. Marine Operations in Korea,* Vol. 2, *The Inchon-Seoul Operation*. Washington, DC: U.S. Marine Corps Historical Branch, 1954–1957.

Mossman, Billy C. *United States Army in the Korean War: Ebb and Flow, November 1950–July 1951*. Washington, DC: U.S. Army, Center of Military History, 1990.

O'Neill, Mark A. "The Other Side of the Yalu: Soviet Pilots in Korea." Unpublished PhD dissertation, Florida State University, 1996.

Paige, Glenn D. *The Korean Decision, June 24–30*. New York: Free Press, 1968.

Pierpaoli, Paul G., Jr. *Truman and Korea: The Political Culture of the Early Cold War*. Columbia: University of Missouri Press, 1999.

Sawyer, Robert K. *Military Advisors in Korea: KMAG in Peace and War*. Washington, DC: Office of the Chief of Military History, U.S. Army, 1962.

Scalapino, Robert A., and Lee Chong-Sik. *Communism in Korea*. 2 vols. Berkeley: University of California Press, 1973.

Simmons, Robert R. *The Strained Alliance: Peking, Pyongyang, Moscow, and the Politics of the Korean War*. New York: Columbia University Press, 1975.

Spanier, John W. *The Truman-MacArthur Controversy and the Korean War*. Cambridge, MA: Belknap, 1959.

Stueck, William W., Jr. *Rethinking the Korean War: A New Diplomatic and Strategic History*. Princeton, NJ: Princeton University Press, 2004.

Suh, Dae-Sook. *Kim Il Sung: The North Korean Leader*. New York: Columbia University Press, 1988.

Truman, Harry S. *Memoirs*. 2 vols. Garden City, NY: Doubleday, 1955–1956.

Tucker, Spencer C., ed. *Encyclopedia of the Korean War*. 3 vols., revised ed. Santa Barbara, CA: ABC-CLIO, 2010.

Van Ree, Eric. *Socialism in One Zone: Stalin's Policy in Korea, 1945–1947*. Oxford: Oxford University Press, 1988.

Cuban Revolution (1953–1959)

Causes

The Cuban Revolution of July 26, 1953–January 1, 1959, toppled the dictatorial regime of Cuban president Fulgencio Batista and brought a Marxist state headed by Fidel Castro. The largest and westernmost island of the West Indies chain, Cuba is about the size of the U.S. state of Ohio. Its location west of Hispaniola and only 90 miles south of Key West, Florida, has necessarily forced it into a close relationship with the United States.

For most of its modern history, Cuba was controlled by Spain. Christopher Columbus claimed Cuba for Spain in 1492. Subsequent Spanish conquistadors and traders recognized the value of Havana as an ideal port, and despite strong native opposition, Spain established its first permanent settlement there in 1511. Within a few decades, Spain had instituted the *encomienda* system, a trusteeship labor arrangement in which natives were assigned to work for a wealthy Spaniard who was given control of a specific area of land. This system aided in Christianizing the natives, structuring the economy, and consolidating Spanish political power. The first African slaves arrived in 1526.

Spain ruled Cuba directly, and the island's governor had almost complete control of all basic government functions as well as of the military. The Spanish exploited the island's natural resources, and the native population suffered considerable abuse. When other Spanish possessions proved more valuable, Cuba came to be chiefly a way station within the empire.

With the emergence of tobacco farming as a profitable enterprise, the Crown used its authority to create a government monopoly over that industry. Growers revolted in the 1720s, but Madrid maintained tight control for almost another century. King Charles III's Bourbon Reforms in the mid-18th century stimulated Cuba's economy and brought liberal ideas to the island. Later in the century, in order to keep the settlers loyal, Spain acquiesced to their requests to ease trade restrictions on sugar, end limits on the importation of slaves, and lower tariffs on Cuban imports.

The Napoleonic Wars of the early 19th century diverted Spain's attention, and the Cuban economy and political sensibility matured under this salutary neglect. Madrid permitted private ownership of land in Cuba for the first time by allowing large estates to be subdivided into sugar and coffee plantations and giving them to established Spanish settlers. By the mid-19th century the Cuban economy was flourishing, with sugar and coffee as the two principal cash crops.

Most Cubans were relatively content with Spanish rule through the first few decades of the 19th century. Nevertheless, the growing and prosperous Creole (locally born Cubans of European descent) aristocracy became increasingly concerned that Madrid would be ineffective in dealing with a large-scale slave rebellion such as that in Haiti. They also came to believe that continued rule by Spain might bring the elimination of slavery, which would present grave economic consequences. Small slave revolts in the 1840s intensified these concerns and encouraged many wealthy landowners to advocate a political connection with the United States.

Cuban Revolution (1953–1959)

Casualties during Fidel Castro-Led Assault on Moncada Barracks (July 26, 1953)	
Insurgents	**Cuban Army**
6 killed, 15 wounded	19 killed, 17 wounded

Approximate Strength of Select Armed Forces in Cuba (1957–1958)	
Castro-Led Insurgents	**Cuban Army**
200–300	30,000–40,000

Approximate Casualty Figures, Operation VERANO (June 28–August 8, 1958)	
Insurgents	**Cuban Army**
76 killed	126 killed, 30 wounded, 240 captured

Approximate Total Casualties, Cuban Revolution (1953–1959)
5,000

Estimated Number of Political Executions in Cuba (1959–1962)
3,200–33,000

Sources: Thomas M. Leonard, *Castro and the Cuban Revolution* (Westport, CT: Greenwood, 1999); Marifeli Pérez-Stable, *The Cuban Revolution: Origins, Course, and Legacy* (New York: Oxford University Press, 2012).

By 1860 many in the Creole elite favored U.S. annexation of Cuba, but a variety of factors, most notably the American Civil War, ended their aspirations. Still, the desire to reform the political relationship with Spain remained and was strengthened by others who wanted equal rights, less centralized power, and gradual emancipation. This reformist movement, combined with the successful independence movement in nearby Santo Domingo, prompted Madrid to explore reform, but the government then ignored the policy recommendations of a commission. This, coupled with new government-levied taxes, demonstrated that Madrid was not serious about reform in Cuba.

In 1868 Creole landowners began the Ten Years' War, the first major effort to bring about Cuban independence. Spain responded forcefully and by 1871 had largely contained the rebellion, which lacked foreign support and was hampered by internal leadership discord. The revolutionaries finally signed a peace treaty in 1878. In the wake of the war, the Crown continued its refusal to undertake political reforms, although it outlawed slavery in 1886.

A new independence movement coalesced under José Martí y Pérez. Working with key figures from the earlier conflict, he spearheaded the Cuban Revolution (Insurrection) that began in 1895. The effort survived Martí's death in the first year of hostilities, and the Cuban revolutionaries made territorial gains until Madrid appointed General Valeriano Weyler y Nicolau as governor-general in 1896. Weyler's harsh policies, including moving civilians to reconcentration camps that caused the deaths of hundreds of thousands from disease and starvation, gave Spain the initiative in the war but also brought an American declaration of war against Spain on April 25, 1898.

The Spanish-American War was a watershed in U.S.-Cuban relations, as it brought greatly enhanced American influence in the island. The U.S. military occupation of Cuba, which occurred in the immediate aftermath of the Spanish-American War, began on January 1, 1899, and ended on May 20, 1902. Although the April 1898 Teller Amendment prohibited U.S. annexation of Cuba, President William McKinley was determined to protect the lucrative U.S. economic investments in Cuba and was uncertain about the ability of Cubans to govern themselves. Also, during the occupation American military officials facilitated the expansion of U.S. economic investments on the island while simultaneously disenfranchising the majority of the Cuban population. At the same time, U.S. officials implemented numerous infrastructure improvements.

As a result of the occupation, the island was a virtual political and economic protectorate of the United States. By the beginning of the 20th century, 60 percent of all rural land in Cuba was owned by U.S. investors and corporations. U.S. economic interests dominated the sugar industry, mining, public utilities, and the railroad network in Cuba. Clearly, the main beneficiaries of U.S. military occupation were U.S. citizens, not Cubans.

Under the terms of the Platt Amendment of March 2, 1901, inserted into the U.S. Army appropriations bill, the United States retained the right to intervene in Cuba to maintain Cuba's independence.

Washington insisted that the Cuban government not negotiate treaties with other nations that might impede Cuban independence and also insisted that the U.S. government had the right to indefinitely maintain naval bases in Cuba. Aware that the U.S. military occupation would not end until it accepted the validity of the Platt Amendment, the Cuban constitutional assembly incorporated it, by a margin of one vote, as an addendum to the Cuban Constitution on June 12, 1901. The Platt Amendment made Cuba a virtual protectorate of the United States and ceded the naval station at Guantánamo Bay to the United States. The U.S. military occupation of Cuba subsequently ended on May 20, 1902.

In 1906 U.S. forces again occupied Cuba following a disputed election and an armed revolt. Self-government returned with José Miguel Gómez, who became president in 1908 following U.S.-supervised elections. U.S. forces returned to Cuba in 1912 to help put down efforts by Cuban blacks to establish a separate republic in Oriente Province.

In 1925 Gerardo Machado y Morales became president of Cuba. Tourism increased dramatically with the construction of American-owned hotels and resorts, but with these came gambling, organized crime, and prostitution. Machado instituted a vigorous public works program but also had to deal with the effects of the worldwide economic depression in 1930 and subsequently adopted repressive measures to deal with the ensuing unrest.

In August 1933 Machado was forced into exile, replaced by Carlos Manuel de Céspedes y Quesada, who was then ousted by the so-called Sergeants' Revolt led by Sergeant Fulgencio Batista. Cuba was then governed by a five-man council (the Pentarchy) until Ramón Grau San Martín was appointed provisional president on September 10. In January 1934 Grau yielded the presidency to Batista, who would control Cuban affairs during the next 25 years.

In 1934 the United States gave up its right to intervene in Cuban internal affairs. Cuba adopted a new progressive constitution in 1940, and Batista was elected president that same year. He abided by the constitution that limited the president to one four-year term and stepped down in 1944, succeeded by Grau. Carlos Prío Socarrás became president in 1948.

On March 10, 1952, however, General Batista seized power in a coup d'état only two months before an election in which nationalist forces were within reach of the presidency. In the context of McCarthyism in America, the destruction of the Cuban democracy by Batista's rightist junta did not generate significant opposition in Washington. Indeed, the United States backed Batista as an ally in the Cold War. For its part, the Cuban authoritarian Right manipulated the West by presenting itself as a bulwark against communism. In practice, the Batista government was actually undermining democracy with its repressive policies. At the same time, the Batista regime did little to improve living standards for poor Cubans, while the middle class and elites enjoyed a close and lucrative relationship with American businesses.

In 1953, Fidel Castro and Ernesto "Che" Guevara led a revolt against Batista. The revolutionaries questioned Cuban dependence on the United States as well as market economy principles. They perceived their movement as part of a rebellion in the developing world against the West and as a natural ally of the communist bloc.

MATTHEW J. KROGMAN, ARTURO LOPEZ-LEVY, AND SPENCER C. TUCKER

Course

The Cuban Revolution (Cuban Insurgency) began in July 1953 and ended with the overthrow of dictator Fulgencio Batista's regime on January 1, 1959. Initially, it was an urban movement incorporating student groups as well as other political entities. Batista's coup d'état in 1952 had sparked widespread popular outrage, and Fidel Castro's movement was only one of a number that sprang up in opposition.

Castro, born in 1926, became an activist and a student leader in Havana and earned a doctorate of law from the University of Havana in 1950. An avowed Marxist, he attempted to establish a law firm that would primarily aid the poor, but it failed financially. He then became involved in political action against the Batista regime, founding an underground organization known as "The Movement."

Castro launched his insurgency on July 26, 1953, leading 165 followers in an assault on the Moncada Barracks at Santiago in an effort to raid its armory. Castro had ordered his men not to fire unless fired upon, but a firefight occurred. The attack ended in failure. The rebels suffered 6 dead and 15 wounded, while the army had 19 dead and 17 wounded. Twenty-two of the rebels captured were subsequently executed without trial. Castro and his brother Raúl escaped but were subsequently taken prisoner. Fidel was tried and sentenced to 15 years in prison; Raúl received a sentence of 13 years. Fidel's trial made him a national political figure, however. In a nearly four-hour-long speech in his defense,

Fidel Castro, leader of the July 26 Movement, and his lieutenants in their guerrilla stronghold in the Sierra Maestra mountains of southeast Cuba, March 14, 1957. (Popperfoto/Getty Images)

Castro told the court, "Condemn me, it does not matter. History will absolve me."

Castro and 25 others were imprisoned in a relatively modern facility on the Isla de Pinos. There Castro renamed his insurgent group the 26th of July Movement in honor of the Moncada Barracks attack. In 1955 following his election as president, Batista succumbed to political pressure and released a number of political prisoners, including Fidel and Raúl Castro. The Castros then left Cuba for Mexico. That June in Mexico City, Fidel met Argentine revolutionary Ernesto "Che" Guevara, who would come to play a large role in the insurgency.

On April 4, 1956, an attempt by hundreds of career army officers to overthrow Batista was suppressed by forces led by Rios Morejon. The leader of the coup attempt, Colonel Ramon Barquin, Cuban military attaché to the United States, was sentenced to solitary confinement for eight years. Other officers received the maximum sentences permissible by law. This event had a devastating effect on army morale and helped ensure that the army would not fight effectively for the Batista regime.

Meanwhile, Fidel Castro was preparing another attempt to overthrow Batista. Following some military training, on November 25, 1956, he and 81 others, including Raúl Castro and Guevara, set sail from Tuxpan, Mexico, for Cuba in the *Granma,* an old yacht they had purchased. They arrived at Playa Las Colcordas on December 2. After coming ashore, the men began the trek to the Sierra Maestra mountains of southeastern Cuba. En route, Batista's soldiers killed the majority; no more than 20 insurgents reached the Sierre Maestra, and it was some time before they were able to link up, aided by sympathetic peasants.

Castro's 26th of July Movement was certainly not the only organization seeking to overthrow the Batista regime. On March 13, 1957, the anticommunist Directorio Revolucionario (Revolutionary Directorate), composed largely of students, assaulted the Presidential Palace in Havana, hoping to kill Batista. The attack ended in failure. Not until 1958 did the 26th of July Movement become the leading Cuban revolutionary organization.

While Castro's insurgents operated in the rural areas of Cuba, Frank País concentrated on mobilizing urban opposition to the Batista regime. The growth of the urban insurgency made it difficult for Batista to eradicate the movement, although País was betrayed to the police and then assassinated after his capture in Santiago in July.

Throughout the last half of 1957, Batista's government forced many opponents into exile, which produced a large expatriate community centered in Miami, Florida. Meanwhile, Castro remained the only opposition leader with an armed force still fighting inside Cuba. At the same time, poorly armed irregulars known as *escopeteros* harassed Batista's soldiers in Oriente Province and assisted Castro by providing intelligence and protecting his supply lines. In February 1958 also, Castro launched a propaganda effort through the establishment of a clandestine radio station.

Batista made several efforts to co-opt the insurgency. In early 1958, he restored civil liberties. He also encouraged the opposition to participate in what he claimed would be open elections. At the same time, the insurgents were greatly aided by an arms embargo imposed by the United States on the Batista regime in March 1958. This especially crippled the Cuban Air Force, which was unable to secure spare parts. Throughout this period Castro only commanded some 200 men, while the Cuban Army numbered 30,000–40,000. The army's numerical advantage was offset by poor training and ineffective leadership.

Castro hoped to be able to topple the regime through a general strike coupled with a military offensive. The nationwide strike began in April 1958 but failed to destabilize the regime, while the insurgents lacked the military strength required for successful large-scale operations. Then in Operation VERANO, Batista sent some 12,000 soldiers under army commander General Eulogio Cantillo into the mountains against the rebels, only to see the latter win a series of small clashes. In one such battle, at La Plata (July 11–21), Castro's forces defeated a government battalion and took 240 prisoners. But on July 29, Castro's forces were badly mauled in the Battle of Las Mercedes. Castro secured a temporary cease-fire on August 1 and during a week of fruitless negotiations succeeded in extracting his men from the government trap.

On August 21, Castro began his own military offensive in Oriente Province, utilizing weapons captured during the government offensive and those smuggled in from abroad by aircraft. By November, Castro's insurgents had succeeded in splitting Cuba in two by closing major roads and rail lines. On December 31, a combined rebel offensive took Santa Clara, capital of Villa Clara Province. Aware of efforts to arrest him and try him as a war criminal, Batista departed Cuba on January 1, 1959, leaving General Eulogio Cantillo in charge of the government.

Castro then initiated negotiations to take Santiago de Cuba. The Cuban Army commander there ordered his soldiers not to fight, and on January 2, 1959, Castro entered Santiago without a shot being fired. At the same time, the Cuban capital of Havana fell to the rebels. Castro himself arrived there on January 8.

Castro established an interim government, with Manuel Urrutia Lleó as interim president on January 3. On February 16 Castro took the office of prime minister, and in December 1976 he also became president.

GATES BROWN AND SPENCER C. TUCKER

Consequences

Fidel Castro's victory was not universally applauded in Cuba. Indeed, during 1959–1966 insurgents in the Escambray Mountains fought the new government but were finally overwhelmed by sheer force of numbers. The U.S. State Department held that during 1959–1962 there were 3,200 political executions in Cuba. Other estimates range as high as 33,000.

The Cuban Revolution ushered in a revolutionary government led by the charismatic Fidel Castro. Initially hailed by democrats worldwide, once the new government demonstrated that it intended to proceed with a major social revolution and an independent foreign policy, U.S. government sympathy rapidly cooled. Nonetheless, the Cuban Revolution marked a turning point in hemispheric relations, giving hope to the region's leftists, providing nightmares to the region's rightists, and completely reorienting U.S. policy toward the rest of the Americas.

The United States was not prepared to deal with the charismatic and doctrinaire Fidel Castro. Washington completely underestimated the profound grievances provoked by American support for the Batista regime. Some of Castro's early measures such as land reform, the prosecution of

Batista's cronies (with no guarantee of due process), and the nationalization of industries were overwhelmingly popular, but at the same time they met stiff U.S. resistance.

Against this backdrop, Castro approached the Soviet Union for support, and in February 1960 a Soviet delegation led by Vice Premier Anastas Mikoyan visited Cuba and signed a trade agreement with Castro's government. The Soviets then began to replace the United States as Cuba's main trade and political partner. Soviet leader Nikita Khrushchev soon promised Cuba new machinery, oil, consumer goods, and a market for Cuban products now subject to American sanctions.

In April 1961 U.S.-Cuban relations collapsed completely, thanks to the abortive Bay of Pigs fiasco sponsored by the U.S. Central Intelligence Agency (CIA). The assault was condemned to failure, given Castro's popularity and the lack of U.S. air support for the rebel force. The botched attack only encouraged closer relations between the Soviet Union and Cuba. Khrushchev subsequently proposed installing nuclear-equipped missiles in Cuba to ensure a better bargaining position with the United States and as a means of offering protection to Cuba. Castro was elated. Khrushchev naively assumed that the missiles could be installed without U.S. detection. U.S. intelligence quickly discovered the activity, however, leading to the Cuban Missile Crisis, the most dangerous confrontation between the two superpowers of the Cold War.

President John F. Kennedy declared a naval quarantine against the island in October 1962. For nearly two weeks the world stood at the edge of a nuclear abyss. In the end, Kennedy and Khrushchev worked out an agreement in which the Soviets withdrew the missiles in return for

U.S. promises not to invade Cuba and to withdraw Jupiter missiles from Turkey.

The end of Kennedy's quarantine did not conclude the strife between Cuba and the United States, however. In addition to an embargo that continues to this day, the United States launched additional covert operations against Castro's government. The most important one, Operation MONGOOSE, included 14 CIA attempts to assassinate Castro. American hostility was reinforced by the Cuban Revolution's transformation from a nationalist rebellion against authoritarianism to a totalitarian state aligned with the Soviet Union, with serious shortcomings in civil and political liberties.

The solution to the Cuban Missile Crisis also created serious strains between Havana and Moscow. Cuba's foreign policy was made in Havana, and therefore Castro refused to accept Moscow's or Beijing's directives. In 1968 he cracked down on a group of Cuban communists, accusing them of working with Soviet agents in Havana. In the end, Castro used the 1968 Soviet intervention in Czechoslovakia against the Prague Spring to broker a compromise by which Cuba preserved its autonomy but promised not to criticize the Soviets publicly. Cuba thus became a member of the Council for Mutual Economic Assistance and received significant additional economic aid from the communist bloc.

In Latin America, the Cuban government actively supported revolutionary movements with leftist or nationalist agendas, especially those that challenged American hegemony in the region. But the 1960s witnessed successive failed Cuban attempts to export revolution to other countries. Che Guevara's 1967 murder in Bolivia concluded a series of subversive projects encouraged by Havana. Cuban revolutionary attempts were part of Cubans' core revolutionary beliefs and also a response to the rupture of diplomatic relations with Havana by all the Latin American countries except Mexico.

From the 1970s to 1990 as part of the Cold War conflict, Cuba played a major role in the international context. A high point of Castro's foreign policy came at the 1979 Sixth Summit of the Non-Aligned Movement in Havana. Cuba became a major conduit of alliance between the developing world and the communist bloc. Havana's diplomatic success and military involvement were accompanied by a massive civilian involvement in aid programs to African, Latin American, and Asian countries in the areas of health and education.

Cuba adopted the foreign policy suited to a medium-sized power. Cuba sent 40,000 troops to Angola to support the pro-Soviet Movimento Popular da Libertação de Angola (Popular Movement for the Liberation of Angola) government there in its struggle against the União Nacional para a Independência Total de Angola (National Union for the Total Independence of Angola) forces, backed by South Africa and the United States. Cuba also dispatched troops to aid the pro-Soviet government of Ethiopia. In all, Cuba deployed a total of more than 300,000 troops or military advisers to Angola, Ethiopia, Congo, Guinea Bissau, Algeria, Mozambique, Syria, and South Yemen. The fight in Southern Africa was ended through a skillfully designed tripartite agreement signed by Cuba, Angola, and South Africa and mediated by the Ronald Reagan administration that led to the independence of Namibia.

Paradoxically, due in part to these Cold War commitments, Cuba missed its best chance to solve its conflict with the United

States. During 1970–1980 the Americans sought serious negotiations with Cuba. This began under the Richard Nixon administration and saw the most promise under the Jimmy Carter administration (1977–1981). Carter demonstrated that he was serious in his desire to improve relations among the nations of the hemisphere and promote human rights. In 1977, Carter went so far as to say that the United States did not consider a Cuban retreat from Angola a precondition for beginning negotiations. Castro, however, insisted on continuing what he defined as "revolutionary solidarity" and "proletarian internationalism."

The Cuban government was interested in negotiations with the Americans but insisted on a radical leftist solution to problems. Castro took significant steps in releasing political prisoners and allowing visits to the island by Cuban exiles as goodwill gestures to the United States. In the international arena, Cuba informed the Americans about the Katanga rebellion in Zaire. Nevertheless, Cuba gave priority to its relations with other revolutionary movements, especially in Africa. In 1977, Castro sent 17,000 Cuban troops to Ethiopia to support dictator Mengistu Haile Mariam in his territorial conflict with Somalia. This development, despite the progress in several bilateral issues, represented a major blow to the prospect of improved Cuban-U.S. relations, as did Castro's support for the Sandinista government of Nicaragua in the 1980s.

A new development came in 1976 in Cuba when Ricardo Boffill, Elizardo Sanchez, and Gustavo Arcos founded the first Cuban human rights group since 1959. A new generation of opposition groups based on strategies of civil disobedience slowly emerged, gaining strength in the 1990s. Equally, during the 1970s Cuban civil society began to emerge from totalitarian ostracism that had reduced its religious communities to a minimum. This evolution continued, and at the end of the 1980s the religious groups were growing at a fast pace.

The collapse of the communist bloc beginning in 1989 was a major catastrophe for Castro's government, as Cuba lost its major benefactors. At the same time, the international community, particularly Latin America and the former communist countries, adopted general norms of democratic governance opposed to the goals and behavior of the Cuban leadership. Without Soviet backing, Cuba adjusted its economy and foreign policy to survive in a world that was no longer safe for revolution. In 1988 Castro withdrew Cuban troops from Angola and reduced the Cuban military presence in the Horn of Africa.

Cuba's gross domestic product fell by almost one-third between 1989 and 1993. The collapse of the Cuban economy was particularly hard on imports, which fell from 8.6 billion pesos in 1989 to about just 2 billion pesos in 1993. In response to the economic collapse, Castro permitted limited private enterprise, allowed Cubans to have foreign currencies, and pushed for foreign investment, particularly in tourism. His reforms, however, did little to stop the economic hemorrhaging. Cuban troops were also withdrawn from wherever they were posted. More than 15 years after the end of the Cold War, Castro remained one of the last leaders of the old-style communist orders. He did not step down until February 2008, when power passed to his brother Raúl.

On December 17, 2014, a political standoff that had spanned more than five decades and 10 U.S. presidents crumbled when U.S. president Barack Obama announced that he planned to normalize relations with Cuba. This came after secret negotiations and followed the release by the United States of three Cuban spies in exchange for a CIA spy and an American prisoner. Although considerable pitfalls remained before the U.S. economic embargo could be lifted and full diplomatic relations were established, this step was nonetheless heralded as a diplomatic breakthrough ending a policy in effect since 1960 that had only hurt the Cuban people.

ARTURO LOPEZ-LEVY
AND SPENCER C. TUCKER

Timeline

1492	Christopher Columbus claims Cuba for Spain.
1511	Diego de Velazquez leads the Spanish conquest of Cuba.
1526	The importation of slaves from Africa to Cuba begins.
1762	
August	During the Seven Years' War, British forces capture Havana, Cuba.
1763	The Treaty of Paris ending the Seven Years' War returns Havana to Spain.
1868–1878	Settlers in Cuba lead the Ten Years' War of Independence. The war ends with Spain promising reforms and greater autonomy, but these pledges are not met.
1886	Slavery is abolished in Cuba.
1895–1898	José Martí y Pérez leads a new war of independence against Spain.
1898	
April 20	The congressional U.S. Teller Amendment prohibits the annexation of Cuba by the United States.
April 25	The United States declares war on Spain and invades and occupies Cuba.
1901	
March 2	The Platt Amendment to a U.S. Army appropriations bill stipulates conditions for the U.S. military withdrawal from Cuba and gives the United States the right to intervene in Cuban affairs.
1902	
May 20	Cuba becomes independent as the Republic of Cuba, but the United States secures a lease on the Guantánamo Bay naval base.

1906–1909	After a disputed election, U.S. forces again occupy Cuba following a rebellion led by José Miguel Gómez, who becomes president in 1908 following U.S.-supervised elections.
1912	U.S. forces return to Cuba to help put down an effort by the Partido Independente de Color to establish an independent black republic in Oriente Province.
1925	
May 20	Gerardo Machado y Morales takes office as president of Cuba. Machado institutes a vigorous public works program but, forced to deal with unrest accompanying the worldwide economic depression, adopts repressive measures.
1933	
August	Machado is forced into exile. He is replaced by Carlos Manuel de Céspedes y Quesada.
September	Céspedes is overthrown in the so-called Sergeants' Revolt, led by Sergeant Fulgencio Batista. Cuba is then governed by a five-man council (the Pentarchy) until Ramón Grau San Martín is appointed provisional president on September 10.
1934	As part of U.S. president Franklin Roosevelt's Good Neighbor Policy, the United States gives up its right to intervene in Cuban internal affairs. It also revises Cuba's sugar quota and changes tariffs to favor Cuba.
January 15	Grau yields the presidency to Batista, who will control Cuban affairs for the next 25 years.
1944	
October 10	Grau succeeds Batista as president of Cuba.
1948	
October 10	Carlos Prío Socarrás becomes president of Cuba.
1952	
March 10	General Batista seizes power in a coup d'état.
1953	
July 26	Fidel Castro leads some 160 revolutionaries in an attack on the Moncada Barracks in Santiago de Cuba.
October 16	Defending his attack on the Moncada Barracks, Fidel Castro delivers in court his impassioned four-hour-long defense speech "History Will Absolve Me."

1954

September	Argentinian revolutionary Che Guevara arrives in Mexico City.
November	Batista dissolves the parliament and is elected constitutional president.

1955

May	Fidel Castro and surviving members of his movement are released from prison under an amnesty.
June	Fidel and Raúl Castro are introduced to Guevara in Mexico City.

1956

November 25	Some 50 insurgents, led by Fidel Castro and including his brother Raúl, Guevara, and Camilo Cienfuegos, sail from Tuxpan, Mexico, in the old yacht *Granma*.
December 2	The yacht *Granma* makes landfall in Oriente Province, Cuba.

1957

January 17	Castro's guerrillas capture an army outpost on the southern coast. Small successes bring increased numbers of recruits.
March 13	The anticommunist Directorio Revolucionario (Revolutionary Directorate), composed largely of Cuban students, mounts an unsuccessful assault on the Presidential Palace in Havana, hoping to kill Batista.
May 28	Fidel Castro's 26th of July Movement overwhelms an army post in El Uvero.
July 30	Cuban revolutionary Frank País, campaigning for the overthrow of Batista, is assassinated by the police following his arrest in Santiago.

1958

February	Raúl Castro opens an insurgent front in the Sierra de Cristal on Oriente's north coast.
March 13	The U.S. government suspends arms shipments to the Batista government, a significant handicap to its military efforts against the rebels especially for the air force, which is now unable to secure spare parts.
March 17	Fidel Castro calls for a general revolt.

April 9	A general strike, organized by the 26th of July Movement, enjoys limited success but fails to paralyze Cuba as Castro had hoped.
May	In Operation VERANO, Batista sends 10,000 troops into the Sierra Maestra to destroy Castro's 300 armed guerrillas.
July 22–21	In the Battle of La Plata, Castro's forces defeat a government battalion and take 240 prisoners.
July 29	Castro's forces are defeated in the Battle of Las Mercedes. Castro is able to secure a temporary cease-fire on August 1 and then succeeds in extracting his men.
August 21	Castro begins his own offensive in Oriente Province. Ultimately the rebels cut Cuba in two, making it difficult for government forces to operate effectively.
December 31	Santa Clara is taken by the insurgents.

1959

January 1	Largely abandoned by his supporters and sensing the inevitable, Batista flees Cuba.
January 2	Batista's commander there having ordered his men not to fight, Castro and his supporters enter Santiago de Cuba. The insurgents also secure Havana at about the same time.
January 7	The United States recognizes the new Cuban regime led by Fidel Castro.
January 8	Fidel Castro returns to Havana in triumph.
February 16	Fidel Castro is sworn in as prime minister of Cuba.
1960	The new Cuban government nationalizes without compensation all U.S.-owned businesses in Cuba.
1961	The Cuban government nationalizes all ecclesiastical properties, including those of the predominant Catholic Church.
	Washington breaks off all diplomatic relations with Havana. The United States sponsors an abortive invasion by Cuban exiles at the Bay of Pigs. Fidel Castro proclaims Cuba a communist state and begins to ally it with the Soviet Union.

1962

January 21	The Organization of American States suspends Cuba over its "incompatible" adherence to Marxism-Leninism.

October 14–28

The Cuban Missile Crisis occurs when, fearing a U.S. invasion, Castro agrees to allow the Soviet Union to deploy nuclear missiles in Cuba. Regarded as the closest the world comes to nuclear war during the Cold War, the crisis is resolved when the Soviets agree to remove their missiles in return for the withdrawal of obsolete U.S. nuclear missiles from Turkey.

2008

February 24

Following Fidel Castro's announcement earlier in the month that he is retiring, Raúl Castro is declared the new president of Cuba.

2014

December 17

Following secret negotiations that involved the Vatican and Canada, U.S. president Barack Obama announces that he plans to normalize relations with Cuba.

SPENCER C. TUCKER

Further Reading

Babun, Teo A. *The Cuban Revolution: Years of Promise.* Gainesville: University Press of Florida, 2005.

Benjamin, Jules R. *The United States and the Origins of the Cuban Revolution.* Princeton, NJ: Princeton University Press, 1992.

Bourne, Peter G. *Fidel: A Biography of Fidel Castro.* New York: Dodd, Mead, 1986.

De la Cova, Antonio Rafael. *The Moncada Attack: Birth of the Cuban Revolution.* Columbia: University of South Carolina Press, 2007.

Díaz-Briquets, Sergio, and Jorge F. Pérez-López. *Corruption in Cuba: Castro and Beyond.* Austin: University of Texas Press, 2006.

Dominguez, Jorge I. *To Make a World Safe for Revolution: Cuba's Foreign Policy.* Cambridge, MA: Harvard University Press, 1989.

English, T. J. *Havana Nocturne: How the Mob Owned Cuba and Then Lost It to the Revolution.* New York: William Morrow, 2008.

Farber, Samuel. *Cuba since the Revolution of 1959: A Critical Assessment.* Chicago: Haymarket Books, 2012.

Farber, Samuel. *The Origins of the Cuban Revolution Reconsidered.* Chapel Hill: University of North Carolina Press, 2006.

Faria, Miguel A. *Cuba in Revolution: Escape from a Lost Paradise.* Macon, GA: Hacienda Publishing, 2002.

Gleijeses, Piero. *Conflicting Missions: Havana, Washington and Africa, 1959–1976.* Chapel Hill: University of North Carolina Press, 2002.

Hansen, Joseph. *Dynamics of the Cuban Revolution: A Marxist Appreciation.* New York: Pathfinder, 1994.

Lazo, Mario. *American Policy Failures in Cuba: Dagger in the Heart.* New York: Twin Circle Publishing, 1970.

Leonard, Thomas M. *Castro and the Cuban Revolution.* Westport, CT: Greenwood, 1999.

Lievesley, Geraldine. *The Cuban Revolution: Past, Present and Future Perspectives.* New York: Palgrave Macmillan, 2004.

Pastor, Robert. *The Carter Administration and Latin America.* Occasional Paper Series Vol. 2, No. 3. Atlanta: Carter Center of Emory University, 1992.

Pérez, Louis A. *Cuba and the United States: Ties of Singular Intimacy.* Athens: University of Georgia Press, 1990.

Pérez-Stable, Marifeli. *The Cuban Revolution: Origins, Course, and Legacy.* New York: Oxford University Press, 2012

Sandison, David. *The Life & Times of Che Guevara.* Sydney: Book Co., 1996.

Smith, Wayne. *The Closest of Enemies: A Personal and Diplomatic History of the Castro Years.* New York: Norton, 1987.

Suchlicki, Jaime. *Cuba: From Columbus to Castro.* Washington, DC: Brassey's, 2002.

Sweig, Julia. *Inside the Cuban Revolution: Fidel Castro and the Urban Underground.* Cambridge, MA: Harvard University Press, 2004.

Thomas, Hugh. *Cuba: The Pursuit of Freedom.* New York: Da Capo, 1998.

Algerian War (1954–1962)

Causes

The Algerian War (also known as the Algerian War of Independence and the Algerian Revolution) was fought between Algerian nationalists known as the Front de Libération Nationale (National Liberation Front, FLN) and the French military between November 1, 1954, and March 19, 1962. The war led to a considerable expenditure of blood and treasure, saw some 1 million Frenchmen serve in the French Army in Algeria, claimed more than a score of French ministries, and brought the end of the French Fourth Republic, replaced by the Fifth Republic. The war also did not bring peace in Algeria.

France had established its control over Algeria more than a century earlier. On June 14, 1830, a French expeditionary force of some 34,000 men commanded by Marshal Louis Auguste Victor, Count de Ghaisnes de Bourmont, landed near Algiers. The pretext for the invasion was the insult to French consul to Algiers Pierre Duval, who had been struck with a flyswatter by Dey Husain in 1827. The French also sought to remove a threat to their Mediterranean trade, but the real reason behind French king Charles X's plan to take Algiers was to shore up his unpopular French government, headed by Prince Jules de Polignac, and enable it to win the 1830 national elections.

Algiers was duly taken on July 5, although Charles X's political gambit failed, as France experienced a revolution on July 28–30. In this July Revolution of 1830, Charles X was forced to abdicate in favor of his cousin Louis Philippe, Duc d'Orléans, who nonetheless decided to continue French military operations in Algeria.

French control was initially largely limited to the coastal areas and cities. A succession of French commanders proceeded to fight a variety of opponents and campaigns in widely differing terrain, from the Atlas Mountains to salt marshes and the *bled* (interior). Beginning in 1835, Abd al-Qadir, emir of Mascara in western Algeria, declared jihad (holy war) and fought the French. Following a number of battles, he was ultimately forced to surrender in December 1847 to French general Thomas Robert Bugeaud de la Piconnerie, who also proved to be an adroit colonial administrator.

By 1847, some 50,000 Europeans had settled in Algeria. French control over the Algerian interior was not accomplished until the Second Empire of Napoleon III (1852–1870), however. European settlement increased following the French defeat in the Franco-Prussian War of 1870–1871 and the German acquisition of Alsace and Lorraine. Many of the French who had lived in the two provinces chose to settle in Algeria rather than be under German rule.

While more Frenchmen immigrated to Algeria, the imbalance between them and the Muslim population ballooned. The Pax Franca brought finis to the tribal wars and disease that had kept the population relatively static. Another factor in the burgeoning Muslim population was the greatly improved medical care that dramatically decreased the infant mortality rate.

Unique among French colonies, Algeria became a political component of France, as the three French departments of Algiers, Constantine, and Oran all had limited representation in the French Chamber of Deputies. Nonetheless, the three Algerian departments were not like those of the Metropole, as only the European settlers, known as colons or *pieds noirs,* enjoyed full rights there. The colon and Muslim populations lived separate and unequal lives. The Europeans controlled the vast majority of the economic enterprises and wealth, while the Muslims tended to be agricultural laborers. Meanwhile, the French expanded Algeria's frontiers deep into the Sahara.

While the colons sought to preserve their status, French officials vacillated between promoting colon interests and advancing reforms for the Muslims. Pro-Muslim reform efforts failed because of political pressure from the colons and their representatives in Paris. While French political theorists debated between assimilation and autonomy for Algeria's Muslims, the Muslim majority were increasingly resentful of the privileged colon status.

World War I helped fuel Algerian Muslim nationalist sentiment, but the first Muslim political organizations appeared in the 1930s, the most important of these being Ahmed Messali Hadj's Mouvement pour le Triomphe des Libertés Démocratiques (Movement for the Triumph of Democratic Liberties, MTLD). World War II brought opportunities for change. Following the Anglo-American landings in North Africa in November 1942, Muslim activists met with American envoy Robert Murphy and Free French general Henri Giraud concerning postwar freedoms but received no firm commitments. However, 60,000 Algerian Muslims who had fought for France were granted French citizenship.

It came as a great shock to the French when pent-up Muslim frustrations exploded on May 8, 1945, during the course of a victory parade approved by French authorities celebrating the end of World War II in Europe. A French plainclothes policeman shot to death a young marcher carrying an Algerian flag, and this touched off a bloody rampage, often referred to as the Sétif Massacre. Muslims attacked Europeans and their property, and violence quickly spread to outlying areas.

The French authorities then unleashed a violent crackdown that included Foreign Legionnaires and Senegalese troops, tanks, aircraft, and even naval gunfire from a cruiser in the Mediterranean. Settler militias and local vigilantes took a number of Muslim prisoners from jails and executed them. Major French military operations lasted two weeks, while smaller actions continued for a month. Some 4,500 Algerians were arrested; 99 people were sentenced to death, and another 64 given life imprisonment. Casualty figures remain in dispute. At least 100 Europeans died. The official French figure of Muslim dead was 1,165, but this is certainly too low, and figures as high as 10,000 have been cited.

In March 1946 the French government announced a general amnesty and released many of the Sétif detainees, including moderate Algerian nationalist leader Ferhat Abbas, although his Friends of the Manifesto and Liberty political party, formed in 1938, was dissolved. The fierce nature of the French repression of the uprising was based on a perception that any leniency would be interpreted as weakness and would only encourage further unrest.

The Sétif Uprising, which was not followed by any meaningful French reform, drove a wedge between the two communities in Algeria. Europeans now distrusted Muslims, and the Muslims never forgave the violence of the repression. French

The Algerian War (1954–1962)

Number of People Killed, Arrested, and Executed, Sétif Uprising (May 8–June 5, 1945)				
	Killed	**Arrested**	**Executed**	
French/Europeans	100+	N/A	N/A	
Algerians	1,165–10,000	4,500	99	

Number of Deaths during the National Liberation Front's Philippeville Offensive (August 20, 1954)		
Colons	**Pro-French Muslims**	**Army of National Liberation**
71	52	134

Casualty and Arrest Figures during the Battle of Algiers (September 30, 1956–September 24, 1957)				
	Killed	**Wounded**	**Arrested**	**Missing**
National Liberation Front	1,000+	Unknown	24,000	3,000
French, Pro-French Forces	300	900	N/A	N/A

Total Deaths, All Causes, The Algerian War (1954–1962)		
Colons	3,000	
Muslims	300,000	
French and Pro-French Forces	18,000	

Sources: Alistair Horne, *A Savage War of Peace: Algeria, 1954–1962* (London: Macmillan, 1977); Roger Trinquier, *Modern Warfare: A French View of Counterinsurgency* (Westport, CT: Praeger Security International, 2006).

authorities did not understand the implications of this. A number of returning Muslim veterans of the war, including Ahmed Ben Bella, now joined the more militant MTLD. Ben Bella went on to form the Organization Speciale and soon departed for Egypt to enlist the support of its leaders.

Genuine political reform proved impossible, as granting full representation to Algeria would have entailed giving it a quarter of the seats in the National Assembly. The result was the compromise Algerian Statute, approved by the French National Assembly in September 1947. For the first time, Algeria was recognized as having administrative autonomy. The heart of the statute, however, was the creation of an Algerian Assembly

consisting of two coequal 60-member assemblies. Although all Algerians were classified as French citizens, the first college included all non-Muslim French citizens and those Muslims French citizens who had been so defined by virtue of military service or education. The second college provided for all other Muslims. A total of 469,023 Europeans and 63,194 Muslims were eligible to vote in the first college, and 1,301,072 Muslims were eligible to vote in the second college. Thus, for all practical purposes, the first college represented the 1.5 million Europeans, and the second represented the 9.5 million Muslims.

The deputies, while elected separately, voted together. To prevent the Muslims from having a majority by securing only one vote in the first college, a two-thirds vote could be demanded by the governor-general or 30 members of the Assembly. Designed to give the Muslims some voice in their governance while ensuring European control, the Algerian Statute proved to be a poor compromise. Still, it might have worked were it not for the fact that the mandatory elections, commencing in April 1948, were rigged. As a result, the period from 1948 to the start of the rebellion in 1954 was marked by increasing bitterness and conflict between the two Algerian communities.

Proindependence Algerian Muslims were emboldened by the May 1954 Viet Minh victory over French forces at Dien Bien Phu during the Indochina War (1946–1954), and when Algerian Muslim nationalist leaders met Democratic Republic of Vietnam president Ho Chi Minh at the Bandung Conference in April 1955, he assured them that the French could be defeated. Ben Bella and his compatriots, having established the FLN on October 10, 1954, began the Algerian War on the night of October 31–November 1.

SPENCER C. TUCKER

Course

Early on November 1, 1954, armed members of the FLN carried out a number of small attacks across Algeria. The French government, which was then dealing with independence movements in neighboring Tunisia and Morocco, had not anticipated a similar development in Algeria. After all, Algeria had been French territory since 1830 (Tunisia had been acquired only in 1881 and Morocco in the period 1904–1911). Unlike Morocco and Tunisia, which were classed as protectorates, Algeria was held to be an integral part

of France. Indeed, for some months the French people and press failed to recognize the significance of what was happening and chose to characterize the rebels as *fellagha* (outlaws).

There were valid reasons for the French to fight in order to retain Algeria. Unlike Indochina, it was in close proximity to France, just across the Mediterranean. The French had largely created modern Algeria, as the deys had only controlled a narrow coastal strip around Algiers itself. There were more than 1 million Europeans living there, and they would be unwilling to concede place to Arab nationalism. Finally, there was the French Army. Its professional soldiers had almost immediately been transferred from Indochina to Algeria. Believing strongly that they had been denied the resources necessary to win the Indochina War (1946–1954) and in the end had been sold out by their government, they were determined that this would not be the case in Algeria.

Ultimately France committed a force of 450,000 men to the war, and upwards of 1 million Frenchmen would serve there. Unlike the Indochina War, this included draftees. As the conflict intensified, French officials sought support from the North Atlantic Treaty Organization (NATO), arguing that keeping Algeria French would ensure that NATO's southern flank would be safe from communism. As a part of France, Algeria was included in the original NATO Charter, but the French government position did not receive a sympathetic response in Washington or in other NATO capitals. Only too late did a succession of French governments attempt to carry out reform.

The FLN goal was to end French control of Algeria and drive out or eliminate the colon population. The FLN was organized in six military districts, or *wilayas,* along rigidly hierarchical lines. Wilaya 4, located near Algiers, was especially important, and the FLN was particularly active in Kabylia and the Aurés Mountains. The party tolerated no dissent. In form and style, it resembled Soviet bloc communist parties, although it claimed to offer a noncommunist and non-Western alternative ideology, articulated by Frantz Fanon. The FLN military arm was the Armée de Libération Nationale (Army of National Liberation, ALN).

Any hope of reconciliation between the two sides was destroyed by a major FLN military operation on August 20, 1954. On that date, its personnel, having infiltrated the port city of Philippeville, killed 71 colons and 52 pro-French Muslims (mostly local politicians), while the French police and military killed 134 ALN troops. On the same day, the ALN attacked and slaughtered European women and children living in the countryside surrounding Constantine while the men were at work. At El-Halia, a sulfur-mining community with some 120 Europeans living peacefully among 2,000 Algerian Muslims, 37 Europeans, including 10 children, were tortured and killed. Another 13 were badly wounded. Several hours later French paratroopers arrived, supported by military aircraft. The next morning they gathered about 150 Muslims together and executed them.

The French administration now allowed the settlers to arm themselves and form self-defense units, measures that the reformist governor-general Jacques Soustelle had earlier vetoed. European vigilante groups are reported to have subsequently carried out summary killings of Muslims. Soustelle reported a total of 1,273 Muslims killed in what he characterized as "severe" reprisals.

The Arab League strongly supported the FLN, while Egypt under President Gamal Abdel Nasser was a source of weapons and other assistance. The French government's grant of independence to both Tunisia and Morocco in March 1956 further bolstered Algerian nationalism. When Israeli, British, and French forces invaded Egypt in the Suez Crisis of 1956, the United States condemned the move and forced their withdrawal. The Algerian insurgents were emboldened by the French defeat. The French now also found themselves contending with FLN supply bases in Tunisia that they could neither attack nor eliminate. Also in 1956, the government of socialist premier Guy Mollet transferred the bulk of the French Army to Algeria.

The major engagement of the war was the battle for control of the Casbah district of Algiers, a district of some 100,000 people in the Algerian capital city. With the guillotining in Algiers in June 1956 of several FLN members who had killed Europeans, FLN commander of the Algiers Autonomous Zone Saadi Yacef received instructions to kill any European between the ages of 18 and 54 but no women, children, or old people. During a three-day span in June, Yacef's roaming squads shot down 49 Europeans. It was the first time in the war that such random acts of terrorism had occurred in Algiers and began a spiral of violence there.

Hard-line European supporters of Algérie Française (French Algeria) then decided to take matters into their own hands, and on the night of August 10, André Achiary, a former member of the French government's counterintelligence service, planted a bomb in a building in the Casbah that had supposedly housed the FLN, but the ensuing blast destroyed much of the neighborhood and claimed 79 lives. No one was arrested for the blast, and the FLN was determined to avenge the deaths.

Yacef, who had created a carefully organized network of some 1,400 operatives as well as bomb factories and hiding places, received orders to undertake random bombings against Europeans, a first for the capital. On September 30, 1956, three female FLN members planted bombs in the Milk-Bar, a cafeteria, and a travel agency. The later bomb failed to go off owing to a faulty timer, but the other two blasts killed three people and wounded more than 50, including a number of children. This event is generally regarded as the beginning of the Battle of Algiers (September 30, 1956–September 24, 1957).

Violence now took hold in Algiers. Both Muslim and European populations in the city were in a state of terror. Schools closed in October, and on December 28 Mayor Amédée Froger was assassinated.

On January 7, 1957, French governor-general Robert Lacoste called in General Raoul Salan, new French commander in Algeria, and Brigadier General Jacques Massu, commander of the elite 4,600-man 10th Colonial Parachute Division, recently arrived from Suez. Lacoste ordered them to restore order in the capital city, no matter the method.

In addition to his own men, Massu could call on other French military units, totaling perhaps 8,000 men. He also had the city's 1,500-man police force. Massu divided the city into four grids, with one of his regiments assigned to each. Lieutenant Colonel Marcel Bigeard's 3rd Colonial Parachute Regiment had responsibility for the Casbah itself.

The French set up a series of checkpoints. They also made use of identity cards and instituted aggressive patrolling and house-to-house searches. Massu was ably assisted by his chief of staff, Colonel Yves Godard, who soon made himself *the* expert on the Casbah. Lieutenant Colonel Roger Trinquier organized an intelligence-collection system that included paid Muslim informants and employed young French paratroopers disguised as workers to operate in the Casbah and identify FLN members. Trinquier organized a database on the Muslim civilian population. The French also employed harsh interrogation techniques of suspects, including the use of torture that included electric shock.

The army broke a called Muslim general strike at the end of January in only a few days. Yacef was able to carry out more bombings, but the French Army ultimately won the battle and took the FLN leadership prisoner, although Yacef was not captured until September 1957. Some 3,000 of 24,000 Muslims arrested during the Battle of Algiers were never seen again. The French side lost an estimated 300 dead and 900 wounded.

The Battle of Algiers had widespread negative impact for the French military effort in Algeria, however. Although the army embarked on an elaborate cover-up, its use of torture soon became public knowledge and created a firestorm that greatly increased opposition in metropolitan France to the war. It should be noted, however, that the French employed torture to force FLN operatives to talk, and some were murdered in the process. The FLN, on the other hand, routinely murdered captured French soldiers and civilian Europeans.

In an effort to cut off the FLN from outside support, the French also erected the Morice Line. Named for French minister of defense André Morice, it ran for some 200 miles from the Mediterranean Sea in the north into the Sahara in the

French paratroopers in the Casbah in Algiers in June 1957. (Nacerdine Zebar/Gamma-Rapho via Getty Images)

south. The line was centered on an 8-foot tall, 5,000-volt electric fence that ran its entire length. Supporting this was a 50-yard-wide "killing zone" on each side of the fence rigged with antipersonnel mines. The line was also covered by previously ranged 105mm howitzers. A patrolled track paralleled the fence on its Algerian side. The Morice Line was bolstered by electronic sensors that provided warning of any attempt to pierce the barrier. Searchlights operated at night.

Although manning the line required a large number of French soldiers, it did significantly reduce infiltration by the FLN from Tunisia. By April 1958, the French estimated that they had defeated 80 percent of FLN infiltration attempts. This contributed greatly to the isolation of those FLN units within Algeria reliant on support from Tunisia. The French subsequently constructed a less extensive barrier, known as the Pedron Line, along the Algerian border with Morocco.

Despite victory in Algiers, French forces were not able to end the Algerian rebellion or gain the confidence of the colons. Some colons grew fearful that the French government was about to negotiate with the FLN, and in the spring of 1958 there were a number of plots to change the colonial government. Colon and army veteran Pierre Lagaillarde organized hundreds of commandos and began a revolt on May 13, 1958. A number of senior army officers, determined that the French government not repeat what had happened in Indochina, lent support. Massu quickly formed the Committee of Public Safety, and Salan assumed its leadership.

The plotters would have preferred someone more frankly authoritarian, but Salan called for the return to power of General Charles de Gaulle. Although de Gaulle had been out of power for more than a decade, on May 19 he announced his willingness to assume authority.

Massu was prepared to bring back de Gaulle by force if necessary and plans were developed to dispatch paratroopers to metropolitan France from Algeria, but this option was not needed. On June 1, 1958, the French National Assembly invested de Gaulle with the premiership; technically he was the last premier of the Fourth Republic. De Gaulle ultimately established a new French political framework, the Fifth Republic, with greatly enhanced presidential powers.

De Gaulle visited Algeria five times between June and December 1958. At Oran on June 4, he said about France in Algeria that "she is here forever." A month later, he proposed 15 billion francs for Algerian housing, education, and public works, and that October he suggested an even more sweeping proposal, known as the Constantine Plan. The funding for the massive projects, however, was never forthcoming. True reform was never realized and in any case was probably too late to impact the Muslim community.

Algeria's new military commander, General Maurice Challe, arrived in Algeria on December 12, 1958, and launched a series of attacks on FLN positions in rural Kabylia in early 1959. The Harkis, Muslim troops loyal to France, guided special mobile French troops called Commandos de Chasse. An aggressive set of sorties deep in Kabylia made considerable headway, and Challe calculated that by the end of October his men had killed half of the FLN operatives there. A second phase of the offensive was to occur in 1960, but by then de Gaulle, who had gradually eliminated options, had decided that Algerian independence was inevitable.

In late August 1959, de Gaulle braced his generals for the decision and then addressed the nation on September 19, 1959, declaring his support for Algerian self-determination. Fearing for their future, some die-hard colons created the Front Nationale Français and fomented another revolt on January 24, 1960, in the so-called Barricades Week. Mayhem ensued when policemen tried to restore order, and a number of people were killed or wounded. General Challe and the colony's governor, Paul Delouvrier, fled Algiers on January 28, but the next day de Gaulle, wearing his old army uniform, turned the tide via a televised address to the nation. On February 1 army units swore loyalty to the government, and the revolt quickly collapsed.

Early in 1961, increasingly desperate Ultras formed a terrorist group called the Secret Army Organization (OAS). It targeted colons whom they regarded as traitors and also carried out bombings in France and attempted to assassinate de Gaulle himself.

The Generals' Putsch of April 20–26, 1961, was a serious threat to de Gaulle's regime. General Challe wanted a revolt limited to Algeria, but Salan and his colleagues (Ground Forces chief of staff General André Zeller and recently retired inspector general of the air force Edmond Jouhaud) had prepared for a revolt in France as well. The generals had the support of many frontline officers in addition to almost two divisions of troops. The Foreign Legion arrested commander of French forces in Algeria General Fernand Gambiez, and paratroopers near Rambouillet prepared to march on Paris after obtaining armored support. The coup collapsed, however, as police units managed to convince the paratroopers to depart, and army units again swore loyalty to de Gaulle.

On June 10, 1961, de Gaulle held secret meetings with FLN representatives in Paris, and then on June 14 he made a televised appeal for the FLN's so-called provisional government to negotiate an end to the war. Peace talks during June 25–29 failed to lead to resolution, but de Gaulle was set in his course. During his visit to Algeria in December, he was greeted by large pro-FLN Muslim rallies and anticolon riots. The United Nations recognized Algeria's independence on December 20, and in a national referendum on January 8, 1962, the French public voted in favor of Algerian independence.

A massive exodus of colons was already under way. Nearly 1 million returned to their ancestral homelands (half of them went to France, while most of the rest went to Spain and Italy). Peace talks resumed in March at Évian, and both sides reached a settlement on May 18, 1962.

WILLIAM E. WATSON AND
SPENCER C. TUCKER

Consequences

The formal handover of power occurred on July 4, 1962, when the FLN's Provisional Committee took control of Algeria, and in September Ben Bella was elected Algeria's first president. The Algerian War claimed some 18,000 French military deaths, 3,000 colon deaths, and about 300,000 Muslim deaths.

The Europeans were encouraged to leave (*la valise ou le cercueil,* meaning "the suitcase or the coffin"), and some 1.5 million did so. Perhaps half relocated in Metropolitan France, and most of the remainder went to Spain or Italy. Some 30,000 Europeans remained in Algeria. Ostensibly granted equal rights in the peace treaty, they instead faced official discrimination by the FLN government and the loss of much of their property. The FLN-led Algerian government, headed by Prime Minister Mohammed Ben Bella, promptly confiscated the colons' abandoned property and established a decentralized socialist economy and a one-party state.

The Harkis, those Algerian Muslims who fought on the French side in the war, suffered terribly. Some 91,000 and their family members settled in France. At least 30,000 and perhaps as many as 150,000 Harkis and their family members, including young children, who remained in Algeria were subsequently butchered by either the FLN or lynch mobs.

Ben Bella's attempt to consolidate his power, combined with popular discontent with the economy's inefficiency, sparked a bloodless military coup by Defense Minister Houari Boumédienne in June 1965. In 1971, the government endeavored to stimulate economic growth by nationalizing the oil industry and investing the revenues in centrally orchestrated industrial development. Boumédienne's military-dominated government took on an increasingly authoritarian cast over the years.

Algeria's leaders sought to retain their autonomy, joining their country to the Non-Aligned Movement, and Boumédienne phased out French military bases. Although Algeria denounced perceived American imperialism and supported Cuba, the Viet Cong in South Vietnam, Palestinian nationalists, and African anticolonial fighters, it maintained a strong trading relationship with the United States. At the same time, Algeria cultivated economic ties with the Soviet Union, which provided the nation with military equipment and training.

When the Spanish relinquished control of Western Sahara in 1976, Morocco attempted to annex the region, leading to a 12-year low-level war with Algeria, which supported the guerrilla movement fighting for the region's independence.

Diplomatic relations with the United States warmed after Algeria negotiated the release of American hostages in Iran in 1980 and Morocco fell out of U.S. favor by allying with Libya in 1984.

In 1976, a long-promised constitution that provided for elections was enacted, although Algeria remained a one-party state. When Boumédienne died in December 1978, power passed to Chadli Bendjedid, the army-backed candidate. Bendjedid retreated from Boumédienne's increasingly ineffective economic policies, privatizing much of the economy and encouraging entrepreneurship. However, accumulated debt continued to retard economic expansion. Growing public protests from labor unions, students, and Islamic fundamentalists forced the government to end restrictions on political expression in 1988.

The Islamic Salvation Front (Front Islamique du Salut, FIS) proved to be the most successful of the new political parties. After victories by the FIS in local elections in June 1990 and national elections in December 1991, Bendjedid resigned, and a new regime under Mohamed Boudiaf imposed martial law, banning the FIS in March 1992. In response, Islamist radicals began a guerrilla war that has persisted to the present, taking a toll of 150,000 or more lives. Although Algeria's military government managed to gain the upper hand in the struggle after 1998, Islamic groups continue to wage war on the state, which maintains control through brutal repression and tainted elections.

ELUN GABRIEL

Timeline

1830

June 14	A French expeditionary force lands near Algiers.
July 5	French forces capture Algiers.

1835 Emir of Mascara in western Algeria Abd al-Qadir declares war on the French.

1847

December	Abd al-Qadir surrenders. France finally subjugates Algeria.

1848 Algeria is recognized as an integral part of France. The colony is opened to European settlers.

1870–1871 The Franco-Prussian War results in the defeat of France. European immigration to Algeria increases in response to the loss of Alsace-Lorraine to the German Empire.

1936 French settlers in Algiers succeed in blocking the Blum-Viollette reform for Algeria.

1937

March — Algerian nationalist Ahmed Messali Hadj forms the Parti du Peuple Algerien (Algerian People's Party, PPA).

1938 — Algerian nationalist Ferhat Abbas forms the moderate Union Populaire Algérienne (Algerian Popular Union).

1940

June — France is defeated by Germany.

1942

November 8 — U.S. and British forces land in Morocco and Algeria.

1945

May 8 — Germany surrenders, ending World War II in Europe.

Independence demonstrations in Sétif, Algeria, turn violent. Some 100 Europeans die, but French reprisals bring as many as 10,000 Muslim deaths.

1946

October — The PPA is replaced by the Mouvement pour le Triomphe des Libertés Démocratiques (Movement for the Triumph of Democratic Liberties, MTLD), with Messali Hadj as president.

1947 — The Organization Spéciale (Special Organization, OS) is formed as a paramilitary arm of the MTLD.

September 20 — The French National Assembly passes the Algerian Statute. All Algerian citizens are offered French citizenship, yet the new Algerian Assembly continues settler domination. Two politically equal 60-member colleges are created, one representing the 1.5 million European settlers, the other for 9 million Algerian Muslims.

1949 — The OS mounts an attack on the Oran central post office, netting 3 million francs.

1952 — French authorities arrest several OS leaders, but Ahmed Ben Bella escapes to Cairo.

1954 — Several members of the OS organize the Comité Révolutionaire d'Unité et d'Action (Revolutionary Committee for Unity and Action, CRUA) to lead the revolt against the French. A subsequent meeting in Switzerland by the CRUA divides Algeria into six administrative districts or Wilaya.

March 13–May 7 — The Siege of Dien Bien Phu in Vietnam ends with the surrender of the French garrison, allowing French politicians to end the Indochina War.

April 21–July 20	An international conference in Geneva, Switzerland, ends the Indochina War.
October 10	The CRUA changes its name to the Front de Libération Nationale (National Liberation Front, FLN).
November	Messali Hadj, under house arrest in Britany, France, founds the Mouvement National Algérien (Algerian National Movement, MNA) as a moderate alternative to the FLN.
November 1	The FLN commences the Algerian War by ordering its military arm, the Armée de Libération Nationale (National Liberation Army, ALN), to attack police and military posts in Aurès and Kabylia with the intent of capturing arms.

1955

January 26	Jacques-Émile Soustelle is appointed governor-general of Algeria and introduces liberal reforms.
February	The ALN targets Muslims cooperating with Europeans, including farmworkers and those attending associated rural schools.
August 20	At Philippeville, ALN operatives kill 71 French citizens and 52 pro-French Algerian Muslims (mostly local politicians). The French authorities kill around 130 of the FLN commandos. On the same day, European women and children are slaughtered in their homes in the countryside surrounding Constantine. At El-Halia 37 Europeans, principally women and children, are slain, and another 13 are badly wounded. French paratroopers kill 150 Muslims.
	The French administration now allows the settlers to arm themselves and form self-defense units, measures that the moderate Soustelle had earlier vetoed. European vigilante groups are reported to have killed 1,273 Muslims in reprisal.

1956

February 1	Socialist Party leader Guy Mollet becomes French premier.
February 9	Soustelle is recalled to Paris. Robert Lacoste replaces him as governor-general of Algeria.
March 2	Morocco is granted independence.

March 20	Tunisia is granted independence. Shortly after receiving independence, both Morocco and Tunisia allow the FLN to establish base camps in their territory.
August 10	A bomb set by Frenchman André Achiary in the Algiers Casbah claims 79 lives.
September 30	Three young Muslim women place bombs in a European milk bar, cafeteria, and travel agency. The latter bomb fails to explode, but the first two kill 3 Europeans and wound 50, including many children. This marks the beginning of the Battle of Algiers.
October 16	The French intercept the ship *Athos,* sailing from Egypt to Algiers and carrying arms for the FLN.
October 22	FLN leader Ben Bella is arrested by French military authorities when the commercial airliner in which he is flying is intercepted and diverted to France.
November 5	French and British forces land at Suez, part of an Israeli-British-French effort to unseat President Gamal Abdel Nasser. This unsuccessful gambit leads Nasser to increase aid to the FLN. It also increases contempt among the professional French military for the French government.
December 14	General Raoul Albin Louis Salan is appointed commander of French forces in Algeria.

1957

January 7	Brigadier General Jacques Massu's 10th Parachute Division commences operations in the Casbah area of Algiers.
May 31	FLN guerrillas massacre 303 Muslim supporters of Messali Hadj's MNA at the village of Melouza. The FLN then blames the massacre on the French.
September	The French complete the Morice Line, a defensive barrier along the border with Tunisia designed to prevent the movement of FLN forces and supplies into Algeria.
September 24	FLN leader in Algiers Yacef Saadi is captured, marking the effective end of the Battle of Algiers.
December	General Salan is appointed commander of French forces in Algeria.

1958

February 8	French aircraft bomb Sakiet Sidi Youssef (Saqiyat Sidi Yusuf) in Tunisia, where the FLN has established a base.

May 13	Demonstrators in Algiers seize government buildings and then demand that Charles de Gaulle be named premier of France.
June 1	De Gaulle is named premier.
June 4	De Gaulle visits Algeria.
September 19	Ferhat Abbas is named head of the Gouvernement Provisoire de la République Algérienne (Provisional Government of the Algerian Republic, GPRA). Establishment of the GPRA is intended to stop de Gaulle from holding a referendum on Algeria gaining autonomous status within the French Community.
October 3	In the course of a speech de Gaulle offers a peace and amnesty agreement to the FLN, which declines. De Gaulle also proclaims the Constantine Plan of economic development to modernize Algeria.
October 8	The Fifth French Republic is established.
December 12	De Gaulle names General Maurice Challe to replace General Salan as commander of French forces in Algeria.

1959

January 8	De Gaulle becomes president of France.
February	Challe begins a series of major offensives against different Wilayas. Culminating in September, these force the FLN/ALN to disperse into small units to avoid capture.
September 16	De Gaulle offers Algeria self-determination with a referendum. This greatly angers the die-hard colons determined to keep Algeria French.
September 19	General Massu is sacked for opposing de Gaulle's Algerian policy.

1960

January 19	Following a speech by de Gaulle, the Algiers insurrection collapses.
January 24	Beginning of the "Week of Barricades," an insurrection in Algiers by those wishing to keep Algeria part of France. French Army paratroopers refuse to fire on the protesters.
April	Challe begins Operation TRIDENT, the final phase of his military offensives against the FLN.
June 25–29	Peace talks fail between the French government and FLN representatives at Melun, France.

December 9–13	De Gaulle visits Algeria.
December 20	The United Nations recognizes Algeria's right to self-determination.

1961

January 25	Those determined to keep Algeria a part of France establish in Madrid the Organisation de l'Armée Secrète (Secret Army Organization, OAS). They begin a series of assassinations in France and Algeria.
April 22	A second attempt to seize power by those determined to keep Algeria a part of France occurs in Algiers. Dubbed the Generals' Putsch, it includes former commanders in Algeria generals Salan and Challe, General André Zeller (former army chief of staff), and General Edmond Jouhaud (former air force inspector general). Aided by a paratroop regiment, they take power in Algiers.
April 25	France explodes an atomic bomb at Raggane in the Sahara. This is done earlier than planned in order to keep the bomb from falling into the hands of the putschists.
April 26	Troops supporting the Generals' Putsch surrender. Challe surrenders, and Zeller is captured. Both are sentenced to 15 years' imprisonment but will be pardoned and reintegrated into the army in July 1968. Salan and Jouhaud escape to lead the OAS.
May 19	OAS operatives explode a bomb in Algiers.
May 20–July 28	Peace talks occur between the French government and the FLN at Évian but end in failure.
September 8	De Gaulle narrowly escapes assassination by the OAS at Pont-sur-Seine, France.

1962

February	OAS bombings and assassinations have killed more than 500 people, but these seriously weaken support for the OAS cause in metropolitan France.
March 7–18	Peace talks between French and FLN representatives at Évian, France, reach agreement.
March 19	A cease-fire agreement goes into effect between the French and the FLN.
April 20	OAS leader Salan is captured in Algiers. He was previously tried and sentenced to death in absentia, but his sentence is subsequently commuted to life imprisonment.

(In July 1968 he is pardoned and in 1982 reintegrated into the army.)

July 1   A referendum is held in France on the issue of independence for Algeria. The vote is some 6 million in favor and only 16,000 opposed.

July 3   Algerian independence is declared. Ben Bella becomes the first Algerian prime minister.

September 27   Ben Bella becomes president of the Republic of Algeria.

SPENCER C. TUCKER

Further Reading

Alleg, Henri. *La Question.* Paris: Éditions de Minuit, 1958.

Aron, Robert. *Les Origines de la guerre d'Algérie: Textes et documents contemporaine.* Paris: Fayard, 1962.

Aussaresses, Paul. *The Battle of the Casbah: Terrorism and Counter-Terrorism in Algeria, 1955–1957.* New York: Enigma Books, 2010.

Danziger, Raphael. *Abd al'Qadir and the Algerians: Resistance to the French and Internal Consolidation.* New York: Holmes and Meier, 1977.

Derradji, Abder-Rahmane. *The Algerian Guerrilla Campaign Strategy & Tactics.* New York: Edwin Mellen, 1997.

Galula, David. *Counterinsurgency Warfare: Theory and Practice.* Westport, CT: Praeger Security International, 1964.

Gillespie, Joan. *Algeria: Rebellion and Revolution.* New York: Praeger, 1960.

Gordon, David C. *The Passing of French Algeria.* London: Oxford University Press, 1966.

Horne, Alistair. *A Savage War of Peace: Algeria, 1954–1962.* London: Macmillan, 1977.

Humbaraci, Arslan. *Algeria: A Revolution That Failed.* London: Pall Mall, 1966.

Kettle, Michael. *De Gaulle and Algeria, 1940–1960.* London: Quartet, 1993.

Leulliette, Pierre. *St. Michael and the Dragon: Memoirs of a Paratrooper.* Boston: Houghton Mifflin, 1964.

Maran, Rita. *Torture: The Role of Ideology in the French-Algerian War.* New York: Praeger, 1989.

Servan-Schreiber, Jean-Jacques. *Lieutenant in Algeria.* Translated by Ronald Matthews. New York: Knopf, 1957.

Sessions, Jennifer. *By Sword and Plow: France and the Conquest of Algeria.* Ithaca, NY: Cornell University Press, 2011.

Smith, Tony. *The French Stake in Algeria, 1945–1962.* Ithaca, NY: Cornell University Press, 1979.

Sullivan, Anthony. *Thomas-Robert Bugeaud: France and Algeria, 1784–1849: Politics, Power, and the Good Society.* Hamden, CT: Archon Books, 1983.

Talbott, John. *The War without a Name: France in Algeria, 1954–1962.* New York: Knopf, 1980.

Trinquier, Roger. *Modern Warfare: A French View of Counterinsurgency.* Westport, CT: Praeger Security International, 2006.

Tucker, Spencer C. "The Fourth Republic and Algeria." Unpublished doctoral dissertation, University of North Carolina at Chapel Hill, 1965.

Watson, William E. *Tricolor and Crescent: France and the Islamic World.* Westport, CT: Praeger, 2003.

Windrow, Martin. *The Algerian War, 1954–62.* London: Osprey, 1997.

Vietnam War (1957–1975)

Causes

The Vietnam War (also known as the Second Indochina War) grew out of the First Indochina War (1946–1954). In 938 the Vietnamese freed themselves from more than 1,000 years of Chinese rule. It remains a source of great national pride that Vietnam then maintained its independence, defeating subsequent Chinese attempts to reestablish control. Vietnam is, however, unique among countries of Southeast Asia in having adopted many Chinese cultural patterns.

The French arrived in the second half of the 19th century, establishing control first over southern Vietnam (Cochinchina) by 1867, then expanding it to central Vietnam (Annam) and the north (Tonkin). The French also dominated Cambodia. In 1887 Paris created the administrative structure of French Indochina. Laos was added in 1893. Technically, only Cochinchina was an outright colony; the others were protectorates, but French officials made all the key decisions.

Nationalism spread in Vietnam after World War I. The French crushed the moderate nationalists, with the result that the more radical Indochinese Communist Party (ICP) took over leadership against the French. In September 1940, the Japanese arrived. Taking advantage of the defeat of France by Germany, Tokyo sent troops and established bases in Vietnam. Japan's move into southern Vietnam in July 1941 brought U.S. economic sanctions that led to the Japanese decision to attack Pearl Harbor.

During World War II, ICP leader Ho Chi Minh formed the Vietnam Independence League (Viet Minh) to fight both the Japanese and the French. By the end of the conflict, with Chinese and American assistance, the Viet Minh had liberated much of Tonkin. The French planned an insurrection against the Japanese, but in March 1945 the Japanese, aware of the plan, arrested all French soldiers and administrators they could find. There was thus a political vacuum at the end of the war, into which Ho Chi Minh moved. On September 2, 1945, in Hanoi, he publicly proclaimed the independence of the Democratic Republic of Vietnam (DRV), to include all of Vietnam.

Acting in accordance with Allied wartime agreements, British forces occupied southern Indochina, and Nationalist Chinese forces arrived in the north. Ho was able to secure the departure of the Chinese, while the British released the French prisoners in the south and allowed them to reestablish their control there. Appeals by Ho to the Soviet Union and the United States fell on deaf ears, and forced into negotiations with the French, he concluded an agreement on March 6, 1946, with French diplomat Jean Sainteny.

In the Ho-Sainteny Agreement, the French recognized the independence of the DRV and agreed to a plebiscite in the south to see if it wished to join the DRV, while Ho allowed the return of some French troops to the north to protect French interests there. The collapse of subsequent talks in France to implement the agreement and distrust between the two sides brought the shelling by the French of the port of Haiphong and then open warfare between the two sides on December 19, 1946.

The Indochina War lasted until 1954. The French had lost the war for all practical purposes with the 1949 communist victory in China, for this gave the DRV's People's Army of Vietnam (PAVN), or as the Americans later called it the North Vietnamese Army (NVA), secure areas for training and supplies. In 1949, in part to win U.S. support, the French government negotiated the Elysée Agreement with ex-emperor Bao Dai. It officially granted independence to Vietnam. The new State of Vietnam (SVN) was, however, a sham, completely dominated by the French until the end of the war.

With the French military defeat in the Battle of Dien Bien Phu in May 1954, the politicians in Paris shifted the blame onto the military and extricated France from the war. The July 20, 1954, Geneva Accords granted independence to Vietnam, Laos, and Cambodia. Vietnam was to be temporarily divided at the 17th parallel, pending national elections in two years to reunify the country. The United States was not a party to the agreement.

In the south, Catholic political leader Ngo Dinh Diem, appointed by Bao Dai as premier of the SVN on June 26, 1954, took charge and brought a semblance of order. His power base rested on some 1 million northern Catholics, many of whom had relocated there after the Indochina War in the regroupment period permitted by the Geneva Accords. Diem solidified his hold on power by moving against and defeating the religious sects and the organized crime syndicate in Saigon known as the Binh Xuyen. A power struggle ensued between Bao Dai and Diem, and in October 1955 Diem staged a referendum in which he called on the people of the south to choose between Bao Dai and himself. Diem won the vote handily and proclaimed the Republic of Vietnam (South Vietnam, RVN), with himself as president. He would hold power in South Vietnam until his assassination in November 1963.

Eager to support this new "democracy" during this Cold War era of containing the spread of communism, U.S. president Dwight D. Eisenhower and Secretary of State John Foster Dulles began sending aid to the new regime. During Eisenhower's last six years as president, U.S. aid to the RVN totaled $1.8 billion. Most of this went to the RVN military budget, with only small sums set aside for education and social welfare programs. The aid thus little affected the lives of the preponderantly rural South Vietnamese populace and therefore provided communist organizers with a powerful propaganda issue with which to generate opposition to the RVN government among the neglected peasantry.

As Diem consolidated his power, U.S. military advisers reorganized the RVN armed forces. Known as the Army of the Republic of Vietnam (ARVN), it was equipped with American weaponry. The U.S. Military Assistance Advisory Group (MAAG) overrode Vietnamese arguments for a lightly armed, highly mobile force capable of combating guerrillas and insisted that the military be organized to fight a conventional invasion from northern Vietnam, as in the recently concluded Korean War (1950–1953) that exerted a psychological hold on the U.S. military.

Fearing a loss and claiming that he was not bound by the Geneva Accords, Diem refused to conduct the scheduled 1956 elections. This jolted veteran communist DRV leader Ho Chi Minh. Ho had not been displeased with Diem's crushing of his internal opposition but was now ready to reunite the country under his sway and believed that he would win the elections.

Northern Vietnam was more populous than southern Vietnam, and the communists were well organized there. The Eisenhower administration backed Diem's defiance of the Geneva Agreements, fortified by the containment policy that sought to halt the spread of communism wherever it threatened; the domino theory, which held that if southern Vietnam were to fall to the communists, the other states of Southeast Asia would surely follow; and the belief that the communists, if they came to power, would never permit a democratic regime (something amply demonstrated by the Soviet-installed communist regimes of Eastern and Central Europe).

When the date for the elections passed, Viet Minh political cadres in the south resumed the armed struggle, this time against the Diem government. The leaders of the DRV faced a dilemma. The north had serious economic problems, for while it contained the bulk of the industry, the south had most of the food. Ruthless moves against small landholders had brought actual rebellion, which, however, was crushed by PAVN troops. Despite its own pressing problems, when the Viet Minh began guerrilla warfare in southern Vietnam, the DRV leadership voted to support it. The ensuing war was extraordinarily costly to the DRV economically and in human casualties, but the desire to reunify the country overrode all other considerations. During the war the north received substantial communist bloc economic and military assistance, especially from the Soviet Union but also from China.

SPENCER C. TUCKER

Course

South Vietnamese president Ngo Dinh Diem's decision not to adhere to the Geneva Accords led to a renewal of fighting, which became the Vietnam War. Various dates have been advanced for its start, from 1954 to as late as 1959. (The U.S. government has settled on 1958.) An insurgency certainly began in earnest in 1957 when Diem moved against the 6,000–7,000 Viet Minh political cadres who had been allowed to remain in southern Vietnam to prepare for the planned 1956 elections. Although this is a matter of some controversy, the Viet Minh in southern Vietnam probably began the insurgency on their own initiative but were subsequently supported by the DRV government.

The insurgents came to be known as the Viet Cong (VC, for "Vietnamese Communists"). In December 1960 they established the National Liberation Front (NLF) of

President of the Republic of Vietnam (South Vietnam) Ngo Dinh Diem rejected the plebiscite called for in the 1954 Geneva Accords, setting the stage for a renewal of fighting in what became the Vietnam War. (Howard Sochurek/The LIFE Picture Collection/Getty Images)

South Vietnam. Supposedly independent, it was completely controlled by Hanoi. The NLF program called for the overthrow of the Saigon government, its replacement by a "broad national democratic coalition," and the "peaceful" reunification of Vietnam.

In September 1959 DRV defense minister Vo Nguyen Giap established Transportation Group 559 in order to send supplies and men south along what came to be known as the Ho Chi Minh Trail, much of which ran through supposedly neutral Laos. The first wave of infiltrators was native southerners and Viet Minh who had relocated in northern Vietnam in 1954. The trail grew increasing complex and sophisticated as time went on, and the resupply effort came to include a naval group that moved supplies south by sea.

Meanwhile, VC sway expanded, spreading out from safe bases to one village after another. The insurgency was fed by the weaknesses of the central government, by communist use of terror and assassination, and by Saigon's appalling ignorance of the movement and the corruption within its government. By the end of 1958 the insurgency had reached the status of conventional warfare in several South Vietnamese provinces. In 1960 the communists carried out even more assassinations, and guerrilla units attacked ARVN regulars, overran district and provincial capitals, and ambushed convoys and reaction forces.

By mid-1961 the Saigon government had lost control over much of rural South Vietnam. Infiltration was as yet not significant, and most of the communist weapons were either captured from the ARVN or left over from the war with France. As had been the case with another American ally, Generalissimo Jiang Jieshi (Chiang Kai-shek) of China, Diem rejected American calls for meaningful reform until the defeat of his enemy and the establishment of full security. He did not understand that the war was primarily a political problem and could be solved only through political means. Diem used 80 percent of his aid funds for internal security. He also estranged himself from the peasants. Little was done to carry out land reform, and by 1961, 75 percent of the land in South Vietnam was owned by 15 percent of the population.

Diem, who practiced the divide-and-rule concept of leadership, remained largely isolated in Saigon from his people, choosing to rely on family members and a few other trusted advisers for counsel. He increasingly delegated authority to his brother Ngo Dinh Nhu and the latter's secret police. Diem resisted U.S. demands that he promote senior officials and military officers on the basis of ability rather than loyalty to him and that he pursue the war aggressively.

By now the John F. Kennedy administration, which took office in January 1961, was forced to reevaluate its position toward the war, but increased U.S. involvement was inevitable, given Washington's commitment to resist communist expansion and the domino theory. In May 1961 Kennedy sent several fact-finding missions to Vietnam. These led to the Strategic Hamlet Program—concentrating the rural population in locations for better defense and isolating South Vietnamese peasants from NLF influence—as part of a general strategy emphasizing local militia defense and to the commitment of additional U.S. manpower. The United States also steadily increased its military presence in South Vietnam. By the end of 1961 U.S. strength there had grown to around 3,200 men, mostly in helicopter units and as advisers.

In February 1962 the United States established a military headquarters in Saigon, when the MAAG was replaced by the Military Assistance Command, Vietnam (MACV) under General Paul D. Harkins to direct the enlarged American commitment. Harkins, who rarely ventured outside of Saigon, agreed with Diem that reforms should await the defeat of the VC. The infusion of U.S. helicopters and additional support for the ARVN by the Kennedy administration probably prevented a VC military victory in 1962, but the VC soon developed tactics to effectively cope with the helicopters, and again the tide of battle turned in the communists' favor.

Meanwhile, Nhu's crackdown on the Buddhist opposition to government policies increased opposition to Diem's rule. A number of frustrated and ambitious South Vietnamese generals now planned a coup, and after Diem rejected repeated calls for reforms, Washington gave the plotters tacit support. On November 1, 1963, the generals overthrew Diem, murdering both him and Nhu. Kennedy, who was shocked at Diem's assassination, was also soon dead. Himself assassinated on November 22, he was succeeded by his vice president, Lyndon B. Johnson.

The United States seemed unable to win the war either with Diem or without him. A military junta now took power, but none of those who followed Diem had his prestige. Coups and countercoups occurred, and much of South Vietnam remained in turmoil. Not until General Nguyen Van Thieu became president in 1967 was there a degree of political stability.

Both sides steadily increased the stakes, apparently without foreseeing that the other might do the same. In 1964 Hanoi took three major decisions. The first was to send south units of its regular army, the PAVN. The second was to rearm its forces in South Vietnam with modern communist bloc weapons, giving the PAVN a firepower advantage over the ARVN, still equipped largely with World War II–era U.S. infantry weapons. The third was to order direct attacks on American installations, provoking a U.S. response.

On August 2, 1964, the first of the so-called Gulf of Tonkin Incidents occurred when DRV torpedo boats attacked the U.S. destroyer *Maddox,* which was gathering electronic intelligence in international waters in the Gulf of Tonkin. A second reported attack two days later on the *Maddox* and another U.S. destroyer, the *Turner Joy,* most certainly never occurred, but Washington believed that this was the case, and this led the Johnson administration to order retaliatory carrier air strikes against DRV naval bases and fuel depots (Operation PIERCE ARROW) on August 5, the start of U.S. air operations over North Vietnam. The Johnson administration also went to Congress to secure what amounted to a blank check to wage war in Vietnam. Congress voted nearly unanimously on August 7 for the Gulf of Tonkin Resolution. Signed into law on August 10, it authorized the president to use whatever force he deemed necessary to protect U.S. interests in Southeast Asia.

Johnson would not break off U.S. involvement in Vietnam, stating privately that he feared possible impeachment if he did so. At the same time, he refused to make the tough decision of fully mobilizing the country for the war and committing the resources necessary to win it, concerned that this would destroy his cherished Great Society social programs.

The ARVN was not faring well against the VC. Communist forces had employed hit-and-run tactics, but in the Battle of Binh Gia (December 28, 1964–January 1, 1965) 40 miles southwest of Saigon, some

Estimated Casualty Statistics of the Vietnam War

	Peak Troop Strength	Killed in Action or Died of Wounds	Wounded	Missing	Captured	Civilian Dead
United States	543,400	47,382	203,678	2,207	7,966	N/A
South Vietnam	1,048,000	225,000	1,170,000	75,000	Unknown	2,000,000
North Vietnam and Viet Cong	300,000	1,100,000	600,000	225,000	127,500	2,000,000
South Korea	48,900	4,407	17,060	N/A	Unknown	N/A
Australia	7,700	423	2,398	6	0	N/A
Thailand	11,600	351	1,358	N/A	Unknown	N/A
New Zealand	550	83	212	N/A	Unknown	N/A

Sources: John S. Bowman, ed., *Facts about the American Wars* (n.p.: H. W. Wilson, 1998); Department of Defense. *Principal Wars in Which the United States Participated: U.S. Military Personnel Serving and Casualties* (Washington, DC: Washington Headquarters Services, Directorate for Information Operations and Reports, 2003); French Press Agency, "Announcement of Vietnamese Government's Release of Casualty Information," April 4, 1995; Michael Lanning, *Inside the VC and the NVA* (New York: Random House, 1992); Bernard C. Nalty, *The Vietnam War* (New York: Smithmark Publishers, 1996); Neil Sheehan, *A Bright Shining Lie* (New York: Random House, 1988); Spencer C. Tucker, ed. *Encyclopedia of the Vietnam War* (Santa Barbara, CA: ABC-CLIO, 1998).

1,800 VC engaged a total of 4,300 supposedly elite ARVN troops in a conventional battle and soundly defeated them. The ARVN suffered 201 killed, 192 wounded, and 68 missing. Five U.S. advisers were also slain. VC killed were 34–200. Both sides saw the battle as a watershed in that well-trained VC forces supplied with modern weapons were capable of fighting and winning large battles. The battle also signaled the beginning of a mix of guerrilla and conventional warfare.

During June 9–13, 1965, two VC regiments totaling some 1,500 men attacked the newly established special forces camp at Dong Xoai in Phuoc Long Province held by 400 Montagnard Civilian Irregular Defense Group troops and 24 U.S. personnel staffing the camp. In their attack, the VC employed AK-47 assault rifles (the first time in the war by a VC unit). Saigon dispatched reinforcements, which were

then ambushed. Some 2,000 ARVN troops were eventually involved fighting the VC. On the ARVN side, the battle claimed 416 killed, 174 wounded, and 233 missing. U.S. forces lost 29 killed or wounded and 13 missing. Some 200 civilians also died. MACV estimated VC casualties at 700, although dead left behind totaled only 134. (Throughout the war MACV and communist casualty claims were always widely different, with each side exaggerating enemy losses.)

The North Vietnamese leadership expected to win the war in 1965. Taking their cue from Johnson's own pronouncements to the American people, they mistakenly believed that Washington would not commit ground troops to the fight. Yet Johnson did just that. Faced with Hanoi's escalation, however, in March 1965 U.S. marines arrived with the mission of protecting the large American air base at Danang, South

Vietnam's second-largest city. The marines' mission soon expanded to seeking out nearby communist forces.

A direct attack on U.S. military advisers at Pleiku in February 1965 led to a U.S. and Republic of Vietnam Air Force (RVNAF) air campaign against North Vietnam, Operation FLAMING DART (February 7–14). The operation targeted PAVN military bases north of the demilitarized zone (DMZ) dividing North and South Vietnam near the 17th parallel.

Johnson hoped to win the war on the cheap, relying heavily on airpower. Known as Operation ROLLING THUNDER (March 2, 1965–October 31, 1968) and paralleled by Operation BARREL ROLL (December 14, 1964–March 29, 1973), the secret bombing of Laos, which became the most heavily bombed country in the history of warfare, the air campaign would be pursued in varying degrees of intensity over the next three and a half years. Its goals were to force Hanoi to negotiate peace and to halt infiltration into South Vietnam.

The bombing resulted in the destruction of more than half of the DRV's bridges, almost all of its large petroleum storage facilities, and nearly two-thirds of its power-generating plants. It also killed some 52,000 Vietnamese. DRV air defenses cost the United States nearly 1,000 aircraft, hundreds of prisoners of war, and hundreds of airmen killed or missing in action. Altogether the U.S. Air Force, U.S. Navy, and U.S. Marine Corps flew almost 1 million sorties (one plane, one mission) and dropped nearly three-quarters of a million tons of bombs. ROLLING THUNDER failed, however, to achieve its stated major political and military objectives.

In the air war, Johnson decided on "graduated response" rather than the massive strikes advocated by the military. He and Secretary of Defense Robert McNamara believed that there was some point at which North Vietnamese leaders would halt their support for the southern insurgency, but what would have been unacceptable to the United States was perfectly acceptable to the DRV leadership. Gradualism became the grand strategy employed by the United States in Vietnam. Haunted by the Korean War, at no time would Johnson consider an invasion of North Vietnam, fearful of provoking a Chinese intervention.

By May and June 1965, with PAVN forces regularly destroying ARVN units, General William C. Westmoreland, who had replaced Harkins in June 1964 as MACV commander, appealed for U.S. ground units, which Johnson committed. As PAVN regiments appeared ready to launch an offensive in the rugged Central Highlands and then drive to the sea, splitting South Vietnam in two, Westmoreland mounted a spoiling attack with Major General Harry W. O. Kinnard's recently arrived 1st Cavalry Division (Airmobile), formed around some 450 helicopters.

In the Battle of the Ia Drang Valley (October 19–November 26), the 1st Cavalry Division won one of the war's rare decisive encounters in what was also the first battle between American regulars and PAVN forces. Although there are conflicting opinions over PAVN commander Chu Huy Man's strategic objective, the outcome may have derailed Hanoi's hopes of winning a decisive victory before full American might be deployed. During the hard-fought battle, Boeing B-52 Stratofortress strategic bombers were called in to provide close ground support. MACV gave casualty figures of 305 killed, while PAVN dead were estimated at 3,561.

Heavy personnel losses on the battlefield, while regrettable, were entirely

VIETNAM WAR, 1964–1967

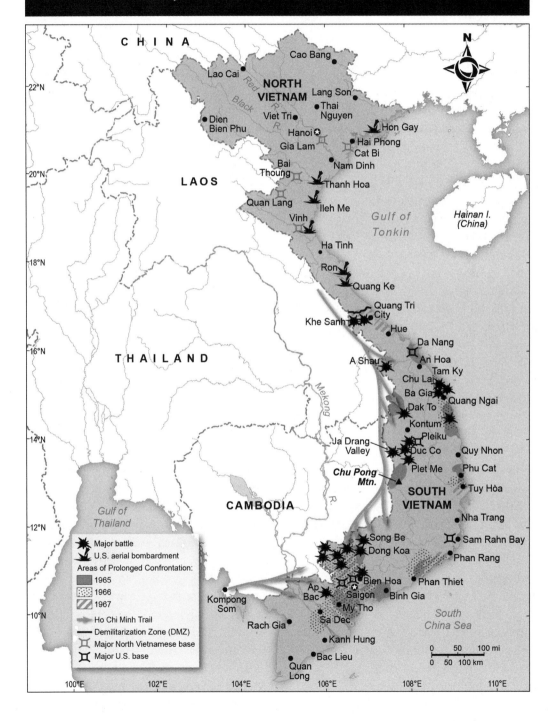

acceptable to the DRV leadership. Ho remarked at one point that the DRV could absorb an unfavorable loss ratio of 10:1 and still win the war. Washington never did understand this and continued to view the war through its own lens of what would be unacceptable in terms of casualties.

From 1966 on Vietnam was an "escalating military stalemate," as Westmoreland requested and received increasing numbers of men from Washington. By the end of 1966, 400,000 U.S. troops were in Vietnam. In 1968, U.S. strength was more than 500,000 men. Johnson also made a major effort to enlist support from other nations. In all, some 40 nations provided some assistance, while the flags of the United States, the Republic of Korea, Thailand, Australia, New Zealand, the Philippines, the Republic of China, and Spain flew alongside the colors of the Republic of Vietnam at MACV headquarters in Saigon. Of the 60,000 troops from other nations, the Republic of Korea provided the greatest number, some 50,000, receiving offset payments from a grateful Johnson administration. This number exceeded the 39,000-man international coalition of the Korean War.

Capturing terrain was not judged important. The goals were to protect the population and kill the enemy. MACV waged attrition warfare and measured success in terms of body count, which in turn led to abuses. During 1966 MACV mounted 18 major operations dubbed "search and destroy," each resulting in more than 500 supposedly verified VC/PAVN dead; 50,000 enemy combatants were supposedly killed in 1966. By the beginning of 1967, the PAVN and the VC had 300,000 men versus 625,000 ARVN troops and 400,000 Americans.

Ultimately more than 2.5 million Americans served in Vietnam, and nearly 58,000

of them died there. At its height, Washington was spending $30 billion per year on the war. Although the conflict was the best-covered war in American history (it became known as the first television war), it was conversely the least understood by the American people.

Hanoi meanwhile had reached a point of decision, with casualties exceeding available replacements. Instead of scaling back, North Vietnamese leaders prepared a major offensive that would employ all available troops to secure a quick victory. Hanoi believed that a major military defeat for the United States would end its political will to continue.

Giap now prepared a series of peripheral attacks, including a modified siege of some 6,000 U.S. marines at Khe Sanh in far northwestern South Vietnam near the DMZ, beginning in January 1968. These were designed to draw U.S. and ARVN forces to the periphery. With U.S. attention riveted on Khe Sanh, Giap planned a massive offensive to occur during Tet, the Vietnamese Lunar New Year holiday. Hanoi mistakenly believed that this massive offensive, called the General Offensive–General Uprising, would lead the South Vietnamese people to rise up and overthrow the RVN government, bringing an American withdrawal. The attacks were mounted against the cities. Although U.S. and South Vietnamese officials believed that an attack was imminent, in a major intelligence blunder they failed to anticipate the timing and strength of the attack, finding it inconceivable that the attack would come during Tet, which would sacrifice public goodwill.

The Tet Offensive began on January 31 and ended on February 24, 1968. Poor communication and coordination plagued Hanoi's effort. Attacks in one province

Smoke from fires in Saigon during the 1968 Tet Offensive in South Vietnam. While the popular uprising anticipated by the Communists did not occur and the offensive was a major military defeat for their forces, it had a tremendous psychological impact and helped turn American public opinion against the war. (National Archives)

occurred a day early, alerting the authorities. Hue, the former imperial capital, was especially hard hit, but within a day 5 of 6 autonomous cities, 36 of 44 provincial capitals, and 64 of 245 district capitals were under attack.

Hanoi's plan failed. ARVN forces generally fought well, and the people of South Vietnam did not support the attackers. In Hue the communists executed 3,000 people, and this horror caused many South Vietnamese to rally to the RVN. Half of the 85,000 VC and NVA troops who took part in the offensive were killed or captured. It was the worst military setback for North Vietnam in the war.

Paradoxically, it was also the communist side's most resounding victory, in part because the Johnson administration and Westmoreland had before Tet trumpeted prior allied successes and encouraged the American people to believe that the war was being won. The intensity of the fighting and heavy casualties came as a profound shock to the American people. They were disillusioned and, despite the victory, turned against the war.

Washington was also shocked by Westmoreland's post-Tet request for an additional 200,000 troops, which Johnson turned down. In June Westmoreland returned to Washington, D.C., to serve as chief of staff of the army, succeeded in Vietnam by his capable deputy General Creighton Abrams. This decision, which had been made in later 1967, was announced shortly after the Tet Offensive and was widely seen by the mass media as a punishment for being caught off guard by the communist assault.

Abrams changed the conduct of the war in fundamental ways. He abandoned Westmoreland's attrition strategy of search-and-destroy tactics and emphasis on body counts. Abrams stressed population security and held that the keys to victory rested on combat operations, pacification, and upgrading South Vietnamese forces. In combat operations he cut back on the multibattalion sweep operations, replacing these with multiple small-unit patrols and ambushes.

At the end of March 1968, meanwhile, Johnson announced a partial cessation of the bombing and withdrew from the November presidential election in the stated hopes of securing a peace settlement. Hanoi persisted, however. In the first six months of 1968, communist forces sustained more than 100,000 casualties, and

the VC was virtually wiped out; 20,000 South Vietnamese, American, and other allied troops died in the same period. All sides now opted for talks in Paris in an effort to negotiate an end to the war.

American disillusionment with the war was a key factor in Republican Richard M. Nixon's razor-thin victory over Democrat Hubert H. Humphrey in the November 1968 presidential election. In his bid to become president, Nixon deliberately and secretly sabotaged the Paris peace talks and also gave the American electorate the false impression that he had a plan to win the war. In fact, with no plan of his own Nixon embraced Vietnamization, which had actually begun under Johnson and involved turning over more of the war to the ARVN.

U.S. troop withdrawals began. Peak U.S. strength of 550,000 men occurred in early 1969; there were 475,000 men by the end of the year, 335,000 by the end of 1970, and 157,000 at the end of 1971. Massive amounts of equipment were also turned over to the ARVN, including 1 million M-16 rifles and sufficient aircraft to make the RVNAF the fourth-largest navy in the world. Extensive retraining of the ARVN was begun, and training schools were established. The controversial counterinsurgency Phoenix Program also operated against the VC infrastructure, reducing the insurgency by 67,000 people between 1968 and 1971, but PAVN forces remained secure in sanctuaries in "neutral" Laos and Cambodia.

Nixon's policy was to limit outside assistance to Hanoi and pressure Hanoi to end the war. For years, American and RVN military leaders had sought approval to attack the sanctuaries. In March 1970 a coup in Cambodia ousted Prince Norodom Sihanouk. General Lon Nol replaced him, and secret operations against the PAVN Cambodian sanctuaries soon began. During a two-month span there were 12 cross-border operations in the so-called Cambodian Incursion. Despite widespread opposition in the United States to the widened war, the incursions resulted in the destruction of considerable communist arms and supplies, raised allied morale, allowed U.S. withdrawals to continue on schedule, and purchased additional time for Vietnamization. U.S. interference in Cambodia also created chaotic conditions that helped the communist Khmer Rouge seize power there in 1976, with dire consequences for the Cambodian people. PAVN forces now concentrated on bases in southern Laos and on enlarging the Ho Chi Minh Trail.

In the spring of 1971 ARVN forces mounted a major invasion into southern Laos, known as Operation LAM SON 719. This overly ambitious operation was designed to cut the Ho Chi Minh Trail and demonstrate the success of Vietnamization. There were no U.S. ground troops or advisers with the ARVN. The operation set back Hanoi's plans to invade South Vietnam but took a considerable toll on the ARVN's younger officers and pointed out serious command weaknesses. In large part due to the bravery of U.S. Army helicopter pilots, about half of the original ARVN force of 15,000 men were able to reach safety. At least 5,000 ARVN troops were killed or wounded, and more than 2,500 were unaccounted for and listed as missing. Additionally, 253 Americans were killed and another 1,149 wounded, although no Americans fought on the ground inside Laos.

By 1972, PAVN forces had recovered and had been substantially strengthened with new weapons, including heavy artillery and tanks from the Soviet Union. The PAVN now mounted a major conventional invasion of South Vietnam. The DRV had 15 divisions. Confident that the United States would not interfere, Hanoi left only 1 division in the DRV and 2 divisions in Laos and committed the remaining 12 to the invasion.

The attack began on March 30, 1972. Known as the Spring or Easter Offensive, it began with a direct armor strike across the DMZ at the 17th parallel and caught the best South Vietnamese troops facing Laos. Allied intelligence misread its scale and precise timing. Hanoi risked catastrophic losses but hoped for a quick victory before ARVN forces could recover. At first it appeared that the PAVN would be successful. Quang Tri fell, and rain limited the effectiveness of airpower.

But in May, Nixon authorized B-52 bomber strikes on Hanoi's principal port of Haiphong and the mining of its harbor. This new air campaign was dubbed Operation LINEBACKER and involved the use of new precision-guided munitions, so-called smart bombs. The bombing cut off much of the supplies for the invading PAVN forces. Allied aircraft also destroyed 400–500 PAVN tanks. In June and July the ARVN counterattacked and then in September regained Quang Tri. The invasion cost Hanoi half its force—some 100,000 men died— while ARVN losses were only a quarter of that, at 25,000.

With both Soviet and People's Republic of China leaders anxious for better relations with the United States in order to obtain Western technology and press the DRV to end the war, Hanoi gave way and switched to negotiations. Nixon's landslide victory against the "peace candidate" George McGovern in the November 1972 presidential election was also likely a major factor in Hanoi's decision to negotiate. Finally, an agreement was hammered out in Paris that December. But President Thieu balked and refused to sign, whereupon Hanoi made the agreements public. A furious Nixon blamed Hanoi for the impasse and ordered a resumption of the bombing, officially known as LINEBACKER II (December 18–29) but also dubbed the December Bombings and the Christmas Bombings. Although 15 B-52s were lost, Hanoi had fired away virtually its entire stock of surface-to-air missiles and now agreed to resume talks.

After a few cosmetic changes, an agreement was signed on January 23, 1973, with Nixon forcing Thieu to agree or risk the end of all U.S. aid. The United States recovered its prisoners of war and departed Vietnam. The Soviet Union and China continued to supply arms to Hanoi, however, while Congress constricted U.S. supplies to Saigon. Tanks and planes were not replaced on the promised one-for-one basis as they were lost, and spare parts and fuel were both in short supply. All of this had a devastating effect on ARVN training, operations, and morale. At the start of 1975, the ARVN had twice the number of combat troops, three times the amount of artillery, and twice the number of tanks as the PAVN. The ARVN also had 1,400 aircraft, but rising oil prices meant that much of this equipment could not be used.

In South Vietnam both sides violated the cease-fire, and fighting steadily increased in intensity. In January 1975 communist forces attacked and quickly seized Phuoc Long Province on the Cambodian border north of Saigon. Washington took no action. The communists next took Ban Me Thuot in the Central Highlands, then in mid-March President Thieu precipitously decided to abandon the northern part of his country. This brought confusion

and then disorder and disaster. Six weeks later PAVN forces controlled virtually all of South Vietnam. Saigon fell on April 30, 1975, to be renamed Ho Chi Minh City. The long war was over at last.

SPENCER C. TUCKER

Consequences

In the war the ARVN had suffered between 220,000 and 313,000 military deaths, while the communist side sustained some 400,000 to 1.1 million. Altogether some 3 million Vietnamese, both military personnel and civilians, had died in the struggle. Much of the country was devastated, and the Vietnamese suffered from the effects of the widespread use of chemical defoliants.

Vietnam was now reunited but under communist rule. In April 1976 general elections occurred for a single National Assembly. It met in June and the next month proclaimed the reunified country the Socialist Republic of Vietnam (SRV), with Hanoi as its capital. Saigon was renamed Ho Chi Minh City. In September 1977 the SRV was admitted to the United Nations. Communist governments also appeared in Laos and Cambodia. Kampuchea (the renamed communist Cambodia) especially suffered. Its 1970 population of some 7.1 million experienced a human catastrophe unparalleled in the 20th century. Cambodia lost nearly 4 million of its people to fighting, famine, and mass murder, perhaps 2.4 million of these murdered by the communist Khmer Rouge.

The new SRV faced staggering problems. These included rebuilding the war-ravaged country, knitting together the two very different halves of the country with their opposing patterns of economic development, and providing for the needs of a burgeoning population. The Vietnamese Communist Party retained its monopoly on power. Indeed, the constitution guaranteed it as the only legal force capable of leading the state and society.

Immediately after the war, the SRV government carried out a political purge in southern Vietnam, although it was nothing like the bloodbath feared and so often predicted by Washington. Thousands of former Republic of Vietnam officials and military officers were sent to Reeducation Camps for varying terms, there to be politically indoctrinated and to undergo varying degrees of physical and mental discomfort, even torture. The government also undertook a program to reduce the urban populations in southern Vietnam, especially Ho Chi Minh City, by far the nation's largest metropolitan area. People had fled to the cities during the war, and perhaps one-third of the arable land lay idle. The government established so-called New Economic Areas to develop new agricultural land and return other areas to cultivation.

The SRV government also sent some 200,000 of its citizens to work in the Soviet Union and Eastern Europe. They sent home an estimated $150 million a year. Finally, the government introduced farm collectivization in southern Vietnam and new regulations that governed business practices. These led to the collapse of light and medium industry. With the economy deteriorating, in 1981 the government introduced an incentive system. Peasants paid fixed rents for the use of the land and were able to sell surplus produce on the private market. Vietnam had no official ties with the United States, though both countries would have benefited economically had such a relationship been established early on.

Meanwhile, relations between the SRV and Kampuchea (Cambodia) deteriorated, the result of traditional animosity between the two countries and Khmer Rouge persecution of its Vietnamese minority and its claims of Vietnamese territory. By 1977 there was serious fighting. The two states became proxies in the developing Sino-Soviet rivalry. Kampuchea was a client state of China, and Vietnam was a client state of the Soviet Union.

In December 1978 the PAVN forces invaded Cambodia, and ultimately there were 200,000 Vietnamese troops there. The Khmer Rouge and other resistance groups fought back, receiving military assistance from China and the United States. Ironically, it was only the Vietnamese occupation that prevented the Khmer Rouge from returning to power and continuing its genocidal policies, and it was only thanks to the Vietnamese invasion that mass killings of Cambodians by the Khmer Rouge were confirmed.

China meanwhile threatened the SRV with force to punish Hanoi for the invasion of Kampuchea and Vietnamese treatment of its large Chinese minority, many of whom fled Vietnam. Indeed, the People's Liberation Army actually invaded Vietnam briefly during February–March 1979, but this brief Sino-Vietnamese War did not force the Vietnamese to quit Cambodia. That came only from the great expense of the operation and its drain on the Vietnamese economy as well as the SRV's attendant isolation in the international community at a time when the nation desperately needed foreign investment. The SRV leadership then decided to quit Cambodia, and by September 1989 all Vietnamese troops had departed.

The SRV continued to maintain an extremely large military establishment. In the mid-1980s it had 1.2 million people under arms, the world's fourth-largest armed force. This figure did not include numerous public security personnel. Military expenditures regularly consumed up to a third of the national budget. This and a bloated government bureaucracy consumed revenues badly needed elsewhere.

By 1986 the economy was in a shambles. Famine—the result of failed farm collectivization and botched currency reform—and rampant inflation took their tolls. An economic growth rate of only 2 percent a year was outstripped by a 3 percent per year birthrate, one of the highest in the world. These developments brought striking changes at the December 1986 Sixth National Communist Party Congress. Among these were material incentives, decentralized decision making, and limited free enterprise. Many of the old hard-line leadership were dropped from the Politburo. Nguyen Van Linh, a proponent of change, became party secretary and the most powerful figure in the state.

Linh had overseen the tentative steps toward a free market economy that had helped southern Vietnam remain more prosperous than northern Vietnam. His reform program, known as Doi Moi (Renovation), produced results. It introduced a profit incentive for farmers and allowed individuals to set up private businesses. Companies producing for export were granted tax concessions, and foreign-owned firms could operate in Vietnam and repatriate their profits with a guarantee against being nationalized. Linh rejected opposition political parties and free elections, however.

Toward the end of normalizing relations with the United States (achieved under President Bill Clinton in 1995), in 1987 the SRV released more than 6,000 military and political prisoners, including generals and senior officials of the former RVN government. Another incentive for the Vietnamese leadership to reach out to the West was the sharp reduction in Soviet aid, which ended altogether in 1991. The conservatives, however, used the collapse of communism in Eastern Europe to halt any movement toward political pluralism.

The effects of the Vietnam War were also profound in the United States. It suffered 58,220 dead and 303,644 wounded (other allied dead totaled nearly 6,000). A significant percentage of the participants suffered from drug addiction and post-traumatic stress disorder. The American military was shattered by the war and had to be rebuilt. Under President Nixon, Congress had done away with the draft and substituted an all-volunteer force. The voting age was also reduced to 18. Congress also moved to curtail the "imperial presidency" with the War Powers Act, which restricted the ability of presidents to wage war without congressional consent.

Inflation was rampant from the failure to face up to the true costs of the war, and there were major social problems. The country also wrestled with an influx of several hundred thousand Vietnamese refugees. The war certainly contributed to a distrust of government and also fractured the Democratic Party, as many blue-collar Democrats saw the party as dominated by antiwar liberals and either joined the Republican Party or became independents. Certainly the war weakened the U.S. commitment to international peacekeeping and institutions. Many questioned U.S. willingness to embark on such a crusade again, at least to go it largely alone. In this sense, the war forced Washington into a more realistic appraisal of U.S. power.

SPENCER C. TUCKER

Timeline

1887	Establishment of French Indochina.
1940	
September	Japanese forces arrive in Indochina.
1945	
September 2	Ho Chi Minh proclaims in Hanoi the establishment of the Democratic Republic of Vietnam (DRV).
1946	
March 6	In the Ho-Sainteny Agreement, the French government recognizes the DRV and agrees to a plebiscite in southern Vietnam as to whether it will join the DRV.
1946–1954	The Indochina War.
1949	
May 8	In the Elysée Agreement, France recognizes that Vietnam is one country in the establishment of the State of Vietnam (SVN).
1950	
December	The United States establishes the Military Assistance Advisory Group (MAAG) in South Vietnam to work with the French forces there.
1954	The United States replaces France as the chief supporter of the SVN.
June 26	Emperor Bao Dai appoints Ngo Dinh Diem premier of the SVN.
July 20	The Geneva Accords officially end the Indochina War. The agreement establishes Vietnam as one country, temporarily divided at the 17th parallel pending national elections to be held in 1956.
1955	
October 26	Diem handily wins a referendum on October 23, 1956, and announces the establishment of the Republic of Vietnam, with himself as president.
1956	Diem refuses to hold the elections called for in the Geneva Accords to reunite Vietnam and is strongly supported in this stand by the Dwight Eisenhower administration in the United States.
1957	A low-level insurgency commences in South Vietnam, led by the communist political cadres who had remained

in South Vietnam to prepare for the planned 1956 elections.

1959

September

People's Army of Vietnam (PAVN, North Vietnamese Army) commander Vo Nguyen Giap establishes the 559th Transportation Group to infiltrate supplies and personnel into South Vietnam. They establish what comes to be known as the Ho Chi Minh Trail through Laos.

1960

November 11

A coup attempt by disgruntled Republic of Vietnam Army (ARVN) leaders fails.

December 20

The communist leadership in South Vietnam establishes the National Front for the Liberation of South Vietnam, better known as the National Liberation Front (NLF). Its military arm, established on December 29, is popularly known as the Viet Cong (VC, for "Vietnamese Communists"). Although claiming to be an independent organization, the NLF is in fact controlled by the DRV government in Hanoi.

1961

May

The John F. Kennedy administration sends a number of fact-finding missions to South Vietnam.

December

U.S. military personnel in South Vietnam number some 3,200.

1962

February 6

The U.S. Military Assistance Command, Vietnam (MACV) replaces the U.S. MAAG in Vietnam.

February 27

Diem survives an assassination attempt when two Republic of Vietnam Air Force (RVNAF) planes bomb the presidential palace.

1963

May 8

Large antigovernment Buddhist protests occur.

November 1

Diem is overthrown in a coup led by ARVN officers and carried out with U.S. government knowledge. Diem and his brother Ngo Dinh Nhu are both assassinated.

November 22

U.S. president John F. Kennedy is assassinated. Vice president Lyndon B. Johnson succeeds him as president.

1964

August 2, 4

The Gulf of Tonkin Incidents occur.

August 5	The United States responds to the Gulf of Tonkin Incidents with the first air strikes of the war against North Vietnam.
August 7	Congress passes the Gulf of Tonkin Resolution, in effect a blank check to President Johnson to wage the war.
December	By the end of 1962 there are some 11,000 U.S. military personnel in South Vietnam.
December 14	Operation BARREL ROLL begins. The U.S. bombing of communist infiltration routes in Laos, it continues until March 29, 1973.

1965

February 7	VC forces mount a direct attack on U.S. military advisory personnel at Pleiku.
February 7–14	In Operation FLAMING DART, U.S. and RVNAF aircraft attack North Vietnamese military positions north of the demilitarized zone (DMZ) at the 17th parallel.
March 2	Operation ROLLING THUNDER begins. The bombing of North Vietnam, it continues with only brief pauses until October 31, 1968.
March 8	U.S. marines arrive in South Vietnam to protect the large U.S. airbase at Danang.
June 9–13	VC forces attack the newly established Dong Xoai Special Forces Camp.
October 19–November 26	In the Battle of the Ia Drang Valley, elements of the U.S. 1st Cavalry Division engage PAVN forces.
December	By the end of the year U.S. military strength in South Vietnam exceeds 200,000.

1966

December	By the end of the year there are 385,000 U.S. military personnel in South Vietnam.

1967

December	By the end of the year there are 485,000 U.S. military personnel in South Vietnam.

1968

January 21–February 24	The communists mount their Tet Offensive throughout South Vietnam by VC and PAVN forces. A military failure, it virtually wipes out VC forces.

February 28	MACV commander General William Westmoreland requests 209,000 additional troops, shocking official Washington.
March 16	U.S. forces massacre at least 347 Vietnamese civilians in the village of My Lai.
March 31	President Johnson announces that he will not seek reelection.
November 6	Republican candidate Richard M. Nixon is elected president of the United States.

1969

January 25	Peace talks open in Paris.
June	U.S. troop strength in Vietnam peaks at 543,000. President Nixon announces his plan for "Vietnamization" to turn over increasing responsibility for the war to the South Vietnamese (actually begun under his predecessor) and promises to reduce U.S. troop strength.

1970

April 30	In an effort to purchase more time for Vietnamization, U.S. forces join the ARVN in an invasion of communist sanctuaries in Cambodia to destroy base camps and supplies there. The forces are withdrawn in June.

1971

February 8–March 29	The ARVN conducts Operation LAM SON 719, a massive incursion against the Ho Chi Minh Trail and communist base areas in Laos that ends in a hasty withdrawal and heavy ARVN casualties.

1972

March 30–October 30	PAVN forces mount a conventional-style invasion of South Vietnam across the DMZ. Known as the Easter or Spring Offensive, it is beaten back by ARVN and U.S. airpower in Operation LINEBACKER. PAVN forces suffer up to 50 percent casualties, ARVN forces about 25 percent.
December 18–29	Frustrated by the failure of a peace agreement, President Nixon orders Operation LINEBACKER II, an attack by U.S. B-52 bombers in the Hanoi-Haiphong area of North Vietnam and also known as the Christmas Bombings.

1973

January 23	A peace agreement is signed in Paris, bringing the U.S. period of the war to a close.

March	The DRV releases U.S. prisoners of war.
August	The U.S. Congress votes to prohibit further U.S. military involvement in Vietnam.

1974

January 4	RVN president Nguyen Van Thieu announces that the war has restarted and that the Paris Peace Accords are no longer in effect.
May	With both sides violating the cease-fire and with renewed fighting, Congress rejects Nixon's request for additional military aid to South Vietnam.
August 9	President Nixon resigns and is succeeded by Vice President Gerald Ford.

1975

January–April	The communist side mounts a major offensive in South Vietnam.
April 30	Communist forces take control of Saigon, officially bringing the long Vietnam War to a close.

SPENCER C. TUCKER

Further Reading

Berman, Larry. *Lyndon Johnson's War: The Road to Stalemate in Vietnam.* New York: Norton, 1999.

Brocheux, Pierre. *Ho Chi Minh: A Biography.* Cambridge: Cambridge University Press, 2007.

Currey, Cecil B. *Victory at Any Cost: The Genius of Viet Nam's General Vo Nguyen Giap.* Washington, DC: Brassey's, 1997.

Dommen, Arthur J. *Conflict in Laos: The Politics of Neutralization.* Revised ed. New York: Praeger, 1971.

Dong Van Khuyen. *The Republic of Vietnam Armed Forces.* Washington, DC: U.S. Army Center of Military History, 1980.

Duiker, William J. *The Communist Road to Power in Vietnam.* 2nd ed. Boulder, CO: Westview, 1996.

Karnow, Stanley. *Vietnam: A History.* New York: Viking, 1983.

Maclear, Michael. *The Ten Thousand Day War, Vietnam: 1945–1975.* New York: St. Martin's, 1981.

McMaster, H. R. *Dereliction of Duty: Johnson, McNamara, the Joint Chiefs of Staff and the Lies That Led to Vietnam.* New York: Harper Perennial, 1998.

McNamara, Robert S., and Brian VanDemark. *In Retrospect: The Tragedy and Lessons of Vietnam.* New York: Vintage Books, 1996.

O'Ballance, Edgar. *The Wars in Vietnam, 1954–1960.* New York: Hippocrene Books, 1981.

Oberdorfer, Don. *Tet! The Turning Point in the Vietnam War.* Baltimore: Johns Hopkins University Press, 2001.

Palmer, Bruce, Jr. *The 25-Year War.* Lexington: University Press of Kentucky, 1984.

Prados, John. *Vietnam: The History of an Unwinnable War, 1945–1975.* Lawrence: University Press of Kansas, 2009.

Pribbenow, Merle L., and William J. Duiker. *Victory in Vietnam: The Official History of the People's Army of Vietnam.* Lawrence: University Press of Kansas, 2002.

Tucker, Spencer C. *Vietnam.* Lexington: University Press of Kentucky, 1999.

Tucker, Spencer C., ed. *The Encyclopedia of the Vietnam War: A Political, Social, and* *Military History.* 4 vols. Santa Barbara, CA: ABC-CLIO, 2011.

Willbanks, James H. *Abandoning Vietnam: How America Left and South Vietnam Lost Its War.* Lawrence: University Press of Kansas, 2004.

Angolan War of Independence (1961–1975)

Causes

The Angolan War of Independence began on February 4, 1961, in an uprising against forced agricultural labor and then became a struggle between three nationalist movements and one breakaway faction against the Portuguese Army for control of the Portuguese Overseas Province of Angola. The war only ended when a leftist military coup overthrew the Portuguese government in Lisbon on April 25, 1974, and declared its intention to grant independence to the Portuguese colonies. A cease-fire was declared in October, and Angola received its independence on November 11, 1975.

In 1482 Portuguese sailors under navigator Diego Cäo landed on the northern coast of Angola and made contact with the African Kongo and Ndongo kingdoms (Angola takes its named from *ngola,* the Ndongo term for "king"). By the beginning of the 16th century the Portuguese had established a number of forts along the Angolan coast, and in 1575 they founded the port city of Luanda. The Portuguese were chiefly interested in the exploitation of Angola's mineral wealth and the slave trade, with the slaves being shipped from Luanda to Brazil. During the centuries of Portuguese colonial settlement there was near-constant warfare with the indigenous tribes, and in 1623–1626 the Portuguese campaigned against and defeated the Ndongos, led by Queen Nzinga. During 1641–1648 the Dutch occupied Luanda and drove the Portuguese from their coastal enclaves.

In 1648 Portuguese forces from Brazil recaptured Luanda and the other coastal forts. By 1671 Ndongo was firmly under Portuguese control. In 1836 the Portuguese abolished the slave trade but not the practice of forced labor. By 1884 the Portuguese had begun to expand their control over the interior. The Congress of Berlin of 1885 officially set Angola's borders, although Angola's present-day borders were not finally settled until after World War I, in 1921. (It is today Africa's seventh-largest country.) The Portuguese Colonial Act of June 13, 1933, recognized the supremacy of the Portuguese over all native peoples. Although blacks could pursue higher education, the act left them at great disadvantage in their own land.

The end of World War II saw a considerable increase in emigration from Portugal to its African colonies, which was encouraged by Portuguese dictator António de Oliveira Salazar. Then on June 11, 1951, the Salazar government changed the status of its colonies to overseas provinces. Although it was possible for Africans to become fully assimilated Portuguese citizens, this was extremely difficult, and Portuguese colonial policy was both suppressive of native rights and economically exploitative. Yet World War II had brought the winds of change throughout Africa, and the days of colonialism were clearly numbered. As with the French and Belgian governments, however, the Portuguese government was determined to hold on to the country's considerable colonial empire.

In 1947 a number of Angolans, notably Viriato da Cruz, established the Movement of Young Intellectuals to promote Angolan history and culture. In 1953 Angolans formed the Partido da Luta Unida dos Africanos de Angola (Party of the United Struggle for Africans in Angola, PLUA), the first Angolan political party to advocate independence from Portugal. The next year Holden Roberto and Barros Necaca founded another independence party, the União dos Povos do Norte de Angola (Union of Peoples of Northern Angola), subsequently renamed the União dos Povos de Angola (Union of Peoples of Angola, UPA). It sought independence for the territory that comprised the former Kingdom of the Kongo, which would include other territory outside Portuguese Angola.

Roberto was born in 1923 in São Salvador, Angola, but moved with his family to Léoipoldville (now Kinhasa) in the Belgium Congo (the present-day Democratic Republic of the Congo) and there graduated from a Baptist missionary school. During the next eight years he worked for the Belgian Finance Ministry in the Congo. In 1951 Roberto visited in Angola, where he witnessed the mistreatment of an old man by the Portuguese authorities, which he said aroused him politically. In December 1958 Roberto represented Angola at the Ghana-sponsored All-African People's Congress.

In 1955, meanwhile, Mário Pinto de Andrade and his brother Joaquin established the Partido Comunista Angolano (Angolan Communist Party, PCA). That December the PCA merged with the PLUA to form the Movimento Popular da Libertação de Angola (Popular Movement for the Liberation of Angola, MPLA). António Agostinho Neto (later the first president of an independent Angola) became its leader.

Born in 1922, Neto was the son of a Methodist minister. Neto studied medicine at the University of Coimbra and the University of Lisbon in Portugal. Arrested in 1951 for his Angolan separatist activities, he was imprisoned by the Portuguese government. Released in 1958, he completed his medical studies and returned to Angola in 1959. Neto was again arrested by the Portuguese in 1960. His political supporters and patients marched to demand his release, and Portuguese soldiers opened fire, killing 30 and wounding 200 in what became known as the Massacre of Icolo e Bengo. Neto was exiled to Cape Verde and then sent to Lisbon, where he was imprisoned. Following international protests, the Portuguese government released him from prison but placed him under house arrest. Neto escaped from this and made his way to Zaire (today the Democratic Republic of the Congo).

The MPLA, based in Brazzaville in the Republic of the Congo before moving its headquarters to Zambia in 1965, was established on a nonracial, nontribal basis, with its goal being the termination of Portuguese rule and the establishment of a Marxist-Leninist state. To accomplish this, the military wing of the MPLA received training in Algeria and later in Soviet bloc countries, from which it also received military assistance.

The granting of independence in 1960 by Belgium to the Congo, renamed Zaire, was a considerable boost to the nascent independence movement in Angola. The MPLA was also able to capitalize on native unrest in Angola, for on January 3, 1961, workers in the cotton fields of the Baixa de Cassanje in the Malanje region mounted a boycott of the Cotonang Company, owned by Portuguese and other foreign investors, to protest both working conditions and pay. In the Baixa de Cassanje Revolt, the workers also burned their identification cards and attacked Portuguese traders. The Portuguese military responded the next day, employing aircraft

The Angolan War of Independence (1961–1975)

Approximate Deaths, Union of Peoples of Angola Raid into Angola (March 15, 1961)	
Black Population	**White Population**
6,000	1,000

Average Approximate Troop Strength (1961–1975)	
Insurgents, All Groups	**Portuguese Forces**
90,000	65,000

Total Approximate Deaths, All Causes, The Angolan War of Independence (1961–1975)		
Insurgents, All Groups	**Portuguese Forces**	**Civilians**
50,000+	4,456	30,000–50,000

Sources: Arthur Jay Klinghoffer, *The Angolan War* (Boulder, CO: Westview, 1980); John A. Marcum, *The Angolan Revolution,* 2 vols. (Cambridge, MA: MIT Press, 1969 and 1978).

dropping bombs that, according to some accounts, included napalm. Estimates of casualties vary considerably, from 400 to 7,000 Angolan blacks killed.

On February 4, 1961, the MPLA began the Angolan War of Independence by undertaking military operations against the Portuguese in northern Angola in an attack against both a police station and the São Paulo prison. Seven policemen died along with 40 of the MPLA attackers, and no prisoners were freed. The MPLA attacked a second prison on February 10. After both attacks the Portuguese authorities came down hard on the blacks, especially in the slums of Luanda, killing hundreds of people.

Spencer C. Tucker

Course

The Marxist MPLA, led by António Agostinho Neto, began the Angolan War of Independence on February 4, 1961. The MPLA operated first from the Republic of the Congo, then from Zaire (present-day Democratic Republic of the Congo), and then back in the Republic of the Congo.

Although the MPLA had 3,000–5,000 fighters, few were actually based in Angola itself. (In 1962 Neto traveled to the United States to request aid from the U.S. government but was turned down by the John F. Kennedy administration because of his Marxist orientation.)

Soon there would be three Angolan independence organizations. The second was the UPA. Led by Holden Roberto, it was based in Zaire. On March 15, several thousand UPA militants crossed into Angola, attacked government outposts, and raided farms and trading centers. Reportedly they killed some 1,000 whites and 6,000 blacks, including women and children. Most of the blacks were contract workers from the Ovimbundu Bantu ethnic group. That the MPLA and the UPA were rivals was shown in the UPA taking prisoner 21 members of the MPLA and then executing them.

In March 1962, Roberto merged his UPA with another Angolan political organization, the Partido Democrático de Angola (Democratic Party of Angola), to form the Frente Nacional de Liberaração de Angola (National Liberation Front of Angola, FNLA). It drew its strength from among the Bakongo tribe of northern Angola and operated chiefly out of Zaire. Roberto received the support of president of Zaire Mobutu Sese Seko when he divorced his wife and married a woman from Mobuto's wife's village. Roberto also received some aid from Israel. On March 27, 1962, he established the Governo Revolucionário de Angola no Exílio (Revolutionary Government of Angola in Exile).

One of Roberto's key lieutenants was Janos Savimbi. Born in 1934 in Munhango, Bie Province, Angola, Savimbi was purposely vague and evasive about his early life. He claimed that he had earned a PhD from the University of Lausanne, Switzerland, and he may have spent two years in Portugal as a medical student. Returning to Angola, Savimbi accepted the post of foreign minister in the FNLA, but he broke with Roberto in 1964 when the latter refused to expand his movement into southern Angola. In 1966 Savimbi founded the União Nacional para a Independência Total de Angola (National Union for the Total Independence of Angola, UNITA). Whereas the FNLA base of support was among the Bakongo people, UNITA was centered in the south among the Ovimbundu and Chokwe peoples.

UNITA's first attack occurred on December 25, 1966, against the Benguela rail line on the border with Zambia. This attack angered the Zambian government, as copper from Zambia was shipped on the line, and as a result it expelled UNITA personnel from the country. Savimbi then relocated to Cairo before returning to Angola a year later. UNITA became the only Angolan insurgent group based in Angola itself but was quite small, with only several hundred fighters.

All three insurgent groups were savaged by Portuguese Army forces, particularly after the latter received helicopters. Portuguese control of the air was an immense advantage, particularly in the largely open eastern part of the country. The Portuguese also carried out resettlement operations, moving the native peoples into government-controlled *dendandas* (defended villages). The Portuguese Army also employed black Angolan troops. Initially these were simply soldiers or noncommissioned officers, but as the war continued a number became officers, although they were limited to junior ranks. By the 1970s the Portuguese finally recognized the deleterious effect of its discriminatory policies on the administration and the military in the colonies and sought to correct these, but it was a case of too little, too late.

The insurgents took heavy casualties but struck back with mines, and they also employed mortars and rockets to attack important Portuguese economic targets such as the Gulf Oil operations in the Cabinda enclave, although without great success. In February 1972, the South African military crossed into Angola and engaged and destroyed MPLA forces in Mexico. Meanwhile, the Portuguese Army forced the MPLA to withdraw from Angola into the Republic of the Congo.

In 1973 Daniel Chipenda, the field commander of the MPLA's Eastern Front, split from the MPLA with some 1,500 followers and formed the Revolta do Leste (Eastern Revolt). Later Chipenda joined the FNLA but then left it to rejoin the MPLA, which he left again in July 1992. Meanwhile, President Julius Nyerere of Tanzania convinced the leaders of the People's Republic of China, which had been aiding the MPLA, to switch their support to the FNLA against the MPLA.

MPLA (Popular Movement for the Liberation of Angola) fighters preparing to ambush Portuguese troops in 1968 during the Angolan War of Independence. (STF/AFP/Getty Images)

The Angolan War reached a stalemate in 1974. The bitterly divided Angolan resistance groups would achieve their goal of independence not because of battlefield success but instead because of a change in the Portuguese government. The economic costs of Portuguese military operations in Angola, as well as in its other colonies of Mozambique and Guinea where it was also fighting insurgencies, were simply staggering. Indeed, by the late 1960s the colonial wars were consuming 50 percent of the national budget. This simply could not be sustained.

On April 25, 1974, young progressive Portuguese Army officers formed into the Movimento das Forças Armadas (Armed Forces Movement) seized power in Lisbon in what became known as the Carnation Revolution. Their new government declared its intention to grant the colonies independence, and a cease-fire was declared that October.

On January 5, 1975, leaders of three principal factions vying for control of Angola—the MPLA, the FNLA, and UNITA—met and agreed to stop fighting each other. They then met with Portuguese government representatives at Alvor, Portugal, beginning on January 10 and agreed on January 15 to set up a coalition government for Angola, with independence for Angola to occur on November 11, 1975. Fighting continued nonetheless, although the Portuguese troops departed Angola on its independence.

SPENCER C. TUCKER

Consequences

Although the Angolan Civil War is usually dated from November 11, 1975, it actually began immediately after the signing of the

Alvor Accords on January 15, 1976, that established a power-sharing arrangement for the new government. Two resistance organizations, the Frente para a Libertação do Enclave de Cabinda (Front for the Liberation of the Enclave of Cabinda, FLEC) and the Revolta do Leste (Eastern Revolt), were excluded from the negotiations and never did adhere to the accords. But the key factor was that the coalition government agreement quickly collapsed amid squabbling by the three major participants: the MPLA, led by António Agostinho Neto; the FNLA, led by Holden Roberto; and UNITA, headed by Jonas Savimbi.

In order to prevent the avowedly Marxist MPLA from taking power, the anti-Marxist FNLA and UNITA formed an alliance. These two groups were supported by Zaire (now the Democratic Republic of the Congo), South Africa, and the United States, the latter through the Central Intelligence Agency. The MPLA enjoyed the support of the Soviet Union and, at its behest, Cuba.

Fighting between the three forces occurred in the Angolan capital of Luanda concurrent with the transitional government assuming office on January 15, 1975. The MPLA was able to wrest control of Luanda from the FNLA, but by March the FNLA had secured control of the northern provinces of Angola and was advancing on the capital from the north. With encouragement from the United States, at the end of April Zaire sent some 1,200 troops into northern Angola to assist the FNLA.

It seemed as if the MPLA would be forced to quit Luanda, but beginning in March, the Soviet Union shipped large amounts of arms to the MPLA. The Soviets also prevailed upon Cuba to assist in training the MPLA forces, and Cuba sent some 500 men with the goal of training 4,800 recruits within three to six months. The Cuban mission was supposed to be a short-term operation of perhaps six months only. Further complicating the mix, the South Africans intervened on behalf of the FNLA in order to protect their own economic interests in Angola and ensure their control of South-West Africa (now Namibia). In Operation SAVANNAH during August 14, 1975–April 30, 1976, South African Defense Force (SADF) troops entered southern Angola, defeated the MPLA forces there, and handed over control of the region to UNITA.

On November 10, 1975, having already defeated the MPLA forces at Porto Quipiri, the FNLA was advancing on Luanda, supported by the Zairians and South Africans, when they encountered the MPLA and Cubans at the strategically located village of Quifangondo, some six miles east of the capital. The advancing force included some 1,000 FNLA troops, 120 mostly white deserters from the Portuguese Army, perhaps 1,200 Zairians, and about 50 South African artillerymen.

With Angola's independence to take effect the next day, November 11, Roberto was determined to take the capital city. The South Africans provided three 5.5-inch (140mm) World War II–era howitzers, while the Zairians contributed two 130 mm guns. South African Canberra bombers were to open the battle with an air strike. Just before the battle, however, the Soviets airlifted Cuban military specialists into Luanda in order to man six BM-21 multiple rocket launchers supplied by the Soviets that had escaped detection by the attackers and were to prove decisive in the battle's outcome.

The South African air strike and the artillery bombardment went as planned, but any advantage was lost in that the ground attack was delayed and then poorly handled. Some 1,000 MPLA troops and 188 Cubans caught the attacking force in the open and unleashed devastating rocket and mortar fire, which destroyed most of the attackers' Panhard armored cars as well as six jeeps mounting recoilless rifles. The rockets outranged the South African and Zairian artillery, and one of the Zairian guns blew up on its first fire as a consequence of poor maintenance. The battle saw hundreds of attackers killed for a reported only one killed and a handful wounded for the defenders. Roberto, who had not been present at the battle, arrived the next morning to discover his men in retreat.

The battle ended any FNLA attempt to take Luanda. By the end of 1975 there were some 25,000 Cuban troops in Angola, and they promptly cleared the FNLA from northeastern Angola. The Zairians and South African gunners withdrew to Ambrizette, where they were evacuated by a South African Navy frigate.

Although the MPLA now held power, with Neto as president, fighting continued. In the Battle of Bridge 14 on December 12, while under enemy fire SDAF engineers rebuilt a bridge over the Bhia River, allowing an SDAF armored column to cross to the other side and rout a far larger Cuban and MPLA force defending the opposite bank. Other inconclusive battles followed before the South African government reached an agreement with the MPLA government under which it would withdraw its forces from Angola in return for an MPLA promise of protection for South African economic interests in Angola. All SDAF forces had departed the country by the end of April 1976.

Alarmed at President Gerald Ford's support for UNITA, on January 27, 1976,

the U.S. House of Representatives overwhelmingly passed an amendment to the Arms Export Control Act (the Senate had approved it earlier) proposed by Senator Dick Clark (D-IA). The Clark Amendment prohibited U.S. aid to private groups engaged in military or paramilitary operations in Angola. Even after passage of the amendment, director of the Central Intelligence Agency George H. W. Bush refused to concede that all U.S. aid to Angola had ceased. Indeed, U.S. ally Israel agreed to step in as a proxy arms supplier for the United States.

On February 8, 1976, MPLA forces and Cuban troops captured the FNLA stronghold of Huambo, forcing Roberto and many of his supporters to seek refuge in Zambia. The United States then switched its support to Savimbi's UNITA. In early June up to 15,000 Cuban troops launched the first of several offensives that year against UNITA. While these operations forced UNITA into southeastern Angola, they failed to defeat it completely, and Savimbi was able to continue insurgent operations. U.S. support for UNITA was now minimal, however, thanks to the Clark Amendment.

Although Marxist-Leninism was the declared official MPLA doctrine, in practice Neto tended to favor a socialist, not communist, model for Angola. In 1977 he violently suppressed an attempted coup by the Organização dos Communistas de Angola (Communist Organization of Angola, OCA), with some 18,000 OCA supporters killed during a two-year span. Neto died in Moscow on September 10, 1979, while undergoing cancer surgery. His birthday is celebrated as National Heroes Day, a public holiday in Angola.

Savimbi's UNITA continued to carry out guerrilla operations against the MPLA and the Cubans, attacking supply convoys and mounting hit-and-run attacks against MPLA bases. The South African government provided some support, and by the early 1980s UNITA controlled the southeastern third of the country. It lacked the resources to defeat the MPLA, however. A stalemate occurred because even with Cuban assistance, the MPLA was unable to completely defeat UNITA.

The MPLA, meanwhile, developed close military ties with the South West Africa People's Organization (SWAPO) in South-West Africa (now Namibia) and the socialist regime in Mozambique as well as with Zambia and the African National Congress in South Africa. In July 1985 the U.S. Congress repealed the Clark Amendment, and the Ronald Reagan administration then supplied UNITA with substantial assistance. Zaire and South Africa served as the major conduits for the U.S. aid.

During December 6, 1983–January 8, 1984, South Africa sent some 2,300 SADF troops on a raid into Angola. Dubbed Operation ASKARI, this sixth SADF foray into Angola was designed to disrupt plans by SWAPO, the liberation movement in South-West Africa, for an offensive in early 1984. The primary battle took place outside Cuvelai during January 3–5, when the SADF defeated a combined Cuban, Angolan, and SWAPO force. The SADF claimed to have killed 324 men of the opposing force while suffering only 21 casualties itself.

On January 30, 1984, Zambian president Kenneth Kaunda invited Republic of South Africa and SWAPO representatives to meet in Lusaka to discuss a truce. With the war in South-West Africa now costing the South African government some $4 million a day and anxious to disengage his country's forces, on January 31 South

African prime minster Pieter Willem Botha announced that he would withdraw his nation's forces from Angola.

On February 23, 1984, representatives of the South African and Angolan governments met in Lusaka, Zambia, and signed a cease-fire agreement. All South African forces were withdrawn from Angola, and the Angolan government agreed that no SWAPO troops or Cubans would be allowed into the vacated territory.

On December 27, 1988, the Cuban government agreed to withdraw its force, which had reached some 50,000 troops, from Angola. The withdrawal was to be completed by July 1991. Still pressed militarily by Savimbi's forces, the Angolan government negotiated a cease-fire with UNITA, and Savimbi himself ran for president in the national elections of 1992, which foreign monitors declared to have been fair. Neither he nor MPLA leader and president José Eduardo dos Santos won the requisite 50 percent, however, and were therefore forced into a run-off, from which Savimbi withdrew, citing electoral fraud. He then resumed the war, much of it financed by the sale of illegally mined diamonds. In 1994 UNITA agreed to a new peace accord, but Savimbi declined the vice presidency offered to him and again took up arms in 1998. On November 20, 1994, UNITA representatives signed the Lusaka Protocol with representatives of the Angolan government as part of an effort to bring to an end the Angolan Civil War.

On February 22, 2002, Savimbi was killed during fighting with MPLA government troops. His death finally made possible a durable cease-fire agreement. UNITA leaders agreed to give up their armed resistance and become the chief opposition party. Although Angola now began to stabilize politically, President dos

Santos refused to institute regular democratic processes, and opposition to the government continued in the northern exclave of Cabinda.

Although Angola has substantial subsoil assets especially in diamonds and oil, this wealth has yet to reach most Angolans. Angola also remains an authoritarian regime, which has been strengthened by a new constitution, with the president and vice president no longer directly elected but chosen instead by the political party that wins the parliamentary elections.

The Angolan Civil War had lasted a quarter of a century and claimed the lives of an estimated half million people. The MPLA, which subsequently abandoned Marxist-Leninism in favor of social democracy, retains power in Angola today.

SPENCER C. TUCKER

Timeline

1482	Portuguese ships commanded by Diego Cäo land on the northern coastline of Angola and encounter the Kongo and Ndongo kingdoms.
1500	In the early 1500s the Portuguese establish a number of coastal forts.
1575	The Portuguese establish the port of Luanda. From there they ship minerals as well as slaves to Brazil.
1623–1626	Portuguese forces defeat the Ndongos, led by Queen Nzinga.
1641–1648	The Dutch occupy Luanda and drive the Portuguese from their coastal settlements.
1648	Portuguese forces from Brazil retake Luanda and other Angolan coastal forts.
1671	The Portuguese control the kingdom of Ndongo.
1836	Portugal abolishes the slave trade but not forced labor in its colonies.
1884	Portugal expands its control into the Angolan interior.
1885	The Congress of Berlin establishes Angola's borders.
1921	Angola's present-day borders are set.
1951	
June 11	Portuguese colonies, including Angola, are recognized as overseas provinces of Portugal.
1956	The Movimento Popular da Libertação de Angola (Popular Movement for the Liberation of Angola, MPLA) is formed with the goal of securing independence. Led by António Agostinho Neto, it receives material assistance from the Soviet Union.

1961   Luanda and northern Angola undergo MPLA-backed
                           rebellions against colonial rule. The Portuguese authori-
                           ties respond with repressive measures.

                           Rebellions beginning on February 4 on the coffee plan-
                           tations against compulsory labor requirements mark the
                           beginning of the Angolan War of Independence. The
                           Portuguese then end the practice of forced labor.

1962   The Frente Nacional para a Libertação de Angola (Na-
                           tional Front for the Liberation of Angola, FNLA) in
                           northern Angola and led by Holden Roberto begins an in-
                           surgency. Zaire and the United States support the FNLA.

1966   The União Nacional para a Indepêndencia Total de
                           Angola (National Union for the Total Independence of
                           Angola, UNITA), formed by Jonas Savimbi in south-
                           ern Angola, becomes Angola's third major nationalist
                           movement.

1974

April 25   Young progressive Portuguese Army officers seize
                           power in Lisbon in the so-called Carnation Revolution.
                           The new government announces its intention to end the
                           wars in Portuguese Africa.

October   A cease-fire goes into effect.

1975

January 15   In a meeting at Alvor, Portugal, the three principal na-
                           tionalist movements of the MPLA, the FNLA, and
                           UNITA agree to the establishment of a coalition gov-
                           ernment. This proves to be brief, as they are unable to
                           resolve their differences.

November 10   In the Battle of Quifangondo, FNLA, Zairean, and South
                           African Defense Force troops attempting to capture Lu-
                           anda are defeated by MPLA and Cuban troops.

November 11   Angola achieves independence. The MPLA unilaterally
                           proclaims the People's Republic of Angola with Neto
                           as president, in effect beginning the Angolan Civil War
                           (1975–2000). The MPLA is supported by the Soviet
                           Union and Cuba, while the FNLA is backed by Zaire,
                           South Africa, and the United States. Cuban forces come
                           to the rescue of the MPLA and defeat the FNLA.

December 12   In the Battle of Bridge 14, South African forces defeat
                           Cuban troops, who enjoy a numerical advantage of three
                           to one.

1976

February   The United Nations (UN) and the Organization of African Unity recognize the MPLA as the legitimate government of Angola.

February 8   MPLA forces and Cuban troops capture the FNLA stronghold of Huambo and force Roberto and many of his supporters to seek refuge in Zambia. The United States then switches its support to Savimbi's UNITA.

1977   A dissident group within the MPLA attempts a coup.

1979

September 10   Following the death of Neto, José Eduardo dos Santos becomes president of Angola.

1983

December 6   South Africa sends some 2,300 troops on a raid into Angola. They are withdrawn on January 8, 1984.

1984   The FNLA announces its withdrawal from military activities.

1986   The United States begins military assistance to UNITA.

1988   South Africa and Cuba reach an agreement to end aid to UNITA and the MPLA, respectively, and also recognize the independence of South-West Africa as Namibia.

1989   The MPLA and UNITA agree to a cease-fire, but it soon comes undone, and fighting resumes.

1990   UNITA controls much of southeastern Angola from its base in Jamba and enjoys considerable support from the Ovimbundu people. It also still receives support from the United States and South Africa.

1991

April   The MPLA repudiates Marxism and Leninism and adopts socialism. A new constitution providing for a multiparty system is then adopted, and the UN brokers yet another peace agreement deal between the MPLA and UNITA.

1992

September   Following an electoral win for dos Santos and the MPLA in multiparty national elections, UNITA rejects the results, and fighting resumes between it and the MPLA.

1994   The Lusaka Peace Agreement is signed between the MPLA and UNITA.

1995	Some 7,000 UN peacekeepers arrive in Angola to oversee the peace agreement.
1996	Both sides in the civil war agree to a government of national unity, with the opposing forces to be formed into a national army. Tensions grow when few UNITA soldiers are incorporated into the new force.
1997	
April	The government of national unity is formed, but UNITA leader Savimbi declines a post and stays away from the inauguration ceremony.
1998	Civil war begins anew.
1999	The UN peacekeeping mission in Angola ends.
2000	UNITA increases its guerrilla war against the MPLA.
2002	
February 22	UNITA leader Savimbi is killed in combat against Angolan government forces.
April 4	A cease-fire is signed between UNITA and the MPLA government side, ending the long Angolan Civil War. It is estimated that half a million Angolans have died in the civil war, and another half million are now facing starvation.
August	UNITA disbands its armed forces.
2003	Isaias Samakuva becomes the new leader of UNITA, now purely a political party.
2004	Angola becomes a major oil-producing state, with over 1 million barrels a day being extracted.
2006	
August	A peace agreement is signed with rebels in the northern Angolan enclave of Cabinda.
2008	
September	The first parliamentary elections in Angola in more than 15 years occur.
2009	
December	Angolan president dos Santos announces that presidential elections will be delayed.
2010	The Angolan parliament changes the constitution, strengthening the presidency and removing the requirement for direct election.

SPENCER C. TUCKER

Further Reading

Abbott, Peter, and Manuel Ribeiro Rodrigues. *Modern African Wars (2): Angola and Mozambique, 1961–74.* Oxford, UK: Osprey, 2013.

Coelho, João Paulo Borges. "African Troops in the Portuguese Colonial Army, 1961–1974: Angola, Guinea-Bissau and Mozambique." *Portuguese Studies Review* 10(1) (2002): 129–150.

George, Edward. *The Cuban Intervention in Angola, 1965–1991: From Che Guevara to Cuito Cuanavale.* New York: Frank Cass, 2005.

Guimaraes, Fernando Andresen. *The Origins of the Angolan Civil War: Foreign Intervention and Domestic Political Conflict.* Basingstoke, UK: Macmillan, 1998.

Hodges, Tony. *Angola from Afro-Stalinism to Petro-Diamond Capitalism.* Bloomington: Indiana University Press, 2001.

Klinghoffer, Arthur Jay. *The Angolan War.* Boulder, CO: Westview, 1980.

Laidi, Zaki. *The Superpowers and Africa: The Constraints of a Rivalry, 1960–1990.* Chicago: University of Chicago Press, 1990.

Marcum, John A. *The Angolan Revolution.* 2 vols. Cambridge, MA: MIT Press, 1969 and 1978.

Schneidman, Witney Wright. *Engaging Africa: Washington and the Fall of Portugal's Colonial Empire.* Lanham, MD: University Press of America, 2004.

Tvedten, Inge. *Angola: Struggle for Peace and Reconstruction.* Boulder, CO: Westview, 1997.

Windrich, Elaine. *The Cold War Guerrilla: Jonas Savimbi and the Angolan War.* Westport, CT: Greenwood, 1992.

Wright, George. *The Destruction of a Nation: United States Policy towards Angola since 1945.* Chicago: Pluto, 1997.

Nicaraguan Revolution (1961–1979)

Causes

Nicaragua experienced a long period of warfare during 1961–1990, first against the rule of the country by the Somoza family and then a civil war against those who had ousted the Somozas. The Republic of Nicaragua is the largest country in the South American isthmus. Honduras lies to the north and Costa Rica to the south, while the Caribbean Sea is on the east and the Pacific Ocean is on the west.

In 1502 Christopher Columbus, sailing for Spain, explored the Miskito coast on the Atlantic side of present-day Nicaragua. The first Spanish settlements were established there in 1524.

The Spaniards took natives as wives and concubines. This led to the ethnic mix of natives and Europeans now known as mestizos. A great many natives died from infectious diseases brought by the Spaniards, however. Britain contested Spain for control of Nicaragua during the Napoleonic Wars (1799–1815). Nicaragua and the other countries of Central and South America freed themselves from Spanish rule following the Napoleonic Wars.

Independent since 1821, Nicaragua has nonetheless experienced its share of political upheaval, war, social unrest, and interventions by the United States. Two political factions, the Conservatives and the Liberals, vied for power. In 1855 the Liberals came to power, and the Conservatives hired an American filibuster, William Walker, to assist their side. He raised a small force, captured Granada, and in 1856 became president. Walker authorized slavery and sought annexation by the United States but was ousted the next year by a coalition of Latin American armies.

The United States became interested in Nicaragua not only for economic reasons but for the possibility of a transisthmian canal that would connect the Atlantic and Pacific Oceans, which was ultimately constructed through Panama. In the ongoing infighting between Conservatives and Liberals, the United States supported the Conservatives and sent warships in November 1909.

In August 1912 Nicaraguan president Adolfo Díaz requested U.S. assistance to put down an insurrection led by dismissed secretary of war General Luis Mena, and U.S. marines arrived and were in Nicaragua until 1933, except for a nine-month period during 1925–1926.

The ensuing Nicaraguan Insurgency of 1927–1933 saw considerable fighting. Conservatives and Liberals had been at loggerheads for decades, and in 1926 Liberal Party leader Juan Bautista Sacasa returned from exile in Mexico and, with assistance from the Mexican government, established a rival government on Nicaragua's east coast. Civil strife commenced in the so-called Constitutional War between the Liberal rebels, led by General José María Moncada, and the government forces, under Conservative Party leader and Nicaraguan president Adolfo Díaz. U.S. president Calvin Coolidge, worried about a communist or Mexican-style revolution in Nicaragua, responded positively to Díaz's request for U.S. military assistance, and the marines returned. Ultimately there were 4,000 U.S. marines in Nicaragua.

On May 4, 1927, U.S. special envoy Henry L. Stimson persuaded Moncada to accept the U.S.-brokered Peace of Tipitapa, whereby the Liberals and Conservatives agreed to U.S.-supervised elections in 1928 and also agreed to give up their arms in return for the creation of a nonpartisan national guard, the Guardia Nacional, to be trained by the marines. The Liberals agreed under a not-so-veiled threat that if they did not disarm, the marines would force their compliance.

All Liberal officers agreed to the Peace of Tipitapa except for Augusto C. Sandino. He and his followers withdrew into the mountains and commenced guerrilla operations against the marines and the Guardia Nacional (National Guard). Numerous engagements followed. One of the largest occurred very early on July 16, 1927, when Sandino led some 800 rebels in an attack on Ocotal, the capital of Nueva Segovia Province in Nicaragua, that was defended by 37 marines and 47 Guardia Nacional personnel. The defenders held off the attackers until daylight, when they were saved by the arrival of marine De Havilland DH-4 aircraft. In the first dive-bombing combat attack in history, the DH-4s drove off the attackers. Some 300 Sandinistas and one marine were killed.

After the Battle of Ocotal, for the most part Sandino avoided pitched battles, choosing to concentrate on hit-and-run attacks against the Guardia Nacional and the marines in the interior. A series of small engagements followed in which the DH-4s proved invaluable, and in January 1928 the marines occupied Sandino's El Chipote base.

In November 1928, 1,500 marines supervised the national elections that saw Liberal candidate General José M. Moncada elected president. Although the marines were able to protect the government and the cities and towns in the western part of Nicaragua as well as supervise the elections of 1928, 1930, and 1932 and train the Guardia Nacional, they could not completely subdue the insurgents or protect lives and property in the Nicaraguan interior.

Under growing pressure from other Latin American countries and the U.S. public and Congress, President Herbert Hoover decided to withdraw the marines. The last marines departed Nicaragua on January 3, 1933. In February 1934 Sandino, who laid down his arms and retired to an agricultural commune in return for amnesty, was treacherously taken by the Guardia Nacional and killed following a meeting at the presidential palace. This deed was carried out on the orders of Guardia commander Anastasio "Tacho" Somoza García.

In December 1936, Somoza seized power. Born in 1896, the son of a wealthy coffee planter, he had been educated in the United States and was fluent in English. Although not president the entire time, Somoza for all practical purposes ruled Nicaragua from December 1936 until he was mortally wounded by an assassin in September 1956. Somoza began a dynasty that lasted 44 years and in effect transformed the country into a family estate. He was succeeded first by his eldest son, Luis Somoza Debayle, who ruled until 1963. The younger son, Anastasio Somoza Debayle, then took over until he was forced to flee Nicaragua in 1979. During their tenure, the Somozas controlled not only the government and the army but also virtually the entire Nicaraguan economy.

The Nicaraguan Revolution (1961–1979)

Approximate U.S. Monetary Aid to Nicaragua

Jimmy Carter Administration (1977–1979)	Ronald Reagan Administration (1981–1986)
$60 million	$132 million

Estimated Losses and Costs, The Nicaraguan Revolution (1961–1979)

Total Killed	Monetary Losses in Nicaragua
45,000	$2 billion

Number of Displaced Nicaraguans, 1979 (Out of a Total Population of 2.8 million)

Homeless/Internally Displaced Persons	Refugees/Exiles
600,000	150,000

Estimated Losses and Costs, The Nicaraguan Civil War (1979–1989)

Total Killed	Monetary Losses
30,000	$2.5 billion

Sources: Robert Pastor, *Exiting the Whirlpool: U.S. Foreign Policy toward Latin America and the Caribbean* (Boulder, CO: Westview, 2001); Thomas W. Walker, ed., *Revolution and Counter-Revolution in Nicaragua* (Boulder, CO: Westview, 1991).

The Somozas were brutal dictators. Using the Cold War to their advantage, they presented themselves as staunch anticommunists in a Latin America that seemed in peril of a communist takeover. Indeed, the United States arranged with the Somoza government to use Nicaragua to train the small force that the John F. Kennedy administration sent against Cuba in the April 1961 Bay of Pigs fiasco.

Dissatisfaction with Somoza family rule and the vast corruption that accompanied it steadily increased. Beginning in May 1959, Nicaraguan insurgents, supported by the Cuban government and opposed to the Somoza regime, began a series of cross-border raids against Nicaragua. These raids increased in 1961 with the formation of the Frente Sandinista de Liberación Nacional (Sandinista National Liberation Front, FSLN). Most were mounted from Honduras, but there were some from Costa Rica. The raids marked the beginning of the Nicaraguan Revolutionary War.

SPENCER C. TUCKER

Course

Various dates are given for the beginning of the Nicaraguan Insurgency or Nicaraguan Revolutionary War. The first of the cross-border raids by Nicaraguans from Honduras backed by Cuba occurred during May–June 1959 and was defeated by the Guardia Nacional under General Anastasio Somoza Debayle, brother of President Luís Somoza Debayle. Other raids, including one mounted from Costa Rica, occurred during January–May and November 1960.

Most historians, however, date the insurgency from the establishment of the

FSLN. Inspired by the 1959 Cuban Revolution and organized on July 26, 1961, by Nicaraguans determined to overthrow the Somoza regime, the FSLN was named for Augusto César Sandino (1895–1934), the charismatic leader of a nationalist rebellion against the U.S. occupation of Nicaragua in the 1920s and 1930s who was subsequently treacherously assassinated by the Guardia Nacional. The Sandinista leaders included Carlos Fonseca, Silvio Mayorga, and Tomás Borge. In 1963 the Sandinistas established an insurgent base in the mountainous Matagalpa region of Honduras from which they carried out cross-border raids into Nicaragua. They made little progress in their efforts to win over the Nicaraguan peasants, however.

Other opposition groups were also active, and during January 22–23, 1967, an attempted coup d'état in Nicaragua by disaffected military officers and civilians was defeated by the Guardia Nacional. On February 5, 1967, Anastasio Somoza Debayle was elected president in an election marked by fraud and violence. His increasingly despotic rule enforced by the Guardia Nacional led to growing opposition.

On December 23, 1972, a major earthquake largely destroyed the city of Managua, killing as many as 10,000 people, injuring another 20,000, and leaving many more homeless. Nicaraguans were outraged at the Somoza family's profiting from construction contracts paid for by international relief funds. The blatant corruption (by 1979 Somoza's net worth was estimated at $700 million) and control of virtually the entire country by the Somoza family strengthened the appeal of the Sandinistas.

When Jimmy Carter became president of the United States in January 1977, human rights became a central focus of U.S. Latin American policy. Somoza felt betrayed by an American president who placed human rights above anticommunism. Nonetheless, the Carter administration pressed Somoza to introduce reforms but had scant success.

The insurgency continued, and following an October 14–17, 1977, raid by the Nicaraguan National Guard across the border to attack Sandinista camps in Costa Rica, the Costa Rican government closed the border with Nicaragua and dispatched troops to police it. Both Costa Rica and Nicaragua accused the other of cross-border violations and appealed to the Organization of American States (OAS), which then dispatched a fact-finding mission to the area to investigate.

On January 10, 1978, Pedro Ramos, a right-wing Cuban American exile, arranged the assassination of the leader of Nicaragua's moderate opposition, Pedro Joaquin Chamorro. Somoza was widely blamed for the murder, which served to unite those opposed to his dictatorship. The radical Sandinistas led the effort and now enjoyed the support of not only Cuba and Costa Rica but also Venezuela and Panama. The OAS also passed a resolution declaring Somoza to be "the fundamental cause" of the Nicaraguan crisis.

On September 9, 1978, Sandinista forces mounted several large attacks in urban areas of Nicaragua. Although the Nicaraguan National Guard quickly counterattacked and drove the insurgents back into the mountains, the fighting was heavy, and the many civilian deaths incurred served to further alienate the population from the Somoza regime.

On May 28, 1979, the opposition to Somoza established a provisional government in San Jose, Costa Rica. The provisional government included social

Nicaraguan urban guerrillas loyal to the Frente Sandinista de Liberación Nacional display a home-made mortar used against the National Guard in Managua in July 1979. (AFP/Getty Images)

democrats, Marxists, and communists. Suspending their sharp ideological differences, the opposition leaders announced a program pledging democracy, political pluralism, and a mixed economy. The next day, May 29, Sandinista forces fighting the Somoza regime began a major military offensive, well supplied with arms from Cuba, Venezuela, Panama, and Costa Rica. In a matter of a few weeks, the Sandinistas controlled most of the major cities and the countryside. The rebels laid siege to Managua beginning on July 10. Somoza went into exile on July 17, and two days later the insurrectionists entered Managua in triumph. Shortly thereafter a Nicaraguan provisional government was established. It enjoyed both widespread popular support and international approval. Unfortunately, the euphoria would prove to be short-lived.

SPENCER C. TUCKER

Consequences

The fighting in Nicaragua had been costly. According to the Inter-American Human Rights Commission, more than 45,000 Nicaraguans had been killed in the effort to overthrow Somoza, and the country had suffered more than $2 billion in economic losses. Faced with a new Nicaraguan government dominated by the Sandinistas, U.S. president Jimmy Carter sought to avoid a confrontation of the kind that had pushed Fidel Castro in Cuba into the Soviet bloc. In September 1979 Carter met with Daniel Ortega, Sergio Ramirez, and Alfonso Robelo, leaders of the new

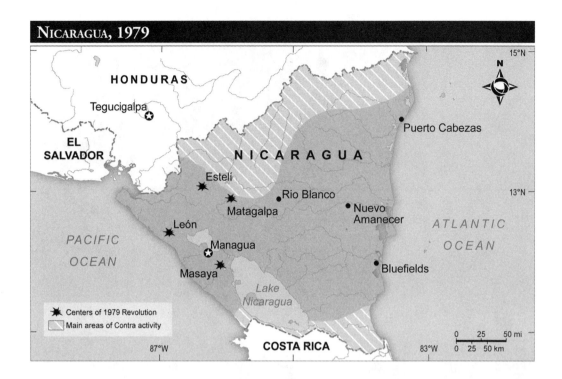

NICARAGUA, 1979

HONDURAS

Tegucigalpa

EL SALVADOR

NICARAGUA

Esteli

Rio Blanco

Matagalpa

León

Nuevo Amanecer

PACIFIC OCEAN

Managua

Masaya

Bluefields

Lake Nicaragua

15°N

Puerto Cabezas

13°N

ATLANTIC OCEAN

★ Centers of 1979 Revolution
▨ Main areas of Contra activity

87°W

COSTA RICA

83°W

0   25   50 mi
0 25 50 km

government. The Carter administration announced that it would not support the ex-Somoza guardsmen now organizing against the government, but the administration also stressed that human rights were a major concern. The Nicaraguan officials expressed support for this position and committed themselves to not aiding the civil conflicts that had begun in Guatemala and El Salvador.

The Sandinistas dominated the government established in July 1979. At first they followed the previously agreed-upon conditions of freedom of expression, political pluralism, and free enterprise. Nonetheless, there was a steady movement to the political Left. By the end of 1980, the moderate leaders had been forced out of the government. The Sandinistas had also stifled freedom of expression and postponed national elections until 1985 at the earliest. The government also forcibly relocated Miskito Indians in

northeastern Nicaragua, provoking armed resistance.

All of this caused considerable unease in Washington. The Carter administration, which had provided $60 million in aid to Nicaragua, suspended this when it discovered that the Sandinistas had indeed shipped arms to the leftist rebels in El Salvador. The Nicaraguan government drew closer to Cuba and the Soviet Union, and by the end of 1981 there were several thousand Cuban and Soviet military and technical advisers in Nicaragua.

Staunch anticommunist Ronald Reagan became U.S. president in January 1981. He soon made Central America a battleground in the Cold War and made Nicaragua a test case for halting Marxist subversion. Pledging U.S. aid for the anti-Sandinista forces, on March 9, 1981, Reagan ordered the U.S. Central Intelligence Agency (CIA) to provide support and training for forces led by Colonel Enrique Bermudez who were already battling the Sandinista government. These forces were known as the Contras.

Reagan faced strong opposition to his policy from the U.S. Congress, but he proceeded nonetheless. From bases in Honduras and Costa Rica, the anti-Sandinista forces raided into Honduras. Contra forces, which grew to a total of some 25,000 men, were led for the most part by former members of the Guardia Nacional and therefore enjoyed little support in Nicaragua, with most of those opposed to the Sandinista government preferring a more centrist course between the Contras and Sandinistas.

On February 21, 1982, Mexican president José López Portillo y Pacheco put forward a plan to end the fighting in Central America. It called for an end to the U.S. intervention in Nicaragua, a reduction in the size of the Nicaraguan armed forces, and a nonaggression pact between Nicaragua and neighboring Central American states. Alarmed by both Reagan's interventionism and the collapse of democracy under the Sandinistas, Mexico, Venezuela, Colombia, and Panama created the Contadora Grouping in January 1983 to search for a purely Latin American solution. This received strong support from Argentina, Brazil, Uruguay, and Peru and from the Democratic Party majority in the U.S. Congress. In December 1983, in the first Boland Amendment, Congress voted to cut off covert military aid to the Contras.

In April 1984, in an operation entirely contrary to international law, the CIA arranged the mining of Nicaraguan coastal waters off the port of Corinto. This brought a strong adverse reaction in the United States and a congressional resolution condemning it, as well as a ban in October on the Defense Department and the CIA as

well as all other U.S. governmental agencies using funds in Nicaragua for military purposes.

On November 4 seven political parties participated in the Nicaraguan general elections, which the Sandinistas won and which observers held to be free and fair. This further undermined Reagan's militant stance.

Also in November, the Reagan administration, fearful that the Soviets were about to ship MiG fighter aircraft to Nicaragua, warned Managua that it would not tolerate such a move. Although no aircraft were delivered, the Nicaraguan government was sufficiently alarmed about the possibility of a U.S. military intervention to move the nation toward a war footing. Then on May 1, 1985, the Reagan administration imposed a total U.S. trade embargo of Nicaragua.

On March 21, 1986, Nicaraguan forces in pursuit of Contra guerrillas crossed into Honduras. Several days of confused fighting followed the initial incursion. News of the fighting was complicated by the reluctance of Honduran officials to admit that the Contras were based in their country. U.S. helicopters ferried Honduran troops to the area, forcing a Nicaraguan withdrawal by March 27.

The United States also established a large military presence in Honduras in order to protect that country against a presumed Nicaraguan invasion, support the Contras in their effort to overthrow the Sandinista regime in Nicaragua, and lend assistance to the Salvadoran military in its counterinsurgency against leftist guerrillas who were backed by Nicaragua. At a reported cost of $30 million, the United States constructed the Palmerola Air Base, near Comayagua, with a 10,000-foot runway capable of handing the large C5-A cargo planes. The United States soon had more than 5,000 troops there. The United States also built a training base near Trujillo to train the Contras and the Salvadoran military. To facilitate these operations, the United States also developed Puerto Castilla in Honduras. Although Honduras was spared civil war, its army did carry out a campaign against leftists, which included extrajudicial killings.

On November 6, 1986, a magazine in Lebanon revealed that the United States had been illegally selling weapons to Iran in order to help secure the release of American hostages held in Lebanon. The proceeds from the arms sales had then been channeled to the Contra rebels fighting the Sandinista regime in Nicaragua, again in violation of U.S. law, such aid having been blocked by the U.S. Congress in the Second Boland Amendment of 1984. Congress approved the Third Boland Amendment in December 1985, cutting off all U.S. assistance to the Contras.

Although much of the Iran-Contra Affair remains unclear even today, in August 1985 Reagan had approved a plan by National Security Advisor Robert McFarlane to sell antitank missiles to Iran via the Israelis in exchange for the release of Americans held in Lebanon. McFarlane's assistants, Rear Admiral John M. Poindexter and U.S. Marine Corps colonel Oliver North, had charge of the operation. Despite reservations by other senior administration officials who were aware of the scheme, Reagan continued it. In all, some 100 tons of missiles and spare parts went to Iran. The plan proved to be only of limited success as far as the hostages were concerned, however; although some were freed, others were soon taken captive to replace them. North, meanwhile, channeled the money from the sales to the Contras.

Reagan initially denied any arms-for-hostages deal. North and his secretary immediately shredded incriminating documents, but some were discovered in North's office that linked the Iranian shipments directly to the Contras. North was fired, and National Security Advisor Poindexter, who had replaced McFarlane, resigned.

A subsequent independent commission criticized the White House for failure to control the National Security Agency. Reagan then admitted to having misled the public in his earlier statements but pled ignorance rather than design. A subsequent congressional inquiry lambasted Reagan but decided that he had not known about the money transfers to the Contras. Vice President George H. W. Bush's involvement remains unclear.

Although North, Poindexter, and a dozen others were subsequently indicted, North and Poindexter were later acquitted on Fifth Amendment technicalities. At the end of his term in office in December 1992, President George H. W. Bush pardoned six other persons implicated in the scandal, including McFarlane and Secretary of Defense Caspar Weinberger.

The fighting in Nicaragua continued. During March 16–17, 1988, Nicaraguan forces crossed into Honduras to attack Contra bases along the border. The Nicaraguan force soon clashed with the Honduran Army. Although the United States rushed troops to Honduras, the Sandinistas withdrew during March 28–31. The Nicaraguans also managed to down a number of CIA-supported aircraft carrying aid to the Contras. Meanwhile, separate peace efforts in 1987 and 1988 went nowhere.

Bush was the U.S. president when the Contra War finally came to an end with the Tesoro Beach Accords in El Salvador on February 14, 1989, between the governments of Costa Rica, El Salvador, Guatemala, Honduras, and Nicaragua. Under the terms of this agreement, all Contra forces were to be disbanded in return for a promise of free elections in Nicaragua, to be held in February 1990. The follow-on Tela Convention in Honduras on August 7 regulated the disbandment of Contra forces under international supervision. Although a few Contra groups initially rejected the agreement, they were ultimately persuaded to participate. All told, the civil war had claimed more than 30,000 lives.

On February 25, 1990, to the surprise of many, in internationally supervised elections the opposition National Opposition Union, led by moderate Violetta Barrios de Chamorro, scored a sweeping triumph, winning the presidential, legislative, and local elections and ousting the Sandinistas from power. Nicaragua has since experienced economic growth and political stability in recent years. Former Sandinista Daniel Ortega, who had led Nicaragua from 1979 to 1990 and has now moderated his political position from Marxist-Leninist to democratic socialist, won the presidential election of November 2006 and was reelected in 2011. The constitution has since been amended to allow him to run for a third term.

SPENCER C. TUCKER

Timeline

1502   In the course of his fourth voyage of discovery, explorer Christopher Columbus, sailing for Spain, explores the Miskito Coast on the Atlantic side of present-day Nicaragua.

1524   The Spaniards establish their first colonial settlements in Nicaragua.

1821   Nicaragua wins independence from Spain.

1855   American filibuster William Walker leads a small volunteer force and captures Granada, and in 1856 he assumes the presidency of Nicaragua. Walker authorizes slavery and seeks annexation by the United States but is ousted in 1857 by a coalition of Latin American armies.

1909   The United States sends warships to Nicaragua to support the Conservatives there.

1912–1933   Nicaraguan president Adolfo Díaz requests U.S. assistance to put down an insurrection. U.S. marines will be in Nicaragua until 1933 except for a nine-month period in 1925–1926.

1956

September 21   Nicaraguan dictator President Anastasio Somoza García is shot and mortally wounded by the poet Rigoberto López Pérez in León. Somoza García dies on September 29 and is succeeded by his son, Luís Somoza Debayle.

1957

May 2–3

Nicaragua and Honduras engage in a border skirmish, ended by Organization of American States mediation.

1959

May 30–June 14

An attempted insurgent invasion of Nicaragua is defeated by the National Guard under General Anastasio Somoza Debayle, brother of President Luís Somoza Debayle. The Nicaraguan government blames Cuba for the invasion.

1960

January 2–May 14

Nicaraguan armed forces turn back insurgent raids mounted from Honduras (January 2, February 29, and May 14) and from Costa Rica (January 9).

November 9–15

Nicaraguan and Costa Rican armed forces cooperate to defeat an insurgent invasion of Nicaragua from Costa Rica. The insurgents are supported by Cuba.

1961

January 27

Honduran rebels, based in Nicaragua, invade Honduras but are then repulsed.

July 26

Nicaraguan insurgents organize in Honduras the Frente Sandinista de Liberación Nacional (Sandinista National Liberation Front). The organization is named for Augusto César Sandino (1895–1934), leader of a nationalist rebellion against the U.S. occupation of Nicaragua in the 1920s and 1930s who was assassinated by the Nicaraguan National Guard.

1963

The Sandinistas establish an insurgent base in the mountainous Matagalpa region of Honduras, then carry out raids across the border into Nicaragua.

1967

January 22–23

An attempted coup d'état in Nicaragua by disaffected military officers and civilians is defeated by the National Guard, commanded by Major General Anastasio Somoza Debayle. On February 5, 1967, Somoza is elected president in an election marked by fraud and violence. His increasingly despotic rule enforced by the National Guard leads to growing opposition.

1972

December 23

A major earthquake strikes Nicaragua, destroying much of Managua and killing as many as 10,000 people. The vast corruption involved in the spending of international relief funds for their own personal use by the Somoza family fuels opposition to the regime.

1977

January

Jimmy Carter becomes president of the United States and makes human rights a priority of his administration, pressing Somoza to undertake reforms but making little headway in that regard.

October 14–17

Following the pursuit into Costa Rica of Sandinista guerrillas by the Nicaraguan National Guard, Costa Rica closes its border with Nicaragua. Both sides appeal to the Organization of American States (OAS), which sends a fact-finding mission.

1978

January 10

Pedro Ramos, a right-wing Cuban American exile, arranges the assassination of Pedro Joaquin Chamorro, leader of Nicaragua's moderate opposition. Somoza is blamed for the murder, which unites those opposed to his dictatorship.

May 28

The opposition to Somoza establishes a provisional government in San Jose, Costa Rica. Their program is based on democracy, political pluralism, and a mixed economy.

May 29

Sandinista forces commence a major military offensive, and in a matter of weeks they control most of the major cities and the countryside.

July 10

The Sandinistas institute a siege of the Nicaraguan capital city of Managua.

July 17

Somoza departs for exile in the United States.

July 19

The Sandinistas enter Managua in triumph, and a provisional government is established that enjoys both widespread popular support and international approval.

September 9

Sandinista forces mount several large attacks in urban areas of Nicaragua. Although the Nicaraguan National Guard quickly counterattacks and drives the rebels back into the mountains, the fighting is heavy, and the many civilian deaths incurred help alienate the population from the government.

1979–1981

Upon coming to power in July 1979, the Sandinista government at first allows freedom of expression, political pluralism, and free enterprise. U.S. president Jimmy Carter seeks to avoid a confrontation that might push the government into the Soviet orbit, as had happened in Cuba. In September 1979 Carter meets with Nicaraguan government leaders Daniel Ortega, Sergio Ramirez, and Alfonso Robelo, and the Carter administration announces that it will not support anti-Sandinista forces. The Nicaraguan officials express their support for human rights and commit to not aiding conflicts in Guatemala and El Salvador.

By the end of 1980, however, the Sandinistas have stifled freedom of expression and postponed national elections. The government also forcibly relocates Miskito Indians in northeastern Nicaragua, provoking armed resistance.

The steady movement of the Nicaraguan government to the Left prompts unease in Washington. At the same time moderates are forced out of the government, which also curtails freedom of expression and postpones elections. The government also moves closer to Cuba and the Soviet Union. By the end of 1981 there are several thousand Cuban and Soviet military and technical advisers in Nicaragua.

Staunch anticommunist and new U.S. president Ronald Reagan takes office in January 1981 and makes Central America a battleground in the Cold War and Nicaragua a test case for halting Marxist subversion.

1981

March 9

President Reagan orders the U.S. Central Intelligence Agency (CIA) to provide support and training for forces led by Colonel Enrique Bermudez who are already battling the Sandinista government. These forces, which grow to some 25,000 men, are known as the Contras.

1982

February 21

Mexican president José López Portillo y Pacheco proposes a plan to end the fighting in Central America. It calls for an end to the U.S. intervention in Nicaragua, a reduction in the size of the Nicaraguan armed forces, and a nonaggression pact between Nicaragua and neighboring Central American states.

1984

April

In an operation entirely contrary to international law, the CIA arranges the mining of Nicaraguan coastal waters off the port of Corinto. This brings a strong adverse reaction in the United States and in the U.S. Congress.

May 24   The U.S. Congress bans further aid to the Contras.

November   Fearing that the Soviets are about to ship MiG fighter aircraft to Nicaragua, Washington warns Managua that it will not tolerate such. No aircraft are delivered, but the Nicaraguan government is sufficiently alarmed about the possibility of a U.S. military intervention to move the nation toward a war footing.

November 4   The Sandinistas win the general elections in Nicaragua, held to be fairly conducted.

1985

May 1   The Reagan administration imposes a total trade embargo on Nicaragua.

December   In the Third Boland Amendment, the U.S. Congress cuts off all U.S. aid to the Contras.

1986

March 21–27   Nicaraguan forces in pursuit of Contra guerrillas cross the border into Honduras. Several days of confused fighting follow, but U.S. helicopters ferry Honduran troops to the area, forcing a Nicaraguan withdrawal.

November 6   The Iran-Contra Affair becomes public when a Lebanese magazine reveals that the United States has been selling missiles to Iran and using the money to pay for aid to the Contras.

1988

March 16–17   Nicaraguan forces cross into Honduras to attack Contra bases along the border. The Nicaraguan forces soon clash with the Honduran Army. Although the United States rushes reinforcements to Honduras, the Sandinistas withdraw during March 28–31.

1989

February 14   On this date the Contra War finally comes to an end with the Tesoro Beach Accords in El Salvador between the governments of Costa Rica, El Salvador, Guatemala, Honduras, and Nicaragua. All Contra forces are to disband in return for a promise of free elections in Nicaragua to be held in February 1990. The follow-on Tela Convention in Honduras on August 7 regulates the disbandment of Contra forces under international supervision. Although a few Contra groups initially reject the agreement, they are ultimately persuaded to participate. The civil war has claimed more than 30,000 lives.

1990

February 25

To the surprise of many, the opposition National Opposition Union, led by moderate Violetta Barrios de Chamorro, wins the Nicaraguan presidential, legislative, and local elections, ousting the Sandinistas from power.

2006

November

Former Sandinista Daniel Ortega, who had led Nicaragua during 1979–1990, wins the Nicaraguan presidential election.

SPENCER C. TUCKER

Further Reading

Black, George. *The Triumph of the People: The Sandinista Revolution in Nicaragua.* Westport, CT: Lawrence Hill, 1981.

Booth, John A. *The End and the Beginning: The Nicaraguan Revolution.* Boulder, CO: Westview, 1982.

Brinkley, Douglas. *The Unfinished Presidency: Jimmy Carter's Journey beyond the White House.* New York: Viking, 1998.

Diederich, Bernard. *Somoza and the Legacy of U.S. Involvement in Central America.* New York: E. P. Dutton, 1981.

Gilbert, Dennis L. *Sandinistas: The Party and the Revolution.* New York: B. Blackwell, 1988.

Grossman, Karl. *Nicaragua: America's New Vietnam?* New York: Permanent Press, 1984.

LaRamee, Polakoff, and Erica Pierre. *Undermining of the Sandinista Revolution.* New York: Palgrave Macmillan, 1999.

Pastor, Robert. *Exiting the Whirlpool: U.S. Foreign Policy toward Latin America and the Caribbean.* Boulder, CO: Westview, 2001.

Selbin, Eric. *Modern Latin American Revolutions.* 2nd ed. Boulder, CO: Westview, 1999.

Walker, Thomas W., ed. *Revolution and Counter-Revolution in Nicaragua.* Boulder, CO: Westview, 1991.

Rhodesian Bush War (1965–1979)

Causes

The Rhodesian Bush War, also known as the Second Chimurenga and the Zimbabwe War of Liberation, was a civil war during which the forces of Rhodesia's white minority government fought black nationalist insurgents serving in the Zimbabwe African National Liberation Army (ZANLA), the military wing of the Zimbabwe African National Union (ZANU) led by Robert Mugabe, and the Zimbabwe People's Revolutionary Army (ZIPRA), the military branch of the Zimbabwe African People's Union (ZAPU) led by Joshua Nkoma. Various dates have been advanced for the start of the war, from 1964 to 1971, while its end date is given either as 1979 or 1980. It seems most appropriate to date the war from the proclamation of Rhodesian independence and end it with the Lancaster House Agreement between the warring parties, which was signed on December 21, 1979.

Rhodesia is a historical region in Southern Africa. Before British colonization there were a number of native kingdoms in the region, which was also a major trade route. This landlocked territory was first settled by British and South African colonists of the British South Africa Company beginning in the 1890s and was named by its settlers after founder and director of the British South Africa Company Cecil Rhodes. The name of Rhodesia became official in 1895 and was recognized by the British government in 1898.

Rhodesia was bisected east-west by the natural border of the Zambezi River. The company designated that territory north of the river as Northern Rhodesia, while that territory to the south was Southern Rhodesia. The two have sometimes been referred to as the Rhodesias.

The prevailing belief was that a referendum in Southern Rhodesia in 1922 would lead to it being incorporated into the Union of South Africa. But negotiations with South Africa produced terms unacceptable to the Rhodesians and a referendum vote rejected this course of action, so in September 1923 Southern Rhodesia became a self-governing British colony. On October 1 the first constitution of the new colony entered into force, with Charles Patrick John Coghlan as premier.

The economy of Southern Rhodesia was centered largely in agriculture and mineral extraction. The chief products were tobacco, copper, and chromium. The economy was thus highly vulnerable to commodity fluctuations.

Southern Rhodesian military units participated in World War II as part of the British Empire forces and distinguished themselves in combat operations in the East Africa and North African campaigns, in Italy, and in Southeast Asia. The Southern Rhodesians suffered the highest per capita loss rate of any British Empire forces, while Southern Rhodesian pilots earned the highest percentage of decorations.

In the aftermath of the war a large number of European settlers arrived in Southern Rhodesia, with some 200,000 immigrating there during 1945–1970. This influx increased their number from some 100,000 to 307,000, and they numbered some 600,000 by 1976.

World War II marked the end of the colonial era, with nationalism sweeping throughout Africa. On August 1, 1953, amid growing calls for independence, the British government created the Federation of Rhodesia and Nyasaland (Central African Federation). It included Southern Rhodesia, Northern Rhodesia, and Nyasaland (present-day Malawi). The British hoped to find a middle ground that would meet the needs of both the white settlers and blacks. The federation failed in this, fueling the demands of black nationalists. Meanwhile, the British government was preparing for majority rule in its African colonies. After a month of visiting in Africa, British prime minister Harold Macmillan on February 3, 1960, addressed the South African parliament and stated Britain's intention to grant independence to its African colonies under black majority rule.

The British government ended the Central African Federation on January 1, 1964. The British expected that the result would be Nyasaland and a united Rhodesia, but the two Rhodesias were very different. Northern Rhodesia had a white population of some 100,000, but most were relative newcomers, nonlandholders, and largely involved in mineral extraction. These factors made them more amenable to black nationalism. As a consequence, the British granted independence to Northern Rhodesia on October 24, 1964. Black nationalists assumed power, changed the name to Zambia, and began the process of Africanization. With its strong white population firmly ensconced in power and resisting majority rule, Southern Rhodesia remained a British colony, as London refused to grant independence without majority rule.

Meanwhile, black nationalists had come to the fore in Southern Rhodesia. The first important Rhodesian black nationalist group was ZAPU, formed in

December 1961 and led by Joshua Nkoma. Born in the Southern Rhodesia province of Matabeleland in 1917, Nkoma had trained as a social worker and had entered politics in 1952, going on to lead a succession of nationalist movements, including the National Democratic Party (NDP), but ZAPU, located in Tanzania, was the most important. Nkomo's imprisonment during 1964–1974 by the government of Prime Minister Ian Smith came to symbolize for the international community the struggle for majority rule in Rhodesia, much as had that of Nelson Mandela in South Africa.

There were several splits in ZAPU. In August 1963 Reverend Ndabaningi Sithole formed the rival ZANU. Born in Nyamandhlovu, Southern Rhodesia, in 1920, Sithole was a member of the Ndau ethnic group. He studied in the United States during 1955–1958 and was ordained a Methodist minister in 1958. The 1964 banning of his book *African Nationalism* led to his entry in politics. Arrested in 1964, he spent the next 10 years in prison along with the man who succeeded him as leader of ZANU, Robert Gabriel Mugabe.

Born in 1924 in the Zvimba District of Southern Rhodesia, Mugabe earned a BA degree from Fort Hare University in South Africa in 1951, then pursued additional studies in education and worked as a teacher in Ghana during 1958–1960. In 1960 Mugabe returned to Southern Rhodesia a Marxist and joined Nkomo's NDP. In December 1961, when the NDP was banned, Mugabe became secretary-general of its successor, ZAPU. Deepening personal and ideological differences with ZAPU led Mugabe to leave the party in 1963; he then became secretary-general of the newly formed ZANU. In 1964 Mugabe was arrested in Southern Rhodesia and imprisoned until 1974, when he

The Rhodesian Bush War (Zimbabwe War of Liberation, 1965–1979)

Estimated Casualties, Nyadzonya Raid (August 9, 1976)

Selous Scouts	ZANLA/FAM Insurgents
4 slightly wounded	1,028 killed

Approximate Military Strength, Opposing Forces (1978–1979)

Rhodesian Security Forces	Insurgents
25,000 soldiers	122,000 guerillas

Estimated Total Deaths, The Rhodesian Bush War (1965–1979)

Rhodesian Security Forces	Insurgents	Black Civilians	White Civilians
1,361	10,000	7,790	1,468

Sources: Peter Abbott and Philip Botham, *Modern African Wars: Rhodesia, 1965–80* (Oxford, UK: Osprey, 1986); Bruce Hoffman, Jennifer M. Taw, and David Arnold, *Lessons for Contemporary Counterinsurgencies: The Rhodesian Experience* (Santa Monica, CA: Rand, 1991).

was released by Prime Minister Smith's white minority government.

Southern Rhodesia had been under white minority rule since 1923. Smith became prime minister on April 13, 1964. Born in Selukwe, Southern Rhodesia, in 1919, he served as a Royal Air Force fighter pilot during World War II, when he was badly wounded. Elected to the Southern Rhodesian parliament in 1948 at only age 29, he resigned in 1961 in protest of the colony's new constitution. The next year he helped form the all-white staunchly conservative Rhodesian Front, which called for full independence without black majority rule. When the Rhodesian Front won the December 1962 parliamentary elections, Smith became deputy prime minister, and on April 13, 1964, he became prime minister. His supporters regarded him as a hero and a man of integrity; his opponents saw him as a narrow-minded racist.

The refusal of the British government to allow the Southern Rhodesia government independence before provision was made for majority rule by its 4.5 million blacks led Smith, strongly supported by the white minority of some 300,000, to unilaterally declare on November 11, 1965, the independence of the Republic of Rhodesia. With international sanctions slow to take effect and with the white minority resistant to any form of meaningful political compromise, black nationalist leaders took up arms to attain their goal of majority rule.

SPENCER C. TUCKER

Course

Although Southern Rhodesia's white leaders attempted to change the country's name to Rhodesia, the British government and the international community refused to recognize either the name change or Rhodesian independence. Indeed, the British government soon applied economic pressure in the hope of compelling the white government of Rhodesia to accept majority rule. This included ending the link between the British pound and the Rhodesian currency, seizing certain Rhodesian economic assets, and banning the import of Rhodesian tobacco. Smith's government retaliated by defaulting on its British-guaranteed debts, which left the British government liable for these. In May 1968, United Nations Security Council Resolution 216 imposed economic sanctions. The U.S. government also banned the export of oil to Rhodesia. This economic pressure on Rhodesia took considerable time to take hold and was of limited success. Rhodesian chromium, a key strategic material, continued to find its way to European and North American buyers throughout the civil war and greatly helped prop up the economy.

Meanwhile, black Rhodesian nationalists had taken up arms. Two insurgent groups bent on achieving majority rule came to the fore. These were ZAPU, led by Joshua Nkoma, and ZANU, led by Reverend Ndabaningi Sithole and later Robert Mugabe. Although united by their overarching political goal of majority rule and their leftist orientation, these two organizations remained bitter rivals throughout the conflict. Their hostility hampered coordination of effort and was grounded in tribal, ideological, and strategic differences. Incapable of reconciling their differences, both organizations mounted a series of limited incursions by small guerrilla units into Rhodesia in the late 1960s.

Mugabe's ZANU was dominated by the Shona ethnic group of eastern Rhodesia. ZANU's military wing was ZANLA. ZANU's leaders sought to follow the military precepts of Chinese Communist leader Mao Zedong (Mao Tse-tung) in basing their insurgency largely on guerrilla warfare in the countryside.

Nkoma's ZAPU drew its strength chiefly from the minority Ndebele people in western Rhodesia. ZAPU's military wing, ZIPRA, commanded by General Lookout Masuku, operated from Zambia to the north of Rhodesia and Botswana

to Rhodesia's west. ZAPU's chief foreign government supporter was the Soviet Union. ZAPU favored the Marxist-Leninist approach of mobilizing urban workers. It adopted the Soviet model of a national liberation struggle, with an emphasis on building up a conventional force in Zambia that would be capable of defeating the Rhodesian regime in open battle.

For much of the 1960s, these black guerrilla campaigns were ineffective. The infiltrators were easily detected and destroyed by Rhodesian security forces. This changed, however, with the collapse of Portugal's African colonial empire. The former Portuguese colony of Mozambique, which had an extensive border with Rhodesia to its east, became independent in 1975. Mugabe's ZANU developed a close relationship with Mozambique's new government led by President Samora Machel, who threw his regime solidly behind the insurgency. The long border between the two countries greatly aided insurgent operations. Operating from secure bases in Mozambique and supported by the People's Republic of China, ZANU became the leading guerrilla force.

ZANU grew more radical politically and underwent a split when Reverend Ndabaningi Sithole, who favored discussions with the Rhodesian government, was challenged by Mugabe on the latter's release from detention by the minority white Rhodesian government of Prime Minister Ian Smith in 1974. Both ZANU groups continued to use that name following their split. ZANLA posed by far the greatest military threat to the Rhodesian government, while ZIPRA, ZAPU's military force, had few fighters within Rhodesia. Meanwhile, the escalating war gave rise to sustained regional and international attempts to secure a negotiated settlement between the Smith regime and ZANU and ZAPU, all of which met failure.

Increasingly benefiting from the training and equipment obtained from the Soviet Union, China, Tanzania, Algeria, and Ghana, ZANU intensified its incursions into Rhodesia, attacking white farmsteads and establishing a base of political support among the rural black population in the northeastern part of the country.

The Rhodesians responded by creating operational sectors that integrated static defenses (free-fire zones and extensive mine belts), population control (food control, martial law, and resettlement programs), and innovative tactical and operational methods. The latter maximized the use of air and ground assets by fusing them into rapid-response fire forces that utilized light helicopters to provide fire support and mobility for light infantry units charged with tracking down and destroying guerrilla units. The fire forces benefited from the Rhodesian military's superior intelligence-gathering apparatus. Elite formations such as the Rhodesian Light Infantry, the Selous Scouts, the Grey's Scouts, and the Rhodesian Special Air Service specialized in patrolling the countryside, tracking down infiltrating guerrilla bands, and vectoring air and ground forces to destroy insurgent units. A joint military operations center, established in 1978, coordinated the efforts of the various branches of Rhodesia's security forces and functioned as a clearinghouse for intelligence collected in the field.

Particularly noteworthy was the Selous Scouts (1973–1980), an elite multiracial all-volunteer special forces regiment of the Rhodesian Army and clearly one of the most effective counterinsurgency forces in history. Named for renowned explorer, hunter, and soldier Frederick Courtney

Selous, they were commanded by Lieutenant Colonel Ronald Reid-Daly. The first racially integrated unit and the first to have black officers in the Rhodesian military, the Selous Scouts trained and lived together and operated in small teams. The unit included turned rebels, which enabled the scouts to more easily adapt to changing enemy tactics. The scouts trained to operate like rebel units, were qualified in all sorts of weapons, and were parachute qualified.

With so many black members, the Selous Scouts could pretend to be their enemy. Probably their most famous operation was the Nyadzonya Raid, carried out some 60 miles inside Mozambique on August 9, 1976. Some 80 Selous Scouts drove into the Nyadzonya ZANLA base camp and opened fire on their unsuspecting enemy. The Selous Scouts claimed at the time to have killed 300 ZANLA and 30 Mozambique Armed Forces personnel, but documentation subsequently captured suggested that 1,028 were killed. The Selous Scouts suffered only 4 men wounded.

Although the Rhodesian forces enjoyed a tactical advantage over the guerrillas throughout the war, military successes alone could not produce a victory in what was fundamentally a political struggle. Smith's regime failed to address the underlying political, social, and economic grievances exploited by the guerrillas in their effort to gain legitimacy or to mobilize the support of the country's black population. Without such a comprehensive strategy, the white government's position deteriorated throughout the late 1970s.

In 1976, under pressure from the leaders of the Frontline States, Nkomo joined his archrival Robert Mugabe to form the Patriotic Front (PF). Following the collapse of Portuguese colonial authority in

Mozambique and Angola, Rhodesia was in effect entirely surrounded by hostile territory except for its southern border with South Africa, which had supported the Smith regime but never officially recognized it. South Africa now scaled back its assistance, recalling the ground troops, helicopters, and aircrews it had loaned to the Smith regime. South African leaders also began to pressure Rhodesia to enter into a dialogue with the guerrillas. Some Rhodesians were to claim that the embittered history between British-dominated Rhodesia and Afrikaner-dominated South Africa was partly behind the South African move. Smith charged in his memoirs that Rhodesia was the "sacrificial lamb" in South African prime minister John Vorster's policy of détente with the black African states. In 1976 the South African and U.S. governments worked together to press Smith to agree to a form of majority rule. Although the Smith government offered more concessions, those proved insufficient to end the war.

Meanwhile, the effects of the economic sanctions were adversely affecting Rhodesia's economy, constraining the ability of government forces to secure fuel and spare parts. Finally, the increasing emigration of whites who could see no end to the war and who found the government's growing demands for military service increasingly burdensome created a serious shortage of military manpower. Ultimately some 70 percent of the Rhodesian army was black.

Rhodesian military action intensified in the final stages of the war, including spectacular cross-border operations that targeted guerrilla camps in Zambia and Mozambique. These were a microcosm of the Rhodesian counterinsurgency effort. In tactical and operational terms, they attested to the Rhodesian security forces' ability

to keep ZANU and ZAPU off balance through a deft combination of air assaults and highly mobile motorized columns of light infantry. The operations resulted in the dispersal of hundreds of guerrillas, the destruction of insurgent supply stocks and weapons, and the erosion of the black nationalists' morale. Strategically and politically, however, the cross-border raids may have positively hurt the Rhodesians by highlighting their flagrant disregard for their neighbors' sovereignty and intensifying international condemnations of the white majority government.

By early 1978, the Rhodesian armed forces were clearly on the defensive. With no more than 25,000 men and with limited air assets, they were not able to defend the country's long borders and had been forced into the defense of key areas (referred to as "vital asset ground") and essential lines of communication to South Africa. Much of Rhodesia became "no-go areas." In desperation, the government resorted to biological warfare, knowledge of which only became public in the 1990s. Water sources along the Mozambique border were deliberately contaminated with cholera and warfarin sodium, and food stocks were laced with anthrax spores. While these had little impact on the insurgents, they led to considerable suffering by the civilian population. Perhaps 10,000 contracted anthrax and 200 died.

The morale of die-hard Rhodesian whites was dealt a particularly harsh blow with the downing on September 3, 1978, of the Air Rhodesia civilian Vickers Viscount airliner *Hunyani* by ZIPRA insurgents with a surface-to-air missile. The insurgents then massacred the survivors, and 56 people died. A second Viscount airliner, the *Umniati,* was similarly downed on February 12, 1979. None of its 59 passengers and crew survived. The insurgent reach was further demonstrated and white Rhodesian morale dealt another serious blow in December 1978 when ZANLA insurgents penetrated the outskirts of Salisbury and, employing rockets and incendiaries, set fire to the country's most heavily defended economic asset, the main oil storage depot. Half a million barrels of petroleum comprising Rhodesia's strategic oil reserve went up in smoke.

The Rhodesian Army continued its efforts to defend vital areas while also carrying out raids into the no-go areas and into neighboring states. In April 1979 Rhodesian special forces raided Nkomo's residence in Lusaka, Zambia, in an attempt to assassinate him. Warned of the attempt (by whom is not known), Nkomo and his family left a few hours before it occurred. In a considerable blow to military morale, in 1979 some special forces units were accused of using counterterrorist operations to carry out ivory poaching and smuggling. Colonel Reid-Daly, commander of the Selous Scouts, was court-martialed and dismissed for insubordination. Support for the insurgents was now growing among the black soldiers of the Rhodesian Army. By late 1979 most of some 122,000 guerrillas inside Zimbabwe were from ZANLA, which also counted another 16,000 outside the country.

By 1978 it was apparent to almost all that a deal had to be struck, but talks failed to bring the two sides to an agreement. Bishop Abel Muzorewa formed a new party, the United African National Council; Sithole had also formed a breakaway party from ZANU, known as ZANU Ndonga. On March 3, 1978, Smith struck an agreement with Muzorewa and Sithole, known as the Internal Settlement. This would lead to the holding of new elections in March 1979 in which black Africans would be in the majority for the first time.

This arrangement did not involve the Patriotic Front, however. Finally, in the September 1979 Lancaster House Agreement, the legal status of the British colony of Southern Rhodesia was restored in preparation for free elections and independence as Zimbabwe.

The Rhodesian Bush War remains a classic case study of a conflict that the counterinsurgents managed to win militarily but lost politically. Lacking the resources and the willingness to engage in civic action programs, Rhodesians made few serious attempts to win the hearts and minds of the rural black population. The failure to do so allowed the insurgents to establish the one aspect of the struggle that mattered the most: the contest for political legitimacy.

SEBASTIAN H. LUKASIK
AND SPENCER C. TUCKER

Consequences

The Rhodesian Bush War claimed 1,361 Rhodesian security forces members and more than 10,000 insurgents killed. It also took the lives of 1,468 white and 7,790 black civilians.

Britain resumed control for a brief period in 1979–1980, when the country was known as Zimbabwe-Rhodesia. The interim government was headed by Bishop Abel Muzorewa, but Robert Mugabe's ZANU dominated. With virtually all its 122,000 fighters outside Rhodesia at the time of the cease-fire in December 1979, ZANU had an immense advantage in the subsequent struggle for political power. Unable to resolve long-standing differences, Reverend Ndabaningi Sithole and Joshua Nkomo registered for the upcoming national elections as ZAPU members, while Mugabe's party campaigned as the ZANU-PF.

A guerrilla reads his rifle serial number to a Patriotic Front Liberation officer on January 3, 1980, prior to entering a cease-fire point during the Rhodesian Bush War. (AFP/Getty Images)

In the Zimbabwe independence elections of February 1980, Mugabe's ZANU-PF was swept into office, while ZAPU failed to win any seats. On April 18, 1980, Zimbabwe was declared independent, with Mugabe as prime minister. ZANU-PF has held power in Zimbabwe ever since.

Opposition to the 1980 election results, which many Zimbabweans saw as a Shona takeover, soon erupted in violence and in the Matabeleland Massacres of January 1983 some 20,000 Matabele were killed. An equal number were interned and tortured in military internment camps. This only ended after Nkomo and Mugabe reached a unity agreement in 1987 that merged ZAPU with ZANU-PF. Nkomo then received a largely ceremonial government position, which he held until his death in July 1999.

In late 1987 the position of prime minister was substituted for that of executive president, which combined the posts of head of state and head of government. Mugabe thus gained more power. The rigged national elections in March 1990 saw another sweeping victory for Mugabe, whose party claimed 117 of the 120 contested seats. In the 1990s workers and students often took to the streets to express their growing dissatisfaction with Mugabe's increasingly authoritarian rule. In 1996, civil servants and many health care workers went on strike over their low salaries. The health of the Zimbabwean people also underwent a considerable decline, and HIV was widespread.

Land reform was a major issue, with whites continuing to hold some 70 percent of the arable land. In 2000 Mugabe moved to forcibly take this land and distribute it among his supporters. Poor management of the process coupled with corruption, droughts, and a drop in external financial support led to a sharp decline in agricultural production, traditionally the country's leading export area. Zimbabwean living standards also fell, and the country faced a persistent health crisis with outbreaks of cholera.

In addition to ruining his country economically and widespread and persistent election fraud, Mugabe has also been accused of extensive human rights abuses. In 2002 the United States imposed a credit freeze on the Zimbabwean government, and in 2002 Zimbabwe was suspended from membership in the Commonwealth of Nations. Mugabe responded by ending his country's membership the next year.

In September 2008, following another election in which the opposition Movement for Democratic Change–Tsvangirai was generally believed to have won a majority of one seat in the lower house of parliament, a power-sharing agreement was reached between Morgan Tsvangirai and President Mugabe whereby Tsvangirai became prime minister. He served in that position from 2009 to 2013. In December 2008, a number of ZAPU members voted to withdraw again from ZANU-PF.

In December 2010, Mugabe threatened to expropriate all remaining privately owned companies in Zimbabwe unless sanctions against his country were lifted. He has also been outspoken in his opposition to LGBT rights. Mugabe was reelected president in 2013, garnering an announced 61 percent of the vote. In 2016 Mugabe continued in power, at the age of 92.

SPENCER C. TUCKER

Timeline

| 1855 | English explorer David Livingstone, exploring Southern Africa, sees the 328-foot waterfall on the Zambezi River. Livingstone names the falls, which today straddles the Zambia and Zimbabwe border, Victoria Falls. The local name is Musi-oa-Tunya (the smoke that thunders). |

1888

| October 29 | Lord Salisbury grants Cecil Rhodes a charter for the British South Africa Company. |

1889

| July | Queen Victoria grants a royal charter to the British South Africa Company in Zimbabwe. |

| October 29 | Rhodes uses an agreement reached with King Lobengula of the Ndebeles as the legal basis for the British South Africa Company in present-day Zimbabwe, modeled after the old East India Company. Its powers include the right to annex and administer land, raise its own police force, and establish settlements within its own boundaries. |

Rhodes persuades King Lobengula to sign away his powers over the Ndebele kingdom in Zimbabwe.

1890–1899	British settlers led by Rhodes march north from South Africa and appropriate vast stretches of arable land.
1895	The new territory is officially named Rhodesia after Cecil Rhodes.
1898	The British government recognizes the name of Rhodesia.
1902	
March 26	Rhodes dies and is buried in a tomb in the Matopos Hills of Rhodesia.
1914–1918	World War I sees fighting in Rhodesia, orchestrated by German colonel Paul Emil von Lettow-Vorbeck.
1923	
September 12	Following the rejection of union with South Africa in a 1922 referendum, the British government annexes Southern Rhodesia as a crown colony.
October 1	The first constitution for the new Colony of Southern Rhodesia comes into force, with Charles Patrick John Coghlan becoming the first premier of Southern Rhodesia.
1939–1945	During World War II, Southern Rhodesian military units earn distinction in fighting in Africa, Italy, and Southeast Asia.
1952	Joshua Nkomo forms and heads the African National Congress, Rhodesia's first black nationalist political party.
1953	
August 1	The British government creates the Federation of Rhodesia and Nyasaland, also known as the Central African Federation. It includes Southern Rhodesia, Northern Rhodesia, and Nyasaland (present-day Malawi).
1962	
December 14	The Southern Rhodesian parliamentary elections are won by the white Rhodesian Front political party, which has called for independence for Southern Rhodesia without immediate black majority rule.
	Kenneth Kaunda forms North Rhodesia's first black-dominated government.
1964	
April 13	Ian Douglas Smith becomes prime minister of Southern Rhodesia and holds that position until November 11, 1965.

October 24	Northern Rhodesia becomes independent as the new state of Zambia. Prime minister Kenneth Kaunda is the first president. Zambia is a single-party state under the slogan "One Zambia, One Nation" until 1991, with Kaunda's socialist United National Independence Party the sole legal political party.
	Joshua Nkomo and Robert Mugabe are jailed in Southern Rhodesia after rivalries in the black nationalist movement become violent.
1965	
November 11	Prime Minister Smith proclaims the independence of the Republic of Rhodesia. Smith holds that post until June 1, 1979.
November 20	The United Nations (UN) Security Council calls for a boycott of Rhodesia.
December 28	The United States bans the sale of oil to Rhodesia.
1966	
April 16	Prime Minister Smith breaks Rhodesian diplomatic relations with Britain.
1968	
May 29	UN Security Council Resolution 253 imposes sanctions on Rhodesia.
1970	
March 17	The United States casts its first veto in the UN Security Council, killing a resolution to condemn Britain for failure to use force to overthrow the white-ruled government of Rhodesia.
1971	Rhodesian bishop Abel Muzorewa forms the African National Council to open negotiations with Prime Minister Smith.
1974	Under pressure from guerrilla groups, Prime Minister Smith releases black leaders for peace talks, but the talks fail.
1976	
March 3	Mozambique closes its border with Rhodesia.
	Black Rhodesian insurgent leaders Joshua Nkomo, exiled in Zambia, and Roger Mugabe, in Mozambique, merge their guerrilla forces in a pact that lasts until 1979.

1977

August 31

Smith, espousing racial segregation, wins the Rhodesian general election with 80 percent of the vote from the overwhelmingly white electorate.

1978

March 3

Smith signs an agreement with moderate black leaders who have pledged to eschew war and bring black majority rule into effect by December 31. Bishop Muzorewa, nationalist Ndabaningi Sithole, and Chief Jeremiah Chirau are to form a transitional government that will pave the way for new elections. Smith agrees to step down following elections in 1979.

1979

January

A new constitution is approved by referendum in which the vast majority of voters are white.

April 10

The first democratic parliamentary elections are held. Bishop Abel Tendekayi Muzorewa's United African National Congress wins 51 seats. The Zimbabwe African National Union (ZANU) led by Ndabaningi Sithole wins 12 seats.

May 29

Bishop Muzorewa is sworn in as the first black prime minister of Zimbabwe-Rhodesia, the name given to the country in the brief period before full independence.

May 31

Zimbabwe proclaims its independence following the British-brokered cease-fire.

June 1

The government of Zimbabwe-Rhodesia takes office under the internal settlement negotiated between the government of Rhodesia and moderate African nationalists. Ian Smith steps down as prime minister, replaced by Josiah Zion Gumede as president and Abel Tendekayi Muzorewa as prime minister.

December 21

The Lancaster House Agreement is signed in London. It ends biracial rule in Zimbabwe-Rhodesia following negotiations between representatives of the Patriotic Front (PF), consisting of the Zimbabwe African People's Union (ZAPU) and ZANU, and the Zimbabwe-Rhodesia government, represented by Bishop Muzorewa and Ian Smith.

1980

March 4

Mugabe's ZANU-PF wins the parliamentary election. Zimbabwe-Rhodesia is then renamed Zimbabwe.

| April 18 | Zimbabwe's formal independence from Britain is proclaimed. Canaan Banana, a Methodist theologian, is president until 1987. Mugabe is prime minister and holds real authority. |

1987

| December 31 | Mugabe is sworn in as Zimbabwe's first executive president. Nkomo rejoins the Zimbabwe government as vice president. Mugabe goes on to establish a dictatorial regime and remains president in 2016. |

SPENCER C. TUCKER

Further Reading

Abbott, Peter, and Philip Botham. *Modern African Wars: Rhodesia, 1965–80.* Oxford, UK: Osprey, 1986.

Baxter, Peter. *Selous Scouts: Rhodesian Counter-Insurgency Specialists.* Solihull, UK: Helion, 2011.

Bhebe, Ngwabi, and Terrence Ranger, eds. *Soldiers in Zimbabwe's Liberation War.* Portsmouth, NH: Heinemann, 1995.

Binda, Alexandre. *The Saints: The Rhodesian Light Infantry.* Johannesburg: 30° South Publishers, 2007.

Brent, W. A. *Rhodesian Air Force: A Brief History, 1947–1980.* Kwambonambi, South Africa: Freeworld Publications, 1987.

Cilliers, Jackie. *Counter-Insurgency in Rhodesia.* Dover, NH: Crom Helm, 1984.

Compagnon, Daniel. *A Predictable Tragedy: Robert Mugabe and the Collapse of Zimbabwe.* Philadelphia: University of Pennsylvania Press, 2011.

Geldenhuys, Preller. *Rhodesian Air Force Operations with Air Strike Log.* Durban, South Africa: Just Done Productions, 2007.

Hill, Geoff. *Battle for Zimbabwe: The Final Countdown.* Cape Town: Zebra, 2003.

Hoffman, Bruce, Jennifer M. Taw, and David Arnold. *Lessons for Contemporary Counterinsurgencies: The Rhodesian Experience.* Santa Monica, CA: Rand, 1991.

Kalley, Jacqueline Audrey. *Southern African Political History: A Chronology of Key Political Events from Independence to Mid-1997.* Westport, CT: Greenwood, 2003.

Kriger, Norma J. *Guerrilla Veterans in Post-War Zimbabwe: Symbolic and Violent Politics, 1980–1987.* New York: Cambridge University Press, 2003.

Lake, Anthony. *The "Tar Baby" Option: American Policy toward Southern Rhodesia.* New York: Columbia University Press, 1976.

Lyons, Tanya. *Guns and Guerilla Girls: Women in the Zimbabwean National Liberation Struggle.* Trenton, NJ: Africa Research and Publications, 2004.

Meredith, Martin. *Our Votes, Our Guns: Robert Mugabe and the Tragedy of Zimbabwe.* New York: PublicAffairs, 2003.

Meredith, Martin. *The Past Is Another Country: Rhodesia, 1890–1979.* London: A. Deutsch, 1979.

Moore, D. S. *Suffering for Territory: Race, Place, and Power in Zimbabwe.* Durham, NC: Duke University Press, 2005.

Moorecraft, Paul, and Peter McLaughlin. *The Rhodesian War: A Military History.* Barnsley, UK: Pen and Sword Military, 2008.

Muzondidya, James. *Walking on a Tightrope: Towards a Social History of the Coloured Community of Zimbabwe.* Trenton, NJ: Africa Research and Publications, 2005.

Norman, Andrew. *Robert Mugabe and the Betrayal of Zimbabwe.* Jefferson, NC: McFarland, 2003.

Nkomo, Joshua. *Nkomo: The Story of My Life.* London: Methuen, 1984.

Nyarota, Geoffrey. *Against the Grain.* Cape Town, South Africa: Struik Publishers, 2006.

Ranger, Terence. *Peasant Consciousness and Guerrilla War in Zimbabwe: A Comparative Study.* Harare: University of Zimbabwe, 1985.

Reid-Daly, Ron, and Peter Stiff. *Selous Scouts: Top Secret War.* Johannesburg: Galago Publishing, 1983.

Rogers, Anthony. *Someone Else's War: Mercenaries from 1960 to the Present.* London: HarperCollins, 1998.

Sibanda, Eliakim M. *The Zimbabwe African People's Union, 1961–87: A Political History of Insurgency in Southern Rhodesia.* Trenton, NJ: Africa Research and Publications, 2005.

Smith, David. *Mugabe.* London: Sphere, 1981.

Smith, Ian. *The Great Betrayal: The Memoirs of Ian Douglas Smith.* London: John Blake Publishing, 1997.

Thomas, Scott. *The Diplomacy of Liberation: The Foreign Relations of the ANC since 1960.* London: I. B. Tauris, 1995.

Wall, Dudley. *Insignia and History of the Rhodesian Armed Forces, 1890–1980.* Durban, South Africa: Just Done Productions, 2009.

Wood, J. R. T. *A Matter of Weeks Rather Than Months: The Impasse between Harold Wilson and Ian Smith; Sanctions, Aborted Settlements and War, 1965–1969.* Victoria, South Africa: Trafford Publishing, 2008.

Wood, J. R. T. *Counter-Strike from the Sky: The Rhodesian All-Arms Fireforce in the War in the Bush, 1974–1980.* Johannesburg, South Africa: 30° South Publishers, 2009.

Wood, J. R. T. *So Far and No Further! Rhodesia's Bid for Independence during the Retreat from Empire, 1959–1965.* Victoria, South Africa: Trafford Publishing, 2005.

Nigerian Civil War (1967–1970)

Causes

The Nigerian Civil War, also known as the Biafra War, of July 6, 1967–January 15, 1970, was fought by the central government of Nigeria in an effort to end the nationalist aspirations of the Igbo (Ibo or Ebo) people of southeastern Nigeria who had declared their independence as the Republic of Biafra on May 30, 1967. Nigeria is Africa's most populous country and is home to more than 500 different ethnic groups speaking as many different languages and marked by religious and cultural differences. Nigeria is bordered by Benin to the west, Cameroon to the east, the Gulf of Guinea to the south, and Niger and Chad to the north. In 1967 Nigeria had a population of some 52.5 million.

Muslims of the linked Hausa and Fulani groups dominate the northern half of Nigeria, known as the Northern Region. The Western Region, which constitutes that part of Nigeria to the south and west of the Niger River, has a majority population of Yoruba people, while the southeastern portion of Nigeria, known as the Eastern Region, is home to a large population of Igbo people.

A number of native kingdoms had ruled the territory of present-day Nigeria, and slavery had been practiced throughout much of Africa. The British government announced in 1807 that it would act to prevent the international trade in slaves. In November 1851 as a part of its antislavery campaign but also as a pretext for making inroads into the Kingdom of Lagos, the British shelled Lagos, ousted the proslavery *oba* (ruler) Kosoko, and established a treaty with more amenable Oba Akitoye.

Britain annexed the Kingdom of Lagos and established it as a crown colony in August 1861. Britain then expanded its influence along the Niger Delta in the 1870s and 1880s. In 1879 the British created the United African Company, later the Royal Niger Company, under the leadership of Sir George Taubman Goldie.

The British territorial holdings received recognition by the other European colonial powers in the 1885 Congress of Berlin. In 1900, with the British controlling virtually all the territory constituting modern Nigeria, the British government took control of the Royal Niger Company, and on January 1, 1901, the territory became a British protectorate. In 1914 the British united the Muslim north and the mostly Christian south under a single administration.

World War I was a considerable boost to nationalism in Africa and Asia, but the colonial populations soon discovered that U.S. president Woodrow Wilson's proclamation in 1918 of the principle of self-determination of peoples applied only to Europeans. World War II had profound impact on Nigeria, which had provided fighting units for British Empire forces. The war also signaled the end of imperialism and heightened Nigerian nationalism.

Following the war, Britain granted more autonomy to Nigeria. British policy favored a federal structure for the rival ethnic regions while at the same time strengthening the preeminence of the Muslim north. In March 1953 in the Nigerian House of Representatives the leading advocate of Nigerian independence and democracy, Anthony Enahoro of the Acton Group

The Nigerian Civil War (1967–1970)

Casualties during Asaba Massacre (October 7, 1967)	
Nigerian Federal Troops	**Nigerian Civilians**
0 killed, 0 wounded	700+ killed, 500+ wounded

Foreign Support and/or Involvement, The Nigerian Civil War (1967–1970)

Nigeria	Biafra
Egypt	France
Great Britain	Portugal
Soviet Union	Czechoslovakia
France	South Africa
Sudan	Tanzania
Chad	Gabon
Niger	Ivory Coast
Syria	Zambia
Saudi Arabia	Rhodesia
Algeria	Spain
Bulgaria	Haiti
United States	
Israel	

Approximate Troop Strength, Opposing Forces (1970)

Nigeria	Biafra
120,000	30,000

Estimated Deaths, All Causes, The Nigerian Civil War (1967–1970)

Nigerian Forces	Biafran Forces	Civilians
25,000–50,000	10,000–20,000	1,930,000–2,930,000

Sources: Herbert Ekwe-Ekwe, *The Biafra War: Nigeria and the Aftermath* (Lewiston, NY: Edwin Mellen, 1990); Eghosa E. Osaghae, *Crippled Giant: Nigeria since Independence* (Bloomington: Indiana University Press, 1998).

(AG) party, proposed Nigerian independence for 1956. The motion was supported by both the AG and the National Council of Nigeria and the Cameroons (NCNC) party. Leader of the Northern People's Congress and the Saraduna of Sokoto, Al-haji Ahmadu Bello, in a countermotion replaced "in the year 1956" with the phrase "as soon as practicable." Another northern member of the House made a motion for adjournment, which was seen by the AG and the NCNC as a delaying tactic. Sharp differences regarding the timing and nature of self-government for Nigeria brought the May 1–5 Kano Riots in the northern city of that name. These clashes between northerners (Yorubas) and southerners (Ibos) claimed many lives and injuries and led to a sharp deterioration in the relationship between the Northern and Southern Regions of the country. Meanwhile, the search for oil, begun in 1908, finally reached fruition in 1956 with the discovery by Sun Oil and British Petroleum of major oil resources in the Eastern Region.

On October 1, 1960, Nigeria became an independent republic within the British Commonwealth. A federal structure of government was installed in 1963. While meant to provide a high degree of autonomy to the different regions of the country, in practice the central federal government dominated affairs. At independence Nigeria was divided into just three regions, but over time it continued to subdivide and reapportion provinces in response to the political demands of smaller ethnic groups. There are now dozens of states.

The country elected rulers democratically until January 1966. Tensions soon arose, with the new weak central government unable to control the discord sparked by the sharp differences that had arisen among the various peoples of the country. During January 15–16, 1966, dissident army officers led by leftists Major Emmanuel Ifeajuna and Major Chukwuma Kaduna Nzeogwu overthrew the government of Prime Minister Sir Abudakar Tafawa Balewa, who was killed in the coup d'état. The coup leaders were unable to bring to power their choice of jailed opposition leader Chief Obafemi Awolowo and turned instead to army head General Johnson Aguiyi-Ironsi, who became chief of state in a military government.

On July 29, 1966, Aguiyi-Ironsi was overthrown and killed in a new military coup. The coup leaders were mostly from the northern Hausa tribe, and their motivations were chiefly ethnic and religious. The new head of state was Lieutenant Colonel Yakubu Gowon. The coup, however, brought increased ethnic tensions and violence and the execution of a number of military officers and civilians, especially those of the southeastern Christian Igbo people, many of whom had held important positions in the government, the army, and commerce. This prompted the flight of many Igbos from the north to their own tribal area in the southeastern part of the country, which only strengthened sectionalism in the country. Southeastern Nigeria was rich in natural resources, especially agriculture and oil.

It was soon clear that tribal tensions might bring the secession of southeastern Nigeria, now led by Oxford University–educated Nigerian Army lieutenant colonel Chukwuemeka Odumegwu Ojukwu. In January 1967, central government leader and northerner Colonel Gowon and Ojukwu met in the Aburi Conference to try to reach a peaceful solution to the crisis. Ojukwu, however, declared himself unhappy with the negotiations, which envisaged a renewed federal structure, and he moved toward secession.

On May 30, 1967, the southeastern region of Nigeria declared itself independent as the Republic of Biafra, with Ojukwu as president. Gowon and the Nigerian central government refused to accept the secession, and Gowon sent the Nigerian Army into Biafra on July 6, beginning the Nigerian Civil War.

SPENCER C. TUCKER

Course

On July 6, Colonel Yakubu Gowon, leader of the Nigerian central government, ordered some 12,000 troops of the Nigerian Army into the breakaway southeastern part of Algeria, which had proclaimed itself the Republic of Biafra and was led by

Lieutenant Colonel Chukwuemeka Odu-megwu Ojukwu, now its president. The invaders were soon driven out. The hast-ily organized Biafran forces then took the offensive, invading the midwestern part of Nigeria and capturing the city of Benia on August 9.

In the ensuing struggle the central gov-ernment of Nigeria enjoyed the advantages of overwhelming manpower and equip-ment resources. In September its reorga-nized forces again took the offensive, and during the course of the next nine months they occupied about half of Biafra. They were finally halted by Biafran forces de-fending their capital city of Umuahia.

In August 1967, Biafran forces launched an offensive across the Niger River and captured Benin City. They then continued west but were stopped at Ore and pushed back to the Niger by the Nigerian 2nd Di-vision under Colonel Murtala Muhammed. At Asaba, the Biafrans withdrew across the Niger to the Biafran city of Onitsha. The Biafrans then blew up the eastern spans of the bridge to prevent the Nigerian govern-ment forces from following.

The federal troops entered Asaba on Oc-tober 5 and soon began ransacking houses and killing civilians, claiming that they were Biafran sympathizers. The city lead-ers called for the inhabitants to assemble on the morning of October 7, hoping to end the violence through a show of support for "One Nigeria." Hundreds of civilians—men, women, and children, many wear-ing ceremonial garb—paraded along the main street, singing, dancing, and chant-ing "One Nigeria." The Nigerian soldiers then separated the men and teenage boys from the women and young children, and in a square at Ogbe-Osawa village, Major Ibrahim Taiwo ordered the men and boys machine-gunned to death. More than 700 were killed (this in addition to those slain earlier), some of them as young as 12 years old, in what is known as the Asaba Massa-cre. Federal troops remained in Asaba for some months, destroying much of the town and committing numerous rapes and other outrages. During October 17–19 in Opera-tion TIGER CLAW, the Nigerian forces cap-tured the major Biafran port city of Calabar.

The Nigerian Civil War was a major problem for the British government, led by Prime Minister Harold Wilson. He called for negotiations and a peaceful settlement, but his government also sought to maintain Nigerian national unity and prevent com-munist inroads in the region, and it agreed to supply arms to the Nigerian central gov-ernment and not to Biafra. Wilson justified this, as Britain was, in his words, a "tra-ditional supplier" of weaponry to Nigeria. This position brought sharp criticism in the House of Commons. Later when the Nigerian government's blockade of Bi-afra brought mass starvation there, parlia-mentary criticism of Wilson became even sharper. Wilson was not alone in arguing, however, that Ojukwu's policy of only al-lowing night relief flights so that he could simultaneously import arms contributed to the humanitarian catastrophe.

The Israeli government, which saw Ni-geria as a major influence in Africa, turned down requests from Biafra for weapons and sold arms to the central Nigerian government. Nigeria also ultimately pur-chased some arms from the Soviet bloc but maintained a generally pro-Western orien-tation. The French government, however, supplied arms to Biafra, leading Wilson in memoirs to sharply criticize President Charles de Gaulle for having prolonged the war. Meanwhile, peace negotiations in May 1968 in London and at Kampala in June failed to produce a settlement.

Biafran soldiers prepare to resist an attack by Nigerian federal troops in southeastern Nigeria on August 16, 1967. The Nigerian Civil War of 1967–1970 claimed an estimated one to two million lives. (AFP/Getty Images)

The United States, at the time very much preoccupied with the Vietnam War in Asia, recognized British predominance in the region and pursued a cautious policy of not selling arms to either side, although some private U.S. citizens did so. Washington did support the British goal of Nigerian unity and pushed for a peaceful resolution of the conflict. The leaders of the Soviet Union also abstained from intervention, clearly seeing the risks of being caught up in an unstable situation. Neither side wanted Nigeria to become a new Cold War battle zone.

As the conflict dragged on the death toll rose dramatically, especially in Biafra from starvation and disease, the result of the Nigerian government decision to employ a total blockade, including foodstuffs, in order to end the secession. The Nigerian government held that employing starvation against an enemy was a legitimate tool of warfare.

In September 1968, Nigerian central government troops again took the offensive. They captured Aba on September 4 and Owerri on September 16 before Biafran forces halted them. Nonetheless, the Nigerians had cut Biafra off from access to the sea, although an airlift of some food and arms was maintained through the Spanish colony of Fernando Po.

During November 15–10, 1968, Biafran forces carried out Operation HIROSHIMA, an unsuccessful attempt to recapture Onitsha on the Niger, which had been lost earlier to Nigerian government forces. In 1969 Biafra adopted one of the most progressive national constitutions in Africa. That February Biafran forces launched a surprise counteroffensive in an effort to reopen access to the sea. They reached the outskirts of Aba on March 3 but were halted there. On April 22, Nigerian Army forces captured the new Biafran capital of Umuahiarri. A stalemate in the fighting then took hold, but much of the Biafran civilian population was now starving as a result of the blockade that included food.

On June 1, 1969, speaking in the town of Ahiara, Ojukwu delivered what became known as the Ahiara Declaration. Drafted by the National Guidance Committee of Biafra, it sought to shame the world and encourage Biafran patriotism. The declaration sharply attacked the British government, accusing "Anglo-Saxons" of sins "against the world" in numerous genocides, including against the Biafran people. It also pointed out the "racist indifference to the suffering of black-skinned noncombatants" and affirmed that Biafrans were "the latest victims of a wicked collusion between the three traditional scourges of the black man—racism, Arab-Muslim expansionism and white economic imperialism." Biafra's struggle was "not a mere resistance" but a "positive commitment to build a healthy, dynamic and progressive state, such as would be the pride of black men the world over."

Also in June, Nigerian government forces, now numbering an overwhelming 180,000 men, began a final offensive to break through the Biafran defenses. During September 2–October 15 the Nigerian forces launched Operation OAU, an effort to capture the remaining Biafran cities. Although the Biafrans were heavily outnumbered, they were able to retain control of Umuahia and eventually recapture the cities of Owerri and Aba.

On January 7, 1970, General Odumegwu Ojukwu launched Operation TAIL-WIND,

the final Nigerian government offensive of the war. The fighting was centered in the towns of Owerri and Uli, both of which fell to the central government forces. On January 9, Ojukwu escaped by air to the Ivory Coast and asylum. On January 15, new president of Biafra Philip Effiong surrendered to Colonel Olusegun Obasanjo, ending the war.

SPENCER C. TUCKER

Consequences

The former Biafra was devastated by the war in terms of infrastructure, wealth, and primarily lives. Its population of 12 million before the conflict was reduced to some 10 million by its end. Most of the 2–3 million deaths were of children lost to starvation as a direct result of the Nigerian government blockade that caused massive food shortages and a lack of medicines. The International Red Cross estimated in September 1968 that 8,000–10,000 people were dying daily. Some scholars have argued that the Biafran War was in fact a genocide for which no perpetrators have been held accountable.

Igbos found themselves unable to recover lost jobs and properties (the Nigerian government claimed that the latter had simply been "abandoned"). Igbos also suffered economically from the Nigerian government decision to institute a new currency, which rendered worthless prewar currency held by inhabitants of the Eastern Region. Chukwuemeka Odumegwu Ojukwu, the former president of the breakaway Republic of Biafra who had fled into exile at the end of the war in 1970, was, however, allowed to return to Nigeria under a special pardon in 1983.

Oil revenues helped with reconstruction in the Eastern Region, although there were accusations of Nigerian government officials diverting resources meant for reconstruction in the former Biafran areas to their ethnic areas. The war also did little to reduce ethnic and religious tensions in Nigeria. Although laws were passed requiring that political parties not be structured along ethnic lines, these have been widely evaded in practice.

Since the civil war, Nigeria has alternated between short periods of democratic government and longer periods of military rule. Strongman president Yakubu Gowon remained in power until 1975; subsequent military rulers of the country included Ramat Mohammed (1975–1976), Olusegun Obasanjo (1976–1979), Muhammad Buhari (1983–1985), Ibrahim Babangida (1985–1993), and Sani Abacha (1993–1998). A civilian, Shehu Shagari, served as president during the years of the Second Nigerian Republic (1979–1983).

The 1970s saw considerable economic growth and development, fueled in large part by the exploitation of the country's considerable oil reserves. Even today the petroleum industry accounts for more than half of the Nigerian gross national product and most of its exports. Unfortunately, the considerable corruption that accompanied this has seen much of the revenue end up in the hands of a few rather than being used for development purposes. There have also been charges that the oil revenues have not been spread equally among the various areas of the country. Mismanagement has also retarded economic development.

Nigeria remained formally nonaligned during the rest of the Cold War years but nonetheless retained cordial relations with the United States and Great Britain. English remains Nigeria's official language. Nigeria also trades extensively with France, West Germany, and other Western nations.

In an effort to demonstrate its important position in Africa, Nigerian leaders have at times taken an important role in African crises, as in opposition to the Republic of South Africa's apartheid policies in the early 1980s. Nigeria's important contributions to the arts have been recognized in Chinua Achebe and Wole Soyinka, the first African Nobel laureate in literature. The current constitution was enacted on May 29, 1999, inaugurating the Nigerian Fourth Republic, which continues today.

Ethnic violence continues and remains a major problem. Especially worrisome is the conflict between Muslims and Christians. Since 2002, Nigeria has experienced attacks that have claimed more than 15,000 lives and resulted in the kidnapping of a number of children by the Islamic extremist Boko Haram group, which seeks to eradicate secular government and create a Muslim state under strict Sharia law in northern Nigeria. There has been considerable international criticism of the central Nigerian government and especially Goodluck Jonathan, Nigerian president during 2010–2015, for the failure to adequately address this threat.

SPENCER C. TUCKER

Timeline

1807	The British government acts to prevent the international slave trade.
1851	
November	As part of an antislavery campaign and as a pretext for making inroads into the Kingdom of Lagos, Britain

	bombards Lagos, ousting proslavery Oba Kosoko and establishing a treaty with the more amenable new ruler, Oba Akitoye.
1879	The British United African Company, later the Royal Niger Company, led by Sir George Taubman Goldie, establishes control of much of Nigeria.
1885	The Congress of Berlin establishes African boundaries and formalizes the British claim to what is known as the "Oil Rivers Protectorate."
1900	The British government assumes the governance of Nigeria.
January 1	The territory constituting Nigeria becomes a British protectorate.
1914	
January 1	The mostly Muslim north and the mostly Christian south are amalgamated, although separately administered, under British governor-general Lord Frederick Lugard.
1918	
January 8	U.S. president Woodrow Wilson proclaims in his Fourteen Points the principle of "self-determination of peoples."
1941	
August 14	In the Atlantic Charter of this date, U.S. president Franklin Roosevelt and British prime minister Winston Churchill pledge self-determination and sovereignty for "all peoples."
1946	The Richards Constitution, named for Nigerian governor-general Sir Arthur Richards, subdivides the Southern Region of Nigeria into Eastern and Western Regions. It also reasserts the British Crown's ownership of "all mineral oils" in Nigeria.
1951	
August	The National Council of Nigeria and the Cameroons (NCNC) party calls for independence in 1956.
1953	
March 31	In the House of Representatives, Nigeria's leading independence and prodemocracy advocate Anthony Enahoro of the Acton Group (AG) party proposes Nigerian independence in 1956. The motion is supported by the AG

and the NCNC. Leader of the Northern People's Congress and the Saraduna of Sokoto, Alhaji Ahmadu Bello, in a countermotion replaces "in the year 1956" with the phrase "as soon as practicable." Another Northern member of the House issues a motion for adjournment, which is seen by the AG and the NCNC as a delaying tactic.

May 1–5	Clashes between Northerners (Yorubas) and Southerners (Ibos) occur in the city of Kano in northern Nigeria, prompted by the differences over self-government. The Kondo Riots claim many lives and make cooperation between the different ethnic groups of Nigeria much more difficult, especially between the peoples of northern and southern Nigeria.
1956	Exploration efforts by Sun Oil–British Petroleum discover major petroleum deposits in the Eastern Region.
1960	
October 1	Nigeria becomes an independent republic within the British Commonwealth.
	Following a referendum, the southern part of the British Cameroons merges with the former French colony of the Republic of Cameroun to form the Federal Republic of Cameroon. The northern part of the British Cameroons votes to join Nigeria.
1966	
January 15–16	Dissident Nigerian Army officers overthrow the government of Prime Minister Sir Abudakar Tafawa Balewa, who is killed in the coup d'état. Unable to bring to power their choice, jailed opposition leader Chief Obafemi Awolowo, the coup leaders turn to army head General Johnson Aguiyi-Ironsi, who becomes chief of state in a military government.
July 29	Aguiyi-Ironsi's government is ousted by another military coup, and he is kidnapped and killed. The coup leaders are mostly from the northern Hausa tribe, and their motivations are chiefly ethnic and religious.
	The new chief of state is Lieutenant Colonel Yakubu Gowon. The coup also brings increasing ethnic tensions and violence and the executions of military officers and civilians, especially those of the southeast, predominantly Christian Igbos (Ibos or Ebos), many of whom had held important positions in the government, the

army, and commerce. A number of survivors flee to their own tribal area, the prelude to the secession of Biafra.

1967

January 4–5	Gowon and Ojukwu meet in the Aburi Conference to try to reach a peaceful solution to the crisis. Ojukwu declares himself unhappy with the negotiations, which envisage a renewed federal structure, and he moves toward secession.
May 27	Gowon announces a planned redistricting of Nigerian federation.
May 30	Ojukwu declares the independence of the Republic of Biafra.
July 6	In Operation UNICORD, Nigerian government forces invade Biafra.
Late July	Nigerian forces capture Bonny Island.
August 9	Biafra, having launched a counteroffensive in the Midwest Region, captures its capital of Benin.
September 20	Creation of the short-lived Republic of Benin in the Northwest Region with its capital at Benin City.
October 1–4	Nigerian forces capture the Biafran capital of Enugu.
October 4–12	The first Nigerian Army invasion of Onitsha occurs.
October 7	The Asaba Massacre takes place. Federal troops, having entered the city of Asaba on the Niger on October 5, accuse its citizens of being Biafran sympathizers, ransack property, and kill a number of civilians. Then on October 7, the soldiers round up men and teenage boys and machine-gun more than 700 of them to death.
October 17–19	In Operation TIGER CLAW, Nigerian forces capture the major Biafran port city of Calabar.
November	The first International Red Cross relief supplies arrive in Biafra.

1968

January 2–March 30	The second Nigerian Army invasion of Onitsha occurs.
March 31	In the Abagana Ambush, Biafran forces ambush a Nigerian force of 200 soldiers, killing 150 of them.
May–June	Peace negotiations in London in May and in Kampala in June fail to produce a settlement.
May 19	Nigerian forces capture Port Harcourt.

June 12	A "Save Biafra" media campaign begins in Great Britain.
July 17	The Israeli Knesset debates Israeli moral obligations regarding the Biafran genocide.
September	Nigerian central government troops again go on the offensive, capturing Aba (September 4) and Owerri (September 16) before the Biafrans halt them. Nonetheless, the Nigerian troops have cut Biafra off from access to the sea, although an airlift of food and arms is maintained through the Spanish colony of Fernando Po.
November 15–29	Operation HIROSHIMA occurs, an unsuccessful Biafran attempt to recapture Onitsha.

1969

February	Biafran forces launch a surprise counteroffensive in an effort to reopen access to the sea. They reach the outskirts of Aba on March 3 but are there halted. A ground stalemate ensues. Much of the Biafran civilian population is now starving as a result of the central government's blockade.
April 22	Nigerian Army forces capture the new Biafran capital of Umuahiarri.
June	Forces of the central Nigerian government, now numbering an overwhelming 180,000 men, begin a final offensive against the Biafran defenses and break through them.
June 1	Speaking in the town of Ahiara, Ojukwu delivers what becomes known as the Ahiara Declaration. Drafted by the National Guidance Committee of Biafra, it is a statement of the principles of the Biafran Revolution that also points out and condemns world acceptance of the Nigerian blockade of food imports into Biafra.
September 2–October 15	Nigerian central government forces launch Operation OAU, an effort to capture the remaining Biafran cities. Although the Biafran forces are heavily outnumbered, they are able to retain control of Umuahia and eventually recapture the cities of Owerri and Aba. The fighting claims more than 25,000 killed on both sides.
September 16	An uprising by the Agbekoyas occurs in the Western Region of Nigeria.

1970

January 7–12	Operation TAIL-WIND occurs. This final Nigerian government offensive of the war, led by General Odumegwu Ojukwu, takes place in the towns of Owerri and Uli, both

of which fall to the central government forces. The new president of Biafra, Philip Effiong, surrenders to Colonel Olusegun Obasanjo.

January 9   Ojukwu escapes by air to the Ivory Coast and asylum.

January 15   Biafra formally surrenders, bringing the war to a close.

SPENCER C. TUCKER

Further Reading

Achebe, Chinua. *There Was a Country.* Penguin, 2012.

Diamond, Larry. *Class, Ethnicity and Democracy in Nigeria: The Failure of the First Republic.* Basingstroke, UK: Macmillan, 1988.

Draper, Michael I. *Shadows: Airlift and Airwar in Biafra and Nigeria 1967–1970.* Aldershot, Hants, UK: Hikoki, 1999.

Dudley, Billy. *Instability and Political Order: Politics and Crisis in Nigeria.* Ibadan, Nigeria: Ibadan University Press, 1973.

Ekwe-Ekwe, Herbert. *The Biafra War: Nigeria and the Aftermath.* Lewiston, NY: Edwin Mellen, 1990.

Falola, Toyin. *The History of Nigeria.* Westport, CT: Greenwood, 1999.

Griffin, Christopher. "French Military Policy in the Nigerian Civil War, 1967–1970." *Small Wars & Insurgencies* 26(1) (2015): 114–135.

Kirk-Greene, A. H. M. *The Genesis of the Nigerian Civil War and the Theory of Fear.* Uppsala, Sweden: Scandinavian Institute of African Studies, 1975.

Levey, Zach. "Israel, Nigeria and the Biafra Civil War, 1967–70." *Journal of Genocide Research* 16(2–3) (2014): 263–280.

Madiebo, Alexander A. *The Nigerian Revolution and the Biafran War.* Enugu, Nigeria: Fourth Dimension Publishers, 1980.

Njoku, H. M. *A Tragedy without Heroes: The Nigeria-Biafra War.* Enugu, Nigeria: Fourth Dimension Publishers, 1987.

Ojiaku, Uche Jim. *Surviving the Iron Curtain: A Microscopic View of What Life Was Like Inside a War-Torn Region.* Baltimore: PublishAmerica, 2007.

Osaghae, Eghosa E. *Crippled Giant: Nigeria since Independence.* Bloomington: Indiana University Press, 1998.

O'Sullivan, Kevin. "Humanitarian Encounters: Biafra, NGOs and Imaginings of the Third World in Britain and Ireland, 1967–70." *Journal of Genocide Research* 16(2–3) (2014): 299–315.

Stremlau, John J. *The International Politics of the Nigerian Civil War, 1967–70.* Princeton, NJ: Princeton University Press, 1977.

Uche, Chibuike. "Oil, British Interests and the Nigerian Civil War." *Journal of African History* 49(1) (2008): 111–135.

U.S. Department of State. *Foreign Relations of the United States 1964–1968,* Vol. 24, *Africa.* Washington, DC: U.S. Government Printing Office, 1999.

Wilson, Harold. *The Labor Government 1964–1970. A Personal Record.* London: Weidenfeld and Nicolson, 1971.

Soviet-Afghan War (1979–1989)

Causes

The Soviet-Afghan War of December 24, 1979–February 15, 1989, was a major military conflict during the Cold War (1947–1991) that had great consequences for both the Soviet Union and Afghanistan. The basic cause of the Soviet-Afghan War was the effort of the Soviets to control the country.

Present-day Afghanistan is bordered by Pakistan to the south and east; Iran to the west; Turkmenistan, Uzbekistan, and Tajikistan to the north; and China to the northeast. Although landlocked, Afghanistan lies at the gateway of Europe and Asia. Afghanistan's geostrategic location has made it the object of would-be conquerors, but it has also suffered from considerable internal strife by contesting factions and tribal groups. Certainly Afghanistan has seen more than its share of warfare during the course of its history. Among notable conquerors of the territory that now constitutes Afghanistan have been Persian king Darius I (the Great) around 500 BCE and Alexander the Great of Macedonia in 330 BCE. The Arabs brought Islam in 642 CE. Mahmud of Ghazni, the most important ruler of the Ghaznavid Empire, conquered both eastern present-day Iran and modern Afghanistan and Pakistan during 997–1030. Genghis Khan and the Mogols took control of Afghanistan in 1219, while Timur (Tamerlane) established the Timurid dynasty in 1370. In the early 16th century, Babur captured Kabul. The area that constitutes present-day Afghanistan was not united as a single country until the 1700s. Islam was firmly established as the country's religion in the 19th century.

The British arrived in the 19th century, as both they and the Russians struggled over control of Afghanistan. The British were especially interested in securing Afghanistan as a buffer to protect their Indian empire. The British efforts in this regard ushered in a series of British-Afghan wars during 1838–1842, 1878–1880, and 1919–1921. As a consequence of the ability of the Afghans to retain their independence, the country has come to be called the "graveyard of empires."

In 1919 Amanullah Khan became emir of Afghanistan. In 1926 he declared Afghanistan a monarchy, with himself as king. Amanullah sought to capitalize on his early popularity to modernize his country through a number of reform measures, including schools for both boys and girls, a change in the centuries-old dress code for women, efforts to limit the power of the Loya Jirga (the grand assembly), and the inauguration of a new constitution that would guarantee civil rights for all Afghans. As would be the case to the present, the reforms were at odds with traditional Afghan practices and brought an armed rebellion in 1924, which was put down.

Beginning in late 1927, Amanullah embarked on an extensive tour of Europe, but growing opposition to his rule and the introduction of Western ways brought his forced abdication on January 14, 1929. After a failed effort to return to power later that year, he went into exile in Europe, dying there in 1960.

Following several other short-tenured rulers, on November 8, 1933, Mohammed Zahir Shah became king and was able to bring a semblance of stability to the country. Afghanistan was neutral in World War II, but after that conflict, in 1947 the British granted independence to the Empire of India. Unable to bridge the hostility between Hindus and Muslims, the British created two states: the predominantly Hindu but secular state of India and the Islamic state of Pakistan. Pakistan enjoys a long porous border with Afghanistan, and that country has frequently sought to influence Afghan affairs.

In September 1953, Afghan Army general Mohammed Daoud Khan, first cousin of the king, became prime minister. Daoud moved Afghanistan toward a close relationship with the Soviet Union. He also introduced a number of social reforms, including more rights for women and their access to higher education and the workforce. In 1961, the close Afghan-Soviet ties brought jet aircraft, tanks, and artillery at the heavily discounted price of $25 million. In January 1965, meanwhile, Afghan communists established the People's Democratic Party of Afghanistan (PDPA), led by Babrak Karmal and Nur Mohammad Taraki.

On July 17, 1973, Daoud seized power from King Mohammed Zahir Shah in a bloodless military coup. Daoud abolished the monarchy and named himself the country's first president. He continued the close Afghan-Soviet ties and in August 1975 secured an agreement whereby the Soviets agreed to provide economic assistance during a 30-year period.

In early 1978, now alarmed over growing Soviet influence, Daoud reduced the number of Soviet advisers in Afghanistan from 1,000 to 200. He also moved, albeit too late and ineffectively, against the Afghan communists. On April 19, 1978, on the occasion of a funeral for prominent leftist political leader Mir Akbar Khyber, up to 30,000 Afghans gathered to hear speeches by Aghan communist leaders Nur Muhammad Taraki, Hafizullah Amin, and Babrak Karmal. Daoud then ordered the arrest of the communist leaders. Taraki was caught after a week, but Karmal escaped to the Soviet Union, and Amin was merely placed under house arrest. Operating from his home and employing his family as couriers, Amin directed planning for a coup d'état against Daoud, who was now unpopular with many Afghans for his authoritarian rule.

On April 26 Daoud placed the Afghan Army on alert, but the next day anti-Daoud military units at Kabul International Airport were nonetheless able to launch the coup attempt. During April 27–28, army units both opposing and loyal to the government battled in and around Kabul. Daoud and most of his family were caught and executed in the presidential palace on April 28, the coup leaders announcing with some understatement that Daoud had "resigned for reasons of health." Soviet involvement in the coup, known as the Saur Revolution, is unclear, but Moscow certainly welcomed the change of government and soon concluded a treaty that renewed assistance to the new Afghan government.

On April 30, the country was renamed the Democratic Republic of Afghanistan (DRA); it would last until April 1992. Then on May 1, Nur Mohammad Taraki assumed the Afghan presidency. He was also the prime minister and secretary-general of the communist PDPA. Hafizullah Amin, who was foreign minister in the new government, was its driving force as the regime rooted out its opponents and embarked on an extensive modernization program that included women's rights and freedom of religion. It also implemented

Soviet-Afghan War Facts and Figures

Approximate Military Death Statistics for the Soviet-Afghan War (1979–1989)			
Died (All Causes)	Soviet Union	Democratic Republic of Afghanistan	Mujahideen
	15,000	26,000	75,000–90,000

Approximate Number of Afghan Civilian Deaths and Refugees/Internally Displaced Persons (1979–1989)	
Civilian Deaths (All Causes)	Refugees/Displaced Persons
1,240,000–2,000,000	8,300,000

Approximate Military Casualty Figures for Operation MAGISTRAL (November 19, 1987–January 10, 1988)			
	Soviet Union	Democratic Republic of Afghanistan	Mujahideen
Killed (All Causes)	320	1,000	1,500–3,000
Wounded	600	2,000	N/A

Sources: Rodric Braithwaite, *Afgantsy: The Russians in Afghanistan, 1979–1989* (New York: Oxford University Press, 2011); Antonio Giustozzi, *War, Politics, and Society in Afghanistan, 1978–1992* (Washington, DC: Georgetown University Press, 2000); Russian General Staff, *The Soviet-Afghan War: How a Superpower Fought and Lost* (Lawrence: University of Kansas Press, 2002).

an extensive land reform program. The majority of Afghan city dwellers either welcomed the reforms or were ambivalent about them. The secular nature of the reforms were, however, highly unpopular with the very religiously conservative Afghans in the countryside, where there was strong sentiment for traditionalist Islamic restrictions regarding women.

On February 14, 1979, U.S. ambassador to Afghanistan Adolph Dubs was taken hostage by Muslim extremists. That same day he was killed in the exchange of gunfire when Afghan security forces and their Soviet advisers stormed the hotel in Kabul where he was being held. The U.S. government protested the Soviet role.

Opposition was now building against the regime, and Afghan Muslim leaders soon declared a jihad against "godless communism." By August 1978 the Taraki regime faced an armed revolt that included the defection of a portion of the army.

On March 15, 1979, the army's 17th Division mutinied at Herat, killing some Soviet citizens there and holding the city for about a week until they were crushed by forces loyal to the government. Nonetheless, the Herat Mutiny (Herat Uprising) resulted in the deaths of between 3,000 and 17,000 people.

On March 27, 1979, Taraki was forced to appoint Amin premier. In these circumstances, in midyear U.S. president Jimmy Carter's administration began Operation CYCLONE, the extension of covert assistance to the conservative Islamic antigovernment mujahideen (freedom fighters, holy warriors) now fighting the Afghan communist government. This program, spearheaded by U.S. national security adviser Zbigniew Brzezinski, aided and trained the mujahideen through the Pakistani Inter-Services Intelligence (ISI). The mujahideen continued to make steady gains in the rural areas of the country.

On September 14, 1979, Amin ousted President Taraki, who was slain in the coup. This change of power was apparently accomplished without Soviet approval, and friction between the Soviets and Amin increased.

As the mujahideen registered steady gains in the countryside against the communist government, Moscow grew increasingly concerned. The Soviet leadership was then committed to the so-called Brezhnev Doctrine, elucidated by Soviet leader Leonid Brezhnev. First employed against the Czech Spring in Czechoslovakia in 1968, it held that the Soviet Union had the right to interfere militarily to prevent the overthrow of a communist government. Moscow was also fearful of the possible impact of an Islamic fundamentalist regime on the large Muslim population of Soviet Central Asia, specifically in the republics bordering Afghanistan. As a consequence, the Soviet leadership moved toward military intervention.

During the last months of 1979, the Brezhnev government dispatched some 4,500 Soviet advisers to assist the DRA while also allowing Soviet aircraft to conduct bombing raids against mujahideen positions. Soviet deputy defense minster Ivan G. Pavlovskii, who had played an important role in the Soviet invasion of Czechoslovakia, opposed a full-scale intervention, but his superior, Defense Minister Dmitrii Ustinov, convinced Brezhnev to undertake it, arguing that this was the only sure means to preserve the Afghan communist regime. Ustinov also postulated a short and victorious intervention. The deciding factor for Brezhnev was apparently Amin's coup and the death of staunch Soviet ally Taraki in September 1979. Beginning in November, the Soviets increased the size of their garrisons at the two air bases in Kabul and began quietly prepositioning forces just north of Afghanistan, most notably the Fortieth Army, composed largely of Central Asian troops.

SPENCER C. TUCKER

Course

On December 24, 1979, Soviet troops invaded Afghanistan. Moscow cited as justification the 1978 Treaty of Friendship, Cooperation and Good Neighborliness between the two countries and claimed that the Afghan government had invited in the Soviet troops. Deputy minister of internal affairs Lieutenant General Viktor S. Paputin commanded the operation. Elements of the 103rd Guards Airborne Division seized strategic installations in Kabul and established an air corridor into the Afghan capital by taking and holding Kabul International Airport. Meanwhile, armored columns of the Soviet's Fortieth Army crossed the border at Kushka in present-day Turkmenistan, with their objective being Kandahar by way of Herat. Other Fortieth Army elements crossed the Amu Daria River at Termez and proceeded toward Kabul along Highway 1.

Having secured the Kabul airport, on December 25 the Soviets began a massive airlift, flying three airborne divisions—the 103rd, 104th, and 105th—to Kabul, while the four motorized rifle divisions moved overland from the north. During December 25–28 the 105th Division occupied Kabul against considerable resistance from elements of the Afghan Army and the local population.

Afghan president Hafizullah Amin and his ministers were cut off in the presidential palace. On December 27 the Soviets attacked the palace, and Amin was killed either in the fighting or by execution. Soviet commander Viktor S. Paputin was

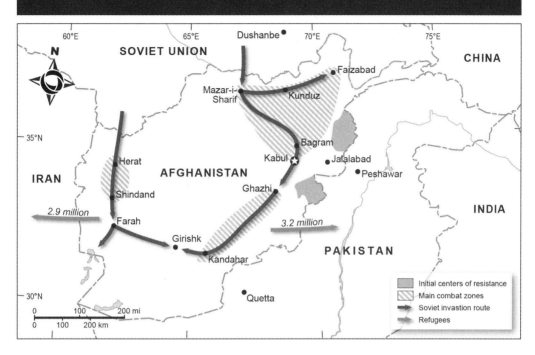

SOVIET INVASION OF AFGHANISTAN, 1979

also killed during the battle. On December 28 the Soviets installed Babrak Karmal, former Afghan vice president and then Afghan ambassador to Czechoslovakia, as president.

The more moderate Karmal attempted without great success to win popular support by portraying himself as a devoted Muslim and an Afghan nationalist. Meanwhile, Soviet forces occupied the major Afghan cities and secured control of the roads.

Unable to meet the Soviets in conventional battle, the mujahideen (freedom fighters, holy warriors) resorted to protracted guerrilla warfare, ambushing Soviet road-bound convoys and laying siege to several Soviet-occupied towns. During February 21–23, 1980, a popular Afghan uprising occurred in Kabul, but Soviet troops crushed it. Some 500 Afghans were killed, and 1,200 others were imprisoned.

The invasion of Afghanistan had immediate adverse international consequences for the Soviet Union. For one thing, it effectively ended détente. Having expended considerable effort to improving relations with the Soviet Union, U.S. president Jimmy Carter felt betrayed by Moscow and reacted swiftly and strongly to the invasion. On December 28 he publicly denounced the Soviet action as a "blatant violation of accepted international rules of behavior." On December 31 he accused Moscow of having lied about the reasons behind its intervention, and on January 3, 1980, he asked the U.S. Senate to delay consideration of the SALT II treaty. On January 23, 1990, in his State of the Union address, Carter warned that the Soviet action in Afghanistan constituted a serious threat to world peace, because should the Soviets be able to control Afghanistan, it would be able to dominate the Persian Gulf and thus be in position to interdict at will the flow of Middle East oil.

Carter then enunciated what became known as the Carter Doctrine, declaring that any effort to dominate the Persian Gulf would be interpreted as an attack on American interests, to be countered by force if necessary. Carter also moved to limit the transfer of technology and the sale of agricultural products, including grain, to the Soviet Union. He imposed restrictions on Soviet fishing privileges in U.S. waters, and he canceled U.S. participation in the 1980 Moscow Summer Games and called on America's allies to do the same.

Carter also called for increased defense spending and registration for the draft, pushed for creation of a rapid-deployment force capable of intervening in the Persian Gulf or other areas threatened by the Soviets, offered increased military aid to Pakistan, moved to enhance ties with the People's Republic of China, and approved expanded covert assistance to the mujahideen. These steps, except for the last, all had but limited impact. Key U.S. allies rejected both economic sanctions and the Olympic boycott. Also, other states, notably Argentina, offset the grain embargo by increasing their own grain sales to the Soviet Union. There was also little interest among the American public for involvement in Afghanistan.

Republican Ronald Reagan, who defeated Carter in the November 1980 presidential election, took an even harder stand toward the Soviet Union, which he characterized as an "evil empire." The Reagan administration poured vast sums of money into a massive military buildup to include development of a missile defense system, the Strategic Defense Initiative, known as "Star Wars" by its critics. This led Moscow to increase its defense spending, a major factor in the subsequent financial collapse of the Soviet Union.

In the spring of 1980 the Soviets mounted offensive operations. The Soviet strategy called for, in order, relieving besieged towns; driving the mujahideen from the towns, roads, and fertile agricultural regions back into the mountains; securing the frontier near the Khyber Pass to prevent the mujahideen from receiving weapons and other military supplies from Pakistan; and attacking and eliminating the mujahideen mountain camps.

The first two phases enjoyed considerable success. The Soviets employed jet aircraft to bomb rebel positions, followed by Mil Mi-24 armored helicopter gunships firing rockets and machine guns. Mil Mi-26 helicopters then ferried assault troops to attack the mujahideen in place.

Although the mujahideen inflicted significant casualties on the Soviets, they themselves suffered heavily and were driven from the towns and into the hills and mountains. The Soviets gradually increased the number of troops in Afghanistan to some 105,000 men, but this number was insufficient to defeat the insurgents. The Soviets never were able to control the mountainous areas where the guerrillas established their bases, nor did the Soviets always enjoy complete control of the fertile valleys, where the mujahideen continued to carry out hit-and-run attacks and secure much-needed Soviet weapons and equipment. The Soviets also were unable to seal the porous frontier with Pakistan, which remained a source of arms and equipment supplied by both Pakistan and the U.S. Central Intelligence Agency (CIA).

Frustrated, the Soviets responded with wanton attacks on villages. They also employed numerous small land mines that

Afghan anti-Soviet resistance fighters with their primitive arms in the mountains of eastern Afghanistan. (AFP/Getty Images)

killed or maimed many innocent civilian victims and, according to some sources, employed biological and chemical weapons in violation of the 1925 and 1972 Geneva protocols. The Soviets also expanded their air bases and brought in additional aircraft and equipment.

The mujahideen remained short of equipment and supplies and were bitterly divided among themselves, thanks to tribal and clan loyalties that prevented them from establishing a unified leadership. In May 1985, however, representatives of seven major mujahideen groups met in Peshawar, Pakistan, to try to establish a united front against the Soviets.

On May 4, 1986, in a bloodless coup engineered by the Soviet Union, Mohammad Najibullah, former head of the Afghan secret police, replaced Karmal as secretary-general of the communist

PDPA. In November 1987, Najibullah was elected president of Afghanistan for a seven-year term.

After meeting with new Soviet leader Mikhail Gorbachev, in October 1986 Najibullah offered the mujahideen a unilateral cease-fire agreement and a limited power-sharing arrangement; the mujahideen rejected these, and the war continued. As with the United States in the Vietnam War, the Soviet leadership found itself committed to waging a war that seemed to offer no acceptable ending.

As the Soviet military increased its offensives, the United States increased its aid to the mujahideen. This included food, vehicles, and weapons. Assistance provided by the CIA ran into the billions of dollars and became one of its most expensive and protracted operations. The most important CIA-supplied weapon was the shoulder-launched ground-to-air Stinger missile. It and the British-supplied Blowpipe proved to be key in defeating Soviet air-to-ground support and especially the Mil Mi-8 and Mil Mi-24 armored helicopter gunships. The seemingly unending war exacted a continued heavy toll as the Afghan fighters defeated several Soviet offensives. As casualties mounted, Moscow came under increased domestic criticism, including that by prominent dissidents such as Andrei Sakharov.

By 1986 the Soviet leadership, now headed by the reformist Gorbachev, began consideration of how it might extricate itself from what many observers characterized as the "Soviet Union's Vietnam." In April 1988, Gorbachev agreed to a United Nations (UN) mediation proposal worked out in Geneva between the warring parties that provided for the withdrawal of Soviet forces to occur during a 10-month period.

The Soviet withdrawal occurred in two phases: the first from May 15 to August 16, 1988, and the second from November 15, 1988, to February 15, 1989. The withdrawal was generally peaceful, with the Soviet military working out cease-fire agreements with local mujahideen insurgent commanders. The agreement allowed Soviet military advisers to remain in Afghanistan and provide aid assistance to the more than 300,000-man DRA Army. Moscow also continued to support the DRA with weapons and equipment totaling some $500 million a month.

SPENCER C. TUCKER

Consequences

The Soviet-Afghan War cost Soviet forces some 15,000 dead; 54,000 wounded, many of them seriously; and 417 missing. Afghan losses can only be approximated, but the best estimates are more than 1 million

Afghan mujahideen combatants and civilians killed and more than 5.5 million displaced, a large number of these relocating in northwestern Pakistan.

Afghanistan itself, fought over during a decade, was devastated by the fighting. Already one of world's poorest countries, after the war Afghanistan ranked, according to the UN, 170th of 174 nations in terms of wealth.

The Soviet-Afghan War was a major military defeat for the Soviet Union. The war had cost the Soviet forces considerable military equipment, seriously damaged the reputation of the Soviet Union's military, and further undermined the legitimacy of the Soviet system. Certainly the war's high financial cost was a major factor in the collapse of the Soviet Union in 1991. The Islamists held this to be the case, with the leader of the Al Qaeda Islamist terrorist organization Osama bin Laden attributing the dissolution of the Soviet Union to God "and the mujahideen in Afghanistan."

Unfortunately, the United States also lost interest in Afghanistan after the Soviet military withdrawal and extended only scant aid to try to influence events in that war-torn nation. The new administration of President William Clinton handed this over to Pakistan and Saudi Arabia. Pakistan quickly took advantage, developing close relations first with warlords and then with the Taliban, a group of radical young Islamists, to secure trade interests and routes. This brought much ecological and agricultural destruction, including the destruction of Afghan forests and the widespread cultivation of opium.

The Soviet Union continued to support the Republic of Afghanistan (1987–1992), and Afghan president Mohammad Najibullah, who declared martial law, increased the role of the PDPA and adopted policies favored by the hard-liners. Many if not most observers concluded that Najibullah would soon be driven from power by the mujahideen. Yet the Afghan Army, which appeared to be on the brink of collapse following the Soviet departure, proved more effective than it had ever been under the Soviets. In July 1989 it inflicted a surprising defeat on the rebel forces at Jalalabad. In October 1990, however, the mujahideen opened a major offensive, taking the provincial capitals of Tarin Kowt and Qalat.

Although they controlled much of the countryside, the mujahideen lacked the heavy weaponry required to secure the cities. Handicapped by the lack of unified command, they were also often at odds with one another. The war appeared to be a stalemate.

Najibullah's government, though it failed to win popular support, territory, or international recognition, remained in power until 1992. A major reason for its collapse was the refusal in 1992 of new Russian president Boris Yeltsin to sell oil products to Afghanistan because it did not want to support communists. The defection from the government side of General Abdul Rashid Dostam and his Uzbek militia in March 1992 further undermined Najibullah's power. On April 16, Najibullah's communist government fell to the mujahideen, who set up a new governing council.

On September 27, 1996, the more Islamic fundamentalist Taliban came to power in Afghanistan and ruled the country as the Islamic Emirate of Afghanistan until December 2001, with Kandahar as the capital. It secured diplomatic recognition from only three states: Pakistan, Saudi Arabia, and the United Arab Emirates. The Taliban enforced Sharia law and sharply curtailed women's rights. The Taliban's harsh policies included the deliberate destruction of

farmlands, tens of thousands of homes, and Afghan archaeological treasures. Hundreds of thousands of Afghans fled their homeland, most to Pakistan and Iran. On September 9, 2001, assassins claiming to be journalists killed Ahmed Shah Masood, head of the Northern Alliance and Afghanistan's most effective insurgent leader.

Widely believed to have been supported by the Pakistani ISI and military, the Taliban also granted safe haven to Saudi citizen bin Laden and his Islamic fundamentalist Al Qaeda terrorist organization. On September 11, 2001, Al Qaeda carried out a devastating attack on the United States. Its operatives commandeered four U.S. commercial airliners and crashed two of them into the twin towers of the World Trade Center in New York City and one into the Pentagon in Washington, DC. The passengers in the fourth plane, believed to be headed for the White House, fought back, and the plane crashed into a field in Pennsylvania. Nearly 3,000 people died in the attacks.

Bin Laden at the time denied responsibility (later he would admit it), but the U.S. government quickly established this. When the Taliban refused to hand over the Al Qaeda leadership, on October 7 U.S. forces supported by those of Britain invaded Afghanistan. Subsequently joined by other countries and working in concert with the Afghan Northern Alliance opposing the Taliban, the government was overthrown on November 27.

Subsequently, the Taliban reemerged as an insurgency movement to fight the American-backed administration of Hamid Karzai and the North Atlantic Treaty Organization International Security Assistance Force. The Afghanistan War that began in 2001, in many ways a legacy of the Soviet-Afghan War, continues.

SPENCER C. TUCKER

Timeline

1926
Amanullah Khan, who came to the throne as emir in 1919, declares Afghanistan to be a monarchy, with himself as king. Enjoying early popularity, Amanullah endeavors to modernize his country and initiates a reform program that includes schools for both boys and girls, a change in the centuries-old dress code for women, and efforts to limit the power of the Loya Jirga, the Afghan national council, with a modern constitution that guarantees civil rights. As would be the case up to the present, this modernization effort clashes with traditional Afghan practices and brings reaction in the form of the Khost Rebellion of 1924, which is put down.

1927–1928
Amanullah travels to Europe.

1929

January 14
Facing growing opposition to his rule, including armed revolt, Amanullah abdicates and goes into exile in India. After an unsuccessful effort to return to power in late 1929, he goes to Europe. He finally settles in Switzerland and dies there in 1960.

1933

November 8
Mohammed Zahir Shah becomes king of Afghanistan and brings a semblance of stability to the country.

1934
The United States formally recognizes Afghanistan.

1947
The Britain grant independence to India, creating two states from the Empire of India: the predominantly Hindu but secular state of India and the Islamic state of Pakistan. Pakistan enjoys a long porous border with Afghanistan and will frequently meddle in its affairs.

1953

September 7
Afghan Army general Mohammed Daoud Khan, first cousin of the king, becomes prime minister and seeks Soviet economic and military assistance. He also introduces a number of social reforms, including more rights for women.

1956
Soviet leader Nikita Khrushchev agrees to assist Afghanistan, and the two countries become allies.

1957
Under Daoud's reforms, Afghan women are allowed to attend university and enter the workforce.

1961	As a result of its close ties with the Soviet Union, Afghanistan acquires jet aircraft, tanks, and artillery, all at the heavily discounted price of $25 million.
1965	
January 1	The communist People's Democratic Party of Afghanistan (PDPA) is formally established, led by Babrak Karmal and Nur Mohammad Taraki.
1973	
July 17	General Daoud Khan overthrows his cousin King Mohammed Zahir Shah in a bloodless military coup, abolishes the monarchy, and names himself the country's first president. As president, Daoud continues the close ties with the Soviet Union.
1975	
August 30	The Soviet Union signs an agreement with Afghanistan in which the latter is to receive economic assistance during a 30-year period.
1978	
January–March	Now alarmed over growing Soviet influence in his country, Afghan president Daoud reduces the number of Soviet advisers from 1,000 to 200.
April 19	Alarmed over the attendance of 30,000 Afghans for speeches by Afghan communist leaders at a funeral for a prominent leftist political leader, Daoud orders the arrest of communist leaders. The effort is haphazard and ineffective. One of these individuals, Babrak Karmal, is simply placed under house arrest. He now directs a coup attempt against Daoud.
April 26	Belatedly aware of the threat against him, Daoud places the Afghan Army on alert.
April 27–28	Anti-Daoud military units at Kabul International Airport are able to launch a coup attempt as fighting erupts in and around Kabul. Daoud and most of his family are caught and executed in the presidential palace on April 28. The coup leaders announce that Daoud has "resigned for reasons of health." This transfer of power to the communists is known as the Saur Revolution.
April 30	Afghanistan is renamed the Democratic Republic of Afghanistan (DRA); it lasts until April 1992.

May 1	Nur Mohammad Taraki assumes the Afghan presidency. He is also the prime minister and the secretary-general of the communist PDPA. The new regime roots out its opponents and embarks on an extensive modernization program that includes women's rights and freedom of religion. It also implements an extensive land reform program. The government is widely supported in the cities but not in the very conservative countryside, with its traditional opposition to secularism and support for restrictions on women's rights.

1979

February 1	U.S. ambassador to Afghanistan Adolph Dubs is taken hostage by Islamic extremists and that same day dies in an exchange of gunfire between Afghan security forces and their Soviet advisers.
March 15–20	Opposition to the DRA government builds, and in the Herat Mutiny (Herat Uprising), soldiers of the Afghan Army's 17th Division mutiny, killing a small number of Soviet citizens and holding the city for five days before the rebellion is crushed. The number of dead in the uprising is variously estimated at between 3,000 and 17,000.
March 27	Taraki is forced to appoint Amin premier.
Midyear	U.S. president Jimmy Carter commences Operation CYCLONE, the Central Intelligence Agency (CIA) program of covert assistance to the conservative Islamic antigovernment mujahideen (freedom fighters, holy warriors) now fighting the Afghan communist government. The program operates through the Pakistani Inter-Services Intelligence (ISI).
September 14	Hafizullah Amin ousts President Taraki, who is slain in the coup. This change of power is apparently accomplished without Soviet approval, and it brings increased friction between the Soviets and Amin.
December 5	The Afghan government signs a friendship treaty with the Soviet Union, building on Soviet economic and military support given to Afghanistan since the early 1950s.
December 12	The Soviet Politbureau's inner circle, fearing an Iranian-style Islamist revolution and wary of Amin's secret meetings with U.S. diplomats in Afghanistan, decides to invade.

December 24	The Soviet Ministry of Defense orders its armed forces into Afghanistan. Elements of the 103rd Guards Airborne Division seize strategic installations in Kabul and establish an air corridor into the Afghan capital, while armored columns of four divisions of the Fortieth Army cross the border with Afghanistan at Kushka and at Termez.
December 27	Amin is killed, either in the fighting or by execution. Soviet commander Viktor S. Paputin is also killed during the battle for the capital of Kabul.
December 28	The Soviets install Babrak Karmal as president. The more moderate Karmal attempts to rally support by portraying himself as a devoted Muslim and Afghan nationalist.
1980	Resistance intensifies, with various mujahideen groups fighting Soviet forces and the DRA Army. In the first six months of the campaign, the Soviets commit more than 80,000 personnel. The United States, Pakistan, and Saudi Arabia provide arms and financial assistance to the mujahideen. The United States also leads a boycott of the Moscow Olympics.
1985	More than 5 million Afghans have now been displaced by the war, with many seeking refuge in Iran or Pakistan. New Soviet leader Mikhail Gorbachev says that he wants to end the war in Afghanistan. In order to bring a quick victory, the resulting escalation of troops to pacify the region leads to the bloodiest year of the war.
May	Representatives of seven major mujahideen groups meet in Peshawar, Pakistan, in an effort to establish a united front against the Soviets.
1986	The CIA begins supplying the mujahideen with Stinger antiaircraft missiles, enabling them to shoot down Soviet helicopter gunships.
May 4	In a bloodless coup engineered by the Soviet Union, Mohammad Najibullah, former head of the Afghan secret police, replaces Karmal as secretary-general of the PDPA.
October	After meeting with Soviet leader Mikhail Gorbachev, Najibullah offers the mujahideen a unilateral cease-fire agreement and limited power-sharing arrangement. They reject this, and the war continues.

1987

November   Najibullah is elected president of Afghanistan for a
                            seven-year term.

1988

April   Gorbachev agrees to a United Nations mediation pro-
                            posal worked out in Geneva between the warring parties
                            that provides for the withdrawal of Soviet forces during
                            a 10-month period. These occur in two phases: the first
                            from May 15 to August 16, 1988, and the second from
                            November 15, 1988, to February 15, 1989.

1989

February 15   The Soviet Union announces the departure of the last
                            Soviet troops. More than 1 million Afghans and 13,000
                            Soviet troops have died in the war. Civil war continues.

1992

April 16   Having launched a major offensive, the mujahideen
                            overthrow Najibullah's communist government. The
                            mujahideen then set up a new governing council.

1996

September 27   The more Islamic fundamentalist Taliban comes to
                            power and rules Afghanistan as the Islamic Emirate of
                            Afghanistan until December 2001, with Kandahar as
                            the capital. It secures diplomatic recognition from only
                            three states: Pakistan, Saudi Arabia, and the United Arab
                            Emirates. The Taliban enforces Sharia law and sharply
                            curtails women's rights. Hundreds of thousands of Af-
                            ghans will flee, most to Pakistan and Iran.

2001

March   Despite widespread international protests, the Taliban
                            carries out its threat to destroy Buddhist statues at Bami-
                            yan, claiming they are an affront to Islam.

September 11   The Taliban had granted safe haven to Saudi Osama bin
                            Laden and his Al Qaeda Islamic terrorist organization.
                            On this date Al Qaeda launches a devastating terrorist
                            attack on the United States, killing nearly 3,000 people.
                            The U.S. government quickly establishes Al Qaeda's
                            responsibility.

October 7   When the Taliban refuses to surrender the Al Qaeda
                            leadership, the United States, supported by the United
                            Kingdom, launches Operation ENDURING FREEDOM, the

invasion of Afghanistan. They are later joined by other forces, including the Afghan Northern Alliance.

November 23   The Taliban is overthrown. Later the Taliban will reemerge as an insurgency movement against the American-backed administration of Hamid Karzai, the North Atlantic Treaty Organization, and the International Security Assistance Force. That war, now fought between the Afghan Army and the Taliban, continues.

SPENCER C. TUCKER

Further Reading

Amstutz, J. Bruce. *Afghanistan: The First Five Years of Soviet Occupation.* Washington, DC: National Defense University Press, 1986.

Barfield, Thomas. *Afghanistan: A Cultural and Political History.* Princeton, NJ: Princeton University Press, 2012.

Borer, Douglas A. *Superpowers Defeated: Vietnam and Afghanistan Compared.* London: F. Cass, 1999.

Bradsher, Henry S. *Afghanistan and the Soviet Union.* Durham, NC: Duke University Press, 1983.

Braithwaite, Rodric. *Afgantsy: The Russians in Afghanistan, 1979–89.* New York: Oxford University Press, 2011.

Crile, George. *Charlie Wilson's War: The Extraordinary Story of the Largest Covert Operation in History.* New York: Atlantic Monthly Press, 2003.

Feifer, Gregory. *The Great Gamble: The Soviet War in Afghanistan.* New York: Harper, 2009.

Galeotti, Mark. *Afghanistan: The Soviet Union's Last War.* London: Frank Cass, 1995.

Giustozzi, Antonio Giustozzi. *War, Politics and Society in Afghanistan, 1978–1992.* Washington, DC: Georgetown University Press, 1999.

Goodson, Larry P. *Afghanistan's Endless War: State Failure, Regional Politics, and the Rise of the Taliban.* Seattle: University of Washington Press, 2001.

Harrison, Selig S., and Diego Cordovez. *Out of Afghanistan: The Inside Story of the Soviet Withdrawal.* New York: Oxford University Press, 1995.

Hauner, Milan. *The Soviet War in Afghanistan: Patterns of Russian Imperialism.* Lanham, MD: University Press of America, 1991.

Hilali, A. *US-Pakistan Relationship: Soviet Intervention in Afghanistan.* Burlington, VT: Ashgate, 2005.

Isby, David C. *Russia's War in Afghanistan.* London: Osprey, 1986.

Judge, Edward, and John W. Langdon, eds. *The Cold War: A History through Documents.* Upper Saddle River, NJ: Prentice Hall, 1999.

Lyon, David. *In Afghanistan: Two Hundred Years of British, Russian and American Occupation.* New York: Palgrave Macmillan, 2009.

MacKenzie, David. *From Messianism to Collapse: Soviet Foreign Policy, 1917–1991.* Fort Worth, TX: Harcourt Brace, 1994.

Prados, John. *Presidents' Secret Wars: CIA and Pentagon Covert Operations from World War II through the Persian Gulf.* Chicago: I. R. Dee, 1996.

Rasanayagam, Angelo. *Afghanistan: A Modern History; Monarchy, Despotism or Democracy? The Problems of Governance in the Muslim Tradition.* New York: I. B. Tauris, 2003.

Riedel, Bruce, *What We Won: America's Secret War in Afghanistan, 1979–89.* Washington, DC: Brookings Institution Press, 2014.

Roy, Olivier. *Islam and Resistance in Afghanistan.* New York: Cambridge University Press, 1990.

Russian General Staff. *The Soviet-Afghan War: How a Superpower Fought and Lost.* Edited by Lester W. Grau and Michael A. Gress. Lawrence: University of Kansas Press, 2002.

Tanner, Stephen. *Afghanistan: A Military History from Alexander the Great.* New York: Da Capo, 2002.

Urban, Mark. *War in Afghanistan.* New York: St. Martin's, 1988.

Yousaf, Mohammad, and Mark Adkin. *Afghanistan, the Bear Trap: The Defeat of a Superpower.* Havertown, PA: Casemate, 2001.

Iran-Iraq War (1980–1988)

Causes

The war between Iran and Iraq of September 22, 1980–August 20, 1988, marked a continuation of the ancient Persian-Arab rivalry fueled by 20th-century border disputes and competition for hegemony in the Persian Gulf and Middle East regions. In the 16th and 17th centuries, Persia (which became Iran in 1935) and the Ottoman Empire had fought to see which would control Mesopotamia (constituting present-day Iraq, Kuwait, and northeastern Syria as well as small parts of southeastern Turkey and southwestern Iran) and the Shatt al-Arab waterway, today Iraq's sole access to the sea.

Modern Iraq came into being in 1920 as a consequence of the defeat of the Ottoman Empire, which was allied with Germany in World War I. At first a British mandate under the League of Nations, Iraq secured independence in 1932. Shortly thereafter on July 4, 1937, Iran and Iraq signed a treaty in Tehran to settle the dispute over the Shatt al-Arab. This set the border between the two states as the low-water mark along that waterway's eastern shore except at Abadan and Khorramshahr, where it would be the deepwater line. This arrangement gave most of the Shatt al-Arab to Iraq and obliged Iran to pay tolls when its ships used the waterway.

Relations between the two states remained cordial for some decades thereafter, and in 1955 both Iraq and Iran joined the U.S.-sponsored Baghdad Pact designed to block communist expansion in the region. On July 14, 1958, however, a nationalist revolution occurred in Iraq. The monarchy was overthrown, and King Faisal II and his family were assassinated. Relations with Iran soured shortly thereafter, as new Iraqi leader Abdul Karim Qassim publicly expressed dissatisfaction with Iran's possession of oil-rich Khuzestan Province, which the Iraqis called Arabistan, that had a large Arab-speaking population. Quassim's regime supported secessionist movements in that province in the hopes of detaching it from Iran.

On July 17, 1968, another Iraqi coup brought the strongly nationalist Ba'ath Party to power. Its leaders were determined that Iraq take first place among the nations of the Arab world. At the same time, Shah Mohammad Reza Pahlavi, a close ally of the United States, was sharply increasing Iranian military spending and flexing Iranian influence in the region. In 1969 the shah unilaterally abrogated the 1979 Shatt al-Arab Treaty, and Iran ceased paying tolls for use of the waterway. The shah claimed that the treaty was unfair to Iran, as most of the world's treaties marking territorial boundaries along waterways set the deepwater mark as the defining line.

Although Iraq threatened war over Iran's action regarding the Shatt al-Arab, it did nothing at the time. Relations remained tense, however, with Iraq increasing its demands for "Arabistan." In 1971, indeed, Iraq, now under the rule of strongman President Saddam Hussein (a Sunni Muslim, with Iraq having a majority Shia Muslim population), broke off diplomatic relations with Iran when it seized the Persian Gulf islands of Abu Musa, Greater Tunb, and Lesser Tunb just before the establishment of the United Arab Emirates.

In retaliation for continued Iraqi agitation over "Arabistan," Iran commenced clandestine support to the large Kurdish minority population of northeastern Iraq, many of whom sought to form an independent Kurdistan. This could be a double-edged sword, however, for Iran, Syria, and Turkey also had sizable Kurdish minorities. Indeed, as might be expected, Iraq retaliated by seeking to stir up Kurdish nationalism in Iran.

During March 1974–March 1975, there were a series of military clashes between Iran and Iraq along their common border in the Kurdish areas. Iran's military was at the time more powerful than that of Iraq, especially in the air, and easily rebuffed the Iraqi ground attacks, which included tanks.

Its relative military weakness vis-à-vis Iran forced Iraq to make concessions to Iran in the Algiers Accords (Algiers Agreement) of March 6, 1975. In it Iraq conceded the deepwater mark for the entire length of the Shatt al-Arab as the boundary between the two countries. Although Iran agreed in return to end its military support of the Iraqi Kurds, most Iraqis regarded the Algiers Accords as a national humiliation. With Iranian support for the Iraqi Kurds ended, however, Saddam Hussein moved against the Kurdish Peshmerga and in a short campaign defeated them. Some 20,000 Kurds perished.

In 1978 there was a brief thaw in relations between the two rival states when Iranian intelligence officers revealed to Hussein a plot by some of his leading military officers against him. In gratitude, Hussein expelled from Iraq Ruhollah Khomeini, the exiled Iranian cleric and leader of the opposition to the shah.

Relations sharply deteriorated again, however, following the Islamic Revolution against the shah of Iran that brought Khomeini to power in that country in February 1979 and the establishment of an Islamist state. The long-standing rivalry between the two nations was now fueled by a collision between the Pan-Islamism and Pan-Shia Islamism of Iran and the Pan-Arab nationalism of Iraq.

Although it is hard to identify just when this began, a series of small cross-border military clashes commenced between the two states, with Iran apparently the chief instigator. Tensions increased when Khomeini rejected Hussein's public embrace of the Islamic revolution in Iran and call for Iraqi-Iranian friendship based on non-interference in each other's internal affairs. Khomeini's call for the overthrow of the Ba'ath government of Iraq and establishment there of an Islamic republic, presumably dominated by the Shiite majority, came as a great shock to Baghdad and was rightly considered by Hussein a major threat to his rule. Indeed, Hussein believed that Shia rioting in Iraq during 1979 and 1980 had been instigated by Iran, and he responded by encouraging rebellion by the Arabs of Iran's Khuzestan Province and the Kurds in Iranian Kurdestan.

Given their long-standing rivalry and conflicting ambitions, it was natural that the leaders of the two states would seek to exploit any perceived weakness in the other. Iran appeared vulnerable following the overthrow of the shah and the establishment of the Islamic Republic. Iran was weakened by its diplomatic isolation and Western economic sanctions imposed in the wake of the Iranian Revolution and the Iran Hostage Crisis, with the seizure of U.S. embassy personnel on November 4, 1979.

The end of ties between Iran and the United States dealt a considerable blow to the U.S.-equipped Iranian military, which was in some disarray and now found itself

Iran-Iraq War (September 22, 1980–August 20, 1988)

Total Estimated Military Casualties	
Iraq	**Iran**
375,000	300,000–1,000,000

Operation KARBALA-5 (January 9–February 25, 1987)	
Dead/Wounded/Captured	
Iraq	**Iran**
20,000	80,000

Sources: Rob Johnson, *The Iran-Iraq War* (Houndmills, Basingstoke, Hampshire, UK: Palgrave Macmillan, 2010); Kenneth M. Pollack, *Arabs at War: Military Effectiveness, 1948–1991* (Lincoln: University of Nebraska Press, 2002).

also handicapped by the lack of access to American spare parts. This situation was particularly damaging to the Iranian Air Force. Iraq would have no such problem with its weaponry, which had been largely acquired from the Soviet Union and communist bloc nations and France.

Hussein saw in this perceived Iranian military weakness a chance to punish Iran for its support of Kurdish and Shia opposition to Sunni domination of Iraq. More important, Hussein, who had never regarded the Algiers Agreement as more than a truce, believed that it was an opportunity for Iraq to gain full control of the Shatt al-Arab as well as secure Khuzestan and to acquire the islands of Abu Musa, Greater Tunb, and Lesser Tunb on behalf of the United Arab Emirates. Hussein also sought to overthrow the Iranian militant Islamic regime. His goals envisioned nothing less than Iraqi territorial expansion that would add greatly to Iraq's petroleum reserves and see Iraq assuming its rightful place as the dominant power in the region.

In early April 1980, heavily armed Shia militants, believed by Baghdad to have been encouraged by Iran, assassinated some 20 Ba'ath Party officials; Deputy Prime Minister Tariq Aziz was wounded

but survived. Hussein responded by executing on April 9 Shia grand ayatollah Mohammad Baqir al-Sadr. This action created outrage throughout the Middle East, especially in Shia Iran. In another affront to Iran, the Baghdad government also confiscated the property of some 70,000 civilians believed to be of Iranian ancestry, although few had direct familial connections in Iran, and expelled them from Iraq. Virtually all were Shia.

On the eve of the war, Iraq could count on an advantage in ground forces, while Iran had the edge in the air. Iraq had a regular army of some 300,000 men, 1,000 artillery pieces, 2,700 tanks, 332 fighter aircraft, and 40 helicopters. The Iranian regular army numbered some 200,000 men. Iran also possessed somewhat more than 1,000 artillery pieces, 1,740 tanks, 445 fighter aircraft, and 500 helicopters.

SPENCER C. TUCKER

Course

The war began on September 22, 1980, when Iraqi forces invaded western Iran. It came as a complete surprise to Iran. Striking on a 300-mile front, Iraqi troops met initial success against the disorganized Iranian defenders. The Iraqis drove into southwestern Iran and secured the far side of the Shatt al-Arab. In November they captured Khorramshahr in Khuzestan Province. In places, the Iraqis penetrated as much as 30 miles into Iran. But Iran is a large country, and the Iraqis moved too cautiously, throwing away the opportunity for a quick and decisive victory. Another factor in their stalled offensive was the rapid Iranian mobilization, especially of the largely untrained but fanatical Pasdaran (Revolutionary Guard Corps) militia.

Recovering from the initial shock of the invasion, the Iranians soon established strong defensive positions. Iran's navy also imposed a blockade of Iraq. On the first day of the war, Iraqi air strikes destroyed much of the Iranian Air Force infrastructure, but most Iranian aircraft survived, and Iraq lacked the long-range bomber aircraft for an effective strategic air campaign against Iran. Indeed, Iranian pilots soon secured air superiority. This enabled the Iranians to carry out ground-support missions by airplanes and helicopters that helped check the Iraqi ground advance.

Far from breaking Iranian morale as Iraqi president Saddam Hussein had hoped, the Iraqi attack served to rally support for the Islamic regime. Ideologically committed Iranians flocked to join the Pasdaran and the army. Within six months, the war had become a protracted stalemate. With both sides having constructed extensive defensive positions, much of the combat came to resemble the trench warfare of World War I.

In January 1982, Jordanian volunteers began arriving to assist the Iraqis, but this had little military impact. Then on March 22, the Iranians launched a major counteroffensive with large numbers of the Pasdaran. Lasting until March 30, it drove the Iraqis back, as far as 24 miles in places.

During April 30–May 20, the Iranians renewed their attacks, again pushing the Iraqis back. The Iranians recaptured Khorramshahr on May 24 and there secured large quantities of Soviet-manufactured weapons. Flush with victory, the Iranians now proclaimed their war aim to be the overthrow of Hussein.

With the war going badly for Iraq, Hussein proposed a truce and the withdrawal of all Iraqi troops from Iranian soil within two weeks. He also declared a unilateral cease-fire. Sensing victory, Iran rejected the proposal and reiterated its demand for Hussein's ouster.

Given the Iranian rebuff and realizing that he had no legitimate hope of retaining his forces in Iran, Hussein now withdrew them back into well-prepared static defenses in Iraq, reasoning that Iraqis would rally to his regime in defense of their homeland. For political reasons, Hussein announced that the withdrawal was to allow Iraqi forces to assist Lebanon, which had been invaded by Israeli forces on June 6, 1982.

Meanwhile, Iranian leaders rejected a Saudi Arabian–brokered peace agreement that would have meant $70 billion in war reparations by the Arab states to Iran and a complete Iraqi withdrawal from Iranian territory. Iranian leaders insisted that Hussein must go, that some 100,000 Shiites expelled from Iraq before the war be permitted to return, and that reparations be set at $150 billion. Iranian leaders probably expected these terms to be rejected and to use the failure of negotiations as justification to continue the war with an invasion of Iraq. Indeed, Ayatollah Khomeini announced his intention to install an Islamic republic in Iraq.

The Iranians now sought to utilize their numerical advantage in a new offensive, Operation RAMADAN, launched on July

Iranian tanks west of the Khaker River in the Dezful area of southern Iran, March 30, 1982, during the Iran-Iraq War. (AFP/Getty Images)

20, 1982. It was directed against Shiite-dominated southern Iraq, with the objective being the capture of Basra, Iraq's second-largest city. Human-wave assaults, caused by a shortage of ammunition, encountered well-prepared Iraqi static defenses supported by artillery. Hussein had also managed to increase substantially the number of Iraqis under arms.

Although the Iranians did register some modest gains, these came at heavy human cost. This was owing in large part to human-wave assaults and such tactics allowing untrained and poorly armed units of boy-soldiers to volunteer to march into Iraqi minefields and clear them with their bodies for the trained Iranian soldiers who would follow. The Iraqi use of poison gas also inflicted many casualties. On July 21, Iranian aircraft struck Baghdad.

Iraq retaliated in August with attacks on the vital Iranian oil-shipping facilities at Kharg Island and there sank several ships.

During September–November, the Iranians launched new offensives in the northern part of the front, securing some territory near the border town of Samar, which Iraq had taken at the beginning of the war. The Iranians also struck west of Dezful and, in early November, drove several miles into Iraq near Mandali. Iraqi counterattacks forced the Iranians back into their own territory. In the southern part of the front, on November 17 the Iranians advanced to within artillery range of the vital Baghdad-Basra Highway.

Iran was now receiving military supplies from such nations as the People's Republic of China, the Democratic People's Republic of Korea (North Korea), and Albania. Iraqi support came from the Soviet Union and other Warsaw Pact states as well as from France, Great Britain, Spain, Egypt, Saudi Arabia, and the United States. Determined to prevent the spread of militant Islamism in the Middle East, President Ronald Reagan in 1982 committed the United States to support Iraq. The United States supplied intelligence information in the form of satellite photography and also furnished economic aid and weapons. Iraq's chief financial backers were Saudi Arabia, Kuwait, and the United Arab Emirates.

In the course of 1983, Iran launched five major offensives against Iraq. Before the first of these, however, during February 2–March 9, the Iraqi Air Force carried out large-scale air attacks against Iranian coastal oil-production facilities, producing the largest oil spill in the history of the Persian Gulf region. Again seeking to utilize their advantage in troop strength, during February 7–16 Iranian leaders launched a ground attack hoping to isolate Basra by cutting the Baghdad-Basra Highway at Kut. They drove to within 30 miles of their objective before being thrown back. The Iraqis claimed they destroyed upwards of 1,000 Iranian tanks.

During April 11–14, the Iranians attacked west of Dezful but failed to make meaningful gains. On July 20, Iraqi aircraft again struck Iranian oil-production facilities. Three days later, the Iranians attacked in northern Iraq but registered few gains. The Iranians mounted a major offensive west of Dezful on July 30 but failed to break through. In the second week in August, however, the Iranians blunted an Iraqi counterattack, with both sides suffering heavy casualties.

In late October the Iranians launched yet another attack in the north to close a salient opened by Iranian Kurdish rebels.

Hussein was disappointed in his hope that the failed Iranian ground offensives and ensuing heavy casualties would make Iran more amenable to peace talks. Indeed, Khomeini restated his determination to overthrow the Iraqi regime.

Believing that more aggressive tactics were necessary to induce Iran to talk peace, Hussein announced that unless Iran agreed to halt offensive action against Iraq by February 7, 1984, he would order major attacks against 11 Iranian cities. Iran replied with a ground attack in the northern part of the front, and Hussein ordered the threatened air and missile attacks to proceed. These lasted until February 22. Iran retaliated in what became known as the War of the Cities. Indeed, there were five such air campaigns during the war.

On February 15, 1984, the Iranians launched a new series of ground offensives. The first fell in the central part of the front and pitted 250,000 Iranian troops against an equal number of Iraqi defenders. In Operations DAWN 5 (February 15–22) and DAWN 6 (February 22–24), the Iranians attempted to take the city of Kut to cut the vital Baghdad-Basra Highway there. The attack carried to within 15 miles of the city before it was halted.

The Iranians enjoyed more success in Operation KHEIBAR (February 24–March 19). This renewed drive against Basra almost broke through. The Iranians did capture part of the Majnoon Islands with their undeveloped oil fields, then held them against an Iraqi counterattack supported by poison gas.

With his forces having benefited from substantial arms purchases financed by the oil-rich Persian Gulf states, on January 28, 1985, Hussein launched the first Iraqi ground offensive since late 1980. It, however, registered only minor gains, and Iran responded with its own offensive, Operation BADR, beginning on March 11. Now better trained, the Iranian Army eschewed the costly human-wave tactics of the past and succeeded in cutting the Baghdad-Basra Highway. Hussein responded to this strategic emergency with chemical weapons attacks and renewed air and missile strikes against 20 Iranian cities, including Tehran.

On February 17, 1986, in a surprise offensive employing commandos, Iranian forces captured the strategically important Iraqi port of Faw, southeast of Basra on the Shatt al-Arab waterway. In January 1987, Iran launched Operation KARBALA-5, a renewed effort to capture Basra. When the operation ground to a halt in mid-February, the Iranians began NASR-4 in northern Iraq, which threatened the Iraqi city of Kirkuk during May–June.

On March 7, 1987, the United States initiated Operation EARNEST WILL to protect oil tankers and shipping lanes in the Persian Gulf. The so-called Tanker War had begun in March 1984 with an Iraqi air attack on strategic Kharg Island and nearby oil installations. Iran retaliated with attacks and the use of mines against tankers carrying Iraqi oil from Kuwait and on any tankers of the Persian Gulf states supporting Iraq. On November 1, 1986, the Kuwaiti government petitioned the international community to protect its tankers. The Soviet Union agreed to charter tankers, and on March 7, 1987, the United States announced that it would provide protection for any U.S.-flagged tankers. This would protect neutral tankers proceeding to or from Iraqi ports, ensuring that Iraq would have the economic means to continue the war.

On the night of May 17, 1987, an Iraqi Mirage F-1 fighter aircraft fired two antiship cruise missiles at a radar contact, apparently not knowing that it was the U.S. Navy frigate *Stark.* Although only one of the missiles detonated, both hit, crippling the ship and killing 37 crewmen and injuring another 50. The crew managed to save the ship, which made port under its own power.

On July 20, 1987, the United Nations (UN) Security Council passed unanimously U.S.-sponsored Resolution 598. The resolution deplored attacks on neutral shipping and called for an immediate cease-fire and the withdrawal of armed forces to internationally recognized boundaries.

During February 1988, the Iraqis launched a renewed wave of attacks against Iranian population centers, and the Iranians reciprocated. These attacks included aircraft and surface-to-surface missiles. Also during February and extending into September, the Iraqi Army carried out a massacre of Kurds in northern Iraq. Known as the al-Anfal (Spoils of War) Campaign, it claimed as many as 300,000 civilian lives and the destruction of some 4,000 villages.

Meanwhile, on April 14, 1988, the U.S. Navy frigate *Samuel B. Roberts,* involved in Operation EARNEST WILL, was badly damaged when it struck an Iranian mine in the Persian Gulf. No one was killed, but the ship nearly sank. On April 18 the U.S. Navy responded with Operation PRAYING MANTIS, its largest battle involving surface warships since World War II and the first surface-to-surface missile engagement in U.S. naval history. U.S. forces damaged two Iranian offshore oil platforms, sank an Iranian frigate and a gunboat, damaged another frigate, and sank three Iranian speedboats for the loss of one helicopter and two marines killed.

By the spring of 1988, Iraqi forces had been sufficiently reorganized to enable them to launch major operations. By contrast, Iran was now desperately short of

IRAN–IRAQ WAR, 1980–1988

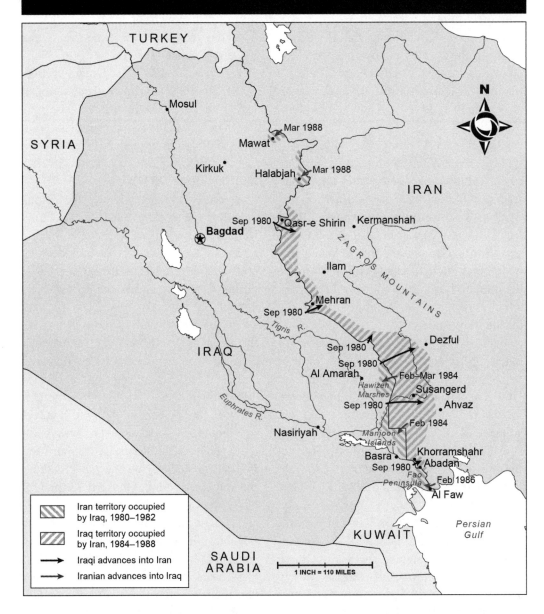

TURKEY

Mosul

SYRIA

Mar 1988

Mawat

Kirkuk

Halabjah   Mar 1988

IRAN

Sep 1980 Qasr-e Shirin   Kermanshah

Bagdad

ZAGROS

MOUNTAINS

Ilam

Sep 1980   Mehran

Tigris R.

Dezful

Sep 1980

Sep 1980

Al Amarah   Feb–Mar 1984

Hawizeh   Susangerd
Marshes

Sep 1980   Ahvaz

Euphrates R.

Feb 1984

Nasiriyah

Majnoon
Islands

Basra   Khorramshahr

Sep 1980   Abadan

Fao   Feb 1986
Peninsula

Al Faw

IRAQ

N

Persian
Gulf

Iran territory occupied
by Iraq, 1980–1982

Iraq territory occupied
by Iran, 1984–1988

Iraqi advances into Iran

Iranian advances into Iraq

KUWAIT

SAUDI
ARABIA   1 INCH = 110 MILES

spare parts, especially for its largely U.S.-built aircraft. The Iranians had also lost a large number of aircraft in combat operations and were less able to mount an effective defense against the resupplied Iraqi Air Force, let alone carry out aerial attacks against a ground attack.

The Iraqis mounted four separate offensives in the spring of 1988, recapturing the strategically important Faw Peninsula, which had been lost in 1986; driving the Iranians away from Basra; and making progress in the northern part of the front. The Iraqi victories came at little cost to themselves, while the Iranians suffered heavy personnel and equipment losses. These Iranian setbacks were the chief factor behind Khomeini's decision to agree to a cease-fire as called for in UN Security Council Resolution 598.

On July 3, 1988, the crew of the U.S. Navy cruiser *Vincennes,* patrolling in the Persian Gulf and believing that they were under attack by an Iranian jet fighter, shot down Iran Air Flight 655, a civilian airliner carrying 290 passengers and crew. There were no survivors. The U.S. government subsequently paid $131.8 million in compensation for the incident. It expressed regret only for the loss of innocent life and did not apologize to the Iranian government. The incident may have served to convince Khomeini of the dangers of the United States actively entering the conflict against Iran, making him more amenable to ending the war.

Both sides accepted a cease-fire agreement on August 20, 1988, bringing the eight-year war to a close.

SPENCER C. TUCKER

Consequences

The long Iran-Iraq War exacted a heavy toll. Estimates of the casualties on both sides vary widely. Total Iraqi casualties, including 60,000 men taken prisoner by Iran during the war, may have numbered about 375,000 (perhaps 200,000 of these killed). This figure does not include the Iraqi Kurds killed by Iraqi government forces during the war. Iran announced a death toll of nearly 300,000 people, but some sources place the actual figure as high as 1 million or more. In financial terms, the war is thought to have cost each side some $500 billion. Both sides suffered damage to their oil production, the chief revenue source for each.

Iraqi leader Saddam Hussein, despite having led his nation into a disastrous war, emerged from the struggle with the strongest military in the Middle East, second only to that of Israel. His power unchallenged in Iraq, he trumpeted a great national victory. The war, however, had put Iraq deeply in debt to its Persian Gulf Arab neighbors. Certainly in the case of Iran, the war helped consolidate popular support behind the Islamic revolution.

The UN-arranged cease-fire of August 20, 1988, merely brought a close to the fighting, leaving both Iran and Iraq to pursue an arms race with each other and with the other states in the region. With UN peacekeepers in place monitoring the border between the two countries, negotiations commenced between Iraq and Iran in Geneva, Switzerland. The talks remained deadlocked for two years after the cease-fire, however, in large part because Iraq refused—in violation of the cease-fire terms—to withdraw its forces from some 3,000 square miles of Iranian territory unless Iran accepted full Iraqi sovereignty over the Shatt al-Arab waterway. For its part, Iran refused to release 70,000 Iraqi prisoners of war it held, twice the number of Iranians held by the Iraqis. Iran also kept in place its naval blockade of Iraq, although Iraqi trade with the neighboring states that had supported it during the war helped negate that.

Iran, meanwhile, had worked to repair relations with a number of states that had supported Iraq in the war. It also undertook an extensive rearmament program, purchasing some $10 billion in arms from abroad, chiefly from the Soviet Union and the People's Republic of China. Iran's new president, Akbar Hashemi Rafsanjani, also reversed Iran's decision not to acquire chemical weapons (in 1993, however, Iran ratified the Chemical Weapons Convention and destroyed its chemical arms). Hussein now believed that Iraq might not be able to win in a renewal of the fighting, and this made him more amenable to a peace settlement.

At the same time, Iraq was deeply in debt. Indeed, Kuwait's refusal to write off the $14 billion debt owed it by Iraq was a key factor in Iraq's decision to invade that nation. Claiming that Kuwait was actually a province of Iraq, Hussein sent his forces into that small state on August 2, 1990. Although Iraqi forces quickly seized control of Kuwait, this development was unacceptable to a number of countries, including the Arab states of Saudi Arabia, Egypt, and Syria as well as many other states as far away as Japan. The United States took the lead in forming a powerful international coalition to drive the Iraqi military from Kuwait.

Hussein now feared that Iran might join the coalition against him, placing Iraq in an impossible military situation. In these circumstances he ended the war with Iran. On August 16, 1990, Hussein agreed to withdraw Iraqi troops from occupied Iranian territory. He also agreed to the deepwater mark of the Shatt al-Arab as the boundary between Iraq and Iran and to the release of prisoners by both sides. The UN peacekeepers were withdrawn shortly thereafter.

The war was at last over. Each side claimed victory, but most analysts consider the war to have been a stalemate, with the outstanding issues unresolved. On December 9, 1991, UN secretary-general Javier Pérez de Cuéllar declared that Iraq's decision to go to war against Iran in 1982 was unjustified, as was Iraq's occupation of Iranian territory and its use of poison gas.

Despite the renewal of diplomatic ties, in the 1990s and early 2000s relations between Iraq and Iran remained strained.

Both sides continued low-level cross-border raids and attacks against the other in an effort to incite revolts, and in 2001 Iran fired 56 Scud missiles at mujahideen targets within Iraq.

In 2003 following Hussein's defiance of UN inspectors searching for (nonexistent) weapons of mass destruction, a U.S.-led coalition invaded Iraq and overthrew Hussein, who was subsequently captured and then tried, found guilty, and executed by the new Iraqi government. Iran was not formally a party in the long 2003–2011 Iraq War, but it was definitely involved in the violence. A Shia-dominated government took power in Iran, and close ties developed between it and Shia Muslim Iran. Iran was active in supporting sectarian violence in Iraq as well as against the coalition troops seeking to restore and maintain order. Nouri al-Maliki, the Shia Muslim prime minister of Iraq during 2006–2014, openly courted Iran. Indeed, in 2005 his government apologized to Iran for having initiated the Iran-Iraq War. His successor, Haider al-Abadi, has, publicly at least, trumpeted a more inclusive policy to include power sharing with the minority Sunni Muslims and Kurds. The occupation of much of northern Iraq by forces of the Muslim extremist Islamic State of Iraq and Syria (ISIS), also known as the Islamic State, led the Iraqi government to call on U.S. military support, to include air strikes. Yet in the spring of 2015 Iraq undertook a military offensive to liberate the city of Tikrit, which had been taken by ISIS. The United States was not informed, and Iranian artillery and advisers participated in the operation, alongside the Iraqi Army and Shia and Sunni militias. Although this operation stalled and the Iraqi government called in American airpower, the developing Iraq-Iran alliance was deeply troubling to Washington as well as to many Kurds and Sunnis. The future of Iraq remained very much a question mark.

Iran, meanwhile, had become something of an international pariah. Its government actively supported terrorist activities in Afghanistan, Yemen, Lebanon, and Israel and supported the Syrian regime of Bashar al-Assad in the Syrian Civil War that began in 2011. Iran also adopted a confrontational posture against the Sunni states of the region while at the same time seeking to secure nuclear weapons. International sanctions brought Iran to the bargaining table, and a series or tortuous negotiations ensued, but it was not clear in 2015 that these would be sufficient to secure a meaningful agreement that would prevent Iran from achieving that end.

SPENCER C. TUCKER

Timeline

1920

July
In the Great Iraqi Revolution of this date, Sunni and Shiite Muslims unite in an important step forward toward the creation of a nation-state and revolt against British rule.

1922
Iraq becomes a British mandate under the League of Nations.

1932

October 2
Iraq is admitted to the League of Nations as a fully independent state.

1937

July 4
Iran and Iraq sign a treaty regarding the Shatt al-Arab waterway, part of their common border.

1955
Both Iran and Iraq join the U.S.-sponsored Baghdad Pact.

1958

July 14
A coup d'état (also known as the 14 July Revolution) occurs in Iraq. Led by Brigadier Abd al-Karim Qasim and Colonel Abdul Salam Arif, it brings to an end the Iraqi monarchy with the assassinations of King Faisal II, his family, and Prime Minister Nuri al-Said.

1968

July 17
A bloodless coup occurs in Iraq, led by General Ahmed Hassan al-Bakr. Saddam Hussein is a major figure in the coup and gradually edges out al-Bakr.

1969
Iranian shah Mohammad Reza Pahlavi unilaterally abrogates the Shatt al-Arab Treaty of 1937.

1971   Iraqi strongman Saddam Hussein breaks off diplomatic relations with Iran after Iran seizes the Persian Gulf islands of Abu Musa, Greater Tunb, and Lesser Tunb.

1974

March   Border clashes begin between Iran and Iraq, lasting until March 1975 and the signing of the Algiers Accord.

1975

March 6   Military weakness relative to Iran leads Iraq to conclude the Algiers Accord, which establishes the deepwater mark of the Shatt al-Arab as the boundary between the two countries.

1979

January 16   In the midst of the Iranian Revolution, Shah Mohammed Reza Pahlavi quits Iran for exile.

February 1   Ayatollah Ruhollah Khomeini returns to Iran from exile, reportedly welcomed by as many as 5 million people in Tehran.

December 2–3   A new constitution is overwhelmingly approved by Iranian voters, confirming Khomeini's hold on power.

1980

September 22   The Iran-Iraq War begins with a full-scale Iraqi attack on Iran. The Iraqis drive into southwestern Iran, securing the far side of the Shatt al-Arab waterway.

September 30   Two Iranian Air Force aircraft bomb the Iraqi Osirak nuclear reactor but inflict only minor damage.

October   Seeking to take advantage of the Iran-Iraq War and secure autonomy, the Kurds in northeastern Iraq expand their insurgency against the government.

November   Iraqi forces capture Khorramshahr in the Iranian province of Khuzestan.

1981

June 7   In Operation OPERA, Israeli aircraft attack and destroy the Iraqi Osirak nuclear reactor. Israeli leaders were determined to prevent any Arab nation from acquiring nuclear weapons. Although strong international condemnation of the Israeli action ensues, there is considerable support for it within the Arab world, which fears a Hussein-led nuclear-armed Iraq bullying its way to regional hegemony. Indeed, if Iraq had achieved nuclear status, this might have given that nation the upper hand in the Iran-Iraq War.

1982

March 22–30	Iranian forces launch a major ground counteroffensive that enjoys considerable success.
April 7–19	A plot is discovered, led by Iranian foreign minister Sadegh Ghotbzadeh and a number of army officers to overthrow the Islamic government of Iran and possibly assassinate Ayatollah Khomeini. Those involved are executed.
April 30–May 20	Iranian forces renew their ground attacks and again push back the Iraqis.
May 24	The Iranians force the surrender of Khorramshahr, which the Iraqis had captured early in the war.
June 10–20	With the war going badly for his country, Iraqi leader Hussein offers a truce and Iraqi troop withdrawal from Iranian soil. Hussein also declares a unilateral cease-fire. Sensing victory, Iran rejects the offer and reiterates its demand for the disposition of Hussein, who now withdraws his troops anyway, into well-prepared static defenses in Iraq, reasoning that Iraqis will rally to his regime in a fight to defend their homeland.
July 20	Iran launches a new ground offensive, Operation RAMADAN, directed against Shia-dominated southern Iraq with the objective of capturing Iraq's second-largest city, Basra. Although the Iranians manage some modest gains, these come at heavy human cost.
July 21	Iranian aircraft strike Baghdad.
August	Iraqi aircraft attack the vital Iranian oil-shipping facilities at Kharg Island and also sink several ships.
September–November	Iran launches new ground offensives in northern Iraq. Iraqi forces drive them back.
November 17	On the southern part of the front, Iranian forces drive to within artillery range of Basra.

1983

February 2–March 9	The Iraqi Air Force carries out large-scale air attacks against Iranian coastal oil-production facilities, creating the largest oil spill in the history of the Persian Gulf region.

February 7–October	Iran launches five major offensives against Iraq, hoping to isolate Basra by cutting the Baghdad-Basra Road at Kut-al-Amara, but the Iranian troops are thrown back.
April 11–14	Iranian forces attack west of Dezful but fail to make meaningful gains.
July 20	Iraqi aircraft again strike Iranian oil-production facilities.
July 23	Iranian ground forces attack in northern Iraq but again register few gains.
July 30	The Iranians mount a major offensive west of Dezful but fail to break through.
August	The Iranians blunt an Iraqi counterattack.
October	The Iranians launch yet another attack in the northern part of the front.

1984

February 7–22	Iraq launches air and missile attacks against Iranian cities. Iran retaliates, in what becomes known as "the War of the Cities." There will be five such air campaigns in the course of the war.
February 15–22	The Iranians launch the first in a series of ground offensives. Known as Operation DAWN 5, it occurs in the central part of the front.
February 22–24	In Operation DAWN 6, the Iranians try to take Kut-al-Amara and cut the vital Baghdad-Basra Road but are halted.
February 24–March 19	Iranian forces enjoy some success in Operation KHEIBAR, a new drive to take Basra. The Iranians capture part of the Majnun (Majnoon) Islands and hold them despite an Iraqi counterattack, which includes the use of poison gas, until near the end of the war.
March	Iraq initiates the so-called Tanker War by attacking Kharg Island, seeking to disrupt Iranian oil shipments.

1985

January 28–March	His forces having benefited from substantial arms purchases financed by the oil-rich Persian Gulf states, Hussein launches the first Iraqi ground offensive since late 1980. It fails to register significant gains, however.
March 11	The Iranians respond with Operation BADR, a successful offensive to cut the Baghdad-Basra Road. Hussein then employs chemical weapons and renewed air and missile attacks against 20 Iranian cities, including Tehran.

1986

February 17	In a surprise offensive, Iranian forces capture the strategically important Iraqi port of al-Faw on the Shatt al-Arab waterway.

1987

January 9–February 19	Iran launches Operation KARBALA-5, a renewed effort to capture Basra in southern Iraq.
March 7	The United States commences Operation ERNEST WILL to protect shipping, especially tankers, in the Persian Gulf.
May 17	On this night, an Iraqi fighter aircraft fires two antiship cruise missiles at a radar contact, apparently not knowing that it is the U.S. Navy frigate *Stark* (FFG-31). Although only one of the missiles detonates, both strike home and cripple the frigate, killing 37 crewmen and injuring another 50; the remaining crew members are able to save the ship.
July 20	The U.S.-sponsored United Nations (UN) Security Council Resolution 598, passed unanimously, condemns attacks on neutral shipping and calls for an immediate cease-fire and the withdrawal of armed forces to internationally recognized boundaries.
February–August	In retaliation for Iranian ground offensives, Hussein renews attacks against Iranian population centers with both aircraft and missiles. Iran retaliates, but Iraq fires many more missiles.
February–September	Iraqi forces massacre Iraqi Kurds. Known as the al-Anfal Campaign, it includes the use of chemical weapons against the Kurdish population, many of whom have sided with Iran in the war. In its entirety, the al-Anfal Campaign claims as many as 180,000 civilian lives and brings the destruction of some 2,000 villages.
April 14	The U.S. Navy-guided missile frigate *Samuel B. Roberts* involved in Operation ERNEST WILL is badly damaged when it strikes an Iranian mine in the Persian Gulf.
April 18	The United States responds to the Iranian mining in Operation PRAYING MANTIS. In the U.S. Navy's largest battle involving surface warships since World War II, its ships and aircraft damage two Iranian offshore oil platforms, sink an Iranian frigate and a gunboat, damage another frigate, and sink three speedboats. U.S. losses are one helicopter and two marines killed.

April–August	The Iraqis mount four separate offensives and recapture the strategically important Faw Peninsula lost in 1986. They also drive the Iranians away from Basra and make progress in the northern part of the front. The Iraqi victories come at little cost to themselves, while the Iranians suffer heavy personnel and equipment losses. These setbacks are the chief factor behind Iranian leader Khomeini's decision to agree to a cease-fire as called for in UN Security Council Resolution 598.
July 3	The U.S. Navy-guided missile cruiser *Vincennes,* on tanker patrol in the Persian Gulf, mistakenly shoots down Iran Air Flight 655, a passenger jet, killing all 290 people on board. The U.S. government subsequently agrees to pay Iran $131.8 million in compensation.
August 20	General war weariness and pressure from other governments induce both sides to accept a cease-fire agreement, bringing the war to a close.

1989

January	Hussein crushes an attempted coup involving dissident Iraqi Army officers.
March 27	King Faud of Saudi Arabia travels to Baghdad and signs a nonaggression pact with Iraq.
July 17	Hussein threatens military action against Kuwait for its overproduction of oil quotas, which has helped drive down the world price. Iraq is heavily in debt as a consequence of its long war with Iran, and Hussein seeks the highest possible price for oil. He also wants Kuwaiti concessions on the considerable sums it owes that country for loans during the war. Hussein also seeks Iraqi control of Bubiyan and Warbah Islands to improve Iraqi access to the Persian Gulf and an end to what he claims is Kuwaiti slant-drilling into the major Iraqi Rumaila oil field. Undergirding all this is Iraq's long-standing claim that Kuwait is simply an Iraqi province.
August 2	Iraqi forces invade and overrun Kuwait, bringing the formation of an international coalition, headed by the United States, to expel them.
August 16	Iraqi leader Hussein agrees to a peace settlement with Iran based on a status quo ante bellum regarding borders with the removal of Iraqi forces from Iranian territory and the release of all prisoners of war.

SPENCER C. TUCKER

Further Reading

Chubin, Shahram, and Charles Tripp. *Iran and Iraq at War.* Boulder, CO: Westview, 2004.

Cooper, Tom. *Iran-Iraq War in the Air: 1980–1988.* Atglen, PA: Schiffer, 2004.

Farrokh, Kaveh. *Iran at War: 1500–1988.* Oxford, UK: Osprey, 2011.

Hiro, Dilip. *The Longest War: The Iran-Iraq Military Conflict.* London: Routledge, 1990.

Johnson, Rob. *The Iran-Iraq War.* Houndmills, Basingstoke, Hampshire, UK: Palgrave Macmillan, 2010.

Karsh, Efraim. *The Iran-Iraq War: 1980–1988.* Oxford, UK: Osprey, 2002.

Murray, Williamson, and Kevin Murray. *The Iran-Iraq War: A Military and Strategic History.* New York: Cambridge University Press, 2014.

Pollack, Kenneth M. *Arabs at War: Military Effectiveness, 1948–1991.* Lincoln: University of Nebraska Press, 2004.

Potter, Lawrence G., and Gary Sick. *Iran, Iraq, and the Legacies of War.* New York: Palgrave Macmillan, 2004.

Rajaee, Farhang. *The Iran-Iraq War: The Politics of Aggression.* Gainesville: University Press of Florida, 1993.

Willet, Edward C. *The Iran-Iraq War.* New York: Rosen, 2004.

Sri Lanka Civil War (1983–2009)

Causes

The Sri Lanka Civil War was fought between the forces of the Democratic Socialist Republic of Sri Lanka and the Liberation Tigers of Tamil Eelam (Tamil Tigers, LTTE), who sought an independent Tamil state. One of the longest conflicts of modern times, it lasted a quarter century, from July 23, 1983, to May 19, 2009.

Sri Lanka, known as Ceylon until 1972, is an island in South Asia. Located just 20 miles off the southern tip of India, it is bordered by the Bay of Bengal to the northeast, the Indian Ocean to the east and south, and the Gulf of Mannar to the west. The island's location and its excellent deep harbors made it of considerable geostrategic importance through World War II.

The ancient kingdoms of Sri Lanka were the object of frequent invasions by neighboring South Asian dynasties. In 1505 the Portuguese arrived. They named the island Ceilão. This was transliterated into English as Ceylon.

By 1517, the Portuguese had constructed a coastal fort and began to expand their holdings. In 1638, the ruler of the Kingdom of Kandy, which comprised western Ceylon and constituted more than a third of the island, concluded a treaty with the Dutch in order to expel the Portuguese who then ruled much of the coast of Kandy. Under the treaty terms, the Dutch were to hand over to the king the areas taken from the Portuguese and would be granted in return a trading monopoly. Both sides failed to honor the agreement, and by 1660 the Dutch controlled virtually all of Kandy.

The British arrived in 1796 during the French Revolutionary War, when they feared that the Dutch might yield Ceylon to the French. The Treaty of Amiens of 1802 between the British and the French awarded the Dutch part of Ceylon to the British. In 1803 British forces invaded the Kingdom of Kandy but were repulsed. A new British invasion in 1815 was successful, and the British crushed armed uprisings in 1818 and 1848. Following World War II, in 1948 Ceylon became a self-governing dominion within the British Commonwealth of Nations.

Ceylon was sharply split along ethnic lines. During the 19th century the British had settled a large number of Tamil laborers from southern India to work on the Ceylonese plantations. While Sinhalese Buddhists comprised some 70 percent of the Sri Lankan population, there was a strong Tamil Hindu minority of some 20 percent concentrated in the northern and eastern parts of the island. The two ethnic groups have separate languages: Sinhala and Tamil. Tamil is the mother tongue of the nation's three largest minorities—the Indian Tamils, the Sri Lankan Tamils, and the Moors—who together numbered about 29 percent of the island's population. Ceylon thus faced sharp differences in ethnicity, religion, and language.

Ceylonese prime minister Solomon Bandaranaike, who held office during 1956–1959, sparked conflict between the Sinhalese and the Tamils by championing the Sinhala language and Buddhism. In June 1956, in the Sinhala Only Act, he made Sinhala the only official language. Bandaranaike also took other actions that exacerbated communal politics. Certainly

The Sri Lankan Civil War (1983–2009)

Approximate Maximum Troop Strength, Opposing and Peacekeeping Forces

Government Forces (2006)	LTTE (2008)	IKPF (1987–1990)
158,000	30,000–35,000	50,000

Peace Talks between Sri Lankan Government and the LTTE (2002–2003)

September 16–18, 2002

October 31–November 3, 2002

December 2–5, 2002

January 6–9, 2003

February 7–8, 2003

March 18–21, 2003

Total Estimated Casualties, Sri Lankan Civil War (1983–2009)

Sri Lankan Government Forces	LTTE	IPKF	Civilians
23,327 killed	27,000+ killed	1,200 killed	40,000+ killed
60,000+ wounded	11,624 captured	N/A	N/A

Sources: William Clarance, *Ethnic Warfare in Sri Lanka and the UN Crisis* (Ann Arbor, MI: Pluto, 2007); Ahmed S. Hashim, *When Counterinsurgency Wins: Sri Lanka's Defeat of the Tamil Tigers* (Philadelphia: University of Pennsylvania Press, 2012).

his policies profoundly impacted Ceylonese politics for decades.

The Tamils responded with civil disobedience, and occasionally this led to riots, which were especially severe in the first half of 1958 (but largely ended when Tamil was granted limited official status in August 1961). On September 26, 1959, Bandaranaike was assassinated, not by Tamils but by a Buddhist radical who believed that the prime minister had not done enough to establish Sinhalese dominance.

The 1960 elections were won by Bandaranaike's widow, Sirimavo Bandaranaike, the world's first female prime minister. She expanded her husband's foreign and domestic policies during two terms in office (1960–1965, 1970–1977). In May 1972 she secured a change in the name of the country from Ceylon to Sri Lanka, which is Sinhalese for "resplendent land,"

and declared it a republic as the Free, Sovereign and Independent Republic of Sri Lanka. A new constitution came into effect in 1978, and the country's name became the Democratic Socialist Republic of Sri Lanka. Buddhism became the state religion, further alienating the predominantly Hindu Tamils.

Prime Minister Bandaranaike also faced an attempt during April 5–June 9, 1971, by the Ceylonese communist party, the Janatha Vimukthi Peramuna (People's Liberation Front, JVP), to seize power. An accidental explosion in a JVP bomb factory tipped off the government and forced the JVP to launch its attempt prematurely. Although the insurgents were for the most part young, poorly armed, and inadequately trained, they were able to seize control of parts of a number of cities, including Colombo.

After several weeks of fighting, the government put down the revolt in the cities, but unrest continued in the rural areas in the southern and central ports of the island. The Soviet Union, India, Pakistan, and Britain all provided military assistance to the government. In order to end the violence, Bandaranaike offered amnesties in May and June 1971, and only the top JVP leaders were tried and sentenced to prison. On June 9 the government officially announced the end of the rebellion, which nonetheless may have claimed 15,000 lives.

Meanwhile, ethnic violence intensified. Reacting to Bandaranaike's politics of ethnic division, politicized Tamil youths began to form and ultimately coopted the moderates. The most important of the extreme nationalist organizations was the LTTE, established on May 5, 1976, and led by Velupillai Prabhakaran. It soon began a campaign of violence against the government, targeting policemen but also moderate Tamils who were willing to negotiate with the government. Prabhakaran subsequently claimed responsibility for the earlier assassination, on July 27, 1975, of Alfred Duraiappah, a prominent Tamil lawyer who was also the mayor of Jaffna and a member of parliament.

Ethnic violence increased, and on the night of May 31–June 1, 1981, an organized mob of Sinhalese burned the Jaffna Public Library, containing more than 97,000 books and manuscripts, including the "Palm Leaf Scrolls," that were of great historical value. This event served to convince many moderate Tamils that the government was not prepared to protect them or their cultural heritage. Although the government responded with a declaration of a state of emergency, this did little to quell the violence.

The accepted starting date for the Sri Lanka Civil War is July 23, 1983, when the LTTE attacked the 15-man Sri Lanka Army checkpoint Four Four Bravo outside the town of Thirunelveli in the Jaffna Peninsula. In their attack the LTTE killed 1 officer and 12 soldiers.

SPENCER C. TUCKER

Course

With the start of the war in the July 23, 1983, attack by the extreme nationalist Tamil organization the LTTE on Sri Lankan Army checkpoint Four Four Bravo, ethnic violence quickly spread. Extremist Sinhalese nationalists carried out pogroms in the capital of Colombo and elsewhere. As many as 3,000 Tamils were killed, and a great many more fled Sinhalese-majority areas in what became known as Black July.

Initially there were a number of Tamil militant groups, but the LTTE gained preeminence through its devastating terrorist acts. These included the Kent and Dollar Farm Massacres, an attack on two small farming communities on November 30, 1984. Hundreds of Sinhalese men, women, and children were attacked during the night as they slept and were hacked to death with axes. Another such action was the May 14, 1985, Anuradhapura Massacre, when LTTE members indiscriminately opened fire and killed or wounded 146 civilians within the Jaya Sri Maha Bodhi Buddhist shrine. Government forces responded in kind the next day with the Kumudini Boat Massacre, when they killed 23 Tamil civilians. Many Tamils rejected the violence of the LTTE terror campaign and its goal of an independent Tamil state. A number agreed to work with the Sri Lankan government as paramilitaries, while others sought to work within the mainstream political parties.

Attempts at peace proved unsuccessful. Talks between the Sri Lankan government and the LTTE in Thimphu in 1985 soon collapsed, and the war continued, with increasing numbers of civilian dead. In 1987 the fighting grew more intense. On April 21, the LTTE exploded a car bomb at the central bus station in Colombo, killing 113 people and wounding many others.

The central government responded by activating reserve forces and on May 26, 1987, mounted Operation VADAMARACH-CHI (LIBERATION). Extending into June, it was a successful effort to secure military control of the Jaffna Peninsula, an LTTE stronghold. With the population of Jaffna city soon in dire straits and with the Tamil population of southern India calling for action, the Indian government of Rajiv Gandhi attempted to send relief supplies. When the Sri Lankan Navy turned back the Indian ships, on June 4 the Indian Air Force mounted Operation POOMALAI, parachuting food and other supplies into the city.

On July 29, Gandhi's government pressured the Sri Lankan government into accepting an Indian "settlement" of the civil war. Signed by Gandhi and Sri Lankan president J. R. Jayewardene in Colombo, the accord included a pledge by the Sri Lankan government to withdraw its troops from the Jaffna area and initiate limited autonomy for the Tamil region of the country. In return, the LTTE was to surrender its arms. When the LTTE rejected this arrangement, the Indian government dispatched troops—the Indian Peacekeeping Force (IPKF) of some 50,000 men—in an effort to disarm the Tamils. This operation, which extended into March 1990 and included an unsuccessful airborne operation against Jaffna, resulted in the deaths of some 1,200 Indian soldiers; several

thousand others were wounded. LTTE casualties are not known. The situation became even more complicated when Sinhalese nationalists initiated a guerrilla-terrorist campaign against the government, which they believed had given up too much to the Tamils and to India.

The religious side of the Sri Lankan Civil War can be seen in the Aranthalawa Massacre, one of the most notorious atrocities of the war. On June 2, 1987, LTTE members stopped a bus close to the village of Aranthalawa in eastern Sri Lanka and massacred 33 Buddhist monks, almost all of them young novices, along with 4 other individuals.

On July 5, 1987, the LTTE mounted its first suicide attack when 21-year-old Vallipuram Vasanthan drove a small truck packed with explosives through the wall of a fortified Sri Lankan Army camp at Nelliady in the Jaffna Peninsula. The ensuing blast killed Vasanthan and 40 soldiers. Suicide attacks became an LTTE trademark, with the organization carrying out hundreds of them in the course of the war.

Despite the presence of the IPKF, the violence grew worse as the Marxist JVP, which had attempted to seize power in 1971, again carried out an armed uprising against the government. The JVP skillfully exploited Sinhalese national opposition to the presence of the Indian peacekeeping troops and began a terrorist campaign against the government of Prime Minister Ranasinghe Premadsa (elected president in December 1988) as well as prominent Sinhalese opposed to their philosophy. The nation underwent a severe test, with many JVP-enforced strikes.

In November 1989 in Colombo, however, government forces killed JVP leader Rohana Wijeweera, and by early 1990 they had either killed or imprisoned the

Tamil fighters cleaning their weapons at a base camp in Jaffna in northern Sri Lanka, March 28, 1986. (AP Photo/J. Wishnetsky)

remaining JVP leadership and arrested some 7,000 of its rank and file. The number of dead from this insurgency is unknown because it had merged with the concurrent struggle against the LTTE. After 1990 the remaining JVP leaders entered into the democratic process, participating in the 1994 parliamentary general election.

Another side note in the Sri Lankan Civil War between the militant Tamils and the Sri Lankan government was the effort by revolutionaries in the Maldives to seize power there. To accomplish that end, they invited in Tamil guerrilla mercenaries. The Maldivian government appealed to India for assistance, and in Operation CACTUS on the night of November 3, 1988, the Indian Air Force airlifted a paratroop battalion from Agra more than 1,200 miles to the Maldives. Landing at Hulule, the paratroopers secured the airfield there and several hours later restored the government at Malé.

In September 1989, the Indian and Sri Lankan governments reached agreement on the withdrawal of the 50,000 Indian troops. This was completed by March 1990. The withdrawal, however, left the majority Tamil populated areas in the hands of the rebels, and fighting continued.

Brief cease-fires were unsuccessful, and in August 1989 the LTTE attacked the previously unaffected and neutral Muslim communities. The Muslims respond with a jihad (holy war) against the Tamils. On December 3, after considerable bloodshed, the LTTE proclaimed a unilateral cease-fire and announced its willingness to conduct peace talks with the Sri Lankan government. The cease-fire did not hold.

Former Indian prime minister Rajiv Gandhi became a casualty of the Sri Lankan Civil War. The LTTE held Gandhi responsible for the dispatch of the IPKF to northern Sri Lanka and the sending of troops to the Maldives to reverse the coup there led by Tamil mercenaries. In 1991 also, Gandhi had imposed direct rule on the south Indian state of Tamil Nadu that had been supporting the LTTE. On May 21, 1991, LTTE suicide bomber Thenmuli Rajaratnam assassinated Gandhi in Srip-erumbudur, where he was campaigning for reelection. A number of others also died in the blast.

On May 1, 1993, an LTTE suicide bomber assassinated Sri Lankan president Ranasinghe Premadasa in Colombo while the president was at a May Day parade. Twenty-three bystanders were also killed, and scores more were wounded. Beginning in September, government forces launched a major offensive against the LTTE, and on October 1 they captured the Tamil Tiger naval base at Kilali and there destroyed some 120 vessels.

In August 1994 Chandrika Kumaratunga became prime minister of a coalition government that bridged both Buddhist extremists and Marxist revolutionaries. That fall she campaigned for the presidency on a pledge to negotiate with the LTTE, and in November 1994 she became the first woman elected president in Sri Lanka. Kumaratunga secured a truce in January 1995. It lasted only three months, ending when the LTTE sank Sri Lankan Navy vessels and shot down two aircraft. On January 31, 1996, an LTTE suicide bomber drove a truck filled with some 440 pounds of explosives into the Central Bank of Sri Lanka building. The ensuing blast killed 91 people and wounded 1,400 others.

On March 6, 1997, LTTE fighters assaulted a Sri Lankan military base and there killed more than 200 soldiers. In the most devastating economic loss of the war, on July 24, 2001, 14 LTTE members carried out a suicide attack on Bandaranaike International Airport. All were killed, but

not before they had destroyed eight Sri Lankan Air Force aircraft and four Sri Lankan Airlines planes. The attack had a major negative impact on Sri Lankan tourism and thus the entire national economy. Compounding the cost of the civil war, on December 26, 2004, in the worst natural disaster in modern times, a giant tsunami, generated by a powerful undersea earthquake in the Indian Ocean, struck the coasts of India, Thailand, Malaysia, Myanmar, the Maldives, Indonesia, Bangladesh, and Sri Lanka. The official death toll was some 225,000 people, with as many as half a million people injured. The Sri Lankan toll was as many as 39,000 dead.

In November 2005 former labor activist Mahinda Rajapaksa was elected president of Sri Lanka. He was determined to use the military to wipe out the LTTE, and on September 26, 2008, the Sri Lankan government launched a major military operation with heavy artillery and air strikes toward Kilinochchi, the town the rebels considered to be their capital. On November 15 government forces captured Pooneryn, a spit of land paralleling the neck of the northern Jaffna Peninsula and a key LTTE stronghold. Control of Pooneryn enabled the Sri Lankan forces to attack the Tamil capital of Kilinochchi from three sides and cut off a Tamil supply route. Also, for the first time since 1993 the government now controlled a land route that would allow easier resupply of its own forces fighting the Tamils.

The government offensive continued, and on December 21 the Sri Lankan troops captured the important LTTE-held town of Paranthan, located on a highway connecting the northern Jaffna Peninsula with the mainland. This brought government forces to within several miles of the former Tamil capital and stronghold of Kilinochchi.

Following several days of heavy fighting, on January 1, 2009, the government secured Kilinochchi. The news prompted celebrations in Colombo and other Sri Lankan cities. The LTTE, meanwhile, moved its operations center to Mullaitivu on the northeastern coast.

On January 25, Sri Lankan Army chief of staff Lieutenant General Sarath Fonseka announced that the army had taken Mullaitivu, ending a dozen years of LTTE rule there. By February the LTTE fighters had been restricted to only about 60 square miles of territory, but an estimated 100,000 civilians were at risk because the government had banned aid workers from the area. On April 26 the government rejected an LTTE offer of a cease-fire but the next day ordered an end to the employment of air and artillery in order to spare civilian casualties. This followed calls by the United Nations (UN), the United States, the European Union, and India for a cease-fire.

On May 16, a Sri Lankan government spokesperson announced that government forces now controlled the entire Sri Lankan coastline, cutting off any escape by sea. President Rajapaksa declared the final defeat of the Tamil rebels, now restricted to a tiny pocket of only some 1.2 square miles. On May 19 in a speech before parliament, Rajapaksa proclaimed victory in the long war. He also announced the death of LTTE leader Velupillai Prabhakaran, whose body was subsequently put on public display by the Sri Lankan military, and declared a national holiday in celebration.

SPENCER C. TUCKER

Consequences

Although the Sri Lankan government claimed a much lower figure, especially regarding the last months of heavy fighting, the UN estimated that the Sri Lankan Civil War had claimed some 80,000–100,000 lives, of whom some 40,000 were civilians. The UN also estimated that some 290,000 civilians had been displaced by the fighting.

With the end of the war, Sri Lankan president Mahinda Rajapaksa, who held office during November 2005–January 2015, oversaw an ambitious economic development program, much of it financed by loans from the People's Republic of China. Perhaps surprising given the duration of the civil war, Sri Lanka has had one of the world's fastest-growing economies. In addition to efforts to reconstruct its economy, the government had by 2015 reportedly resettled more than 95 percent of those civilians displaced by the fighting. The vast majority of former LTTE combatants who had been imprisoned were also returned to civilian society. Unfortunately, there has been little progress on such contentious matters as reaching a political settlement with elected Tamil representatives and holding accountable those individuals on both sides in the civil war alleged to have committed human rights violations.

During the war the UN had repeatedly called on the Sri Lankan government and the LTTE to make protection of civilians a priority, but little to nothing was done. After the war, with many claims of rape, especially by Sri Lankan security forces, there have been repeated calls for investigations into war crimes and atrocities.

On March 31, 2011, UN secretary-general Ban Ki-moon released a report commissioned in 2010. It concluded that "a wide range of serious violations of international humanitarian and human rights law were committed by the government of Sri Lanka and the LTTE, some of which would amount to war crimes and crimes against humanity." The government was held responsible for the killing of civilians, including the shelling of hospitals and humanitarian objects in no-fire zones, the denial of humanitarian assistance, forced displacement, and torture. The LTTE was held responsible for using civilians as human shields, killing civilians attempting to flee, firing from civilian installations, forcibly recruiting children, employing forced labor, and carrying out indiscriminate suicide attacks. Despite strong opposition from the Sri Lankan government, in March 2014 the UN Human Rights Council voted to open an international inquiry into such charges and on June 25 appointed three international experts to advise the investigation. The Sri Lankan government and army commanders claim that they have nothing to hide.

SPENCER C. TUCKER

Timeline

1505	Portuguese soldier and explorer Lourenço de Almeida arrives. The Portuguese call the island Ceilão, which is transliterated into English as Ceylon.
1517	The Portuguese establish a coastal fortification in the Ceylonese Kingdom of Kandy.
1660	By this date the Dutch control virtually all of the Ceylonese Kingdom of Kandy.
1796	The British arrive in Ceylon and take possession from the Dutch.
1802	The Treaty of Amiens between Britain and France awards Ceylon to the British.
1818, 1848	The British crush two rebellions against their rule in Ceylon.
1948	Ceylon becomes a self-governing dominion within the British Commonwealth.
1956–1959	Ceylon prime minister Solomon Bandaranaike creates conflict with the minority Hindu Tamils when he embarks on a program of championing the Sinhala language and Buddhism. Tamil civil disobedience often leads to riots.
1971	
April 5–June 9	The communist Janatha Vimukthi Peramuna (People's Liberation Front, JVP) attempts to seize power in Sri Lanka and seizes parts of a number of cities, including Colombo. The government is able to put down the revolt, which may have cost 15,000 lives.
1972	
May 22	Ceylon officially becomes the Republic of Sri Lanka.

1976

May 5 — The militant Tamil organization the Liberation Tigers of Tamil Eelam (Tamil Tigers, LTTE) is established. Led by Velupillai Prabhakaran, it soon commences a program of violence against the Sri Lankan government.

1978

September 7 — The Republic of Sri Lanka officially becomes the Democratic Socialist Republic of Sri Lanka.

1981

May 31–June 1 — An organized Sinhalese mob burns the Jaffna Public Library containing more than 97,000 books and manuscripts, among them important Tamil documents.

August 17 — The Sri Lankan government declares a state of emergency.

1983

July 23 — The Sri Lankan Civil War begins with an LTTE attack on army outpost Four Four Bravo outside the town of Thirunelveli, killing 13 members of the Sri Lankan military. Sinhalese mobs respond by indiscriminately killing as many as 3,000 Tamils in what comes to be known as Black July.

1984

November 30 — Members of the LTTE kill hundreds of Sinhalese men, women, and children in the Kent and Dollar Farm Massacres.

1985

May 14 — LTTE militants kill 146 civilians at the Jaya Sri Maha Bodhi Buddhist shrine. The Sri Lankan Army retaliates the next day, killing 23 Tamil civilians in the Kumudini Boat Massacre.

1987

April 21 — LTTE operatives detonate a car bomb at the central bus station in Colombo, killing 113 people and wounding many others.

May 26 — Having activated reserve forces, in Operation VADAMA-RACHCHI (LIBERATION) the Sri Lankan central government sends troops against the city of Jaffna, an LTTE stronghold, in northern Sri Lanka. With the population of the city in dire straits, Indian prime minister Rajiv Gandhi, under pressure from the Tamil population of southern India to act, attempts a relief mission. When Indian ships are turned back by the Sri Lankan Navy, on June 4, 1987, in Operation POOMALAI (FLOWER GARLAND), the Indian Air Force parachutes food and other supplies into the city.

July 5

Twenty-one-year-old LTTE member Vallipuram Vasanthan drives a small truck packed with explosives through the wall of a fortified Sri Lankan Army camp at Nelliady in the Jaffna Peninsula. The ensuing blast kills him and 40 soldiers. Suicide attacks now become an LTTE trademark, with the organization carrying out hundreds of them during the war.

July 29

The Indian government pressures Sri Lanka to accept a "settlement" in the civil war. Signed by Indian prime minister Rajiv Gandhi and Sri Lankan president J. R. Jayewardene in Colombo, the accord includes a Sri Lankan government pledge of the withdrawal of its troops from the area of the Tamil stronghold city of Jaffna and limited autonomy for the Tamil region of the country. In return, the LTTE is to surrender its arms. When the LTTE rejects this arrangement, the Indian government sends a peacekeeping force of some 50,000 men in an effort to disarm the Tamils. This operation, which extends into early 1990, results in the deaths of some 1,200 Indian soldiers and an unknown number of LTTE members.

1987–1989

The Marxist JVP, which had attempted to seize power in 1971, again carries out an armed uprising against the government, skillfully stressing Sinhalese nationalism against the presence of Indian peacekeeping troops and carrying out a terrorist campaign. Thousands of people are killed.

In November 1989 in Colombo, government forces kill JVP leader Rohana Wijeweera, and by early 1990 the government has either killed or imprisoned the remaining JVP leadership and arrested some 7,000 of its rank and file. The number of dead in the insurgency is unknown, because it merges with the concurrent struggle against the Tamil separatists.

1988

November 3

Revolutionaries in the Maldives invite in Tamil guerrilla mercenaries from Sri Lanka to mount a coup d'état. The Maldivian government appeals to India for assistance, and in Operation CACTUS on the night of November 3, 1988, the Indian Air Force airlifts a paratroop battalion from Agra more than 1,200 miles to the Maldives. Landing at Hulule, the paratroopers secure the airfield and several hours later restore the government at Malé.

1989

September

The Indian and Sri Lankan governments agree to a withdrawal of the some 50,000-strong Indian Peacekeeping Force from the northern and eastern provinces of Sri Lanka. Completed by March 1990, the withdrawal leaves this part of Sri Lanka in the hands of the Tamil rebels.

1990

August

The LTTE mounts attacks on the previously unaffected and neutral Muslim communities. The Muslims respond with a jihad (holy war) against the Tamils.

December 3

The LTTE proclaims a unilateral cease-fire and announces its willingness to conduct peace talks with the Sri Lankan government.

1991

May 21

In retaliation for his intervention in the Sri Lankan Civil War, LTTE suicide bomber Thenmuli Rajaratnam assassinates former Indian prime minister Rajiv Gandhi in Sriperumbudur, India. A number of others also die in the blast.

1993

May 1

An LTTE member wearing a suicide vest assassinates Sri Lankan president Ranasinghe Premadasa at the May Day parade in Colombo. Twenty-three others also die in the blast, and scores are wounded.

September–October

The Sri Lankan government launches a major offensive against the LTTE. On October 1 government troops capture the Tiger naval base at Kilali and there destroy some 120 vessels.

1995

January

A truce between the LTTE and the Sri Lankan government lasts only three months.

1996

January 31

An LTTE suicide bomber drives a truck containing an estimated 440 pounds of explosive into the Central Bank of Sri Lanka building in Colombo. The ensuing blast kills 91 people and wounds 1,400 others.

1997

March 6

LTTE members assault a Sri Lankan military base and there kill more than 200 soldiers.

2001

July 24

The LTTE carries out a suicide attack on Bandaranaike International Airport, destroying eight Sri Lankan Air Force aircraft and four Sri Lankan Airlines planes. This attack sharply affects tourism and has a major financial impact on the economy.

2004

December 26

In the worst natural disaster in modern times, a giant tsunami, generated by a powerful undersea earthquake in the Indian Ocean, strikes the coasts of Sri Lanka, India, Thailand, Malaysia, Myanmar, the Maldives, Indonesia, and Bangladesh. The official death toll reaches some 225,000 people, with as many as half a million injured. The disaster triggers the single greatest international relief effort in history.

2008

September 26

In a major escalation of the quarter-century-long civil war, the Sri Lankan government launches a major military operation toward Kilinochchi, the town that the LTTE considers its capital. The operation includes artillery fire and air strikes.

November 15

Sri Lankan government forces capture Pooneryn, a key LTTE stronghold paralleling the neck of the northern Jaffna Peninsula. Control of Pooneryn will enable Sri Lankan forces to attack the Tamil capital of Kilinochchi from three sides and cut an LTTE supply route. For the first time in the civil war since 1993, the government controls a land route that will allow easier resupply for its forces.

December 31

Government forces secure the important northern town of Paranthan, located on a highway connecting the northern Jaffna Peninsula with the mainland. This brings government forces within several miles of the former Tamil capital and stronghold of Kilinochchi.

2009

January 1

Government forces capture Kilinochchi, the former capital and LTTE stronghold, prompting celebrations in Colombo and other Sri Lankan cities. The LTTE moves its operations center to Mullaitivu on the north-eastern coast.

January 25	Sri Lankan Army chief of staff Lieutenant General Sarath Fonseka announces on television that government forces have captured the LTTE stronghold of Mullaitivu.
February 9	A suicide bomber, hiding among refugees who have fled the fighting in Mullaitivu, kills at least 20 soldiers and 6 civilians at a checkpoint.
April 27	The government orders an end to combat operations in northern Sri Lanka, and a spokesman for the president's office announces that troops have been ordered not to use heavy weapons, including aircraft and artillery, in order to spare civilian casualties. This comes one day after the government had rejected a cease-fire offer by the LTTE and announced that it would continue fighting until the rebels surrender. The United Nations (UN), the United States, the European Union, and India have all called for a cease-fire. A UN refugee official states that as many as 100,000 civilians may be in peril.
May 16	A spokesman announces that the Sri Lankan military now controls the entire Sri Lankan coastline, cutting the LTTE off from any possible escape by sea. President Mahina Rajapaksa declares that Sri Lankan forces have "finally defeated" the Tamil rebels, who are now reportedly restricted to a tiny pocket only some 1.2 square miles in area that is being pounded by artillery fire.

Many civilians have been killed in the relentless government shelling of the last rebel enclave, which has drawn sharp international protests. More than 17,500 civilians have fled the area in the last few days. |
| May 19 | In a speech before the Sri Lankan parliament, President Mahina Rajapaksa announces victory in the long-running civil war against the LTTE. He also announces the death of Tamil leader Velupillai Prabhakaran, whose body is subsequently put on public display by the Sri Lankan military. Rajapaksa declares a national holiday in celebration. Since the beginning of the rebellion in 1983, the fighting has claimed the lives of an estimated 70,000–80,000 people. |

SPENCER C. TUCKER

Further Reading

Amato, Edward J. "Tail of the Dragon: Sri Lankan Efforts to Subdue the Liberation Tigers of Tamil Eelam." Unpublished master's thesis, U.S. Command and General Staff College, Fort Leavenworth, Kansas, 2002.

Balasingham, Adele. *The Will to Freedom: An Inside View of Tamil Resistance.* Mitcham, UK: Fairmax Publishing, 2003.

Bandarage, Asoka. *The Separatist Conflict in Sri Lanka: Terrorism, Ethnicity, Political Economy.* New York: Routledge, 2004.

Bullion, Alan J. *India, Sri Lanka and the Tamil Crisis, 1976–1994: An International Perspective.* London: Pinter, 1995.

Clarance, William. *Ethnic Warfare in Sri Lanka and the UN Crisis.* Ann Arbor, MI: Pluto, 2007.

Deegalle, Mahinda, ed. *Buddhism, Conflict and Violence in Modern Sri Lanka.* London: Routledge, 2006.

Dissanayaka, T. D. S. A. *War or Peace in Sri Lanka.* Mumbai, India: Popular Prakashan, 2005.

Dixit, J. N. *Assignment Colombo.* Delhi: Konark Publishers, 2002.

Gamage, S., and I. B. Watson. *Conflict and Community in Contemporary Sri Lanka.* New Delhi: Sage, 1999.

Gunaratna, Rohan. *Indian Intervention in Sri Lanka: The Role of India's Intelligence Agencies.* Colombo, Sri Lanka: South Asian Network on Conflict Research, 1993.

Gunaratna, Rohan, Alok Bansal, M. Mayilvaganan, and Sukanya Podder. *Sri Lanka: Search for Peace.* New Delhi: Manas Publications, 2007.

Hashim, Ahmed S. *When Counterinsurgency Wins: Sri Lanka's Defeat of the Tamil Tigers.* Philadelphia: University of Pennsylvania Press, 2012.

Hoole, R., D. Somasundaram, K. Sritharan, and R. Thiranagama. *The Broken Palmyra: The Tamil Crisis in Sri Lanka; An Inside Account.* Claremont, CA: Sri Lanka Studies Institute, 1990.

Johnson, Robert. *A Region in Turmoil.* New York: Reaktion, 2005.

Mohan, Rohini. *The Seasons of Trouble: Life amid the Ruins of Sri Lanka's Civil War.* New York: Verso Books, 2014.

Narayan Swamy, M. R. *Tigers of Lanka: From Boys to Guerrillas.* Delhi: Konark Publishers, 2002.

Rotberg, Robert I. *Creating Peace in Sri Lanka: Civil War and Reconciliation.* Washington, DC: Brookings Institution Press, 1999.

Thiranagama, Sharika. *In My Mother's House: Civil War in Sri Lanka.* Philadelphia: University of Pennsylvania Press, 2011.

Weiss, Gordon. *The Cage: The Fight for Sri Lanka and the Last Days of the Tamil Tigers.* New York: Bellevue Literary, 2012.

Winslow, Deborah, and Michael D. Woost. *Economy, Culture, and Civil War in Sri Lanka.* Bloomington: Indiana University Press, 2004.

Persian Gulf War (1991)

Causes

The chief cause of the Persian Gulf War was the Iraqi invasion of and refusal to withdraw from Kuwait. On July 17, 1990, Iraqi president Saddam Hussein, dictator since 1979, threatened military action against Kuwait for its overproduction of oil quotas that had helped drive down the world price of oil. Iraq was heavily in debt as a consequence of the Iran-Iraq War (1980–1988) and wanted the price of oil to be as high as possible. Hussein also sought concessions on the vast sums that Iraq owed to Kuwait for loans during the war. He wanted to secure control of Bubiyan and Warbah Islands to improve Iraqi access to the Persian Gulf and end what he claimed was Kuwaiti slant drilling into the major Iraqi Rumaila oil field. Undergirding all this was Iraq's long-standing claim that Kuwait was an Iraqi province.

In mid-July 1990, American spy satellites detected Iraqi forces massing along the Kuwaiti border. The intent was unknown, but U.S. analysts assumed that it was most likely a show of force by the Iraqis to extract concessions from Kuwait. After all, Kuwait was hardly in a position to resist militarily. U.S. policy was in any case unclear, and Washington had tacitly supported Iraq in its war with Iran, providing intelligence information. However, for some time Washington had been concerned over Iraq's expanding nuclear industry and its development of chemical and biological weapons, which had been employed in the war against Iran as well as against Kurds within Iraq itself.

On July 25 new U.S. ambassador to Iraq April Glaspie, a career diplomat and skilled Arabist, met for the first time with Hussein, who was accompanied by Iraqi deputy prime minister Tariq Aziz. Glaspie delivered mixed messages on behalf of the George H. W. Bush administration that seemed, at least to the Iraqis, to allow Hussein operational freedom in the Persian Gulf.

Although there are differing accounts of what transpired in the meeting, apparently Glaspie stated that the United States did not take a stand on Arab-Arab conflicts, such as Iraq's border dispute with Kuwait. She also stressed that the differences should be settled by peaceful means. Hussein also informed Glaspie that an upcoming meeting in Jeddah, Saudi Arabia, between Iraqi and Kuwaiti officials would be followed by substantive discussions to be held in Baghdad involving Kuwaiti crown prince Shaikh Sa'ad Abdallah. Hussein probably believed that any move against Kuwait would not be challenged by the United States, certainly not by war. For its part, the U.S. State Department did not believe that Hussein would actually mount a full-scale invasion of Kuwait. Washington expected at most only a limited incursion to force the Kuwaitis to accede to Iraq's demands regarding the price of oil. As Glaspie was to state subsequently, all of Washington underestimated Hussein's ambition.

With Iraq Army divisions now on the Kuwaiti border, on July 31 Iraqi and Kuwaiti officials met in Jeddah. There Iraq presented Kuwait with a list of demands, including the writing off of some $12–14 billion in loans extended to Iraq during the

Estimated Casualty Statistics of the Persian Gulf War

	United States	Other Coalition Forces	Iraq
Force strength	541,000	252,500	361,000
Killed in action or died of wounds	147	87	40,000
Wounded	467	830	120,000
Captured (later released)	21	Unknown	71,204
Missing/Deserted	52	Unknown	100,000
Civilian dead	N/A	N/A	3,500
Military postwar dead (uprisings, health-related, etc.)	N/A	N/A	5,000
Civilian postwar dead (uprisings, health-related, etc.)	N/A	N/A	130,000

Sources: Michael Clodfelter, *Warfare and Armed Conflict: A Statistical Reference to Casualty and Other Figures, 1618–1991* (Jefferson, NC: McFarland, 1992); Carl Conetta, "The Wages of War: Iraqi Combatant and Noncombatant Fatalities in the 2003 Conflict," *Project on Defense Alternatives,* October 20, 2003; Department of Defense, *Principal Wars in Which the United States Participated: U.S. Military Personnel Serving and Casualties* (Washington, DC: Washington Headquarters Services, Directorate for Information Operations and Reports, 2003); John G. Heidenrich, "The Gulf War: How Many Iraqis Died?," *Foreign Policy*, no. 90 (Spring 1993): 108–125; Iraq Coalition Casualty Count, http://icasualties.org; Project on Defense Alternatives, http://www.comw.org//pda; "The Unfinished War: A Decade since Desert Storm," CNN, 2001, http://www.cnn.com/TRANSCRIPTS/0101/16/cgs.00.html.

Iran-Iraq War, giving up control of some territory along their common border, and leasing the islands of Bubiyan and Warbah to Iraq in order to facilitate the shipment of Iraqi oil.

With Kuwait rejecting the Iraqi demands, on August 2, 1990, four elite Iraqi Republican Guard divisions invaded Kuwait and seized key military installations, including air bases as well as airports. Another division of commandos and special forces employed small craft and helicopters to assault Kuwait City. The invasion caught the Kuwaitis by surprise. Despite the tensions leading up to the invasion, the Kuwaiti government had not expected an invasion, and its far smaller forces were not on alert. Within two days the Iraqis had seized full control, and on August 8 Iraq formally announced the annexation of Kuwait as its 19th province.

On news of the Iraqi invasion, President Bush had immediately convened the National Security Council, the Central Intelligence Agency (CIA), and the military leadership headed by chairman of the Joint Chiefs of Staff (JCS) General Colin Powell. U.S. Central Command (CENTCOM) commander General H. Norman Schwarzkopf was also present. Washington was concerned about Kuwait but also about the stranglehold that Iraq might now have over Kuwait's neighbor, Saudi Arabia, which had the world's largest oil reserves. Bush and others of his generation saw Hussein's aggression as a challenge akin to that of Adolf Hitler and made much of the supposed contrast between dictatorship (Iraq) and democracy (Kuwait). Powell and other officers who had fought in Vietnam, however, resisted waging another unpopular war in a faraway country. Most certainly,

Iraqi Invasion of Kuwait, August 2–3, 1990

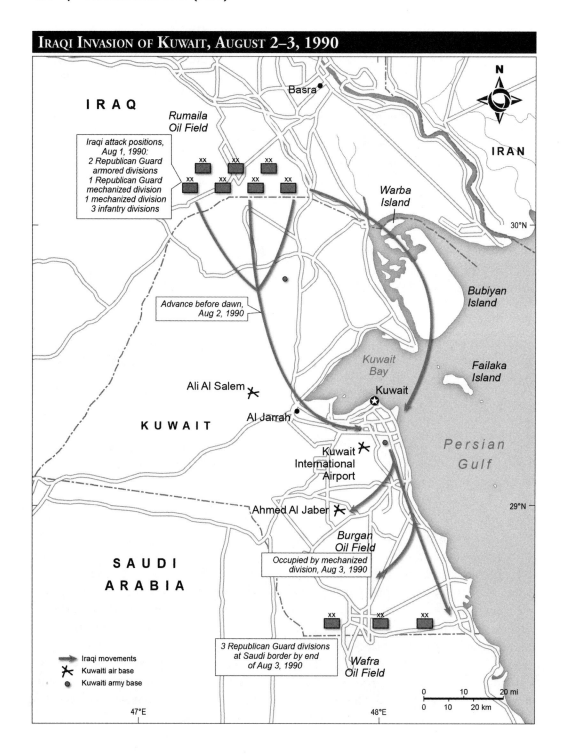

IRAQ

Basra

Rumaila
Oil Field

Iraqi attack positions,
Aug 1, 1990:
2 Republican Guard
armored divisions
1 Republican Guard
mechanized division
1 mechanized division
3 infantry divisions

IRAN

Warba
Island

30°N

Bubiyan
Island

Advance before dawn,
Aug 2, 1990

Kuwait
Bay

Failaka
Island

Ali Al Salem

Al Jarrah

KUWAIT

Kuwait

Persian
Gulf

Kuwait
International
Airport

Ahmed Al Jaber

29°N

Burgan
Oil Field

Occupied by mechanized
division, Aug 3, 1990

SAUDI
ARABIA

Iraqi movements
Kuwaiti air base
Kuwaiti army base

3 Republican Guard divisions
at Saudi border by end
of Aug 3, 1990

Wafra
Oil Field

0   10   20 mi
0   10   20 km

47°E

48°E

the Pentagon overestimated Iraq's military prowess.

On August 2, the United Nations (UN) Security Council passed Resolution 660 condemning the Iraqi invasion. UN Resolution 661 of August 6 called for sanctions against Iraq. On August 8, President Bush ordered the deployment of forward forces to Saudi Arabia in Operation DESERT SHIELD. The air, ground, and naval units were sent to bolster the Saudis and to demonstrate U.S. resolve in support of diplomacy.

The buildup of forces was massive. CENTCOM directed the U.S. effort. The U.S. Army provided the bulk of the forces, including armor, infantry, and airborne units from the United States and Europe. The marines also contributed two divisions, while offshore there were two carrier battle groups with full complements of aircraft and a U.S. Marine Corps fleet force. The U.S. Air Force deployed several wings of combat aircraft as well as transports and support units.

President Bush deserves considerable credit for forging an impressive international coalition and then holding most of the Arab states in it by keeping Israel out. Allied support arrived in the form of an armored division and two armored brigades from Britain and a light armored division from France. Saudi Arabia, Syria, and Egypt also provided troops, and Czechoslovakia sent a chemical decontamination and detection unit. Other nations furnishing military assistance were Argentina, Australia, Bahrain, Belgium, Canada, Denmark, Germany, Greece, Italy, Kuwait, the Netherlands, Norway, Oman, Poland, Portugal, Qatar, Spain, and the United Arab Emirates. Other nations including Japan furnished financial, medical, and logistical support. Altogether, the

U.S. Army general H. Norman Schwarzkopf directed the highly successful international military coalition that drove Iraqi forces from Kuwait in the Persian Gulf War in 1991. (Gilles Bassignac/Gamma-Rapho via Getty Images)

force in theater numbered some 665,000 troops. Opposing them, Hussein in January 1991 deployed an Iraqi force of some 546,700 men, 4,280 tanks, 2,880 armored personnel carriers, and 3,100 artillery pieces. General Schwarzkopf commanded the combined coalition forces.

When Hussein refused to yield, Operation INSTANT THUNDER began early on the morning of January 17, 1991.

SPENCER C. TUCKER

Course

The Persian Gulf War opened with an air campaign dubbed INSTANT THUNDER that lasted from January 17 to February 24, 1991. It was a massive air offensive directed at targets in Baghdad and throughout Iraq. The operation commenced with stealth bombers and fighters and cruise missiles destroying the Iraqi air defense network. Large numbers of Iraqi aircraft were destroyed on the ground, and Hussein ordered the remaining aircraft to fly to Iran.

INSTANT THUNDER moved through four phases. The first was destruction of Iraqi air defenses and offensive aircraft, along with communications, transportation, and nuclear, biological, and chemical production capacity. The second was to cut off those Iraqi forces not in the area of Kuwait from reinforcing there. The third was the destruction and demoralization of Iraqi forces in Kuwait. The final phase was preparation for the ground offensive. In retaliation, Hussein launched Scud missiles against targets in Saudi Arabia and Israel in an attempt to draw Israel into the war and split the coalition of Arab states against him.

Washington responded by dispatching Patriot antiaircraft missiles from Germany to Israel. Much was made at the time of the ability of these antimissile missiles to intercept and destroy Scuds in flight. This claim was later shown to be largely false. A major objective of the air campaign was to eliminate the highly mobile Scud force, but this was not achieved. At the same time, airpower inflicted tremendous casualties on the dug-in Iraqis, and the capital of Baghdad came under heavy attack. The Fairchild A-10 "Warthog" ground-attack aircraft proved highly effective against Iraqi armor, destroying several hundred tanks during the course of the war.

With his forces now being seriously degraded by coalition airpower and determined to begin what he threatened would be "the mother of all battles," Iraqi president Saddam Hussein ordered his

commanders to attack across the Saudi border. Only at Khafji did such a battle occur, but during January 29–31 it was beaten back by Saudi and Qatari forces and U.S. marines supported by artillery and airpower.

In only a few days the coalition had established absolute air supremacy over the battlefield. Iraq possessed nearly 800 combat aircraft and an integrated air defense system controlling 3,000 antiaircraft missiles, but it was unable to win a single air-to-air engagement, and coalition aircraft soon destroyed the bulk of the Iraqi Air Force. Air superiority ensured success on the ground. The air campaign also destroyed important Iraqi targets along the Saudi border. Night after night B-52s dropped massive bomb loads in classic attrition warfare, and many Iraqi defenders were simply buried alive.

Operation DESERT STORM, the ground war, began at 4:00 a.m. on February 24, 1991, Iraqi time (February 23 in the United States). Coalition commander General H. Norman Schwarzkopf had mounted an elaborate deception to convince the Iraqis that the coalition was planning an amphibious assault against Kuwait. This feint pinned down a number of Iraqi divisions. In reality, Schwarzkopf had planned a return to large-scale maneuver warfare, which tested the U.S. Army's new Air-Land Battle concept.

Schwarzkopf's campaign involved three thrusts. On the far left, 200 miles from the coast, the XVIII Airborne Corps of the 82rd Airborne Division and the 101st Airborne Division (Airmobile), supplemented by the French 6th Light Armored Division and the U.S. 24th Infantry Division (Mechanized) and 3rd Armored Cavalry Regiment, were to swing wide and cut off the Iraqis at the Euphrates River, preventing resupply or retreat. The center assault, the mailed fist of VII Corps, was to be mounted some 100 miles inland from the coast. It consisted of the heavily armored coalition divisions: the U.S. 1st and 3rd Armored Divisions, the 1st Cavalry Division, the 1st Infantry (Mechanized) Division, and the British 1st Armored Division. VII Corps's mission was to thrust deep, engage, and then destroy the elite Iraqi Republican Guard divisions. The third and final thrust was to occur on the coast. It consisted of the U.S. 1st Marine Expeditionary Force of two divisions, a brigade from the U.S. 2nd Armored Division, and allied Arab units and was to drive on Kuwait City.

On February 24, coalition forces executed simultaneous drives along the coast while the 101st Airborne Division established a position 50 miles behind the border. As the marines moved up the coast toward Kuwait City, they were hit in the flank by Iraqi armor. In the largest tank battle in the history of the U.S. Marine Corps, the marines, supported by coalition airpower, easily defeated the Iraqis. The battle was fought in a surreal day-into-night atmosphere caused by the smoke of oil wells set afire by the retreating Iraqis.

As the marines, preceded by a light Arab force, prepared to enter Kuwait City, Iraqi forces fled north with whatever they could steal. Thousands of vehicles and personnel were caught in the open on the highway from Kuwait City and were pummeled by air and artillery along what became known as the Highway of Death. The coalition now came up against an Iraqi rear guard of 300 tanks covering the withdrawal north toward Basra of four Republican Guard divisions. In perhaps the most lopsided tank battle in history, the Iraqi force was defeated at a cost of only one American death.

Lieutenant General Frederick Franks, commander of VII Corps to the west, angered Schwarzkopf by insisting on halting on the night of February 24 and concentrating his forces rather than risk an advance through a battlefield littered with debris and unexploded ordnance and subject to the possibility of casualties from friendly fire. When VII Corps resumed the advance early on February 25, its problem was not the Iraqis but the supply of fuel; because of the speed of the advance, the M1s needed to be refueled every eight to nine hours.

The afternoon of February 27 saw VII Corps engaged in some of its most intense combat. Hoping to delay the coalition, an armored brigade of the Medina Republican Guard Division established a six-mile-long skirmish line on the reverse slope of a low hill, digging in their T-55 and T-72 tanks. The advancing 2nd Brigade of the 1st Armored Division came over a ridge, spotted the Iraqis, and took them under fire from 2,500 yards. The American tankers used sabot rounds to blow the turrets off the dug-in Iraqi tanks. The battle was the largest single armor engagement of the war. In only 45 minutes, U.S. tanks and aircraft destroyed 60 T-72, 9 T-55 tanks, and 38 Iraqi armored personnel carriers.

Allied tanks, especially the M1A1 Abrams and the British Challenger, had proved their great superiority over their Soviet counterparts, especially in night fighting. Of 600 M1A1 Abrams that saw combat, not one was penetrated by an enemy round. Conversely, the M1A1's 120mm gun proved lethal to Iraqi main battle tanks. It could engage the Iraqi armor at 3,000 meters (1.86 miles), twice the Iraqis' effective range, and its superior fire control system could deliver a first-round hit while on the move. Overall,

A U.S. Army M1A1 Abrams main battle tank from the 3rd Brigade, 1st Armored Division, moves across the desert in northern Kuwait during Operation DESERT STORM, February 28, 1991. (DOD Photo/Alamy Stock Photo)

the coalition maneuver strategy bound up in the AirLand Battle concept worked to perfection. As VII Corps closed to the sea, XVIII Corps to its left, with a much larger distance to travel, raced to reach the fleeing Republican Guard divisions before they could escape to Baghdad.

In only 100 hours of ground combat, coalition forces had liberated Kuwait. On February 28 President Bush stopped the war. He feared the cost of an assault on Baghdad and was also concerned that Iraq might then break up into a Kurdish north, a Sunni Muslim center, and a Shiite Muslim south. Bush wanted to keep Iraq intact to counter a resurgent Iran.

SPENCER C. TUCKER

Consequences

The war was declared at an end at 8:01 a.m. on February 28 local time. With the air portion, the war had lasted just 43 days. In the 100-hour ground war, coalition forces liberated Kuwait, but the war was

halted earlier than many thought should have been the case. President George H. W. Bush feared Arab opposition and a fragmented Iraq unable to stand against a resurgent Iran if U.S. forces were to move on Baghdad. Chairman of the JCS General Colin Powell had no taste for the further slaughter of Iraqis and world reaction to this. Iraq thus escaped with its best Republican Guard troops largely intact.

Iraqi military might had been vastly overrated, and its ground forces had fallen easy prey in the desert to coalition airpower and highly mobile and advanced ground forces supported by superior intelligence and logistics. The war was among the most lopsided conflicts in history. Iraq lost 3,700 tanks, more than 1,000 other armored vehicles, and 3,000 artillery pieces. The victors lost 4 tanks, 9 other combat vehicles, and 1 artillery piece. The coalition sustained 500 casualties (150 dead), many of these from accidents and friendly fire, while Iraqi casualties totaled between

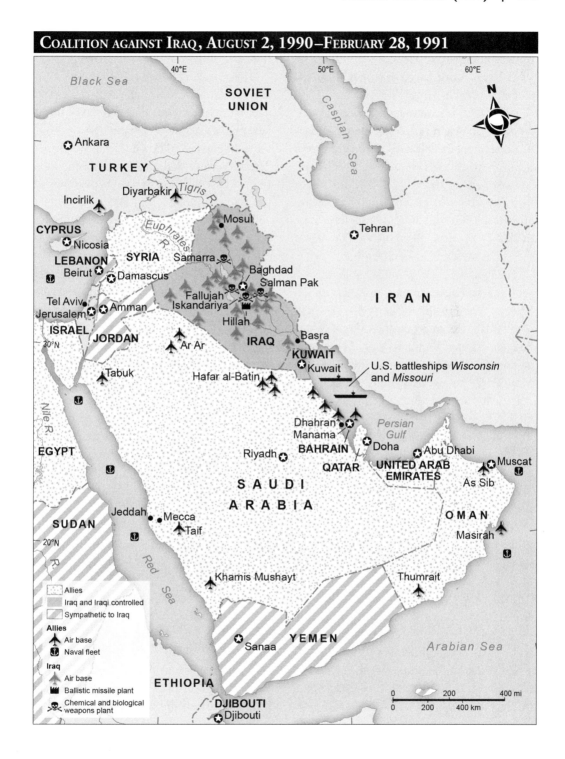

COALITION AGAINST IRAQ, AUGUST 2, 1990–FEBRUARY 28, 1991

Black Sea

SOVIET UNION

Caspian Sea

40°E   50°E   60°E

N

Ankara

TURKEY

Incirlik

Diyarbakir

Tigris R.

Mosul

Tehran

CYPRUS

Nicosia

Euphrates R.

LEBANON

SYRIA

Samarra

Baghdad

Salman Pak

IRAN

Beirut

Damascus

Fallujah

Iskandariya

Tel Aviv

Jerusalem

Amman

Hillah

Basra

ISRAEL

JORDAN

Ar Ar

IRAQ

KUWAIT

30°N

Tabuk

Kuwait

U.S. battleships Wisconsin and Missouri

Hafar al-Batin

Nile R.

Dhahran

Manama

Persian Gulf

EGYPT

Riyadh

BAHRAIN

Doha

Abu Dhabi

Muscat

QATAR

UNITED ARAB EMIRATES

As Sib

SAUDI ARABIA

OMAN

Jeddah

Mecca

Masirah

Taif

20°N

SUDAN

Red Sea

Khamis Mushayt

Thumrait

Allies

Iraq and Iraqi controlled

Sympathetic to Iraq

Allies

Air base

Naval fleet

Iraq

Air base

Ballistic missile plant

Chemical and biological weapons plant

ETHIOPIA

YEMEN

Sanaa

Arabian Sea

0   200   400 mi

0   200   400 km

DJIBOUTI

Djibouti

25,000 and 100,000 dead, with the best estimates being around 60,000. Eighty thousand Iraqis were taken prisoner. Perhaps an equal number simply deserted.

CENTCOM commander General H. Norman Schwarzkopf concluded a cease-fire agreement that allowed the beaten Iraqis to fly their armed helicopters. The March 3 agreement at the Safwan airfield established a no-fly zone for Iraqi fixed-wing aircraft north of the 36th parallel to protect the Kurds, but no such prohibition protected the Shiite Muslims in southern Iraq.

The war marked a remarkable renaissance of American military power from the Vietnam War era and the early 1970s. President Bush declared that the United States had ended the Vietnam War Syndrome, and he trumpeted a "New World Order." In May 1992, an overwhelming majority of Americans answered in the affirmative to a Gallup Poll question as to whether liberating Kuwait was worth a war.

The conflict saw the apparent triumph of new technology, with the increasing use and success of precision-guided munitions. Claims of Patriot missile successes in shooting down Iraqi Scud missiles were grossly exaggerated, but other new weapons systems, especially the M1 Abrams tank and stealth and attack aircraft, performed very well. Other nations took notice. The leaders of the People's Republic of China, whose own military establishment greatly resembled that of Iraq, began a robust modernization program.

Within U.S. forces, some 40,000 female military personnel served in theater during the war, and while they were technically excluded from combat, many were in harm's way, as seen by the 11 killed in the war (3 others succumbed to accidents). The war drew attention to the increasing vulnerability of women in the military during combat but in fact did not slow their movement into combat roles.

Thousands of veterans of the war complained afterward of unexplained illnesses and extreme fatigue. The Veterans Administration was slow to respond to symptoms that came to be called Gulf War Syndrome. Theories were wide-ranging, but the most likely cause appears to have been exposure to toxic chemicals.

The war ended probable Iraqi pressure on oil prices through the threat of military intervention in Saudi Arabia. Kuwait, the object of the war, had been restored to independence, although a massive and costly cleanup effort would be required to deal with the environmental disaster caused by the deliberate release of oil into the Persian Gulf and the torching of Kuwaiti oil fields by withdrawing Iraq troops. Much damage would have to be repaired in Kuwait itself, all to be funded by Iraqi reparations. Kuwait was little changed politically. This was hardly a war for democracy against dictatorship as Bush had trumpeted, and Kuwait remained securely under the control of the affluent.

The employment of Western military forces in the Middle East, even if they were allied with those from Arab states, fueled Muslim extremism and brought the birth of the Al Qaeda terrorist organization. Its founder, the wealthy Saudi Osama bin Laden, had been outraged at the Saudi Arabian government's decision to allow American armed forces into the desert kingdom. Al Qaeda was to play a major role in bringing about the Iraq War of 2003.

Saddam Hussein, hardly humbled by the outcome of the conflict, remained firmly in power, his intransigence intact. He constantly stymied the work of the United Nations Special Commission observers sent to Iraq to ensure compliance with the UN resolutions outlined in the cease-fire agreement and in Security Council Resolution 687. To many foreign observers, Hussein appeared to be bent on efforts to revive his weapons of mass destruction (WMD) programs, making UN searches of possible facilities for these as difficult as possible. The Iraq War of 2003 revealed that no such sites existed, with Hussein having apparently engaged in a game of cat and mouse as a means to shore up his regional power. Hussein also managed to divert some of the revenues from the UN-authorized Oil for Food Program, using these monies to keep himself in power and partially rebuild the Iraqi military. Meanwhile, the bulk of the Iraqi people suffered from the immense damage to Iraq's infrastructure inflicted during the air war.

Hussein was not long in wreaking vengeance on those who had risen against him, especially the Kurds in northern Iraq and the majority Shiites in the south of the country. These populations, who had risen up in support of coalition forces, now found themselves at Hussein's mercy. The United States, Britain, and France were forced to maintain air assets in the region and use these to enforce no-fly zones in the north and south and from time to time carry out air strikes or fire Tomahawk cruise missiles from ships. The coalition was forced to institute Operation PROVIDE COMFORT for the Kurds, with safe havens

and designated refugee areas. A no-fly zone established in the south along the 32nd parallel came only in 1992, however. Operation NORTHERN WATCH and Operation SOUTHERN WATCH continued until the Iraq War, but Kurds and especially the Shiites were bitter over what they regarded as a betrayal by the coalition in 1991. This manifested itself during the 2003 Iraq War.

The Persian Gulf War also did not translate, as many had hoped and President Bush had claimed, into a new era in the Middle East. The Israeli-Palestinian issue remained unresolved. Indeed, the Bush administration seems to have had no broad plan for Iraq or the region apart from evicting Iraq from Kuwait. By weakening Iraq, the United States had strengthened Iran, its chief rival for regional dominance and the major state sponsor of terrorism in the region. (Iran also benefited directly militarily, as the bulk of the Iraqi Air Force was flown to Iran early in the conflict and remained there afterward.)

Disillusionment in the region with the United States found expression a decade later in 2003, when President George W. Bush took the United States into war with Iraq for a second time. This time there was no broad Arab support. While the new war removed a cruel dictator from power, Iraq descended into sectarian violence, and the problems of the Middle East appeared as intractable as ever.

SPENCER C. TUCKER

Timeline

1990

July 1   Iraqi president Saddam Hussein threatens military action against Kuwait. He wants relief on the debts owed that country by Iraq as a consequence of its war with Iran (1980–1988), claims that Kuwait has driven down the price of oil by exceeding its quota, and seeks to end

	slant drilling by Kuwait into southern Iraq. Behind all this is Hussein's desire to annex Kuwait.
Mid-July	U.S. spy satellites detect Iraqi forces massing along the Kuwaiti border, but the intent is unclear, and the State Department assumes that this is at most a demonstration to extract concessions from Kuwait.
July 25	New U.S. ambassador to Iraq April Glaspie meets for the first time with Hussein and Iraqi deputy prime minister Tariq Aziz. Hussein misleads her about upcoming plans, but Glaspie says that the crisis between Iraq and Kuwait is an Arab-to-Arab matter.
July 31	With Iraq Army divisions having moved to the Kuwaiti border, Iraqi and Kuwaiti officials meet in Jeddah, Saudi Arabia. Iraq presents Kuwait with a list of demands, including the writing off of some $12–14 billion in loans to Iraq extended during the Iran-Iraq War, giving up control of some territory along their common border, and leasing the islands of Bubiyan and Warbah to Iraq in order to facilitate the shipment of Iraqi oil.
August 1	Kuwait rejects Iraqi demands, and negotiations break down.
August 2	Four elite Iraqi Republican Guard divisions invade Kuwait and seize its key military installations. Kuwait requests U.S. military assistance, but within two days the Iraqi military has overrun all of Kuwait. In a 14 to 0 vote, the United Nations (UN) Security Council passes Resolution 660, calling for an immediate cease-fire and Iraqi withdrawal from Kuwait.
August 2–7	The U.S. Central Command (CENTCOM) at MacDill Air Force Base has responsibility for military operations in the Middle East and develops a plan to send 200,000 American troops to defend Saudi Arabia from an Iraqi attack should military aid be requested. General H. Norman Schwarzkopf, commander in chief of CENTCOM, begins work to implement the plan.
August 5	U.S. president George H. W. Bush announces that Iraq will not be allowed to absorb Kuwait.
August 6	Saudi Arabian king Fahd meets with U.S. secretary of defense Richard Cheney and requests military assistance to defend his kingdom against a possible Iraqi attack.

	The UN Security Council in a vote of 13 to 0 passes Resolution 661 prohibiting the importation of all Iraqi and Kuwaiti goods, imposing economic sanctions on Iraq, and preventing the transfer of funds to Iraq and occupied Kuwait.
August 7	Operation DESERT SHIELD begins. This includes the dispatch of U.S. troops, aircraft, and ships to defend Saudi Arabia against possible Iraqi attack. Other nations also respond.
August 8	The Iraqi government formally declares Kuwait to be Iraq's 19th province.
August 9	The UN Security Council unanimously (15 to 0) passes Resolution 662, declaring the Iraqi annexation of Kuwait null and void.
August 12	Iraqi president Saddam Hussein seeks to tie the Iraqi invasion of Kuwait to the Arab-Israeli dispute by declaring that Iraq will withdraw from Kuwait if Israel withdraws from the occupied territories and Syria withdraws from Lebanon, all in accordance with UN Security Council resolutions.
August 18	The UN Security Council unanimously (15 to 0) passes Resolution 664, calling on Iraq to immediately withdraw from Kuwait. UN secretary-general Javier Pérez de Cuéllar announces plans to send envoys to Iraq to discuss the release of foreigners detained by the Iraqi government.
August 21	Syria joins Egypt in its commitment to defend Saudi Arabia in the event of an Iraqi invasion.
August 25	The UN Security Council approves (13 to 0, with 2 abstentions) Resolution 665, authorizing naval forces in the Persian Gulf to enforce the embargo against Iraq.
September 5	Iraq calls for the removal of the leaders of Saudi Arabia and Egypt.
September 13	The UN Security Council votes (13 to 2) to approve Resolution 666, which imposes controls over humanitarian food aid to Iraq and directs its agencies to determine the necessity for aid and the means of distribution.
September 16	The UN Security Council unanimously (15 to 0) approves Resolution 667, which condemns the Iraqi violation of diplomatic compounds in Kuwait and

	demands the immediate release of foreign nationals held in Kuwait.
September 24	The UN Security Council unanimously approves (15 to 0) Resolution 669, which requires an examination of requests from foreigners trapped in Iraq and Kuwait and recommendations to the Security Council on prospective action.
September 25	The UN Security Council passes (14 to 1) Resolution 670, which tightens sanctions against Iraq, including a prohibition on all air transportation to that country.
October 2	Amnesty International publishes a report detailing widespread Iraqi arrests, torture, and summary executions of Kuwaiti citizens.
October 29	The UN Security Council passes (13 to 2) Resolution 674, condemning Iraq for mistreatment of foreign nationals and demanding their immediate release.
November 6	The Bush administration declares its intention to double American forces in the Persian Gulf from 200,000 to 400,000 personnel.
November 19	Iraq augments its forces in Kuwait by 100,000 men.
November 28	The UN Security Council unanimously passes (15 to 0) Resolution 677, which condemns Iraq's occupation of Kuwait and destruction of Kuwaiti civil records.
November 29	The UN Security Council passes (12 to 2, with 1 abstention) Resolution 678, authorizing "all means necessary" after January 15, 1991, to ensure the removal of Iraqi forces from Kuwait. This resolution essentially permits an international coalition to go to war with Iraq if it does not end its Kuwaiti occupation by that date.
December 6	Under considerable international pressure, the Iraqi government decides to release foreign nationals held since August 2.

1991

January 9	In an effort to avoid armed conflict, U.S. secretary of state James Baker meets with Iraqi foreign minister Aziz. Baker presents a letter from President Bush essentially demanding that Iraq leave Kuwait, but Aziz refuses to deliver it to Iraqi president Hussein.
January 12	The U.S. Congress formally authorizes the use of force against Iraq.

January 15	The UN Security Council calls for immediate withdrawal of Iraqi forces to comply with UN Resolution 678.
January 17	With the expiration on January 15 of the UN Security Council deadline for an Iraqi withdrawal from Kuwait, forces of the international coalition assembled in the Persian Gulf region commence an air assault on Iraqi military, communications, and command and control positions in both Kuwait and Iraq, initiating the Persian Gulf War. This occurs at 2339Z hours on January 16 (Z time is Greenwich mean time or 2:39 a.m., January 17, local time. Baghdad is soon under heavy attack.
	Iraq responds by beginning the destruction of Kuwaiti oil fields by setting wellheads on fire, starting at the Wafra oil field and then moving north.
January 19–23	Iraq releases some 4–11 million barrels of oil into the Persian Gulf from the Sea Island oil terminal eight miles offshore and from several tankers in what is by far the largest oil spill in history.
February 15	Iraq pledges to comply with the UN Security Council resolutions regarding Kuwait if Israel withdraws from the occupied territories and Iraq will have a say in who governs Kuwait. The Arab countries in the coalition reject the Iraqi conditions.
February 23	Iraq declares that it will withdraw from Kuwait but according to the peace plan put forward by the Soviet Union.
	Iraqi forces intensify the destruction of Kuwaiti oil wells.
February 24	Beginning of the coalition ground assault on Kuwait and southern Iraq.
February 25	The U.S. Army 101st Airborne Division severs a key highway in the Euphrates Valley, isolating Iraq's reserves from supporting combat units in Kuwait and southern Iraq. An Iraqi counterattack fails to arrest the coalition momentum.
	Iraq declares that it will withdraw from Kuwait in accordance with UN Security Council Resolution 660.
	In the most deadly such attack of the war, an Iraqi Scud missile strikes a U.S. barracks in Saudi Arabia, killing 28 and wounding 98 others.

February 26	Iraqi forces depart Kuwait City.
February 28	Almost exactly 100 hours after commencement of the ground war and with U.S. and allied forces having entered Iraq and poised for a major invasion, U.S. president George H. W. Bush orders an end to the war. Iraq agrees to a cease-fire. Much of the Iraqi Republican Guard escapes. Bush's decision not to pursue Iraqi forces to Baghdad and topple President Saddam Hussein's regime is criticized by some, but the White House contends that getting rid of Hussein was not the coalition's stated purpose and that such an action would cause Arab nations to withdraw from the coalition and likely lead to chaos in Iraq, as indeed is the case in the U.S.-led invasion of Iraq in 2003.
March 1	Following public encouragement from the United States and fully expecting American and coalition support, Shiite Arabs in southern Iraq begin a revolt against the Iraqi government of Saddam Hussein. The revolt rapidly spreads.
March 2	The UN Security Council passes (11 to 3, with 1 abstention) Resolution 686, which defines the terms of the Persian Gulf War cease-fire. These include Iraq's release of prisoners of war and those detained before the war, formal renunciation of annexation of Kuwait, restitution for damages caused by the invasion, and the prompt disclosure and mapping of minefields. Coalition forces would then be withdrawn from Iraq once all conditions had been met.
March 3	At Safwan Airfield, Iraq, Iraqi military representatives meet with coalition leaders and accept all demands put to them.
March 4	Kurds in northern Iraq rebel against the Baghdad government, commencing with the occupation of Rania near Sulaymaniyah. The Kurds take oil-rich Kirkuk on March 20.
April 2	The UN Security Council passes (12 to 1, with 2 abstentions) Resolution 687, which demands the restoration of Kuwaiti sovereignty, validates all previous UN resolutions, demands Iraqi surrender of all weapons of mass destruction (WMD) and missiles with a range of more than 100 miles, and calls for the appointment of a UN commission to oversee the destruction of WMD

and long-range missiles. A search for WMD and long-range missiles begins along with the destruction of Iraqi chemical weapons.

April 6   The Iraqi government accepts UN terms for a formal cease-fire. The provision that allows Iraqi forces the use of helicopters for humanitarian purposes facilitates the brutal Iraqi suppression by Iraqi forces of the revolts of the Kurds and Shias. General Schwarzkopf, who had agreed to the helicopter use, later admits to having been taken in by the Iraqis.

The UN Security Council passes (10 to 3, with 2 abstentions) Resolution 688, which condemns Hussein's regime for brutalizing its people, especially the Kurds and Shias. The resolution requires Iraq to allow international aid organizations to provide humanitarian assistance. Operation PROVIDE COMFORT commences on April 6.

April 9   The UN Security Council unanimously passes (15 to 0) Resolution 689, which establishes an Observer Mission to monitor the permanent cease-fire.

April 11   The UN Security Council announces that Operation DESERT STORM is over.

SPENCER C. TUCKER

Further Reading

Amos, Deborah. *Lines in the Sand: Desert Storm and the Remaking of the Arab World.* New York: Simon and Schuster, 1992.

Atkinson, Rick. *Crusade: The Untold Story of the Persian Gulf War.* Boston: Houghton Mifflin, 1993.

Baker, James A, III, with Thomas M. DeFrank. *The Politics of Diplomacy: Revolution, War, and Peace, 1989–1992.* New York: Putnam, 1995.

Blair, Arthur H. *At War in the Gulf: A Chronology.* College Station: Texas A&M University Press, 1992.

Bush, George, and Brent Scowcroft. *A World Transformed.* New York: Knopf, 1998.

Dunnigan, James F., and Austin Bay. *From Shield to Storm.* New York: William Morrow, 1992.

Freedman, Lawrence, and Efraim Karsh. *The Gulf Conflict, 1990–1991: Diplomacy and War in the New World Order.* Princeton, NJ: Princeton University Press, 1993.

Goodman, A. Sue. *Persian Gulf War, 1990–1991: Desert Shield/Desert Storm.* Maxwell Air Force Base, AL: Air University Library, 1991.

Hess, Gay R. *Presidential Decisions for War: Korea, Vietnam, and the Persian Gulf.* Baltimore: Johns Hopkins University Press, 2001.

Hilsman, Roger. *George Bush vs. Saddam Hussein: Military Success! Political Failure?* Novato, CA: Lyford Books, 1992.

Marolda, Edward J., and Robert J. Schneller Jr. *Shield and Sword: The U.S. Navy and the Persian Gulf War.* Washington, DC: Naval Historical Center, 1998.

Record, Jeffrey. *Hollow Victory: A Contrary View of the Gulf War.* Washington, DC: Brassey's, 1993.

Romjue, John L. *American Army Doctrine for the Post–Cold War.* Washington, DC: Military History Office and U.S. Army Training and Doctrine Command, 1997.

Scales, Robert H. *Certain Victory.* Washington, DC: Office of the Chief of Staff, United States Army, 1993.

Schubert, Frank N., and Theresa L. Kraus, eds. *Whirlwind War: The United States Army in Operations Desert Shield and Desert Storm.* Washington, DC: U.S. Army Center for Military History, 1994.

Schwarzkopf, H. Norman. *It Doesn't Take a Hero.* New York: Bantam Books, 1992.

Tucker, Spencer C., ed. *Persian Gulf War Encyclopedia: A Political, Social, and Military History.* Santa Barbara, CA: ABC-CLIO, 2014.

United States Department of Defense. *Conduct of the Persian Gulf War: Final Report to Congress.* Washington, DC: Department of Defense, 1992.

Watson, Bruce W., ed. *Military Lessons of the Gulf War.* Novato, CA: Presidio, 1991.

Yugoslav Wars (1991–1999)

Causes

The causes of the Yugoslavian Wars began in the formation of the first Yugoslav state in 1918. The Kingdom of the Serbs, Croats, and Slovenes that emerged at the end of World War I had a plurality of Serbs scattered throughout much of its territory. These included the population of the Kingdoms of Serbia and Montenegro as well as the Serbian populations of Bosnia and Croatia. Many of these Serbs regarded the new state as theirs by right of their sacrifices made during the war against the Central Powers.

The assertion of Serbian authority and rights often came at the expense of the non-Serbian population. Many Bosniaks (Bosnian Muslims), Croats, and Slovenes had served in the Austro-Hungarian Army during the war and thus were regarded as former enemies by the Serbs. Serbian domination belied the ideal of Yugoslavism, which regarded all South Slavs as being essentially the same people. Serbs held leading positions in the government, military, and police. The monarch was from the Serbian Karageorgevich dynasty. To emphasize the dominant position of the Serbs, the constitution of the new state, essentially an updated version of the Serbian Constitution of 1903, was enacted on Vidovdan (St. Vitus Day), June 28, 1921, the Serbian national holiday and the seventh anniversary of the Sarajevo assassination.

The predominance of the Serbs in the government alienated much of the non-Serbian populations. The Croats, who constituted the second-largest element in the population, were especially disaffected. King Alexander attempted to denationalize the country in 1929 by redrawing the borders of administrative districts to vary the population and adopted the name Yugoslavia for the country. This had little effect. Nor did the 1939 Sporazum, which granted the Croatian parts of the country some autonomy, alleviate the problem.

The German and Italian attack on Yugoslavia in April 1941 demonstrated how deep the divisions among the Yugoslav nationalities had become. Most Serbian units in the Yugoslav armed forces resisted the invaders. Many Croatian units did not. Yugoslavia dissolved into the German-sponsored Nezavisna Država Hrvatska (Independent State of Croatian, NDH) and a German-sponsored Serbian state. Bulgarian, German, Hungarian, and Italian forces occupied the rest of the country. The atrocities of the ruling party in the NDH, the Ustashe, directed against the Serbian populations of Bosnia and Croatia soon led to Serbian resistance. At the same time, mainly Serbian units of the Royal Yugoslav Army bypassed during the invasion coalesced with local Serbs in Bosnia and Croatia into a force known as the Chetniks. A nonnationalist resistance force led by Tito (Josip Broz) and the Yugoslav Communist Party known as the Partisans became active after the German invasion of the Soviet Union on June 22, 1941.

A multisided civil war ensued among the Chetniks, Partisans, and Ustashe. Adding another dimension to the fighting were occupation forces. Smaller units of various origins—including Montenegrin nationalists (Greens), Slovene Home Guards, Kosovo Albanian units, and even a Russian

Cossack unit—participated in the general chaos. While fighting occurred throughout the country, the epicenter of the conflict was Bosnia, which was nominally a part of the NDH. There, all sides committed horrific atrocities, and all sides suffered considerable military and civilian casualties.

The surrender of the Italians in September 1943 and the withdrawal of the Germans in the fall of 1944 left the Partisans to dominate Yugoslavia. The NDH held on until May 9, becoming the last of the German European allies in World War II to fall. Vengeful Partisans pursued the remnants of the Chetniks, Ustashe, and others, massacring around 70,000 of them near Bleiburg in southern Austria. A legacy of nationalist hatred remained.

After the war, the new communist regime sought to erase the nationalist legacy. This meant the imposition of communist ideology in place of nationalism. This also meant the establishment of a federal government, with six republics: Serbia, Croatia, Slovenia, Bosnia-Herzegovina, Macedonia, and Montenegro. The Tito regime also carved two autonomous regions—Kosovo, with a predominately Albanian population, and Vojvodina, with a mixed population—out of Serbian territory. They were intended to some degree to dilute Serbian influence and prevent Serbian domination of the new Yugoslavia. Overt expressions of nationalism were forbidden in this second Yugoslavia. The Tito regime succeeded to some degree in developing and maintaining the idea of Yugoslavia as an independent communist state. Only in 1971 did Croatian intellectuals attempt to emphasize their particularism. The regime soon suppressed this Croatian Spring. This incident demonstrated that nationalist sensibilities, although muted, persisted in Tito's Yugoslavia.

Tito's death in May 1980 began the revival of nationalism and, with it, the slow unraveling of the second Yugoslavia. Several problems beset the post-Tito government. In place of the dictatorial leadership of Tito was a council consisting of the presidents of the six republics and two autonomous regions. Chairmanship of this council rotated on a yearly basis. This arrangement precluded the rapid and decisive exercise of executive power.

During the 1980s, the Yugoslav economy foundered. The cost of imported gas and oil soared. Yugoslav production faltered. One well-known failure was the Yugo, a cheap car exported to the United States. Without the adequate repair and supply infrastructure to maintain it, exports plummeted. Another problem for the country was the 1989 failure of communism throughout Eastern Europe. This brought the validity of the ruling ideology in Yugoslavia into question.

As the post-Tito Yugoslavia faced economic and political crises, nationalism reemerged. Soon after Tito's death, the majority Albanian population of Kosovo began to raise demands for the elevation of their autonomous region to the status of a republic. Under Tito, the Kosovo Albanians had achieved important economic and political gains in Kosovo.

Serbs, however, had long regarded Kosovo as the heartland of their nationalist mythology. Even though by 1980 they were in the distinct minority, they considered Kosovo to be an important part of their identity. They perceived the demands of the Kosovo Albanians for a republic as a threat to Serbian identity. Although federal authorities quashed the demands for a Kosovo republic in 1981, many Serbs remained concerned that their domination of that region was in peril. In 1986, a

Estimated Casualties and Perpetrators Indicted for War Crimes in Bosnia

Category	Number
Casualties	200,000
Refugees	1.2–2 million
Casualties due to the Siege of Sarajevo	11,000
Injuries due to the Siege of Sarajevo	50,000
Average number of shell impacts per day in Sarajevo during the siege	327
Number of United Nations fatalities	12
Number indicted by International Criminal Tribunal for the Former Yugoslavia (ICTY)	161
Number of concluding proceedings	126
Number indicted that have been sentenced	64

Source: Department of Public Information, "Bosnia and Herzegovina—UNMIBH—Facts and Figures," United Nations, http://www.un.org/en/peacekeeping/missions/past/unmibh/facts.html.

group from the Serbian Academy of Sciences published a memorandum claiming that the Serbian population of Kosovo and Croatia was under threat of extermination. The rhetoric grew even more extreme the next year, when a Communist Party official from Serbia, Slobodan Milosevic, told a Serbian crowd in Kosovo that "no one [meaning the Kosovo Albanian police] should dare to beat you." He implied that the Yugoslav government was then replacing the Tito-era consideration for the Kosovo Albanians with the restoration of Serbian privilege in Kosovo. This performance elevated Milosevic to the leadership of the Serbian nationalists. For him, Serbian nationalism became a vehicle to Yugoslav political power.

By 1989, Milosevic had taken over control of the Serbian Communist Party. That same year, he ousted the leaders of the communist parties of Kosovo and Vojvodina and installed his allies in their places. This gave him control of three seats in the rotating presidency, together with the ready acquiescence of Montenegro. With four presidential seats under Milosevic's

power, the specter of a Serbian-ruled Yugoslavia appeared again.

This situation was unacceptable to the Croats and Slovenes. These two republics also resented that their greater economic prosperity helped to fund Serbian political power through the federal system. They both declared their independence on June 25, 1991, and the war was on.

RICHARD C. HALL

Course

The Yugoslav Wars were a series of conflicts resulting from years of increasing ethnic antagonism in the former nation of Yugoslavia. The outbreak of hostilities was precipitated by the death of communist leader Tito in 1980 and the subsequent collapse of the Cold War and communism.

Under Tito's regime, small-scale ethnic clashes and religious rivalries were quickly and forcefully suppressed. Following Tito's death, a nationalistic movement supplanted the League of Communists in Yugoslavia, and Slobodan Milosevic gained power. On May 8, 1989, Milosevic was elected president of Serbia. He soon established control over the autonomous regions of Kosovo and Vojvodina. Together with control of Montenegro, this gave him effective domination of the eight-member Yugoslav Executive Council established as an executive body after Tito's death in 1980. As it became clear that Milosevic was intent on Serbian authority over the entire region, Croatia and Slovenia declared their independence from Yugoslavia on June 25, 1991. Consequently, the Bosnian Serbs, led by Milosevic and Radovan Karadzic, launched a campaign of ethnic cleansing against the Muslim and Croat population.

On June 27, 1991, the Yugoslav Army failed to quell the insurgent Slovenian forces with tank and infantry assaults. At about the same time, fighting began between Croats and local Serbs in the Krajina region of Croatia. Slovenia's war for independence lasted only a month, with fewer than 70 deaths reported. Milosevic decided to cut his losses in Slovenia. In any event, Slovenia did not contain a significant Serbian population. Croatia, however, was different. Around 12 percent of the population of Croatia was Serbian. Croatian secessionist forces pitted against Serb rebels (supported by the Yugoslav Army) continued fighting for another six months, with roughly 10,000 reported deaths. On December 19, 1991, rebel Serbs declared independence in the Krajina region, which constituted almost a third of Croatia.

The center of the Serb-Croat struggle was the city of Vukovar, a Croatian stronghold at the confluence of the Vukar and Danube Rivers. Vukovar held out for 87 days but was eventually overrun on November 17 by Croatian Serb and Yugoslav Army forces. The city was, for all practical purposes, destroyed. Perhaps 2,000 Croats, defenders and civilians, died in the

fighting for Vukovar; 800 were missing, and 22,000 fled the city. The devastation here is said to have been the worst in Europe since World War II. By September the Yugoslav Army had taken about one-third of Croatia. Perhaps 250,000 Croats and other non-Serbs fled, many of them forced from their homes by the Serbs.

On January 3, 1992, the United Nations (UN) successfully brokered a cease-fire agreement between the Croatian government and rebel Serbs. After many subsequent breaches, the UN Protection Force installed 14,000 peacekeeping troops in Croatia. That installation was eventually expanded to include help in the delivery of humanitarian aid for those affected by the ongoing hostilities.

The fighting then shifted to Bosnia. On December 21, local Serb leaders in Bosnia and Herzegovina declared a new republic independent from Bosnia. On March 3, the Bosnian Muslim and Croat population voted for independence in a referendum denounced by Bosnian Serbs.

On April 6, 1992, Bosnian Serbs attempted to seize possession of Bosnia's capital city of Sarajevo. Fighting broke out between Bosnian government forces and the rebel Serbs, and war ensued. The Bosnian Serb attack on Sarajevo failed due to the resistance of the mainly Muslim (Bosniak) Bosnian government forces. The Bosnian Serbs then imposed a siege from the hills around Sarajevo. In May, UN sanctions were implemented against Serbia for support of rebel Serbs in Croatia and Bosnia.

As heavy fighting continued throughout January 1993, the Serbian rebel siege of Sarajevo continued. The UN and European Union (EU) peace negotiations failed, while war broke out in Bosnia once more—this time between Muslims and

A Bosnian soldier returns fire in downtown Sarajevo as he and civilians come under fire from Serbian snipers on the roof of a hotel, April 6, 1992. The civilians were part of a crowd of some 30,000 people taking part in a peace demonstration. (Mike Persson/AFP/Getty Images)

Croats, who fought over the remaining 30 percent of Bosnia not already claimed by the Bosnian Serbs. On April 13, 1993, the North Atlantic Treaty Organization (NATO) began air patrols over Bosnia to enforce a UN ban on flights in the region.

On February 6, 1994, A Serbian rebel mortar shell exploded in Sarajevo's central marketplace, killing 68 people and wounding hundreds of others. The attack brought sharp international condemnation. In retaliation, U.S. jets operating under NATO shot down four Serbian aircraft violating the no-fly zone as hostilities continued to escalate in the region. This marked the first time that NATO had used force since its inception in 1949. On March 18, 1994, Bosnian Muslims and Croats signed a U.S.-brokered peace agreement. On April 10, NATO launched its first air strikes against the Serbs in Banja Luka.

Bosnian Serbs and the Bosnian government signed a truce facilitated by former U.S. president Jimmy Carter on January 1, 1995. However, when the agreement expired four months later, the Muslim-led government refused to renew the terms, and fighting escalated once more. Serbs continued to assail Sarajevo, while on May 26, 1995, NATO air strikes created a crisis situation in which 350 UN peacekeepers were taken hostage by Bosnian Serbs. The Serbian government (in a bid to improve relations with the West) helped to arrange the hostages' release. The massacre of some 8,000 Bosniak men and boys after Bosnian Serb forces led by Ratko Mladic overran Srebrenica on July 11, 1995, provided added incentive for the resolution of the fighting.

In Operation STORM, launched on August 4, 1995, U.S.-trained Croat forces undertook the offensive against the Croatian Serb troops in the Krajina. The Croats rapidly overran the Serbian positions. In the aftermath of this operation, most of the Serbian population left or was expelled from the Krajina, where it had lived since the beginning of the 18th century. Then on August 28, NATO launched a massive bombing campaign on Bosnian Serb positions. Of 3,515 sorties flown, 2,470 involved attacks on 48 target complexes. These attacks enabled Croat and Bosniak forces to proceed against the Bosnian Serbs. By September 21, 1995, the Croats and Bosniaks had taken about half of Bosnia. Both sides were now exhausted and ready to talk.

Hosted by the United States, peace talks began on November 1, 1995, at the Begrime Conference Center near the Wright-Patterson Air Force Base in Dayton, Ohio. While Serbian president Milosevic claimed support for the peace talks, Serbian general Mladic proclaimed that he would fight the terms of the forthcoming peace accord. As the talks continued, the first NATO peacekeeping troops arrived in Sarajevo.

On December 14, the Dayton Agreement was signed in Paris, France. The terms of the agreement granted 51 percent of Bosnia to the Bosnian-Croat federation and 49 percent to the Serbs. After signing the Dayton Agreement, Yugoslavia was granted looser sanctions, still affecting much of its economy (trade, tourism, industrial production, and exports of final products) but allowing its citizens to exit Yugoslavia, for a limited time. While the Dayton Agreement officially ended the war, as Serbs withdrew occupation forces in the region granted to the Bosnian-Croat federation, they destroyed what little was left intact in the aftermath of the conflict, and sporadic fighting continued.

Fighting then erupted in Kosovo in 1998. A collapse of Albanian government authority in 1997 led to the looting of stores of Albanian Army weapons and munitions. The next year, the Kosovo Liberation Army made use of these weapons against Serbian authorities in Kosovo. The Serbs responded with brutality. NATO undertook a bombing campaign against the Serbs in February 1999, the first time NATO had conducted a military campaign against a sovereign nation and the first military operation for the German Air Force since World War II. All the NATO powers took part to some degree, including Greece, the government of which opposed the war. In all, NATO aircraft flew some 38,000 sorties. Although no NATO lives were lost in the bombing campaign, it is estimated that as many as 1,500 Serb civilians were killed.

In response, in Operation HORSESHOE the Serbs attempted to force much of the Albanian population out of Kosovo. Finally on June 10, 1999, the Serbs agreed to withdraw from Kosovo. NATO forces assumed responsibility for the country in Operation JOINT GUARDIAN.

Following U.S. bombing of Kosovo in 1999 and the winding down of the war, Milosevic remained in power despite being declared a war criminal. He was finally brought to justice in 2000, and his trial began at The Hague on September 26, 2002. Milosevic died of an apparent heart attack on March 11, 2006, before a verdict could be rendered. On July 26, 2008, Karadzic was captured and subsequently sent to The Hague. On May 26, 2011, Serbian authorities apprehended Mladic and sent him to The Hague Court for trial.

On February 17, 2008, Kosovo declared its independence from Serbia. While most European states and the United States recognized this, Serbia and Russia have not.

RICHARD C. HALL

Consequences

The Yugoslavian Civil War was a series of horrific disasters for the people living there. These conflicts tore apart what had been a stable and even at times prosperous country. Prewar Yugoslavia had even achieved sufficient international acclaim to successfully host the 1984 Winter Olympics. The cost in lives for the wars remains unclear. At least 200,000 people died. Hundreds of thousands more were displaced from their homes. In addition, uncounted numbers of people suffered from deprivation, psychological problems, and rape. Much of Bosnia especially sustained great material damage. Finally, the concept of Yugoslavism, which emphasized the essential cultural and political unity of the South Slavic peoples of Southeastern Europe, suffered a blow from which it is unlikely to soon recover.

The death, devastation, and displacement caused by the fighting did not affect the lands of Yugoslavia evenly. The most grievously distressed region was Bosnia-Herzegovina. Before 1991, this republic was the most ethnically diverse of all the Yugoslav republics, with about 44 percent Bosniaks (Bosnian Muslims), 31 percent Serbs, and 17 percent Croats. It also had the highest percentage of self-professed "Yugoslavs" of any republic. Before the war, this population was distributed fairly evenly throughout Bosnia.

Around 150,000 Bosnians died in the war, although any casualty figures lack precision. The majority of these victims were Bosniaks. One of the most horrific instances of loss of life occurred during the first two weeks of July 1995 at Srebrenica, when units of the Serb Army of the Republika Srpska, led by General Ratko Mladic and assisted by the paramilitary group from Serbia known as the Scorpions, rounded up and killed a reported 8,372 Bosniak men and boys in the region of Srebrenica. Much infrastructure was also destroyed in the fighting, including many mosques and Catholic and Orthodox churches. The famous Old Bridge (Stari Most) in Mostar was also destroyed by deliberate Croat tank cannon fire, although it has since been rebuilt.

Among the casualties was the concept of a multinational Bosnia. The ethnic cleansing carried out by all sides, especially the Serbs, has concentrated the Bosniak, Croat, and Serbian populations in their own ethnic enclaves. It has also increased the Muslim, Catholic, and Orthodox identities of these groups. The division of Bosnia into a Bosniak-Croat federation and a Serbian Republic by the Dayton Agreement of 1995 is unlikely to overcome these differences anytime soon. As a result, the federal Bosnian state with its two components is unlikely to gain economic and political stability. Any inclusion in wider European organizations such as NATO or the EU remains only a remote possibility. An EU military force is stationed in Bosnia to enforce the peace.

Another area that endured significant death and destruction from the Yugoslavian Civil War was Croatia. Here, the losses were confined to three distinct areas. In the southwest, the medieval city of Dubrovnik suffered considerable material damage while blockaded by Serbian and Montenegrin forces in the fall of 1991. In eastern Croatia (Slavonia) during the same time, the city of Vukovar endured many civilian and military casualties while under siege by the Serbs. Many of its buildings were destroyed in the fighting. The Serbs massacred many survivors when they took the city on November 18, 1991. Most of the consequences for Croatia occurred in the traditional Serbian areas known as the Krajina. Serbs had settled this area as a part of the Habsburg Military Frontier in the early 18th century. They constituted around 12 percent of the population of the Croatian republic.

During Operation STORM in August 1995, most of the Serbian civilian population fled from their homes or were driven out by the Croatian Army into the Serbian-held areas of Bosnia and Serbia itself. The 200-year-old presence of Serbs in south-central Croatia was ended in a week. The independent Croatian state became much less ethnically diverse.

For some time after 1995, Croatia remained something of an international pariah because of the ethnic cleansing. Only after the death of wartime leader Franjo Tudjman in 1999 did Croatia begin to seek to restrain its nationalist self-righteousness. It began to detain internationally indicted war criminals and sought inclusion in European organizations. Croatia joined NATO in 2009 and entered the EU in 2013.

The outbreak of fighting in Yugoslavia in 1991 raised hopes in Kosovo that Serbian rule might come to an end. An underground Kosovo assembly proclaimed independence in the fall of 1991, but the presence of Serbian security forces prevented any action. Resentment over the failure of the Dayton Agreement to address the Kosovo issue helped to revive the Albanian cause. At the same time, the Serbian government, under pressure due to the losses in Bosnia and Croatia, became more determined than ever to retain Kosovo. The repetition of the same tactics of brutality toward the civilian population and ethnic cleansing that the Serbs had employed in Bosnia helped to focus the sympathies of the outside world on the Kosovo Albanians.

As a result, NATO intervened and carried out a bombing campaign against Serbia. This caused considerable destruction and some loss of life. After the Serbs withdrew from Kosovo, NATO assumed control there. Kosovo remained under UN control from 1999 until its unilateral declaration of independence in 2008.

The efforts that Slobodan Milosevic took in 1999 to ensure Serbian control of Kosovo and Yugoslavia ended in the loss of Serbian control of both. The actions and atrocities committed by some Serbian groups during the fighting in Bosnia and Croatia cast a shadow of international opprobrium. The behavior of Serbian forces in Kosovo did little to alleviate these impressions. After the separation of Kosovo in 2008, Serbia was reduced to little more than the pre-1912 state plus Vojvodina, which remains nominally autonomous. With the election of a pro-European government in 2008, the Serbs finally began to seek out internationally indicted war criminals as a preliminary step to an application to the EU.

For Macedonia, the consequences of the Yugoslavian Civil War were mixed. Macedonia declared independence from Yugoslavia on September 8, 1991. While no Yugoslav component challenged this, two problems did confront the new state. The Greeks objected to the name of the state and its use of certain symbols.

They considered the name "Macedonia" as a provocation indicating designs on the northern Greek province of the same name. As a result, the Greeks obstructed Macedonian admission to international bodies such as NATO. The other problem concerned the status of the Albanian minority within the new state. The Albanians, who constitute at least a quarter of the population, were emboldened by the Albanian success in Kosovo to seek greater access to economic and political power in Macedonia. A brief war ensued in 2001. NATO peacekeepers enforced a cease-fire. EU peacekeepers remain. Because of Greek embargoes, economic development still lags in Macedonia. Macedonia achieved a precarious independence but not international acceptance or internal stability.

Montenegro and Slovenia actually benefited from the collapse of Yugoslavia. At first Montenegro, the smallest of the Yugoslav republics, sided with Serbia in the wars. In April 1992, Montenegro and Serbia declared themselves the components of a new Yugoslav federation. Montenegrin enthusiasm for the war and the new Yugoslavia waned, however, as the fighting dragged on and as EU investment money became available. Montenegro's Adriatic coast attracted much foreign interest. NATO's bombing campaign in 1999 hit some Montenegrin targets and further eroded the ties between Montenegro and Serbia. In 2003, a looser union between Serbia and Montenegro replaced Yugoslavia. In 2006, Montenegrins voted for independence. With the declaration of independence on June 3, 2006, for the first time since 1918 an independent Montenegrin government ruled the country. The coastline of the country has sustained extensive development. The country seeks admission to the EU and NATO. The smallest Yugoslav republic has gained some prosperity along with its restored independence.

The biggest winner in the Yugoslavian Civil War was Slovenia. The most developed republic of Tito's Yugoslavia fought a brief war in August 1991 against the Yugoslav Army. At a low cost in lives and material, the Slovenes preserved the independence they had declared on June 25, 1991. After the withdrawal of federal forces, Slovenia maintained a distance from events in the rest of Yugoslavia. Slovenia established good commercial and political relations with the rest of Europe. In 2004, Slovenia became the first of the former Yugoslav republics to join both NATO and the EU.

The Yugoslavian Civil War was a horrible tragedy for most of the former state of Yugoslavia. The exact number of dead and displaced will probably never be clear, but perhaps 200,000 citizens of the state perished as it fell apart. At least 2.5 million people were internal or external refugees. The trauma inflicted on the survivors in Bosnia and Croatia will endure for a long time. For Serbia, these wars meant physical destruction, territorial retreat, and international humiliation. Everywhere the concept of Yugoslavism was also a casualty. Cultural, economic, and political unity in Southeastern Europe will now likely only occur in the context of a greater European union. Ironically, for Montenegro the wars meant the restoration of independence lost in 1918. For Kosovo and Macedonia, the collapse of Yugoslavia led to political independence for the first time in their histories. For Slovenia, they opened a new era of political independence and economic development.

RICHARD C. HALL

Timeline

1917

July 20

A meeting of the Serbian parliament in exile on the island of Corfu calls for a unified south Slav state to be a constitutional monarchy under the Karageorgevich dynasty of Serbia and known as the Kingdom of Serbs, Croats, and Slovenes.

1919

December 1

The Kingdom of Serbs, Croats, and Slovenes is formally established, with its capital in Belgrade.

1929

October 3

Seeking to combat local nationalism in favor of a wider Slav nationalism, King Alexander I proclaims a royal dictatorship and officially changes the name of the Kingdom of Serbs, Croats, and Slovenes to the Kingdom of Yugoslavia.

1930

June 27

Fearful of a threat to their territorial integrity, Yugoslavia, Romania, and Czechoslovakia (the "Little Entente" powers) sign a comprehensive treaty of alliance.

1941

April 6–21

The German military, supported by Italian and Hungarian forces, invades and conquers Yugoslavia.

1944

October 20

The Soviet Red Army and the Partisan forces, having begun their Belgrade Offensive in September, liberate the capital city.

1945

March 8

A coalition Yugoslav government is formed in Belgrade with Tito (Josip Broz) as premier. King Peter II agrees not to return until after an election can be organized. Tito is firmly in control and determined to create a communist state, backed in this by some 800,000 Partisans.

November 29

The Yugoslav Constituent Assembly formally deposes King Peter II and proclaims the Federal People's Republic of Yugoslavia. Tito is in full control and eliminates all opposition elements.

1963

April 7

A new constitution is approved by the Yugoslav parliament, with Tito to be president for life. On his death, the parliament will select future presidents who will be limited to no more than two four-year terms. The new constitution also renames the state the Socialist Federal Republic of Yugoslavia.

1973

February 21

A new federal Yugoslav Constitution is enacted. It recognizes the sovereign status of the republics making up Yugoslavia and gives both them and the provinces the right to veto federal legislation. The republics constituting the country are Bosnia and Herzegovina, Croatia, Macedonia, Montenegro, Serbia (which includes the autonomous provinces of Vojvodina and Kosovo), and Slovenia.

1980

May 4

Yugoslav president Tito dies.

1989

May 9

Slobodan Milosevic becomes president of Serbia. A staunch Serbian nationalist, he heightens tensions in the already restive Yugoslav republics by seeking to reverse the Constitution of 1973 and secure Serbian control over all of Yugoslavia.

1990

July 2

Ethnic Albanian Kosovo declares itself independent of Serbia. On July 5 the Serbian government declares this unconstitutional, dissolves the government and parliament of Kosovo, and assumes direct control of the province.

October

The large Serb minority living in Croatia forms the Serbian Autonomous Oblast of Krajina (SAO Krajina).

December 22

Slovenia declares its independence from the Socialist Federal Republic of Yugoslavia.

1991

April 1

The SAO Krajina, consisting of those areas of Croatia where Serbs are the majority, votes to secede and join Serbia. In May, Serbs living in the SAO Krajina vote overwhelmingly in support.

June 25

Slovenia and Croatia declare their independence.

September 25

United Nations (UN) Security Council Resolution 713 imposes an arms embargo on all of the former Socialist Federal Republic of Yugoslavia.

October 22	Led by Premier Alija Izetbegovich, Bosnia and Herzegovina declare independence from Yugoslavia.
October 24	Serbs living in Bosnia and Herzegovina, who constitute some 31 percent of its population, abandon the central tripartite government that has been ruling the country and form the Assembly of the Serb People of Bosnia and Herzegovina.
November 17	The UN Security Council unanimously supports peace-keeping operations in war-torn Yugoslavia, requested by both Serbia and Croatia. The occupied territories are to be recognized as UN Protected Areas, and the UN Protection Force replaces the Yugoslav Army.
November 18	Serbian forces take the besieged Croatian city of Vukovar.
November 22	In the Serbian province of Kosovo, the shadow Kosovo Assembly organizes a referendum on independence for the province. Despite widespread violence and harassment by Serbian security forces, some 90 percent of ethnic Albanians turn out and vote 98 percent in favor of independence.

1992

January 9	The self-proclaimed Serb Assembly in Bosnia and Herzegovina proclaims the Serbian Republic of Bosnia and Herzegovina, which becomes the Republika Srpska in August 1992.
January 15	States of the European Community recognize the independence of Slovenia and Croatia.
February 21	UN Security Council Resolution 743 authorizes a UN Protection Force for war-torn Yugoslavia.
February 29–March 1	With the Serbs having left the central assembly, the Socialist Republic of Bosnia and Herzegovina follows the example of Slovenia and Croatia and organizes a plebiscite on the matter of leaving the Yugoslav federation. On February 29–March 1, 1992, with the Serbs boycotting the referendum, the Bosniaks (Bosnian Muslims, who comprise 43 percent of the population) and Croats (17 percent) vote overwhelmingly in favor of independence.
April 6	The Republic of Bosnia and Herzegovina declares independence. The United States and a number of European governments recognize the new republic, but the

	declaration of independence brings the Bosnian War of April 6, 1992–December 14, 1995.
May	At the end of May the UN imposes economic sanctions on Serbia for its support of its fellow nationalists in Bosnia. Nonetheless, by the summer of 1992 the Bosnian Serbs have employed their significant military superiority, especially in heavy weapons, to secure control of more than 60 percent of Bosnian territory.
June	The Croats demand recognition for their area, Herceg-Bosna. When the Bosnian central government rejects this, the war becomes a three-way affair, with Croats and Serbs fighting the Bosniaks.
August 13–14	Meeting in extraordinary session, the UN Human Rights Commission unanimously passes a resolution condemning the policy of forced expulsions practiced by the Serbs against Muslims and Croats in Bosnia as ethnic cleansing.
October	To help ensure the safety of humanitarian operations, the UN Security Council imposes a no-fly zone over Bosnia.

1993

April 12	When the Serbs violate the UN-imposed no-fly zone with helicopters, the North Atlantic Treaty Organization (NATO) begins Operation DENY FLIGHT to enforce the no-fly zone over Bosnia-Herzegovina. It remains in effect until December 20, 1995.
May	Croatian forces launch a war against the Bosniaks and lay siege to the city of Mostar. The Bosniaks are poorly armed, but by fighting a largely defensive war they manage to hold off their opponents.
	The UN declares Sarajevo and five other Muslim enclaves to be safe areas under its protection.
August	NATO declares its readiness to respond with air strikes in the event that UN safe areas, including Sarajevo, come under siege. This action temporarily ends the Serb stranglehold on Sarajevo.

1994

February 5	In Sarajevo a mortar shell fired by Serbian forces who have besieged the city for 22 months explodes in the Central Marketplace, killing as many as 68 people and wounding hundreds of others. The attack brings sharp international condemnation.

February 19	Serbian forces withdraw the majority of their heavy artillery from the vicinity of Sarajevo following a NATO threat to bomb Serbian positions after the devastating Serb attack on Sarajevo's Central Marketplace. For a short time, there is a lull in the fighting.
February 28	U.S. F-16 fighter aircraft assigned to NATO shoot down four Yugoslav fighter jets over Bosnia-Herzegovina in response to Serbian violation of the Bosnian no-fly zone imposed by NATO in April 1993. The engagement is the first military strike by NATO in its 45-year history.
March	With increasing U.S. government involvement in peace efforts, an agreement is reached between the Bosnian government, Bosnian Croats, and the government of Croatia to establish a federation between Muslims and Croats in Bosnia. Fighting between these two groups now ends. Their united forces soon conquer the small Autonomous Province of Western Bosnia.
April	NATO employs air strikes against Bosnian Serb forces to halt a Serb attack on the eastern enclave and UN safe area of Gorazhde. In the spring of 1994 the United States, Russia, Britain, France, and Germany establish a five-nation Contact Group in an effort to broker a settlement between the federation and the Bosnian Serbs.
August	New fighting having erupted, an economic embargo of Serbia is declared, and NATO responds to Serb attacks by expanding the area for its air strikes into Serb-controlled Croatia.
December	With the help of former U.S. president Jimmy Carter, all sides agree to a four-month cessation of hostilities, but on the expiration of the truce the fighting resumes.

1995

February 13	A UN war crimes tribunal charges 21 Serb military officers with crimes against humanity and genocide.
May	Bosnian Serb forces renew attacks on Sarajevo and threaten the safe area of Srebrenica.
	Bosnian Serb forces respond to NATO air strikes by taking hostage more than 350 UN peacekeepers of the 24,000 sent to Bosnia to stop the fighting. Serbia helps secure their release.
July 13–18	Units of the Serb Army of the Republika Srpska, led by General Ratko Mladic and assisted by the paramilitary

group known as the Scorpions, kill a reported 8,372 Bosniak men and boys in the region of Srebrenica in Bosnia and Herzegovina. In response to the fall of the safe areas of Srebrenica and Zhepa, U.S. president William J. Clinton insists that NATO and the UN make good on their commitment to protect the remaining safe areas. The allies agree and threaten broad-based air strikes if the remaining safe areas in Bosnia, including Gorazhde, Tuzla, Bihach, and Sarajevo, are attacked again.

August 4–7	Operation STORM begins on August 7 when the Croatian Army, reequipped and trained by the United States, attacks the Serb-held territory of Krajina, taken from Croatia by the Serbs in 1990. By August 7 the Croats are firmly in control of the Krajina, forcing a mass exodus of 150,000 Serbs who had lived there. A UN cease-fire then goes into effect.
August 29–September 14	With Serb forces testing the NATO ultimatum by launching attacks against the Bosnian safe areas of Zhepa, Bihach, and Sarajevo, NATO responds with Operation DELIBERATE FORCE. It follows a Bosnian Serb mortar attack on Sarajevo on August 28 that kills 37 civilians. The 11 days of air strikes constitute the largest military operation by NATO to this point.
October	A cease-fire goes into effect.
November 1–21	Peace talks take place at Wright Patterson Air Force Base near Dayton, Ohio.
December 14	In Paris the leaders of Bosnia, Croatia, and Serbia formally sign the Dayton Accords, officially ending the wars in Bosnia and Croatia. The Muslim-Croat federation receives control of 51 percent of the territory, while the Serbs receive 49 percent. All three parties agree to a union in which each side would have control over its own defense, security, and taxes.
December 16	NATO launches Operation JOINT ENDEAVOR, its largest military operation to date, in order to support the Bosnia Peace Agreement. Ultimately it sees the deployment of some 60,000 NATO troops, including 20,000 from the United States (supported by an additional 12,000 U.S. troops of other nations). This force is reduced to a 24,000-strong international stabilization force in 1997. The Bosnian War, which has lasted three and a half years, has claimed about 100,000 lives and displaced as

many as 2 million people, creating the largest refugee crisis in post–World War II Europe.

1996

April 22

The Kosovo War begins when the secret Kosovo Liberation Army (KLA) carries out a series of attacks against Serbian security personnel throughout the province. The Yugoslav Army responds to the KLA attacks with force, attacking base areas.

1998

June

Following a major Yugoslav Army military operation in Kosovo in May, NATO launches Operation DETERMINED FALCON, an air demonstration across the Yugoslav borders. President Milosevic then concludes an agreement with Russian Federation president Boris Yeltsin to cease offensive military operations and begin negotiations, but Milosevic and Rugova meet only once. The United States is now clearly backing the KLA.

October 25

A cease-fire agreement is brokered. U.S. diplomats attempt to hammer out a deal in which the Yugoslav Army will halt its attacks, NATO peacekeeping troops will enter the province, and the KLA will drop its bid for independence finally produces agreement on a cease-fire. The Kosovo Verification Mission is established with unarmed observers. The inadequacy of this effort is soon apparent, as the violence increasingly shifts to urban areas. It includes assassinations and bombings by both sides.

1999

January 15

The so-called Rachak Massacre occurs in which a number of ethnic Albanians are found murdered, their bodies mutilated.

March 12–June 11

With the Serbs intransigent, NATO carries out a bombing campaign. With NATO actively considering the dispatch of ground troops (U.S. president William J. Clinton is, however, opposed), in early June 1999 Finnish president Martii Ahtisaari, former Russian prime minister Viktor Chernomyrdin, and London banker Peter Castenfelt convince Milosevic to back down and accept a peace agreement that will end the war and halt the NATO bombing campaign.

March 18

Contentious, plodding talks occur at Rambouillet, France, between the parties during February–March

1999, with NATO secretary-general Javier Solana acting as a go-between. On March 18 Albanian, U.S., and British representatives to the talks sign the Rambouillet Accords. This agreement calls for the autonomy of Kosovo, the development of democratic institutions, and the protection of human rights. This is to be guaranteed by an invited international civilian and military force. The Serb and Russian delegations refuse to sign the agreement, however. The Serbian counterproposal is so extreme as to be rejected even by Serbia's Russian ally.

June 9   NATO and the Federal Republic of Yugoslavia formally sign a peace agreement that will admit a military presence (the Kosovo Force) within Kosovo under the UN but incorporating NATO forces.

June 11   NATO troops enter Kosovo in Operation JOINT GUARDIAN as the Yugoslavian Army exits the province.

SPENCER C. TUCKER

Further Reading

Allen, Beverly. *Rape Warfare: The Hidden Genocide in Bosnia-Herzegovina and Croatia.* Minneapolis: University of Minnesota Press, 1996.

Almond, Mark. *Europe's Backyard War: The War in the Balkans.* London: Heinemann, 1994.

Armatta, Judith. *Twilight of Impunity: The War Crimes Trial of Slobodan Milosevic.* Durham, NC: Duke University Press, 2010.

Benson, Leslie. *Yugoslavia: A Concise History.* New York: Palgrave, 2001.

Finlan, Alastair. *The Collapse of Yugoslavia, 1991–1999.* Oxford, UK: Osprey, 2004.

Gagnon, Valère Philip. *The Myth of Ethnic War: Serbia and Croatia in the 1990s.* Ithaca, NY: Cornell University Press, 2004.

Glenny, Misha. *The Fall of Yugoslavia: The Third Balkan War.* London: Penguin, 1996.

Goldstein, Ivo. *Croatia: A History.* Montreal, Quebec: McGill-Queen's University Press, Hurst Publishers, 1999.

Hagan, John. *Justice in the Balkans: Prosecuting War Crimes in the Hague Tribunal.* Chicago: University of Chicago Press, 2003.

Hall, Richard C. *War in the Balkans: An Encyclopedic History from the Fall of the Ottoman Empire to the Breakup of Yugoslavia.* Santa Barbara, CA: ABC-CLIO, 2014.

Magas, Branka. *The Destruction of Yugoslavia: Tracking the Breakup, 1980–1992.* New York: Verso, 1993.

Meštrović, Stjepan Gabriel. *Genocide after Emotion: The Postemotional Balkan War.* New York: Routledge, 1996.

Naimark, Norman M., and Holly Case. *Yugoslavia and Its Historians: Understanding the Balkan Wars of the 1990s.* Stanford, CA: Stanford University Press, 2003.

Nation, R. Craig. *War in the Balkans, 1991–2002.* Carlisle, PA: Strategic Studies Institute, U.S. Army War College, 2003.

Oliver, Ian. *War & Peace in the Balkans: The Diplomacy of Conflict in the Former Yugoslavia.* New York: I. B. Tauris, 2005.

Pavlović, Aleksandar. *The Fragmentation of Yugoslavia: Nationalism and War in the Balkans.* New York: St. Martin's, 2000.

Philips, John. *Macedonia: Warlords and Rebels in the Balkans.* New Haven, CT: Yale University Press, 2004.

Rogel, Carole. *The Breakup of Yugoslavia and Its Aftermath.* Westport, CT: Greenwood, 2004.

Rogel, Carole. *The Breakup of Yugoslavia and the War in Bosnia.* Westport, CT: Greenwood, 1998.

Sell, Louis. *Slobodan Milosevic and the Destruction of Yugoslavia.* Durham, NC: Duke University Press, 2002.

Silber, Laura, and Allen Little. *Yugoslavia: Death of a Nation.* New York: Penguin, 1998.

Tanner, Marcus. *Croatia: A Nation Forged in War.* New Haven, CT: Yale University Press, 1997.

United States Central Intelligence Agency. *Balkan Battlefields: A Military History of the Yugoslav Conflict, 1990–1995.* Washington, DC: Central Intelligence Agency, 2002.

Contributors

Dr. Gates Brown
Assistant Professor
Department of Military History
U.S. Army Command and General Staff
  College
Fort Leavenworth, Kansas

Dr. Phillip Deery
Professor of History
Victoria University
Melbourne, Australia

Dr. Elun Gabriel
Associate Professor and Department
  Chair, History
St. Lawrence University
Canton, New York

Dr. Richard C. Hall
Chair
Department of History and Political
  Science
Georgia Southwestern State

William H. Kautt
Professor of Military History
U.S. Army Command and General Staff
  College
Fort Leavenworth, Kansas

Dr. Arne Kislenko
Associate Professor of History
Ryerson University
Toronto, Canada

Matthew J. Krogman
Independent Scholar

Arturo Lopez-Levy
Lecturer, PhD Candidate
Josef Korbel School of International
  Studies
University of Denver

Dr. Sebastian H. Lukasik
Assistant Professor of Comparative
  Military History
U.S. Air Force Air University
Montgomery, Alabama

Dr. Paul G. Pierpaoli Jr.
Fellow
Military History, ABC-CLIO, Inc.

Dr. Jennie Purnell
Associate Professor of Political
  Science
Boston College

Dr. Annette Richardson
Independent Scholar

Dr. Spencer C. Tucker
Senior Fellow
Military History, ABC-CLIO, Inc.

Dr. William E. Watson
Professor of History and Chair of the
  History Department
Immaculata University

Lawton Way
Independent Scholar

Index